UNDERSTANDING THE CULTURE

UNDERSTANDING THE CULTURE

A SURVEY OF SOCIAL ENGAGEMENT

JEFF MYERS

UNDERSTANDING THE CULTURE
Published by Summit Ministries
P.O. Box 207
Manitou Springs, CO 80829

In cooperation with
David C Cook
4050 Lee Vance Drive
Colorado Springs, CO 80918 U.S.A.

Integrity Music Limited, a Division of David C Cook
Brighton, East Sussex BN1 2RE, England

The graphic circle C logo is a registered trademark of David C Cook.

The website addresses recommended throughout this book are offered as a resource
to you. These websites are not intended in any way to be or imply an endorsement
on the part of David C Cook, nor do we vouch for their content.

Details in some stories have been changed to protect the identities of the persons involved.

Unless otherwise noted, all Scripture quotations are taken from the ESV® Bible (The Holy Bible,
English Standard Version®), copyright © 2001 by Crossway, a publishing ministry of Good News
Publishers. Used by permission. All rights reserved. Scripture quotations marked KJV are taken
from the King James Version of the Bible. (Public Domain.); NIV are taken from the Holy Bible,
NEW INTERNATIONAL VERSION®, NIV®. Copyright © 1973, 2011 by Biblica, Inc.® Used by
permission. All rights reserved worldwide. NEW INTERNATIONAL VERSION® and NIV® are
registered trademarks of Biblica, Inc. Use of either trademark for the offering of goods or services
requires the prior written consent of Biblica, Inc.; RSV are taken from the Revised Standard Version
of the Bible, copyright 1952 [2nd edition, 1971] by the Division of Christian Education of the National
Council of the Churches of Christ in the USA. Used by permission. All rights reserved.

The author has added italics to Scripture quotations for emphasis.

Library of Congress Control Number 2016956968
ISBN 978-1-4347-0989-9
eISBN 978-1-4347-1108-3

© 2017 Summit Ministries

Printed in the United States of America
First Edition 2017

7 8 9 10 11 12 13 14 15 16

091421

CONTENTS

ACKNOWLEDGMENTS

I am so grateful for the Verdoorn Family Foundation's generosity toward this project. Their vision and ongoing encouragement were extraordinary. Summit's founder, Dr. David Noebel, has been such an encouragement, and I dedicate this volume to David and his wonderful wife, Alice, and their family.

Our Summit team is amazing. Jason Graham and Tosha Payne pored over each chapter and gave helpful feedback. Amanda Bridger and David Knopp helped keep the project organized. Karl Schaller kept things moving along on the publishing and marketing side. Jeff Wood, Eric Smith, and Aaron Atwood took on significant extra work to "hold down the fort" while I wrote and edited. Joey Amadee spent hundreds of hours preparing a digital delivery system to significantly expand the book's reach and impact. Every person on the Summit team has helped by reading chapters, giving feedback, providing encouragement, and praying. *Understanding the Culture* is a true example of teamwork in action.

As I wrote on cultural issues, the following people's research and input were invaluable: Kevin Bywater, John Stonestreet, Dr. Paul Boling, Dr. Glenn Sunshine, Paige Gutacker, Jay Watts, Dr. Sean McDowell, Robert Gagnon, Eric Teetsel, Darrow L. Miller, Dr. Rouven Steeves, and Marc Levin, Esq.

A "who's who" of subject matter experts checked various chapters for accuracy and logic. These experts included Dr. Stephen J. Grabill, Dr. Glenn Sunshine, Dr. Chris Leland, Dr. Kathy Koch, John Stonestreet, Scott Klusendorf, Dr. Sean McDowell, Atty. Jeffrey Ventrella, Dr. Ryan Anderson, Dr. Mike Adams, and Rob Schwarzwalder.

My editors—Robert Hand, John Stonestreet, and Dr. David Hare—did a wonderful job making the text more readable and engaging with the content in an immensely helpful way.

I'm grateful to the entire team for the tireless effort to help me craft the best edition of *Understanding the Culture*. Nevertheless, wherever this volume may be found deficient, that responsibility lies solely with me.

Jeff Myers, PhD, President
Summit Ministries

PREFACE

How to Use the Summit Worldview Library

Noted Christian writer and teacher Del Tackett has said that the Summit Worldview Library needs to be the core in every high school, college, and seminary today. Colson Center president John Stonestreet has said that this series should have a place in every Christian's home library. Why is this series so important for Christian students and adults in all walks of life to use often in today's complex world? Perhaps seeing how the trilogy came together will help explain:

- *Understanding the Faith: A Survey of Christian Apologetics*—**the first book in the series enables Christians to better understand theology and apologetics.** *Understanding the Faith* is a fast-track, fast-paced theological education for those who want to understand God and his world in a profound way and share their faith intelligently with unbelievers. Theology and apologetics aren't just academic exercises for pastors and church leaders; we are all "ambassadors for Christ" (2 Cor. 5:20) charged with giving "reason[s] for the hope" we have in him (1 Pet. 3:15). Pressing questions about life and faith deserve thoughtful answers.

- *Understanding the Times: A Survey of Competing Worldviews*—**the second book in the series gives Christians insight into the battle other worldviews are waging against Christ and inspires newfound confidence in the breadth and depth of a biblical Christian worldview.** By providing trusted, documented insight into the six major worldviews that drive the global events of our day, *Understanding the Times* helps Christians "[understand] the times" in which they live so they can know what to do in response to the critical issues they're facing today (1 Chron. 12:32).

- *Understanding the Culture: A Survey of Social Engagement*—**the third book in the series shows Christians how to transform culture.** With a firm foundation in biblical theology, apologetics, and worldview, Christians have something vital to say about every significant issue of our day. The depth and creativity of Christian thought on today's events should inspire tremendous confidence in communicating biblical truth to friends, loved ones, and associates. In John 8:32, Jesus said we can "know the truth, and the truth will set [us] free." Entire nations are in bondage to bad ideas, but believers can proclaim the truth—boldly, intelligently, and practically—that can set people free.

As a result, the Summit Worldview Library is eminently useful for students, teachers, pastors, businesspeople, public leaders, and others who want their faith to make an impact on twenty-first-century society.

CHAPTER 1

1

INTRODUCTION

1. LIFE IS MORE THAN RAISIN RUGBY

Job 12:7 says, "Ask the beasts, and they will teach you." As odd as it seems, I once learned an important life lesson from chickens. Several years ago my wife and I purchased a home in the country. Naturally, we decided to get chickens. We didn't expect them to arrive in the mail, but they did—via a package about the size of a frozen dinner.

Housed in a box in our laundry room, the chicks provided endless hours of entertainment for our children. One day while fixing lunch, I heard an unbelievable racket emanating from the laundry room. Rushing in, I found my two-year-old daughter dropping raisins into the box. One chick discovered a raisin, grabbed it in his beak, and bolted. The others gave chase. Another stole the raisin and lit out, his fellows in hot pursuit.

Wow, raisin rugby, I thought.

Then I realized my daughter had actually dropped a *handful* of raisins into the box, more than enough for each chick to have one. Yet none of them noticed, consumed as they were with competing fiercely for that first raisin. These chicks couldn't contemplate abundance, even with raisins raining down on them. They had only one thought in their raisin-sized brains: others have it; I want it; I must take it.

We aren't as different from these chicks as we might like to think. Since the fall of humanity, we tend to be takers, not givers. God, on the other hand, gives generously. One of the first things Scripture reveals about him, in fact, is how he desired the abundance and flourishing of humans and the world. He equipped us to be fruitful and bring joy to his creation and one another. Tragically, like those rugby chickens, our first parents chose to be stingy, jealous, and selfish. Humanity has followed suit ever since.

In God's offer of redemption, however, we're given another chance. Christ provides the grace and opportunity to have our identities changed back from being takers to being the givers he created us to be. When that happens to individuals, communities, and even nations, cultures are transformed for the good.

> Christ provides the grace and opportunity to have our identities changed back from being takers to being the givers he created us to be.

Understanding the Culture is the third book in a trilogy. In book 1, *Understanding the Faith*, we got to know who God is based on the Bible, and what his plan for the world looks like. In book 2, *Understanding the Times*, we grappled with how the biblical Christian worldview compares to other prominent worldviews, and in so doing, we found it to be more intelligible, reasonable, and livable than the other philosophies of our age.

In this book, we turn our attention to the needs of the world around us and ask whether the Bible really speaks to the pressing issues of our age. You will *not* find in these pages a manual with clever plans for saving humanity. It's actually the opposite. This book is an invitation to stop playing God and start engaging the world around us based on his intended design for it and for us. It isn't enough to merely start caring. We must care *well*.

Most people are concerned about what is going on in the world around them, or at least they say they are. But the form our caring takes betrays what we really believe. If the homeless ask us for money, do we give it and drive away, do we give them a meal, do we engage them in a conversation about what they really need, do we refer them to a homeless shelter, or do we walk away and in the next election vote for a government-entitlement program to help the poor?

Ideas have consequences because we act on them. We all live based on what we believe to be true. Christians must act on biblical ideas not just in our personal conduct but also in the big issues of our day, such as life, marriage, military force, the economy, and justice.

As we seek to make a difference, we're standing on the shoulders of giants. It's hard to imagine where our world would be today without Christians applying biblical ideas over the centuries. The question we face is this: Are such ideas still relevant? We can agree that Christians ought to be nice people. If you met a group of young men in a dark alley, for example, it ought to make a difference if they were coming from a Bible study.[1] But does this suggest that we ought to apply the Bible's teachings at a cultural level? Should we *try* to shape culture? Should society put up with our trying to do so?

If the primary identifying characteristic of Christians is pleasantness, then being nice ought to be the primary goal of our lives. But if what the Bible reveals about why we're here on this planet is actually true, then being caring people is much more than smiling and checking boxes on a do-gooder list. Rather, Christian caring ought to be the very best kind of caring. It ought to unleash human ingenuity. It ought to point the way for people to be reconciled to God. It ought to restore people to a high capacity of bearing God's image. It ought to bring glory to the Creator. So how does Christian caring start?

> Christian caring ought to be the very best kind of caring. It ought to restore people to a high capacity of bearing God's image.

2. CHRISTIAN CARING STARTS WITH GOOD DECISIONS

All cultures, including ours, are products of people's decisions, both good and bad. Jim Clifton, chairman and CEO of Gallup, argues that people make between ten and twenty thousand small decisions a day. Multiply this by the US population, and people make an estimated *quadrillion* decisions (that's a one followed by fifteen zeros) every year in America alone.[2] Our personal legacy is the sum of our decisions over a lifetime. By extension, our *cultural* legacy results from the interaction of everyone's decisions.

Our decisions have an enormous influence. Think about what you're doing right now: reading a book. Books influence the world largely because a man named Johannes Gutenberg had ideas about their importance. He acted on those ideas by inventing a printing system that used movable type to rapidly reproduce words on the printed page. His innovations changed the world.

Gutenberg's genius as an inventor was just the beginning of the story. Gutenberg saw printing as a means of rapidly spreading God's truth. He hoped that the printing press would "win every soul that comes into the world by her word no longer written at great expense by hands easily palsied, but multiplied like the wind by an untiring machine."[3]

Because Gutenberg's press was based on the design of wine presses he had seen in his region of Germany, wine became his figure of speech for the impact he hoped his invention would have:

> Yes … it is a press, certainly, but a press from which shall flow in inexhaustible streams the most abundant and most marvellous liquor that has ever flowed to relieve the thirst of men! Through it, God will spread his Word. A spring of pure truth shall flow from it: like a new star it shall scatter the darkness of ignorance and cause a light hithertofore unknown to shine amongst men.[4]

Think of it. A few modifications to a wine press enabled ideas to be disseminated rapidly. It dramatically changed learning and made it nearly impossible to suppress viewpoints those in power didn't like. No wonder Gutenberg has been named "man of the millennium."[5] The book you hold in front of you is a direct result of one man's invention. The ready availability of the written word is still changing the world.

Many people today no longer read the printed page but use computer devices of some

> The book you hold in front of you is a direct result of one man's invention. The ready availability of the written word is still changing the world.

sort, like tablets or smartphones. In their most basic form, computers are nothing but complex arrangements of glass, plastic, silicone, and various metals. Every part comes from the earth, from sand on the seashore to minerals found deep underground. Without mining, oil exploration, information theory, engineering, intricate manufacturing systems, and a well-developed system of economic exchange, we might very well be scratching drawings on a cave wall, not texting on smartphones.

As it is, the spread of ideas enabled by technology continues to grow by leaps and bounds. The computing power in your cell phone is more than NASA (the National Aeronautics and Space Administration) possessed when *Apollo* landed on the moon in 1969. That microchip hidden in the musical greeting card you got on your birthday has more computing power than all the Allied forces in World War II possessed in 1945. Your PlayStation or Xbox contains more computing power than a multi-million-dollar military supercomputer in 1997.[6]

The real genius of technology is its ability to extend power to those who, without it, would have no power at all. People now use handheld devices to exchange money, run businesses, and even deploy social media in revolt against undemocratic regimes. Without millions of decisions from people all over the world, you wouldn't be reading right now. You probably wouldn't even know how to read. You might not even have lived past infancy.

Clearly, we must learn to make good decisions about the natural world, technology, economics, and so forth. Christian caring starts with good decisions, but that's not the whole picture. In fact, if we just focus on good decision making, we'll miss the picture entirely.

3. CHRISTIAN CARING STARTS WITH SEEING THE BIG PICTURE

As we've seen, good decisions can lead to good results. But bad decisions have an impact as well. People can use perfectly good computers to destroy the dignity and reputations of others, enable more efficient traffic in illegal drugs, or disseminate child pornography. One or two isolated bad decisions probably won't hurt much. Eating a whole bag of potato chips won't really hurt either, unless it becomes a daily habit. Over time, though, patterns emerge that move us like a swift river current. For a while we make our decisions, but inevitably our decisions begin making us. As the prophet Joel cried out, "Multitudes, multitudes, in the valley of decision! For the day of the LORD is near in the valley of decision" (Joel 3:14). Decisions matter.

Perhaps you've wondered about the impact your decisions have. Is it possible to somehow rise above your circumstances and gain a fuller sense of what your life means?

Entrepreneur Sir Richard Branson thinks he knows how to help you do it, and as long as you're willing to pay $250,000, you can sign up to ride in one of his Virgin Galactic spaceships for a six-minute view of Earth from sixty-eight miles above its surface.[7] Justin Bieber, Ashton Kutcher, and Paris Hilton are among nearly seven hundred people who have purchased tickets as of this writing and await the day when Virgin Galactic completes testing and begins passenger flights.[8]

On their trip aboard a Virgin Galactic spaceship, the lucky few will be strapped in a specially designed aircraft and propelled to an altitude of fifty thousand feet. According to Virgin Galactic, once released from the "mother ship," there is a "brief moment of quiet" followed by "a wave of unimaginable but controlled power." And then

> you are instantly pinned back into your seat, overwhelmed but enthralled by the howl of the rocket motor and the eye-watering acceleration which, as you watch the read-out, has you traveling in a matter of seconds, at almost 3000 mph, 4 times the speed of sound. As you hurtle through the edges of the atmosphere, the large windows show the cobalt blue sky turning to mauve and indigo and finally to black. You're on a high, this is really happening, you're loving it…. The rocket motor has been switched off and it is quiet. But it's not just quiet, it's QUIET…. What's really getting your senses screaming now though, is that the gravity which has dominated every movement you've made since the day you were born is not there any more…. After a graceful mid-space summersault you find yourself at a large window and what you see … is a view that you've seen in countless images but the reality is so much more beautiful … and produces emotions that are strong but hard to define. The blue map, curving into the black distance is familiar but has none of the usual marked boundaries. The incredibly narrow ribbon of atmosphere looks worryingly fragile. What you are looking at is the source of everything it means to be human, and it is home.[9]

As a Virgin Galactic customer, you'll briefly glimpse something only 555 humans have seen prior to the advent of commercial space travel: continents, oceans, and the blue tint of the earth's atmosphere.[10]

Certainly, some people are signing up for the thrill because they have excess wealth. According to Virgin Galactic's website, though, the company's mission eclipses mere thrill seeking or luxury travel. It provides a window into what is really important in life. "We think it will be actually something of a transformative experience," says Virgin Galactic CEO George Whitesides. "Once the engine shuts off, the cabin will be devoid of any mechanical noise from the inside and any atmospheric sound from the outside, so people will be able to make a deep and organic connection with the universe and the planet. It should be an extraordinary moment."[11]

Maybe the visionaries behind Virgin Galactic genuinely think space travel as a consciousness-raising experience will improve lives. Or perhaps their sales pitch seeks to make customers feel less guilty about spending $250,000 on a six-minute experience rather than using that money to improve the lives and situations of starving and destitute people here on Earth. What you think the big picture is makes all the difference in the world.

For many of the first astronauts, seeing Earth from space resulted in something much more than a "connection with the universe and the planet." Colonel Jim

> **What you think the big picture is makes all the difference in the world.**

Irwin, one of only twelve men to actually land and walk on the moon's surface, said of his experience, "I felt the power of God as I'd never felt it before."[12] For Irwin, seeing the earth from space turned his thoughts not toward creation's fragility but toward the majesty of the creator.

4. CHRISTIAN CARING STARTS WITH WHAT GOD CARES ABOUT—PEOPLE

From a biblical perspective, people are at the heart of what God cares about. The earth's atmosphere, the majesty of the oceans, and the beauty of the landscape take on significance because of God's image bearers. People matter most in a biblical worldview. To many, though, this kind of talk is pure folly. Edwin A. Burtt, an American philosopher who grew up as the son of missionaries to China and later rejected his faith, said gloomily, "The ultimate accommodation necessary in a wise plan of life is acceptance of a world not made for man, owing him nothing, and in its major processes quite beyond his control."[13]

Was Burtt right? Is there no plan behind creation? You might be surprised at how many scientists disagree with him and hold that some intelligent force fine-tuned the universe to contain all the properties that make intelligent life inevitable. As Albert Einstein affirmed, "The harmony of natural law ... reveals an intelligence of such superiority that, compared with it, all the systematic thinking and acting of human beings is an utterly insignificant reflection."[14]

> People matter most in a biblical worldview.

Embracing the **anthropic principle** (*anthro* means "pertaining to humanity"), many scientists argue that we can observe the universe only because it exists in a way that allows us as observers to exist. Robert Jastrow, an agnostic astrophysicist instrumental in NASA's development, wrote, "The anthropic principle is the most interesting development next to the proof of the creation, and it is even more interesting because it seems to say that science itself has proven, as a hard fact, that this universe was made, was designed, for man to live in. It's a very theistic result."[15]

If Einstein was right that there is intelligence behind the universe, and if Jastrow was right that the universe is the way it is so that humanity can exist, then any view of the world that diminishes the importance of people is missing the most important fact about our existence here.

> *Anthropic Principle:* the theory that the universe contains all the necessary properties that make the existence of intelligent life inevitable.

Understanding that importance isn't always easy, of course. In some ways, being unable to see people from space would be a relief. We wouldn't be confronted with starvation or crime or abuse. We wouldn't feel the pain of watching those we care about undergoing chemotherapy or cowering in fear as mortar shells screamed overhead. But we wouldn't see the majesty of humanity either—the joy of seeing the smile on a child's face, the thrill of watching a couple fall in love or a son or daughter receive an acceptance letter from college, or the exhilaration of hearing that a loved one has overcome a long-held fear.

The biblical witness is that people are made in the image of God and are central to his plan. This changes what we care about and why. We still care about the planet not because we see humans as a cancer but because focusing on people is to care about what God cares about.

5. Why We Should Care about What God Cares About

If there truly is a God who has always existed, and who at specific points in time created matter and the universe, then it is reasonable to ask why our creator made us.

As we've seen in the previous books in this series, Christianity is intellectually sound. There is strong evidence that the universe is a product of design, that the Bible accurately reveals who this designer is, and that it points us to how we might come to know him. In this book, we'll see that once these and other biblical ideas took hold, the world rapidly began to change for the better.

> The biblical witness is that people are made in the image of God and are central to his plan. This changes what we care about and why.

Up until a couple of hundred years ago, life went on as it had for millennia. Widespread poverty reigned well into the eighteenth century. Deplorable working conditions, starvation, and disease were part of life for most people. Then something changed, and quickly. The amount of wealth in the world increased rapidly, as did the standard of living, safety, and health of people around the world. It wasn't "accidental or a matter of luck," author Sylvia Nasar points out, "but the result of human intention, will, and knowledge."[16]

What economist Cleon Skousen referred to as the "5,000-year leap" dramatically improved conditions for humanity, advancing people toward prosperity more in the past two hundred years than in the previous five thousand.[17] Today's US economy is thirty times bigger than it was two hundred years ago.[18] Prosperity is spreading, and people around the world are rapidly being lifted out of poverty. According to the World Bank, extreme poverty has dropped in half just in the last generation, from 36 percent of the world's population to 18 percent.[19]

We don't have to go into outer space to see what has happened and why. Beyond the bustle of daily life, something really important is going on in the human race. Every religious tradition has explanations for it, for how we got here and what we ought to do. Some say it's because of enlightened thinking. Others say it's because of revolution against illicit power. Still others say it's because we're achieving higher consciousness.

> Prosperity is spreading, and people around the world are rapidly being lifted out of poverty. Extreme poverty has dropped in half just in the last generation.

Yet few worldviews can account fully for the dark side of progress as well. While we gain the ability to alleviate suffering and pursue stability for unprecedented numbers of people, humanity has also developed unprecedented means of destroying itself. If we want to account for all of reality, we must not ignore this. We need to know what is really real.

When people talk about the nature of reality, they're engaging in an area of study philosophers call **metaphysics**. In Greek, the word *metaphysics* means "beyond the natural things" (*meta* means "beyond"; *physics* means "natural things"). In grappling with what is ultimately real, people tend to ask five questions. We analyzed these questions in the first two books in this trilogy, but they're worth reviewing briefly here:

Metaphysics: the branch of philosophy that seeks to understand the nature of ultimate reality.

1. Origin. Where did we come from? Some say God created us to bear his image. Others say humans evolved through random-chance processes. And there are many more views as well. They can't all be right, but which are wrong?

2. Identity. Who are we? What is a human being? Does every human being have intrinsic worth and dignity, or are worth and dignity determined by external factors, skills, and attributes? And if there is something wrong with us, what is it and how do we fix it?

3. Meaning. What is real and true, and how do we know? What is life all about? Is there purpose to our lives, or must we contrive it somehow? Is reality real or an illusion? Why do humans not only exist but also wonder about why they exist?

4. Morality. How should we live? Are there rules for the good life? Who makes them? Are they true for all times and all cultures, or do they depend on our circumstances? Is morality based on feelings? Does morality change if our feelings change?

5. Destiny. What happens next? Where is history headed? Is there an afterlife? How do we explain what is wrong with the world—the poverty, injustice, pain, and sickness? Should we try to fix things or merely look forward to a life beyond this one?

These five questions are ultimate in the sense that everyone answers them, if not with their minds, then by the way they live. Their answers form their **worldview**.

Everyone answers these ultimate questions, if not with their minds, then by the way they live. Their answers form their worldview.

Even among those who believe the Bible, differing answers can lead to cultural conflict (the Reformation, for example). One such conflict took place in the twentieth century between varying groups of Christians based on specific theological understandings. It so shaped the way Christians today think about cultural engagement that it would be hard for us to answer the question about how Christians should be involved in society without first understanding what transpired.

6. THE CONTROVERSY: FUNDAMENTALISM VERSUS LIBERALISM

When Shane Claiborne walks onstage, the audience sees a skinny white guy with dreadlocks and a dry sense of humor and hears his message about separating from society. "Jesus taught that his followers … should not attempt to 'run the world,'" he says.[20] For Claiborne, Christians are citizens of heaven alone. We should have no allegiance to an earthly kingdom. The best we can do is form an alternative, a community that's attractive enough to make people want to join us.

In short, reform is hopeless. It's time to bail out.

Claiborne's approach may be new, but his message is not. More than one hundred years ago, a prominent evangelist named Dwight L. Moody explained his message as follows: "I look upon this world as a wrecked vessel. God has given me a life-boat, and said to me, 'Moody, save all you can.'"[21] The world is passing away, Moody thought, and nothing is of ultimate value except ensuring that people go to heaven when they die. As brilliant and innovative as Moody was, his view was certainly not the way the majority of Christians in history saw it. How did this kind of thinking come about?

At the turn of the twentieth century, there was widespread concern that American Protestantism was becoming liberal. America's greatest universities, founded largely as Christian institutions, were being run by people who denied doctrines such as the holiness of God, the divinity of Christ, and the truth of the Scriptures. Fanning these flames, a New York City pastor named Walter Rauschenbusch published *A Theology for the Social Gospel*, which defined *sin* as "selfishness" and implied that salvation would come by ushering in the kingdom of God through good works that changed society.[22]

> The world is passing away, Moody thought, and nothing is of ultimate value except ensuring that people go to heaven when they die.

Rauschenbusch openly identified himself as a socialist, which inevitably caused concern that he had rejected biblical orthodoxy and embraced Darwinian evolution and communism. The reaction was immediate and intense. If this new **social gospel** was in any way replacing the true gospel, there were a good many Christians who wanted to stay far away from it. It wasn't that they didn't care about the culture—many of them were politically active, such as social-reform-minded Democrats William Jennings Bryan, three-time candidate for president, and William Bell Riley, pastor of First Baptist Church, Minneapolis, and founder of what is now the University of Northwestern, where Billy Graham got his start.

Rather, many thought Rauschenbusch and others like him were offering a false form of salvation. In response, theology professors A. C. Dixon and R. A. Torrey decided to set forth what they saw as the basic principles of Christianity in a series of twelve volumes titled The Fundamentals: A Testimony to the Truth. A wealthy businessman named Lyman Stewart funded the series, and the Bible Institute of Los Angeles (B.I.O.L.A., now called Biola University) published it.[23] Well-known theologians of the time, including James Orr, B. B. Warfield, and C. I. Scofield, wrote featured essays, and copies were distributed free to pastors, missionaries, and Christian educators.

> *Social Gospel:* a late eighteenth-century, early nineteenth-century postmillennial movement popular among liberal Protestants that sought to eradicate social evils like poverty and racism in the belief that this would usher in the second coming of Christ.

Out of the publication of The Fundamentals rose a new movement, **fundamentalism**, which George Marsden defined as "militantly anti-modernist evangelicalism."[24] Fundamentalists strongly sensed a responsibility to bring maturity to the American theological landscape and also, in some senses, to be the "older brother" who helped American culture avoid self-destruction.

Unfortunately for its adherents, the fundamentalist movement unraveled as a consequence of relentless attacks in the culture, exhaustion, and infighting. The sense of fierce theological independence that gave fundamentalism its start made it difficult for its leaders to form a cohesive movement.[25] In the 1930s, the fundamentalist coalition, which had included Baptists, Presbyterians, and Congregationalists, began splintering along doctrinal lines. Many of the movement's leaders embraced a new doctrine called **dispensational premillennialism**, which argued that the end of all things was coming and that the anti-Christ would soon rise. One sign of this, they argued, was that churches would discard their doctrinal beliefs in pursuit of a misguided sort of unity, the Interchurch World Movement, often derisively called **ecumenism** by fundamentalists.[26] To dispensational premillennialists, there was only one reasonable response: leave such churches and "be separate from them" (2 Cor. 6:17).[27] Continued association was a sign of being secretly wed to liberal doctrines.[28]

> *Fundamentalism:* an early twentieth-century Protestant movement that sought to defend orthodox Christianity against the challenges of liberalism, modernism, and Darwinism by requiring strict adherence to a set of "fundamental" doctrines.

> *Dispensational Premillennialism:* an eschatological doctrine that establishes a sequence of events for the end times, asserting that the anti-Christ will soon rise, the second coming of Christ is imminent, and all things will culminate in a millennial reign of Christ.

These conflicts are still with us today. Churches are still forfeiting essential doctrines. Mockery of biblical doctrines is common. Many churches have become proxies of one political party or another or have endlessly divided themselves through increasingly fine doctrinal distinctions. Pastors are still openly living lifestyles that contradict biblical teachings about marital purity. Where do we go from here?

7. THE RISE OF CHRISTIAN CONSERVATISM

Out of the cultural conflict between liberalism and fundamentalism rose a new movement of Protestant Christians who claimed a born-again experience, believed the Bible is true, and were involved in like-minded churches. They called themselves the "new evangelicals." In the 1950s, Christian leaders who wanted to see orthodox Christianity more effectively engage the culture formed the National Association of Evangelicals, with Harold Ockenga as president. Joining the organization were Carl F. H. Henry and other evangelicals who held to conservative positions on the truth of Scripture and were strongly critical of liberal theology and **Secularism**.[29] This new

> *Ecumenism:* the push to foster unity among various Christian traditions that disagree on key doctrinal issues.

tradition became the largest religious movement in the United States, constituting up to 47 percent of the population in 2005 before decreasing to 25 percent by 2014.[30]

But then the 1960s happened. The Vietnam War. Drugs. The sexual revolution. Rebellion against authority. Though only a small percentage of the population actually participated in it, their numbers were large enough to shift American culture in a very different direction. This is especially true of the sexual revolution, which led to the 1973 Supreme Court decision *Roe v. Wade*, legalizing surgical abortion on demand.

> *Secularism:* an atheistic and materialistic worldview that advocates a public society free from the influence of religion.

Without a strong sense of what Christian cultural engagement involved, **evangelicalism** seemed incapable of responding to these trends. For example, the organization producing this book (Summit Ministries) took an immediate stand against the *Roe v. Wade* decision through the publication of David Noebel's book *Slaughter of the Innocent*. Yet other evangelical groups were neutral or even viewed abortion favorably, at least at first. Shortly after the *Roe v. Wade* decision, the Southern Baptist Convention's Baptist Press celebrated the decision for having "advanced the cause of religious liberty, human equality and justice."[31] Today the Southern Baptist Convention is strongly pro-life, as is the larger evangelical Christian community, but at the time, evangelicals struggled to figure out how to respond to cultural issues.

> *Evangelicalism:* a mid-twentieth-century Protestant movement that sees the essence of Christianity as the gospel: salvation comes by grace through faith in the saving work of Jesus Christ.

Then an evangelical ran for president. Not only was he a self-proclaimed born-again Christian, but he was also a Sunday school teacher in a Baptist church and an honored military veteran. His name was Jimmy Carter. In the wake of the Nixon Watergate scandal, the nation was craving a president whose honesty and decency seemed above reproach. Carter was elected handily.

Things immediately started going wrong. Carter's approach to economic issues seemed to make things worse, not better. Gas prices skyrocketed. Inflation was out of control. And the people he put in charge of social policy were quite liberal in their viewpoints. For example, the Carter administration formed the Department of Education, which immediately began taking steps that, for many evangelicals, threatened the freedom of parents to educate their children in Christian schools. All of these actions left America dispirited.

> *Moral Majority:* a late twentieth-century political and religious movement founded by Jerry Falwell to further Christian ideals through conservative politics—namely, promoting laws that restrict abortion on demand and protect religious expression in public education.

One Virginia pastor had had enough. He set about forming a network of patriotic, concerned Christians to respond to the drift away from Christianity that he perceived in America. The pastor's name was Jerry Falwell, and his organization was called the **Moral Majority**. Millions of people joined, and the effect was immediate. Falwell's organization and similar groups got behind the presidential candidacy of former California governor Ronald Reagan. Before an audience of fifteen thousand Christian leaders in Dallas, Texas, Reagan said, "I know this is a non-partisan gathering, and so I know that you can't endorse me, but I only brought that up because I want you to know that I endorse you and what you're doing."[32]

> To many people, Reagan was a hero who changed the course of history.

The overwhelming popularity of Ronald Reagan enabled conservatives to enact many parts of their agenda, primarily lowering the federal income-tax rate and strengthening foreign policy. The effect was dramatic: lower unemployment, lower inflation, and increased economic growth. To many people who remember that era, Reagan was a hero who changed the course of history.

8. THE END OF CHRISTIAN CONSERVATISM AS A MASS MOVEMENT

The influence of Christian conservatism continued through the turn of the century, even though it waned in the 1990s as it faced unrelenting criticism from cultural elites in both political parties and the media. Despite a vague sense that Christian conservatism had run its course, the movement largely succeeded in accomplishing many of its aims, which included obtaining restrictions to abortion on demand and establishing a system of Christian schools and colleges across the country, some of which became quite large, including Liberty University, which Jerry Falwell founded during the Moral Majority days. Groups like the Christian Action Council, cofounded by theologian Harold O. J. Brown and former US surgeon general C. Everett Koop, not only inspired the pro-life movement but also helped establish a network of crisis pregnancy centers that opposed abortion yet still offered counseling and practical support to women with unwanted pregnancies.[33]

> *Two-Kingdoms Theology:* based on an idea expressed by Martin Luther, two-kingdoms theology distinguishes between the kingdom of God (i.e., the church) and the kingdom of humanity (i.e., the state), contending that Christians should not promote their religious views outside the kingdom of God.

In the first decade of the twenty-first century, though, evangelicalism began to splinter for at least three reasons. First, there was a growing resistance to the way Christians were involved in the culture. Mostly, the movement was seen as too political. Separationists like Shane Claiborne held this view, as well as a small yet influential group of Presbyterian theologians who embraced what is known as the **two-kingdoms theology**. According to this view, Martin Luther's distinction between the kingdom of heaven and the kingdom of humanity actually represents the kingdom of the church and the kingdom of the world, and therefore the Bible's teachings are relevant only to the life of the church, not to civil government. Says Michael Horton, one of the two-kingdom theologians: "The central message of Christianity is not a worldview, a way of life, or a program for personal and societal change; it is a gospel."[34]

The second reason evangelicalism began to splinter has less to do with a well-thought-out theological position than with a loss of enchantment among those in the rising generation.

LifeWay researcher Ed Stetzer found in 2007 that of those who regularly attended youth group as teens, only about 30 percent regularly attended church as twentysomethings.[35] Saying they needed a break from church, young adults seemed to stop seeing the Christian faith as important to their everyday lives. Christian Smith, a sociologist at the University of Notre Dame, has suggested that most young people who claim to be Christian have very shallow roots. Their primary theological beliefs are that God loves them and wants them to be happy, a view he calls **moralistic therapeutic diesm**.[36] To this way of thinking, God is a kindly grandfather who gives us treats and chuckles at our naughty antics.

> *Moralistic Therapeutic Deism:* a term coined by sociologist Christian Smith in reference to the shallow beliefs of many young Christians in the twenty-first century; the belief that God loves everyone and wants them to be happy.

The third reason evangelicalism began coming apart is a rebranded reemergence of an old heresy called **gnosticism**. In this view, what we do in this world is really irrelevant because ultimate reality is not physical but spiritual. In the early days of the church, after Jesus's resurrection, gnostics went so far as to proclaim that Jesus didn't really appear in the flesh, because they saw the physical world as evil, and appearing in the flesh would have meant that Jesus participated in evil. Early church leaders condemned gnosticism as a radical and dangerous misunderstanding of the gospel. John the apostle stated very strongly that anyone who "does not confess [that] Jesus [came in the flesh] is not from God" (1 John 4:3). Still, in modern times, discouragement with the way things are going has led many people, including many Christians, to flirt with the idea that the physical world is unimportant.

> *Gnosticism:* a second-century heretical Christian movement that taught that the material world was created and maintained by a lesser divine being, that matter and the physical body are inherently evil, and that salvation can be obtained only through an esoteric knowledge of divine reality and the self-denial of physical pleasures.

Today, whether because of embarrassment at Christian political involvement, theological shallowness, or a rising sense that what we do in the physical world doesn't matter, evangelical Christianity in America is declining in both popularity and influence. In fact, in 2009 Michael Spencer predicted in a widely read *Christian Science Monitor* op-ed that evangelicalism would collapse within a decade.[37] Others, however, have taken issue with such a dire assessment, pointing out that while less committed believers seem to be moving away from orthodoxy, the number of committed evangelicals remains steady. Still, it's hard to see churches being converted into playhouses, libraries, skate parks, and nightclubs and not wonder whether Spencer's predictions are coming true.

In this book, our aim is not to "save" evangelical Christianity. Rather, we wish to see the difference it would make if we consistently applied a biblical worldview to today's perplexing issues. To do this, we'll need to explore a middle way between the secular idea that the physical world is all there is and that the spiritual world is irrelevant, and the gnostic idea that the physical world is irrelevant because only the spiritual world is ultimately real. The approach we'll test rests on the ideas that both the physical and the spiritual matter to God. As a spiritual being, God made creation and proclaimed it "good."

The gospel doesn't deny or trivialize any aspect of our fallen humanity but offers us full restoration. In other words, as the Colson Center's John Stonestreet observes, we're not saved from our humanness but to it.[38] The revered thirteenth-century theologian Thomas Aquinas put it this way: "Grace does not destroy nature, but completes it."[39]

At the outset, we readily admit that in addition to the opposition Christianity faces in the world, there are significant differences among Christians themselves. Such categories as "born-again" or "evangelical" or "fundamentalist," even though they are often used in a derogatory fashion, are not monolithic. They include people of all races and political persuasions, as well as a bewildering array of theological beliefs. Undoubtedly, the majority of evangelicals describe themselves as politically conservative, but even this category defies description when it comes to issues like the appropriate level of government intervention, taxes, the best way to care for the poor, foreign policy, and so forth.

> **Might there be a way to bring Christians together across long-drawn theological lines to focus on how to help everyone flourish in our culture without abandoning firm adherence to biblical truth?**

Today the question for many Christians is whether it is even possible to be actively concerned about what is happening in the world without resorting to blunt political force on the one hand or seemingly pious separation on the other. Is it possible for Christians to care about culture without implying that we are somehow responsible for bringing about God's kingdom on Earth? Might there be a way to bring Christians together across long-drawn theological lines to focus on how to help everyone flourish in our culture without abandoning firm adherence to biblical truth?

These are not easy questions. But the answer to each question is yes. Let's examine why.

9. What Are the Biblical Reasons for Caring?

As Christians, we want to care about what God cares about. From Scripture we can discern that God cares about his glory, that we bear his image, and that we love our neighbor as ourselves. He cares about a great deal more, of course, but from these three principles we can build a faithful biblical response to the most pressing issues of our age.

God Cares about His Glory

In the New Testament, the Greek word for "glory" is *doxa*, which means "good reputation" or "honor." Saint Augustine defined *glory* as "*clara notitia cum laude*," or "brilliant celebrity with praise."[40] God's glory is so immense that all of nature proclaims it. Psalm 19:1 says, "The heavens declare the glory of God, and the sky above proclaims his handiwork." In the world to come, God's glory will sustain us. Revelation 21:23 says of heaven, "The city has no need of sun or moon to shine on it, for the glory of God gives it light, and its lamp is the Lamb."

Sin has caused humans to fall short of God's glory (Rom. 3:23).[41] Even worse, in our sin, we attempt to exchange the glory of God for created images (Ps. 106:20; Rom. 1:23).[42] Because of God's grace, though, we may rejoice in the hope of the glory of God (Rom. 5:2),[43] and we can look forward to freedom from bondage to corruption (Rom. 8:21).[44]

Jesus Christ made this redemption possible. He is, according to Scripture, the glory of God. Hebrews 1:3 says, "He is the radiance of the glory of God and the exact imprint of his nature, and he upholds the universe by the word of his power."

It is in and for his glory that Jesus Christ calls us and equips us for great things. Second Peter 1:3 tells us that "[God's] divine power has granted to us all things that pertain to life and godliness, through the knowledge of him who called us to his own glory and excellence." This is why 1 Corinthians 10:31 says, "So, whether you eat or drink, or whatever you do, do all to the glory of God."

God Cares That We Bear His Image

In the very name God gave himself, YHWH (Gen. 2:4),[45] he shows himself to be the maker of covenants and the rescuer of his people. These are relational attributes, and it makes sense because God is a relational God. Right from Genesis 1:26–28[46] the Bible portrays God as a king who, instead of erecting statues of himself, as kings in the Near East were known to do, created image bearers—living, breathing humans to serve as stewards of his creation.[47]

Humanity has a special place in God's creation. In the biblical narrative, human beings are divinely created to bear the *imago Dei*, the well-known Latin term for "image of God." As opposed to pagan creation stories in which only the supreme ruler bears God's image, there is in Scripture a sense in which *all* human beings bear God's image.[48] And the very nature of God's plan for human beings was, according to the biblical text, "*very good*." In Hebrew, the phrase is **tob meod** (pronounced "tōve MAY-odd"), which refers to something so exceedingly, abundantly, and immeasurably good that happiness is the natural result.[49]

> *Tob Meod:* a Hebrew phrase translated as "very good"; the very best thing possible; the ultimate superlative of good.

Your *being*, who you are as an image bearer of God, precedes any action you may take. We call people human *beings*, not human *doings*, for a reason. That humans specially bear God's image and aren't mere playthings for the gods is the single biggest distinguishing characteristic between the Judeo-Christian conception of humanity and all others. According to this view, human beings are actually distinct and inherently valuable persons regardless of size, level of development, environment, or degree of dependency.[50] They have a definable *essence*.[51]

> That humans specially bear God's image and aren't mere playthings for the gods is the single biggest distinguishing characteristic between the Judeo-Christian conception of humanity and all others.

So what does this have to do with caring? It's simple. Each and every person bears God's image. If God cares enough about people to impart his image to them, how could we justify caring any less? Unfortunately, we humans often abuse the image of God by inviting others to worship *us* rather than the Creator. As Dave Kinnaman and Gabe Lyons write in *UnChristian*, this is a major problem for the rising generation:

By a wide margin, [according to a Pew survey,] the top life priorities of eighteen- to twenty-five-year-olds are wealth and personal fame. Objectives like helping people who are in need, being a leader in the community, or becoming more spiritual have much less traction among young Americans than they do among older adults.[52]

Luton First, sponsor of Britain's National Kids' Day, corroborated these findings in a survey that asked British schoolchildren under age ten, "What do you think is the very best thing in the world?" The number one reply was "Being a Celebrity," followed by "Good Looks" and "Being Rich." "God" was the tenth—and last—response on the list.[53]

> *Narcissism:* **the love of or obsession with oneself; selfishness; self-centeredness.**

The term for this obsessive self-focus is **narcissism**, which is derived from a Greek myth about a boy who fell in love with his own reflection. In their book *The Narcissism Epidemic*, Jean Twenge and Keith Campbell lay the blame at the feet of endlessly repeated mantras, such as "You are special," and ask whether this blatant promotion of self-love has the potential to become pandemic among young adults.[54]

Narcissism is a personal problem that morphs into a cultural problem that Twenge and Campbell say leads to vanity, materialism, uniqueness [that we are better than others], antisocial behavior, relationship troubles, entitlement, and self-centered religion and volunteering.[55] The last item on this list, religion and volunteering, should shake us up. Even good things become bad when the goal is boosting self-admiration.[56] When we fail to bear God's image, or bear it badly, even our good deeds can contribute to the overall level of evil. As Isaiah 64:6 states, "We have all become like one who is unclean, and all our righteous deeds are like a polluted garment. We all fade like a leaf, and our iniquities, like the wind, take us away."

> **When we fail to bear God's image, or bear it badly, even our good deeds can contribute to the overall level of evil.**

God Cares That We Love Our Neighbors

The first two things God cares about—his glory and his image—lead to the third thing he cares about: that we love our neighbors. Scripture says we're to love our neighbors *to the glory of God*. We read in Romans 15:7 that we should "welcome one another as Christ has welcomed you, for the glory of God." The word *welcome* in Greek is *proslambanō*, which implies inviting someone into the life of something. In other words, God is glorified when we personally care for those around us. Scripture reminds us that our ability to serve in this way comes only through God's power and only so that Christ may be glorified (1 Pet. 4:10–11).[57]

> **God is glorified when we personally care for those around us.**

That God is glorified when we care for those around us is no minor point in Scripture. In fact, it's a central feature of God's plan. In the Old Testament, Leviticus 19 is just one passage that speaks of how we should love our neighbors *because of who God is*:

When you reap the harvest of your land, you shall not reap your field right up to its edge, neither shall you gather the gleanings after your harvest. And you shall not strip your vineyard bare, neither shall you gather the fallen grapes of your vineyard. You shall leave them for the poor and for the sojourner: I am the LORD your God.

You shall not steal; you shall not deal falsely; you shall not lie to one another. You shall not swear by my name falsely, and so profane the name of your God: I am the LORD.

You shall not oppress your neighbor or rob him. The wages of a hired worker shall not remain with you all night until the morning. You shall not curse the deaf or put a stumbling block before the blind, but you shall fear your God: I am the LORD.

You shall do no injustice in court. You shall not be partial to the poor or defer to the great, but in righteousness shall you judge your neighbor. (vv. 9–15)

Notice the motivation God gave the people: *I am the Lord your God.* It's because God is glorious that the Israelites were to serve, and this service applied to everything from agriculture to business contracts to dealing with employees to poverty care to legal matters.

Loving our neighbors is the clear, unequivocal response to the reality that they are image bearers of God. In Matthew 22, Jesus was asked about the great commandment in the Law of Moses. He replied, "You shall love the Lord your God with all your heart and with all your soul and with all your mind. This is the great and first commandment. And a second is like it: You shall love your neighbor as yourself. On these two commandments depend all the Law and the Prophets" (vv. 37–40). Our love for God will be evident by how richly and fully we love our neighbors.

> **Our love for God will be evident by how richly and fully we love our neighbors.**

This is a whole Bible truth. The apostle Paul reiterated many key Old Testament commands and makes it clear that obedience to them is part of the way we are to proclaim the gospel. From our economic structures to our personal conduct, Scripture clearly ties everything we do back to glorifying God, bearing God's image, and loving our neighbors.

Consider, for example, Romans 13:

Owe no one anything, except to love each other, for the one who loves another has fulfilled the law. For the commandments, "You shall not commit adultery, You shall not murder, You shall not steal, You shall not covet," and any other commandment, are summed up in this word: "You shall love your neighbor as yourself." Love does no wrong to a neighbor; therefore love is the fulfilling of the law.

Besides this you know the time, that the hour has come for you to wake from sleep. For salvation is nearer to us now than when we first believed. The night is far gone; the day is at hand. So then let us cast off the works of darkness and put on the armor of light. Let us walk properly as in the daytime, not in orgies and drunkenness, not in sexual immorality and sensuality, not in quarreling and jealousy. But put on the Lord Jesus Christ, and make no provision for the flesh, to gratify its desires. (vv. 8–14)

If redeemed people don't care for others by loving them as neighbors, who will? The Christian writer C. S. Lewis believed that the humility of serving our neighbors is part of displaying God's glory: "The load, or weight, or burden of my neighbour's glory should be laid on my back, a load so heavy that only humility can carry it, and the backs of the proud will be broken."[58] Lewis went on to say that

> the dullest and most uninteresting person you can talk to may one day be a creature which, if you saw it now, you would be strongly tempted to worship, or else a horror and a corruption such as you now meet, if at all, only in a nightmare. All day long we are, in some degree, helping each other to one or the other of these destinations.... Next to the Blessed Sacrament itself, your neighbour is the holiest object presented to your senses.[59]

> *Shalom:* from the Hebrew for "peace, prosperity, and wellness"; a concept that implies harmony in creation and with one's neighbors as well as a right relationship with God.

Scripture repeatedly emphasizes the connection between our neighbors' well-being and our love for God through the concept of **shalom**—peace, wellness, prosperity, tranquillity, and contentment. At the very heart of *shalom* is neighborliness: We should wish *shalom* for others as well as ourselves. In fact, God told the Israelites in captivity that their *shalom* would be secured as they worked to secure *shalom* for those around them, even their captors (Jer. 29:7).[60]

But seeking the good of our neighbors, which is contrary to our sin nature, must involve repentance, redemption, and renewal. If it doesn't, the good we do may end up *looking* like caring even though it is actually narcissism. We may have the best of intentions but end up doing more harm than good.

10. How We Ought to Care

Biblical caring focuses on attributes that Scripture itself admonishes us to pursue. We'll look at three of these attributes: wisdom, worthiness, and words.

Godly Caring Is Based on Wisdom

Wisdom is central to the Scripture's vision of human flourishing. However, many people find it theologically baffling because wisdom seems to have more to do with what we might

> Wisdom is central to the Scripture's vision of human flourishing.

call *common grace*—the grace of God that is available to all people so that they might live well in God's creation—than with *saving grace*, the grace available to the redeemed. It's possible for a person to be wise in a particular area, such as developing an artistic ability, and foolish in rejecting God. Scripture's Wisdom Literature—Job, Psalms, Proverbs, Ecclesiastes, and the Song of Solomon—reveals four distinct meanings of wisdom:

- Skill in a craft; technical expertise (e.g., metal worker, skilled warriors, sailors, farmers, priests, scribes, judges, counselors)

- Intelligence; shrewdness, such as the academic wisdom of Solomon (1 Kings 4:29);[61] and the scheming or cunning of Pharaoh (Exod. 1:10)[62] or David (1 Kings 2:6, 9)[63]

- Good sense; moral understanding—the ability to apply knowledge prudently to life

- Understanding the fundamental issues of life—this top level recognizes that the essence of wisdom is theological ("the fear of the Lord")

In outlining how to live well, the Wisdom Literature is guided by four assumptions:

- The universe is ordered, and life proceeds according to a fixed order.

- This order is teachable and learnable.

- By learning the order in the universe, the individual is handed an instrument with which to determine and navigate his or her way through life.

- The source and foundation of the order in the universe is God himself.

We should, according to the book of Proverbs, pursue a life of wisdom even though it costs everything we have (Prov. 4:7).[64] Normally, wisdom's rewards are straightforward. We reap what we sow. If we develop the right character and make right decisions, we'll be successful. If we cultivate poor character and make poor decisions, on the other hand, our lives will be a disaster.

Yes, as we see in Job and Ecclesiastes, things don't always work out as expected. We're affected by the presence of evil, by our own limitations, and by the poor decisions others make. But the Bible still encourages us to live according to the principles of wisdom and encourage others to do so as well.

> **Normally, wisdom's rewards are straightforward. We reap what we sow.**

Godly Caring Is Based on Worthiness

Scripture focuses on what it means to live a worthy life. The apostle Paul tells us in Philippians 1:27, "Only let your manner of life be *worthy* of the gospel of Christ." He went on to say, "Finally, brothers, whatever is true, whatever is honorable, whatever is just, whatever is pure, whatever is lovely, whatever is commendable, if there is any excellence, if there is anything *worthy* of praise, think about these things" (4:8).

The word *worthy* in Greek is *axios*, which means "to be recognized as fitting." It's the root word of the English word *axis*, as in the axis on which the world turns.[65] A worthy life is based on such virtues as prudence, charity, hope, and faith, around which the world of humanity turns.[66]

The biblical approach to virtue is very different from the self-help psychologies that focus on *our* happiness, *our* health, and *our* spiritual awareness rather than on how we can live to glorify God by loving our neighbors.

From a biblical view, there is a relationship between an individual's mental outlook and his or her belief about God, Christ, salvation, and eternal life. When we focus on core virtues that are truly worthy, our souls, spirits, hearts, and minds grow. Self-centeredness, on the other hand, shrinks us.

> A virtuous person will literally lead out of the overflow of a worthy life.

Christians explain that a virtuous life is possible because God, through Christ, forgives our sins, heals our sinful human nature, and replaces our guilty consciences with the fruit of his Spirit. The fruit of the Spirit comes from the work of the Holy Spirit in our lives, and it is always outward focused. A virtuous person will literally lead out of the overflow of a worthy life.

Godly Caring Is Based on Words

Twenty miles into my first marathon, I hit a wall. With only 6.2 miles to go, I suddenly felt as if I might topple over. Along that last part of the route, however, volunteers stood cheering, holding signs, and offering words of encouragement. By the time I hit the home stretch, I was so energized that I sprinted to the finish. It might not have looked like I was running very fast, but I felt as if I were flying. The cheering of the crowd breathed life into me at just the right moment.

Words can bring life. Proverbs 18:21 says, "Death and life are in the power of the tongue, and those who love it will eat its fruits." Well-spoken words of encouragement enrich us. "A word fitly spoken is like apples of gold in a setting of silver," as Proverbs 25:11 observes. You can probably recall a specific time in which someone gave you a blessing, even if it was as simple as "Good job! Keep going!" Words can also bring death. I once conducted a study of grown-ups who related stories of teachers who'd had a bad influence on them. Stunningly, the people in my study—many of whom had been out of school for thirty or forty years—could remember *word for word* nasty things the bad teachers had said, words that in effect became a curse on their lives.

We owe it to our fellow citizens to speak the truth as we understand it. To not do so is to violate at least three scriptural principles:

1. "Do not withhold good from those to whom it is due, when it is in your power to do it" (Prov. 3:27).

2. "Rescue those who are being taken away to death; hold back those who are stumbling to the slaughter. If you say, 'Behold, we did not know this,' does not he who weighs the heart perceive it? Does not he who keeps watch over your soul know it, and will he not repay man according to his work?" (24:11–12).

3. "Open your mouth for the mute, for the rights of all who are destitute" (31:8).

As we speak the way God designed us to speak, we bear his image well. And when we do that, we can live with wisdom and show ourselves to be worthy in a way that blesses other people. It enables us to be like members of the ancient Israelite tribe of Issachar, who understood the times and knew what Israel ought to do (1 Chron. 12:32).[67] Because they had understanding and used words wisely, they were apparently seen as leaders in the nation.

Words are important to the gospel, which is a spoken message. The apostle John even called Jesus "the Word" (John 1:1).[68] And much attention is devoted throughout the New Testament to living and speaking in a way worthy of him. Ed Stetzer put a spin on an old adage attributed to Saint Francis of Assisi: "Preach the Gospel, and *since it's necessary*, use words."[69] As we live wisely, walk worthily, and speak words of life, we prepare the ground in which the seeds of the gospel can grow. Caring, then, is at the very heart of what it means to live the Christian life.

11. What You'll Learn in This Book

It's a daunting task to apply a biblical worldview to the issues of our culture. We'll almost certainly have our disagreements—both theological and political—along the way. But our task isn't to come up with point-by-point policy prescriptions for today's ills. It is to develop a method of applying our faith to the culture.

This said, here's a little overview of what we'll focus on in this volume:

> As we live wisely, walk worthily, and speak words of life, we prepare the ground in which the seeds of the gospel can grow.

- What culture is, how it's fashioned, and how Christians in the past have shaped culture.

- How to become a shaper of culture who thinks and speaks clearly and logically.

- What biblical principles look like when applied to tough issues, such as technology; the arts and entertainment; abortion; euthanasia; bioethics; sexuality (including pornography and same-sex attraction, marriage, politics, creation care, poverty care, tolerance, persecution, religious liberty, justice, the use of force, and community renewal).

Whew. That's quite a list. Along the way it may seem overwhelming. Even as I write I sometimes feel that there are too many issues with too many angles for me to effectively care about. That's why I'm trying to keep my eye firmly on the baseline of *shalom*, because, as we saw earlier, *shalom* means pursuing the peace, tranquillity, and prosperity of our communities. *Shalom* is the connection between the way we bear God's image and the way we care for our neighbors' well-being.

This doesn't mean that all of our neighbors will be grateful. It's very likely that Christians alive today—no matter where they are in the world—will be mocked, denied rights and freedoms, and even physically persecuted for their beliefs. "In the world you will have tribulation,"

Jesus said (John 16:33).[70] God calls us to stand for truth and fight against evil and injustice. Our central question is not "Could I be harmed by this belief or action?" but "How can I pursue *shalom* so people can live in prosperous harmony with one another in a way that glorifies God?" Even if we go to our graves feeling that all our efforts have been in vain, we aren't to worry, because we have this encouragement from Jesus: "Take heart; I have overcome the world" (John 16:33).

12. GIVERS, NOT TAKERS

As we saw at the beginning of this chapter, we humans base our lives on what we believe to be true. If we believe the Bible, we ought to find ourselves increasingly becoming givers, not takers. In my book *Handoff*, I told an old story of a man who visited a farmer friend. As the men sat on the porch rocking back and forth, two of the farmer's dogs got into a fight. Startled, the visitor asked, "Aren't you going to stop them?"

"Nah, they'll stop soon enough. They fight all the time."

"Which one wins?" asked the visitor.

"Whichever one I feed the most," the farmer replied.[71]

With every action, we either feed or starve the two competing sides of our nature, the giver side or the taker side. Those who feed the "taker" ultimately live miserable lives. They don't build anything of enduring value, they don't leave others better off, and they don't rescue the perishing. Those who cultivate the "giver," on the other hand, learn to build and deposit and grow. They gain favor with God and man. When difficulty chips away at them, it only reveals a deeper beauty. When it comes to facing difficult issues, takers wilt quickly and slink away; givers take on challenges willingly. Takers tolerate people; givers shape them. Takers grow needier; givers become more generous. Takers fill their houses with junk; givers fill their lives with memories.

> With every action, we either feed or starve the two competing sides of our nature, the giver side or the taker side. Takers grow needier; givers become more generous.

You and I develop into givers or takers through the endless choices we make every day. Of course, we can't solve every problem in the world or we'll get burned out. But the solution to burnout is not to back away; it is to engage biblically. Author Parker Palmer says that burnout "results from trying to give what I do not possess.… It does not result from giving all I have: it merely reveals the nothingness from which I was trying to give in the first place."[72] Only when we have a clear sense of who God is and what he thinks can we truly care about others.

> Only when we have a clear sense of who God is and what he thinks can we truly care about others.

So let's get to it. As C. S. Lewis said in his famous sermon "The Weight of Glory," "The cross comes before the crown and tomorrow is a Monday morning. A cleft has opened in the pitiless walls of the world, and we are invited to follow our great Captain inside."[73] Let's open the door and go on in, first by discussing what culture actually is, how it's created, and how Christians in the past have shaped it.

ENDNOTES

1. Thanks to Dennis Prager for this brilliant example from a debate—"Can We Be Good without God?"—with atheist professor Jonathan Glover at Oxford University, March 3, 1993. Prager asked, "If you, Professor Glover, were stranded at the midnight hour in a desolate Los Angeles street and if, as you stepped out of your car with fear and trembling, you were suddenly to hear the weight of pounding footsteps behind you, and you saw ten burly, young men who had just stepped out of a dwelling coming toward you, would it or would it not make a difference to you to know that they were coming from a Bible study?" Of this exchange, Ravi Zacharias said, "Amidst hilarious laughter in the auditorium, Glover conceded that it would make a difference." See Ravi Zacharias, *The Real Face of Atheism* (Grand Rapids: Baker Books, 2004), 135–36.

2. Jim Clifton, *The Coming Jobs War* (New York: Gallup Press, 2011), 46.

3. Johannes Gutenberg, quoted in Alphones de Lamartine, *Memoirs of Celebrated Characters*, 2nd ed. (London: Richard Bentley, 1854), 308.

4. Johannes Gutenberg, quoted in Lamartine, *Memoirs of Celebrated Characters*, 319–20.

5. Agnes H. Gottlieb and Henry Gottlieb, *1,000 Years, 1,000 People: Ranking the Men and Women Who Shaped the Millennium* (New York: Kodansha, 1998), 2.

6. Michio Kaku, "What Happens When Computers Stop Shrinking?," Salon.com, March 19, 2011, www.salon.com/2011/03/19/moores_law_ends_excerpt/.

7. "Fly with Us: Ready to Become an Astronaut?," Virgin Galactic, accessed July 2, 2016, www.virgingalactic.com/human-spaceflight/fly-with-us/; "The Virgin Galactic Space Experience," Galactic Experiences by DePrez, accessed July 2, 2016, www.galacticexperiencesbydeprez.com/experience.shtml.

8. Lauren James, "Stars Head for the Stars: Justin Bieber Joins the Virgin Galactic Party," Contactmusic.com, June 7, 2013, www.contactmusic.com/justin-bieber/news/justin-bieber-space-virgin_3708279; "Why We Go: Exploring Space Makes Life Better on Earth," Virgin Galactic, www.virgingalactic.com/why-we-go/.

9. "Welcome to Virgin Galactic," Virgin Galactic, accessed July 2, 2016, http://sites.virtuoso.com/virgingalactic/virgingalactic/documents/vg_overview.pdf.

10. "Human Spaceflight," Virgin Galactic, accessed July 2, 2016, www.virgingalactic.com/human-spaceflight/.

11. George Whitesides, quoted in Robert Lamb, "How High Will Virgin Galactic Fly?," DNews, August 2, 2010, http://news.discovery.com/space/how-high-will-virgin-galactic-fly.htm.

12. Jim Irwin, quoted in John Noble Wilford, "James B. Irwin, 61, Ex-Astronaut; Founded Religious Organization," *New York Times*, August 10, 1991, www.nytimes.com/1991/08/10/us/james-b-irwin-61-ex-astronaut-founded-religious-organization.html.

13. Edwin A. Burtt, *Types of Religious Philosophy* (New York: Harper and Brothers, 1939), 353. Clearly, the humanist has no patience with the anthropic principle, which contends that the world was tailored for human existence. For an excellent defense of this principle, see Roy Abraham Varghese, ed., *The Intellectuals Speak Out about God: A Handbook for the Christian Student in a Secular Society* (Washington, DC: Regnery, 1984).

14. Albert Einstein, *Ideas and Opinions*, ed. Cal Seelig, trans. Sonja Bargmann (New York: Three Rivers Press, 1982), 40.

15. Robert Jastrow, interview by Bill Durbin, in "A Scientist Caught between Two Faiths," *Christianity Today* 26, no. 13 (August 1982): 17.

16. Sylvia Nasar, *Grand Pursuit: The Story of Economic Genius* (New York: Simon and Schuster, 2011), xiii.

17. W. Cleon Skousen, *The Five Thousand Year Leap* (Franklin, TN: American Documents Publishing, 2009), 4.

18. Partha Dasgupta, *Economics: A Very Short Introduction* (Oxford, UK: Oxford University Press, 2007), 17. Growth in this sense is measured by the per-capita gross domestic product (GDP), which refers to the total of all goods and services produced, divided by the number of people, and adjusted for inflation.

19. Poverty statistics for 1990 and 2010, respectively. See World Bank Group, *Prosperity for All: Ending Extreme Poverty* (Washington, DC: World Bank, 2014), 1, http://siteresources.worldbank.org/INTPROSPECTS/Resources/334934-1327948020811/8401693-1397074077765/Prosperity_for_All_Final_2014.pdf.

20. Shane Claiborne and Chris Haw, *Jesus for President: Politics for Ordinary Radicals* (Grand Rapids: Zondervan, 2008), 167.

21. Richard S. Rhodes, ed., *Dwight Lyman Moody's Life Work and Gospel Sermons* (Chicago: Rhodes and McClure, 1907), xi.

22. Walter Rauschenbusch, *A Theology for the Social Gospel* (New York: Macmillan, 1917), 15, 97–99.

23. Paul W. Rood, "The Untold Story of *The Fundamentals*," *Biola Magazine* (Summer 2014), http://magazine.biola.edu/article/14-summer/the-untold-story-of-the-fundamentals/.

24. George M. Marsden, *Fundamentalism and American Culture: The Shaping of Twentieth-Century Evangelicalism, 1870–1925* (New York: Oxford University Press, 1980), 5.

25. Joel A. Carpenter, *Revive Us Again: The Reawakening of American Fundamentalism* (New York: Oxford University Press, 1997), 13–15.

26. Carpenter, *Revive Us Again*, 39–40.

27. Second Corinthians 6:17: "Therefore go out from their midst, and be separate from them, says the Lord, and touch no unclean thing; then I will welcome you."

28. The doctrine of separation from theological liberalism grew into what is called *secondary separation*, in which associating with people who associate with liberals is considered a sign of a person's liberalism. So if you have a friend who has a friend who is theologically liberal, you might be a liberal yourself.

29. Carpenter, *Revive Us Again*, 148–50, 199.

30. Gallup survey, 1991–2005, cited in Frank Newport and Joseph Carroll, "Another Look at Evangelicals in America Today," December 2, 2005, Gallup, www.gallup.com/poll/20242/Another-Look-Evangelicals-America-Today.aspx. According to the Pew "US Religious Landscape Study" conducted between 2007 and 2014, American evangelicals stand at 25.4 percent of the population. See Alan Cooperman et al., "America's Changing Religious Landscape," Pew Research Center, May 12, 2015, www.pewforum.org/2015/05/12/americas-changing-religious-landscape/.

31. Quoted in Tom Strode, "Roe, Legalizing Abortion in 1973, Caused Baptists to Embrace Life," Baptist Press, January 18, 2013, www.bpnews.net/39549.

32. Ronald Reagan, campaign speech transcript, "National Affairs Campaign Address on Religious Liberty," Dallas, Texas, August 22, 1980, http://americanrhetoric.com/speeches/ronaldreaganreligiousliberty.htm.

33. Some of the positive impact of theologians who embraced Christian conservatism may be seen in the obituary written of Harold O. J. Brown by John D. Woodbridge. See Woodbridge, "Harold O. J. Brown 1933–2007," *First Things*, July 10, 2007, www.firstthings.com/web-exclusives/2007/07/harold-oj-brown.

34. Michael Horton, *Christless Christianity: The Alternative Gospel of the American Church* (Grand Rapids: Baker Books, 2008), 105.

35. LifeWay Research, 2007, in Scott McConnell, "LifeWay Research Finds Reasons 18- to 22-Year-Olds Drop Out of Church," LifeWay, August 7, 2007, www.lifeway.com/Article/LifeWay-Research-finds-reasons-18-to-22-year-olds-drop-out-of-church.

36. Christian Smith, *Soul Searching: The Religious and Spiritual Lives of American Teenagers* (New York: Oxford University Press, 2005), chap. 4.

37. Michael Spencer, "The Coming Evangelical Collapse," *Christian Science Monitor*, March 10, 2009, www.csmonitor.com/Commentary/Opinion/2009/0310/p09s01-coop.html.

38. John Stonestreet, personal conversation with the author, August 21, 2013.

39. Thomas Aquinas, *St. Thomas Aquinas Philosophical Texts*, trans. Thomas Gilby (Oxford, UK: Oxford University Press, 1951; Whitefish, MT: Kessinger, 2003), 16.2.928.

40. *Catholic Encyclopedia*, s.v. "Glory," www.catholic.org/encyclopedia/view.php?id=5201.

41. Romans 3:23: "All have sinned and fall short of the glory of God."

42. Psalm 106:20: "They exchanged the glory of God for the image of an ox that eats grass"; Romans 1:23: "[They] exchanged the glory of the immortal God for images resembling mortal man and birds and animals and creeping things."

43. Romans 5:2: "Through [Christ] we have also obtained access by faith into this grace in which we stand, and we rejoice in hope of the glory of God."

44. Romans 8:21: "The creation itself will be set free from its bondage to corruption and obtain the freedom of the glory of the children of God."

45. Genesis 2:4: "These are the generations of the heavens and the earth when they were created, in the day that the LORD God made the earth and the heavens."

46. Genesis 1:26–28: "God said, 'Let us make man in our image, after our likeness. And let them have dominion over the fish of the sea and over the birds of the heavens and over the livestock and over all the earth and over every creeping thing that creeps on the earth.' So God created man in his own image, in the image of God he created him; male and female he created them. And God blessed them. And God said to them, 'Be fruitful and multiply and fill the earth and subdue it, and have dominion over the fish of the sea and over the birds of the heavens and over every living thing that moves on the earth.'"

47. While the plural reference in "let us" (Gen. 1:26; cf. 3:22; 11:7) is open to interpretation, polytheism is not an option. All the verbs in Genesis 1 with God as subject are singular in the Hebrew.

48. See Kenneth J. Turner's chapter, "Teaching Genesis 1 at a Christian College," in J. Daryl Charles, ed., *Reading Genesis 1–2: An Evangelical Conversation* (Peabody, MA: Hendrickson, 2013). Not all theistic religions teach that humans bear God's image. Islam, for example, does not. The Quran consistently refers to people as slaves of Allah. See, just as a starting point, surahs 2:23, 90, 186, 207; 3:15, 20, 30, 61, 79, 182; 4:172; 6:18, 88; 7:128, 194; 8:51; 9:104; 10:107; 14:11; and 15:49. The Arabic word is *abd*, which means "one who is totally subordinated." Badru Kateregga says, "The Christian witness, that man is created in the 'image and likeness of God,' is not the same as the Muslim witness." See Badru D. Kateregga and David W. Shenk, *Islam and Christianity: A Muslim and a Christian in Dialogue* (Nairobi: Uzima Press, 1980), 100, available on *The World of Islam: Resources for Understanding*, 2.0 (Global Mapping International, 2009), CD-ROM, 5350.

49. See "*meod*" (Strong's no. 3966, Hebrew), and "*tob*" (Strong's no. 2896a, Hebrew), in Robert L. Thomas, ed., *New American Standard Exhaustive Concordance of the Bible; Hebrew-Aramaic and Greek Dictionaries*, rev. ed. (Nashville: Holman Bible Publishers, 1981).

50. These four points—size, level of development, environment, and degree of dependency—form an acronym, SLED, which in turn forms an extremely strong argument against elective abortion. See Scott Klusendorf, "How to Defend Your Pro-Life View in 5 Minutes or Less," Life Training Institute, accessed July 4, 2016, http://prolifetraining.com/resources/five-minute-1/.

51. See chapter 12 of R. Scott Smith, *In Search of Moral Knowledge: Overcoming the Fact-Value Dichotomy* (Downers Grove, IL: IVP Academic, 2014), in which he reviews the sometimes complicated but deeply compelling arguments of the philosopher Edmund Husserl about how we can know reality because people and ideas have definable essences that present themselves in a consistent way that others can understand.

52. Andrew Kohut et al., *How Young People View Their Lives, Futures, and Politics: A Portrait of Generation Next* (Washington, DC: Pew Research Center, 2007), 12, cited in David Kinnaman and Gabe Lyons, *UnChristian: What a New Generation Really Thinks about Christianity … and Why It Matters* (Grand Rapids: Baker Books, 2007), 45.

53. Luton First, National Kids' Day survey, 2006, cited in "Being a Celebrity Is the 'Best Thing in the World,' Say Children," *Daily Mail*, December 18, 2006. www.dailymail.co.uk/news/article-423273/Being-celebrity-best-thing-world-say-children.html.

54. Jean M. Twenge and W. Keith Campbell, *The Narcissism Epidemic: Living in the Age of Entitlement* (New York: Atria Books, 2009), 16, 260.

55. Twenge and Campbell define each of the points in this list: (1) *Vanity*—"an obsession with appearance"; (2) *materialism*—"an insatiable desire to acquire possessions"; (3) *uniqueness*—"a strong desire to stand out, to be unique and different"; (4) *antisocial behavior*—"a belief that a person's needs take precedence, and a willingness to act aggressively to ensure that those needs are met"; (5) *relationship troubles*—"using relationships to look and feel powerful, special, admired, attractive, and important"; (6) *entitlement*—"a person's belief that he or she deserves special treatment"; and (7) *religion and volunteering*—"using church and community service as ways of boosting self-admiration." See Twenge and Campbell, *Narcissism Epidemic*.

56. See Peter Greer, *The Spiritual Danger of Doing Good* (Bloomington, MN: Bethany House, 2013), in which the author warns that service can lead to either burnout or pride, and risks the kind of Phariseeism that Jesus criticized so severely.

57. First Peter 4:10–11: "As each has received a gift, use it to serve one another …: whoever speaks, as one who speaks oracles of God; whoever serves, as one who serves by the strength that God supplies—in order that in everything God may be glorified through Jesus Christ."

58. C. S. Lewis, *The Weight of Glory: And Other Addresses* (New York: HarperOne, 1980), 45.

59. Lewis, *Weight of Glory*, 45–46.

60. Jeremiah 29:7: "Seek the welfare of the city where I have sent you into exile, and pray to the LORD on its behalf, for in its welfare you will find your welfare."

61. First Kings 4:29: "God gave Solomon wisdom and understanding beyond measure, and breadth of mind like the sand on the seashore."

62. Exodus 1:10: "Come, let us deal shrewdly with [the Israelites], lest they multiply, and, if war breaks out, they join our enemies and fight against us and escape from the land."

63. First Kings 2:6, 9: "Act therefore according to your wisdom, but do not let [Joab's] gray head go down to Sheol in peace.… Now therefore do not hold [Shimei] guiltless, for you are a wise man. You will know what you ought to do to him, and you shall bring his gray head down with blood to Sheol."

64. Proverbs 4:7: "The beginning of wisdom is this: Get wisdom, and whatever you get, get insight."

65. HELPS Word-studies, s.v. "*axios*," Helps Ministries, 2011, cited in Bible Hub, http://biblesuite.com/greek/516.htm.

66. Paul Vitz refers to secular authorities who now consider virtue a thing worth pursuing. He says, "Peterson and Seligman list six core virtues, and it is not hard to provide the familiar Christian [fruit of the Spirit—Gal. 5:22–23] or Greco-Roman names for them. Their explanation of wisdom and knowledge is very close to the traditional virtue of prudence; humanity is close to charity; courage, justice, and temperance have not changed their names; and their sixth core virtue, transcendence, is not far from hope and faith." Paul C. Vitz, "Psychology in Recovery," *First Things*, March 2005, 20, www.firstthings.com/article/2005/03/psychology-in-recovery.

67. First Chronicles 12:32: "[The men] of Issachar … had understanding of the times [and knew] what Israel ought to do, 200 chiefs, and all their kinsmen under their command."

68. John 1:1: "In the beginning was the Word, and the Word was with God, and the Word was God."

69. Ed Stetzer, "Preach the Gospel, and Since It's Necessary, Use Words," *The Exchange: A Blog by Ed Stetzer*, June 25, 2012, www.christianitytoday.com/edstetzer/2012/june/preach-gospel-and-since-its-necessary-use-words.html. Emphasis added.

70. John 16:33: "I have said these things to you, that in me you may have peace. In the world you will have tribulation. But take heart; I have overcome the world."

71. Jeff Myers, *Handoff: The Only Way to Win the Race of Life* (Dayton, TN: Legacy Worldwide, 2008), 29.

72. Parker Palmer, *Let Your Life Speak: Listening for the Voice of Vocation* (San Francisco: Jossey-Bass, 2000), 49.

73. Lewis, *Weight of Glory*, 45.

CHAPTER 2

2

WHAT IS CULTURE?

1. DOES CULTURE MATTER?

Culture happens when humans interact with the world. Everyone *participates* in culture. Some even help *create* it. In history, small groups of culture creators committed to a well-defined set of principles have exerted a very large influence in the lives of others, for better or for worse. "In the Christian

> Culture happens when humans interact with the world. Everyone *participates* in culture. Some even help *create* it.

view, then, human beings are, by divine intent and their very nature, world-makers," says sociologist James Davison Hunter.[1]

Ernest Gordon's *To End All Wars* is a moving example of how Christians can shape culture even amid unimaginable circumstances. Gordon was a prisoner in one of the cruelest places on Earth: a squalid and terrifying World War II Japanese prison camp called Chungkai.

Chungkai was filthy, disease ridden, and inhumane. Prisoners frequently died from starvation, disease, overwork, beatings, shootings, beheadings, or hopelessness. One man, Dusty, was mockingly hung on a tree to die like the Savior he professed. Deprived of their humanity, the prisoners adopted a beastly survival-of-the-fittest mind-set. Death meant nothing, and life meant little more. Gordon, a member of the elite Scottish Highlanders, described it this way: "Death called to us from every direction. It was in the air we breathed, the food we ate, the things we talked about. The rhythm of death obsessed us with its beat—a beat so regular, so pervasive, so inescapable that it made Chungkai a place of shadows in the dark valley."[2]

But two events, according to Gordon, changed everything. First, word spread of a prisoner who, in the name of Christ, offered his own food and stayed by the side of his bunkmate to nurse him back from the brink of death. His bunkmate survived, but he did not. In the second incident, a guard threatened to randomly execute the prisoners serving a work detail until someone confessed to stealing a missing shovel. A Christian stepped forward and confessed, saving the lives of the others. The enraged guard beat the man, crushing his skull. The others watched in horror, helpless to assist the man who had given his life for theirs. A later recount showed no shovels missing.

> **"Death called to us from every direction. It was in the air we breathed, the food we ate, the things we talked about."**

From a purely pragmatic viewpoint, these deaths were a foolish waste. But in the camp, they led to a new attitude of "You first" rather than "Me first." Christian volunteers changed gangrenous bandages and bathed hideous wounds. Life regained some of its meaning. Even the experience of death changed as prisoners stopped piling bodies, instead electing chaplains to conduct honorable funerals for the fallen.

Out of this restored humanity grew a stunning culture. The prisoners formed a library and taught courses in everything from math to philosophy to languages (nine of them). They staged plays. Having retrieved six violins from a vandalized relief shipment, they formed an orchestra and held concerts.

> **From a purely pragmatic viewpoint, these deaths were a foolish waste. But in the camp, they led to a new attitude of "You first" rather than "Me first."**

The overall camp conditions hadn't changed. Frightful diseases still claimed lives. Food was still scarce and nauseating. But the *culture* had changed. Sacrifice had brought meaning out of misery. Gordon wrote,

Death was still with us—no doubt about that. But we were slowly being freed from its destructive grip. We were seeing for ourselves the sharp contrast between the forces that made for life and those that made for death. Selfishness, hatred, envy, jealousy, greed, self-indulgence, laziness and pride were all anti-life. Love, heroism,

WHAT IS CULTURE?

self-sacrifice, sympathy, mercy, integrity and creative faith, on the other hand, were the essence of life, turning mere existence into living in its truest sense. These were the gifts of God to men.[3]

What Gordon described was culture. He and a handful of others refused to accept the environment that had been forced on them. Despite their horrifying conditions, they were able to shape something beautiful. Along the way, they transformed a place of hatred, cowardice, and greed into a place of love, heroism, and self-sacrifice.

A worldview that denies suffering, submits to fate, or coldly envisions a world of mere survival of the fittest is unable to explain a story like Gordon's. In fact, such a story would be incomprehensible if there weren't something so profoundly worth living for that even the fear of death could not conquer it. But the message of the Christian worldview is that something like this indeed exists. Whether in a remote outpost of the Roman Empire or a forgotten prisoner-of-war camp in Asia, the Christian worldview doesn't ignore culture or stand aloof from it. It transforms it.

While the assertion that Christianity can positively influence culture seems self-evident, it is the subject of great controversy. Some wonder whether Christianity should have anything to do with culture. Others are skeptical because so many culture-change efforts end badly. Still others wonder whether anyone can really change cultures to begin with, or should even try to. Maybe we should all just mind our own business.

> **The Christian worldview doesn't ignore culture or stand aloof from it. It transforms it.**

What Christians should do with culture is such a big question that it will take three chapters to answer it. In this chapter, we'll define *culture*. In the next chapter, we'll examine how Christians in other times and places have interacted with culture. Following that discussion, we'll spend a chapter outlining a plan by which we can engage culture faithfully, especially in relation to the difficult issues we face in our own time.

For readers who love to look "under the hood" to see what makes the engine of culture run, these three chapters will be an exciting, eye-opening journey. Some readers, though, will be impatient to get to the issues that form the bulk of this book. I understand the impatience, but if we don't understand what culture is and how it can be changed, we risk damaging the very societal tissue on which we presume to operate with a healing touch.

2. CAN WE CHANGE CULTURE, AND SHOULD WE EVEN TRY?

Nearly everyone agrees that we have problems in our society today. In fact, despite stunning advances in technology and medicine, most people think our culture has gotten worse, not better.[4]

The question isn't whether bad things are happening—they are—but what we should do in response. In one of my presentations, I suggested that Christians ought to try to engage culture. Afterward a pastor approached me to express disagreement. He was polite and respectful but still firmly insisted that Christians ought to *avoid* engaging with culture. Later in the day, he gave me a two-page list of Bible verses illustrating his point. Here's a sample:

- "My son, walk not thou in the way with them; refrain thy foot from their path" (Prov. 1:15).

- "Enter not into the path of the wicked, and go not in the way of evil men" (4:14).

- "Go from the presence of a foolish man, when thou perceivest not in him the lips of knowledge" (14:7).

- "Wherefore come out from among them, and be ye separate, saith the Lord" (2 Cor. 6:17).

His list contained all of the verses he could find that warn believers not to walk with unbelievers. Of course, the danger that this world will pull us toward idolatrous ideas and lead us to forfeit our faith is very real. Many people have lost their bearings because they were influenced by others who didn't share their convictions. The Old Testament king Solomon, who authored the Proverbs on this pastor's list, was one of them. He married many wives and began following their various religions (1 Kings 11). He began ruling as a very wise young man; he ended his life regretful and confused (see the book of Ecclesiastes). This pastor's point is well taken.

Yet it's a big mistake to assume that culture is always a bad thing we must avoid. As we saw in chapter 1, there are also many other biblical injunctions that call us to intentionally involve ourselves in culture. Indeed, God will hold to account those who see wrong taking place and do nothing about it (Prov. 24:11–12).[5] Even the apostle Paul, from whose Corinthian letter the pastor quoted ("Come out from among them, and be ye separate"), famously discussed and debated with nonbelievers in Athens, Greece (Acts 17:16–34). He even quoted from their own poets and philosophers. Paul knew their culture and, in fact, used it as a platform from which to preach the gospel.

> It's a big mistake to assume that culture is always a bad thing we must avoid. Indeed, God will hold to account those who see wrong taking place and do nothing about it.

The Old Testament is full of examples of culture shapers as well. Joseph became a leader in Egypt. Moses started the nation of Israel. Esther influenced the king and protected her people, the Jews. Daniel and his friends learned Babylon's literature and language and attained influence that they used for godly purposes.

Looking at the Bible as a whole gives a very strong impression that God wants us to engage the culture. Further, we need to engage culture for its long-term good rather than merely to fix problems in the short term. The prophet Jeremiah, speaking for God, told the Jewish captives in Babylon to stop hoping for a quick escape and instead to "seek the welfare of the city where I have sent you into exile" (Jer. 29:7).[6]

Let me illustrate with an odd example. Several years ago I lived in the countryside, where my wife and I were close friends with the family on the neighboring property. One day as I was leaving for work, the neighbor's dog shuffled up to me whimpering. Apparently he had tried to take a bite out of a porcupine and got a mouthful of quills for his effort.

No problem, I thought. *I'll just yank them out.* But hypersensitive to his own pain, the dog became distraught and tried to bite me. Not until he had received a sedative from the traveling veterinarian were we able to get him to relax enough so we could remove the quills. Soon the delicate procedure was complete, the dog finished his "nap," and everything returned to normal. Never again did the chastened hound bother any creature that looked remotely like a porcupine, including skunks (thankfully). From that day forward, he chased nothing but squirrels.

"Quill removal" is a common approach to culture. It stems from reacting more to the symptoms than the problems causing those symptoms. If we can extract a few irritating quills, we think, everything will be fine. For instance, some might say, "If we can just get excessive government out of our lives, then we'll live well." Others say, "If we can just crack down on crime, then we'll be able to flourish." Still others, however, identify exactly the opposite kind of quills: "If we can just get the government to remedy economic and racial injustice, we'll be free to live good lives." Lots of people have a quill or two or four they would like pulled from our culture. Some of these pet projects—forgive the pun—include reforming education, regulating behavior, cleaning up popular culture, employing technology more efficiently, fighting for justice, and protecting the environment. The list is almost endless.

But what if the attacks on culture are less like quills embedded in the skin and more like some sort of cancer flowing through the bloodstream? If so, taking a painkiller and dealing with surface wounds might, in spite of welcome temporary relief, cause us to miss the healing that's possible only by treating the source of the pain.

Just as easy as putting salve on surface wounds, perhaps even easier, is pretending that the something or someone "out there" is actually causing the problems we face. We can't expect nonbelievers to act like believers, but if God's revelation in the Bible is the source of truth, we ought to seek to influence culture by living out that truth as much as possible. This is for the good of others as well as for our own good.

> **If God's revelation in the Bible is the source of truth, we ought to seek to influence culture by living out that truth as much as possible.**

Here's why. Many worldviews, because they don't have a category for personal sin and guilt, see all problems as external, not internal. *If we could stop those few bad people "out there" from having their way*, they think, *our problems would be solved.* Protests calling for the overthrow of the wealthy are a good example. We don't have as much money as we want, they say, because the rich took it. The answer? Revolution. Express anger, and change will come. As the popular 1990s Canadian band Nickelback sang in an album they hoped would launch their comeback,

> *What do we want? We want the change.*
> *And how're we gonna get there? Revolution.*[7]

For those in pain, revolution seems to promise immediate relief. But culture change takes time. As culture commentator Andy Crouch phrases it, "The only thing you can do with Rome in a day is burn it."[8] Plus, if the problem lies within our own souls, lashing out through revolt won't make things turn out the way we want them to. What if, as the Christian

---

worldview teaches, the problem isn't only "them" but also "us"? Well, then, we're back to the cultural drawing board, aren't we?

Snarling at our problems won't change them. Nor will attacking them one by one. Instead, we need to become students of culture, understanding its elements and discerning its underpinnings so our solutions actually restore health rather than merely stave off the ravages of disease. Let's start by seeking to understand what culture is in the first place.

3. WHAT IS CULTURE ANYWAY?

> *Culture:* the way of life for a group of people; the culmination of human communication and willful activity in a particular civilization.

Business guru John Kotter knows a lot about shaping organizational cultures in the business world, and he knows it isn't easy. "Here is the problem," he says. "First, virtually no one clearly defines what they mean by 'culture,' and when they do they usually get it wrong. Second, virtually no one has read the original research that shows why culture—when clearly defined—is so important, how it is formed, and how it changes."[9]

This is true beyond the business world, in culture as a whole. We need to understand what **culture** is and how it's formed if we want to understand why we should change it—or how.

According to professor Kevin Vanhoozer, "Culture refers to everything that humans do voluntarily as opposed to involuntarily (e.g., by nature, reflex, or instinct)."[10] Andy Crouch's definition is even simpler. *Culture*, he says, "is what we make of the world."[11] The poet T. S. Eliot, in *Notes towards the Definition of Culture*, defined *culture* as "that which makes life worth living. And it is what justifies other peoples and other generations in saying, when they contemplate the remains and the influence of an extinct civilisation, that it was worth while for that civilisation to have existed."[12]

Cultures are complex things. As James Davison Hunter points out, culture is what gives us a sense of what we should or should not do. Cultures develop over a long period of time, and cultural ideas harden into institutions. These institutions give certain people status and power, which they use to keep things the way they are.[13]

Hoping for cultural change does not, in itself, change anything. Those who want change must have a deep knowledge of what culture is and how it got that way. In his landmark volume on the history of intellectual influence, sociologist Randall Collins says most of the large-scale cultural change that has taken place was the result of just a few dozen philosophers, artists, and religious leaders who operated in influential intellectual networks.[14]

> *Cultural Anthropologist:* one who studies the cultural details of society, such as social institutions, language, law, politics, religion, art, and technology.

Those who study culture are called **cultural anthropologists**. Often their work deals with minute aspects of distant cultures. But in a sense, we ought to all be cultural anthropologists so we can discern culture's power in our lives and find ways to breathe life into it, as Ernest Gordon and his fellow prisoners did at Chungkai prison camp.

Cultural anthropologists know that seemingly small elements of culture have the power to define what we think is normal. Here's an example of how a small decision in the economic realm helped create a large change in a whole culture. In the mid-1800s in England, it was important to have cheap sugar for tea. When Samuel Wilberforce, the bishop of Oxford, gave a speech in Parliament announcing that "cheap sugar means cheap slaves," people began considering the possibility that saving a few shillings on sugar was putting human lives at risk.[15] In a nation where believers had, a generation before, succeeded in abolishing the slave trade and slavery (largely through the efforts of Samuel Wilberforce's father, William Wilberforce), Wilberforce's words stripped away the excuses people made that led to misery on plantations far away. Wilberforce knew that what we *ignore* can influence culture just as much as what we attend to.

Also consider what happened during a six-and-a-half-minute segment at the 2013 MTV Video Music Awards, which *Rolling Stone* said changed pop culture forever.[16] In that short span of time, the once-innocent child actor and singer Miley Cyrus sang "We can't stop" while simulating sexual intercourse with another singer, Robin Thicke.

> What we *ignore* can influence culture just as much as what we attend to.

In previous times the performance might have surprised those in the audience and merited nothing but a black-and-white photo in newspapers. Through the television broadcast and replays on YouTube, though, millions of people read news reports about the event and viewed the performance itself. A line had been crossed, much to the delight of the narcissistic, young performer.

Two months after Cyrus's performance, Queen Latifah presided over the first-ever televised same-sex, mass wedding during the Grammy Awards, accompanied by Macklemore's award-winning rap ballad "Same Love." By the standards of what has constituted marriage for the past two thousand years, this should have been viewed as far more shocking than Cyrus's vulgarity. But because it was carried out tastefully—with fully clothed performers and no indecent gestures—the cultural commentators who had a fit about Cyrus's performance were nearly mute about Latifah's.

Latifah officiated the first televised same-sex mass wedding, and America yawned. As John Stonestreet and Sean McDowell later noted in reference to this incident, "In terms of cultural significance, silence either signifies irrelevance or complete victory. This silence was deafening."[17] It was no big deal. These two performances may, looking back, seem like trivial cultural moments. Because technology enabled people all over the world to view them, though, they redefined what we think of as normal and caused people to believe in—and even celebrate—something that just a few years ago would have been unthinkable.

> Latifah officiated the first televised same-sex mass wedding, and America yawned.

How do cultural acts like these gain such power? After all, viewers could have seen Cyrus and Latifah as pathetically shallow people desperate for attention. They could have just shrugged and changed the channel. But that's not what happened. And once we understand something about the nature of human community and the elements that make up culture, we may understand why.

4. WHERE DOES CULTURE COME FROM?

Humans create culture. As far as we can tell, this isn't true with any other creatures. Lots of animals communicate. They have social organization. Some have advanced language. Prairie dogs, for instance, use different kinds of chirps to describe various predators, such as hawks or coyotes. This language is so advanced, says Con Slobodchikoff, who has studied prairie-dog language for thirty years, that in one-tenth of a second, prairie dogs can use vocal calls to say something as specific as, "Tall thin human wearing blue shirt walking slowly across the colony."[18]

> **Only human beings use the spoken word to permanently alter their surroundings for their own benefit. The spoken word creates culture.**

For humans, though, speech is the most significant way we communicate. As Walter Ong said, "Man communicates with his whole body, and yet the word is his primary medium. Communication, like knowledge, flowers in speech."[19] Other creatures communicate through vocalizations, posture, and even blushing. Humans do this too. But only human beings use the spoken word to permanently alter their surroundings for their own benefit. The spoken word creates culture.[20]

The use of spoken language is universal among human communities. One of the early cultural anthropologists focusing on spoken language, Edward Sapir, wrote in 1921,

> There is no more striking general fact about language than its universality. One may argue as to whether a particular tribe engages in activities that are worthy of the name of religion or of art, but we know of no people that is not possessed of a fully developed language. The lowliest South African Bushman speaks in the forms of a rich symbolic system that is in essence perfectly comparable to the speech of the cultivated Frenchman.[21]

Human beings use spoken language to link themselves to the surrounding environment, to regulate their behavior in community, and even to develop higher mental processes.[22]

Human use of spoken language is different from other animals not only on the level of what our mouth-and-tongue structure make possible but also on the level of the purpose to which it is put. Animal communication can be quite advanced, but it always seems to be on the level of *signs*. A sign is a stimulus (a unit of sensory input that rouses the organism to action) announcing that which it is a part of. Thunder, for example, is a sign of an advancing storm. Spoken language does make use of signs, of course, but it primarily revolves around *symbols*. A symbol is a stimulus as well, but the relationship with the thing to which it refers is not as clear as the relationship between thunder and a storm. Rather, it is based on the agreement of human users. For example, a nation's flag symbolizes not only what its government does but all that its culture represents to those who participate in it.

When as few as two of us begin to use spoken language to communicate, we develop ways of understanding the world that make sense to us, that organize our perceptions of the world, and that allow us to change our environment based on the agreements we've made. Over time, even the natural things in our environment become symbols to us. Mountains symbolize majesty. A burbling brook symbolizes peace. An elk with a full set of antlers symbolizes strength. These things may have little symbolic meaning in and of themselves, but when we conceive of them in a certain way, it changes the way we think and communicate. Mountains don't just change what we think of as majestic; our developing sense of majesty changes how we see mountains.

For several decades Ken Myers has read widely and thought deeply about cultural change. Starting out as a reporter and producer for public radio, Myers developed a highly regarded audio magazine called the *Mars Hill Audio Journal*, in which he interviews authors and thinkers who discuss everything from science to literature to theology, all in the service of coaxing Christians below life's surface into the fascinating and dramatic world of ideas. The *Mars Hill Audio Journal* has become a cultural phenomenon in and of itself. Its subscribers might number only in the thousands, as opposed to the millions who view television, read magazines, or pick up newspapers, but those thousands are some of the most influential Christian thought leaders in the world.

Mars Hill Audio Journal subscribers trust Myers's insights about culture. These insights are possible, Myers says, because he pays attention to six aspects of culture rather than just the one or two most other people consider.[23]

> When we use spoken language to communicate, we develop ways of understanding the world that make sense to us, that organize our perceptions of the world, and that allow us to change our environment based on the agreements we've made.

1. Artifacts. An **artifact** is an object made by a human being. Artifacts include material things such as cars and buildings but also less tangible yet very real things such as literary forms and styles of design. Artifacts may seem like mere "things," but as we interact with them, our habits change. Digital technology, for example, is an artifact common all over the world. It has changed the way we communicate. Social media websites, email, and texting have also changed the nature of manners. It is now considered normal, for example, to look at our phones when we receive a text message, even if doing so interrupts an important conversation. Text messaging has literally changed the conventions of how we converse with one another.

> *Artifact:* any man-made thing, both tangible (e.g., works of art and technology) and intangible (e.g., literary forms and philosophical concepts).

But other artifacts have had an even more enduring impact. In chapter 1, we talked about Gutenberg's invention of a printing press with movable type. Who could have predicted how much this would change the world? Certainly not the kings and queens and religious leaders whose authority was eventually challenged by the books Gutenberg and others printed. More people learned to read. More books became available. Previously squelched thoughts spread like wildfire. The "official" version of events was challenged, and no one could stop it.

> Artifacts may seem like mere "things," but as we interact with them, our habits change.

On the surface, life in literate households seemed to change very little. Below the surface, though, everything had changed. A house where the works of Martin Luther were read may have looked like all the other houses in the neighborhood, but what its occupants read changed what they believed, how they spent their time, whom they associated with, and what they talked about. They regarded the Catholic Church no longer as the repository of all truth but, in fact, as an institution that must be opposed. In a very real way, the artifact of the printing press made the Reformation possible.

2. Institutions. The sorts of institutions we develop as human communities end up organizing their own sorts of behaviors. Consider the *New York Times*, a newspaper with a daily circulation of around a million readers. That's a lot of subscribers, but compared to all of the other newspapers available and the billions of people living on the planet, it isn't really that vast. And yet the *New York Times* is considered to be the "newspaper of record" in the industry. It has become an **institution**. If an event isn't reported in the *Times*, the decision makers in politics, culture, and business don't view it as relevant. Hundreds of millions of people pay attention to the decision makers of the world who read this particular newspaper. This is the true influence of the *Times*. Over the years certain institutions develop symbolic significance that makes the actions of those institutions seem more important.[24]

> *Institution:* any organization of cultural significance that preserves or promotes cultural features (e.g., schools, sports leagues, and country clubs).

The category of institutions also includes churches (and the various doctrines and movements that go along with them), schools (including the associated knowledge, their history, and their sports traditions), sports leagues, governmental agencies, country clubs, social organizations, and neighborhood associations that we join, cheer for, and support, and that set the rules and establish expectations. In America, the National Football League (NFL) is an important institution governing culture. During football season, millions of people schedule their week around the games featuring their favored teams. Advertisers make it possible to broadcast the games at no charge and in turn use the time allotted to shape the tastes, perceptions, and buying habits of the audience.

At a deeper level, people use analogies from football to structure the way they think about everything else, including the way they do business. In America, throwing a "hail Mary" pass becomes a way to describe taking a great risk in the hopes of gaining a potentially large reward. In cultures without exposure to American football, or without any sense of what the Ave Maria (the Hail Mary prayer) is in the Catholic Church, such an analogy makes no sense at all.

The institutions we embrace determine what kinds of people we accept as heroes; what sort of trash talk we tolerate; what kinds of products we view as cool; how we understand competition; how we relate to coworkers, friends, and family; what sorts of clothing we buy; what constitutes masculinity or femininity; what kinds of foods we eat; what we see as the rules of combat; and so much more. If we take this and multiply it by the hundreds of thousands of institutions in America alone, we can see that the institutions of society have a far-reaching effect on how we understand culture.

3. Practices. The third aspect of culture Myers emphasizes is common **practices**, such as celebrating holidays; attending weddings, funerals, and awards shows; going on vacations; and voting in elections. I once traveled to a predominantly Catholic country during the observance of All Saints' Day. Coming from a nation with a lot of Catholics but where Catholicism is far from dominant, I was stunned to see the entire nation's system of commerce shut down—restaurants, offices, taxis, everything. The only people working, with few exceptions, were the non-Catholics. Christmas Day is similar in the United States. Every culture has traditional observances that express what is important to people.

> *Practice:* any traditional activity or observance by which people express the value of certain cultural features (e.g., holidays, weddings, and funerals).

For example, what we think is proper in forming family relationships shows up in how we conduct weddings. Funerals display how we view death. High school dances and socials shape how we view courting rituals and the transition from adolescence into adulthood. Birthday parties reinforce the emphasis we put on individuals as opposed to the community. We might not even think twice about the practices we engage in, but they, too, affect culture at a deep level.

4. Beliefs. The deeply held **beliefs** of a group of people—about things like the value of human life, heaven and hell, what makes a person a hero, how family members should relate to one another, how we should behave at school or work or church, and what makes something right or wrong—affect how a culture develops.

> *Belief:* any idea that a person or group holds as a common understanding or conviction.

Some friends of mine were on a flight with a group of teachers visiting from another country who were experiencing their first trip to the United States. The flight attendant announced that several members of the military were on board and asked the passengers to thank them for their service. Everyone clapped heartily.

The non-Americans looked quizzically at my friends. "Why are they doing this?" they asked.

"Because members of the military are heroes," my friends replied.

Their guests found this stunning. In their country, members of the military are often brutal individuals who coerce others and force them to pay bribes. The flight attendant might as well have said, "We have lots of mean bullies on the flight today. Let's show them our appreciation."

It took quite a while for these guests to regain a positive view of America. This, in turn, must have been baffling for their American hosts, who clearly appreciated the sacrifices members of the military make. Beliefs usually come to the surface only when we interact with people who have different ones. Yet they deeply affect our culture.

5. Moods, styles, "ethos." To use another American example, there are big differences between the cosmopolitan, fast-paced style of living in large cities, such as New York, Chicago, and Los Angeles, and the more measured pace of middle America. Those living in the western part of the country are thought to value rugged individualism, while city dwellers tend to accept limits to their freedom as the price of the good life. We often talk of "red state" versus "blue state," with red states tending to elect a higher percentage of conservative politicians, and blue states tending to elect a higher percentage of liberal ones. But even these differences tend to be urban versus rural. Regional differences, such as Texas swagger, Yankee ingenuity, Hawaii surfer attitude, Kansas common sense, and North Carolina gentility, are all examples of cultural moods.

> *Ethos:* from the Greek word for "character," *ethos* refers to the moods or styles of a particular group of people that form cultural distinctives.

Ethos is a Greek word referring to what we think of as good—certain moods and styles that form our cultural distinctives. *Ethos* is hard to pin down, but it's real. A bumper sticker that says "American by birth, Southern by the grace of God" will elicit a smile and nod in Alabama but probably a smirk or frown in Rhode Island. Even the code of honor differs from northern to southern states.

In one study, male students were instructed to fill out a questionnaire. They also provided saliva samples and were told that their blood-sugar levels would be monitored throughout the experiment. In reality, researchers planned to monitor the students' cortisol and testosterone levels before and after the experiment to gauge their reactions.

After the students completed their questionnaires, they walked down a hallway to turn them in. But one of the researchers deliberately bumped into them on the way and uttered a rude remark. Following the incident, the participants provided another saliva sample. Young men from a southern culture were significantly more likely to have elevated cortisol and testosterone levels, indicating that they viewed the rude remark as an insult to their honor and were instinctively preparing to fight. Young men from a northern culture, on the other hand, dismissed the insult as an indication that the other person was a jerk, and little more.[25]

How did this significant difference in response to an insult come about? Through parental training? School? It's hard to say. Likely, these young men picked up a sense of how they should respond to acts of aggression from the attitudes, remarks, and habits of those around them. They didn't even realize they were doing it. Moods, styles, and "ethos" are deeply embedded aspects of culture.

6. Metabeliefs. Myers's sixth aspect of culture refers to the intuitive sense—or "gut instinct"—of what life is about. Metabeliefs display a posture toward creation. For instance, people's sense of why we're here and how we ought to act toward other people and creation forms a highly significant aspect of culture. Once, on a wild van ride through the streets of Manila in the Philippines, I noticed that drivers didn't seem to mind if another vehicle cut directly in front of them.

> People can live their entire lives without considering what their metabeliefs are or how they were formed, but such beliefs affect their actions every day.

"In America," I observed, "that would have gotten a very angry response and perhaps a certain hand gesture." My driver shrugged and replied that in the Philippines, a crowded country, you have a right to the space you occupy and nothing more. Americans, on the other hand, tend to believe they have a right to where they currently are *as well as where they are going*. If you step in their way or cut in line or move in front of them in traffic, they'll be angry.

This sense of a "right" is a **metabelief**—a belief about which beliefs are worth having and how we ought to act in certain situations. People can live their entire lives without considering what their metabeliefs are or how they were formed, but such beliefs affect their actions every day.

These six aspects of culture sensitize us to how cultures actually operate. That's important. As cultural anthropologists, we need to understand the way subtle experiences affect the way we live and interact with others.

> *Metabelief*: the intuitive sense of being, purpose, and posture toward other people and creation.

These six aspects reveal why Miley Cyrus's and Queen Latifah's performances were so powerful as culture shapers. They were *artifacts* in programs that have become *institutions* in and of themselves. These performances spread rapidly through both traditional and non-traditional media, introducing new *practices* that celebrated *beliefs* supported by a cultural *mood* of wanting to be edgy and cool and proposing a new *metabelief* for followers of pop culture to consider: tastefulness is everything. Cyrus's performance was tasteless and therefore bad; Latifah's was tastefully done and therefore good, regardless of the values either artist promoted.

Some will take issue with this particular example. But we can all agree that culture-shaping events are taking place around us every day. We would probably also admit that we rarely contemplate their effects. Think about what we're encouraged to pay attention to when we watch television or go to the movies. When future generations judge whether it was worthwhile for our civilization to have existed, is this the evidence we want them to consider? Obviously there are things in every society to be proud of, but if we look at it objectively, there is much to be ashamed of as well. The measure of a trivial culture is not only that its people don't care but also that they don't care that they don't care.

It takes a great deal of discernment to evaluate what is happening in the culture and how it ought to be viewed from a Christian worldview. Christians are always wondering how to respond to the culture around them. Should they condemn it? Should they admonish those who produce it? Should they, perhaps, just ignore it? As it turns out, these are questions Christians have been wrestling with for more than two thousand years.

> It takes a great deal of discernment to evaluate what is happening in the culture and how it ought to be viewed from a Christian worldview.

5. What Should Christians Do about Culture?

In 1949, a theologian named H. Richard Niebuhr delivered a series of lectures on Christian-cultural engagement for the Alumni Foundation at Austin Presbyterian Theological Seminary. In 1951, Niebuhr turned his lectures into an influential book called *Christ and Culture*.[26] Some people like the book; others don't. Those who like it think it helpfully describes how Christians have engaged with culture through the centuries. Those who dislike it say Niebuhr's framework is too simplistic. But if we don't go too far with it, Niebuhr's description of five Christian approaches to culture can help us see where Christians have agreed and disagreed about culture in the past, and how we might be able to transform culture even though we may be in exile, as the Jews were when the prophet Jeremiah instructed them to settle in and become a blessing to their captors (Jer. 29:4–7).[27]

With these caveats in mind, let's take a look at Niebuhr's description of five distinct approaches to culture that Christians have taken throughout the centuries.

1. Christ *against* culture. The first approach Niebuhr discussed is based on 1 John 2:15–17,[28] which instructs Christians not to love the world, emphasizing that the love of the Father is not in those who love the world and that the world will pass away. Those who hold the Christ-against-culture view, according to Niebuhr, believe the world "is the region of darkness, into which the citizens of the kingdom of light must not enter; it is characterized by the prevalence in it of lies, hatred, and murder.… It is a culture that is concerned with temporal and passing values, whereas Christ has words of eternal life."[29]

Historically, the Christ-against-culture approach originated with the church father Tertullian, for whom, according to Niebuhr, "avoidance of sin and fearsome preparation for the coming day of judgment seem[ed] more important than thankful acceptance of God's grace in the gift of his Son."[30] Today the Christ-against-culture view is common among groups with a Mennonite, Amish, or Quaker tradition.

> Those who hold the Christ-against-culture view believe the world "is the region of darkness, into which the citizens of the kingdom of light must not enter."

As with most of the other Christian approaches to culture, the Christ-against-culture view is an important restraint against the worship of the state and worldly power. People holding this view have played an important role in opposing corrupt institutions, such as chattel slavery, and forming new institutions that have challenged the authority of the old ones. And yet these groups didn't achieve cultural reform on their own. They formed the first line of resistance, Niebuhr pointed out, but others who didn't hesitate to get involved were the ones who brought about the actual change.[31] After all, people who have withdrawn from culture have a hard time understanding their neighbors, and it's hard to love a neighbor you don't understand.

A modern version of Christ against culture, the "**Benedict Option**," is gaining traction among Christians discouraged with the direction of culture. In the AD 400s, Saint Benedict's parents sent him to Rome to complete his education. Shocked by the city's decadence, Benedict fled into the wilderness to form an alternative community. Ultimately, Rome collapsed, but these Benedictine communities survived and preserved culture. Journalist Rod Dreher says,

> *Benedict Option:* the belief that Christians should remove themselves from culture and establish alternative communities to separate themselves from the sinfulness of human culture.

Rome's collapse meant staggering loss. People forgot how to read, how to farm, how to govern themselves, how to build houses, how to trade, and even what it had once meant to be a human being. Behind monastery walls, though, in their chapels, scriptoriums,

WHAT IS CULTURE?

and refectories, Benedict's monks built lives of peace, order, and learning and spread their network throughout Western Europe.[32]

According to Dreher, the Benedictine monasteries were the bases from which European civilization once again emerged. He points to similar communities today, such as Clear Creek Abbey in Oklahoma, a center for Benedictine thought centered around a monastery, and Eagle River, Alaska, an orthodox community formed around a church. Other examples include the Simple Way community in Philadelphia and the Homestead Heritage community near Waco, Texas.

2. Christ *of* culture. The Christ-of-culture view tends to hail Jesus as the Messiah of a particular culture. People who see America as God's chosen people, a "new Israel," for example, would fit this view. So would others in history like John Locke, Immanuel Kant, and Thomas Jefferson, who tried to show that the life of reason forms a uniquely good culture on which Jesus would certainly put his stamp of approval.[33] In the twentieth century, president Woodrow Wilson represented a progressive view of the Christ-of-culture perspective in promoting America as a nation that, because of its enlightened and advanced state, ought to serve the world by helping other nations become like it was. Said Wilson, it is the American duty to "stand shoulder to shoulder to lift the burdens of mankind in the future and show the paths of freedom to all the world."[34]

> The Christ-of-culture view tends to hail Jesus as the Messiah of a particular culture.

Richard Niebuhr stated that the church father who most aligned with this view was Peter Abélard (1079–1142), a scholar who thought that the tension between the church and the world was really due to "the church's misunderstanding of Christ" as somehow opposed to the life of reason.[35]

Many societies have formed around the thought that their unique cultural expression was an especially Christian one. Such groups as the Dutch Reformed and the Scottish Presbyterians comingled their ethnic identity with their religious one; the truly good person, it was thought, would represent both. Others who embrace the Christ-of-culture view, though, aren't as concerned about a specific cultural tradition as they are about removing Christianity's rough edges and seemingly harsher claims. They want people to think of Christians as those who represent the uplifting morality and love of Jesus, not those who embrace biblical claims or commands.[36] Christianity embodies that which is nice and reasonable, they believe. Let's not get too much into the details.

On the good side, the Christ-of-culture view is usually focused on maintaining a good culture and is well meaning in its desire to identify Jesus with what people in a society believe to be "their finest ideals, their noblest institutions, and their best philosophy."[37] There is a downside, however. Many bad things have been done based on the assumption that our culture is uniquely blessed of God and therefore should be spread

> On the good side, the Christ-of-culture view is usually focused on maintaining a good culture. But many bad things have been done based on the assumption that our culture is uniquely blessed of God.

abroad. Examples in history are numerous, such as the belief among European nations that they were exercising kindness by taking over developing nations and imposing their values on them, often with uncalled-for harshness. In nations like South Africa, this resulted in the policy of apartheid, which officially diminished the value of nonwhites and led to a racially oppressive society.

3. Christ *above* culture. The Christ-above-culture view proposes that, as Richard Niebuhr phrased it, "the fundamental issue does not lie between Christ and the world, important as that issue is, but between God and man."[38] In a world of sin, what does God require? He requires that believers obey him in all their actions, relationships, and work. The focus is on one's personal relationship with God. The culture is chock-full of sin, and the goal is not to change it but to point people to God.

> The goal of the Christ-above-culture view is not to change the culture but to point people to God.

Historically, the church father whom Niebuhr identified most closely with the Christ-above-culture view was Clement of Alexandria, who set forth the view in his book *The Instructor* that the goal of Christianity was primarily to improve the souls of people so that they could live more virtuous lives.[39] Personally, I encountered this view while attending graduate school at a traditionally Baptist university. Not being too familiar with Baptist theology, I found my professors' personal self-control and temperance admirable, but their lack of interest in applying the Bible to their courses was perplexing. To them, mixing Christianity and scholarship would pollute Christianity. The two didn't mix. While Baptist beliefs vary widely, the Baptist view to which I was exposed thought it untoward to bring Christ into the educational process except when it came to encouraging students to live personally pious lives.

On the good side, the Christ-above-culture view keeps one's focus on the many paradoxes of Christianity in the world, such as believers being *in* the world but not *of* the world, God being both immanent and transcendent, and Christians living in the temporal world while realizing that it's not our eternal home. In the same way as two halves of a pitched roof lean on each other and, through tension, create strength, the Christ-above-culture view enables Christians to cooperate with nonbelievers in making a good society while not losing their faith's distinctiveness.

The downside is significant, though. What happens if relying on nonbelievers to make a good society actually results in a society that is *against* Christ? This happens in history more often than we might like to admit. For example, Erwin W. Lutzer tells the story of how Christians became complicit in Nazi Germany's rise. After World War I, Germany was beset by runaway inflation, crime, and decadence. The Nazis brought the currency back under control, instituted nationalized health care, established training schools, controlled crime, and embarked on ambitious public-works programs.[40] Supportive of making Germany stronger, many Christians failed to heed the warnings that Adolf Hitler was a bad man with bad intentions for the nation.

> The downside of this view is that relying on nonbelievers to make a good society can result in a society that is *against* Christ.

The pastor Martin Niemöller once attended a meeting in which Hitler said, "You confine yourself to the Church. I'll take care of the German people." Niemöller, at the end of the conversation, said to Hitler, "You said that 'I will take care of the German people.' But we too, as Christians and churchmen, have a responsibility toward the German people. That responsibility was entrusted to us by God, and neither you nor anyone in this world has the power to take it from us."[41] That evening Gestapo thugs ransacked Niemöller's rectory, and a few days later, a bomb exploded in his church. Niemöller was ultimately imprisoned, accused of using his pulpit to speak "with malicious and provocative criticism ... of a kind calculated to undermine the confidence of the People in their political leaders."[42]

Looking back, we can easily see that a synthesis between Nazism and Christianity was impossible. One would win and the other lose. But why wasn't this more obvious at the time? Going along with laws specifying building codes and traffic patterns might be perfectly reasonable, but can we really have a firm basis for such commands as helping the poor and refraining from stealing, even when it costs us greatly, apart from God's eternal law?

4. Christ and culture in *paradox*. As Christians, our place in the world does seem odd. As Andy Crouch puts it, we're both immigrants and missionaries at the same time.[43] The Christ-and-culture-in-paradox view focuses on trying to reconcile the tension between Christ having made all things new and yet things in the world being as they have been since the fall. Our righteousness is as "filthy rags," Scripture says (Isa. 64:6 NIV), and yet we're called to deeds of righteousness. God has revealed himself in Christ, and yet we see as though through a glass darkly (1 Cor. 13:12 KJV). Essentially, the Christ-and-culture-in-paradox view says that culture must be important—otherwise, why would God leave us here?— but it is also broken and cannot be fixed apart from the power of Christ redeeming the people who make up culture.

Niebuhr identified the Christ-and-culture-in-paradox view with the church father Marcion, for whom the world was "stupid and bad, crawling with vermin, a miserable hole, an object of scorn."[44] Humans may have achieved great things, but compared to who God is, our work is pretty meaningless. We might be proud of the majestic buildings in our town's business district, but from outer space, they don't appear very different from the neighboring shanties.[45]

> The Christ-and-culture-in-paradox view says that culture must be important because God left us here, but it is also broken and cannot be fixed apart from the redemptive power of Christ.

As you can imagine, one of the main goals of the Christ-and-culture-in-paradox view is to find those who are influential in the culture and witness to them in the hope that their culture-shaping power might be used to promote Christ. Star athletes, musicians, and business leaders who come to faith in Christ are trumpeted, and young people are encouraged to attain positions of influence so they can have a stronger platform from which to proclaim the gospel.

Many different Christian traditions have tried to resolve this paradox. Most conclude that culture cannot draw us closer to God, but God can enable us to live wisely and "do faithfully and lovingly what culture teaches or requires us to do."[46]

On the good side, the Christ-and-culture-in-paradox view speaks openly of the struggle of being isolated from the culture because of the strangeness of our beliefs, and it highlights how good the good news is in saving us from corruption. People who embrace the paradox have made substantial contributions in history, such as separating the branches of government and making them accountable to one another to hold back the power of sin.

Still, the Christ-and-culture-in-paradox view can lead to a sort of hopelessness in relation to culture. If heaven is our goal, and the best thing that can happen to us is that we'll die and be united with God, then what is the point in investing intentionally in our culture here on Earth? What we do here may help our personal spiritual development, the thinking goes, but shaping culture is sort of a waste of time.

5. Christ, the *transformer* of culture. The finished work of Christ is available to us here and now in bringing the newness of redemption to every aspect of culture. That's the hope the Christ-the-transformer-of-culture view expresses. Beginning with a strong view of creation, which was, to Niebuhr, "a kind of prologue to the one mighty deed of atonement,"[47] it acknowledges that humanity's fall into sin has corrupted, warped, twisted, and misdirected us.[48] And yet it also calls us to restore culture to what is good rather than replacing it with something different. Niebuhr called people who hold this view "conversionists": "For the **conversionist**, history is the story of God's mighty deeds and of man's responses to them. He lives somewhat less 'between the times' and somewhat more in the divine 'Now' than do his brother Christians."[49]

> *Conversionist:* someone who acknowledges the fallen nature of humanity but recognizes the transforming power available through the redemptive work of Christ to restore culture to what is good rather than replacing it with something that is different.

An early Christian tract from ancient Rome called "The Letter to Diognetus" described it this way: "What the soul is in the body, that are Christians in the world."[50]

Christ-the-transformer-of-culture focuses on applying God's love to everything. This helps avoid a self-centered focus on what God does for me and also avoids watering down the Bible's teachings to make culture seem better. As Saint Augustine wrote in *Confessions*, "Let thy works praise thee, that we may love thee; and let us love thee that thy works may praise thee."[51] Augustine also said,

> Temperance is love keeping itself entire and incorrupt for God; fortitude is love bearing everything readily for the sake of God; justice is love, serving God only, and therefore ruling well all else, as subject to man; prudence is love making a right distinction between what helps it towards God and what might hinder it.[52]

A life of love isn't a life of unreason, Niebuhr observed. Rather, it redeems reason from idolizing itself.

The promise of being able to transform culture based on a Christian worldview is an exciting one, but it seems like such a huge project. Can it actually work? If so, how?

6. Transforming Culture

Of all the views of culture, the Christ-the-transformer-of-culture view most neatly fits the biblical sequence of creation, fall, redemption, and restoration. It enables Christians to focus on loving God with all their being, bringing the law of love to bear in every aspect of culture. This includes areas people don't ordinarily think are related to "spiritual" things, such as mathematics, logic, natural science, fine arts, and technology. In each of these areas, we teach the world what God has taught us, which is to "trace out His designs and humbly to follow His ways," as Niebuhr phrased it.[53]

> The Christ-the-transformer-of-culture view most neatly fits the biblical sequence of creation, fall, redemption, and restoration, enabling Christians to focus on loving God and bringing the law of love to bear in every aspect of culture.

What steps might we take to participate in transforming culture in this way? I suggest three: see culture as part of our Christian mission, take culture seriously, and create new culture.

Step 1: See culture as part of our Christian mission. A common temptation among Christians is to keep faith locked securely inside church. Certainly the opponents of Christianity would like to see it kept there. But even when there is no opposition, many Christians seem strangely reluctant to acknowledge that what Jesus says is relevant everywhere: at work, in politics, in the arts, and anywhere else.

In *The Last Christian on Earth*, Os Guinness imagines, in an allegory reminiscent of C. S. Lewis's *Screwtape Letters*, a conversation between two demons about how to conquer civilization through **secularization**—that is, through stripping away the spiritual aspect of life. According to Guinness, secularization is complete not when people fail to believe in God but when they see such belief as increasingly irrelevant.[54] "Once that happens," one demon says to another in Guinness's allegory, "whatever faith is left is limited and inconsequential, and lacks the mental and moral muscle to resist us."[55]

> *Secularization:* the movement of a culture away from religious identification and values as religion loses cultural relevance and significance.

This fictional demon has uncovered a disturbing hole in Christianity's defenses: it is possible to believe *every fact* about Christianity but also to be secularized to the point of acting as if those facts simply don't matter. The danger is not that brilliant arguments will dismantle Christianity but that people will turn away with a stifled yawn.

If Christ is the transformer of culture, then what he says is relevant to everything, everywhere. J. Gresham Machen, a professor at Princeton Theological Seminary and one of the founders of Westminster Theological Seminary in Philadelphia, expressed it this way:

> The Christian cannot be satisfied so long as any human activity is either opposed to Christianity or out of all connection with Christianity. Christianity must pervade not merely all nations, but also all of human thought. The Christian, therefore,

cannot be indifferent to any branch of earnest human endeavor. It must all be brought into some relation to the gospel. It must be studied either in order to be demonstrated as false, or else in order to be made useful in advancing the Kingdom of God.[56]

> If Christ is the transformer of culture, then what he says is relevant to everything, everywhere.

To hold this view, though, we must distinguish between the *structure* of creation, which is good, and the *direction* it often takes in a fallen world.[57] Our temptation when we see the evil and corruption in the world around us is to condemn the *structure* of cultural ideas and artifacts rather than the uses to which they're put. Though ideas are complicated and exceptions may abound, the Christ-the-transformer-of-culture view assumes that when the truly good happens in culture, it is *because* of Christ, not in spite of him.

Step 2: Take culture seriously. Often Christians are tempted not only to *accommodate* a shallow culture but to *imitate* it by baptizing it with sentimentalism. An entire industry has been developed to imitate popular artwork (while decorating it with Bible verses), music (while scrubbing away all profanity and innuendo), and so forth. Sometimes the purpose is to create a platform for the gospel. Other times, quite honestly, it's a way of getting Christians to buy things they might not otherwise buy.

The biggest problem with accommodation is that it not only leads to cheesy commercial products but also fails to take culture seriously. It assumes that culture's value is in how quickly it can be mutated into a platform from which to preach a sound-bite version of the gospel. It is revolution minus the obscenity. Unfortunately, hard experience shows that there is no perfect song that will win the hearts of the world, and no perfectly stated meme on Facebook that will instantly silence doubters. We shouldn't be looking for an angelic appearance on national television.

> Francis Schaeffer—along with his wife, Edith—developed an approach to Christian engagement that didn't ignore art, music, and culture but incorporated them into his teaching to bring out valuable truths.

One example of taking culture seriously is a J. Gresham Machen's student at Westminster Theological Seminary, Francis Schaeffer. In 1955, Schaeffer acquired a lodge in the Swiss Alps and named it L'Abri (French for "the Shelter"). Along with his wife, Edith, he developed an approach to Christian engagement that didn't ignore art, music, and culture but incorporated them into his teaching to bring out valuable truths, much as the apostle Paul did with the Athenian leaders at Mars Hill (Acts 17:16).[58] Andy Crouch describes Schaeffer's approach this way:

> He treated culture not as something to be condemned and avoided, but as a valuable dialogue partner that offered access to the reigning philosophical assumptions of the time, along with clues to the best way to convince skeptical moderns that the gospel was indeed the most compelling account of reality.[59]

As Crouch points out, God didn't isolate his chosen people, Israel, from other nations. Today we have a similar opportunity to take culture seriously. Let's not make the mistake of viewing our neighbors as accidents of proximity, or truth as something to be compromised rather than revealed.

Step 3: Create new culture. Andy Crouch says, "The only way to change culture is to create more of it."[60] But how do we do this? After all, as T. S. Eliot pointed out, "Culture is the one thing that we cannot deliberately aim at."[61]

Creating culture—or, as we describe it in this book, *shaping* culture—is a difficult thing for Christians to do. It's often easier for Christians to focus on propositions proving that God's truth is true, or that his moral standards are the right ones. But God's truth is no less true in the realms of art, music, and other expressions of beauty than it is in propositions. Law professor David Skeel, drawing on the work of Harvard professor Elaine Scarry, makes the case that beauty can create a desire for truth as much as anything else can:

> [According to Scarry,] "the beautiful person or thing incites in us the longing for truth." It "prompts the mind to move chronologically back in the search for precedents and parallels, to move forward into new acts of creation, to move conceptually over, to bring things into relation, and does all this with a kind of urgency as though one's life depended on it." In this sense, beauty is not itself truth, but it sharpens our commitment to truth. Beauty often inspires a sense of conviction, which is, to quote Scarry again, "so pleasurable a mental state … that ever afterwards one is willing to labor, struggle, wrestle with the world to locate enduring sources of conviction—to locate what is true."[62]

When future generations consider whether the civilization we created was worthwhile, they will consider as much evidence from the realm of beauty as they consider from the realms of truth and goodness.

Beauty is important to God. As Crouch notes in examining Genesis 2, the original garden of Eden was a place of gold and onyx and bdellium, a tree gum that "hardened into translucent white balls that were prized as jewelry as well as perfume."[63] The description of the new heavens and new earth is similarly beautiful, with the heavenly city being described as bedecked with jewels and paved with gold. But such jewels are the product of culture, and they happen only when humans find them and shape them. Similarly, gold becomes beautiful when humans extract it from the ground, remove its impurities, and shape it. Crouch concludes, "Culture, then, is the furniture of heaven."[64]

God is an artist. So are we. And not just those of us gifted in producing paintings and sculptures and music and jewelry. Believers are daily invited to conduct masterful symphonies of grace by rescuing those wandering in misery and restoring the lost to the way of truth. Some of us do this by making paintings. Others do it through athletic pursuits, intellectual works, or practical inventions, or by starting creative new ministries or companies. It is artists

> Shaping culture is a difficult thing for Christians to do. But beauty can create a desire for truth as much as anything else can.

who lead the way, picturing beauty—and even brokenness—in a way that reminds us that we are image bearers of God who are fallen and for whom the promise of redemption means a season of refreshing and the promised restoring of all things (Acts 3:19–21).[65]

Believers are daily invited to conduct masterful symphonies of grace by rescuing those wandering in misery and restoring the lost to the way of truth.

Christianity is culture shaping. It always has been. As sociologist Rodney Stark frames it, what caused Christianity to rise in significance since the time of Christ wasn't trickery or the abuse of power, as is often assumed, but its core doctrines, which "prompted and sustained attractive, liberating, and effective social relations and organizations."[66]

7. Conclusion

The Old Testament often uses the Hebrew word *derek*, "the way," to describe a direction-filled life. For example, Deuteronomy 10:12[67] instructs us to "walk in all [God's] ways," and Isaiah 40:3[68] says to "prepare the way of the Lord." The implication is that there is a right way and a wrong way to live. There is a way of wisdom and a way of foolishness. There is a way of life and a way of death.

> *Derek:* from the Hebrew for "the way," *derek* refers to the overall direction of a person's life.

Which way should we go? If Christ is indeed a transformer of culture, then regardless of our level of skill or vocational expertise, we ought to imitate *him*, not *it*. Our surrender is to God, not to our circumstances. The hope of heaven isn't first and foremost a call to escape from the world but a source of power by which we may do a great deal of earthly good. If we do this to God's glory, bearing his image and loving our neighbors, it's a vision that can inspire those around us as well as generations yet to be born.

In spite of their disagreements, proponents of various views of culture all agree that ultimately everything comes from God. The question, really, is how much sin has effectively ruined God's work, and what we ought to do about it now. Three-quarters of a century ago, two men who are now famous, J. R. R. Tolkien and C. S. Lewis, strolled over the grounds of Magdalen College in Oxford, England, late at night, discussing the relationship between God and humanity, truth and lies. Lewis contended that the myths he was studying as a scholar were ultimately "lies and therefore worthless."

"'No,' said Tolkien. 'They are not lies.'"[69] Tolkien went on to explain that myths are stories that ring true because they are grasping for fulfillment through Christianity.[70] Humans may distort thoughts and thus pervert them into lies, but it is from God that all good ideas originate. As Humphrey Carpenter relates the conversation through pieced-together recollections of the two men, Tolkien explained that "not merely the abstract thoughts of man but also his imaginative inventions must originate with God, and must in consequence reflect something of eternal truth."[71]

> Understanding how God is at the root of culture enables us to appreciate it more and even shape it.

As they walked, Tolkien asked Lewis a life-changing question: Is it possible that Christianity is the great story behind all great stories? Soon after, Lewis committed his life to Christ. His resulting books inspire and give confidence to people even today. Understanding how God was at the root of culture enabled Lewis to, in turn, appreciate culture all the more and even shape it through his own fiction and nonfiction works.

This book invites you into a journey of shaping culture. Our goal in examining the key issues of our day from a Christian perspective is not to lock down the "right" answers beyond a shadow of doubt but to find ways in which obeying God will enable us to be culture shapers who bring joy and flourishing to an often hopeless world. In the next chapter, we'll scour history for examples of how it can be done, examining the incredible lives of Christians who, operating from a biblical worldview, significantly shaped culture, especially in morality, human value, and freedom.

ENDNOTES

1. James Davison Hunter, *To Change the World: The Irony, Tragedy, and Possibility of Christianity in the Late Modern World* (New York: Oxford University Press, 2010), 3.

2. Ernest Gordon, *To End All Wars: A True Story about the Will to Survive and the Courage to Forgive* (Grand Rapids: Zondervan, 1963), 72.

3. Gordon, *To End All Wars*, 105–6.

4. "Executive Summary," Daniel Cox, Juhem Navarro-Rivera, and Robert P. Jones, "Citizenship, Values, and Cultural Concerns: What Americans Want from Immigration Reform," PRRI, March 21, 2013, http://publicreligion.org/research/2013/03/2013-religion-values-immigration-survey/.

5. Proverbs 24:11–12: "Rescue those who are being taken away to death; hold back those who are stumbling to the slaughter. If you say, 'Behold, we did not know this,' does not he who weighs the heart perceive it? Does not he who keeps watch over your soul know it, and will he not repay man according to his work?"

6. Jeremiah 29:7: "Seek the welfare of the city where I have sent you into exile, and pray to the LORD on its behalf, for in its welfare you will find your welfare."

7. Nickelback, "Edge of a Revolution," *No Fixed Address* © 2014 Republic.

8. Andy Crouch, *Culture Making: Recovering Our Creative Calling* (Downers Grove, IL: InterVarsity, 2008), 58.

9. John Kotter, "The Key to Changing Organizational Culture," *Forbes*, September 27, 2012, www.forbes.com/sites/johnkotter/2012/09/27/the-key-to-changing-organizational-culture/.

10. Kevin Vanhoozer, "What Is Everyday Theology? How and Why Christians Should Read Culture," in Kevin J. Vanhoozer, Charles A. Anderson, and Michael J. Sleasman, eds., *Everyday Theology: How to Read Cultural Texts and Interpret Trends* (Grand Rapids: Baker Academic, 2007), 21.

11. Crouch, *Culture Making*, 23.

12. T. S. Eliot, *Notes towards the Definition of Culture* (New York: Harcourt, Brace, 1949), 26.

13. This is a very brief, simplified summary of James Davison Hunter's theory of what culture is and how it changes, which he outlines in eleven propositions in *To Change the World*, 32–47.

14. See Randall Collins, *The Sociology of Philosophies: A Global Theory of Intellectual Change* (Cambridge, MA: Belknap, 1998).

15. Samuel Wilberforce, *Cheap Sugar Means Cheap Slaves: Speech of the Right Reverend, the Lord Bishop of Oxford, in the House of Lords, February 7th, 1848, Against the Admission of Slave Labour Sugar on Equal Terms with Free Labour Produce* (Ithaca, NY: Cornell University Library, 1848).

16. Katy Kroll, "Twerk It Out: Miley and Robin's VMA Performance, One Year Later," *Rolling Stone*, August 22, 2014, www.rollingstone.com/tv/news/miley-cyrus-robin-thicke-vma-performance-one-year-later-20140822#ixzz3PWIkeupN.

17. Sean McDowell and John Stonestreet, *Same-Sex Marriage: A Thoughtful Approach to God's Design for Marriage* (Grand Rapids: Baker Books, 2014), 79.

18. Con Slobodchikoff, interview by Erica Johnson, *The Current*, CBC Radio, June 2014, quoted in "Prairie Dogs' Language Decoded by Scientists," CBC News, June 21, 2013, www.cbc.ca/news/technology/prairie-dogs-language-decoded-by-scientists-1.1322230.

19. Walter J. Ong, *The Presence of the Word: Some Prolegomena for Cultural and Religious History* (New Haven: Yale University Press, 1967), 1.

20. See Alvin M. Liberman, "The Speech Code," in George A. Miller, ed., *Communication, Language, and Meaning: Psychological Perspectives* (New York: Basic Books, 1973), 128–29.

21. Edward Sapir, *Language: An Introduction to the Study of Speech* (New York: Harcourt, Brace, 1921), 21–22.

22. Frank E. X. Dance and Carl E. Larson, *Speech Communication: Concepts and Behavior* (New York: Holt, Rinehart, and

Winston, 1972).

23. Ken Myers originally presented this list at a lecture on culture at the Association of Classical and Christian Schools (ACCS) 2008 Conference, "Recovering Truth, Goodness, and Beauty," Austin, Texas, June 26–28, 2008. I've included it here with my commentary, gleaned in part from "ACCS—Ken Myers on Culture," *Mark's Blog*, Every Good Path, July 23, 2008, www.everygoodpath.net/ACCSKenMyersCulture.

24. How institutions develop this kind of cultural significance is a large part of the argument James Davison Hunter makes in *To Change the World*. See specifically "An Alternative View of Culture and Cultural Change in Eleven Propositions," 32–47.

25. Dov Cohen et al., "Insult, Aggression, and the Southern Culture of Honor: An Experimental Ethnography," *Journal of Personality and Social Psychology* 70, no. 5 (1996): 945–60, http://deepblue.lib.umich.edu/bitstream/handle/2027.42/92155 /InsultAggressionAndTheSouthernCulture.pdf.

26. H. Richard Niebuhr, *Christ and Culture* (New York: Harper and Row, 1951).

27. Jeremiah 29:4–7: "Thus says the LORD of hosts, the God of Israel, to all the exiles whom I have sent into exile from Jerusalem to Babylon: Build houses and live in them; plant gardens and eat their produce. Take wives and have sons and daughters; take wives for your sons, and give your daughters in marriage, that they may bear sons and daughters; multiply there, and do not decrease. But seek the welfare of the city where I have sent you into exile, and pray to the LORD on its behalf, for in its welfare you will find your welfare."

28. First John 2:15–17: "Do not love the world or the things in the world. If anyone loves the world, the love of the Father is not in him. For all that is in the world—the desires of the flesh and the desires of the eyes and pride of life—is not from the Father but is from the world. And the world is passing away along with its desires, but whoever does the will of God abides forever."

29. Niebuhr, *Christ and Culture*, 48.

30. Niebuhr, *Christ and Culture*, 52.

31. Niebuhr, *Christ and Culture*, 67–68.

32. Rod Dreher, "Benedict Option: A Medieval Model Inspires Christian Communities Today," *American Conservative*, December 12, 2013, www.theamericanconservative.com/articles/benedict-option/.

33. Niebuhr, *Christ and Culture*, 83.

34. Woodrow Wilson, "Address at Arlington National Cemetery: 'Closing a Chapter,'" June 4, 1914, American Presidency Project, www.presidency.ucsb.edu/ws/?pid=65379.

35. Niebuhr, *Christ and Culture*, 91.

36. Niebuhr, *Christ and Culture*, 99. Some examples of portraying Jesus as a moral teacher rather than as God in the flesh include Immanuel Kant's idea of the kingdom of God being instead "the kingdom of ends"; Alfred Lord Tennyson's "Parliament of Man and Federation of the World"; Thomas Jefferson's dream of humankind being united "under the bonds of charity, peace, common wants and common aids"; as well as Albert Ritschl's use of the term "brotherhood of man" instead of "kingdom of God."

37. Niebuhr, *Christ and Culture*, 103.

38. Niebuhr, *Christ and Culture*, 117.

39. Niebuhr, *Christ and Culture*, 125.

40. Erwin W. Lutzer, *When a Nation Forgets God: Seven Lessons We Must Learn from Nazi Germany* (Chicago: Moody, 2010), 42–47.

41. Lutzer, *When a Nation Forgets God*, 24.

42. Lutzer, *When a Nation Forgets God*, 27.

43. Crouch, *Culture Making*, 49.

44. Marcion, quoted in Niebuhr, *Christ and Culture*, 168.

45. Richard Niebuhr described it this way: "Before the holiness of God as disclosed in the grace of Jesus Christ there is no distinction between the wisdom of the philosopher and the folly of the simpleton, between the crime of the murderer and his chastisement by the magistrate.... One might say that comparisons between the highest skyscrapers and the meanest hovels are meaningless in the presence of Betelgeuse." Niebuhr, *Christ and Culture*, 152–53.

46. Niebuhr, *Christ and Culture*, 175.

47. Niebuhr, *Christ and Culture*, 191.

48. Niebuhr, *Christ and Culture*, 194.

49. Niebuhr, *Christ and Culture*, 195.

50. "Letter to Diognetus," chap. 6, in Paul Pavao, "Letter to Diognetus," Christian History for Everyman, 2014, www.christian -history.org/letter-to-diognetus.html.

51. Augustine, *Confessions*, 12.33.48.

52. Niebuhr, *Christ and Culture*, 214–15.

53. Niebuhr, *Christ and Culture*.

54. Os Guinness, *The Last Christian on Earth: Uncover the Enemy's Plot to Undermine the Church* (Ventura, CA: Regal,

2010), 69. Craig Gay's work on this point has been very influential in my thinking. The thesis of his book *The Way of the (Modern) World* is that the irrelevance of God is embedded in "modern institutions and habits of thought" and that "we are tempted to live as though God did not exist, or at least as if his existence did not practically matter." Craig Gay, *The Way of the (Modern) World: Or, Why It's Tempting to Live as If God Doesn't Exist* (Grand Rapids: Eerdmans, 1998), 2.

55. Guinness, *Last Christian on Earth*, 61.

56. J. Gresham Machen, "Christianity and Culture," *Princeton Theological Review* 11, no. 1 (1913): 6, http://scdc.library.ptsem.edu/mets/mets.aspx?src=BR1913111&div=1&img=6.

57. See Albert M. Wolters, *Creation Regained: Biblical Basics for a Reformational Worldview* (Grand Rapids: Eerdmans, 2005), chap. 5.

58. Acts 17:16: "While Paul was waiting for [Silas and Timothy] at Athens, his spirit was provoked within him as he saw that the city was full of idols."

59. Crouch, *Culture Making*, 86.

60. Crouch, *Culture Making*, 67.

61. Eliot, *Notes towards the Definition of Culture*, 17.

62. Elaine Scarry, *On Beauty and Being Just* (Princeton, NJ: Princeton University Press, 1999), 30–31, quoted in David Skeel, *True Paradox: How Christianity Makes Sense of Our Complex World* (Downers Grove, IL: InterVarsity, 2014), 84. Scarry is a professor of English and American literature and language at Harvard University.

63. Crouch, *Culture Making*, 165.

64. Crouch, *Culture Making*, 170.

65. Acts 3:19–21: "Repent therefore, and turn back, that your sins may be blotted out, that times of refreshing may come from the presence of the Lord, and that he may send the Christ appointed for you, Jesus, whom heaven must receive until the time for restoring all the things about which God spoke by the mouth of his holy prophets long ago."

66. Rodney Stark, *The Rise of Christianity: A Sociologist Reconsiders History* (Princeton, NJ: Princeton University Press, 1996), 211.

67. Deuteronomy 10:12: "Now, Israel, what does the LORD your God require of you, but to fear the LORD your God, to walk in all his ways, to love him, to serve the LORD your God with all your heart and with all your soul."

68. Isaiah 40:3: "A voice cries: 'In the wilderness prepare the way of the LORD; make straight in the desert a highway for our God.'"

69. Humphrey Carpenter, *The Inklings: C. S. Lewis, J. R. R. Tolkien, Charles Williams, and Their Friends* (London: Allen and Unwin, 1978), 43.

70. Alister McGrath calls the ancient myths Lewis studied "narrated worldviews" to distinguish them from the idea of myth as a thing that is untrue and yet something many people believe nonetheless. Alister McGrath, lecture at Summit's C. S. Lewis conference in Oxford, England, October 7, 2013.

71. Carpenter, *Inklings*, 43.

CHAPTER 3

CHRISTIANITY AND CULTURE: A HISTORY

1. DOES CHRISTIANITY BENEFIT CULTURE OR DESTROY IT?

The Jesus cult is evil. It poisons our culture by weakening our resolve to fulfill our destiny.

No, this is not a conclusion one of today's new atheists have drawn, though it sounds like something the late Christopher Hitchens might have said. After all, Hitchens publicly argued that Christianity is the product of "crude, uncultured human mammals" who trafficked in humans, promoted slavery, and engaged in "indiscriminate massacre."[1] Rather, this conclusion was drawn by early Romans, who blamed Christianity for the demise of Rome's peace, happiness, and productivity. It was a widespread criticism that the early Christian philosopher Augustine refuted in a book-length work called *City of God*.[2]

Christianity has always had its critics. Some were professors of mine. In working through my bachelor's, master's, and doctoral degrees, I had probably forty different instructors. All but two of them treated Christianity as either irrelevant or bad. Of course, Christianity didn't come up in every class. I don't remember talking about it in badminton. And, gratefully, none of my instructors were openly scornful, like the mocking Professor Radisson in the movie *God's Not Dead*.[3]

Instead, my professors most often expressed their distaste for Christianity by simply omitting it from the discussion. Their silent dismissal, punctuated by the soft nuance of lightly skeptical class readings and the occasional wry remark, led my classmates and me to believe that Christianity had nothing positive to contribute to the world and that those who seemed devout, such as America's founding fathers, merely pretended to be so out of political or social expedience.

A couple of my professors, however, were frequently openly hostile to Christianity. As a new Christian, I was torn about how to respond. On the one hand, their objections seemed petty, a sort of grown-up version of the middle-school-age wail "You're ruining my life!" On the other hand, their arguments clearly contained a grain of truth. No one could plausibly claim that Christians have been nothing but angelic over the past two millennia. Yes, bad people have claimed to know Jesus, but what did this have to do with me? Was I continuing their crimes merely by deciding to follow Christ?

> People all over the world, based on their understanding of Christian teachings, have beneficially shaped and transformed culture.

Looking back, it seems to me that these professors tolerated Christianity only as a private belief. This chapter, though, makes just the opposite case: that Christianity ought to be taken seriously as a positive culture-shaping force. People all over the world, based on their understanding of Christian teachings, have taken culture-shaping actions that beneficially transformed human rights, the rights of women and children, education, medicine, charity, science, and the arts.

And yet the personal actions of individual Christians aren't enough to transform culture by themselves. Those actions must be based on something deeper and more enduring.

2. RIGHT BELIEFS—NOT JUST ACTIONS—ENABLE CHRISTIANS TO CHANGE THE WORLD

In the previous chapter, we saw that culture is what humans voluntarily do.[4] It's what we make of the world.[5] Culture makes life worth living and shows future generations that our existence was worthwhile.[6] In that discussion, I also claimed that Christians have enormously influenced culture by promoting that which is good, true, and beautiful. This chapter proves it.

Christians have changed the world. Though in almost all cases they acted out of their personal giftings and convictions rather than by church authority or patronage, there is something about the Christian religion that has made it uniquely helpful as a culture-shaping force. A person's **religion**—"a set of beliefs concerning the cause, nature, and purpose of the universe"[7]—has a big effect on how he or she influences culture. Religious belief is to culture what an artistic style, such as impressionism, is to painting. A painting is the product of an artist's beliefs about the universe, combined with skill. Similarly, our individual religious beliefs guide what we think should or shouldn't be done in the world around us.

> *Religion:* a system of belief that attempts to define the nature of God and how human beings can understand and interact with the divine; any system of belief that prescribes certain responses to the existence (or nonexistence) of the divine.

Some religions downplay belief and instead focus on practice. What we *think about* is not as important as what we *do*. Islam and Judaism are like this. In Christianity, though, belief precedes practice. The apostles emphasized this repeatedly. Consider Paul's letter to the Roman believers. After writing eleven chapters on what they ought to believe, he finally began instructing them in what to do in light of his teaching. And to the church at Philippi, Paul wrote, "Have this *mind* among yourselves, which is yours in Christ Jesus" (Phil. 2:5). Jesus calls Christians to not just obey God but to love him with all their hearts, souls, minds, and strength and, *on that basis*, to love their neighbors as themselves (Luke 10:27).[8] Jesus said that people who don't act rightly are in error because their *beliefs* are wrong. He called those who focus on outward acts while nursing wrong beliefs "whitewashed tombs" (Matt. 23:27).[9] He also said that "out of the abundance of the heart [the] mouth speaks" (Luke 6:45).

To put it philosophically, Christianity places **orthodoxy** ("sound doctrine") before **orthopraxy** ("sound practice"). Lots of religions teach "Thou shalt not kill," but Jesus told his audience in the Sermon on the Mount that the real offense was being *angry* or *insulting* others (Matt. 5:22).[10] With few exceptions (such as the distinction between murder and premeditated murder), laws judge what people *do*, not how they think or feel about it. Acting according to properly applied laws can keep a culture from devolving into anarchy, but it cannot in the same way make a culture better. This isn't to say that law is

> *Orthodoxy:* sound doctrine.

> *Orthopraxy:* sound practice.

somehow an inferior pursuit. As Martin Luther King Jr. said, "It may be true that the law cannot make a man love me; religion and education will have to do that. But it [can keep] him from lynching me, and I think that's pretty important also."[11] Still, believing rightly is the difference between avoiding murder, which is a culture-sustaining thing to do, and actively helping, protecting, educating, and loving people, which is culture shaping.

Christians expect one another to act rightly, of course, but they do so because they expect right actions to flow from right belief, not because they feel obligated merely to obey a list of commands. If we know something about beliefs, we can trace back why one person shaped culture in a positive way, and another shaped it destructively. We'll also be able to respond with understanding when we see that most people, ourselves included, embrace both right and wrong beliefs. As we increasingly measure our beliefs against what is true, correct any erroneous beliefs, and align our actions with those corrected beliefs, we'll grow more skillful in shaping our own lives, the culture, and even future generations.

One more important note by way of introduction: strictly speaking, *people* hold beliefs; *institutions* do not. Institutions often attract people who share, emphasize, and encourage certain beliefs, but individuals—or several people working together who hold similar beliefs—are the ones who actually live out those beliefs. When it comes to changing culture, we should focus on living out—and helping other people live out—those *beliefs* that come from Scripture. We should also identify the *people in history* who lived out those beliefs in ways that brought life to culture by freeing millions from slavery, alleviating suffering, eliminating ignorance, and ending oppression.

> *Category Mistake:* a fallacy that presents things belonging to one particular category as if they belong in another category.

It's a logical fallacy to confuse institutions and people. To say, "Christians in the past have done amazing things; therefore, Christianity as an institution is awesome, and since I'm a Christian, I'm awesome too," is what's known as a **category mistake**. It's also an enormous turnoff to those who might otherwise accept Christianity's belief system. We're each responsible to believe and live out our beliefs. As Kevin Vanhoozer says, "It is impossible to construct a culture-free Christianity. The Christian faith is incarnational, after all, and even God became not a generic but a culturally located human being. Jesus' followers can do no less."[12]

But that doesn't mean we shouldn't examine Christians from other times and places. We have much to learn from them. In this chapter, the creative and prolific work of a professor of history, Dr. Glenn Sunshine, will aid us greatly. His many books and articles highlight the ways little-known people in history, operating from the standpoint of the Christian faith, have exerted a profound influence on the culture. If you like, you can explore Professor Sunshine's work in more detail by following the Internet links included in the source notes. Also, the work of sociologist Rodney Stark is compelling to both academics and a popular audience. Some of his books are cited in the endnotes and are well worth reading. I also like Alvin Schmidt's *How Christianity Changed the World* and Vishal Mangalwadi's *The Book That Made Your World*.

So back to my professors for a moment. Were they right to deride or ignore Christianity? Is it true that Christianity has lacked any positive influence in history, or were my professors missing something that could help us better understand both our faith and the world in which we live? Let's find out.

3. HOW CHRISTIANS ACTING ON BIBLICAL BELIEFS ADVANCED HUMAN RIGHTS

The story of the Bible is that people have value just by virtue of being human. Further, these rights are held *equally*. As humans we're made in God's image (Gen. 1:26–27).[13] Old Testament law instructed the nation of Israel to treat people fairly and admonished judges to uphold the rights of those who were often treated as socially lower in value, such as women, slaves, and the poor (Exod. 23:6–9).[14]

Jesus treated people with dignity as image bearers of God. For instance, during his ministry, women gained an unheard-of stature. Women followers supported his ministry. They were the last to leave the cross, the first to arrive at the empty tomb, and the first to see the risen Christ. The apostle Paul, while often criticized for a presumed low view of women, considered at least twelve women as coworkers in his ministry (Acts 16:14–15, 40; Rom. 16:1–4, 6, 13, 15; 1 Cor. 1:11; Phil. 4:2; Col. 4:15).[15] This was unprecedented at the time, since women were either ignored or shunned in religious conversation. As Jesus demonstrated, the good news is available to all, regardless of gender or status (Gal. 3:27–29).[16]

Treating people with dignity is at the heart of **human rights**. From the perspective of a Christian worldview, humans are all made in the image of God, all are under sin, and all are saved only by the work of Christ on the cross. This places all of us on equal spiritual and moral footing before God. These beliefs have generated such a profound influence on human rights that Glenn Sunshine flatly states, "We owe our entire idea of human rights to Christianity."[17]

> *Human Rights:* the standards of conduct based on moral principles that express the dignity of humanity; those rights that are inherent to every human being just by merit of being human.

The concept of human rights developed during what we now call the Middle Ages, when theologians began seriously examining the implications of applying Scripture to the conversation about human rights. God gave us life, they realized. And the right to life is so important in Scripture that the punishment for unjustly taking another person's life was to forfeit one's own life (Gen. 9:6).[18] They also reasoned that God established the principle of freedom when he made our first parents (2:16)[19] and that it would be wrong to arbitrarily take away the liberty God himself granted.

For more than a thousand years after Plato's death, his **theory of forms** dominated the conversation about rights. In the same way a tree or a chair is just a representation of an eternal reality, what mattered for people was their eternal form, not their status in material reality. A person's rights in the physical world weren't seen as all that important. In the thirteenth century, though, a Franciscan friar named William of Ockham (1280–1349) argued that Plato's idea of universal forms was wrong and that rights ought to be grounded in what actually exists in physical reality, such as property. William reasoned that by giving Adam and Eve the right to enjoy the fruits of their labors,

> *Theory of Forms:* a type of philosophical idealism formulated by Plato positing that everything we experience in this world is simply an imperfect instantiation of an eternal and perfect ideal that exists in the world of the forms.

God had, in effect, given them the right to property. Later scriptures specifically forbidding theft ("Thou shalt not steal") and the telling of untruths to gain a material advantage over others ("Thou shalt not bear false witness") reinforced William's view (Exod. 20:15–16 KJV).

Hundreds of years later, John Locke (1632–1704) developed the idea that life, liberty, and property are inalienable rights. Yet Locke's thoughts didn't come out of thin air. In his

Two Treatises of Government, Locke put forth detailed arguments that the rights of human beings were derived from the creation account in Genesis. Many other early thinkers like Locke based their ideals of equality and human rights on their understanding of biblical teaching.

Christians aren't the only ones who make this argument. Jürgen Habermas, Europe's most prominent public intellectual, said the following in a now-famous interview:

> Egalitarian universalism, from which sprang the ideas of freedom and social solidarity, of an autonomous conduct of life and emancipation, of the individual morality of conscience, human rights and democracy, is the direct [legacy of] the Judaic ethic of justice and the Christian ethic of love. This legacy, substantially unchanged, has been the object of continual critical appropriation and reinterpretation. To this day, there is no alternative to it. And in light of the current challenges of a postnational constellation, we continue to draw on the substance of this heritage. Everything else is just idle postmodern talk.[20]

As an atheist, Habermas wasn't saying that he *believes* the Judeo-Christian tradition, only that it is the historical source of our ideas about human rights. Any secular attempt to find a new source will merely build on its legacy.

Christianity is unique in its emphasis on human rights. Glenn Sunshine says,

> Some religious and philosophical traditions have ideas similar to Christian ideas of equality, though in practice they never produced societies that recognized universal human rights. It took Christianity centuries of biblical and theological reflection to develop fully these ideas, though early Christians certainly put them into practice even when the theological concepts had not yet been articulated. You do not see anything similar in other cultures, religions, or philosophies.[21]

> "Conversionary Protestants [were] a crucial catalyst initiating the development and spread of religious liberty, mass education, mass printing, [and other] innovations ... that made stable representative democracy more likely."

Further, Christianity's tradition of human rights and equality isn't limited to Western nations, such as those in Europe and North America. It also includes Africa, Asia, Latin America, and Oceania (e.g., nations such as Australia, New Zealand, and Malaysia). Political scientist Robert Woodberry found, after extensive research, that "conversionary Protestants" (i.e., missionaries) were "a crucial catalyst initiating the development and spread of religious liberty, mass education, mass printing, newspapers, voluntary organizations, most major colonial reforms, and the codification of legal protections for nonwhites.... These innovations fostered conditions that made stable representative democracy more likely."[22]

One example of Christianity's unique influence outside the West is Krishna Mohan Bannerjee, an Indian student who converted to Christianity in 1832 through the mentorship of a British missionary and made it his life's work to oppose the caste system, polygamy,

CHRISTIANITY AND CULTURE: A HISTORY

idolatry, the practice of forcing girls to be child brides, and **suttee** (or sati), the custom of burning a woman alive on the funeral pyre of her husband. Bannerjee led many of his people to faith in Christ through his work, which focused on finding traditional Hindu ways of opposing practices destructive of human rights and equality.[23]

Another believer whose work illustrates Christianity's global influence is Chiune Sugihara, a Japanese diplomat to Lithuania who, upon hearing that the Nazis were slaughtering Jews, began issuing visas allowing Jews to "transit" through Japan on their way to somewhere else, even though there was no "somewhere else." Sugihara chose to obey his conscience rather than the directive his government gave him not to issue the visas. He wrote visas by hand at a rate of three hundred per day for more than a month as World War II was heating up, and he saved between six thousand and ten thousand Jews from the Holocaust.[24]

> *Suttee:* an ancient Hindu practice of burning a widow alive on the funeral pyre of her deceased husband.

The Christian tradition of defending human rights and promoting equality is vast, and even the best academic scholars widely acknowledge it. As it turns out, this tradition ignited fruitful opposition to an institution nearly as old as humanity itself: the institution of slavery.

4. How Christians Acting on Biblical Beliefs Brought About the Abolition of Slavery

Slavery has been common everywhere and at all times throughout history. The ancient Hebrews had slaves, but on the basis of the belief that everyone bears the image of God (Gen. 1:26–27),[25] they treated their slaves in a markedly different fashion, establishing laws to provide for their care and protection. (These laws are clearly spelled out in Exodus 11, 12, and 21; Leviticus 19, 22, and 25; and Deuteronomy 5, 15, 16, and 21.) In a way the ancient Hebrews couldn't have foreseen, the application of these principles of law in later times changed the trajectory of history, making it possible not only to treat slaves more humanely but also, ultimately, to abolish the institution of slavery altogether in those nations most strongly influenced by the laws.

In the New Testament, the apostle Paul greeted slaves using terms of equality, such as *kinsmen, fellow prisoners,* and *fellow workers* (e.g., Rom. 16:9).[26] Equality of slaves is found throughout the New Testament and is based on the belief that all are one in Christ Jesus, no matter their role in life (1 Cor. 12:13; Gal. 3:28; Col. 3:11).[27] Paul, for example, commanded Philemon to treat the slave Onesimus as a brother (Philem. v. 16).[28] Revelation 18:11–13[29] condemns trading humans as "cargo," echoing Ezekiel 27:13.[30] First Timothy 1:9–10[31] condemns "enslavers" who forced humans into slavery.

> Throughout history, based on the unalienable right to liberty and grounded in the doctrine that every human bears God's image, Christianity has been the driving force behind the abolition of slavery.

Throughout history, based on the unalienable right to liberty and grounded in the doctrine that every human bears God's image, Christianity has been the driving force behind the abolition of slavery.

Even during those times when people believed Aristotle's conception that some humans were "living tool[s]" and thus slaves by nature,[32] early church leaders went against the grain of the culture and promoted slaves to high offices. Onesimus, the bishop of Ephesus in the early second century, was a former slave (his name, which means "useful," marked him as a slave, and many Christian traditions hold that this was the same Onesimus about whom the apostle Paul spoke in his letter to Philemon). Two early Roman Catholic popes (Pius I and Callixtus I) had also been slaves.

Many records exist of Christians, both individually and through churches, purchasing slaves at market to set them free. In the sixth century, Saint Eligius purchased British and Saxon slaves in lots of fifty or one hundred specifically to give them their freedom. Baptized Christian slaves were also routinely freed.

Early Christians opposed the slave trade as well and sometimes took direct action against it. Augustine of Hippo (a city in North Africa), who wrote *City of God*, penned a letter speaking of the "practice of performing acts of mercy" by setting slaves free from slave ships and from wherever the slavers had hidden them.[33]

It's true that some early Christians, while recognizing the evils of slavery, didn't call for its abolition. Many, including Augustine, thought slavery resulted from sin and had to be tolerated as such. John Chrysostom saw the institution of slavery as sin but didn't advocate abolition. Origen called for a return to the Old Testament practice of releasing slaves after six years. On the other hand, Gregory of Nyssa, Acacius of Amida, and Saint Patrick all argued for the complete abolition of slavery. It was such a widespread and accepted practice during this period—and still is in parts of the world relatively untouched by a biblical ethic[34]—that it took a long time for people to fully recognize slavery as evil.

By a long time, I mean four to seven hundred years after Christ, in the Middle Ages. As Europe became Christianized, slavery began to disappear. Explicit laws against slave trading were formed as early as the seventh century. Many of these laws were designed to protect Christians from slavery, and since almost everyone was considered to be a Christian, this meant that slavery was essentially abolished on the continent, apart from Muslim prisoners captured and enslaved as spoils of war.

In the 1400s, however, the Portuguese began exploring the coast of Africa looking for places they could colonize, and slavery once again reared its ugly head. Because the African coastal kingdoms were too powerful for them to colonize, the Portuguese bought slaves from these kingdoms (captives taken from other African people groups) and transported them to Brazil and other island colonies. When Spain annexed Portugal in 1580, it took over the slave trade. It seems odd that Spain and Portugal, as Catholic countries, would permit slavery in direct violation of Catholic teaching on the subject. Yet in spite of four different popes condemning the Atlantic slave trade in the fifteenth and sixteenth centuries, the practice continued.

British merchants had traded slaves for decades, but in 1713, the slave-trade issue was thrown into the British government's lap through the Treaty of Utrecht, which ended the War of the Spanish Succession and gave England a monopoly on the transatlantic slave trade to Spain's colonies in America. Opposition grew among Quakers and other Dissenters from the Church of England, such as Anabaptists and Puritans. Among those who publicly advocated the abolition of slavery were John Wesley and the early Methodists, Olaudah Equiano (a former slave),[35] Thomas Clarkson, Granville Sharp, James Ramsay, Hannah More,[36] and William Wilberforce.

In 1787, a group called the Society for Effecting the Abolition of the Slave Trade was formed. One of its supporters was Josiah Wedgwood, a wealthy and widely respected potter whose designs were the equivalent of popular clothing designers today.[37] Wedgwood produced a cameo—a piece of jewelry—picturing an African in chains kneeling, with the words "Am I not a man and a brother?" Wedgwood donated hundreds of these cameos for the society to distribute and thus sparked a wildly successful fashion trend, all in the cause of opposing slavery. Thomas Clarkson, an abolitionist who wrote the definitive history of the slave trade's abolition movement, described the impact of the image inscribed on the cameos:

> Some [people] had them inlaid in gold on the lid of their snuff-boxes. Of the ladies, several wore them in bracelets, and others had them fitted up in an ornamental manner as pins for their hair. At length the taste for wearing them became general; and thus fashion, which usually confines itself to worthless things, was seen for once in the honourable office of promoting the cause of justice, humanity and freedom.[38]

Largely because of the groundswell of support for those suffering in slavery but also through clever political maneuvering, Wilberforce was able to successfully persuade Parliament to outlaw the slave trade. Shortly before Wilberforce's death, slavery itself was actively abolished throughout the British Empire by means of an agreement in which the government compensated slave owners for the loss of their "property."

Inspired by what was happening in England, many Christians in America—joined by freethinkers like Benjamin Franklin—also began championing the abolition of slavery. These abolitionists included Harriet Beecher Stowe, Frederick Douglass (contrary to what is often said of him),[39] Harriet Tubman, and many others.

As improbable as it seems today, the story of slavery's abolition began as a theological issue. The abolitionists believed that all humans bore God's image and were therefore equal in his sight. This led naturally to the belief in the rights to liberty and property. The law of the nations wasn't God's law. It needed to be changed, and the abolitionists set about the task with fervor. The same love of freedom also birthed a new era of rights and dignity for women and children. Let's take a look at that next.

> The abolitionists believed that all humans bore God's image and were therefore equal in his sight.

5. How Christians Acting on Biblical Beliefs Secured the Basis for Women's and Children's Rights

Christianity has done more for women's rights than any other movement in history. Christianity sprouted in the seedbed of the Roman Empire, whose soil was nourished with the blood of the innocent. To say that Rome was distinctly anti-woman is an understatement. Families typically kept all their healthy boys and their oldest healthy girl. Other daughters were left to die as infants. Surgical abortion was available, and women often died from it or were left maimed. Surviving girls were typically married off at age twelve and were pressured into remarriage when widowed.

Christians opposed these practices. They took in abandoned infants, condemned surgical abortion, allowed girls to remain unmarried until they were ready, and provided support for widows. Welcomed by the church rather than shunned, women converted to Christianity at a far higher rate than men and rose to positions of leadership.[40] Unsurprisingly, this led to a surplus of Christian women who, in marrying pagan men, provided the early church "with a steady flow of secondary converts," as Rodney Stark drily phrased it.[41] Also, because they accepted rather than rejected all children, Christians gained a distinct population advantage in producing the next generation.

> **Christianity's acceptance of women's dignity led to cultural innovations all over the world.**

Furthermore, Christianity's acceptance of women's dignity led to cultural innovations all over the world. In India, for example, it was only when Parliament forced the British East India Company to allow Christian missionaries into India that the practice of suttee was questioned. It took decades, but these missionaries, together with indigenous Christians like Krishna Mohan Bannerjee, eventually succeeded in having this gruesome practice banned.[42]

In China, traditional culture held that tiny feet were a mark of status and beauty for women. In many parts of China, the feet of little girls were bound tightly to prevent them from growing. This broke the toes and bones in the arches of their feet, leaving many girls nearly crippled. In the 1600s, the Manchu emperors (who were not ethnically Chinese) tried and failed to stop the practice. In the late 1800s, however, Chinese Christian women, such as medical doctor Shi Meiyu, began agitating against this abuse of young girls and women and were eventually successful in making the practice illegal.[43] Meiyu also exerted a transformational influence on China through her work in medicine and public health and the help she provided to opium addicts.[44]

Historically in most cultures, women were often denied educational opportunities. Christian missionaries and indigenous Christian leaders changed that in country after country. In Japan, Nitobe Inazō, a scholar with five doctoral degrees and an innovator in Japan's agricultural advancement, founded Tokyo Christian Women's University and became its first president.[45] Tsuda Umeko, a Japanese woman educated in the United States, became the private tutor of prime minister Ito Hirobumi's children. She had such an influence on securing the right of women to education that Tsuda College, the most prestigious private women's college in Japan, is named in her honor.[46]

Pandita Ramabai, based on her evangelical Christian beliefs, dedicated herself to breaking down the caste system in India. In the midst of the 1897 famine and plague, Ramabai started the Mukti Mission (*mukti* means "salvation" in Marathi, the local language). By 1900, the mission was caring for two thousand girls, who studied literature, physiology, botany, and practical arts such as printing and carpentry. Girls at the mission were required to be involved in social causes, and the resulting impact was immense.[47]

> **It was Christians, not Secularists, who helped secure rights for women based on a conviction that men and women are equal in the sight of God.**

During the Industrial Revolution in England, children were often treated as slaves, working long hours in dangerous conditions in factories and mines and denied education and proper nutrition. Young girls were often forced into prostitution. Christian reformers, such as John Wood, a devout Christian and the owner of a cloth mill, led by example, limiting the workday and establishing a church and school as part of his operation. Others, such as Anglican priest George Bull and member of Parliament Michael Sadler, fought against a legislative system reluctant to intervene in economic matters, helping secure more reasonable work hours and some form of education for affected children.[48]

It was Christians, not Secularists, who helped secure rights for women based on a conviction that men and women are equal in the sight of God. Their work started the women's movement two thousand years ago. The same impulse that elevated women, children, and slaves also elevated common people through education, as we shall see next.

6. How Christians Acting on Biblical Beliefs Established Modern Education

Social philosopher Thomas Sowell once pointed out, tongue in cheek, that "each new generation born is in effect an invasion of civilization by little barbarians, who must be civilized before it is too late."[49] Failing to educate even one generation can set a nation's progress back one hundred years. Because Christianity is a belief and thought system before it is a set of practices, Christians have always valued the life of the mind. Wherever Christians have gone, schools have followed.

> Christians have always valued the life of the mind. Wherever Christians have gone, schools have followed.

In medieval times, Europe was in serious decline. The population was dwindling. Civil authority was collapsing. Education was in ruins. Who saved it? Irish monks.[50] The Celtic revival from the fifth through the ninth centuries preserved and restored many aspects essential to a thriving culture, particularly education. In the AD 500s, an Irish monk named Saint Columbanus embarked on a *perigrinatio*, a pilgrimage from which he expected never to return. He sailed first to Britain and then to France and ultimately to Switzerland and Italy, establishing monasteries along the way. These monasteries focused on literacy and learning, and many became homes to celebrated libraries. One of Columbanus's monasteries, Luxeuil, is

> *Perigrinatio:* a pilgrimage from which one does not expect to return.

known to have sent out sixty-three missionaries who, in turn, established one hundred other monasteries that carried on Columbanus's educational work.[51]

The success of the French king Charlemagne's (circa 747–814) military campaigns in the late 700s and early 800s brought stability to the European continent. While Charlemagne's legacy is undoubtedly mixed, one of his successes was convincing the scholar Alcuin of York (735–804) to educate his own children and establish a liberal-arts-oriented educational system for the area under his control. This area became known as the Carolingian Empire. Alcuin is credited with preserving many of the texts we have today from the classical period. He established schools throughout Europe with a standardized curriculum and reformed the copying of textbooks by developing a new style of handwriting. Alcuin also had a direct influence on Charlemagne himself, convincing him, among other things, to stop forcing pagans to convert to Christianity under the threat of execution.[52]

As Europe moved into the second millennium, higher education was increasingly centered in cathedral schools, such as those Alcuin developed. These schools became the first universities and were so closely connected with the church that their students and faculty were considered members of the clergy.

In the late Middle Ages, Geert Groote from the Netherlands established the Brethren of the Common Life, an organization promoting literacy and offering people access to materials they could use to live better Christian lives. As a result of these efforts, schools sprang up across Europe,[53] educating people like Pope Adrian VI, Cardinal Nicholas of Cusa, Rudolph Agricola, Desiderius Erasmus, and Martin Luther. In the 1600s, August Hermann Francke (1663–1727), convinced that Christian education was the only way to counter moral depravity, began an educational movement that Johann Julius Hecker (1707–1768) carried on, which ultimately established hundreds of schools throughout Prussia, a German kingdom that at one time encompassed much of Europe.[54] The king of Prussia, Frederick the Great, liked these schools so much that he signed a comprehensive compulsory-education law in 1763, paving the way for the modern idea of compulsory education.[55] While this had the unfortunate result of tying school and state together, thus ensuring that schools would become more secular as the state did, it shows the enormous influence of early Christians—indeed, deeply devout Christians—in forming what we now assume to be a universal right to education.

> **Protestants formed primary schools in the belief that Bible knowledge was essential to preparing citizens who would hold the government in check.**

In America, as in Europe, schools were founded almost entirely by churches or other Christian organizations. Some of America's most famous schools, such as Harvard, William and Mary, Yale, Princeton, and Brown, were all founded as Christian institutions. Yet Christianity's influence wasn't just in higher education. Protestants formed primary schools in the belief that Bible knowledge was essential to preparing citizens who would hold the government in check. The Bible wasn't the only text in these schools, but its teachings were thought to be the basis for both virtuous living as well as a prosperous society.

Even the development of America's public schools was a profoundly biblical enterprise. Benjamin Rush, the father of American public education, argued that the Bible was the single most important text students could study, since its principles were the basis for character and good citizenship.[56]

Christianity's focus on education also spread around the world, as missionaries founded what, in many parts of the world, became the first primary, secondary, and postsecondary schools. William Carey, in India, made advances in botany, astronomy, women's rights, medicine, banking, and industry. In addition, he mastered several Indian languages and translated classical Indian literature into English. Carey was far more than a teacher, however. He brought the first printing press to India and developed typefaces for Indian languages, translating all or part of the Bible into forty-four of them and developing grammars and dictionaries for seventy-three languages along the way.[57]

Indigenous Christians in other nations also exerted a great deal of influence in education. In addition to Krishna Mohan Bannerjee, Shi Meiyu, Tsuda Umeko, Pandita Ramabai, and Nitobe Inazō, whom we've already discussed, we could also include Joseph Hardy Neesima in Japan, one of the most important educators of the Meiji period (Japan's era of modernization); Fei Qihao, who narrowly survived the Boxer Rebellion in China and helped start the Young Men's Christian Association (YMCA) there; Zhang Fuliang, who established rural schools in China in the early twentieth century; and H. L. Zia, who became China's first major Christian author.[58]

With its focus on education, it's only natural that Christianity contributed substantially to the development of modern medicine. Let's discover how this happened.

7. How Christians Acting on Biblical Beliefs Formed the Practice of Modern Medicine

In addition to starting schools wherever they went, Christians also established hospitals. Because they believed that caring for the body was an important part of bearing God's image, early Christians tended the sick during epidemics when everyone else, including physicians, fled. Cyprian, the bishop of Carthage, and Dionysius, the bishop of Alexandria, documented accounts of Christians staying behind and nursing the sick, often forfeiting their own lives in the process. The same thing happened during the Black Death in Europe from 1347 to 1351, when the mortality rate among the clergy was higher than that of the general population because they risked their lives to care for the afflicted.

Why would Christians care for the sick knowing they might lose their own lives? Clearly, they took literally Jesus's teaching about loving their neighbors (Mark 12:31)[59] and caring for the sick (Matt. 25:34–40).[60] They were convinced that the same Jesus who instructed them to care for bodily needs would care for their souls in the afterlife once their own bodies gave out, just as he had promised (John 14:1–3).[61] They didn't fear death.

> Because they believed that caring for the body was an important part of bearing God's image, early Christians tended the sick during epidemics when everyone else, including physicians, fled.

Throughout the Middle Ages, care of the seriously ill fell to Christian religious institutions. These institutions were most often associated with monasteries, though groups of Christian laypeople (nonclergy) ran some of them. Even as medical care became increasingly secularized, the Catholic Church continued to establish hospitals, as did the Moravian Brethren and Pietists at Halle. Sir Thomas Percival (1740–1804), a Dissenter who had studied theology prior to becoming a physician, helped create the field of occupational health and wrote an influential book on medical ethics. One of the American founders we discussed earlier, Benjamin Rush, was a physician whose faith clearly inspired his work.[62] Today the medical personnel of hospitals founded by Catholics, Methodists, Baptists, and other Christian denominations continue the tradition of living out their faith in practical ways.

In addition to the gospel and education, Christian missionaries took modern medicine with them to the mission field. While colonial governments invested little effort in helping natives, missionaries saw providing medical care as part of their calling. They opened hospitals and arranged for local Christians to receive medical training at Western universities. The Methodist missionary Gertrude Howe, for example, prepared a number of Chinese women for entrance into the University of Michigan. Of these, Kang Chang and Shi Meiyu, who, as we talked about earlier, was influential in establishing women's rights in China, received their medical degrees.[63] Establishing hospitals and training nurses became an important part of their work.

It only makes sense that the same impulse to care for the sick would motivate Christians to also care for the poor. This led Christians to establish modern systems of charity.

8. HOW CHRISTIANS ACTING ON BIBLICAL BELIEFS INSTITUTED PRINCIPLES OF MODERN CHARITY

Christians, taking principles directly from the Bible, transformed concepts of both charity and responsibility for others in the Western world. Jesus strongly encouraged his followers to take care of those in need, even if doing so would be "politically incorrect" (see, for example, the parable of the good Samaritan, in which the "unclean" Samaritan did the right thing when the Jewish religious leaders did not). Jesus drew on Old Testament principles of caring for the widow, the orphan, and the sojourner and also criticized Jews for practicing these principles only within their own community. Following Jesus's admonition, early Christians gave to those in need, Christian or not, and even went so far as to fast for days at a time to save money to give to the destitute.[64]

> *Mercy:* receiving forgiveness rather than the punishment one deserves.

> *Charity:* the act of voluntarily giving time, money, and other resources to help those who are in need.

This behavior was unthinkable in many parts of the pagan world. In fact, the satirist Lucian mocked Christians for their charitable impulse. To the pagan way of thinking, **mercy** and **charity** were vices, not virtues. Referencing the work of historian Edwin A. Judge, Rodney Stark explains:

> Classical philosophers regarded mercy and pity as pathological emotions—defects of character to be avoided by all rational men. Since mercy involves providing *unearned* help or relief, it was contrary to justice. Therefore [according to Judge,] "mercy indeed is not governed by reason at all," and humans must learn "to curb the impulse"; "the cry of the undeserving for mercy" must go "unanswered."… Judge continued: "Pity was a defect of character unworthy of the wise and excusable only in those who have not yet grown up."[65]

Instead of charity, wealthy Romans practiced "patronage," taking in poor individuals only in exchange for public acknowledgment of their virtue for having done so.

By contrast, Christianity teaches that mercy is a primary virtue. God is merciful and expects us to be merciful as well. Not only that, but Christians also worship a God who actually *loves* people. This in turn motivates them to be loving: "We love because he first loved us" wrote the apostle John (1 John 4:19). The idea that pleasing God involves loving one another was an entirely new concept in the ancient world. Perhaps even more revolutionary was the principle that Christian love and charity should be extended beyond boundaries of family and tribe, even to enemies, and while expecting nothing in return (Luke 6:27–36).[66]

By some accounts, Christian charity was deeply threatening to Rome. In trying to return Rome to its pagan roots after the death of the emperor Constantine, Julian the Apostate complained, "These impious Galileans [i.e., Christians] feed not only their own poor, but ours as well, while no one in need looks to temples."[67] He tried, without success, to get pagan temples to engage in charity so as to win back people's allegiance from Christianity.

In the Middle Ages, individual and corporate charity grew dramatically. Monasteries, lay confraternities (religious brotherhoods), guilds, churches, and wealthy individuals all supported the poor by feeding the hungry, caring for the sick, and providing for widows and orphans. Christians further shaped culture in the realm of charity by inventing new social services, such as paying dowries so poor women could marry (a ministry started by Nicholas of Patara, known today as Saint Nicholas, on whom the story of Santa Claus is based). The convictions and creativity of Christians brought about such an enduring change in culture that today in the West even nonbelievers take it as a moral obligation to help those less fortunate. This impulse gave rise to such organizations as the Young Men's Christian Association (YMCA), the Young Women's Christian Association (YWCA), the Salvation Army, the Red Cross, and the United Way, as well as World Vision, Compassion International, Samaritan's Purse, and the International Justice Mission.

Christian beliefs about God, creation, and Scripture motivated Christians to start schools, hospitals, and relief organizations. Though it's surprising to some, these same beliefs also inspired Christians to develop the modern scientific enterprise. Here's how.

> God is merciful and expects us to be merciful as well. Not only that, but Christians also worship a God who actually loves people. This in turn motivates them to be loving.

9. How Christians Acting on Biblical Beliefs Built the Foundations of Modern Science

Science and religion are often imagined to be at odds with each other, but in reality they are complementary ways of knowing. Rabbi Lord Jonathan Sachs—the former chief rabbi of Great Britain, a distinguished professor at three universities, and a member of the House of Lords—says, "Science takes things apart to see how they work. Religion puts things together to see what they mean."[68]

Wondering *why* the world works the way it does is what led early scientists to explore *how* it works. The result was science as we know it today. Nobel Prize–winning physicist Steven Weinberg, no fan of religion, admits, "The Protestant Reformation of the early sixteenth century set the stage for the great scientific breakthroughs of seventeenth-century England."[69]

> Modern science came about not as a rebellion against the Christian faith but as an outworking of it.

Sociologist Rodney Stark goes even further. Of the fifty-two active scientists who made the most significant contributions during the Scientific Revolution, only one was an atheist, he says. More than 60 percent were devout Christians.[70] Modern science came about not as a rebellion against the Christian faith but as an outworking of it. This is startling to those who believe the anti-theist narrative that science is both a rebellion against and superior to Christianity.

So exactly how did Christianity bring about modern science? In their book *The Soul of Science*, Nancy Pearcey and Charles Thaxton explain that Christianity provided the greenhouse in which science could develop and that other worldviews did not, though they had plenty of opportunity to do so. Pearcey and Thaxton identify seven Christian convictions that enabled the scientific impulse to flourish:[71]

> 1. **Nature is real and valuable enough to study** (as opposed to the ancient Greek belief that nature was transient and therefore relatively unimportant).
>
> 2. **Nature is good, but it isn't God** (as opposed to animistic religions that leave nature alone because it's the exclusive abode of the gods).
>
> 3. **Nature is orderly** (as opposed to religions that teach that the world is unpredictable because it is ruled by a pantheon of unruly and unpredictable gods).
>
> 4. **Nature's laws can be precisely stated and understood** (as opposed to ancient religions that taught that creation was too mysterious to be consistently known).
>
> 5. **Humans can discover nature's order** (as opposed to the ancient Eastern belief that nature was not the product of a rational mind and therefore not subject to rational thinking).
>
> 6. **Detailed observation is possible and important** (as opposed to Aristotle's thinking that if an object's purpose was understood, detailed observation of it was unnecessary).
>
> 7. **The universe is rationally intelligible because God is rationally intelligent** (as opposed to philosophies that trust limited human intelligence as the only kind that really exists).

If the universe is a "theatre" of God's glory, as John Calvin eloquently phrased it, then studying the world points us directly to God.

Interestingly, these assumptions made the study of the natural world both theological as well as scientific. God cares about what he has made, and so should we. If the universe is a "theatre" of God's glory, as John Calvin eloquently phrased it,[72] and if scientific inquiry is a process of "thinking God's thoughts after him," or as Johannes Kepler famously expressed, "[sharing] in his own thoughts,"[73] then studying the world points us directly to God.[74]

Ancient Greeks tended to reason *about* the world. Beginning in the twelfth century, though, scientists informed by their Christian beliefs decided to look *at* it. The effect was that scholars, such as the unfortunately named Robert Grosseteste (his last name may be translated "fat head") (1170–1253), developed methods for observing aspects of nature and identifying from those observations a universal law that could be used to understand other aspects. The focus on induction, deduction, experimentation, and observation formed a strong basis for the later development of the **scientific method**.[75]

Roger Bacon (1214–1294), one of Grosseteste's students at Oxford and later a Franciscan priest, further developed the scientific process of observation and experimentation. He called for the use of mathematics, as well as direct observation, to describe the world. This led to the study of natural philosophy and natural theology, which in turn became the building blocks for natural science and laid the foundation of the Scientific Revolution.[76] A few hundred years later, Francis Bacon (1561–1626) (probably from the same family line as Roger Bacon) codified what we think of as the scientific method. Bacon was a devout Anglican, and Christianity's teachings on God, humanity, and the natural world were important influences on his thinking about science.

> *Scientific Method:* a process of empirical inquiry that seeks to understand the phenomena of the physical world through hypothesizing, observing, measuring, experimenting, predicting, and testing.

Along with Francis Bacon, the principal leaders of the Scientific Revolution in the sixteenth to eighteenth centuries were almost all devout Christians. Nicolaus Copernicus (1473–1543) was a churchman who originally undertook astronomy to determine the date of Easter more reliably. Johannes Kepler (1571–1630) was a devout Lutheran who thought of astronomy as a form of theology.[77] Galileo Galilei (1564–1642), for all his well-publicized spats with the Catholic Church, exerted a great deal of effort to prove that the Bible supported the idea that the earth was not the center of the universe. Sir Isaac Newton (1642–1727), though unorthodox in many ways, saw himself as a Christian and wrote more about theology than he did about physics. Similarly, Robert Boyle (1627–1691), referred to as the "father of modern chemistry," was a devout Christian so concerned about the rise of "irreligion" that he wrote *The Christian Virtuoso*, a manifesto on how to be fully Christian as a scientist.[78]

Christian involvement in science has formed an unbroken chain right up to the present time. For example, Leonhard Euler (1707–1783) was a physicist and mathematician whose discoveries were so numerous that physicists and mathematicians today joke that to avoid naming everything after Euler, they are forced to name discoveries and theorems after the first person to rediscover them *after* Euler. Along with his work in math and physics, however, Euler also wrote works defending biblical inspiration and arguing for the importance of Christianity as a foundation for science.[79]

> Along with Francis Bacon, the principal leaders of the Scientific Revolution in the sixteenth to eighteenth centuries were almost all devout Christians.

James Clerk Maxwell (1831–1879), considered the third most important physicist in history next to Newton and Einstein, was another devout

Christian who saw his work as an expression of his faith. The dominant view of science in Maxwell's day was **positivism**, which discounts revelation and says that empirical observation, logic, and mathematical analysis *alone* are valid ways of knowing. Maxwell, who believed in biblical authority and miracles, saw science as a religious calling and even involved himself in debates on the philosophy of science.[80]

Many famous scientists of the twenty-first century are also Christians. For instance, Francis Collins, a physician and geneticist who headed up the Human Genome Project and is currently the head of the National Institutes of Health, claims a Christian faith and sees his work as an expression of that faith. His book *The Language of God: A Scientist Provides Evidence for Belief* focuses on providing scientific evidence for God's existence.

In summary, early scientists' beliefs about God, creation, and Scripture undergirded the development of modern science. Biblical beliefs took into account nature's value, goodness, orderliness, precision, discoverability, accessibility, and intelligibility. They gave curious people permission—indeed, a mandate—to explore creation's wonders. Not only that, but they also enabled believers to see the beauty of creation. This led some Christians, in a very different but equally profitable direction, to contribute to culture through the arts.

> *Positivism:* the idea that sensory experience, interpreted through logical thinking, forms the only basis for knowledge.

10. How Christians Acting on Biblical Beliefs Shaped the Arts

Most of the West's greatest art is about Christian themes. Icons, religious paintings, the Madonnas that Renaissance artists painted and sculpted, and even the deep symbolism of Muiredach's Irish High Crosses[81] were all designed to reveal Christian truths. Musical works such as Bach's *St. Matthew Passion* and Handel's *Messiah* were among thousands written for, or even commissioned by, churches or religiously inclined civil authorities to induce a worshipful attitude among the faithful. Religious themes also dominate great works of literature, such as Dante's *Divine Comedy* and Milton's *Paradise Lost*, and even later works, such as Lew Wallace's *Ben-Hur: A Tale of the Christ* or Henryk Sienkiewicz's *Quo Vadis*. One can hardly travel in Europe without being captivated by architecture designed to display God's glory, whether the Cathedral of Notre-Dame in Paris; the Hagia Sophia in Istanbul, Turkey; or Saint Peter's Basilica in Rome.

> *Postmodernism:* a skeptical worldview, founded as a reaction to modernism, which is suspicious of metanarratives and teaches that ultimate reality is inaccessible, knowledge is a social construct, and truth claims are political power plays.

But the influence of the biblical worldview shapes art in ways that go well beyond depictions of Christian people or ideas. This is especially important to recognize amid today's aggressive attempts to "disrupt bourgeois fantasies about art," as Glenn Ward phrased it, describing the way Postmodernists believe privileged people hijack art to create an idealistic view of reality.[82] **Postmodernism, which teaches that ultimate reality is**

inaccessible, may seem clever and cutting edge, but why is it that master works of art aren't being produced today as they were hundreds of years ago? Why did a previous age give us Michelangelo's *David*, while our age's "famous" works include Marcel Duchamp's 1917 display of a urinal, titled *Fountain*, symbolizing that everything is waste to be flushed away?[83]

In the previous section on science, we explored the idea that because the world came from God, studying nature can lead us back to God. The term for this idea, developed in the medieval cathedral schools, is **platonic humanism**. Artists, like philosophers and theologians, believed that observing the world *as it is* helps us understand the mind of the Creator and thus makes us want to depict the world as it really is.

> *Platonic Humanism:* the idea that because the world came from God, studying the world can lead us back to God.

This change of mind-set transformed art. Earlier medieval art, such as the sculptures at Chartres Cathedral carved in the late twelfth and early thirteenth centuries, featured elongated figures with stylized clothing falling in parallel folds. This changed abruptly in the mid-thirteenth century, as we can see in the mortuary chapel of Naumburg Cathedral in Germany.[84] This new, realistic approach to art would continue to develop through the late Middle Ages, leading ultimately to the astonishing art of Jan van Eyck in Flanders and the work of the great Renaissance masters.

As Jonathan Hill explains in *What Has Christianity Ever Done for Us?*,

> It was the emphasis on the intrinsic spirituality of nature that helped to lead Western art, during and after the Renaissance, to the pursuit of realism which has been a central feature of art ever since. In Asia, the visual arts remained more stylized— which is why the Chinese were so astounded by a picture of the Virgin Mary that they thought the image must be somehow real. The laws of perspective, for example, were unknown to the Chinese, who simply depicted more distant objects above closer ones. But in Renaissance Europe, these laws and other aids to accuracy were discovered, allowing artists to achieve far more realistic images. Moreover, the interest in accuracy spurred artists and others to investigate the human body in more detail, providing an incentive to the study of anatomy and medicine.[85]

Art was seen not just as frilly ornamentation or a means of showcasing an artist's skill but also as a means of vividly displaying how the divine touches our everyday experiences, transforming medicine as well as art.

Christian beliefs have shaped music as well. Unlike many other religions, Christianity is a singing faith. This melodic impulse inspired artists to use what they created for worship to form the expectations of the role of music—and how it ought to be performed—in all of society. You've probably heard plainsong chants (sometimes

> Art was seen as a means of vividly displaying how the divine touches our everyday experiences.

called *Gregorian chant* after Pope Saint Gregory the Great) and noticed that while they are hauntingly beautiful, they lack musical accompaniment. They are *monophonic*, meaning that they consist of a melody without a harmony. Gradually, church musicians developed an increasingly complex *polyphony* that required sophisticated systems of musical notation. These systems of notation, along with the forms of music developed for churches, formed the scaffolding on which the platform of classical music was built.

> Western music is related to the deep structure of the biblical narrative. It mirrors the glory of creation, the tension of the fall, and the resolution of redemption.

The basic format of Western music, which begins in harmony, progresses into tension, and then releases the tension through melodic resolution, is actually related to the deep structure of the biblical narrative. It mirrors the glory of creation, the tension of the fall, and the resolution of redemption. We might think this is a universal pattern in music, but listening for a few minutes to musical patterns common in other parts of the world, such as Buddhist chanting, will show that it is not.

Similarly, Western literature often displays Christian themes, such as the horror of sin, the honor of self-sacrifice, and the glory of redemption. Aside from obvious greats like Dante, John Bunyan, or John Milton, authors as diverse as Fyodor Dostoyevsky, T. S. Eliot, Walker Percy, Flannery O'Connor, and G. K. Chesterton all explored the human predicament from a perspective shaped by their Christian beliefs.

It's also perhaps worth noting that even popular culture mimics the forms that emerged from Christian beliefs. In the Marvel Comics movie *Thor*, for example, Thor's belligerence and arrogance lead to his being stripped of power and sent into exile.[86] He's restored to power only when he learns humility and self-sacrifice, plainly based in Jesus's teaching that "Greater love has no one than this, that someone lay down his life for his friends" (John 15:13). This is dramatically different from the Thor of Norse mythology, in which a proud, warlike attitude was the ideal.[87] Today a character who remains proud and refuses to serve others wouldn't be considered a hero. This is just one example of how thoroughly the ideas of Christian virtue have shaped even surface aspects of our culture.

> Christian influence in the arts runs so deep that most people don't realize they're being affected by it every day.

Christian influence in the arts runs so deep that most people don't realize they're being affected by it every day. But this may be said of other areas of Christian engagement as well. Many of the aspects of modern society that we appreciate in our moments of curiosity or need came about because someone used his or her skill to reflect a firm belief in God, the Bible, and God's plan for redeeming the world through Jesus Christ.

11. CONCLUSION

Christians have wielded a weighty influence on nearly every aspect of Western culture and on other cultures around the world. Most probably didn't realize how their contributions would shape culture for generations to come. So it is with us. History's culture shapers influenced the world *because* of their Christian faith, not in spite of it. We, too, ought to choose to live in a way that makes life more worthwhile for others.

As we celebrate the genius of our forebears, we must also acknowledge their flaws as part of the story of this sin-wrought world. They were quirky. They sometimes held notions we would consider bizarre. They may have been hard to get along with. Some authors ignore these rough edges and make these heroes of the faith seem superhuman. This isn't helpful. Nor is it helpful to obsess about their warts, as some historians do, and miss the larger picture of how they bore God's image and pursued their callings with passion. Our goal isn't to just admire them; it is to imitate them. Great Christians of the past surely wrestled with fear and doubt and arrogance and anger and jealousy and meanness, as all of us do. And yet God used them to shape culture.

This leads us to the next question: Could God also use *us* to shape our own culture? The answer to that question is yes. How it might be so is what we'll examine in the next chapter.

> **Christians of the past surely wrestled with fear and doubt and arrogance and anger and jealousy and meanness, as all of us do. And yet God used them to shape culture.**

ENDNOTES

1. Christopher Hitchens, *God Is Not Great: How Religion Poisons Everything* (New York: Twelve, 2007), 102.

2. See T. M. Moore, *Culture Matters: A Call for Consensus on Christian Cultural Engagement* (Grand Rapids: Brazos, 2007), 22–24.

3. *God's Not Dead*, directed by Harold Cronk (Pure Flix Productions, 2014).

4. Kevin Vanhoozer, "What Is Everyday Theology? How and Why Christians Should Read Culture," in Kevin J. Vanhoozer, Charles A. Anderson, and Michael J. Sleasman, eds., *Everyday Theology: How to Read Cultural Texts and Interpret Trends* (Grand Rapids: Baker Academic, 2007), 21.

5. Andy Crouch, *Culture Making: Recovering Our Creative Calling* (Downers Grove, IL: InterVarsity, 2008), 23.

6. T. S. Eliot, *Notes towards the Definition of Culture* (New York: Harcourt, Brace, 1949), 26.

7. Dictionary.com, s.v. "religion," http://dictionary.reference.com/browse/religion.

8. Luke 10:27: "You shall love the Lord your God with all your heart and with all your soul and with all your strength and with all your mind, and your neighbor as yourself."

9. Matthew 23:27: "Woe to you, scribes and Pharisees, hypocrites! For you are like whitewashed tombs, which outwardly appear beautiful, but within are full of dead people's bones and all uncleanness."

10. Matthew 5:22: "I say to you that everyone who is angry with his brother will be liable to judgment; whoever insults his brother will be liable to the council; and whoever says, 'You fool!' will be liable to the hell of fire."

11. Martin Luther King Jr., "Towards Freedom," speech at Dartmouth College, May 23, 1962, www.dartmouth.edu/~mlk/towards_freedom_mlk.pdf.

12. Vanhoozer, *Everyday Theology*, 34.

13. Genesis 1:26–27: "God said, 'Let us make man in our image, after our likeness. And let them have dominion over the fish of the sea and over the birds of the heavens and over the livestock and over all the earth and over every creeping thing that creeps on the earth.' So God created man in his own image, in the image of God he created him; male and female he created them."

14. Exodus 23:6–9: "You shall not pervert the justice due to your poor in his lawsuit. Keep far from a false charge, and do not kill the innocent and righteous, for I will not acquit the wicked. And you shall take no bribe, for a bribe blinds the clear-sighted and subverts the cause of those who are in the right. You shall not oppress a sojourner."

15. Acts 16:14–15: "One who heard us was a woman named Lydia, from the city of Thyatira, a seller of purple goods, who was a worshiper of God. The Lord opened her heart to pay attention to what was said by Paul. And after she was baptized, and her household as well, she urged us, saying, 'If you have judged me to be faithful to the Lord, come to my house and stay.' And she prevailed upon us"; Acts 16:40: "[Paul and Silas] went out of the prison and visited Lydia."; Romans 16:1–16: "I commend to you our sister Phoebe, a servant of the church at Cenchreae, that you may welcome her in the Lord in a way worthy of the saints, and help her in whatever she may need from you, for she has been a patron of many and of myself as well. Greet Prisca and Aquila, my fellow workers in Christ Jesus, who risked their necks for my life.… Greet Mary, who has worked hard for you.… Greet Rufus, chosen in the Lord; also his mother, who has been a mother to me as well.… Greet Philologus, Julia, Nereus and his sister, and Olympas, and all the saints who are with them"; 1 Corinthians 1:11: "It has been reported to me by Chloe's people that there is quarreling among you, my brothers"; Philippians 4:2: "I entreat Euodia and I entreat Syntyche to agree in the Lord"; Colossians 4:15: "Give my greetings to the brothers at Laodicea, and to Nympha

and the church in her house."

16. Galatians 3:27–29: "As many of you as were baptized into Christ have put on Christ. There is neither Jew nor Greek, there is neither slave nor free, there is no male and female, for you are all one in Christ Jesus. And if you are Christ's, then you are Abraham's offspring, heirs according to promise."

17. Glenn Sunshine, research paper provided for this chapter, March 17, 2014. Sunshine is a professor of early modern European history at Central Connecticut State University.

18. Genesis 9:6: "Whoever sheds the blood of man, by man shall his blood be shed, for God made man in his own image."

19. Genesis 2:16: "The LORD God commanded the man, saying, 'You may surely eat of every tree of the garden.'"

20. Jürgen Habermas, *Time of Transitions* (Malden, MA: Polity, 2006), 150–51.

21. Sunshine, research paper submitted for this chapter.

22. Robert D. Woodberry, "The Missionary Roots of Liberal Democracy," *American Political Science Review* 106, no. 2 (May 2012): 244–45.

23. Glenn Sunshine, "Krishna Mohan Bannerjee (1813–1885)," *Christian Worldview Journal*, March 25, 2013, www .colsoncenter.org/the-center/columns/call-response/19458-krishna-mohan-bannerjee-1813-1885.

24. Glenn Sunshine, "Chiune Sugihara (1900–1986)," *Christian Worldview Journal*, February 25, 2013, www.colsoncenter .org/the-center/columns/call-response/19313-christians-who-changed-their-world.

25. Genesis 1:26–27: "God said, 'Let us make man in our image, after our likeness. And let them have dominion over the fish of the sea and over the birds of the heavens and over the livestock and over all the earth and over every creeping thing that creeps on the earth.' So God created man in his own image, in the image of God he created him; male and female he created them."

26. Romans 16:9: "Greet Urbanus, our fellow worker in Christ, and my beloved Stachys."

27. First Corinthians 12:13: "In one Spirit we were all baptized into one body—Jews or Greeks, slaves or free—and all were made to drink of one Spirit"; Galatians 3:28: "There is neither Jew nor Greek, there is neither slave nor free, there is no male and female, for you are all one in Christ Jesus"; Colossians 3:11: "Here there is not Greek and Jew, circumcised and uncircumcised, barbarian, Scythian, slave, free; but Christ is all, and in all."

28. Philemon 1:16: "No longer as a bondservant but more than a bondservant, as a beloved brother—especially to me, but how much more to you, both in the flesh and in the Lord."

29. Revelation 18:11–13: "The merchants of the earth weep and mourn for her, since no one buys their cargo anymore, cargo of gold, silver, jewels, pearls, fine linen, purple cloth, silk, scarlet cloth, all kinds of scented wood, all kinds of articles of ivory, all kinds of articles of costly wood, bronze, iron and marble, cinnamon, spice, incense, myrrh, frankincense, wine, oil, fine flour, wheat, cattle and sheep, horses and chariots, and slaves, that is, human souls."

30. Ezekiel 27:13: "Javan, Tubal, and Meshech traded with you; they exchanged human beings and vessels of bronze for your merchandise."

31. First Timothy 1:9–10: "Understanding this, that the law is not laid down for the just but for the lawless and disobedient, for the ungodly and sinners, for the unholy and profane, for those who strike their fathers and mothers, for murderers, the sexually immoral, men who practice homosexuality, enslavers, liars, perjurers, and whatever else is contrary to sound doctrine."

32. See Aristotle, *Nicomachean Ethics*, 8.11.

33. Augustine, Letter 10 to Alypius, para. 7, in *Augustine: Political Writings*, eds. E. Margaret Atkins and Robert J. Dodaro (Cambridge, UK: Cambridge University Press, 2001), 46.

34. Walk Free Global Slavery Index, in Max Fisher, "This Map Shows Where the World's 30 Million Slaves Live. There Are 60,000 in the U.S.," *Washington Post*, October 17, 2013, www.washingtonpost.com/news/worldviews/wp/2013/10/17 /this-map-shows-where-the-worlds-30-million-slaves-live-there-are-60000-in-the-u-s/.

35. Glenn Sunshine, "Olaudah Equiano (1745–1797)," *Christian Worldview Journal*, May 5, 2014, www.colsoncenter.org/the -center/columns/call-response/21700-olaudah-equiano-c1745-1797-christians-who-changed-their-worlds.

36. Glenn Sunshine, "Hannah More (1745–1833)," *Christian Worldview Journal*, April 6, 2015, www.colsoncenter.org/the -center/columns/changed/22783-christians-who-changed-their-world-hannah-more-1745-1833.

37. Glenn Sunshine, "Josiah Wedgwood (1730–1795)," *Christian Worldview Journal*, February 27, 2012, www.colsoncenter .org/the-center/columns/indepth/17482-josiah-wedgwood-1730-1795.

38. Thomas Clarkson, *History of the Rise, Progress, and Accomplishment of the Abolition of the African Slave Trade by the British Parliament* (London: John W. Parker, 1839), 417.

39. Frederick Douglass was a minister in the African Methodist Episcopal Church. His remarks against Christianity are often cited as evidence that he had turned against the faith of his youth, but Douglass himself distinguished clearly between the "Christianity of Christ" and the "White Christianity" he felt was both hypocritical and cruel. See "People of Faith: Frederick Douglass," *This Far by Faith: African-American Spiritual Journeys* (Blackside and the Faith Project, 2003), www.pbs.org/thisfarbyfaith/people/frederick_douglass.html.

40. Rodney Stark, *The Rise of Christianity: A Sociologist Reconsiders History* (Princeton, NJ: Princeton University Press, 1996), 128.

41. Stark, *Rise of Christianity*, 128.

42. Sunshine, "Krishna Mohan Bannerjee."

43. Glenn Sunshine, "Shi Meiyu (1873–1954)," *Christian Worldview Journal*, April 15, 2013, www.colsoncenter.org/the -center/columns/call-response/19567-shi-meiyu-1873-1954.

44. Sunshine, "Shi Meiyu."

45. Glenn Sunshine, "Nitobe Inazō (1862–1933)," *Christian Worldview Journal*, January 28, 2013, www.colsoncenter.org/the -center/columns/call-response/19162-christians-who-changed-their-world.

46. Glenn Sunshine, "Tsuda Umeko (1864–1929)," *Christian Worldview Journal*, February 18, 2013, www.colsoncenter.org /the-center/columns/call-response/19271-tsuda-umeka-1864-1929.

47. Glenn Sunshine, "Pandita Ramabai (1858–1922)," *Christian Worldview Journal*, March 11, 2013, www.colsoncenter.org /the-center/columns/call-response/19375-pandita-ramabai-1858-1922.

48. Penelope Carson, "Child Labor: White Slavery," *Christian History* 53 (January 1997), www.christianitytoday.com/history /issues/issue-53/child-labor-white-slavery.html.

49. Thomas Sowell, *A Conflict of Visions: Ideological Origins of Political Struggles*, rev. ed. (New York: Basic Books, 2007), 167.

50. While much has been written about the Irish, Thomas Cahill's *How the Irish Saved Civilization: The Untold Story of Ireland's Heroic Role from the Fall of Rome to the Rise of Medieval Europe* (New York: Anchor Books, 1996) is perhaps the most widely read, or at least the most well known.

51. Glenn Sunshine, "St. Columbanus (540–615)," *Christian Worldview Journal*, October 17, 2011, www.colsoncenter.org/the -center/columns/indepth/17053-st-columbanus-540-615.

52. Glenn Sunshine, "Alcuin of York (735–804)," *Christian Worldview Journal*, November 7, 2011, www.colsoncenter.org/the -center/columns/indepth/17122-alcuin-of-york-c735-804.

53. Glenn Sunshine, "Geert Groote (1340–1384)," *Christian Worldview Journal*, November 28, 2011, www.colsoncenter.org /the-center/columns/indepth/17204-geert-groote-1340-1384.

54. Frank Schnorbus, "Whose Children? Rethinking Schools and Education," *Home School Researcher* 30, no. 1 (2014): 1–6.

55. Schnorbus, "Whose Children?"

56. Glenn Sunshine, "Benjamin Rush (1745–1813)," *Christian Worldview Journal*, December 12, 2011, www.colsoncenter.org /the-center/columns/indepth/17245-benjamin-rush-1745-1813.

57. Glenn Sunshine, "William Carey (1761–1834)," *Christian Worldview Journal*, January 2, 2012, www.colsoncenter.org/the -center/columns/indepth/17309-william-carey-1761-1834.

58. Glenn Sunshine, "Joseph Hardy Neesima (1843–1890)," *Christian Worldview Journal*, January 14, 2013, www.colsoncenter.org /the-center/columns/call-response/19091-christians-who-changed-their-world; "Fei Qihao (1879–1953)," *Christian Worldview Journal*, May 27, 2013, www.colsoncenter.org/the-center/columns/call-response/19793-christians-who-changed-their-world; "Zhang Fuliang (1889–1984)," *Christian Worldview Journal*, October 7, 2013, www.colsoncenter.org/the-center/columns/call -response/20510-christians-who-changed-their-world; and "H. L. Zia (1873–1916)," *Christian Worldview Journal*, August 26, 2013, www.colsoncenter.org/the-center/columns/call-response/20277-christians-who-changed-their-world.

59. Mark 12:31: "The second [commandment] is this: 'You shall love your neighbor as yourself.' There is no other commandment greater than these."

60. Matthew 25:34–40: "The King will say to those on his right, 'Come, you who are blessed by my Father, inherit the kingdom prepared for you from the foundation of the world. For I was hungry and you gave me food, I was thirsty and you gave me drink, I was a stranger and you welcomed me, I was naked and you clothed me, I was sick and you visited me, I was in prison and you came to me.' Then the righteous will answer him, saying, 'Lord, when did we see you hungry and feed you, or thirsty and give you drink? And when did we see you a stranger and welcome you, or naked and clothe you? And when did we see you sick or in prison and visit you?' And the King will answer them, 'Truly, I say to you, as you did it to one of the least of these my brothers, you did it to me.'"

61. John 14:1–3: "Let not your hearts be troubled. Believe in God; believe also in me. In my Father's house are many rooms. If it were not so, would I have told you that I go to prepare a place for you? And if I go and prepare a place for you, I will come again and will take you to myself, that where I am you may be also."

62. Sunshine, "Benjamin Rush."

63. Sunshine, "Shi Meiyu."

64. See, for example, Kent D. Berghuis, "Fasting through the Patristic Era," chap. 3 in *Christian Fasting: A Theological Approach* (Richardson, TX: Biblical Studies Press, 2007).

65. E. A. Judge, "The Quest for Mercy in Late Antiquity," in *God Who Is Rich in Mercy: Essays Presented to D. B. Knox*, eds. P. T. O'Brien and D. G. Peterson (Sydney, Australia: Macquarie University Press, 1986), 107–21, quoted in Stark, *Rise of Christianity*, 212.

66. Luke 6:27–36: "I say to you who hear, Love your enemies, do good to those who hate you, bless those who curse you, pray for those who abuse you. To one who strikes you on the cheek, offer the other also, and from one who takes away your cloak do not withhold your tunic either. Give to everyone who begs from you, and from one who takes away your goods

do not demand them back. And as you wish that others would do to you, do so to them. If you love those who love you, what benefit is that to you? For even sinners love those who love them. And if you do good to those who do good to you, what benefit is that to you? For even sinners do the same. And if you lend to those from whom you expect to receive, what credit is that to you? Even sinners lend to sinners, to get back the same amount. But love your enemies, and do good, and lend, expecting nothing in return, and your reward will be great, and you will be sons of the Most High, for he is kind to the ungrateful and the evil. Be merciful, even as your Father is merciful."

67. Quoted in John Foster, *Church History: The First Advance, AD 29–500* (London: SPCK, 1977), 28.

68. Jonathan Sachs, *The Great Partnership: Science, Religion, and the Search for Meaning* (New York: Schocken Books, 2011), 2.

69. Steven Weinberg, *To Explain the World: The Discovery of Modern Science* (New York: Harper Perennial, 2015), 253.

70. Rodney Stark outlines his methodology in "God's Handiwork: The Religious Origins of Science," chap. 2 in *For the Glory of God: How Monotheism Led to Reformations, Science, Witch-Hunts, and the End of Slavery* (Princeton, NJ: Princeton University Press, 2003), 160–63. Of the fifty-two scientists Stark examined, half were Catholic and half were Protestant. Only two, Edmund Halley and Paracelsus, qualified as skeptics, and Halley was probably, Stark concludes, an atheist.

71. This brief list, which I've summarized, is wonderfully explained, illustrated, and footnoted in Nancy R. Pearcey and Charles B. Thaxton, *The Soul of Science: Christian Faith and Natural Philosophy* (Wheaton, IL: Crossway Books, 1994), 21–37.

72. John Calvin, *Institutes of the Christian Religion*, trans. Henry Beveridge (Grand Rapids: Christian Classics Ethereal Library, 2002), 5.8; 6.1; 14.20, www.ntslibrary.com/PDF%20Books/Calvin%20Institutes%20of%20Christian%20Religion.pdf.

73. Johannes Kepler, letter to Herwart von Hohenberg, 1599, quoted in Philip G. Ryken, *Christian Worldview: A Student's Guide*, Reclaiming the Christian Intellectual Tradition, ed. David S. Dockery (Wheaton, IL: Crossway, 2013), 59.

74. The term for this idea, *platonic humanism*, arose in the cathedral schools we discussed earlier in the section on education. See Glenn Sunshine, "Robert Grosseteste (1170–1253)," *Christian Worldview Journal*, April 30, 2012, www.colsoncenter.org/the-center/columns/indepth/17711-robert-grosseteste-c1170-1253.

75. Sunshine, "Robert Grosseteste."

76. Glenn Sunshine, "Roger Bacon (1214–1294)," *Christian Worldview Journal*, June 4, 2012, www.colsoncenter.org/the-center/columns/indepth/17899-roger-bacon-ca-1214-1294.

77. Glenn Sunshine, "Johannes Kepler (1571–1630)," *Christian Worldview Journal*, June 25, 2012, www.colsoncenter.org/the-center/columns/indepth/18026-johannes-kepler-1571-1630.

78. Glenn Sunshine, "Robert Boyle (1627–1691)," *Christian Worldview Journal*, July 9, 2012, www.colsoncenter.org/the-center/columns/indepth/18094-robert-boyle-1627-1691.

79. Glenn Sunshine, "Leonhard Euler (1707–1783)," *Christian Worldview Journal*, July 23, 2012, www.colsoncenter.org/the-center/columns/indepth/18168-leonhard-euler-1707-1783.

80. Glenn Sunshine, "James Clerk Maxwell (1831–1879)," *Christian Worldview Journal*, August 13, 2012, www.colsoncenter.org/the-center/columns/indepth/18282-james-clerk-maxwell-1831-1879.

81. Glenn Sunshine, "Muiredach (Late 9th–Early 10th Century)," *Christian Worldview Journal*, March 19, 2012, www.colsoncenter.org/the-center/columns/indepth/17534-muiredach-late-9th-early-10th-century.

82. Glenn Ward, *Teach Yourself Postmodernism* (Chicago: McGraw-Hill, 2003), 51.

83. Stephen R. C. Hicks, *Exploring Postmodernism: Skepticism and Socialism from Rousseau to Foucault* (Tempe, AZ: Scholargy, 2004), 196.

84. Glenn Sunshine, "The Naumburg Master," *Christian Worldview Journal*, April 16, 2012, www.colsoncenter.org/the-center/columns/indepth/17652-the-naumburg-master.

85. Jonathan Hill, *What Has Christianity Ever Done for Us? How It Shaped the Modern World* (Downers Grove, IL: InterVarsity, 2005), 37.

86. *Thor*, directed by Alan Taylor (Burbank, CA: Marvel Studios, 2013).

87. Glenn Sunshine, "The Gospel and the Avengers," *Christian Worldview Journal*, May 26, 2014, www.colsoncenter.org/the-center/columns/call-response/21799-the-gospel-and-the-avengers; "The Gospel and the Avengers, Part 2," *Christian Worldview Journal*, June 16, 2014, www.colsoncenter.org/the-center/columns/call-response/21911-the-gospel-and-the-avengers-part-2; and "The Gospel and the Avengers, Part 3," *Christian Worldview Journal*, June 23, 2014, www.colsoncenter.org/the-center/columns/call-response/21945-the-gospel-and-the-avengers-part-3.

CHAPTER 4

4

CHRISTIANITY AND CULTURE: A PLAN

1. WHAT IT MEANS TO SHAPE CULTURE

Most people would think there is no hope for a kid like Pete. Abandoned by his father and often homeless with a mentally ill mother, Pete had to fend for himself. Finding food became an obsession. Still, Pete persevered, earning a university degree, getting married, and building a business.

But he could never seem to get a handle on his weight. Gaining ten pounds a year, Pete ultimately tipped the scales at 416 pounds.

When Pete Thomas was chosen in 2005 to be a contestant on the long-running reality-TV show *The Biggest Loser*, his life changed dramatically. Within nine months Pete had lost 185 pounds.[1] To keep the weight off, he wisely built an accountability structure around himself, mainly by offering exercise boot camps and giving motivational speeches in front of crowds who would be able to see whether he was staying fit.

Watching Pete and the other contestants on *The Biggest Loser* is a case study in transformation. Millions tune in at the beginning of a season to witness the exhaustion, pain, and insecurity related to excess weight. They stay tuned in to watch those same contestants confront their fears and shed the pounds that threaten their lives.

Unfortunately, once the show ends, some contestants find themselves unable to maintain their success and return at least partially to the bad habits that caused them to become overweight in the first place. The ones who keep the weight off, like Pete, do so in two ways: they *avoid* bad habits, and they *pursue* good ones. In fact, one might say that engaging desirable habits is their main way of escaping bad ones.

> Christians who engage a culture that is exhausted, in pain, and fighting insecurity, rather than trying to escape it, can have an enormously positive influence. Yet where do we start?

Culture is like that. What we've seen so far in this book is that Christians who engage a culture that is exhausted, in pain, and fighting insecurity, rather than trying to escape it, can have an enormously positive influence. Yet it's hard. Even if we're motivated and surround ourselves with other talented people who are motivated as well, where would we even start?

Some think we need to start with politics. Change the laws, and people will change accordingly, the thinking goes. Certainly, laws can discourage negative behavior, but they can't really inspire people to be and do their best. This doesn't mean politics is insignificant and unworthy of our time. It's popular today to avoid political involvement because we believe that politics is downstream from culture, and we can't make a difference politically until culture changes. But that's like saying, "I can't eat healthier until I lose weight," or "I'll start a business when I have enough customers." Though the water temperature may not be perfect, that shouldn't stop us from diving in.

Diving in is what this chapter is about. It outlines a two-part plan for becoming culture shapers. First, we'll talk about how to develop a *posture* of engagement by learning to read, write, and share culture with others. Second, we'll establish a *direction* of engagement based on the biblical flow of history from creation, through the fall, and toward redemption.

2. Posture: Reading, Writing, and Sharing

Just as martial artists develop a stance from which a variety of movements are possible, having a strong sense of what is actually true about God, the world, and our relationship to God allows us to assume a thoughtful stance, or posture, of engagement from which we can spring into action in a variety of ways.

In chapter 2, we saw that culture is made up of artifacts, institutions, practices, beliefs, styles, and metabeliefs.[2] In chapter 3, we studied the lives of dozens of culture shapers who, by acting on biblical principles, changed the course of history. What we haven't yet discussed, though, is how you and I might become culture shapers ourselves.

Developing a versatile posture of engagement is important because, as T. S. Eliot pointed out, culture isn't something we can "deliberately aim at."[3] It's unlikely, in fact, that the culture shapers we studied in chapter 3 woke up in the morning and said, "I need to get out of bed so I can create some culture today." Rather, as John Baillie observed, they shaped culture as "a by-product of something immeasurably more to be treasured."[4] Namely, it was a by-product of their desire to know God and please him.

Before we get into our discussion of reading, writing, and sharing culture, here are a few snapshots of what a faithful posture of engagement should look like:

A faithful posture of engagement is thoughtful. Few people think about what culture is, how it's created and sustained, and what effect it has on us. We eat food without thinking about where it comes from, use cell phones without thinking about what makes them work, and absorb popular culture with half our minds tied behind our backs. We shouldn't. "See to it," the apostle Paul wrote, "that no one takes you captive through hollow and deceptive philosophy" (Col. 2:8 NIV). Christians are not to be intellectually passive.

A faithful posture of engagement is intentional. We have to know what is good and develop a strategy for going after it. Changing it for the better isn't something that happens by accident. As G. K. Chesterton said, "A dead thing can go with the stream, but only a living thing can go against it."[5] This book is an invitation to a new kind of life, a life of going against the flow so we may have a shaping influence on the world around us.

> This book is an invitation to a new kind of life, a life of going against the flow so we may have a shaping influence on the world around us.

A faithful posture of engagement is long term. In the same way a sculpted piece of marble can last hundreds of years beyond the artist's own lifetime, the artifacts, institutions, practices, beliefs, styles, and metabeliefs we cultivate tend to have an influence far beyond our own lifetimes. As bestselling author Peter Senge explained it in *The Fifth Discipline*,

> The cathedral builders of the Middle Ages labored a lifetime with the fruits of their labors still a hundred years in the future. The Japanese believe building a great organization is like growing a tree; it takes twenty-five to fifty years. Parents of young children try to lay a foundation of values and attitude that will serve an adult twenty years hence. In all of these cases, people hold a vision that can be realized only over the long term.[6]

Are we building on the work of those who came before us? Are our own works worth building on in the future? These are questions culture shapers ask as they seek a faithful posture of engagement.

A faithful posture of engagement is proactive. If what we've understood in previous chapters about the Christian worldview is true, we ought not to content ourselves with being bystanders. We need to analyze how culture is transmitted from one generation to another.[7] We need to stop passing on bad habits and start passing on good ones. We need to be involved. We need to seek ways to live out our God-given design as stewards of his world.

> **Thoughtfulness, intentionality, long-term thinking, and proactivity are all part of a faithful posture of engagement.**

Thoughtfulness, intentionality, long-term thinking, and proactivity are all part of a faithful posture of engagement. If we're committed to these things, we can be prepared to approach culture in three essential ways. First, we *contemplate* culture; that is, we become culturally literate so we can accurately read what is happening around us. Second, we *cultivate* culture by living with virtue, awareness, and wisdom. Third, we *enter into community* by involving ourselves with people who challenge us to do our best. Let's look at each of these aspects.

Contemplating Culture

If you want to understand how to use a complicated piece of machinery, you have to read the directions. If you can't or won't read them, you could hurt yourself or others. Culture is the same way. Being culturally illiterate is dangerous. Kevin Vanhoozer says,

> Cultural illiteracy is harmful to our spiritual health. Christians need to know how to read culture because, first, it helps to know what is forming one's spirit. It helps to be able to name the powers and principalities that vie for the control of one's mind, soul, heart, and strength. Christians need to become culturally literate, second, so that they can be sure that the scripts they perform in everyday life are in accord with the Scriptures—the story of what God is doing in Jesus Christ through the Spirit to give meaning and life to the world—rather than some other story. Finally, Christians need to become culturally literate because we need to know where we are in the drama of redemption.[8]

Cultural literacy is more than just scanning culture with our eyes. As Dr. Ted Baehr from Movieguide points out, just as we teach kids grammar so they can use and understand language well, we need to teach them the grammar of cultural engagement, a structure that, if we understand it well, opens up a whole new level of communication.[9]

> *Cultural Literacy:* the knowledge and understanding of a culture that enables individuals to engage and influence that culture.

What we're talking about isn't a disengaged kind of contemplation. Catholic priest Richard John Neuhaus was highly regarded as a social commentator among Protestants and Catholics alike. A liberal social activist in his early days, Neuhaus became known for winsomely advocating a conservative approach to life and society. In his article "Telling the World Its Own Story," Neuhaus

CHRISTIANITY AND CULTURE: A PLAN

commented on serving for several years as a liaison between Dr. Martin Luther King Jr. and civil rights groups in the northeastern United States. He recalled a common saying of Dr. King's: "Whom you would change, you must first love, and they must know that you love them."[10]

We must love what we hope to change. We don't ordinarily think of contemplation as something that involves love, but it does. If we really want to get to know a person, we must love him or her first. Knowledge is the same way. As philosopher Esther Lightcap Meek puts it, "We love in order to know. Love, not bare information amassing, should characterize the way we relate to the world."[11]

Neuhaus specifically related the idea of loving to such activities as the arts, music, and academic work in history and physics and the sciences: "If we make a difference in any of these things, we must come to them and to the people involved in them with love, with a vision of a more excellent way, with a proposal—imposing nothing, only proposing."[12] Cultural anthropologists are not disinterested observers. Only when we care, and show it, will culture open its secrets to us.

Not only must we love culture to understand it, but our love must fuel curiosity. If you've ever fallen in love, you know what it means to say, "I want to know everything there is to know about you!" You love the mystery of the person, but at the same time, you feel compelled to peel back the layers, to somehow enter into the mystery through understanding.

Culture reveals itself through what cultural anthropologists call **texts**, which are "maps and scripts that orient us in life and give us a sense of direction."[13] These texts include not only what books and films and works of art *say* but their structure as well. Our Western idea of a song, for example, has a sequence that establishes

> *Texts:* a culture's media (e.g., books, movies, and works of art).

equilibrium, develops tension, and then resolves it. This structure, as much as the message, affects our engagement. Television programs operate with a similar structure, explaining the world in which the characters operate, creating a tension the characters must deal with, and then resolving that tension. Even the tension itself has a structure to it. Our favorite songs have "hooks" that keep us listening. Television programs create plot "spikes" that raise the level of tension just before a series of commercials to increase the likelihood that viewers will stay tuned in.

Those who've studied the Christian worldview can immediately see that the equilibrium-tension-resolution sequence common to popular culture closely mimics the creation-fall-redemption structure of the Bible's story of the world. We aren't just watching a story; we're living it. And the tension we feel is of living in a culture that isn't as it ought to be. We long for ultimate redemption.

Contemplating culture means avoiding the temptation to numb ourselves to this tension. Rather, we should be like the Mars rover, probing and exploring our culture, reading it as we would a text. Vanhoozer says,

> Readers of culture ought to be able to answer the following questions: Who made this cultural text and why? What does it mean and how does it work? What effect does it have on those who receive, use, or consume it? Perhaps the essential feature of a cultural text is the world it projects: its proposal about what it is to be human.[14]

As Vanhoozer suggests, we need to contemplate what is *behind* the cultural text we're seeking to understand, as well as what is *in* it and in *front* of it.[15] Looking at what is *behind* the

> **We need to contemplate what is *behind* the cultural text we're seeking to understand, as well as what is *in* it and in *front* of it.**

text means thinking about how it is communicated. How does it grab our attention? Does it do so with excellence?

Thinking about what is *in* the text means contemplating its message. What is this text telling us about what is actually true? For example, when a magazine airbrushes its models to remove evidence of their physical imperfections, what is it saying about the good life, the value of people, and what it means to be beautiful?

To think about what is in *front* of a text is to ponder its purpose—where it's headed. What problem is it trying to solve? What kind of anxiety is it trying to relieve? To what end is it drawing us?

Being able to think well about culture is important. But being literate doesn't just mean being able to understand what other people are saying. It also means making ourselves understood. We need to learn to read culture, yes, but we must also learn to write it.

Cultivating Culture

Writing culture requires a high level of intellectual engagement. To be honest, this isn't something Christians are particularly known for. In the 1950s Harry Blamires, a student of C. S. Lewis's at Oxford University, sounded the alarm: "There is no longer a Christian mind."[16]

In the last hundred years or so, at least, Christians have been known instead for emphasizing a personal *feeling* of connection with God rather than thinking robustly about what is going on in the world around them. While there's nothing wrong with a focus on personal conversion—indeed, Scripture describes it as central to salvation—encouraging people to act out of emotion and not reflection can have long-lasting negative consequences. As philosopher J. P. Moreland related in his book *Love Your God with All Your Mind*,

> Obviously, there is nothing wrong with the emphasis of these movements on personal conversion. What was a problem, however, was the intellectually shallow, theologically illiterate form of Christianity that came to be part of the populist Christian religion that emerged. One tragic result of this was what happened in the so-called Burned Over District in the state of New York. Thousands of people were "converted" to Christ by revivalist preaching, but they had no real intellectual grasp of Christian teaching. As a result, two of the three major American cults began in the Burned Over District among the unstable, untaught "converts": Mormonism (1830) and the Jehovah's Witnesses (1884).[17]

An inability to gracefully and coherently write culture makes people think that Christianity has little to say about what's important. This in turn frustrates Christians, who often respond by going to battle, metaphorically speaking, against those they perceive as dismissive. As Rod Dreher puts it, "Culture is hard; culture war is much easier and more emotionally gratifying."[18]

So what exactly are we cultivating? Three attributes that undergird and continually reinforce one another: virtue, awareness, and wisdom.

Virtue. Virtue results from cultivating our souls to the point where our actions naturally match our beliefs. Andrew Kern, founder and president of the CiRCE Institute, notes that this involves being respectful people who "[cultivate] good taste" and appreciate the "greatness of wisdom and virtue."[19] Many people think of education as something we submit to only so we can get ahead. According to Kern, though, we should be asking not "What can I do with this learning?" but "What will this learning do to me?"[20] Learning changes us, and the virtuous person is committed to being changed for the better.

Awareness. True virtue doesn't separate us from the world. Instead, it makes us more skillful in engaging it. One year I watched the Super Bowl with a group of friends that included a well-known Olympic athlete. My athlete-friend seemed to pay only scant attention to the game as he visited with people, played with his children, and helped with food preparations. And yet when anything happened in the game, he seemed to instantly understand what occurred and why. He paid better attention with 10 percent of his focus than I did with 100 percent of mine. Living in a community with a significant number of professional athletes, I'm starting to realize that success in athletics requires a high level of sensory awareness, which in turn can lead to success in many other areas of life.

> True virtue doesn't separate us from the world. Instead, it makes us more skillful in engaging it.

Wisdom. Virtue and awareness combine to produce what Aristotle called *prudence*, or practical wisdom. Wisdom deepens our experience with everything around us. In his book *Culture Matters*, T. M. Moore relates a conversation he had with classical guitarist Phil Keaggy. The way Moore described the effect of Keaggy's music on him displays how the twin headlights of a desire for virtue and strong sensory awareness illuminate the path to wisdom:

> I would say … your [Phil's] music, at least my experience of it, tends to tap into some affections that I don't normally experience—wonder, majesty, pain—and teaches me how to feel those things. This is really important to me, because as I exercise those affections listening to your music I find they are more readily available to me in other areas of my life—when I come into the presence of God's glory, when I'm worshipping him, or when I'm called on to minister to someone in some new or unexpected way.[21]

Most people don't think this deeply about music. If they did, they might experience the connection between virtue and awareness that produces wisdom, not mere amusement.

Together, virtue, awareness, and wisdom generate the kind of curiosity and learning that bridges the gap between what we believe and what we do. They span the gulf between seeing what culture looks like and recognizing the areas in which we ourselves can shape culture.

It turns out that cultural leaders acknowledge this unique combination of contemplation and cultivation as an important key to real-world success. Robert Thomas operates a leadership think tank that's part of one of America's largest business-consulting companies and is perhaps best known for his book *Crucibles of Leadership* (a crucible is a reference to a container in which alchemists in the Middle Ages would melt lead over intense heat in the belief that it would transform into gold). For his book, Thomas interviewed eighty-eight leaders in business, government, the military, social movements, and the performing arts, focusing on those who had a "proven ability to grow and sustain organizations in times of trial."[22] He concluded that what set these leaders apart was *not* talent, though talent is important. Rather, it was their approach to *learning*. Outstanding leaders, Thomas discovered, are ambitious about learning from their experiences and the experiences of others.[23]

> **Culture shapers hang around places where culture is birthed. They take risks and get into the fray.**

Culture shapers are driven to know more. They hang around places where culture is birthed, ask questions, meet people, and practice their own skills. They take risks, try things themselves, and evaluate their experiences so they can improve. They get into the fray.

Entering into Community

If you want to be a great author, you've got to read great authors and then try your hand at writing. But there is one more step: you have to share your work with others. Sharing your work with mentors not only helps you improve but also enlists others as cheerleaders and perhaps even champions for your work. If you want to shape culture, you've got to share. As Os Guinness expresses it, "Individual ideas certainly have a logic of their own, but when ideas are linked together and framed as a set of ideas, as in a worldview, and when they are lived out in conjunction with others, they form an even stronger character and social shape. Such ideas have inevitable cultural consequences."[24]

In other words, if you want to achieve the excellence and focus necessary to generate good culture, you have to find out where culture is formed and go there. The infamous bank robber Willie Sutton, when asked why he robbed banks, said, "Because that's where the money is." He was on to something. If you want money, you have to go where people work with it. If you want to make spectacular food dishes, you have to be around great chefs. If you want to shape culture, you must walk alongside those who shape it. Culture-shaping ability isn't something we're born with. It's something we find in relationship to others.

A famous example of such culture-creating community is the **Inklings**, a group of Oxford scholars that included C. S. Lewis, J. R. R. Tolkien, Charles Williams, Owen Barfield, Hugo Dyson, and others at various times. The members gathered at places like the Eagle and Child pub in Oxford to read their work and invite critique. Sometimes they just gathered to talk and debate and commiserate about their difficulties.[25] In his novel *The Place of the Lion*, Williams wrote, "Much was possible to a man in solitude…. But some things were possible only to a man in

> **Inklings: an informal group of Oxford scholars who met in the 1930s and 1940s to discuss and develop literary works.**

companionship, and of these the most important was balance. No mind was so good that it did not need another mind to counter and equal it, and to save it from conceit and blindness and bigotry and folly."[26] It's hard to imagine that he didn't have the Inklings in mind when he penned these thoughts.

The principle of culture-creating community is true at a deep level, even explaining how cultural organisms as large as nations grow and develop. There is a family-like aspect to it, people gathering around common beliefs and generating good ideas. Nations aren't just political districts. They are like family reunions for ideas. In fact, the Mandarin word for "nation," *guójiā*, literally means "kingdom family."

I recognize that all this may seem very theoretical, but the impact is very real. Demonstrating how this is so has been the life work of a sociologist named Randall Collins. In his book *The Sociology of Philosophies*, we can gather at least three insights about the kind of community that can help us become shapers of culture.

(1) **Find a group that challenges you.** "The history of philosophy is to a considerable extent the history of groups."[27] These groups aren't crowds. They're close-knit gatherings of people who are friends, who engage in vibrant discussion, and who influence others across generations. "Creativity is not random among individuals," Collins says. "It builds up in intergenerational chains."[28]

(2) **Don't worry if your group is small.** Those who influence the course of events, Collins found, are few in number (as few as 150 people in the whole course of history).[29] The key is that the group members have to be willing to think hard and mentor others, and have the emotional energy to develop "**cultural capital**" (enduring ideas that capture the imagination). The most successful groups develop their ideas in the context of opposition. They enter into social struggles that force them to perform their best, just like a sports team entering a tournament of champions.

> *Cultural Capital*: a culture's enduring and significant ideas.

(3) **Bring the group with you in everything you do.** Intellectual creativity often requires people to work alone for sustained periods of time, but ultimately individuals are their best when the group is present in their consciousness even when they're alone.[30] In fact, says Collins, it is when a culture creator is alone that the intellectual community of which he or she is a part is of paramount importance.

Culture shaping germinates through contemplation, emerges into the light through cultivation, and flowers in community. Even though there are billions of people on the planet, those who actually shape culture operate in small groups committed to working innovatively with one another in mind, mentoring others, and generating work that captures people's imaginations. Operating in this way postures us for culture change.

> Culture shaping germinates through contemplation, emerges into the light through cultivation, and flowers in community.

It can do this, however, only when the deep structure of the world—the reality of creation, the tragedy of the fall, and the promise of redemption—informs the direction we're heading in. It is to this sequence, and how it shapes us so we may shape culture, that we now turn.

3. Direction: Develop a Map and Get Moving

Cultures are always moving and changing—sometimes for the good, sometimes for the bad. They require constant alertness. Some think they can withdraw from society and have a neutral impact on the culture as long as they're not hurting others. Not so. "Not to act is to act."[31] Throughout history, evil has just as often been due to the good things people have *failed* to do as much as the bad things they've done. Being superficial and self-centered isn't necessarily benign. As Amos Elon suggested in his introduction to Hannah Arendt's book about the trial of the Nazi war criminal Adolf Eichmann, "Evil comes from a failure to think."[32] After observing how very little the plain and undistinguished Eichmann cared about the consequences of his actions, Arendt realized that evil often cloaks itself in ordinariness. She called it the "banality of evil."[33]

> "Not to act is to act." Throughout history, evil has just as often been due to the good things people have *failed* to do as much as the bad things they've done.

Today people think of the Nazi regime as the prototype of aggressive evil, but the true picture ought to confront the leisurely live-and-let-live mind-set we find ourselves embracing. We picture Hitler as a constantly scheming madman, but as Albert Speer, Hitler's architect and close companion, described it, the reality is that Hitler was a superficial, cynical man who wasted his time on trivial pursuits.

In his book *Inside the Third Reich*, written during the twenty-year sentence he served for his crimes, Speer said that Hitler usually appeared late morning, around eleven o'clock. He worked for a couple of hours and then hosted a long luncheon, followed by a walk to the teahouse for tea, coffee, cake, and cookies, during which his company of hangers-on would listen absently to one of his lengthy monologues. This ended around six in the evening, with dinner served at eight, followed by a movie.[34] Said Speer, "No one took the trouble to raise the conversation above the level of trivialities" during these events that "dragged on in monotonous, wearing emptiness," after which everyone went home "dead tired, exhausted from doing nothing" and "vacant from the constant waste of time."[35]

According to Speer's accounts, "Hitler scarcely ever said anything about the Jews, about his domestic opponents, let alone about the necessity for setting up concentration camps. Perhaps such topics were omitted less out of deliberate intention than because they would have been out of place amidst the prevailing banality."[36] Rather than talk about anything substantive, Hitler "made fun of his closest associates" and "spoke disparagingly of everything and everyone," displaying his contempt for those around him and what was happening in the world.[37]

> We picture Hitler as a constantly scheming madman, but the reality is that Hitler was a superficial, cynical man who wasted his time on trivial pursuits.

One wonders whether insight into this aspect of Hitler's character was what convinced the German pastor Dietrich Bonhoeffer of the thorough-going evil of the Nazi regime. In his letters from prison, Bonhoeffer wrote, "Have there ever been people in history who in their time, like us, had so little ground under their feet, people to whom every possible alternative open to them at the time appeared equally unbearable, senseless, and contrary to life?"[38]

Today, while the majority of people say they believe in God, most live as if his existence has little effect on daily life. Whether or not there is a God who cares about how we live our lives is seemingly irrelevant to the masses.[39] Belief in belief is more important than belief in God.[40]

> **Today, while the majority of people say they believe in God, most live as if his existence has little effect on daily life.**

But what we believe about the answers to life's ultimate questions shapes us at a level far deeper than we might like to admit. As John Stonestreet from the Colson Center often remarks, "A worldview is not so much the one you have; it's the one that has you." Do we live as if Jesus *really has* risen from the dead and redeemed us, or do we live as if our *belief* in him is all that really matters? The difference isn't as subtle as it initially appears. Do we realize that we live in a world God has made, or are we trying to fit God into a world *we* have made? It's one thing to be constantly obsessed with taking our own spiritual pulse to see if we're still alive, and yet another to *really live* as restored, renewed, reconciled image bearers of God.

> **Do we live as if Jesus *really has* risen from the dead and redeemed us, or do we live as if our *belief* in him is all that really matters?**

Through its metanarrative of creation, fall, and redemption, the Bible explains our enormous capacity for changing things, why we often change things for the worse, and how things might actually change for the better. Let's explore the difference this biblical structure makes to culture creators.

Creation

Every culture has its creation stories. The creation account in the Bible isn't just a story, though. The portrayal of God in Genesis 1 confronts the pagan gods and popular creation stories the Hebrews would have been familiar with, such as the Enuma Elish, the Egyptian Memphite creation myth, and the Phoenician cosmogony of Philo of Byblos. The Hebrew account is clear: Yahweh is an altogether different kind of God, far superior to his would-be rivals.[41] We can see this in at least eight ways:

(1) **The universe has a divine origin.** The universe had a beginning and has not existed eternally.[42]

(2) **God is spirit.** He isn't like the embodied, sexually active, power-hungry, petty pagan gods.[43]

(3) **Creation is not God.** The sun, moon, and sea were viewed as gods in ancient Near East creation stories, but in the biblical narrative, they are just creations.[44]

(4) Creation was made perfect. God's Spirit hovered over the waters, superintending every aspect of creation. The pagan stories offer up a creation full of imperfections.[45]

(5) Creation resulted from God speaking. The universe is the product not of a divine power struggle but of a spoken command. God created everything out of nothing with words.[46]

(6) God organized creation in a structured and orderly way. In Genesis 1, plants and animals were created "according to their kinds," not as bizarre forms common in the pagan texts.[47]

(7) Humanity has a special place in creation. Human beings aren't slaves of the gods but are divinely created beings bearing God's image regardless of their level of wealth or power.[48]

(8) God rested after his creative work. God enjoys and takes pleasure in his creation, and he even created space and time in which to enjoy it. This is in stark contrast to the perpetual restlessness of the pagan gods.[49]

Taken together, these facets of the biblical account of creation provide a strong framework for cultural engagement. Bearing God's image, we have a spiritual capacity to create and relate. We can also use our words to bring ideas into being.

There's one more important point to add from Genesis 2, which offers a close-up view of the creation of human beings. In this account, God placed humans in a garden to work and tend it, which is a task of culture creation in itself. The creation account exalts *work*, not ease. That it takes thousands of hours of intensive concentration and practice to master a subject isn't a bad thing to God.[50] Those who would bear God's image must be prepared to engage in concentrated effort.

> Bearing God's image, we have a spiritual capacity to create and relate.

The garden God created for the man and woman was what experts might refer to as a rich biosphere of purposeful interaction. Our first parents had a model of what they were to produce, the skill to do it, and God's personal guidance. It was a sort of innovation lab through which to create substantial new value.[51] This value was to be spread throughout all the earth (Gen. 1:28).[52]

Fall

In the biblical account in Genesis 3, Satan[53] tempted the man and woman with the knowledge of good and evil. Seemingly, the serpent offered something to the man and woman that was proper for only God to know (v. 22).[54] Perhaps it had something to do with claiming for themselves the authority to *define* good and evil. It was a temptation to replace God.

> *Sin:* any action or inaction that violates the will of God.

By attempting to take matters into their own hands, our first parents departed from the good way. They fell into **sin**. First, their sin was an act of *unbelief*, a refusal to trust God and even a desire to believe the opposite of what he said. Second, it was a desire for *autonomy*. The man and woman wanted to be wise on their own terms rather than on God's. Third, it was an act of *irresponsibility*. Although Adam knew the serpent's nature (since he had observed its characteristics and named it), he lost courage and gave in to lies rather than fight for the truth. Fourth, Adam and Eve's sin was an act of *rebellion*, purposely going against what God said was best. In the end, sin was less about the fruit and more about the man and woman saying, "God, we don't think your plan is as good as you think it is. *We want what we want, and we want it now.*"

This picture of sin is familiar to us today. We still bear the image of a mighty and loving God, but because of sin, our efforts often spiral into abuse of our God-given capacities, leading to death (Gen. 4–11). After the fall, people *craved* evil (6:5),[55] and even after being rescued from slavery in Egypt, "everyone did what was right in his own eyes" (Judg. 17:6).[56] Sin is a parasite in the human bloodstream.

To make matters worse, humans often attempt to explain away our fallenness. Abraham Maslow wrote, "As far as I know we just don't have any intrinsic instincts for evil."[57] Carl Rogers said, "I see members of the human species, like members of other species, as essentially constructive in their fundamental nature, but damaged by their experience."[58] Christianity disagrees with these rationalizations and insists that the fall actually happened and affects us so deeply that our attempts at self-repair only make matters worse. "For all tables are full of filthy vomit, with no space left" (Isa. 28:8). We are shattered, and like Humpty Dumpty, nothing we do will put us back together.

Because of the fall, humanity's ideas about how to save ourselves are part of the problem, not part of the solution. In his classic essay on culture, J. Gresham Machen wrote,

> False ideas are the greatest obstacles to the reception of the gospel. We may preach with all the fervor of a reformer and yet succeed only in winning a straggler here and there, if we permit the whole collective thought of the nation or of the world to be controlled by ideas which, by the resistless force of logic, prevent Christianity from being regarded as anything more than a harmless delusion. Under such circumstances, what God desires us to do is to destroy the obstacle at its root.[59]

This kind of teaching may seem melancholic, but it's the first step in the right direction. Spiritual warfare is real. And if we want to win, we need to know the Enemy's tactics.

As Kevin Bywater, director of the Summit Oxford Study Centre in Oxford, England, points out, the most effective way to undermine your enemy is to send out false information about your intent.[60] In Genesis 3, the serpent told the man and woman, "You will be like God." But, in fact, they already *were* like God. By getting them to doubt God's word, the serpent disrupted their culture-shaping mission. Satan tried a similar technique on Jesus during his forty-day sojourn in the wilderness (Matt. 4:1–11).[61] He twisted the Scriptures to put God on trial rather than to sustain trust in him.

> Christianity insists that the fall actually happened and affects us so deeply that our attempts at self-repair only make matters worse.

In 2 Timothy 2, the apostle Paul told Timothy not to "have anything to do with foolish and stupid arguments" (v. 23 NIV). We are, instead, to put on God's armor (Eph. 6:10–18):[62] truth, righteousness, readiness, faith, and salvation. Wearing this armor enables us to stand firm as image bearers of God.

Human efforts to create culture have often led to arrogance and violence. If the story ended there, we might be utterly suspicious of our ability to create culture. We would rightly be concerned that our efforts are doing more harm than good. But in the biblical account, humanity's unraveling is the beginning of restoration.

Redemption

While the first three chapters of the Bible, Genesis 1–3, provide a clear picture of God's creation and humanity's fall, the last three chapters of the Bible, Revelation 20–22, provide a clear picture of his redemption. God replaces fallen creation with a new heaven and new earth (21:1).[63] Darkness is replaced with eternal light (v. 25).[64] The sorrow and pain of spiritual and physical death disappears (v. 4).[65] The curse is no more (22:3).[66] Redemption makes all things new. Here's the difference it makes:

Redemption breaks sin's grip on the world. In the 1950s, professor Solomon Asch conducted a simple experiment showing how one person committed to the truth could break the spell of falsehood. Asch brought study participants into his lab and put them in a group with others they thought were participants but were actually Asch's assistants. Asch then revealed two cards, one with a single line on it and the other with lines of three different lengths labeled "A," "B," and "C." Asch asked each of his assistants to guess which line on the second card was closest in length to the line on the first card. The answer was clearly "B," but each of the assistants, on his instructions, asserted that it was "A." The real participant answered last. Fully 75 percent of these participants conformed at least once to the incorrect answer the others gave.

In a separate trial, though, Asch had one of his assistants give an incorrect but different answer from the other assistants (for example, guessing "C" when the correct answer was "B" and all the other confederates answered "A."). He found that having one single dissenter reduced conformity to the incorrect answer from 75 percent to between 5 and 10 percent.[67] *All it took was one other person going against the grain to inspire the research participants to give the correct answer.* Perhaps this is why Scripture says that wisdom comes with many advisers (Prov. 15:22).[68]

> As redeemed image bearers, we have the opportunity to break sin's grip by speaking the truth of God's good news in our culture.

Redemption breaks sin's spell and turns back time "till everything that has happened has unhappened," as the poet Czeslaw Milosz put it.[69] This is compellingly portrayed in J. R. R. Tolkien's *The Two Towers*, where Gandalf breaks Grima's spell over Théoden, king of Rohan. When the king's evil adviser is banished, frail Théoden is restored to the powerful warrior he once was.[70] As redeemed image bearers, we have the opportunity to break sin's grip by speaking the truth of God's good news in our culture.

Redemption makes it possible to be discerning without being cynical. Peer pressure exerts an enormous influence on us. Studies show that pressure from others (celebrities or other people with whom we fear to disagree, for example) over time leads dissenting individuals to, as philosopher Miriam Solomon puts it, "change their minds and, perhaps as important, *not* to share their knowledge of contrary evidence."[71] This leads to **groupthink**, which ironically means the group is not thinking at all. Group members unthinkingly go along with what they think the most powerful group members want.

> *Groupthink:* a psychological phenomenon that occurs when a group reaches a bad decision because it finds itself striving for unity over reason.

Cynicism can break the stranglehold of groupthink but can't replace it with anything positive. As C. S. Lewis drily noted in *The Abolition of Man*, "A hard heart is no infallible protection against a soft head."[72] Redemption, on the other hand, replaces bad thinking with good thinking. It holds us fast to the truth in two ways. John Stonestreet explains: "It's what Paul says in II Corinthians 5, the love of Christ *compels* us and *constrains* us. The Greek word there is like this funnel, *the love of Christ should be the thing that holds us fast, and shoots us forward.*"[73] Redemption focuses on the good, true, and beautiful without conforming to cultural habits that are common to the world but are not of Christ (Rom. 12:1–2).[74]

Learning how redemption applies to the world around us involves a lifelong process of growing in discernment. It's what a good education—one focused on God's truth—is all about. As the literary giant Samuel Johnson said, "The supreme end of education … is expert discernment in all things—the power to tell the good from the bad, the genuine from the counterfeit; and to prefer the good and the genuine to the bad and the counterfeit."[75]

> Redemption focuses on the good, true, and beautiful without conforming to cultural habits that are common to the world but are not of Christ.

At a practical level, you can grow in discernment by asking the right questions when you encounter cultural claims of truth:

- *What* do they want you to do?

- *Why* do they want you to do it?

- To what *motives* do they appeal?

- *How* do they make their case persuasive?

- Can they really *deliver* what they promise?

- What is *best*?

Redemption aligns our emotions with the truth. Earlier I criticized Christians who focus on feeling rather than thinking. Redemption enables us to do both well. Redemption relieves us of dry rationality, freeing us to *feel* rightly. Often people see *thought* as objective and rational and *feeling* as subjective and irrational. But this doesn't account for the full experience of redemption. It's impossible to read the Bible without encountering sanctified expressions of great feeling, whether joy at God's presence, anger at evil, shame over sin, or gratitude over forgiveness.

Unredeemed people experience emotions, of course. But as the apostle Paul put it in Galatians 5:22–23,[76] because of Christ's work on the cross, we can cultivate the fruit of the Spirit: "love, joy, peace, patience, kindness, goodness, faithfulness, gentleness, self-control." Each of these reflects a deeply emotional response to God's goodness.[77]

> Through the Holy Spirit we're empowered to train our emotions to respond to truth, not error.

Like all good fruit, though, they result from cultivation, not from happenstance. And such fruit not only *results* from accepting the truth; it enables us to *experience* truth more deeply than we might otherwise.

Through the Holy Spirit we're empowered to train our emotions to respond to truth, not error. We can, with humility and thoughtful awareness, learn to balance and aim our emotions to draw out truth. As Adam Pelser observes,

> We can learn to "see" the suffering of others through the eyes of compassion, to become angry at significant injustices (and only at significant injustices), to take pleasure in and wonder at that which is truly beautiful, to find amusing that and only that which is truly funny (as opposed to jokes that are demeaning, hateful, or disgusting), and to feel appropriately contrite for our sins.[78]

Redemption enables us not only to know that the truth exists but also to feel deeply what it means that sin's power is canceled, and death is defeated.

Redemption makes true creativity possible. Steve Jobs, the founder of Apple Computer and the cofounder of Pixar Animation Studios, knew more about creating culture, in technology at least, than just about anyone else. After Jobs's death, biographer Walter Isaacson revealed that Jobs drew his inspiration not from giving people what they said they wanted but from imagining whole new worlds of technological possibility. In other words, he didn't wish to imitate culture; he wished to transform it. Jobs said,

> Some people say, "Give the customer what they want." But that's not my approach. Our job is to figure out what they're going to want before they do. I think Henry Ford once said, "If I'd asked customers what they wanted, they would have told me, 'A faster horse.'" People don't know what they want until you show it to them. That's why I never rely on market research. Our task is to read things that are not yet on the page.[79]

The great culture creators of all time understood this. In chapter 1, we saw this with the example of Johannes Gutenberg's invention of a printing press with movable type. In chapter

3, we looked at the example of Josiah Wedgwood's cameo, designed to give people a stylish means of declaring their opposition to slavery.

Largely because of technology, we live in a world where such innovations can accelerate rapidly. Just a few years ago, a company called Uber became a multi-billion-dollar company by arranging for people to use their own personal vehicles as taxis and earn extra income. It's a free-market innovation in which people must serve well (and be pleasant to serve) in order to succeed. Uber is now a bigger transportation company in terms of market value than Delta Airlines or FedEx.[80]

> The great culture creators of all time understood that their job was to figure out what customers were going to want before they did.

Earlier we talked about how successful culture creators operate in networks of like-minded innovators. Uber couldn't have succeeded without other innovative companies, such as PayPal, which made it safe to make financial transactions on the Internet. Uber's success also relies on smartphone creators, providers of mobile Internet and phone service, and mapping programs using GPS data. Tens of thousands of people, each working on their own ideas for their own reasons, combined to reshape the market. None of them could have done it alone.

Later in this book, we'll talk about other innovations, such as a phone company that enables people in developing countries to use their cell phones to make transactions that avoid risky banks and work around dictators attempting to control them by controlling the currency. We'll also look at people who are using architecture to restore human value, city planning to make it easier for people to interact with one another, and asset-based community development to help struggling communities solve their own problems.

You can get started with your own innovations by asking four questions John Stonestreet and coauthor Warren Cole Smith pose in *Restoring All Things*:[81]

1. What is good in our culture that we can promote, protect, and celebrate?

2. What is missing in our culture that we can creatively contribute?

3. What is evil in our culture that we can stop?

4. What is broken in our culture that we can restore?

We don't have to be powerful elites to seek answers to these questions. Uber blew past all the elite Fortune 500 transportation companies before those companies even knew what was happening. Airbnb, which arranges for people to rent out spare bedrooms, has outpaced most large hotel companies in market value. Tiny pro-life ministries like Live Action are giving fits to the huge and lavishly funded proabortion company Planned Parenthood. Everyday people living redemptively become culture shapers in ways that often seem impossible.

> Everyday people living redemptively become culture shapers in ways that often seem impossible.

Let's review: Earlier in this chapter, we saw that culture shaping begins with a posture of engagement. As image bearers of God, we can read, write, and share culture. Yet because of the fall, we're prone to believe lies about God, the world, and humanity that threaten to destroy culture and must be resisted by wearing God's armor. Fortunately, redemption through Jesus Christ protects what is good, fixes what is broken, stops what is evil, and contributes what is missing.

Even in a world where Christ died and rose from the dead, we still face challenges that would stop us from shaping culture as we ought.

4. THE CHALLENGES OF CULTURAL ENGAGEMENT

Innovation is never without risks. Just as a printing press with movable type could be used to print lies and Internet technology makes it possible to view and transmit horrible things, culture can be shaped for good and ill. This makes it important to be aware of barriers that might stop us from living in the truth and power of Jesus Christ. Following are three potential barriers that threaten to shape *us* even as we try to shape the culture around us.

Fear

Christians far too often fail to act because of fear of what others will think. Change is controversial, and there are always those who benefit from keeping things as they are. In chapter 17, I'll tell the story of a city council friend of mine who once tried to pass common-sense regulations for strip clubs to protect women and children, only to find out the clubs were owned by mafioso, who resented the intrusion and used bullying to try to stop it. My friend's situation is extreme, but it illustrates that many people *like* things the way they are and will resist change at all costs.

Fearing what others think is *never* condoned in Scripture. God calls his people to have

> **Christians far too often fail to act because of fear of what others will think.**

courage (Deut. 31:6–8; Josh. 1:6; 2 Chron. 32:7; Ps. 27:14),[82] to speak up for those who cannot speak for themselves (Esther 4:14; Prov. 24:11–12; 31:8),[83] and to proclaim his message of redemption (Col. 3:16; Heb. 13:15; 1 Pet. 3:15).[84]

Friendly Fire

> *Mere Christianity:* based on the work of C. S. Lewis, mere Christianity is the idea that Christians can, and should, work together around their shared beliefs in essential doctrines.

Few people realize that beloved author C. S. Lewis was an infantryman in the trenches in World War I. Once, a British shell fell short of the enemy and landed in his trench, obliterating the man next to him and splattering Lewis with shrapnel he carried the rest of his life. He quite literally carried within his body the wounds caused by friendly fire. Perhaps this was in the back of Lewis's mind as he developed his idea of "**mere Christianity**," a way of bringing bickering Christian traditions together around what they could all agree on.

It hurts to be shot at. But as a friend of mine, who is an air force general, says, "If you're not taking flak, you're not over the target." It's good to know we're over the target, but it's painful to realize that being on the front lines puts us in danger of shots fired by our own side as well as the enemy's. We expect nonbelievers to criticize us, but when we encounter criticism from believers whose support would mean so much and who could make such a difference by walking alongside us, we need to do a gut check to ensure we're on the right track.

Getting Too Close

To shape culture we have to get close to it, but how close can we get without being hurt? Respected hip-hop artist Lecrae is familiar with this dilemma. As the owner of a record label and performing concerts with major sponsors like McDonald's,[85] Lecrae has attained a level of influence that has positioned him to share his faith with artists working in a form that often glorifies abusive sex, drugs, and violence. Admittedly, this is the cutting edge of cultural engagement, and Lecrae has his critics. But he says, "When you have good community like I have, close people who encourage you to keep going …, you say, 'It's worth it.' And, 'God is real. He's here for me.'"[86]

Perhaps an even more controversial Christian invasion of culture is XXXchurch, a ministry that helps men and women overcome pornography addiction. It also ministers to people in the adult-entertainment ministry, which looks glamorous on the outside but is rife with disrespect and abuse on the inside. To do their ministry, XXXchurch volunteers attend pornography-industry conventions to hand out Bibles and pray with people. They say,

> We believe that Jesus meets people where they are. We don't subscribe to the belief system that God only loves those who live the way we or religion think they should live. We believe that it is when Jesus meets, loves and accepts us where we are, no matter[,] that place that we are transformed by that crazy kind of love.[87]

Many would draw the line at this kind of ministry. We respect people who sell their belongings and travel halfway around the world to minister to people enslaved to false religions in other countries, but reaching out to people who produce porn? It's like hand-to-hand combat.

This is precisely the point: we can't reach the culture from afar, but when we get close, we're tempted by the very sins we're trying to stand against. So how do we respond to people called to minister in the areas we find repugnant? And from the other perspective, how do we treat people who criticize *us* for exercising our own cultural callings?

> We can't reach the culture from afar, but when we get close, we're tempted by the very sins we're trying to stand against.

At the same time, we may reach a place where we have to say, "Enough is enough." It's a question of wisdom. It would probably not be wise, for instance, for a recovering alcoholic to minister in bars. In the same way, a person who struggles with a pornography addiction would probably be unwise to go to a porn convention to share his faith.

Engaging rather than escaping culture requires constant discernment, whether we're examining a political issue or scanning magazines in the checkout line at the grocery store. But is there a time when culture becomes so corrupt that we must choose holiness and withdraw? Absolutely. Here are four questions that serve as guides for knowing where to draw the line:

> Is there a time when culture becomes so corrupt that we must choose holiness and withdraw? Absolutely.

1. Do you know how culture is affecting you? Dr. Ted Baehr is called to minister in the movie industry, a place rife with narcissism, sexual brokenness, materialism, and superficiality. Ted told me,

> In the wake of the Columbine High School massacre [a 1999 school shooting in which two students killed twelve students and a teacher], CBS president Leslie Moonves put it quite bluntly: "Anyone who thinks the media has nothing to do with this is an idiot." The major medical associations have concluded that there is absolutely no doubt that those who are heavy viewers of violence demonstrate increased acceptance of aggressive attitudes and aggressive behavior. "Do not be misled: 'Bad company corrupts good character'" (1 Cor. 15:33).[88]

It is human nature to deny that we're affected by what takes place around us. If you struggle with being honest, you're probably in too deep.

2. Are you making excuses? Second Peter 2:19[89] talks of those who promise freedom but themselves are slaves of corruption. Watching movies we ought not watch because we're "looking for how they portray different worldviews," or habitually listening to degrading music to "better understand the culture" are two examples I often hear from people who lazily absorb culture and try to appear noble about it. It's wrong and they know it. If you're making excuses, you're probably in too deep.

3. Are you losing your sense of distress? At one point during his ministry, the apostle Paul visited Athens, a tremendously corrupt and vile culture in his day. Scripture says in Acts 17:16 (NIV) that Paul was "greatly distressed" by what he saw. If you ever get to the point where sin doesn't bother you, you're probably in too deep.

> Effective culture shapers grow in virtue, awareness, and wisdom as they carry out their mission. They immerse themselves in community and challenge one another as "iron sharpens iron."

4. Are you trying to do it by yourself? Our capacity for self-deception knows no bounds. Many years ago a well-known pastor and founder of a large church in Colorado was discovered to have been visiting a gay prostitute. The question on the lips of many observers was, "How did he think he could get away with it? He's one of the most recognizable pastors in America." The answer is, as John Stonestreet bluntly puts it, "Sin makes you dumb. It makes you so dumb that you will deceive yourself."[90] We need people who will look us in the eye and tell us when we're acting like idiots. Scripture says, "Faithful are the wounds of a friend" (Prov. 27:6). If you're engaging culture all by yourself, you're probably in too deep.

Effective culture shapers grow in virtue, awareness, and wisdom as they carry out their mission. They immerse themselves in community and challenge one another as "iron sharpens iron" (Prov. 27:17).[91] This encourages them through fear, sustains them through friendly fire, and enables them to continue exerting an influence without being compromised by the very aspect of culture they're trying to shape.

5. CONCLUSION

The central message of this book is that we're called to overcome fear and engage the culture. Christians in the past have had a profound influence on the world for what is good and true by doing this, and it's our calling as well. But as this chapter makes clear, our influence is only as good as our ability to cultivate virtuous habits of engagement. John Stonestreet offers an example that hits close to home:

> Let's say you're out on a boat and someone puts a gun to your head and says either your iPhone or your daughter is going overboard. Which one is it going to be? We would obviously throw the phone overboard. But that's not really where I am tested. Instead, every single day, I have to choose between putting down my phone to pick up my kids or putting down my kids to pick up my phone. These everyday choices shape our loyalties, and the danger is becoming more loyal to *something* than to *someone*.[92]

Every choice, every day matters. Journalist Ross Douthat says,

> To make any difference in our common life, Christianity must be *lived*—not as a means to social cohesion or national renewal, but as an end unto itself.… Anyone who would save their country should first look to save themselves. *Seek first the kingdom of God and his righteousness, and all these things will be added to you.*[93]

Christians who influence culture learn to be in the world but not of it, a reference to Jesus's prayer for his disciples just before going to the cross (John 17:16–18). They bring truth to bear. They are persistent. They relentlessly focus on excellence. And things change in their wake.

In the last few years, a discussion has arisen about where we should start engaging the culture. Do we start at the grass roots, with everyday people, or is change only possible from the top? There is a third way: *grasstops*. I don't know who came up with the idea, but I first heard about it from Warren Smith, vice president of mission advancement at the Colson Center. Change happens where the grass roots meet the top. We pursue excellence at the highest level God has given us the capacity to pursue. We seek to network with other influencers. And we trust that the lives of everyday people will be changed as a result.

> Christians who influence culture learn to be in the world but not of it. They bring truth to bear. They are persistent. They relentlessly focus on excellence. And things change in their wake.

To use an analogy that is closer to Scripture, the light of the gospel isn't a lesser light that only illuminates the path of those nearest to it. Nor is it a spotlight shining on the actions of a few while hiding all else in shadow. It's like the light of the sun ruling the day, shining light everywhere so that even those who are completely lost may find their way. In the light of the sun, the darkness and all that prosper therein must flee. And so it is as we seek to influence culture in the only truly enduring fashion: by shining the Light of the World on it.

> We seek to influence culture in the only truly enduring fashion: by shining the Light of the World on it.

ENDNOTES

1. "Pete Thomas Bio," Pete Thomas.com, accessed July 8, 2016, http://petethomas.com/pete-thomas-bio/.

2. Ken Myers originally presented this list at a lecture on culture at the Association of Classical and Christian Schools (ACCS) 2008 Conference, "Recovering Truth, Goodness, and Beauty," Austin, Texas, June 26–28, 2008; see also "ACCS— Ken Myers on Culture," *Mark's Blog*, Every Good Path, July 23, 2008, www.everygoodpath.net/ACCSKenMyersCulture.

3. T. S. Eliot, *Notes towards the Definition of Culture* (New York: Harcourt, Brace, 1949), 17.

4. John Baillie, *What Is Christian Civilization?* (Oxford, UK: Oxford University Press, 1945), 51.

5. G. K. Chesterton, *The Everlasting Man*, in *The Collected Works of G. K. Chesterton,* vol. 2, eds. George J. Marlin, Richard P. Rabatin, and John L. Swan (San Francisco: Ignatius, 1986), 388.

6. Peter M. Senge, *The Fifth Discipline: The Art and Practice of the Learning Organization* (New York: Doubleday, 2006), 196.

7. Theologian Kevin Vanhoozer describes the artifacts and habits of culture as units or "memes" (from the Greek term *mimesis* or "imitation"). Kevin Vanhoozer, "What Is Everyday Theology? How and Why Christians Should Read Culture," in Kevin J. Vanhoozer, Charles A. Anderson, and Michael J. Sleasman, eds., *Everyday Theology: How to Read Cultural Texts and Interpret Trends* (Grand Rapids: Baker Academic, 2007), 30.

8. Vanhoozer, *Everyday Theology*, 34.

9. See, for example, the Ted Baehr interview on Dr. James Dobson's *Family Talk,* www.movieguide.org/news-articles/dr-ted -baehr-family-talk-dr-james-dobson.html.

10. Martin Luther King Jr., quoted in Richard John Neuhaus, "Telling the World Its Own Story," Wilberforce Forum, July 2001, Catholic Education Resource Center, www.catholiceducation.org/en/religion-and-philosophy/apologetics/telling-the -world-its-own-story.html.

11. Esther Lightcap Meek, *A Little Manual for Knowing* (Eugene, OR: Cascade Books, 2014), 17.

12. Neuhaus, "Telling the World Its Own Story."

13. Vanhoozer, *Everyday Theology*, 29.

14. Vanhoozer, *Everyday Theology*, 48.

15. Kevin Vanhoozer says, "Paul Tillich, a leading theologian of culture, said that the best way to understand a particular culture or even epoch is to discover its greatest anxiety (i.e., the focus of a negative concern) and its greatest hope (i.e., the focus of what Tillich called 'ultimate concern,' or simply 'religion'). We begin to understand others and groups of others, then, when we begin to understand what concerns them and why." Vanhoozer, *Everyday Theology*, 19.

16. Harry Blamires, *The Christian Mind: How Should a Christian Think?* (London: SPCK, 1963), 3.

17. J. P. Moreland, *Love Your God with All Your Mind: The Role of Reason in the Life of the Soul* (Colorado Springs, CO: NavPress, 1997), 23. Incidentally, the third cult to which Moreland refers is Christian Science, which arose in 1866 and is unrelated to the Burned Over District.

18. Rod Dreher, "'Duck Dynasty' vs. Dante," *American Conservative,* January 19, 2015, 25.

19. "Principles of Classical Education," CiRCE Institute, accessed July 9, 2016, www.circeinstitute.org/principles-classical -education.

20. "Principles of Classical Education," CiRCE Institute.

21. T. M. Moore, interview with Phil Keaggy, 2001, in T. M. Moore, *Culture Matters: A Call for Consensus on Christian Cultural Engagement* (Grand Rapids: Brazos, 2007), 62.

22. Robert J. Thomas, *Crucibles of Leadership: How to Learn from Experience to Become a Great Leader* (Boston: Harvard Business School, 2008), xiii.

23. Thomas, *Crucibles of Leadership*, xii, 6–7.

24. Os Guinness, *Renaissance: The Power of the Gospel However Dark the Times* (Downers Grove, IL: IVP Books, 2014), 75.

25. See Humphrey Carpenter, *The Inklings: C. S. Lewis, J. R. R. Tolkien, Charles Williams, and Their Friends* (London:

HarperCollins, 1978).

26. Charles Williams, *The Place of the Lion* (Grand Rapids: Eerdmans, 1950), 187.

27. Randall Collins, *The Sociology of Philosophies: A Global Theory of Intellectual Change* (Cambridge, MA: Belknap, 1998), 3.

28. Collins, *Sociology of Philosophies*, 6.

29. Collins, *Sociology of Philosophies*, 76.

30. Collins, *Sociology of Philosophies*, 7.

31. Attributed to Dietrich Bonhoeffer in Eric Metaxas, *Bonhoeffer: A Four-Session Study on the Life and Writings of Dietrich Bonhoeffer* (Nashville: Thomas Nelson, 2014), 59.

32. Amos Elon, "Introduction: The Excommunication of Hannah Arendt," in Hannah Arendt, *Eichmann in Jerusalem: A Report on the Banality of Evil* (New York: Penguin, 2006), xiv.

33. Adolf Eichmann, one of the organizers of the Holocaust, escaped from Germany after the war and was captured in Argentina fifteen years later. Put on trial in Jerusalem, Eichmann was found guilty of war crimes and executed in 1962. Arendt's book details the trial of Eichmann, one of the most evil men ever to have lived. What startled Arendt, and what led to her writing a book about her experiences, is not how wicked Eichmann appeared, but how ordinary—and even thoughtless—he was. At its root, evil is not white-hot wickedness. It is, rather, trite, unimaginative, and dull. As word and thought defying as it is, Arendt decided, there is a banality of evil. See Arendt, *Eichmann in Jerusalem*, 252.

34. This is a description of the time Hitler spent at his retreat in the mountains in Austria, the Berghof, but it's a fair representation of Hitler overall, since he spent more time there than at his office in Berlin and planned many of his major campaigns from there. Albert Speer, *Inside the Third Reich: Memoirs* (New York: Simon and Schuster, 1970), 89–90.

35. Speer, *Inside the Third Reich*, 90, 91.

36. Speer, *Inside the Third Reich*, 94.

37. Speer, *Inside the Third Reich*.

38. Dietrich Bonhoeffer, *Dietrich Bonhoeffer Works*, vol. 8, *Letters and Papers from Prison* (Minneapolis: Augsburg Fortress, 2009), 38.

39. This prevailing idea, Secularism, was a major focus of the book David Noebel and I wrote titled *Understanding the Times* (Colorado Springs, CO: David C Cook, 2015). Secularism, at root, doesn't claim that there is no God. It just claims that belief in God is pointless; we must take charge of our own destinies.

40. In his very important book on Secularism, professor Craig Gay wrote, "Still, under modern conditions the decision *to* believe has a way of eclipsing the object *of* belief, and often seems to give way to subjectivism." Craig M. Gay, *The Way of the (Modern) World: Or, Why It's Tempting to Live as If God Doesn't Exist* (Grand Rapids: Eerdmans, 1998), 198.

41. See Kenneth J. Turner, "The Kind-ness of God: A Theological Reflection of *Mîn*, 'Kind,'" in *Genesis Kinds: Creationism and the Origin of Species*, eds. Todd C. Wood and Paul A. Garner (Eugene, OR: Wipf and Stock, 2009), 31–64; and Kenneth J. Turner, "Teaching Genesis 1 at a Christian College," a research paper submitted directly to the author and subsequently published in *Reading Genesis 1–2: An Evangelical Conversation*, ed. J. Daryl Charles (Peabody, MA: Hendrickson, 2013), chap. 6.

42. Turner, "Teaching Genesis 1," in *Reading Genesis 1–2*.

43. Turner, "Kind-ness of God," in *Genesis Kinds*, 31–64.

44. Turner, "Kind-ness of God," in *Genesis Kinds*.

45. Turner, "Teaching Genesis 1," in *Reading Genesis 1–2*.

46. Turner, "Kind-ness of God," in *Genesis Kinds*, 31–64.

47. Turner, "Kind-ness of God," in *Genesis Kinds*.

48. Turner, "Teaching Genesis 1," in *Reading Genesis 1–2*.

49. Turner, "Teaching Genesis 1," in *Reading Genesis 1–2*.

50. Malcolm Gladwell referred to what he called the "10,000-hour rule," the number of hours of intensive concentration and practice it takes to master a subject. If you worked at it eight hours a day, it would take you three and a half years to get that kind of experience. For more information, see Malcolm Gladwell, *Outliers: The Story of Success* (New York: Little, Brown, 2008).

51. For the sake of emphasizing the point, I'm intentionally using language that parallels how business leaders today describe innovation. See, for example, Jeff Dyer, Hal B. Gregersen, and Clayton M. Christensen, *The Innovator's DNA: Mastering the Five Skills of Disruptive Innovators* (Boston: Harvard Business School, 2011).

52. Genesis 1:28: "God blessed [Adam and Eve]. And God said to them, 'Be fruitful and multiply and fill the earth and subdue it, and have dominion over the fish of the sea and over the birds of the heavens and over every living thing that moves on the earth.'"

53. The serpent is referred to as one of the wild creatures God made (Gen. 3:1), which would be consistent with the curse about crawling on the belly (v. 14). Many indicators—including the serpent's actions and the curse against him in Genesis 3:14–15—support the New Testament identification of the serpent with Satan (Rom. 16:20; Rev. 12:9; 20:2).

54. Genesis 3:22: "The LORD God said, 'Behold, the man has become like one of us in knowing good and evil. Now, lest he

reach out his hand and take also of the tree of life and eat, and live forever'—therefore the LORD God sent him out of the garden."

55. Genesis 6:5: "The LORD saw that the wickedness of man was great in the earth, and that every intention of the thoughts of his heart was only evil continually."

56. Judges 17:6: "In those days there was no king in Israel. Everyone did what was right in his own eyes."

57. Abraham Maslow, quoted in Ira David Welch, George A. Tate, and Fred Richards, eds., *Humanistic Psychology: A Source Book* (Buffalo: Prometheus Books, 1978), 190.

58. Rollo May, Carl Rogers, and Abraham Maslow, eds., *Politics and Innocence: A Humanistic Debate* (Dallas: Saybrook, 1986), 12.

59. J. Gresham Machen, "Christianity and Culture," *Princeton Theological Review* 11, no. 1 (1913): 7.

60. Kevin Bywater, personal conversation with the author, November 3, 2014.

61. Matthew 4:1–11: "Jesus was led up by the Spirit into the wilderness to be tempted by the devil. And after fasting forty days and forty nights, he was hungry. And the tempter came and said to him, 'If you are the Son of God, command these stones to become loaves of bread.' But he answered, 'It is written, "Man shall not live by bread alone, but by every word that comes from the mouth of God."' Then the devil took him to the holy city and set him on the pinnacle of the temple and said to him, 'If you are the Son of God, throw yourself down, for it is written, "He will command his angels concerning you," and "On their hands they will bear you up, lest you strike your foot against a stone."' Jesus said to him, 'Again it is written, "You shall not put the Lord your God to the test."' Again, the devil took him to a very high mountain and showed him all the kingdoms of the world and their glory. And he said to him, 'All these I will give you, if you will fall down and worship me.' Then Jesus said to him, 'Be gone, Satan! For it is written, "You shall worship the Lord your God and him only shall you serve."' Then the devil left him, and behold, angels came and were ministering to him."

62. Ephesians 6:10–18: "Be strong in the Lord and in the strength of his might. Put on the whole armor of God, that you may be able to stand against the schemes of the devil. For we do not wrestle against flesh and blood, but against the rulers, against the authorities, against the cosmic powers over this present darkness, against the spiritual forces of evil in the heavenly places. Therefore take up the whole armor of God, that you may be able to withstand in the evil day, and having done all, to stand firm. Stand therefore, having fastened on the belt of truth, and having put on the breastplate of righteousness, and, as shoes for your feet, having put on the readiness given by the gospel of peace. In all circumstances take up the shield of faith, with which you can extinguish all the flaming darts of the evil one; and take the helmet of salvation, and the sword of the Spirit, which is the word of God, praying at all times in the Spirit, with all prayer and supplication. To that end keep alert with all perseverance, making supplication for all the saints."

63. Revelation 21:1: "Then I saw a new heaven and a new earth, for the first heaven and the first earth had passed away, and the sea was no more."

64. Revelation 21:25: "[Heaven's] gates will never be shut by day—and there will be no night there."

65. Revelation 21:4: "[God] will wipe away every tear from their eyes, and death shall be no more, neither shall there be mourning, nor crying, nor pain anymore, for the former things have passed away."

66. Revelation 22:3: "No longer will there be anything accursed, but the throne of God and of the Lamb will be in it, and his servants will worship him."

67. Solomon E. Asch, "Effects of Group Pressure upon the Modification and Distortion of Judgments," in *Documents of Gestalt Psychology*, ed. Mary Henle (Berkeley, CA: University of California Press, 1961), 222–36.

68. Proverbs 15:22: "Without counsel plans fail, but with many advisers they succeed."

69. Czeslaw Milosz, "This World," in *Facing the River: New Poems* (Manchester, UK: Carcanet, 1995), 58.

70. J. R. R. Tolkien, *The Two Towers*, The Lord of the Rings (Boston: Houghton Mifflin, 1965), 116–26.

71. Miriam Solomon, "*Groupthink* versus the *Wisdom of Crowds*: The Social Epistemology of Deliberation and Dissent," *Southern Journal of Philosophy* 44, no. S1 (Spring 2006): 31.

72. C. S. Lewis, *The Abolition of Man* (New York: HarperOne, 2001), 14.

73. John Stonestreet, "Moving Worldviews to Living Well," presentation at Summit Ministries' Teach for Eternity conference, Orlando, Florida, October 2013.

74. Romans 12:1–2: "I appeal to you therefore, brothers, by the mercies of God, to present your bodies as a living sacrifice, holy and acceptable to God, which is your spiritual worship. Do not be conformed to this world, but be transformed by the renewal of your mind, that by testing you may discern what is the will of God, what is good and acceptable and perfect."

75. Samuel Johnson, quoted in James Boswell, *Boswell's Life of Johnson*, ed. Charles Grosvenor Osgood (New York: Charles Scribner and Sons, 1917), xviii.

76. Galatians 5:22–23: "The fruit of the Spirit is love, joy, peace, patience, kindness, goodness, faithfulness, gentleness, self-control; against such things there is no law."

77. Adam Pelser, "Irrigating Deserts: Thinking with C. S. Lewis about Educating for Emotional Formation," *Christian Scholar's Review* 44, no. 1 (Fall 2014): 27–44. For a fuller treatment of how the fruit of the Spirit applies to vocation, see Dallas Willard and Gary Black Jr., *The Divine Conspiracy Continued: Fulfilling God's Kingdom on Earth* (New York: HarperOne, 2014).

78. Pelser, "Irrigating Deserts," 27–44.

79. Steven Jobs, in Walter Isaacson, *Steve Jobs* (New York: Simon and Schuster, 2011), 567.

80. Joel Stein, "Baby, You Can Drive My Car, and Do My Errands, and Rent My Stuff …," *Time*, January 29, 2015, http://time.com/3687305/testing-the-sharing-economy/.

81. See Warren Cole Smith and John Stonestreet, *Restoring All Things: God's Audacious Plan to Change the World through Everyday People* (Grand Rapids: Baker Books, 2015), 25–26.

82. Deuteronomy 31:6–8: "Be strong and courageous. Do not fear or be in dread of [these nations], for it is the LORD your God who goes with you. He will not leave you or forsake you. Then Moses summoned Joshua and said to him in the sight of all Israel, 'Be strong and courageous, for you shall go with this people into the land that the LORD has sworn to their fathers to give them, and you shall put them in possession of it. It is the LORD who goes before you. He will be with you; he will not leave you or forsake you. Do not fear or be dismayed'"; Joshua 1:6: "Be strong and courageous, for you shall cause this people to inherit the land that I swore to their fathers to give them"; 2 Chronicles 32:7: "Be strong and courageous. Do not be afraid or dismayed before the king of Assyria and all the horde that is with him, for there are more with us than with him"; Psalm 27:14: "Wait for the LORD; be strong, and let your heart take courage; wait for the LORD!"

83. Esther 4:14: "If you keep silent at this time, relief and deliverance will rise for the Jews from another place, but you and your father's house will perish. And who knows whether you have not come to the kingdom for such a time as this?"; Proverbs 24:11–12: "Rescue those who are being taken away to death; hold back those who are stumbling to the slaughter. If you say, 'Behold, we did not know this,' does not he who weighs the heart perceive it? Does not he who keeps watch over your soul know it, and will he not repay man according to his work?"; Proverbs 31:8: "Open your mouth for the mute, for the rights of all who are destitute."

84. Colossians 3:16: "Let the word of Christ dwell in you richly, teaching and admonishing one another in all wisdom, singing psalms and hymns and spiritual songs, with thankfulness in your hearts to God"; Hebrews 13:15: "Through [Christ] then let us continually offer up a sacrifice of praise to God, that is, the fruit of lips that acknowledge his name"; First Peter 3:15: "In your hearts honor Christ the Lord as holy, always being prepared to make a defense to anyone who asks you for a reason for the hope that is in you; yet do it with gentleness and respect."

85. Brooke Obie, "Hip-Hop's Spiritual Son Lecrae Speaks," *Ebony*, June 18, 2013, www.ebony.com/wellness-empowerment/the-spiritual-life-hip-hops-spiritual-son-lecrae-speaks-967/2#axzz3Qswtg2yE.

86. Lecrae, quoted in Obie, "Hip-Hop's Spiritual Son."

87. XXXchurch, "Our Approach," accessed July 9, 2016, http://xxxchurch.com/theindustry#our-approach.

88. Ted Baehr, quoted in Jeff Myers, *From the President's Desk* (blog), *Summit Journal* 13, no. 4 (April 2013): 2.

89. Second Peter 2:19: "They promise … freedom, but they themselves are slaves of corruption. For whatever overcomes a person, to that he is enslaved."

90. Stonestreet, "Moving Worldviews to Living Well."

91. Proverbs 27:17: "Iron sharpens iron, and one man sharpens another."

92. Stonestreet, "Moving Worldviews to Living Well."

93. Ross Douthat, *Bad Religion: How We Became a Nation of Heretics* (New York: Free Press, 2012), 293.

CHAPTER 5

5

THINKING AND SPEAKING CLEARLY

1. Engaging a Culture That Wants to Hurt Us

Comfortable as leader of the scouting organization Boy Rangers, the refreshingly wholesome Jefferson Smith received a call out of the blue asking him to fill the seat of a recently deceased senator. Suddenly thrust into the national spotlight, Smith tried to make the most of his position by proposing legislation to establish a national camp for boys. Unfortunately, the land selected for the camp was the very same plot that a group of corrupt politicians—including the other senator from his state, Senator Paine—had designated for the Willet Creek Dam project, from which these senators stood to gain financially. Smith had unknowingly picked a fight with Washington's most powerful people.

That's the no-good-deed-goes-unpunished story line of Frank Capra's classic film *Mr. Smith Goes to Washington*. More than seventy years after the film was released, the ongoing problem of political corruption makes the story line sound like something from today's headlines. Especially realistic is the way the entrenched political boss in the movie, Jim Taylor, took advantage of Smith's naïveté to attack him with false accusations and negative media coverage.

But in the *Mr. Smith* story, Smith fought back. Taking the Senate floor to clear his name, Smith exercised his privilege as a senator to hold a filibuster, refusing to yield the floor until his innocence could be proved. Desperate to get Smith out of public view before the truth came to light, the secretly corrupt Senator Paine brought baskets of telegrams onto the Senate floor calling for Smith to step down:

> **Paine:** There it is, there's the gentleman's answer. Telegrams, five thousand of them, demanding that he yield the floor. I invite the Senate to read them. I invite my colleague to read them. The people's answer to Mr. Jefferson Smith.

> **Smith:** (Seizing handfuls of telegrams at random and sagging in despair): "I guess this is just another lost cause, Mr. Paine. All you people don't know about lost causes. Mr. Paine does. He said once they were the only causes worth fighting for, and he fought for them once, for the only reason that any man ever fights for them. Because of just one plain, simple rule, "Love thy neighbor," and in this world today, full of hatred, a man who knows that one rule has a great trust. You knew that rule, Mr. Paine, and I loved you for it, just as my father did. And you know that you fight for the lost causes harder than for any others. Yes, you'd even die for them, like a man we both know, Mr. Paine. You think I'm licked. You all think I'm licked. Well, I'm not licked and I'm going to stay right here and fight for this lost cause even if this room gets filled with lies like these, and the Taylors and all their armies come marching into this place. Somebody'll listen to me—some—

With that, Smith fainted. The senators fell silent. Paine rose, his face blank, and headed for the cloakroom. As other members tried to revive Smith, a shot rang out. In the cloakroom Paine struggled with several men trying to wrest a revolver out of his hand to keep him from committing suicide. Tearing himself loose, Paine rushed into the chamber:

> **Paine:** (Crying out, as the senators and spectators stare[d] in shocked silence): "Expel *me!* Not him. *Me!* Willet Dam is a fraud! It's a crime against the people who sent me here—and *I* committed it! Every word that boy said is the truth! I'm not fit for office! I'm not fit for any place of honor or trust in this land! Expel *me*—!"[1]

THINKING AND SPEAKING CLEARLY

In the end, justice was done, and Smith and the Boy Rangers continued happily ever after. Today's viewers, though, find Capra's story line unrealistic. The idea that the truth would come to light and the wrongdoers would confess and slink remorsefully away makes for good theater, but that's not typical of real life. This is a world in which men and women spend a lifetime building a good reputation, only to have it shattered in minutes by careless media personalities; a world in which powerful fat cats cast mindless votes that saddle future generations with unbearable debt; in which government cronyism profits the greedy at the expense of tens of millions who struggle from paycheck to paycheck. Good people suffer. Evildoers prosper.[2]

> The idea that the truth would come to light and the wrongdoers would confess and slink remorsefully away makes for good theater, but that's not typical of real life.

And it isn't just in politics. Many who have spoken up for their Christian convictions have suffered shame or even forfeited their livelihoods. In 2015, the city of Atlanta's esteemed fire chief, Kelvin Cochran, an African American man who fought his way out of poverty and established a remarkable career, was fired for expressing his biblical views on sexual morality and traditional marriage in a guide he had written for a private Bible study.[3] Chief Cochran wasn't the first, and he won't be the last. No wonder so many people are drawn to the parts of the Christian message that promise an escape from it all.

And yet rather than hide away from culture, we're called to advance. That we live in evil times is no excuse for doing otherwise. Ephesians 5:15–16 says, "Look carefully then how you walk, not as unwise but as wise, making the best use of the time, because the days are evil." Evil days are a given. The only variable is whether we'll make the most of them.

Engaging in a culture that could hurt us requires strong convictions and an unshakable trust in God. It's a call to speak the truth with thoughtful, well-formed arguments presented persuasively through loving dialogue. This chapter is a how-to manual for four aspects of engagement: think, argue, persuade, dialogue. Let's begin with clear thinking.

> Engaging in a culture that could hurt us requires strong convictions and an unshakable trust in God.

2. Why We Should Think, and Think Well

This book is based on two previous books, the first of which, *Understanding the Faith*, outlines a Christian worldview and answers its most prominent criticisms. The second book, *Understanding the Times*, compares Christianity with other worldviews and shows the Christian worldview's robustness against its most vocal opponents. Both previous books, and this one, argue that the Christian worldview is the most accurate reflection of the truth. Having revealed himself in nature and in Scripture, God enables us to obtain eternal salvation and also to be ambassadors of his redemption. Revelation enlivens truth in our minds and hearts, showing us how to really live.

Truth is to be understood in two ways: with our *minds* (Rom. 12:2)[4] and with our *hearts* (Heb. 4:12).[5] We believe that truth can be tested. The authors of *Making Sense of Your World* suggest four tests:[6]

1. The test of reason. Is it reasonable? Can it be logically stated and defended?

2. The test of the outer world. Is there some external, corroborating evidence to support it?

3. The test of the inner world. Does it adequately address the everyday relationships, crises, victories, blessings, and disappointments we experience in our world?

4. The test of the real world. Are its consequences good or bad when applied in any given cultural context?

These four tests assume we can think clearly not only about the world around us but also about spiritual truth. Clear thinking is based on logic, an idea derived from the Greek word *logos*, which is often translated "word" but more accurately means "to express thoughts based on universal principles of reasoning or thinking." The study of logic has deep roots going back thousands of years. One early source for the logos is Plato's dialogue *Euthyphro*, in which he demonstrated that the essence of things (in this case piety and justice) can be known because universal, unchanging forms actually exist in the spiritual realm.[7]

> We are bound by the laws of logic as surely as we are bound by the law of gravity.

Plato's student Aristotle rejected his teacher's idea of abstract universal forms but still believed that logic was a valid universal tool by which humans could reason consistently. Sometime later, the Jewish philosopher Philo (born 15–10 BC, died AD 45–50), seeking to harmonize Greek philosophy with Jewish thought, personalized the idea of the logos, referring to it as the "eldest or firstborn Son of God" and even the "man of God" or "heavenly man."[8] His personalization of logic turned out to be truer than he knew: the apostle John described Jesus as the Word (Logos) of God (see John 1).

Whatever the origin, logos proposes that logic and rational thought exist first in the mind of God, who applies them consistently and impartially in our human experience. We are bound by the laws of logic as surely as we are bound by the law of gravity. If universal principles of reasoning don't exist, or cannot be discovered, there is little point in seeking to know the truth and communicate it. If universal principles of reasoning do exist, though, and we can know them, it's possible for us to think well enough and communicate clearly enough to reach out to our fellow humans no matter what culture we're from or what subject we're talking about.

> To reason well, we must take words and language seriously.

With this brief overview in our pockets, let's look at two ways logic is worked out in our lives: through clear definitions and critical thinking.

The Art of Reasoning Involves the Clear Definition of Words

Logic is the art of formulating conclusions and outlining the reasons supporting those conclusions. Together, these conclusions and the reasons that support them is called an

argument. Many people think the word *argument* is just another word for *quarrel*, but this isn't so. Arguments are merely groups of statements (**premises**) supporting a conclusion.

To reason well, we must take words and language seriously. As the apostle John argued in John 1:1, Jesus Christ is the Logos of God. His words have the power to create. Only God can create something out of nothing, but because humans bear his image, we can also use words to create. Proverbs 18:21 says, "Death and life are in the power of the tongue, and those who love it will eat its fruits."

Logic: the study of orderly thinking; the art of formulating conclusions and outlining the reasons supporting those conclusions.

A properly used word is a well-defined word. This is especially true of terms like *justice* or *modesty* or *respect*, which are notoriously hard to pin down. The goal of defining words is not to make them robotic but to make them clear enough that rational people who aren't other wise influenced by prior commitments may understand what is meant. Good definitions must be as clear as possible, not vague or fuzzy. Good definitions must also avoid being too broad (it's unhelpful, for example, to answer the question "When will you be home?" by saying "Later"). Finally, good definitions must not be ambiguous. Their intended meanings must be as plain as possible. When politicians proclaim that their opponents are engaged in a "war on women," for example, they are intentionally using an ambiguous definition of *war* to imply, without having to provide an explanation, that their opponents are acting evilly.

Argument: a set of premises supporting a conclusion.

Premise: a basic statement in an argument that is used as support for a conclusion.

Unsurprisingly, not everyone who defines words is doing so in the service of clear thinking. Some people define words *persuasively*, attempting to get their hearers to adopt their point of view. It's okay to try to persuade others, but it's sketchy to use definitions to make people think an issue is settled without making valid arguments for it. This is what happens, for example, when someone who thinks same-sex marriage is wrong is called a "homophobe"—someone who fears homosexuality. Such a definition is used to make it seem that the person's convictions are, in fact, a mental disorder. Clear thinkers, though, seek to use definitions in a *lexical* (derived from the Greek for "word") fashion, reflecting the common use of a word in a language precisely enough that their hearers are able to think more clearly about what is being discussed.

Language is ambiguous. Words and definitions aren't precise in the way scientific formulas are, and they may even change over time. This is why we must seek clear definitions that reduce uncertainty in our communication with others.

As we'll see, many people take advantage of language's inherent ambiguity to manipulate their hearers' emotions, desires, or needs. Saying things like "Rich people aren't paying their fair share" uses words vaguely to evoke feelings of resentment. After all, what would a "fair share" be? Who gets to decide?

Critical Thinking: the process of analyzing and evaluating arguments for validity and soundness.

Often language is manipulated through euphemisms to avoid offending the easily offended.[9] Sometimes this leads to a more accurate use of words (*flight attendant* rather than *stewardess*, for example). Other times it leads to a cynical use (for instance, *undocumented alien* rather than *illegal immigrant*).

To reason well we must define words as clearly as possible, in a way that makes our meanings plain and rises above claims of bias or manipulation.

The Art of Reasoning Involves Critical Thinking

The term **critical thinking** describes the kind of thinking that enables people to cut through ambiguity to make meaning clear. The textbook *Critical Thinking: A Student's Introduction* defines this term as follows:

> Critical thinking is the general term given to a wide range of cognitive skills and intellectual dispositions needed to effectively identify, analyze, and evaluate arguments and truth claims; to discover and overcome personal preconceptions and biases; to formulate and present convincing reasons in support of conclusions; and to make reasonable, intelligent decisions about what to believe and what to do.[10]

This is a good example of a clear and thorough definition. It takes an ambiguous word and explains it in terms of its outcome—namely, the ability to effectively evaluate arguments and present clear reasons on which good decisions may be based.

Richard Paul and Linda Elder from the Center for Critical Thinking say that critical thinking is important as a method for countering four false beliefs that often muddle the reasoning process:[11]

- **False belief no. 1:** It's true if *I* believe it.

- **False belief no. 2:** It's true if *we* believe it.

- **False belief no. 3:** It's true if I *want* to believe it.

- **False belief no. 4:** It's true if it serves my vested *interest* to believe it.

Embracing any one of these four false beliefs makes truthful communication almost impossible. They cut against understanding, empathy, honesty, clarity, and true persuasion. Paul and Elder put it this way:

> The human mind is often myopic, inflexible, and conformist, while at the same time highly skilled in self-deception and rationalization. People are by nature highly egocentric, highly sociocentric, and wantonly self-interested. Their goal is not truth but advantage. They have not acquired their beliefs through a rational process. They are highly resistant to rational critique. Blind faith, fear, prejudice,

and self-interest are primary organizers of much human thinking. Self-delusion, in conjunction with lack of self-command, characterize[s] much human thinking. A highly compromised integrity is the result.... Without a long-term transformation of the mind, little can be done to produce deeply honest thought.[12]

This gloomy assessment shouldn't shock Christians who realize sin's effects. Rather, it ought to renew our own commitment to deep, honest thinking as God's image bearers. Here are eight characteristics of good critical thinking:

1. **Clarity**—to make one's meaning as plain as possible

2. **Precision**—to make important distinctions in a way that scts apart alternatives

3. **Accuracy**—to present exact information

4. **Relevance**—to state premises and conclusions simply, on topic, and without unwarranted assumptions

5. **Consistency**   to avoid contradictions in thought or actions

6. **Completeness**—to make arguments that are not superficially stated or ignorant of opposing points of view

7. **Fairness**—to be as impartial as possible and open about biases

8. **Courage**—to maintain a humble yet charitable attitude

Concealing the truth or manipulating others for selfish gain violates our created image. Also, as communication scholar Em Griffin points out, avoiding manipulation can make us more persuasive because people are more likely to agree if they know we truly love them and are putting their needs ahead of our own egos.[13]

> Avoiding manipulation can make us more persuasive because people are more likely to agree if they know we truly love them and are putting their needs ahead of our own egos.

3. WHY WE SHOULD ARGUE, AND ARGUE WELL

If we're committed to using words accurately and thinking critically, we needn't be afraid of arguing. Arguments can be made positively, and we can "always being prepared to make a defense to anyone who asks you for a reason for the hope that is in you ... with gentleness and respect" (1 Pet. 3:15).[14] With this in mind, let's take a look at the art of argumentation.

> Good arguers habitually evaluate their own arguments by asking probing questions.

What Good Arguments Look Like (and How to Use Them)

A good argument satisfies the characteristics of good critical thinking by being accurately drawn from true premises (*deduction*) or formed from a general principle that accurately summarizes what has happened in the real world (*induction*). I'll expand on these concepts later in the chapter, but for now, just keep in mind that good arguers habitually evaluate their own arguments by asking questions like these:

- Are the premises true?

- Does the reasoning correctly lead to the conclusion?

- Are the reasons *relevant* to the conclusion?

- Have I committed any logical fallacies?

- Is the argument complete and fair?

They also learn to refute *bad* arguments by showing that

- the premises are false,

- the reasons given don't sufficiently lead to the conclusion drawn,

- the reasons aren't *relevant* to the conclusion,

- the conclusion is reached through logical error, or

- the argument isn't complete or fair.

Let's dig a little deeper with illustrations and examples of how this is done.

Earlier we saw that an argument is a group of statements supporting a conclusion. Many things people think are arguments aren't actually arguments. For example, reports of information, personally held beliefs, or illustrations are not, strictly speaking, arguments. They may explain why a person might hold something to be the case, but they do not actually argue that it *is* the case.

As an example of a nonargument, for instance, consider President Obama's 2015 State of the Union address, in which he advocated a minimum-wage increase. He said, "To everyone in this Congress who still refuses to raise the minimum wage, I say this: If you truly believe you could work full time and support a family on less than $15,000 a year, try it. If not, vote to give millions of the hardest working people in America a raise."[15] Clearly, the president believes the minimum wage is too low and that a full-time minimum-wage worker would earn around $15,000 a year. He might even think his illustration of asking members of Congress to "try it" is clever, but none of these things constitutes an argument.

For his statement to constitute an argument, he would have to clearly outline his premises in a way that sufficiently, completely, and fairly leads to the conclusion without logical errors.

Obviously, meeting the criteria for a good argument in the time constraints of a televised speech is difficult. But it's not impossible. In his 1995 State of the Union address, former president Bill Clinton made his case for an increase in the minimum wage as follows:

> I know that a lot of you have your own ideas about tax relief, and some of them I find quite interesting. I really want to work with all of you. My test for our proposals will be: Will it create jobs and raise incomes; will it strengthen our families and support our children; is it paid for; will it build the middle class and shrink the under class? If it does, I'll support it. But if it doesn't, I won't.
>
> The goal of building the middle class and shrinking the under class is also why I believe that you should raise the minimum wage. It rewards work. Two and a half million Americans, … often women with children, are working out there today for $4.25 an hour. In terms of real buying power, by next year that minimum wage will be at a 40-year low. That's not my idea of how the new economy ought to work.
>
> Now, I've studied the arguments and the evidence for and against a minimum wage increase. I believe the weight of the evidence is that a modest increase does not cost jobs and may even lure people back into the job market. But the most important thing is, you can't make a living on $4.25 an hour, especially if you have children, even with the working families tax cut we passed last year. In the past, the minimum wage has been a bipartisan issue, and I think it should be again. So I want to challenge you to have honest hearings on this, to get together, to find a way to make the minimum wage a living wage.[16]

Granted, Clinton's statement took two minutes instead of thirty seconds, but it clearly outlined his criteria, gave reasons, and drew a conclusion while calling for cooperation with a clearly defined goal.

As we prepare to make good arguments, it's important to understand that arguments may be divided into two types, deductive and inductive.

Deductive arguments are those in which the conclusion is "deduced" from the premises. If the premises are true, the conclusion is necessarily true. Generally speaking, deductive arguments move from the general to the specific. If the general principles are true, the specific conclusions must be also. Deductive arguments follow a format like this:

> *Deductive Argument:* **any argument built on generally accepted premises necessarily leading to a conclusion.**

Major premise

Minor premise

Conclusion

This format of making an argument is called a **categorical syllogism**. It is the most recognizable of many types of syllogisms, probably because of this common example:

Categorical Syllogism: a deductive argument that confers a conclusion from exactly two premises.

All men are mortal.
Socrates is a man.
Therefore, Socrates is mortal.

Here are two examples of categorical syllogisms:

Argument by elimination:

Argument by Elimination: a deductive argument in which the first premise presents all possible scenarios, while the second rules out all unreasonable scenarios, and the conclusion is reached by a process of elimination.

Either Kay walked to the store or she drove to the store.
Kay did not walk to the store.
Therefore, Kay drove to the store.

Argument by definition:

All uncles are male.
Bill is an uncle.
Therefore, Bill is a male.

Argument by Definition: a deductive argument in which a premise establishes a specific definition, while another premise establishes a subject's association with that definition.

In these examples, if the major and minor premises are true, then the conclusion must be true as well.

Deductive arguments can be either valid or invalid. An argument whose form is such that *if* the premises are true, the conclusion must be true is said to be a **valid argument**. This confuses people because it's possible for the premises to be *false* but the *form* of the argument to still be valid. For example,

All toasters are items made of gold.
All items made of gold are time-travel devices.
Therefore, all toasters are time-travel devices.[17]

Valid Argument: a properly formed argument.

Obviously, these premises aren't true, and yet the argument is properly formed. If the premises were true, however, the conclusion could not be false.

A **sound argument** is a valid argument in which the premises are true and lead to a true conclusion. Because the premises are true, the conclusion cannot be false.

Sound Argument: a valid argument with true premises.

An **inductive argument** "induces" the conclusion from the premises. Whereas deductive arguments take a general principle and draw a specific conclusion, inductive arguments take specific instances and form a general principle. For instance:

THINKING AND SPEAKING CLEARLY

Most of the people I have met from Tennessee have been friendly.
Therefore, it's likely that most Tennesseans are friendly.

Or an inductive argument may take a *predictive* form in which guesses are made regarding future events based on information from past events:

> *Inductive Argument:* any argument built on specific premises leading to a probable conclusion.

Most winters in Minnesota have been cold.
Therefore, next winter in Minnesota will probably be cold.

It may also take a *statistical* form, which allows for probability rather than certainty:

Eighty percent of the students at Biscayne College are Protestants.
Sam is a student at Biscayne College.
Therefore, Sam is probably a Protestant.

> *Argument from Analogy:* an inductive argument that uses a comparison between similar subjects in order to reach a conclusion.

Other forms of this argument include the **argument from analogy** (drawing a conclusion based on comparisons). An argument from analogy would be something like this: "The best ideas are like tress. The more deeply rooted they are, the stronger they become."

Inductive arguments can be either strong or weak. A strong inductive argument is one where the conclusion *probably* follows from the premises. The more likely the conclusion, the greater the argument's strength. If the premises are true and the conclusion follows with strength, it's called a **cogent argument**.

> *Cogent Argument:* a clear and convincing inductive argument in which the premises lead to a highly probable conclusion.

What Bad Arguments Look Like (and How to Avoid Using Them)

Ernest Hemingway was once asked what it takes to be a great writer. He replied, "In order to be a great writer a person must have a built-in, shockproof crap detector."[18] It's true in other areas as well. If you're a teacher, you have to be able to quickly discern whether your students are just filling exam space with words or actually offering reasoned arguments. If you're a news editor, you must be able to know whether your reporter's work is hitting the real issues.

It's also true in general life. To not be fooled by every argument we hear, we must be able to discern whether arguments that sound good or even knock us back on our rear ends are actually true. Carl Sagan, though an atheist who found religion insulting, hit the nail on the head when he said that if we don't practice tough habits of thinking, "we cannot hope to solve the truly serious problems that face us—and we risk becoming a nation of suckers, a world of suckers, up for grabs by the next charlatan who saunters along."[19]

The term **fallacy** refers to mistakes that make arguments invalid, unsound, weak, or ineffective. There is no exhaustive list of fallacies. Following are some of the more common ones to avoid if you wish your arguments to be taken seriously.

Fallacy: a mistake in reasoning that renders an argument invalid, unsound, weak, or ineffective.

Ad hominem. *Ad hominem* means "against the man" and represents an argument based on a personal attack. For example, "Bob claims that marijuana does not interfere with a person's ability to do his job on a construction site, but we all know that Bob was a regular marijuana user in college." Unless the arguer proves that Bob's facts are wrong or that his arguments are based on impaired reasoning, accusations of his past marijuana use aren't relevant to the argument and would be ad-hominem fallacies.

Ad Hominem: a fallacy in which an argument attacks a person rather than supporting or disproving a conclusion.

Attacking the motive. Similar to the personal attack, it's a fallacy to say that a person's vested interests are what make his or her argument wrong. For example, "Ted has argued that there is an almost total lack of transitional forms in support of biological evolution; but of course Ted believes that because he is a creationist." Whether Ted is a creationist may help us predict the arguments he seeks to make, but it lacks relevance as to whether the claims he makes are true.

Attacking the Motive: a fallacy in which an argument attacks a person's vested interest in the conclusion instead of the person's conclusion.

Tu quoque (Too KWO-kwee). Tu quoque is also called the look-who's-talking fallacy. In this fallacy, an argument is rejected because the person doesn't practice what he or she preaches. Admittedly it's hard to take exercise advice from an out-of-shape person, but just because the person doesn't personally heed the advice doesn't necessarily mean his or her advice is wrong.

Tu Quoque: a fallacy in which a person's conclusion is rejected because he or she doesn't live as if the conclusion is true.

Scare tactics. In the scare-tactic fallacy, a person is threatened physically or otherwise if he or she doesn't accept the arguer's conclusion. For example, "You ought to take my advice; after all, I have been a big financial supporter of your ministry." Scare tactics are used all the time on the international stage. In the ongoing conflict between Russia and the Ukraine, Russia warned in 2015 that Ukrainians taking up arms to defend themselves would "worsen the crisis" between them.[20] This is a scare tactic because the crisis would be worse only if Russia responded with force. The argument was like a bully saying, "If you defend yourself, you're going to force me to start fighting you."

Scare Tactics: a fallacy in which an argument's strength is built on the fear of negative consequences for not agreeing with its conclusion.

Appeal to pity. An appeal-to-pity fallacy tries to evoke feelings of pity rather than making actual arguments. For example, a woman in Great Britain who weighed 350 pounds said she was obese because healthy food is too expensive and she can only afford to buy junk food. She claimed she needed more taxpayer money to lose weight and suggested that she should be reimbursed for every pound she loses.[21]

Appeal to Pity: a fallacy in which an argument tries to evoke an emotional response rather than establish logical support for its conclusion.

Bandwagon. The bandwagon fallacy asserts that a person should accept a claim because it's popular, not because it's based on sound reasoning or evidence. For example, "A group of three thousand scientists has said that climate change is caused by humans, so you should believe it too." Of course, such a group might have good reasons for believing something, but to focus on the number who believe it rather than the reasons is to commit a logical fallacy.

Bandwagon: a fallacy in which an argument appeals to popular support of a conclusion instead of building a case for that conclusion.

Straw man. In the straw-man fallacy, an arguer distorts an opponent's argument to make it easier to attack. For example, "Representative Clyde opposes the bill to limit carbon emissions; therefore, she must think climate change really poses no serious threat to the environment."

Straw Man: a fallacy in which an argument is misrepresented in a way that makes it easier to refute.

Red herring. The term *red herring* supposedly originated from hunters using a strong-smelling fish to distract hounds from chasing an animal the hunters didn't want chased. In a red-herring argument, an arguer tries to sidetrack the discussion by raising an irrelevant issue and then claiming that the original matter has been settled by the diversion. In a humorous moment in *Transformers*, the character Sam Witwicky uses a red-herring argument, combined with an appeal to pity (and probably several other fallacies as well), when arguing that his teacher should give him a higher grade on his oral report:

Red Herring: a fallacy in which an irrelevant issue is raised in an argument in order to avoid the issue at hand.

> Look, can you do me a favor—can you look out the window for a second? See my father? He's the guy in the green car? Let me tell you about a dream, a boy's dream, and a man's promise to that boy. He looked him in the eye and said, "Son, I'm gonna buy you a car, but I want you to bring me two thousand dollars and three A's." Okay, I got the two thousand and two A's. Okay, here's the dream. Your B minus? Pfff! Dream gone. Kaput. Sir, just ask yourself: What would Jesus do?[22]

In 2015, philosopher Justin McBrayer published an op-ed piece in the *New York Times* calling for better moral training of American public-school students.[23] Thousands of people commented on the article, and millions forwarded it through social media. One critic of McBrayer made an argument that perfectly illustrates the red-herring fallacy. In response to McBrayer's claim that new national standards wrongly teach students that morality is a matter of opinion, not fact, professor Adam Laats responded in a post, saying, "Most teachers-in-training are not activists; they are not classroom scientists. Rather they are job-seekers who hope mostly to avoid controversy and prove their classroom competence."[24]

> *Equivocation:* a fallacy in which a key word in an argument is used ambiguously or in two different senses.

> *Begging the Question:* a fallacy in which a premise of an argument merely assumes what the conclusion is trying to prove.

> *Inappropriate Appeal to Authority:* a fallacy in which an argument is built upon the testimony of an individual who is not an authority on the subject at hand.

> *Appeal to Ignorance:* a fallacy in which an argument asserts that a proposition must be true simply because it has not been proven false (or vice versa).

McBrayer wasn't arguing that teachers are conspiring to undermine morality but that new national standards, by confusing students about the difference between facts and opinions, did students a disservice. Laats's response missed McBrayer's point about moral facts, made an unrelated argument about whether teachers are conspiring to harm students' values, and claimed the unrelated argument proves that new national standards do not in fact teach students that there are no moral facts. It's classic red herring.

Equivocation. Equivocation is a logical fallacy in which a key word in the argument is used in two different senses, and the success of the argument depends on this shift in meaning. After arguing that computers in the future will be intellectually superior to people, the late atheist writer Victor J. Stenger wrote, "If the computer is 'just a machine,' so is the human brain."[25] Exactly what constitutes a "machine" is the entire issue in question. Demonstrating that computers are machines with brain-like characteristics in no way demonstrates that brains are machine-like computers.

Begging the question. The begging-the-question fallacy, also called *circular reasoning*, assumes in a premise what the arguer is trying to prove in the conclusion. For example, "The Bible says God exists; everything the Bible says is true because God wrote it; therefore, God exists." For this to be a valid argument, the arguer would need to demonstrate that the Bible is accurate in its verifiable claims and therefore ought to be considered reliable in the claims it makes that aren't verifiable.

Inappropriate appeal to authority. We rely on authorities to help us judge things to be true or false based on their expertise. Appealing to expert authorities is usually a legitimate form of inductive argument. The appeal to authority becomes *illegitimate*, though, when the arguer appeals to a source who is not a genuine authority, has a reason to deceive, is inaccurate, is generally unreliable, comments out of context, contradicts general findings, or makes extravagant claims. For example, when people quote noted astronomer Carl Sagan's statement that "the cosmos is all that is or ever was or ever will be,"[26] they are inappropriately appealing to authority, because such a claim isn't something anyone, even an astronomer, could actually know to be true based on available evidence.

Appeal to ignorance. The appeal-to-ignorance fallacy says a claim must be true because no one has proved it false, or it's false because no one has proved it true. In explaining his vision for future computers, Victor Stenger said, "If there is anything we do that computers cannot, be patient. In time they will do it better, if it is worth doing at all."[27] His claim was an appeal to ignorance in two ways. First, he based it on future events and thus couldn't be proved false. Second, he was saying that contrary claims were false because they failed to show that what computers cannot do is actually worth doing.

> *False Dilemma:* a fallacy in which a problem is presented as having only two solutions when there is at least one other possibility.

False dilemma. In the false-dilemma fallacy, an arguer poses a false either-or choice. Arguing that Christians should support government programs, Craig Watts says,

> Some politicians who identify themselves as Christians claim the only way the poor should be helped is by voluntary contributions. To use tax dollars to help them is "theft" and "using other people's money," they argue. Oddly, they don't seem to think that using tax dollars for crop subsidies, energy subsidies, surveillance apparatus or weapons systems constitute[s] theft. The hypocrisy is clear.[28]

In this instance, Watts created a false dilemma by assuming that politicians' opposition to government subsidies for the poor is hypocritical unless they oppose all government subsidies. But that the government should spend the money on the poor instead of other things is exactly what he was obligated to prove if he wished to make a cogent argument.

Loaded question. In the loaded-question fallacy, the arguer asks a question that contains an unwarranted presupposition. For example, the question "Have you stopped beating your wife yet?" forces a yes-or-no response in which a yes answer presupposes that the man has beaten his wife in the past, and a no answer presupposes that he still does so. It isn't fair.

> *Loaded Question:* a fallacy in which a question presupposes an unjustified assumption.

False cause. In a false-cause fallacy, an arguer claims, without sufficient evidence, that one thing is the cause of another. There are three versions of this fallacy. The *post-hoc* version assumes that one event is the cause of another event because it precedes it (for example, a friend of mine

> *False Cause:* a fallacy in which a cause-and-effect connection is assumed without sufficient evidence for that connection.

said, "The doctrine of the rapture must be true because that's why I came to Christ"). The *correlation problem* occurs when two events are correlated and one is therefore assumed to be the cause of the other (for example, the old joke about the husband who says to his wife, "Whenever anything bad has happened to me, you've been there for me … I'm beginning to think you're bad luck"). The third version is *oversimplified cause*, which asserts that a complex happening has only one cause (for example, the statement "Rome fell because of the rise of Christianity" is suspect because something as complicated as the fall of a civilization likely has many causes).

> *Hasty Generalization:* a fallacy in which a certain quality of a part is assumed to be a quality of the whole.

Hasty generalization. The hasty-generalization fallacy occurs when the arguer says that because part of a thing has a certain quality, *all* of that thing has that quality. In his argument against conservativism, for example, the author Sam Tanenhaus wrote, "What conservatives have yet to do is confront the large but inescapable truth that movement conservatism is exhausted and quite possibly dead."[29] The very next election showed that his inductive argument was based on too small of a sample: conservatives won most of the key electoral contests.

> *Slippery Slope:* a fallacy in which a claim is made with insufficient evidence that if a certain action is taken, it would eventually lead to dire consequences.

Slippery slope. The slippery-slope fallacy happens when an arguer contends without sufficient evidence that if a certain action is taken, it will lead to more extreme consequences and eventually to disaster. For example, "If the government bans assault weapons, then they will ban shotguns and even handguns, and we'll live in a police state with no protection for our families."

> *Weak Analogy:* a fallacy in which a comparison is made between things that aren't comparable in relevant respects.

Weak analogy. A weak-analogy fallacy is when an arguer compares things that aren't really comparable in relevant respects, such as "Making people without children pay school taxes is like making people who don't smoke pay taxes on cigarettes." It's a weak analogy because cigarettes are a product not everyone uses, but education benefits everyone in the community by helping prepare children to be good, productive citizens.

> *Fallacy of Division:* a fallacy based on the assumption that because a whole has a certain characteristic, then so must its parts.

Division and composition. In the **fallacy of division**, the claim is made that because a whole has a certain characteristic, each part of the whole has that characteristic (for example, "Our football team is the best team; therefore, each of our players must be the best player in his position"). In the **fallacy of composition**, the claim is made that because each part of something has a certain characteristic, the whole

THINKING AND SPEAKING CLEARLY

thing must have that characteristic. (For example, "Our political party's candidates are the best in this election; therefore, our party is the best.")

Just because someone arrives at a conclusion based on logical fallacies doesn't mean the conclusion is false, however; it just means that the conclusion isn't merited based on the arguments given. New arguments must be made that don't take shortcuts. True principles don't need tricky techniques to show themselves to be true.

> *Fallacy of Composition:* a fallacy based on the assumption that because parts of a whole have certain characteristics, then so must the whole.

4. WHY WE SHOULD PERSUADE, AND PERSUADE WELL

Persuasion is "the act of influencing the mind by arguments or reasons offered, or by anything that moves the mind or passions, or inclines the will to a determination."[30] To persuade others to reach truthful conclusions requires trust and credibility as well as clear definitions and logical arguments. Jesus is described in Luke 2:52 as increasing in wisdom and stature and favor as a young man.[31] Similarly, even if God specially gifts us for some great cause, we still need to grow in favor with others. How do we do this?

> To persuade others to reach truthful conclusions requires trust and credibility as well as clear definitions and logical arguments.

Building Trust and Credibility

Good persuasion takes a high level of credibility. Credibility comes from the root word *credo* for "I believe"[32] We become credible when we live consistently with what we say we believe. A lack of credibility leads to a lack of trust. In his book *The Speed of Trust*, business-man Stephen Covey says,

> Simply put, trust means *confidence*. The opposite of trust—distrust—is *suspicion*. When you trust people, you have confidence—in their integrity and in their abilities. When you distrust people, you are suspicious of them—of their integrity, their agenda, their capabilities, or their track record.[33]

Building trust has practical benefits. In his book, Covey demonstrates that when business relationships are built on trust, they can develop more quickly and at a lower cost. Conversely, when trust is low, the process of reaching agreement slows down and the costs go up, because it takes time and expensive attorneys to devise the complicated contracts they need to protect their interests.[34]

The philosopher Aristotle developed a three-part test for credibility.[35] The first part, Aristotle said, is *ethos*—demonstrating that you are a good person. People are watching. Do you display good character? The second part, *pathos*, or passion, is based on how your

---

hearers are led to feel emotion by your approach. Does your message engage them? The third part of credibility is based on a word we've already discussed, *logos*. Are your arguments well constructed based on proper evidence?

Pygmalion Effect: a psychological effect whereby the confidence of an arguer makes the persuasion of those listening more likely.

Credible people, to Aristotle, are those who can effectively share their passion with others and do so based on good arguments. But there is one more subtle aspect to this kind of credibility. Credibility is as much an *attitude* on the part of the persuader as it is an *event* for those being persuaded. Researchers call this the **Pygmalion effect**, based on an ancient Greek myth about a sculptor whose love for the statue he created moved the goddess Aphrodite to bring it to life. In the *Harvard Business Review*, J. Sterling Livingston wrote,

> Contrary to what might be assumed, the high expectations of superior managers are based primarily on what they think about themselves—about their own ability to select, train, and motivate their subordinates.… If [managers] have confidence in their ability to develop and stimulate subordinates to high levels of performance, they will expect much of them and will treat them with confidence that their expectations will be met. But if they have doubts about their ability to stimulate subordinates, they will expect less of them and will treat them with less confidence.[36]

So while we want those we're persuading to be convinced of our character, to find our arguments moving, and to see the logic in what we're saying, there is also a self-fulfilling-prophesy aspect to persuasion: people are unlikely to be convinced if we aren't convinced ourselves.

Forming a Persuasive Message

Let's say you have the opportunity to make a presentation to your local city council encouraging members to pass a bill that fights sex trafficking. You've got all your points prepared, but how do you present them in the best way? In the 1940s, a researcher named Alan Monroe tested lots of different ways of organizing persuasive messages. He found that one format is significantly more likely than others to move people to action. There are five steps to Monroe's motivated sequence, and I will describe and illustrate with examples of how it might be used to support a presentation opposing sex trafficking:[37]

1. Attention. Get the attention of your audience using a story, a shocking example, a dramatic statistic, or a memorable quotation. For example, "We thought the Civil War ended slavery in America, but we were wrong."

2. Need. Audiences are moved to action by their needs. People won't buy a bottle of water unless they're thirsty. Focus on the "thirst" by making your point relevant to your audience. For example, "Sex trafficking occurs when young women are held captive emotionally and forced to meet the sexual desires of others. It isn't just a problem out there. It's a problem here in our own community."

3. Satisfaction. Offer a specific, workable solution the people in your audience can actually imagine implementing. For example, "Fortunately, there are legal powers we can give to our police department to effectively fight this travesty."

4. Visualization. Help your audience see what will happen if the solution is implemented. For example, "Imagine making our community a place where young women feel safe and protected."

5. Action. Ask your audience for a specific action. For example, "I am asking you today to pass a law based on the codes put together by expert attorneys who are skilled at fighting sex trafficking."

Turning Hostility into Agreement

It's hard to imagine community leaders not wanting to do something about an issue like sex trafficking. On many other issues, however, you'll encounter opposition. This is true even if your arguments are clearly defined, logically supported, and persuasively organized. Here are some suggestions for turning hostility into agreement:

Avoid fear appeals. Studies show that fear is an effective appeal only if there is a way for people to act to reduce their fear.[38] And while fear can lead people to accept certain beliefs and attitudes, positive appeals are more likely to change intentions and behavior.[39]

> While fear can lead people to accept certain beliefs and attitudes, positive appeals are more likely to change intentions and behavior.

Don't insist on being acknowledged as right. People are most likely to be persuaded if they believe they're persuading themselves rather than feeling as if they're being compelled to admit they're wrong. Persuasion expert Elliot Aronson says,

> Self-persuasion is almost always a more powerful form of persuasion (deeper, longer lasting) than more traditional persuasion techniques—that is, than being directly persuaded by another person, no matter how clever, convincing, expert, and trustworthy that other person might be—precisely because in direct persuasion, the audience is constantly aware of the fact that they have been persuaded by another.[40]

Don't take shortcuts. I remember someone who disagreed with my political viewpoint telling me, "Your candidate is scary." I dropped the point. Clearly the other person wasn't interested in hearing what I had to say. But this didn't mean I had been persuaded. Shaming people into believing something or making them feel that their view is uncool doesn't really persuade them. Compelling people to stop arguing doesn't mean they're persuaded that you're right. In fact, people silenced in this way are as likely to switch back to their previous opinions as if they never changed them in the first place.[41] An old saying applies here: "A man convinced against his will is of the same opinion still."

Understand the source of the resistance. Why do people resist change? To answer this, we need to understand what change actually means to people. Generally speaking, people don't resist change, per se. Rather, they resist loss of status, security, and comfort. It may be the case that what they're resisting is uncertainty, not change. In fact, resistance to change can actually be a good trait: it keeps people from going along "just because," and it opens up new ways of thinking about an issue.[42] Encourage them to explore why they find it so difficult to agree and ask how you can help.

Make your message personally relevant. The personal relevance of a message affects whether people accept it. In a study of students considering whether or not a university-wide exam required for graduation was a good idea, researchers discovered that students told they would be required to take the exam were more likely to consider the strength of the argument than those told the implementation of the exam was ten years away.[43]

Enlist help. Actual *feedback* is more important in persuading a person to accept an argument than that person's *belief* that the argument is persuasive.[44] Say something like "Why don't you take this argument to your friends and see if they have any good responses; then share them with me."

Avoiding Propaganda and Manipulation

Propaganda is mass persuasion that involves manipulating symbols to control people's impressions.[45] Propaganda is a dangerous form of pseudo-persuasion because it manipulates people's prejudices so that the decisions they arrive at seem voluntary but in reality are not.

Propaganda: any biased, selective, misleading, or manipulating information circulated with the goal of changing opinions and influencing action toward a particular position or cause.

The most famous examples of propaganda come from World War II, where posters the German government produced made Jewish people appear evil. And it wasn't just the bad guys who resorted to propaganda. Unfortunately, American posters designed to heighten opposition to Japan's war efforts incited hatred of Japanese people inside America.

Persuasion enlightens an audience to the truth. *Manipulation* deceives an audience and keeps people from seeing the truth.

As I've taught the art of persuasion over the years, many students have asked, "But isn't *all* persuasion a form of propaganda? After all, when I make arguments to get someone to do something, even if my intentions and strategies aren't evil, am I not still trying to manipulate a person to my point of view?" Tragically, many people refrain from persuading others to do what's right because they're afraid of unethical manipulation.

Let's sort out the difference between persuasion and manipulation. *Persuasion* involves arranging ethical arguments to enlighten an audience to the truth. *Manipulation* involves arranging ethical or unethical arguments to deceive an audience and keep people from seeing the truth. True persuasion isn't just getting people to do what we *want*; it's getting people to do what's right. Persuasion can be a godly, biblical thing to do as long as you follow certain criteria:

- **Is what you're saying true, to the best of your knowledge?** Ephesians 4:25 advises, "Therefore, having put away falsehood, let each one of you speak the truth with his neighbor, for we are members one of another."

- **Does your message encourage an emotionally healthy response?** Ephesians 4:27 cautions, "Give no opportunity to the devil."

- **Are you seeking the good of others?** Matthew 20:28 says, "The Son of Man came not to be served but to serve, and to give his life as a ransom for many."

- **Are you treating others as you would wish to be treated?** Luke 6:31 states, "As you wish that others would do to you, do so to them."

- **Are you appealing to righteous motives?** In Matthew 18:6, Jesus said, "Whoever causes one of these little ones who believe in me to sin, it would be better for him to have a great millstone fastened around his neck and to be drowned in the depth of the sea."

- **Are you leading others to better obey God?** Culture shapers need to focus on helping people obey God. In fact, it's part of the Great Commission. Matthew 28:18–20 says, "Jesus came and said to [his disciples], 'All authority in heaven and on earth has been given to me. Go therefore and make disciples of all nations, baptizing them in the name of the Father and of the Son and of the Holy Spirit, teaching them to observe all that I have commanded you.'"

Propaganda operates by isolating people from the truth. Having the opportunity to talk about the truth breaks its spell. As French philosopher Jacques Ellul put it, "Propaganda ceases where simple dialogue begins."[46] All types of clear thinking and speaking, in fact, begin with dialogue. We must learn to dialogue, and dialogue well.

5. Why We Should Dialogue, and Dialogue Well

Most persuasion doesn't take place in speeches. Someone is unlikely to say, "Will you give me a thirty-minute speech about why you believe in God?" Such persuasion is more likely to occur in the context of a dialogue (from *dia-* and *logos*, literally to "think and talk through"). Today, persuasion is just as likely to happen at a coffee shop as in a lecture hall.

> People who dialogue well *listen* as much as they *talk*. Their goal isn't just to be right. It's to learn—and help others learn—the truth.

People who dialogue well *listen* as much as they *talk*. Their goal isn't just to be right. It's to learn—and help others learn—the truth. As Ralph G. Nichols and Leonard A. Stevens put it, "The talker cannot learn for the listener. 'Telling' doesn't equate with teaching, and 'getting told' certainly doesn't equate with learning."[47]

Here's an example Greg Koukl shares in his book *Tactics*:

> "Are any of you in the room God?" The professor scanned the audience slowly, looking for takers. No hands went up.
>
> "God knows 'TRUTH,'" she continued, writing the word in all capital letters on the board. "All truth is God's truth. God is truth. But you are not God. Therefore, you only know 'truth.'" She then scrawled in lower case this secondary and substandard take on reality next to the superior version that is forever out of reach for mere humans.
>
> She paused for a moment, letting her point sink in, then closed. "Have a nice day," she said, and dismissed the class.
>
> It was a brilliant piece of rhetorical wizardry. Students were too busy taking notes and worrying whether or not this would be on the test to think carefully about what had been stolen from them or the ruin this foreshadowed for their faith.
>
> The professor's assertions teemed with confusion. What does "TRUTH" mean? Omniscience? That couldn't be her meaning. That God knows everything and we do not is a trivial observation, hardly a revelation even for college freshmen.
>
> Does she mean we can't know things in the way God knows them, that we don't see the world the way he does? Again, not particularly profound.
>
> No, the professor was going after the conviction in "modernist" circles that human beings can actually know something like absolute truth—knowledge they can count on. Instead, she is saying that we mortals inhabit a kind of knowledge twilight where the outlines of reality are vague and indistinct, robbing us of all confidence that anything we think we know is actually so.[48]

What would you do if you were in this class? Clearly, you've not been invited to give a formal refutation. The best approach, Koukl suggests, is to ask questions. Something like this might be appropriate:

> Professor, I'm confused about your comments. Is this insight you've offered true or false? I don't think you'd knowingly teach us something false, so you must think it [is] true. And that's what confuses me. What kind of "truth" would that be? It couldn't be *TRUTH*, because you're not God. So it must be *truth*. But if this is just your personal perception of reality, why should any of us take you seriously? We have our own perceptions. Since none of us has *TRUTH*, who's to say who is right and who is wrong? Can you clear this up for me?[49]

> **Those who dialogue well use tactics to navigate the way toward truth.**

Tactics is Koukl's term for navigating the way toward truth through dialogue. It's especially important in situations where we feel we ought to say something but don't want to make people mad or appear to them

THINKING AND SPEAKING CLEARLY

as extreme. When someone says something you think needs to be challenged, Koukl says, you have about a ten-second window to get information, buy time, and steer things in a productive direction.

Koukl offers a strategy he calls the "Columbo tactic," named after Lieutenant Columbo, a brilliant TV detective who disarmed bad guys with questions.[50] You can start a dialogue by simply asking, "Do you mind if I ask you a question?" Questions display an interest in the person asked, educate you on the other person's perspective, and allow you to make progress on a point without being pushy. Never make a statement when a question will do the job. Consider questions like these:

What do you mean by that? This question requests clarification and helps ensure that the dialogue is based on good definitions of the terms being discussed.

> Never make a statement when a question will do the job.

How did you come to that conclusion? When someone makes an assertion, the ideas on the table are theirs, not yours. It's not your duty to prove them wrong; it's their duty to prove them right. Is what the person claiming possible, plausible, and probable? Is it an argument or just an opinion? Find out by asking clarifying questions instead of trying to win your case.

Can I take some time to think about it? Just because someone demands an answer right now doesn't mean you're obligated to give one. Once you understand the other person's point of view, you can work to respond later, on your own, when the pressure is off.

Have you considered this? Can you help me understand? Take the conversation to the next level by going on the offensive without *being* offensive. Do this by asking questions that *expand* the conversation rather than *narrow* it. Be alert to people who try to drive toward the conclusion too quickly by pinning you down to a one-word answer. For example, if someone says, "That may be true for you, but it's not true for me," you could reply, "When I say something is true, I mean to say that it applies to all people, everywhere. By saying that it's not true for you, what you're really saying is that I'm wrong. Can you help me understand where I've gone wrong and what reasons you have for saying that?"

Very few people can be clever "on command." It takes a lot of knowledge and skill to be quick on your feet. Be curious, ask thoughtful questions, and then go study some more and return with other questions.

> Be curious, ask thoughtful questions, and then go study some more and return with other questions.

The Columbo tactic doesn't so much answer questions as it directs people away from knee-jerk reactions. Once you've done this, the next step is to identify the flaws in wrong views and take the opportunity to inject truth. Koukl offers some examples:

Ideas that commit suicide. Some ideas, in their very expression, refute themselves. For example: "There is no truth." (Is this statement true?) "You can't know anything for sure." (Are you sure about that?)[51] Ask if the claim applies to itself. Is truth true?

Taking the roof off. *Taking the roof off* means looking inside an idea to see if it is as true on the inside as it appears on the outside. Many bad arguments, if applied consistently, move toward an unreasonable destination.[52] For example, someone might say, "The school should not punish so-and-so for cheating. Jesus would forgive." Disagreeing would seem unforgiving. But as Koukl says, you can take the roof off and get to the heart of the person's basic argument by asking, "Are you saying that the school should never punish *any* wrongdoing?"

Steamroller. Have you ever tried to discuss truth with someone whose forceful personality seems to roll over everyone else? It's hard to know what motivates steamrollers. Maybe they're just being controlling. Maybe they're prejudiced. Perhaps they're in rebellion.[53] The best response is to try to stop them. "Whoa. I feel like whenever I try to bring something up, I don't really have the opportunity to finish my thought." If that doesn't work, just drop it. Always be known as a person who keeps your calm and refuses to respond to rudeness with rudeness.

> Always be known as a person who keeps your calm and refuses to respond to rudeness with rudeness.

Rhodes Scholar. Ask the other person to supply reasons for saying something. There's a difference between *informing* and *educating*. As Koukl phrases it, "When an article tells you *why* he holds his view, you have been educated."[54] When someone says, "Scholars agree with me," ask, "Can you tell me which scholars agree and what reasons they give?"

Just the facts, ma'am. Some time ago in a discussion, a person asked, "How does it affect your marriage if I'm married to my same-sex partner?" The question made it seem that I was somehow reserving a right for myself that I wasn't willing for others to have. I recalled Koukl's point about a TV detective named Joe Friday who often interrupted witnesses' tirades by saying, "Just the facts, ma'am."

> Dialogue takes practice. Work on becoming a good ambassador, a person who is ready, patient, reasonable, tactical, clear, fair, honest, humble, attractive, and dependent on God.

Many challenges to Christianity are based on bad information. Ask yourself, "What claim is this person making? Is it factually accurate?" If you're not sure, you can go back to the question, "How did you come to that conclusion?" In the instance of the question I was asked about marriage, I realized that the person hadn't really made an argument to support the claims that the definition of marriage should be expanded, that same-sex relationships should be called marriage, or even that marriage ought to be about us and what we want. Just asking a question that puts me on the defensive doesn't mean the person has made a valid argument. Instead of *answering* the question, ask something like "What argument are you making exactly?" or "Can you share with me the facts that support your argument?"

Dialogue takes practice. But as you work on the things you've learned in this chapter, such as clarifying definitions, making logical arguments, organizing your thoughts, and asking probing questions, you'll improve. Keep truth in perspective. As Koukl says, "If they want to go, let them leave.… But don't let them leave empty-handed." Be a good ambassador, a person who is ready, patient, reasonable, tactical, clear, fair, honest, humble, attractive, and dependent on God.[55]

6. Conclusion

Persuasion takes time and trust. Public repentance as Senator Paine modeled in *Mr. Smith Goes to Washington* is rare. Yet while conclusions like these happen only in movies like *Mr. Smith*, the movie portrayed many truths we can apply in our own lives. To paraphrase the Roman orator Quintilian, our goal is to be good people speaking well.[56] Following are some of the takeaways from the Jefferson Smith character that can help us shape culture in credible, even admirable, ways.

Goodness. Senator Smith had a strong moral core. He knew corruption when he saw it because he had a wholesome, honest understanding of truth. Romans 12:2–3 says,

> Do not be conformed to this world, but be transformed by the renewal of your mind, that by testing you may discern what is the will of God, what is good and acceptable and perfect. For by the grace given to me I say to everyone among you not to think of himself more highly than he ought to think, but to think with sober judgment, each according to the measure of faith that God has assigned.

Along with cultivating our ability to think well and speak clearly, it's important that you and I stay focused on the Christian virtues of holiness, justice, and love. Scott Rae and Kenman Wong observe that being holy should improve our moral standards and behavior. We should treat employees better. We should seek to be just without being harsh. We should love without showing favoritism or being permissive.[57] At the end of the day, how we treat people, more than whether our points are well argued, wins them to the truth.

> At the end of the day, how we treat people, more than whether our points are well argued, wins them to the truth.

Genuineness. Even in the midst of great pressure, Senator Smith remained humble and honorable. First Peter 2:12 says, "Keep your conduct among the Gentiles honorable, so that when they speak against you as evildoers, they may see your good deeds and glorify God on the day of visitation." Genuinely representing truth makes truth attractive. And as persuasion expert Robert Cialdini says, "People prefer to say yes to those they like."[58]

Grit. Senator Smith refused to compromise what he knew was true, even under immense pressure. He possessed a quality called *grit*, which is the tendency to work "strenuously toward challenges, maintaining effort and interest over years despite failure, adversity, and plateaus in progress."[59] Grit gets people through tough times. One study found that West Point military academy cadets who persevered through their training weren't necessarily the most physically fit or self-disciplined.[60] Grit, the study found, is what got them through. Further, grit was found to be a community virtue. Charles Duhigg summarized as follows: "To succeed, they need a keystone habit that creates a culture—such as a daily gathering of like-minded friends—to help find the strength to overcome obstacles."[61]

Goodness, genuineness, and grit aren't qualities we possess on our own. We need others. Hebrews 10:23–25 says, "Let us hold fast the confession of our hope without wavering, for he who promised is faithful. And let us consider how to stir up one another to love and good works, not neglecting to meet together, as is the habit of some, but encouraging one another, and all the more as you see the Day drawing near."

Mr. Smith Goes to Washington is more fairy tale than reality, but its call to be open hearted and clear minded, not hard bitten and cynical, is one worth heeding. "Speaking the truth in love" is how we grow up in Christ (Eph. 4:15).

ENDNOTES

1. *Mr. Smith Goes to Washington*, directed by Frank Capra (Culver City, CA: Columbia Pictures, 1939).

2. It's nothing new that evildoers often prosper while those doing good deeds are punished. See the lament of Asaph in Psalm 73.

3. Todd Starnes, *Atlanta Fire Chief: I Was Fired Because of My Christian Faith*, FoxNews.com, January 7, 2015, www.foxnews .com/opinion/2015/01/07/atlanta-fire-chief-was-fired-because-my-christian-faith.html.

4. Romans 12:2: "Do not be conformed to this world, but be transformed by the renewal of your mind, that by testing you may discern what is the will of God, what is good and acceptable and perfect."

5. Hebrews 4:12: "The word of God is living and active, sharper than any two-edged sword, piercing to the division of soul and of spirit, of joints and of marrow, and discerning the thoughts and intentions of the heart."

6. W. Gary Phillips, William E. Brown, and John Stonestreet, *Making Sense of Your World: A Biblical Worldview* (Salem, WI: Sheffield, 1996), chap. 3.

7. Plato, *Five Dialogues: Euthyphro, Apology, Crito, Meno, and Phaedo*, 2nd ed., ed. John M. Cooper, trans. G. M. A. Grube (Indianapolis: Hackett, 2002).

8. NET Bible, s.v. "*Logos*," http://classic.net.bible.org/dictionary.php?word=LOGOS.

9. This is commonly called, with ironic euphemism, *political correctness*.

10. Gregory Bassham et al., *Critical Thinking: A Student's Introduction*, 5th ed. (New York: McGraw-Hill, 2013), 1.

11. Richard Paul and Linda Elder, *The Thinker's Guide to Fallacies: The Art of Mental Trickery and Manipulation* (Dillon Beach, CA: Foundation for Critical Thinking Press, 2006), 7.

12. Paul and Elder, *Thinker's Guide to Fallacies*, 7–8.

13. Emory A. Griffin's book *The Mind Changers: The Art of Christian Persuasion* (Carol Stream, IL: Tyndale, 1976) is a classic text in persuading people Christianly and is well worth reading.

14. First Peter 3:15: "In your hearts honor Christ the Lord as holy, always being prepared to make a defense to anyone who asks you for a reason for the hope that is in you; yet do it with gentleness and respect."

15. Barack Obama, "Address before a Joint Session of the Congress on the State of the Union," January 20, 2015, www.presidency .ucsb.edu/ws/index.php?pid=108031.

16. William J. Clinton, "Address before a Joint Session of the Congress on the State of the Union," January 24, 1995, *Public Papers of the Presidents of the United States: William J. Clinton* (Washington, DC: Government Printing Office, 1996), 82.

17. "Validity and Soundness," *Internet Encyclopedia of Philosophy*, accessed September 19, 2016, www.iep.utm.edu/val-snd.

18. Ernest Hemingway, quoted in Neil Postman and Charles Weingartner, *Teaching as a Subversive Activity* (New York: Dell, 1969), 3.

19. Carl Sagan, *The Demon-Haunted World: Science as a Candle in the Dark* (New York: Ballantine Books, 1996), 38–39.

20. "Ukraine Conflict: Battles Rage Ahead of Minsk Talks," BBC News Europe, February 10, 2015, www.bbc.com/news/world-europe-31357588.

21. Lucy Waterlow, "It's Not Easy Being Overweight and on Benefits, Says 25 Stone Mother-of-Two Who Wants *More* Money from the Government to Help Her Diet," *Daily Mail*, September 24, 2014, www.dailymail.co.uk/femail/article-2768442/It-s-not -easy-overweight-benefits-says-25-stone-mother-two-wants-MORE-money-government-help-diet.html#ixzz3S13ob6MK;

Katherine Timpf, "350-Pound Woman: I'm Obese Because I Don't Get Enough Taxpayer Money," *National Review Online*, September 25, 2014, www.nationalreview.com/article/388887/350-pound-woman-im-obese-because-i-dont-get-enough-taxpayer-money-katherine-timpf.

22. *Transformers*, directed by Michael Bay (Glendale, CA: DreamWorks SKG, 2007).

23. Justin P. McBrayer, "Why Our Children Don't Think There Are Moral Facts," *Opinionator* (blog), *New York Times*, March 2, 2015, http://opinionator.blogs.nytimes.com/2015/03/02/why-our-children-dont-think-there-are-moral-facts/.

24. Adam Laats, "Alert: Public Schools Teach Nihilism!," *I Love You but You're Going to Hell* (blog), March 3, 2015, http://iloveyoubutyouregoingtohell.org/.

25. Victor J. Stenger, *Not by Design: The Origin of the Universe* (Buffalo: Prometheus Books, 1988), 189.

26. Carl Sagan, *Cosmos* (New York: Ballantine, 2013), 1.

27. Stenger, *Not by Design*, 188.

28. Craig M. Watts, "Hating the Poor but Loving Jesus?," Red Letter Christians, September 10, 2013, www.redletterchristians.org/hating-poor-loving-jesus/.

29. Sam Tanenhaus, "Conservatism Is Dead: An Intellectual Autopsy of the Movement," *New Republic*, February 17, 2009, https://newrepublic.com/article/61721/conservatism-dead.

30. Noah Webster, *An American Dictionary of the English Language* (London: Black, Young, and Young, 1828), s.v. "persuasion."

31. Luke 2:52: "Jesus increased in wisdom and in stature and in favor with God and man."

32. Douglas Harper, Online Etymology Dictionary, 2001–2016, s.v. "credo," www.etymonline.com/index.php?term=credo&allowed_in_frame=0.

33. Stephen M. R. Covey, *The Speed of Trust: The One Thing That Changes Everything* (New York: Free Press, 2006), 5.

34. Covey, *Speed of Trust*, 13.

35. Aristotle *On Rhetoric: A Theory of Civic Discourse*, trans. George A. Kennedy (New York: Oxford University Press, 1991), 36–39.

36. J. Sterling Livingston, "Pygmalion in Management," *Harvard Business Review*, January 2003, https://hbr.org/2003/1/pygmalion-in-management/ar/1.

37. I've summarized and added examples of the five steps outlined in Alan H. Monroe, *Principles and Types of Speech* (Glenview, IL: Scott, Foresman, 1949), 308–10.

38. R. F. Soames Job, "Effective and Ineffective Use of Fear in Health Promotion Campaigns," *American Journal of Public Health* 78, no. 2 (February 1988): 163–67.

39. Kenneth Beck, "The Effects of Positive and Negative Arousal upon Attitudes, Belief Acceptance, Behavioral Intention, and Behavior," *Journal of Social Psychology* 107 (April 1979): 239–51.

40. Elliot Aronson, "The Power of Self-Persuasion," *American Psychologist* 54, no. 11 (November 1999): 875–84.

41. Anthony Pratkanis and Elliot Aronson use the term *peripheral persuasion* to refer to superficial cues about a position's attractiveness rather than actual arguments. Peripheral persuasion often secures immediate but shallow agreement that can easily change when well-formed counterarguments are presented. See Anthony Pratkanis and Elliot Aronson, *Age of Propaganda: The Everyday Use and Abuse of Persuasion*, rev. ed. (New York: Henry Holt, 2001), 38–39.

42. Eric B. Dent and Susan Galloway Goldberg, "Challenging 'Resistance to Change,'" *Journal of Applied Behavioral Science* 35, no. 1 (March 1999): 25–41; Dianne Waddell and Amrik S. Sohal, "Resistance: A Constructive Tool for Change Management," *Management Decision* 36, no. 8 (1998): 543–48.

43. Richard E. Petty and John T. Cacioppo, "The Effects of Involvement on Responses to Argument Quantity and Quality: Central and Peripheral Routes to Persuasion," *Journal of Personality and Social Psychology* 46, no. 1 (1984): 69–81.

44. Charles R. Berger, "Influence Motivation and Feedback regarding Influence Outcomes as Determinants of Self-Persuasion Magnitude," *Journal of Personality* 40, no. 1 (March 1972): 62–74.

45. Pratkanis and Aronson, *Age of Propaganda*, 11. See also Jacques Ellul, *Propaganda: The Formation of Men's Attitudes* (New York: Vintage, 1973). Ellul said that propaganda is largely a modern technique made possible by psychological and sociological insights into what moves people. Propaganda makes people feel they are part of a mass movement while, in fact, isolating them from the truth.

46. Ellul, *Propaganda*, 6.

47. Ralph G. Nichols and Leonard A. Stevens, *Are You Listening?* (New York: McGraw-Hill, 1957), 43.

48. Gregory Koukl, *Tactics: A Game Plan for Discussing Your Christian Convictions* (Grand Rapids: Zondervan, 2009), 112–13.

49. Koukl, *Tactics*, 113.

50. Koukl, *Tactics*, 46–48.

51. Koukl, *Tactics*, 108.

52. Koukl, *Tactics*, 146.

53. Koukl, *Tactics*, 157–58.

54. Koukl, *Tactics*, 167.

55. Koukl, *Tactics*, 191, 199–200.

56. See Quintilian, *Institutes of Oratory*, bk. 2, chap. 15. Available online at http://rhetoric.eserver.org/quintilian/2 /chapter15.html.

57. Scott B. Rae and Kenman L. Wong, *Beyond Integrity: A Judeo-Christian Approach to Business Ethics*, 2nd ed. (Grand Rapids: Zondervan, 2004), 121–26.

58. Robert B. Cialdini, "The Science of Persuasion," *Scientific American*, January 2001, 79.

59. Angela L. Duckworth et al., "Grit: Perseverance and Passion for Long-Term Goals," *Journal of Personality and Social Psychology* 92, no. 6 (June 2007): 1087–88. See also Charles Duhigg, *The Power of Habit: Why We Do What We Do in Life and Business* (New York: Random House, 2014), 124.

60. Duckworth, "Grit," 1094–96.

61. Duhigg, *Power of Habit*.

6

TECHNOLOGY

1. Is Technology Neutral?

After my speech to a group in Singapore, a young man asked, "You said that there is a biblical-worldview approach to everything. How does a biblical worldview apply to computer programming?" He assumed that things like computers are "neutral" because they can convey any idea without any bias toward one or another. Thus, they'd have no particular relationship with any worldview. As you'll see, I don't view technology as neutral. Technology moves us to think and act in certain ways and not in others. It always has an effect.

Interestingly, the evening before this conversation, I had dinner with a businessman who shared about a company enabling people in developing countries to use text messaging to trade cell-phone minutes with one another. Because of this simple feature, cell-phone minutes essentially become an alternate form of currency in many countries. People who live hours away from the nearest bank are able to save minutes and use them to make purchases and even start businesses. For those typically at risk of being stolen from or taken advantage of, it's an alternative way to get ahead.

This simple innovation has been helpful for millions of people, and yet there are even larger implications. Much of the world's population lives in countries where corrupt leaders fuel their power by printing more money, which drives down the value of the currency and forces people to live day to day, unable to save for the future. After all, who wants to save money when that money might be worthless by next week? For people in countries stuck with corrupt leaders, cell-phone minutes provide a way to avoid the unstable national currency. People can move beyond just staying alive and actually trade without government interference. They can accumulate capital, protect their investments, and exercise their God-given creativity with less help from the international aid community.

"So," I explained to this young man, "while technology is not neutral, and it can be used for good or ill, there is definitely a way to develop technology that reflects a biblical worldview. You can use it to help people better bear God's image."

> **Technology isn't neutral; it changes our lives in *bad* ways as well as *good* ones.**

Nearly everyone in the world benefits from technology. Technology makes our lives easier, safer, more comfortable, and more secure. Yet an uncritical acceptance of technology is dangerous. Technology isn't neutral; it changes our lives in *bad* ways as well as *good* ones. On a large scale, easy access to the Internet makes our financial and military systems vulnerable to cyberattack. On a personal level, the technology that enables parents to conceive also introduces a host of questions about cloning, "leftover" embryos, "designer babies," and surrogacy. Technology can prolong life but also brings up questions about end-of-life intervention. When it comes to technology, *what is possible* isn't the same as *what is good*. Technology can't answer questions like "To what degree and under what circumstances should we interfere with life and death?" and "Should living as long as possible be our top value?"

> **Wisdom: the ability to think and act with good judgment.**

Having more information doesn't necessarily make us wiser, and **wisdom**—not just knowledge—should be our goal. The late theologian Howard Hendricks often quoted these words: "When God measures a man, he puts the tape around the heart, not the head."

Unfortunately, cultures come to see *what is possible* as *what is expected*. But if we believe we're justified in using any technology we have to its greatest extent, then our unquestioned assumptions about technology shape our view of just about everything else.[1] As we'll see, our assumptions about technology affect our daily habits and how we use time. They affect how we relate to others when we're with them and how we use our down time. They affect how we take in and use information. Ultimately, our assumptions about technology affect the values we pass on to the next generation.

Despite its critical importance, technology is so much a part of our lives that its impact can seem invisible. Indeed, technology itself is often invisible. We have to intentionally examine what it is and how it works in our lives. We'll begin by looking at what the problem is, and then we'll discuss why and how Christians should care about technology. And finally we'll propose ways to be culture shapers based on a biblical worldview when it comes to the realm of technology.

2. THE BENEFITS AND DRAWBACKS OF TECHNOLOGY

What Is Technology?

The word **technology** comes from the Greek word *tekhne*, for "art or craft." *Tekhnelogia* is a discourse about, or systematic treatment of, an art or technique. When we focus on the techniques of something—for example, the techniques of persuasion—we're focusing on *how* we're persuading others, not *what* we're persuading them to do.

It's important to understand the breadth of this definition. If technology is focused on *technique—how* we do what we do—then technology isn't just about our iPhones. It's also about the air-conditioning unit we forget is quietly humming in the background, the processes that produced the fabric in the clothes we're wearing, the design of the chairs we're sitting on, and even the colors and graphics of the billboards, vehicles, websites, and media advertisements calling for our attention.

> **Technology:** the application of techniques employed to solve human problems.

Technology has always been a part of human life. Adam and Eve's son Cain developed techniques for growing crops, while their son Abel developed techniques for raising sheep. The biblical description of Noah's ark offers a stunning example of technology. Roman aqueducts still standing today are a fascinating example of engineering technology.

Yet it wasn't until the Middle Ages in Europe that technological growth became focused on making work easier and more productive. For example, the first waterwheels appeared in the 600s in Irish monasteries. Initially used for grinding grain, waterwheels were quickly adapted to a wide range of additional tasks: cleaning newly woven cloth, powering bellows and trip hammers in blacksmith shops, sawing lumber, and making paper.[2] In areas without easy access to rivers, windmills were designed to do the same tasks.

Other technological innovations in the Middle Ages included the heavy-wheeled plow, the horseshoe, the horse collar, the scythe, the chimney, the blast furnace, the suction pump, the grinding wheel, the wheelbarrow, the horizontal loom, the cog, the compass, the hourglass, the mechanical clock, eyeglasses, soap, the wine press, and plate armor.[3] Many of these were invented specifically to improve work conditions for laborers.

Because technology is such a broad topic, we need a way to narrow our discussion. So in this chapter, we'll focus on the ever-present, urgent, and personal technology in our lives: smartphones and other devices, search engines, apps, and the Internet. The broad term for this is **information technology**, which communication professor Quentin Schultze defines as "all computer-based technologies that enable people to collect, store, access, and exchange information of any kind, including personal messages communicated via the

> **Information Technology:** the use of computer systems for collecting, storing, accessing, and retrieving data.

Internet."[4] In discussing information technology, we must also address the **cyberculture** it generates.[5] This cyberculture daily expands to become a larger and larger part of culture itself.

Cyberculture: **the modern values, habits, and social conditions brought about by the widespread use of the Internet.**

When I first tried to find figures for this book, I found an infographic that said that *every passing minute* 204,166,667 email messages were sent, YouTube users uploaded forty-eight hours of new video, Twitter users sent more than one hundred thousand tweets, and Instagram users shared 3,600 new photos.[6] There's no way to have the most up-to-date figures in a book like this, but I think it's safe to say that the numbers are even higher now.[7]

As information technology becomes a bigger part of our overall culture, it reveals a good side and a not-so-good side.

The Good Side

Many of our gadgets, innovations, and inventions are great gifts. Information technology has improved medical care, lowered the cost of necessary goods, improved security, increased comfort, and made it possible for people to accomplish more and know more in less time, at less expense, and with less back-breaking labor.

Personally, information technology has profoundly changed the way I work. The shift was gradual. In the early nineties, my graduate school began encouraging students to use email to share ideas with a vast network of scholars. Though initially I mainly used it to correspond with my long-distance girlfriend, soon the Internet was putting hard-to-find information at my fingertips, reuniting me with long-lost acquaintances, and facilitating daily interaction with people around the globe.

Information technology drove down the cost of communication for several businesses I started. Whereas I initially sent a paper newsletter to thousands of people at a cost of thousands of dollars a month, the Internet made it possible to communicate with ten times as many people for just a few dollars a month. Today the cost of delivering information is so low that most of us expect information to be both free *and* fast. Not long ago, people didn't expect free shipping or two-day delivery. Now we can often instantly download what we purchase from the Internet or even use 3-D printers to make a product we once had to order. These are all benefits of rapid technological development.

Information technology has taken my teaching to a new level as well. Students interact through webinars and chatrooms. In the leadership classes I teach, I often have one thousand students a year who watch lectures online, have their papers graded and questions answered by a facilitator on the Internet, and join me for Q-and-A webinars.

Today the cost of delivering information is so low that most of us expect information to be both free *and* fast.

Moreover, text messaging, Voxer, Snapchat, FaceTime, and other communication tools are evolving so rapidly that the list is almost outdated even as I write it. With these applications, or apps, I can stay in touch with my family and staff in ways that were nearly impossible just a few years ago.

Finally, technology may be useful in helping students learn. Research has found a positive relationship between learning and technology.[8] Many of you are reading this book right now using an ereader, which makes information as easy to understand as reading something in print and can increase your ability to apply what you're learning.

The Not-So-Good Side

And yet, all is not well. Information technology seems as if it can provide a miracle cure for our problems, but there are downsides.

First, too much information can be distracting. For example, as of 2009, the cost of "information overload" and interruptions to people's workdays, such as looking at the latest video they've been forwarded or checking out someone's Twitter feed, was around $900 billion a year in lost productivity.[9] Doubtless it's even more now. In addition, most states have passed laws against texting and driving because distracted driving kills thousands and injures hundreds of thousands each year.[10] The misuse of technology isn't the only thing that distracts us, however. Sometimes even its proper use can distract us. One study found that even though students took more notes when they typed them on a laptop, they actually remembered less than when they took notes by hand. Researchers speculated that since most people can't write as fast as they type, writing notes by hand forces them to listen more carefully and summarize what they're hearing. This "heavy 'mental lifting'" helps them understand and remember what they're hearing.[11] So while technology can help reading in some cases, when people use it to take notes it seems to detract from learning.

> Information technology seems as if it can provide a miracle cure for our problems, but there are downsides.

Second, information technology can hurt the depth of communication. Many people seem to have lost the ability to talk face-to-face.[12] Cleverly worded social-media posts and edited photographs have replaced transparency and vulnerability. Text messaging allows more frequent communication with friends and family, but the messages are usually shorter and less substantive. Once we're used to short, shallow, fast messages, we have less tolerance for in-depth communication. It's common to see people ignore everyone in their actual physical surroundings because they're so focused on trivial communication with those at a distance. In 2015, one man died after walking off a cliff while looking at his smartphone.[13]

Third, information technology can make us more narrow minded. While information technology makes it theoretically possible to acquire knowledge about a lot of things, it also makes it possible to listen to only the music we're interested in, watch only programs that directly relate to our interests, and communicate only with people when and if we want to. Information technology doesn't create intolerance; it exposes it and enables it. It gives us the illusion that we're in control of the world and don't have to bother with the inconvenience of different views or people. It makes us feel that it's okay to treat others rudely or even shut them out completely.

> Information technology can hurt the depth of communication. Many people seem to have lost the ability to talk face-to-face.

And, finally, there is the largest problem of all. Access to technology 24-7 steals innocence by constantly exposing us to degrading, demeaning, perverse content. Technology has enabled the incredible growth of pornography, exploitation, the hook-up culture, and the sex-trafficking industry. What we used to find disgusting just seems normal now. It's sad. We'll discuss these problems, and the overall sexual brokenness in our modern culture, in chapter 9.

> **Information technology doesn't create intolerance; it exposes it and enables it. It makes us feel that it's okay to treat others rudely or even shut them out completely.**

In short, here's the risk with technology: if we fail to cultivate habits of the heart, such as discernment, moderation, wisdom, humility, authenticity, and diversity, we risk losing a sense of what it means to bear God's image well and, in the process, lose sight of what the good life is and what it means to be human.[14] Technology doesn't *make* us do anything, but it can seduce us away from the path that leads to God's best for our lives. Let's take a closer look at how technology tempts us.

Technological Temptations

Respected Massachusetts Institute of Technology (MIT) professor and psychoanalyst Sherry Turkle has been studying technology's effects on people for more than thirty years. "My concerns have grown," she writes. "These days, insecure in our relationships and anxious about intimacy, we look to technology for ways to be in relationships and protect ourselves from them at the same time."[15] Our "machine dream," she says, "is to be never alone but always in control."[16] Turkle's book *Alone Together: Why We Expect More from Technology and Less from Each Other* tells two stories: "today's story of the network, with its promise to give us more control over human relationships, and tomorrow's story of sociable robots, which promise relationships where we will be in control, even if that means not being in relationships at all."[17]

> **Technology doesn't *make* us do anything, but it can seduce us away from the path that leads to God's best for our lives.**

Technology's promise of putting us fully in control of a life that is easier, more productive, and more connected must be tempered by an understanding of who we are and how we were created primarily for the purpose of loving God and our neighbors. Here are some of the temptations of technology that research has revealed:

> **Technology tempts us to think that "elsewhere" is a better place and "others" would be better companions than the ones we're with.**

1. Information technology tempts us to lose focus. Because so many technologies are available to us all of the time, it's easy to find ourselves working, texting, surfing the Internet, listening to music, and trying to pay attention to a conversation all at the same time. Nearly one-third of seventh to twelfth graders say they multitask "most of the time" by simultaneously doing homework, watching TV, sending instant messages, talking on the phone, surfing the web, and listening to music.[18] Not only can multitasking be physically dangerous, as in the case of texting while driving, but it can also be relationally damaging, such as when a person develops a pattern of texting in the presence of others.[19] Technology tempts us to think that "elsewhere" is a better place and "others" would be better companions than the ones we're with.[20]

Studies now show that although we think multitasking makes us more efficient, the opposite is true.[21] Multitaskers don't perform as well on any of the tasks they're trying to do simultaneously as they do when they give focused attention to each task individually. It takes more effort than we realize to switch productively from one task to another. And yet the stimulation of feeling productive and clever produces neurochemicals that offer a sort of high that deceives us into thinking we're productive.[22] This chemical response actually produces a physical craving for the kind of stimulation multitasking gives us. Our brains actually rewire to *require* this sort of craving. Turkle says, "As we try to reclaim our concentration, we are literally at war with ourselves."[23] Ultimately we find it difficult to pay attention to anything at all because we're multitasking in our minds. Writer Linda Stone calls this "continuous partial attention," noting that "we are so accessible, we're inaccessible."[24]

> Studies now show that although we think multitasking makes us more efficient, the opposite is true.

2. Information technology tempts us to isolate ourselves. Though on the surface, technology seems to facilitate communication, it can actually divide us by helping us avoid those who aren't like us. As psychologist Kathy Koch often points out, we don't even have to ask other people questions—we can just ask Siri or Google.[25] The vast array of television channels and online forums target specific audiences and make it possible for us to hear from and interact with only those who have the exact same interests we do. Granted, it's a welcome relief to feel understood by people who are like us and to avoid the stress of communicating with those who aren't. But this can actually impoverish us. Consider the way it changes our everyday interactions:

- Rather than shopping at the corner market, people roam the aisles of twenty-four-hour megastores, hardly making eye contact with others, or shop online in the comfort of their own homes.

- People sit with others in close physical proximity, but their attention is entirely on the little screens in front of them rather than on one another. They can also stay home from church but watch it on the Internet and enjoy simulcast events at home rather than in a crowded church or theater where they might have to talk with people.

- Neighbors move from the front porch to the back deck, from the living room to the TV room.

- Music becomes a means of isolating rather than uniting people.

- Special-interest groups and political groups stop cooperating for the common good and devolve into forums for vicious attacks.

How long can good people survive this level of fragmentation? How long can a good *culture* survive it? The cry of the populace is "Leave me alone." Perhaps the ultimate hell is that their wish will be granted. One wonders whether the collapse of our civilization will occur not through an explosive conflict but through a deafening silence. We all just walk away. Alone.

> One wonders whether the collapse of our civilization will occur not through an explosive conflict but through a deafening silence. We all just walk away. Alone.

Technology does make some kinds of connections stronger. According to sociologists, weak ties—connections between people who are acquaintances or second-level contacts (friends of friends or associates of family members)—explain all sorts of things, from how people get job referrals to why they feel they have mysterious illnesses.[26] Information technology increases our number of weak ties. Consider, for instance, the number of Facebook "friends" you have versus the number of actual friends you have. But technology claims so much of our time and attention for weak-tie relationships that it's harder today to maintain "strong-tie" relationships with family and close friends. In fact, we may even lose the *ability* to have the kinds of interactions that keep strong-tie relationships strong. For instance, studies show that the Internet and cell phones help us communicate more frequently with those we care about most, but they also tend to lower the probability of face-to-face visits in the home.[27]

> Information technology seems to improve communication with people who aren't central to our lives but *damage* communication with those who truly are central.

Ironically, information technology seems to improve communication with people who aren't central to our lives but *damage* communication with those who truly are central, such as loved ones and those in our communities.[28] Barry Wellman and his colleagues even suggest that having multiple computers in the home interferes with family relationships, creating "post-familial families" where family members interact with their devices rather than with each other.[29]

3. Information technology tempts us to be superficial. God designed person-to-person communication to be profoundly meaningful. We were made to connect with others and with God himself. Every aspect of our bodies and minds is involved. The spoken word is directly linked to our breathing, gestures, posture, and physical closeness.[30] In some ways, the spoken word is even more intimate than physical contact because physical contact is exterior to exterior, whereas human communication is interior to interior, from one heart and mind to another. We were wired for relational intimacy.

Communication technology permits us to observe more and communicate less. Our communication ability is anemic, even though technology offers a remedy. Do words fail you? You can borrow some clever lines from a movie or song or repost a meme expressing thoughts with which you agree. A few years ago I participated in a documentary about media addiction called *Captivated*.[31] Interviewed in the film was Emory University professor Mark Bauerlein, whose confrontationally titled book *The Dumbest Generation* makes the case that growing wealth and technological advancement have stunted intellectual growth. Bauerlein observes that "all the occasions and equipment for learning are in place, but [people use] them for other purposes.... No cohort in human history ... has experienced so many technological enhancements and yielded so little mental progress."[32]

Superficiality erodes the deep historical connection that guides our interactions and informs our collective consciousness. Like hikers lost in a snowstorm, we find ourselves disoriented by a blizzard of information. Librarian of Congress James Billington has noted that if we lose our sense of the past, we lose a sense of who we are to a "world of motion without memory, which is one of the clinical definitions of insanity."[33]

Superficiality also changes our relationships with others. As Sherry Turkle says of the networking made possible by information technology, "Networked, we are together, but so lessened are our expectations of each other that we can feel utterly alone. [We] risk [seeing] others [only] as objects to be accessed ... for the parts we find useful, comforting, or amusing."[34]

> Superficiality erodes the deep historical connection that guides our interactions and informs our collective consciousness.

4. Information technology tempts us to give in to evil. Deception is one kind of evil that new technology has made more common. Jeana Frost of Boston University and the Massachusetts Institute of Technology found that about 20 percent of online daters admit to deception. When asked, however, how many other online daters they thought were lying (an interviewing tactic that probably gets closer to the truth about their own behavior as well as the behavior of others), that number jumped to 90 percent.[35]

But there is an even deeper evil still: technology as an object of worship. Humans have always been tempted to believe that technology will save us. Consider this over-the-top assessment from Secular Humanist philosopher Paul Kurtz:

> We have virtually conquered the planet, explored the moon, overcome the natural limits of travel and communication; we stand at the dawn of a new age.... Using technology wisely, we can control our environment, conquer poverty, markedly reduce disease, extend our life span, significantly modify our behavior, alter the course of human evolution and cultural development, unlock vast new powers, and provide humankind with unparalleled opportunity for achieving an abundant and meaningful life.[36]

Some devotees of technology seem almost religious in their enthusiasm. In at least one case, this devotion has morphed into an actual religion called **Terasem**. The founder of Terasem is Martine Rothblatt, a corporate pioneer who founded Sirius XM satellite radio in 1990.

> *Terasem*: a cyber-religion, founded by Martine Rothblatt, that teaches that human beings will someday be able to attain immortality by downloading data from their brains (i.e., mind files) and uploading this information into some form of robot.

Rothblatt believes that humans can secure immortality by uploading and storing "mindfiles" until robot technology advances sufficiently to recreate personal consciousness. By downloading their mindfiles into robots, people will be able to "live" forever even after they're dead. Loraine Rhodes, who runs Terasem's educational nonprofit, admits, "Some people call it the rapture of the nerds."[37] But Rothblatt is deadly serious: "For us," she says, "God is in-the-making by our collective efforts to make technology ever more omnipresent, omnipotent and ethical. When we can joyfully all experience techno immortality, then God is complete."[38]

If such enthusiastic worship of technology leaves you feeling bewildered, you're not alone. Based on the Bible's teachings about the sin nature, you might expect technology to feed humankind's destructive tendencies as well as its noble ones. And it has. The Nazis were among IBM's first customers, using rudimentary computers to streamline their genocidal plans.[39] Nuclear research promised energy in abundance but resulted in bombs powerful enough to obliterate all living things. Movies that entice the viewer with a promise of relationship also generate innocence-stealing lust. Chemical substances that promise bliss rob addicts of life purpose.

> **Technology feeds humankind's destructive tendencies as well as its noble ones.**

Industry pioneers fantasized that communication technology would lead to global harmony. The reality, however, isn't so pretty. Nations the world over have used technology to communicate dehumanizing messages, such as "Jews are not persons," "Babies are not persons," and "Those who resist communism are not persons." The consequences? According to historian R. J. Rummel, almost 170 million persons were killed at the whim of governments in the "first eighty-eight years" of the twentieth century.[40]

Technology manufactures the vehicle and hands humanity the keys. If the past is any guide to the future, we may be careening toward our own demise. We thought technology would accelerate wisdom and caring, but what if it actually destroys itself and us in the process?

3. WHY SHOULD CHRISTIANS CARE?

It's one thing to say that technology leads to problems. It's another to think that Christians should have a greater concern about this than other people. I think they should, and in the balance of this chapter, I hope to show why. Here are five reasons Christians, as culture shapers, ought to lead the way in calling for deeper thinking about technology's potential and pitfalls:

(1) The Christian worldview unmasks technology's illusion of neutrality. Technology is never passive. It *does* things, but it also *undoes* other things.[41] According to Neil Postman, author of the bestselling and brilliantly named book on technology *Amusing Ourselves to Death*, "New technologies alter the structure of our interests: the things we think *about*. They alter the character of our symbols: the things we think *with*. And they alter the nature of community: the arena in which thoughts develop."[42] As Sherry Turkle puts it, "We make our technologies, and they, in turn, make and shape us."[43]

> **Technology is never passive. It *does* things, but it also *undoes* other things.**

Many people argue that technology is passive. It isn't good or bad; it just *is*. Postman disagreed. He said that "embedded in every tool is an ideological bias, a predisposition to construct the world as one thing rather than another, to value one thing over another, to amplify one sense or skill or attitude more loudly than another."[44] Even as simple a technology as a stethoscope proclaims, "Medicine is about disease, not the patient. And, what the patient knows is untrustworthy; what the machine knows is reliable."[45] A stethoscope is just a tool that enables doctors to gather information and diagnose disease, and yet it generates a way of thinking about people and about the world. It redefines the way people see themselves and the power of medicine.[46]

Technology can lead to either good or bad changes, or both at the same time. But technology is never neutral.

French philosopher Jacques Ellul went even further. He suggested in his prophetic 1954 book *The Technological Society* that technology develops its own internal logic to serve its own needs, and when we submit to it rather than master it, we do so at our own peril. Technology, in its pretense of neutrality, tends to eliminate moral considerations altogether. Technology is known by "its refusal to tolerate moral judgments," he said. "It is absolutely independent of them and eliminates them from its domain. Technology never observes the distinction between moral and immoral use."[47]

> Technology, in its pretense of neutrality, tends to eliminate moral considerations altogether.

Technology alters our assumptions about what is possible and valuable.[48] It makes arguments about what is in the human interest and promises to reshape us. With a focus on bearing God's image and being reshaped into the image of his Son, Jesus Christ (Gal. 4:19; Eph. 4:15),[49] Christians can provide the moral core that distinguishes between a society that uses technology wisely and one that doesn't.

(2) The Christian worldview reminds us that we are stewards of creation, not masters of it as the use of technology sometimes leads us to believe. Technology causes us to see creation as an appliance to be used rather than a resource to be stewarded. Again, it isn't that technology is all bad. As Neil Postman noted, technology is both a friend that "makes life easier, cleaner, and longer" and an enemy that threatens to destroy our humanity by creating "a culture without a moral foundation" and undermining "certain mental processes and social relations that make … life worth living."[50]

Technology becomes an enemy of creation when we develop what Quentin Schultze calls "information-intensive, technique-oriented habits" that shape our values.[51] These habits lead us to think that we're clever enough to impose our will on creation and solve every problem.[52]

The problem isn't that technology adds to our values in a negative way but that it changes them altogether by encouraging us to view ourselves, others, and the world around us as instruments to do our bidding.[53] Noninstrumental values, such as moderation, discernment, and humility, become things to be used rather than states to aspire to for their own sake.[54] Though we would never say it aloud, we start thinking things like *How can I show myself to be humble so I can get what I want? How can I be friendly so I can get what I want?* and *How can I be neighborly so I can get what I want?*

Moreover, information technology enables us to believe that our relationship with the world has little to do with our physical surroundings. After a while, the virtual world seems to us to be the real one, while the real world becomes virtually irrelevant.

Technology has also changed our relationship to time and space. Time-saving devices like smartphones were supposed to buy us time, but instead they've erased its value. It's not that we can't get away from our work; it's that technology has blurred the distinction between work and leisure. Ultimately, as Sherry Turkle puts it, "All the time in the world [is] not enough."[55]

Unless we're careful, technology can encourage us to think of creation not as something we steward but as something to be taken from, used, and made into our own image. The Christian worldview helps restore balance by reminding us that we are here to serve God by stewarding creation, not to become God by mastering it.[56]

> Unless we're careful, technology can encourage us to think of creation not as something we steward but as something to be taken from, used, and made into our own image.

(3) The Christian worldview helps redeem the use of technology. In many ways, relating to technology is the defining concern of our times. In *Alone Together*, Sherry Turkle describes a disturbing situation in which an elderly woman became so engrossed with a robot doll called My Real Baby that she started ignoring her two-year-old great-granddaughter. While the young girl clamored for attention, the woman cradled the robot and spoke to it, saying things like, "Sweetie … you are my sweetie pie! Yes, you are."[57]

Frankly, Turkle's description of the encounter is creepy. While dolls may be helpful for comforting ill children or adults with diseases like dementia, this elderly woman seemed to have lost track of what was real and what wasn't. But we're guilty too; we increasingly find it difficult to distinguish between what is real and what is simulated. For example, we experience real emotions when watching movies we know to be scripted, staged, lighted, acted, and edited. This is a startling change for our society. As Turkle puts it, "The meaning of the computer presence in people's lives [today] is very different from what most expected in the late 1970s.… We are moving from a modernist culture of calculation toward a postmodernist culture of simulation."[58]

In the past, Christians intentionally engaged with the technologies of their day in ways that both reflected a Christian worldview and made life better for whole cultures. Based on the belief that Adam and Eve were given responsibilities prior to the fall (Gen. 2:15),[59] work was seen not as a necessary evil but as a positive good. But after the fall, work became drudgery (Gen. 3:17–20).[60]

The monastic leaders we talked about in chapter 3 responded to work's drudgery by arguing that if an animal could do it rather than a human, it should, and if a machine could do it, even better. Eliminating repetitive, mindless work allows humans to focus on higher pursuits. Thus, many early monasteries became nurseries for technological innovation. There is a stark difference between the Christian worldview and other worldviews during this fertile period of imagination: many other cultures actually had more advanced technology, but the elites used it as a plaything rather than a way to make the lives of everyday people better.

A Christian worldview grapples with what to do not only with the technology we have but also with what the technology we have does to us. Both issues are important. We cannot use technology to live better lives unless we have a clear sense of what it means to live well.

(4) The Christian worldview helps restore the humanity that technology tends to diminish. Neil Postman identified three types of cultures that engage with technology. The first type is *tool-using cultures*—those that invented tools to make life easier (e.g., windmills) or to carry political or religious meaning (e.g., cathedrals).[61] The second level is *technocracies*—cultures in which nonintegrated tools, such as the mechanical clock or the printing press, became central to thought and society.[62] The third level is *technopolies*—those societies that submit "all forms of cultural life to the sovereignty of technique and technology."[63] Our society, Postman believed, is a **technopoly**. "The Technopoly story is without a moral center," he wrote. "It puts in its place efficiency, interest, and economic advance."[64]

> *Technopoly:* a term coined by Neil Postman that refers to any culture that assumes technology is the highest human good.

In a technopoly, talk of sin and evil or even transcendent good gives way to the "theology of expertise."[65] People stop asking *why* and focus only on *how*. A technopoly thinks of human value based on what people can *do* rather than who they *are*. Its adherents struggle to answer the ultimate questions in life, such as where we come from, who we are, what is right and wrong, what is the purpose of life, and where we're going both as a society and beyond this life.[66]

Technopoly also changes our personal habits in ways that diminish our sense of self. Who are you when no one is texting you? Sometimes when I've been on a long flight, I wonder whether anyone needed me during those two quiet hours. Did anyone text? Did anyone email? Did anyone respond to my Facebook post? If they didn't, do I still exist as a relevant person?

After a while, we become uncomfortable without our devices. One thirteen-year-old told CNN, "When I get my phone taken away, I feel kind of naked."[67] People "need to be connected in order to feel like themselves."[68]

The answer to technopoly is to hit the reset button and begin seeing one another, once again, as persons rather than as a bundle of economic interests whose value is in how efficiently we convert human ingenuity into practical benefits. Our value to God and people doesn't change based on whether people in cyberspace need us. We literally need to put down our devices, look others in the eye, and do unto them as we would want them to do unto us. This is a desperately needed message.

> Our value to God and people doesn't change based on whether people in cyberspace need us. We literally need to put down our devices, look others in the eye, and do unto them as we would want them to do unto us.

(5) The Christian worldview confronts technology's dumbing-down effect on communication and community. Have you ever been in a room where two people are so into each other, whispering and giggling together, that they totally ignore everyone around them? That's what it's like to others when we're engaged with a handheld device. I remember visiting a college campus in the South, where on a long walk between buildings, all the people I passed—and there were dozens of them—were either listening to music or looking at their devices. Ironically, promoters of that university like to talk about their strong "community." What I experienced, though, was a bunch of people plugged in but tuned out. As strong a tradition as southern hospitality is, it couldn't withstand the pressure of obsessive technological connection.[69]

God, on the other hand, is all about relationship. He is trinity, one God made manifest in three persons: God the Father, God the Son, and God the Holy Spirit. This relationship in the Godhead closely relates to how we ought to act in the world. Matthew 28:19 says, "Go therefore and make disciples of all nations, baptizing them in the name of the *Father* and of the *Son* and of the *Holy Spirit*." As God's image bearers, we, too, are built for relationship.

But in a technological society, *environment* is decoupled from *awareness*, and inhabitants are encouraged to engage or disengage as they wish.[70] We've talked about how technology hampers our relationships with those in our surrounding environment, but it also hampers our relationships with the weak-tie contacts we're paying so much attention to on our smartphones. We text others, and like a genie, we make them appear on command. If they don't appear, we impatiently text someone else. Our attitude is "Are you paying attention to me? If not, then I'm not paying attention to you either."

Strictly speaking, our communication isn't the cause of this relational breakdown. Yet, as we saw earlier, technology redefines the boundaries of what is acceptable public behavior. Says Sherry Turkle, "In every era, certain ways of relating come to feel natural. In our time, if we can be continually in touch, needing to be continually in touch does not seem a problem or a pathology but an accommodation to what technology affords. It becomes the norm."[71]

> **Technology facilitates self-centeredness and discourages other-centeredness.**

Technology facilitates self-centeredness and discourages other-centeredness. A study of more than fourteen thousand college students over the past thirty years has shown a dramatic decline in empathy corresponding with the rise in information technology. Today's college students are significantly less likely than those from thirty years ago to say that it's valuable to understand other people's feelings.[72] A "selfie" isn't just a way of taking a picture. It's a cultural movement in which each person thinks the world revolves around him- or herself.

Part of our lack of empathy may be self-protective. Who hasn't been in a conversation that was interrupted by one participant stopping to reply to a text message? On a handful of occasions, I've found myself saying, "I have a call coming through from someone I promised to talk to," and the other person replied, "Of course. I understand." Earlier in my life, stopping one conversation to begin another would have been viewed as rude. Now we see it as rude to oppose it. To use Turkle's memorable phrase, "Mobile technology has made each of us 'pauseable.'"[73] We often choose to ignore our immediate surroundings to pay attention to what our technology demands of us. By doing so, we're actually alone much of the time we're together. In fact, we become disoriented about what it means to be alone and what it means to be together in the first place.[74]

Obi-Wan Kenobi told Luke Skywalker, "Use the force."[75] "God," in *Star Wars*, is a force to manipulate. The Bible's worldview couldn't be more different. According to the Bible, God is a person who loves all the persons he has created (John 3:16).[76] We *use* things. We *love* people. Will we use technology to serve the people God loves or to replace them? In times like these, a biblical worldview is more important than ever.[77]

4. WHAT SHOULD CHRISTIANS DO?

Information technology brings up some big questions. Christians ought to care, but what should we *do* differently? Certainly we should be filled with hope, because Christ has won the victory over sin (Heb. 2:14).[78] We should look expectantly to the future, knowing that Christ's kingdom will have no end (Luke 1:32–33).[79] But in a world that doesn't see technology as a problem, how do we live wisely, let alone search for a solution? Here are four ideas:

(1) **Bear God's image as a restorer.** In Genesis 1:1,[80] we learn that God is creation's architect and artist. According to medieval theologian Hugh of St. Victor, as God's image bearers, humans need technological knowledge just as much as they need theology, math, physics, economics, ethics, and politics. We see very little of this kind of thinking in cultures that didn't have a similar Christian tradition.[81] Says Vishal Mangalwadi,

> As God's image bearers, humans need technological knowledge just as much as they need theology, math, physics, economics, ethics, and politics.

> Asia and Africa did not lack ability. But ability alone does not produce liberating technology. Jesus said that people are like sheep in need of good shepherds. Without shepherds, slavery will remain the norm—from the women in Jinja to the untouchables in India. Nonbiblical cultures need more than technology; they need a philosophy that values people.[82]

As we've already seen, a biblical worldview enabled people in the Middle Ages to improve technologies, make the lot of workers better, and make goods more readily available. A desire to improve the lot of workers based on a biblical worldview was behind many inventions that changed the world, including the invention and improvement of the steam engine by Thomas Newcomen, a lay pastor who tried to help the workers in his congregation, and James Watt, a Scottish Presbyterian.[83]

We can bear God's image today by creating technologies that help restore people to their image-bearing capacity. We can make life better for people, much as the company we talked about at the beginning of this chapter transformed life in developing countries through software that enables people to use cell-phone minutes as a form of currency.

> We can bear God's image today by creating technologies that help restore people to their image-bearing capacity.

(2) Bear God's image as a renewer. James K. A. Smith, in his book *Desiring the Kingdom*, says we are shaped more by our loves than by our ideas.[84] According to Smith, "Our love is aimed from the fulcrum of our desire—the habits that constitute our character, or core identity. And the way our love or desire gets aimed in specific directions is through practices that shape, mold, and direct our love."[85]

When Smith speaks of practices that shape our love, he is referring to things we can regularly do to grow by renewing our deepest beliefs about God and our calling in the world. Craig Dykstra says in *Growing in the Life of Faith*, "[Christian Practices] are means of grace, the human places in which and through which God's people come to faith and grow in maturity in the life of faith."[86]

Over the centuries, Christians have developed such practices as worshipping God and praying together, telling the Bible's story, confessing sins, giving liberally, suffering together, and celebrating holidays.[87] These practices, and others such as the art of hospitality, help form us into virtuous men and women whose foundation is unshaken by rapid change. Consider how the disciplines in the following list can help us move away from being self-concerned, comfort-driven, stressed-out consumers to being producers of the good, true, and beautiful.

> *Idol:* any image or substitute representation of God used as an object of worship.

Confession. If reading this chapter hasn't caused you to feel convicted about your technology use, start over. There is hardly a person alive who isn't tempted to worship the **idol** of technology. We cannot be restored to God without first repenting of our habit of letting other gods take his place. To have true worship, we must give up false worship.

Prayer. Prayer is a conversation with God. When we lose our ability to converse with other people, our prayer life undoubtedly suffers. Prayer isn't talking aloud to ourselves. It isn't superficial or about trying to compel God to give us what we want. True prayer helps us let go of the illusion that we're in control, lament our fallenness, ask God to give us what we need to accomplish his will through Jesus Christ, and express thankfulness for his good gifts. Through prayer we can become more humble, balanced, and focused on others.

Sabbath. On the seventh day of creation, God rested. Taking a Sabbath rest from our devices reminds us that technology cannot replace basic habits like sleep, a healthy diet, and exercise.[88] Interestingly, the latest research confirms the wisdom of God's call to rest. John

> God's unexpected invitation to rest helps us remember that he, not our constant access to technology, sustains us.

Jonides, a professor of psychology and neuroscience, says that exposure to "softly fascinating" environments, such as an engagement with the natural world, can lead to improved working memory and attention.[89] Educational learning expert Kevin Washburn summarizes this finding by saying, "When students seem mentally tired, a walk outside may be the best instructional activity."[90]

God's unexpected invitation to rest helps us remember that he, not our constant access to technology, sustains us. Sabbath keeping isn't a duty; it's a practice full of quiet reflection, delight, renewal, and whimsy.

Calendar keeping. For much of the church's history (and in many Christian traditions today), the people of God have together recognized a different orientation to time. Two common Greek words for "time" in the New Testament are *chronos*, which refers to *clock* time, and *kairos*, which refers to *opportunity* time. *Kairos* cannot be measured; it is always "now." Make the most of every *kairos*, the apostle Paul wrote (Eph. 5:16).[91] In God's economy, temporal *minutes* are valuable because they're potential *moments* of eternal significance. The church calendar marks many holidays (holy days) and seasons, such as Advent, Lent, and Easter, to provide the opportunity of stepping away from clock time to experience the rhythms of eternity. Through these observances we can focus on what is most important and be renewed through waiting, listening, and hoping.

(3) **Bear God's image as a relater.** As we've seen, God is personal and relational. He is in an eternal relationship *within himself* through the Trinity. From the beginning, he has related with his image bearers, even walking with Adam and Eve in the garden (Gen. 3:8).[92] Right from the beginning of creation, God was revealed to be *Yahweh Elohim*, "the LORD God" (Gen. 2:4).[93] He is not only the creator-God *(Elohim)*; he's also the personal God of Israel *(Yahweh)*, the maker of covenants and the rescuer of his people.[94] John 1:1 tells us, "In the beginning was the Word."[95] God is a personal God. He shows up. He's clear. He's direct. God also communicates with us by listening. In conversations recorded in the Bible, God asked questions and listened as people spoke to him. In the Gospels, Jesus asked hundreds of questions.

> In God's economy, temporal *minutes* are valuable because they're potential *moments* of eternal significance.

As God's image bearers, we too can use words to create, encourage, build community, and reach out to others, including those isolated by the fallout of information technology. To do this, we must bury lying, gossip, and verbal abuse and resurrect words of blessing, grace, and hope. Proverbs 15:23 says, "To make an apt answer is a joy to a man, and a word in season, how good it is!"

As image bearers, we need to ask whether our technology use is deepening our connection with others or keeping it at a surface level. We also need to ask whether we're using technology in a way that keeps the spotlight on God's truth. Randall Niles is an attorney and educator who cofounded AllAboutGOD.com. He believes that Christians can change their orientation to information technology by using it to communicate worthy messages:

> As God's image bearers, we too can use words to create, encourage, build community, and reach out to others, including those isolated by the fallout of information technology.

> Whether we like it or not, social networks and other media tools will play a crucial role in the delivery of spiritual information—both truth and deception. If

we're not engaged in the online marketplace of spiritual ideas, we will miss one of the greatest opportunities for the Great Commission.[96]

Spreading truth is something Christians have used technology to do since at least the time of Johannes Gutenberg, who, as we discussed earlier, invented movable type and the printing press out of an explicit desire to spread knowledge of the Bible.[97]

Here are a few specific ways we can bear God's image as relaters:

Awareness. We can refuse to let technology get in the way of being aware of other people and their thoughts and needs. Technology should never get in the way of true friendship.[98] Friendship is more than hanging out. It's mutual caring—being another's confidant by choice. In his bestselling book *The Friendship Factor*, Alan Loy McGinnis says that "friendship is the springboard to every other love."[99]

Alliances. Navigating between complete acceptance of information technology and complete rejection of it is difficult. There are two ways we can err, and each reflects the consequences of sin for relationships. First, we can err through **sins of commission**—engaging in ridicule, lying, and gossip. Second, we can err through **sins of omission**—failing to listen when we ought to, failing to speak as we should, or tuning others out instead of offering hope and encouragement. Says Quentin Schultze, "With our sins of omission and of commission, we are symbolic predators in the communication jungles of a fallen world."[100] Thus, we cannot succeed alone. If you haven't already done so, consider forming an alliance of friends to read relevant scriptures or a book about life in modern society, such as Neil Postman's *Technopoly* or Marva Dawn's *Unfettered Hope*. Discuss. Pray together. Commit to better bearing God's image in relation to what you study.

> *Sin of Commission:* the failure to avoid what God commands us to avoid (e.g., theft, gossip, and adultery).

> *Sin of Omission:* the failure to act as God commands us to act (e.g., loving and forgiving others).

Accountability. We need accountability. Sadly, technology can accelerate our fallenness. It tempts us to waste time on superficial pursuits or, worse, to explore pornography or other evils that destroy our innocence and cause severe relational decay. We need others—parents, teachers, mentors, grandparents, siblings, friends—to be honest with us about our own technological practices. Are we using technology to distract ourselves from worthier pursuits? Are we using technology to avoid reality or hide from inconvenience? Give a handful of trusted people permission to be honest with you about what they see, and receive their critiques with a humble spirit and gracious attitude (striving not to be quick to defend yourself but quick to listen, as James 1:19 says).[101]

(4) Bear God's image as a repairer. When God completed creation, he announced it as "very good" (Gen. 1:31).[102] As a free, wise, moral agent, God knows what is right and good

(Gen. 2:17; 3:22).[103] Indeed, his nature is the very definition of *good*. Scripture shows him to be gracious and merciful, taking care of the needs of human beings even after they transgressed his law. God, in his mercy, is also focused on repairing what was broken in the fall. Through Christ's death on the cross, God repaired our broken relationship with him (Col. 1:21–22).[104] In Amos's prophecy about God's people returning to him, Amos referred to God as the repairer of breaches (Amos 9:11).[105]

God encourages his people to be repairers as well. When the enemies of Israel destroyed Jerusalem's walls, God sent the prophet Nehemiah to oversee the repairs so the people would no longer live in disgrace (Neh. 2:17).[106] In addition to repairing broken walls, we're also called to repair broken relationships (Matt. 18:15; Gal. 6:1).[107]

Here are some steps we can take to reflect God's image as repairers:

We must actively repair the lack of discernment that traps us in an unwise use of technology. Once when I took my son on a cross-country airline flight, an inappropriate video came on the screen. I asked my son to avert his gaze, but after a few moments, he blurted, "I just can't keep my eyes from looking at it." The images *were* riveting. They were also poisoning our souls. When I realized that the way our family used technology was damaging our souls, I began an ongoing process of repairing that damage. That's why we use accountability programs, such as Covenant Eyes and XXXchurch, to help us avoid impure content. Each program sends reports of our online activity to trusted mentors, offering us the opportunity to engage in "soul repair work" and commit to remaining whole. Knowing how often we make bad decisions in our brokenness also encourages us to take preventive measures, such as reading PluggedIn.com reviews to decide what to watch and listen to. As God's image bearers, each of us must learn to use discernment.

We must actively repair the thoughtlessness that makes our technology use destructive. This requires asking hard questions like these:

- What does this technology *undo*? Is it worth undoing?

- What does this technology free us from? Is that something from which we *should* be set free?

- In what ways does this technology bring us closer together or distance us from one another?

- What does this technology seem to suggest humans are for?

- How does this technology affect how I think of myself?

The point of these questions isn't to eliminate our need for thoughtfulness but to require it. Repairing the

> Adopt all new technology with a clear view of the proper degree of its use, as well as whether it leads to a good end.

damage from technology is hard work, and each of us has much more to repair than we probably imagine we do.

The most important question to ask ourselves before adopting any new technology is not "Can I?" but "Should I?" Understanding what technology does *to* us, not just what it does *for* us, is critical. Adopt all new technology with a clear view of the proper degree of its use, as well as whether it leads to a good end.

To think clearly about technology, we must ask, "What does the good life look like?" If the best we can come up with is "What I'm doing now," our vision may be too small. When God repairs something, it's better than it was to begin with. The goal of repairing isn't just to zero out destructive influences; it's to embrace the biblical idea of a good life—a life of community, forgiveness, peace, and purpose—in a whole new way.

We must actively repair our obsession with the new. In modern society, part of our brokenness is that we so easily become obsessed with owning the latest, most popular technology. Technology has a deep effect on us. As Sherry Turkle says, "We have to love our technology enough to describe it accurately. And we have to love ourselves enough to confront technology's true effects on us."[108] Repairing this kind of brokenness requires us to be proactive, to stop thinking that newer is automatically better. We need to get in the habit of thinking and evaluating the potential impact *before* we adopt a new technology. It may not be wise to buy the latest computer or smartphone or upgrade to the newest software just because we can. It's best to pause and ponder our motives. Ask, "Will this newer technology make things better not just for me but for others? Is it truly a need, or is it just a desire for something new and different? What part of the good life will I gain or lose by possessing it?"

Discerning how we ought to live in a world of technology comes down to bearing God's image as restorer, renewer, relater, and repairer. These four attributes aren't just a checklist; they're a posture toward God, creation, and others. As we make our way through this book, such a posture should help us uncover new ways to think God's thoughts after him and serve as his ambassadors.[109]

5. Conclusion

Technology can be a great good. Whether it harnesses energy to ease the pain of human labor or reinvents the idea of money using cell phones, technology makes life better for nearly everyone. Around the world, people are rising out of poverty. Though there are always ups and downs, over time technology has made possible an unprecedented growth in wealth.[110] Technology is the lever that has enabled the world to move.

> We'll always face a tension between developing new technologies that express God's redemptive power and avoiding the kind of fascination with them that threatens to turn them into destructive idols.

And yet, as we have seen, technology can also diminish the fervor with which we bear God's image. We'll always face a tension between developing new technologies that express God's redemptive power and avoiding the kind of fascination with them that threatens to turn them into destructive idols.

What enables us to keep our balance is remembering who we are in God's story. We aren't here on this planet just to survive. We are God's image bearers. Though we're all broken because of the fall, redemption through Christ is open to us, and we look toward the hope of the resurrection. Meanwhile, however, as Summit's alumni director Paige Gutacker puts it, "all is not presently well." Our hearts are turned in on themselves, and technology magnifies our brokenness as well as our created selves. As long as life endures, we'll always need God's grace to attend to the "habits of our high-tech hearts."[111]

ENDNOTES

1. How we view life is often referred to as our *worldview*, which I've defined in this series as "a pattern of ideas, beliefs, convictions, and habits that help us make sense of God, the world, and our relationship to God and the world."

2. Andrew I. Wilson, "Machines, Power, and the Ancient Economy," *Journal of Roman Studies* 92 (October 2002): 1–32.

3. If you're interested in more information, lots of websites talk about medieval inventions. Most are run by hobbyists who enjoy re-creating medieval times. For example, see "Medieval Inventions," www.medieval-life-and-times.info/medieval -life/medieval-inventions.htm.

4. Quentin J. Schultze, *Habits of the High-Tech Heart: Living Virtuously in the Information Age* (Grand Rapids: Baker Academic, 2002), 16.

5. Schultze places his thought here within a well-known framework: "As Jacques Ellul argued, this technological-mindedness is essentially a faith in *la technique*, the means of efficiency and control." Schultze, *Habits of the High-Tech Heart*, 18.

6. For more statistics, source information, and references, see the infograph at "Data Never Sleeps," Domo, 2012, http://visual.ly /data-never-sleeps.

7. How big is the Internet? If each byte of data (the size of one letter or number) were the size of the largest bacteria (0.5 mm), the amount of data YouTube users upload each day would be about twenty-one terabytes (a terabyte is one thousand gigabytes), enough to wrap around the sun three times. See Doug Camplejohn, "How Much Data Is on the Internet?," *Fliptop Blog*, accessed July 12, 2016, http://blog.fliptop.com/blog/2011/05/18/how-much-data-is-on-the-internet/.

8. Ryan T. Gertner, "Effects of Multimedia Technology on Learning" (master's thesis, Abilene Christian University, 2011), http://acu.edu/technology/mobilelearning/documents/research/effects-of-technology-on-learning.pdf.

9. Jonathan B. Spira and Cody Burke, *Intel's War on Information Overload: A Case Study* (New York: Basex, 2009), 1, http://iorgforum.org/wp-content/uploads/2011/06/IntelWarIO.BasexReport1.pdf.

10. US Department of Transportation and National Highway Traffic Safety Administration, "Distracted Driving 2014," in *Traffic Safety Facts Research Note: Summary of Statistical Findings*, DOT HS 812, 260 (Washington, DC: NHTSA, 2016), https://crashstats.nhtsa.dot.gov/Api/Public/ViewPublication/812260.

11. Pam A. Mueller and Daniel M. Oppenheimer, "The Pen Is Mightier Than the Keyboard," *Psychological Science*, April 23, 2014, cited in Cindi May, "A Learning Secret: Don't Take Notes with a Laptop," *Scientific American*, June 3, 2014, www.scientificamerican.com/article/a-learning-secret-don-t-take-notes-with-a-laptop/.

12. Paul Barnwell, "My Students Don't Know How to Have a Conversation," *Atlantic*, April 22, 2014, www.theatlantic.com /education/archive/2014/04/my-students-dont-know-how-to-have-a-conversation/360993/.

13. "Distracted Man Who Fell to His Death from San Diego Cliff Identified," FoxNews.com, December 28, 2015, www.foxnews.com/us/2015/12/28/distracted-man-who-fell-to-his-death-from-san-diego-cliff-identified.html.

14. Schultze, *Habits of the High-Tech Heart*, 20.

15. Sherry Turkle, *Alone Together: Why We Expect More from Technology and Less from Each Other* (New York: Basic Books, 2011), xii.

16. Turkle, *Alone Together*, 157.

17. Turkle, *Alone Together*, 17.

18. Ulla G. Foehr, *Media Multitasking among American Youth: Prevalence, Predictors and Pairings* (Menlo Park, CA: Henry J. Kaiser Family Foundation, 2006), 7, http://kff.org/other/media-multitasking-among-american-youth -prevalence-predictors/.

19. See, for example, Rebecca A. Clay, "Mini-Multitaskers," *Monitor on Psychology* 40, no. 2 (February 2009), www.apa.org /monitor/2009/02/multitaskers.aspx; Christine Rosen, "The Myth of Multitasking," *New Atlantis*, www.thenewatlantis.com /publications/the-myth-of-multitasking.

20. Catherine Steiner-Adair says, "In any given moment, with a buzz or a ping, our devices summon us and we are likely to respond, allowing ourselves to be pulled away from our immediate surroundings and anyone in them, into the waiting world of elsewhere and others." Catherine Steiner-Adair, with Teresa Barker, *The Big Disconnect: Protecting Childhood and Family Relationships in the Digital Age* (New York: HarperCollins, 2013), 4.

21. Turkle, *Alone Together*, 163. Further, regarding multitasking, Sherry Turkle observes, "I notice, along with several of my colleagues, that the students whose laptops are open in class do not do as well as the others." See also Jim Taylor, "Technology: Myth of Multitasking," *Psychology Today*, March 30, 2011, www.psychologytoday.com/blog/the-power-prime/201103 /technology-myth-multitasking.

22. Turkle, *Alone Together*.

23. Turkle, *Alone Together*, 296.

24. Linda Stone, "Continuous Partial Attention," *Linda Stone* (blog), 2014, https://lindastone.net/qa/continuous-partial -attention/.

25. Kathy Koch, "Screens' Influence on Students' Connection and Character," conference speech, Fort Worth, Texas, July 7, 2015, https://naums.sched.org/event/2swE/lunch-and-general-session.

26. Mark S. Granovetter, "The Strength of Weak Ties," *American Journal of Sociology* 78, no. 6 (May 1973): 1360–80.

27. This conclusion is reached in Miller McPherson, Lynn Smith-Lovin, and Matthew E. Brashears, "Social Isolation in America: Changes in Core Discussion Networks over Two Decades," *American Sociological Review* 71, no. 3 (June 2006): 353–75, based on the research of Jeffery Boase et al., *The Strength of Internet Ties* (Washington, DC: Pew Internet and American Life Project, 2006), and other studies.

28. New articles are coming out on this all the time. See, for example, Lee Rainie and Kathryn Zickuhr, "Chapter 4: Phone Use in Social Gatherings," in *Americans' Views on Mobile Etiquette* (Washington, DC: Pew Research Center, 2015), www.pewinternet.org/files/2015/08/2015-08-26_mobile-etiquette_FINAL.pdf; Guy Winch, "How Cellphone Use Can Disconnect Your Relationship," *Psychology Today*, January 13, 2015, www.psychologytoday.com/blog/the-squeaky-wheel/201501 /how-cellphone-use-can-disconnect-your-relationship.

29. Research cited in Barry Wellman et al., "Connected Lives: The Project," in Patrick Purcell, ed., *Networked Neighbourhoods: The Connected Community in Context* (London: Springer, 2006), 172.

30. See, for example, Marcel Jousse (1978), cited in Walter Ong, *Orality and Literacy: The Technologizing of the Word* (New York: Routledge, 2012), 34.

31. *Captivated: Finding Freedom in a Media-Captive Culture*, directed by Phillip Telfer (Gunn Productions/Media Talk 101, 2012).

32. Mark Bauerlein, *The Dumbest Generation: How the Digital Age Stupefies Young Americans and Jeopardizes Our Future* (New York: Penguin, 2008), 36–37.

33. James Billington, "The Future Face of Russia" (lecture, January Series, Calvin College, Grand Rapids, Michigan, January 15, 1999), quoted in Quentin J. Schultze, *Communicating for Life: Christian Stewardship in Community and Media* (Grand Rapids: Baker Academic, 2000), 52.

34. Turkle, *Alone Together*, 154.

35. Survey conducted by Jeana Frost and MIT, cited in Robert Epstein, "The Truth about Online Dating," *Scientific American Mind* (February/March 2007): 30, www.scientificamerican.com/article.cfm?id=the-truth-about-online-da.

36. Paul Kurtz, *In Defense of Secular Humanism* (Amherst, NY: Prometheus Books, 1983), 40.

37. Loraine Rhodes, quoted in Jessica Roy, "Rapture of the Nerds," *Time*, April 17, 2014, http://time.com/66536/terasem -transcendence-religion-technology/.

38. Martine Rothblatt, quoted in Roy, "Rapture of the Nerds."

39. See Edwin Black, *IBM and the Holocaust: The Strategic Alliance between Nazi Germany and America's Most Powerful Corporation* (New York: Crown, 2001). For the author's overview, see the *New York Times* review, Gabriel Schoenfeld, "The Punch-Card Conspiracy," March 18, 2001, www.nytimes.com/books/01/03/18/reviews/010318.18schoent.html.

40. R. J. Rummel, *Death by Government* (New Brunswick, NJ: Transaction, 1994), 9.

41. Neil Postman, *Technopoly: The Surrender of Culture to Technology* (New York: Vintage Books, 1993), 5.

42. Postman, *Technopoly*, 20.

43. Turkle, *Alone Together*, 263.

44. Postman, *Technopoly*, 13.

45. Postman, *Technopoly*, 100.

46. Postman, *Technopoly*, 111.

47. Jacques Ellul, *The Technological Society* (New York: Vintage Books, 1964), 97.

48. Sherry Turkle, *Life on the Screen: Identity in the Age of the Internet* (New York: Simon and Schuster, 1995), 22.

49. Galatians 4:19: "My little children, … I am again in the anguish of childbirth until Christ is formed in you!"; Ephesians 4:15: "Rather, speaking the truth in love, we are to grow up in every way into him who is the head, into Christ."

50. Postman, *Technopoly*, xii.

51. Schultze, *Habits of the High-Tech Heart*, 18.

52. Schultze, *Habits of the High-Tech Heart*, 19.

53. Schultze, *Habits of the High-Tech Heart*, 27.

54. Schultze, *Habits of the High-Tech Heart*, 19.

55. Turkle, *Alone Together*, 13.

56. See, for example, Genesis 2:15: "The LORD God took the man and put him in the garden of Eden to work it and keep it." The Hebrew words for "work" and "keep" imply "to serve." See also Matthew 20:16: "The last will be first, and the first last"; Mark 10:45: "Even the Son of Man came not to be served but to serve, and to give his life as a ransom for many"; and Philippians 2:5–7: "Have this mind among yourselves, which is yours in Christ Jesus, who, though he was in the form of God, did not count equality with God a thing to be grasped, but emptied himself, by taking the form of a servant, being born in the likeness of men."

57. Turkle, *Alone Together*, 117.

58. Turkle, *Life on the Screen*, 20.

59. Genesis 2:15: "The LORD God took the man and put him in the garden of Eden to work it and keep it."

60. Genesis 3:17–20: "To Adam [God] said, 'Because you have listened to the voice of your wife and have eaten of the tree of which I commanded you, "You shall not eat of it," cursed is the ground because of you; in pain you shall eat of it all the days of your life; thorns and thistles it shall bring forth for you; and you shall eat the plants of the field. By the sweat of your face you shall eat bread, till you return to the ground, for out of it you were taken; for you are dust, and to dust you shall return.' The man called his wife's name Eve, because she was the mother of all living."

61. Postman, *Technopoly*, 23.

62. Postman, *Technopoly*, 28.

63. Postman, *Technopoly*, 52.

64. Postman, *Technopoly*, 179.

65. Postman, *Technopoly*, 90.

66. Postman, *Technopoly*, 162.

67. Quoted in Chuck Hadad, "Why Some 13-Year-Olds Check Social Media 100 Times a Day," CNN.com, October 13, 2015, www.cnn.com/2015/10/05/health/being-13-teens-social-media-study/.

68. Turkle, *Alone Together*, 176.

69. Sherry Turkle puts it this way: "We are too quick to celebrate the continual presence of a technology that knows no respect for traditional and helpful lines in the sand." Turkle, *Alone Together*, 162.

70. Turkle, *Alone Together*, 13.

71. Turkle, *Alone Together*, 177.

72. Sara H. Konrath, Edward H. O'Brien, and Courtney Hsing, "Changes in Dispositional Empathy in American College Students over Time: A Meta-analysis," *Personality and Social Psychology Review* 15, no. 2 (May 2011): 180–98, http://psr.sagepub.com/content/15/2/180.abstract.

73. Turkle, *Alone Together*, 161.

74. Turkle, *Alone Together*, 329n2.

75. "Star Wars: Episode IV–A New Hope," *Star Wars*, directed by George Lucas (Lucasfilm/Twentieth Century Fox, 1977).

76. John 3:16: "God so loved the world, that he gave his only Son, that whoever believes in him should not perish but have eternal life."

77. John 13:34: "[Jesus said,] 'Just as I have loved you, you also are to love one another.'"

78. Hebrews 2:14: "Since therefore the children share in flesh and blood, [Christ] himself likewise partook of the same things, that through death he might destroy the one who has the power of death, that is, the devil."

79. Luke 1:32–33: "[Jesus] will be great and will be called the Son of the Most High. And the Lord God will give to him the throne of his father David, and he will reign over the house of Jacob forever, and of his kingdom there will be no end."

80. Genesis 1:1: "In the beginning, God created the heavens and the earth."

81. Glenn Sunshine, "Hugh of St. Victor (1096–1141)," *Christian Worldview Journal*, January 30, 2012, www.colsoncenter.org/the-center/columns/indepth/17398-hugh-of-st-victor-1096-1141.

82. Vishal Mangalwadi, *The Book That Made Your World: How the Bible Created the Soul of Western Civilization* (Nashville: Thomas Nelson, 2011), 114.

83. Glenn Sunshine, "Thomas Newcomen (1664–1729) and James Watt (1736–1819)," *Christian Worldview Journal*, February 13, 2012, www.colsoncenter.org/the-center/columns/indepth/17439-thomas-newcomen-1664-1729-and-james -watt-1736-1819.

84. James K. A. Smith, *Desiring the Kingdom: Worship, Worldview, and Cultural Formation* (Grand Rapids: Baker Academic, 2009), 80.

85. Smith, *Desiring the Kingdom*.

86. Craig R. Dykstra, *Growing in the Life of Faith: Education and Christian Practices*, 2nd ed. (Louisville, KY: Westminster John Knox, 2005), 43.

87. The original list appeared in Craig Dykstra, "No Longer Strangers," *Princeton Seminary Bulletin* 6, no. 3 (November 1985): 197. This is a representative sampling from the list of fourteen "practices that appear consistently throughout the tradition and that are particularly significant for Christians today," in Dykstra, *Growing in the Life of Faith*, 42–43.

88. Alvaro Fernandez, "Evidence of Emerging Technology to Assess and Train Cognitive and Emotional Functioning" (presentation, "Learning and the Brain: Using Brain Research to Raise IQ and Achievement," San Francisco, February 17–20, 2010).

89. John J. Jonides, "Better Cognition through Training and Interaction with the Environment" (presentation, "Learning and the Brain: Using Brain Research to Raise IQ and Achievement," San Francisco, February 17–20, 2010).

90. Kevin D. Washburn, "Guest Blog: Report from the Learning and the Brain Conference," Edutopia.org, March 6, 2010, www.edutopia.org/kevin-washburn-learning-brain-intelligence-factors.

91. Ephesians 5:16: "[Make] the best use of the time, because the days are evil."

92. Genesis 3:8: "[Adam and Eve] heard the sound of the Lord God walking in the garden in the cool of the day, and the man and his wife hid themselves from the presence of the Lord God among the trees of the garden."

93. Genesis 2:4 refers to the Lord God, using both his name as creator (Elohim) and his name as relator (Yahweh): "These are the generations of the heavens and the earth when they were created, in the day that the Lord God made the earth and the heavens."

94. YHWH is a *tetragrammaton* (Greek for "four letters"), which in Hebrew means "to be." Pronounced "Yahweh," YHWH is the name of God that refers to his nature as divine warrior.

95. The word for "word" here is *logos*, which, as we saw in the previous chapter, refers to the expression of a thought and is the root word for our word *logic*.

96. Randall Niles, "Viewpoint: Web 2.0," notes provided for Summit Ministries' summer student notebook, 2013.

97. Glenn Sunshine, "Johannes Gutenberg (c. 1398–1468)," *Christian Worldview Journal*, January 16, 2012, www.colsoncenter .org/the-center/columns/indepth/17348-johannes-gutenberg-c1398-1468.

98. According to a study by Miller McPherson, Lynn Smith-Lovin, and Matthew Brashears, the number of Americans who said they have no one with whom to discuss important matters has tripled since 1985. See McPherson, Smith-Lovin, and Brashears, "Social Isolation in America."

99. Alan Loy McGinnis, *The Friendship Factor: How to Get Closer to the People You Care for* (Minneapolis: Augsburg, 1979), 9.

100. Schultze, *Communicating for Life*, 59.

101. James 1:19: "Know this, my beloved brothers: let every person be quick to hear, slow to speak, slow to anger."

102. Genesis 1:31: "God saw everything that he had made, and behold, it was very good. And there was evening and there was morning, the sixth day."

103. Genesis 2:17: "Of the tree of the knowledge of good and evil you shall not eat, for in the day that you eat of it you shall surely die"; Genesis 3:22: "The Lord God said, 'Behold, the man has become like one of us in knowing good and evil."

104. Colossians 1:21–22: "You, who once were alienated [from God] and hostile in mind, doing evil deeds, he has now reconciled in [Christ's] body of flesh by his death, in order to present you holy and blameless and above reproach before him."

105. Amos 9:11: "In that day I will raise up the booth of David that is fallen and repair its breaches and raise up its ruins and rebuild it as in the days of old."

106. Nehemiah 2:17: "[Nehemiah] said to [the people], "You see the trouble we are in, how Jerusalem lies in ruins with its gates burned. Come, let us build the wall of Jerusalem, that we may no longer suffer derision."

107. Matthew 18:15: "If your brother sins against you, go and tell him his fault, between you and him alone. If he listens to you, you have gained your brother"; Galatians 6:1: "If anyone is caught in any transgression, you who are spiritual should restore him in a spirit of gentleness."

108. Turkle, *Alone Together*, 243.

109. Philip G. Ryken, *Christian Worldview: A Student's Guide*, Reclaiming the Christian Intellectual Tradition, ed. David S. Dockery (Wheaton, IL: Crossway, 2013), 59. Second Corinthians 5:20 says, "Therefore, we are ambassadors for Christ, God making his appeal through us. We implore you on behalf of Christ, be reconciled to God."

110. According to the World Bank, extreme poverty has dropped in half just in the last generation, from 36 percent of the world's population to 18 percent. World Bank Group, *Prosperity for All: Ending Extreme Poverty* (Washington, DC: World Bank, 2014), 1, http://siteresources.worldbank.org/INTPROSPECTS/Resources/334934-1327948020811/8401693-1397074077765 /Prosperity_for_All_Final_2014.pdf.

111. Schultze, *Habits of the High-Tech Heart*.

CHAPTER

7

7

THE ARTS AND ENTERTAINMENT

1. THE BIG STORY VERSUS LOTS OF LITTLE STORIES

"Mia, this is the finest senior paper I've read in several years."

Mia blushed, subconsciously glancing behind her as her classmates filed out of the room, hoping a little that they hadn't heard her professor's remark, and a little that they had.

"I think you need to do something with it. I really do," the professor continued. Tapping the sheaf of papers Mia now held close, she stressed, "This, *this* is a *movie*. No doubt in my mind. It's a screenplay."

Inspired, Mia had moved to Los Angeles after graduation to pursue her dream of being a screenwriter. That was four months ago. Her professor's remarks echoing in her tired mind, Mia coaxed her little four-cylinder beater through the streets to the cramped apartment she shared with a revolving group of girls. She worked long days at a restaurant that had "seen better days," as she ruefully described it. One day, she hoped, she'd remember all of this with a fond sigh.

In Hollywood, Mia was one of thousands of others who, it seemed, were just days away from their big break. At first she spent every spare minute clacking away on her laptop at the corner coffee shop she'd sworn to make famous one day by casually mentioning it in an interview.

Mia's first break came just a couple of weeks after arriving in town. Right in the midst of wrangling snappiness out of a weary dialogue passage, her phone buzzed. A text from Mia's roommate read, "U wanna be in a movie tmro? Friend says need xtras."

A minivacation, Mia thought. "Sure," she replied.

The next day, dressed in period garb and chatting happily on command, Mia and her friend strolled down the street, over and over again. There were thirty others in the scene, but that didn't bother Mia one bit.

Being an extra was hard work, but through dedication Mia managed to abide the hours of waiting, waiting, waiting. She could make more flipping burgers, but this was *research*, Mia told herself. Plus, she had seen the movie's star, Cash Upton, *only fifty yards away*, his tall frame and handsome face occasionally visible through the gaggle of camera operators and sound techs and makeup artists. Since then, she had been on the set of two movies and a television show. The unfinished screenplay nagged at her, but what could compare with the thrill of being on set when a director called "Action"?

Late to work from a film set earlier that day, Mia threw on her apron and scurried to a table of waiting customers. "Welcome to Hollywood!" she enthused, immediately recognizing it would be hard to win over what appeared to be an exhausted and grumpy tourist family. Fortunately, the family's young son broke the ice.

"Are you in the movies?" he asked as Mia took their drink order.

"Well, sort of," Mia hinted with a grin. "I'm working on a screenplay and am taking small parts in the meantime."

"Who have you worked with?" asked the father, perking up.

"A few weeks ago I was in a film with Cash Upton."

"Cash Upton? No way," said the kid, his eyes shining. Mom and dad nodded. *Hollywood magic*.

It was well after midnight when Mia finally pulled into a parking spot and switched off the car ignition. She looked around, relieved that no teenagers were standing on the corner. She made it one block to her apartment and trudged up three flights of stairs.

Home at last, she thought, putting her key in the lock. It didn't work. *That's odd*. She texted her roommate: "Key won't work and no one's here. What's up?"

Two minutes later: "Evicted. Will sort it out in AM."

What a pain. Mia guessed that in the confusion of roommates moving in and out, no one had paid the rent. The landlord responded by changing the lock. Was this legal?

And then a jolt: "My laptop!" she texted back, practically shrieking. No reply.

Late that night, shivering in her car, Mia didn't know whether to cry or scream. Her *whole life* was on that laptop. She hadn't worked on her screenplay in weeks, but still. *Tomorrow morning the dream begins anew*, she assured herself.

Silence washed over her for a few minutes. Mia shifted in the driver's seat and closed her eyes. Bzzz. Another text: "U wanna be in a movie tmro?"

Oh, good. They needed her. "Yep," she replied and then closed her eyes, smiling.

2. The Entertainment Culture

Our entertainment-driven culture tempts all of us, like Mia, to put the bigger story of our lives on hold while we accept bit parts in other people's stories. Derived from a Latin word meaning "to keep people in a certain frame of mind," **entertainment** adds much joy to our lives. Increasingly, though, people find themselves trapped in a perpetual cycle of seeking amusement, which is an altogether different thing. *Muse* means "to think." *A* means "without." **Amusement**, *then, is entertainment without thought.*

> *Entertainment:* an activity designed to hold the interest and attention of an audience.

In *Amusing Ourselves to Death*, the late Neil Postman described how an obsession with amusement hurts us personally and culturally. He illustrated this by comparing two dystopian worlds, George Orwell's *1984*, with its dark tale of the all-seeing Big Brother, and Aldous Huxley's *Brave New World*, in which people embrace oppression with the help of a fictional drug called *soma*

> *Amusement:* the state of being entertained without inspiring thought.

(which Huxley described as "all the advantages of Christianity and alcohol, [with] none of their defects"[1]):

> What Orwell feared were those who would ban books. What Huxley feared was that there would be … no one who wanted to read one.… Orwell feared that the truth would be concealed from us. Huxley feared the truth would be drowned in a sea of irrelevance. Orwell feared we would become a captive culture. Huxley feared we would become a trivial culture.… In short, Orwell feared that what we hate will ruin us. Huxley feared that what we love will ruin us.[2]

Ignorance. Apathy. Triviality. Ruin. A grim picture of modern life, to be sure. But Postman was not the only one concerned. Respected film critic Michael Medved, after years of reviewing movies, wondered why the public had such a high tolerance for mediocre and debauched entertainment. He concluded bluntly, "The true sickness is in the soul."[3]

We don't set out to become soul sick. I don't know anyone who says, "I'm going to aspire to a life of hazy complacency." Rather, we cross the line between entertaining relaxation and amusement addiction without realizing we've done so. Like Mia, we're tripped up by alluring obstacles and bloated by our appetite for the easy and insubstantial. To paraphrase the famed critic Malcolm Muggeridge, our entertainment wasn't invented to make us shallow; rather, it emerges out of our shallowness.

But perhaps shallowness is a symptom of a deeper problem: we're afraid. We're afraid we won't find what we're looking for in life. We're afraid of not being needed or desired. We're afraid there is no "out there" out there. As we critically examine the entertainment culture, we're faced with a choice: Will we passively absorb whatever our culture offers, or will we fight for meaningful lives?

It's tempting to turn this chapter into a pessimistic rant against modern culture. But my sincere hope is to offer an eye-opening perspective on the entertainment culture within a larger focus on how to really *live*, not just merely be *alive*. May it not be said of us at the end of our days, as Oliver Wendell Holmes Sr. lamented, "Alas for those that never sing, but die with all their music in them!"

> *Art:* a physical, visual, or auditory expression of human creativity, skill, and imagination (e.g., paintings, music, plays, and musicals).

We *can* rise above everyday triviality and reach this goal. But first we need to know what we're up against. A battle of worldviews rages in the entertainment culture. Christians must learn to care and be clear on what that caring should look like.

The Choice before Us

Art is essential to the human experience. Painting, sculpture, music, and literature deepen the meaning of our lives if we're patient and thoughtful enough to learn their ways. But the entertainment culture transmutes the arts into something to numb us rather than bring us alive. A popular band from my own growing-up years sang,

> *With the lights out, it's less dangerous*
> *Here we are now: entertain us*
> *I feel stupid and contagious*
> *Here we are now: entertain us.*[4]

The singer, Kurt Cobain, ended his own life in despair. Yet his fans live on; most are now in their thirties and forties. Known for their sarcasm and cynicism, they grew up and found jobs, were married, had children, and entered mainstream life. With every new generation, though, the angst comes roaring back. Each generation wonders, *Is this life all there is?*

> Is this life all there is? The Christian worldview has an answer: let Christ peel back the layers of fallenness and bring healing, not just to release us from the pain but to give us purpose.

The Christian worldview has an answer: let Christ peel back the layers of fallenness and bring healing, not just to release us from the pain but to give us purpose. It's risky to embrace this truth. As John Piper says, "If our single, all-embracing passion is to make much of Christ in life and death, and if the life that magnifies him most is the life of costly love, then life is risk, and risk is right. To run from it is to waste your life."[5]

The arts ought to not just be colorful ornaments hung on an otherwise dreary life. From a biblical perspective, they point to God, unlock deep truths about humanity, and enlarge life itself in the process. How the arts do this, and how they have been hijacked, is a fascinating subplot in Christian history.

How the Arts Became Amusement

The arts is one of the most enduring aspects of human culture. Among our most ancient artifacts are sculptures, paintings, mosaics, works of architecture, and manuscripts of plays, stories, and songs. In the biblical narrative, the Scriptures repeatedly refer to the Hebrews as a musical people. Genesis 4:21 tells of an instrument called a *kinnor* invented by Jubal, a forerunner of the Israelite people. The warrior-poet King David was gifted in its use. Some versions of Scripture call it a *harp*, but the Greek word for this instrument, *kithara*, is where we get our word *guitar*.[6]

> The arts point to God, unlock deep truths about humanity, and enlarge life itself in the process.

The ancient Hebrews knew how to have a good time. One of the three tithes God instructed ancient Israelites to pay was the festival tithe, in which they were to annually sell animals and spend the proceeds on "whatever you desire—oxen or sheep or wine or strong drink, whatever your appetite craves. And you shall eat there before the LORD your God and rejoice, you and your household" (Deut. 14:26–27). People rarely think the God of the Old Testament wanted people to throw big parties, but it's right there in the text.

Unfortunately, in a fallen world, the arts often become grotesque. Israel's Canaanite neighbors hosted orgies in which they burned babies alive in a furnace sculpted to resemble the god Molech, masking the infants' screams with music.

Greek culture featured complex narratives, robust plays, and athletic events. Ancient philosophers, such as Plato, believed that training in the arts, especially music, would lead to a life of moderation, self-restraint, and harmony for the soul. People who have a "good beginning in play" can develop habits of order, he said, and such habits can help preserve the state.[7]

The Romans inherited these traditions, though their cultural artifacts degraded as the empire disintegrated. Gladiators fought to the death in coliseums, wild animals ate political prisoners and other undesirables (Christians) in front of an approving crowd, and sexually explicit parades marked public holidays.

> The highest and best of Western art has Christianity's fingerprints all over it.

The highest and best of Western art has Christianity's fingerprints all over it. Shakespeare liberally quoted the Bible and trusted his audience's understanding of it to grasp his subtle allusions. The very structure of Western music follows the biblical pattern of creation, fall, and redemption. So, too, great literature reminds us of the horror of sin, the honor of self-sacrifice, and the glory of redemption pictured in a story's ultimate resolution.

During the **Age of Enlightenment**, the world began to change. According to Nancy Pearcey, a professor of Christian worldview, somewhere along the way, people began thinking of truth as being like two stories of a building: *lower-story truth*, based on demonstrably true facts, and *upper-story truth*, based on subjective and culturally relative values.[8] Upper-story truth was seen as idealistic and based on feelings and moral preferences. Lower-story truth was seen as enlightened and knowable, based on scientifically known facts.[9] The two views of truth were considered separate—one was sacred, the other secular.

> *Formalism:* an artistic movement that emphasized the formal elements of art, such as line, color, space, and volume.

Enlightenment thinkers, Pearcey says, thought lower-story truth was most important; real truth was what could be known through reason (*rationalism*). Art, on the other hand, was an upper-story concern—frilly and insubstantial. Anything that couldn't be measured through the factual language of science was second class. There were three main responses to this thinking. Artists who decided to *join* the trend developed **formalism**, using art to communicate objective formal elements, such as line, color, space, and volume.[10] Artists who decided to *fight* this trend developed **romanticism**, a movement of pure feeling and emotion. Artists who decided to *ignore* this trend developed **realism**, which says that art is just supposed to show what *is*. It isn't supposed to be *about* something or make us *feel* anything.

> *Romanticism:* an artistic movement that emphasized the emotional elements of art and rejected the more traditional artistic elements, such as order, harmony, and balance.

> *Realism:* an artistic movement that emphasized portraying the world truthfully without embellishment, exaggerated emotion, or romantic idealism.

Splitting the secular and sacred makes it hard to see art as something that enables us to better understand God and the world. Artists tend to see their work either as an ethereal withdrawal from the world or as a stiff embrace of its cold meaninglessness.[11] Not many people find cold meaninglessness attractive. Withdrawal attracts a larger audience, but only because it takes peoples' minds off reality. This is no less a problem.

Christians reacted to this secular-sacred split in two ways. Says screenwriter Brian Godawa, those fearful of the uncontrolled emotional influence of the arts became "cultural anorexics." In their wariness, they lost touch with the delightful side of being God's image bearers. Others became "cultural gluttons" who reveled in art's escapism.[12] While the cultural anorexics looked on disapprovingly, the cultural gluttons retorted, in the immortal words of the hippie Jesus movement singer-songwriter Larry Norman, "Why should the devil have all the good music?"[13]

> Splitting the secular and sacred makes it hard to see art as something that enables us to better understand God and the world.

As more entertainment options emerged, art devolved into amusement, a morphine drip of distraction for a culture in chronic pain. But this, according to Ravi Zacharias, is the way cultures decline. At first art imitates life, then life imitates art, and then life draws its very reason for existence from the arts.[14]

When they hear about the change in approaches to art in the past few hundred years, many people wonder, *Why is this a big deal? Can't we just enjoy our entertainment and leave it at that?* Perhaps you're wondering this as well. What is the big deal? Does amusement really hurt us?

> **At first art imitates life, then life imitates art, and then life draws its very reason for existence from the arts.**

What Amusement Does to Us

Amusement can help relieve stress and bring us happiness. But it also produces four lingering effects that can damage us in the long term. It can enslave our affections, make us restless, destroy contentment, and make us angry. Let's look at each of these concerns.

1. The amusement culture enslaves our affections. We're designed to experience God's love as the basis of true companionship as we take on the task of forming and filling the earth. Our brains are wired to learn, and our bodies are made to move in response. When we see something new, a cluster of cells in our brains recognizes that thing so we can recall it when we see it again. When two things are experienced together, such as smelling a favorite dish and eating it, the two memories become linked.

An obsession with amusement can turn our design against us, changing our affections. When we experience something like shooting people in a violent video game or viewing a movie scene in which verbal insults result in violence, our memories link to what we're seeing, and our bodies respond accordingly. Violent content usually doesn't *cause* such behavior, but it *primes* it. An amusement culture gives us hair triggers.[15]

An amusement culture also changes our affections by deadening our moral responsiveness, especially in the area of sexuality. God designed sexual activity to link emotion and reason inside the loving relationship of marriage, forming a shared memory on which an enduring relationship may be built. All other sexual activity, including watching pornography, separates sex and love while linking sex to pleasurable sensations in the brain. In short, it forms an addiction. As Rollo May predicted in *Love and Will*, this leads, ironically, to apathy and the loss of erotic desire.[16] When sex and love are separated, sexuality becomes a way to *use* others rather than *serve* them. As an example, a Princeton University study showed that viewing pictures of scantily clad women activated the "tool-use part" of men's brains, causing them to view women as objects to be used rather than as people to be loved.[17]

> **God designed sexual activity to link emotion and reason inside the loving relationship of marriage, forming a shared memory on which an enduring relationship may be built.**

Some think violent video games are wrong because they lead to violence and that pornography is wrong because it leads to sex crimes. But there are other concerns. The truth is, few people play violent video games and then commit acts of violence. Rather, their affections gradually shift from companionship to defiance, from respect to disrespect, from helpfulness to aggression, from other-centeredness to self-centeredness.

Similarly, very few people who view pornography commit sex crimes. Rather, their affections gradually shift from relationship to guilt, from guilt to frustration, from frustration to a demand for control, from control to blaming others for what they cannot control, and from blame to abusive words and actions.

> Unfulfilled desire reminds us that we were made for another world. When the sacred and secular are split, however, unfulfilled desire is seen as something to be gratified only physically.

C. S. Lewis said that unfulfilled desire reminds us that we were made for another world.[18] When the sacred and secular are split, however, unfulfilled desire is seen as something to be gratified only physically. Hungry? Eat *now*. Thirsty? Drink *now*. Tired? Sleep *now*. Lustful? Satisfy it *now*. The only caveat is not to hurt anyone else, as if that's possible.

But God didn't create us to meet our needs in isolation, and trying to go it alone only makes things worse, not better. One tech company invented a robot companion that gives its "owner" affection without the complication of a real relationship. But this only turns our souls' desire to connect with another person into self-gratifying obsession. MIT professor Sherry Turkle muses,

> The questions for the future are not whether children will love their robot companions more than their pets or even their parents. The questions are rather, What will love be? And what will it mean to achieve ever-greater intimacy with our machines? Are we ready to see ourselves in the mirror of the machine and to see love as our performances of love?[19]

> If the real world is a sacred place, not a secular one, then to view our desires as merely physical is to live halfheartedly.

If the real world is a sacred place, not a secular one, then to view our desires as merely physical is to live halfheartedly. This was C. S. Lewis's point in his sermon "The Weight of Glory": "We are half-hearted creatures, fooling about with drink and sex and ambition when infinite joy is offered us, like an ignorant child who wants to go on making mud pies in a slum because he cannot imagine what is meant by the offer of a holiday at the sea. We are far too easily pleased."[20]

2. The amusement culture makes us restless. Attention is one of our most valuable currencies. We never have more than twenty-four hours in a day. Journalist Maggie Jackson writes, "Nothing is more central to creating a flourishing society built upon learning, contentment, caring, morality, reflection, and spirit than attention. As humans, we are formed to pay attention. Without it, we simply would not survive."[21]

The amusement culture clamors for our limited attention. Breaking-news alerts make it seem as if everything is urgent and worthy of our attention. This clamor, says theologian Craig Gay, "makes the world appear to be nothing but an endless jumble of events through which it is difficult, if not impossible, to discern anything beyond the relatively base motivations of lust, calculated self-interest, and the will to power."[22] According to journalism professor John Sommerville, the twenty-four-hour news cycle actually makes us dumber because when everything seems urgent, it's difficult to distinguish what is really important.[23] The demand to be informed replaces the desire to grow wise.[24]

> The twenty-four-hour news cycle actually makes us dumber because when everything seems urgent, it's difficult to distinguish what is really important.

Even our devices make us restless. Who hasn't logged on to their laptop or iPad or smartphone while in bed waiting to go to sleep? In recent years, studies have shown that using blue-light-emitting electronic devices before bedtime can make it harder to sleep, negatively affecting health and alertness. Even after eight hours of sleep, those using such devices were sleepier and less alert.[25]

Also, the constant demand for attention makes us self-centered. We begin feeling it's the *obligation* of others to grab our attention, and if they don't, it's their fault, not ours. Radio host John Stonestreet has seen the effect of an entertainment mentality on the audiences he addresses. Known as a compelling communicator, Stonestreet nonetheless says,

> One of the great issues I encounter when I get up to speak is not "I wonder if he has anything to say"; it's that if they don't think I'm entertaining they assume I have nothing to say.... Not all the really good stuff in life comes through entertainment. It might be that *you're* not entertained well, not that some guy isn't entertaining. *You* might be the one that's broken.[26]

We're broken. We're restless. I know I am. Even as I try to write this chapter, I find it impossible to resist toggling over to check Facebook or email. If something isn't happening "right now," if there aren't enough "likes" in response to what I think is a clever Facebook post, I tend to feel pushed to the margins of meaning. I'm restless by nature. The amusement culture makes it worse.

3. The amusement culture destroys contentment. Contentment is the virtue of being calm and satisfied rather than always demanding more. Contentment isn't afraid of the silence that occurs when nothing much is happening. Rather, it sees this silence as a good and natural part of life.

As we discussed in chapter 4, one of the most basic psychological patterns of our lives is equilibrium, tension, and resolution. We strive for equilibrium, but tensions arise that demand a release. Jeremy Begbie, who teaches at the University of Cambridge in England, thinks the good life involves comfort with God's rhythms, including the rhythm of silence. "Music is remarkably instructive here," he observes, "because more

> Contentment is the virtue of being calm and satisfied rather than always demanding more.

than any other art form, it teaches us how not to rush over tension, how to find joy and fulfill-ment through a temporal movement that includes struggles, clashes and fractures. The temptation is to pass over what needs to be passed through."[27]

When we're comfortable with life's rhythms, we realize we don't have to frantically make something happen every moment. Quiet moments are good. They lead to a calm happiness. Practicing content-ment is hard, though, in an amusement culture where silence is nothing more than a space that marketers hav-en't yet figured out how to fill.

> When we're comfortable with life's rhythms, we realize we don't have to frantically make something happen every moment. Quiet moments are good.

In radio and television, silence is a sign that some-thing's broken. A disc jockey permitting a gap between songs or commercials has committed an unforgivable mistake. We see silence as bad, Begbie says, "presumably because we think nothing happens in silence. Silence is void, emptiness, blank space."[28] Silence makes us feel alone, and we hate being alone.

As comedian and social commentator Louis CK observes,

> Sometimes when things clear away … you're not watching anything … you're in your car, and you start going, "Oh no, here it comes … I'm alone." It starts to visit on you.… That's why we text and drive. I look around, pretty much 100 percent of the people driving are texting. And everybody's murdering each other with their cars. But people are willing to risk taking a life and ruining their own because they don't want to be alone for a second.[29]

Psychologist Mihaly Csikszentmihalyi has found that because we're desperate to fill the empty, quiet moments, we're four times more likely to spend our free time watching TV than doing things we enjoy more, such as working on hobbies or playing sports. Puzzled, Csikszentmihalyi asks, "Why would we spend four times more time doing something that has less than half the chance of making us feel good?[30]

> Silence makes us feel alone, and we hate being alone.

It's a great question, but one it seems we're too preoc-cupied to answer. Americans spend approximately eleven hours a day, on average, using digital media.[31] Much of this time is spent on the Internet, and the bulk of Internet use is spent on social media.[32] Yet 60 percent of people in a 2013 *Time* magazine poll said that using social media didn't make them happier.[33] Social-media sites like Facebook make us feel more connected, but studies show that as our networks of friends grow broader, they also grow shallower, making us feel lonely.[34]

We need a change of attitude. In music, the proper use of silence makes a work more profound.[35] When all our spaces are filled with noise, though, we come to expect that tensions will be immediately resolved in a predictable way, and when they aren't, we become impatient. That's why we gravitate toward music and other forms of entertainment that allow us to escape from reality rather than embrace it. Silence and stillness block our escape, uncomfortably reminding us of how empty we are. As John Davies (1569–1626), a poet and contemporary of William Shakespeare, memorably expressed it,

We that acquaint ourselves with every zone,
      And pass both tropics and behold the poles,
When we come home, are to ourselves unknown,
      And unacquainted still with our own souls.[36]

The amusement culture tricks us into thinking that as long as things are happening, we're fulfilling our purpose. Everyone else is in constant demand—why aren't you?

> **The amusement culture tricks us into thinking that as long as things are happening, we're fulfilling our purpose.**

If being in demand makes us important, then celebrities are the most important people. What rock stars and actors think seems more important than what we think, even if they aren't very informed. Experts are tolerated; celebrities are celebrated. No wonder schoolchildren think that "being a celebrity" is "the very best thing in the world."[37]

4. The amusement culture makes us angry. Chinese researchers studied seventy million posts and found that angry tweets were far more likely to be retweeted than tweets expressing joy, sadness, or disgust.[38] The Internet makes us madder and meaner. One study found that preteens who left behind their devices for five days were more tuned in to how others felt.[39] If *not* having the devices makes us *more* relational, then what is risked by *having* them becomes clear. They dull our sensitivity toward others.

Whether our devices have anything to do with it or not, our culture is growing angrier. The president of the National Association of Scholars, Peter Wood, says the anger epidemic is "more flamboyant, more self-righteous, and more theatrical than anger at other times in our history. It often has the look-at-me character of performance art."[40] We're becoming, Wood concludes, "a culture that celebrates anger."[41] Even what's supposed to be funny seems angry. Comedian Steve Carell admitted, "It's not like I want to put sunshine and lollipops into the world.… But I do believe there's been a turn toward an uber-cynical point of view, and it's borderline mean."[42]

There are, of course, good uses of humor, sarcasm, and ridicule.[43] The amusement culture, however, twists them into cynicism, suspicion, and distrust in ways that affect us both spiritually and physically. Proverbs 14:30 says, "A tranquil heart gives life to the flesh, but envy makes the bones rot." The Hebrew word for envy is often translated "anger." It's an unsettled, bitter feeling toward others. According to neuroscientist Caroline Leaf says, research has shown that 75–98 percent of mental and physical illnesses come from our thought lives. Toxic thinking leads to stress, eroding our body's natural ability to heal.[44]

> **The anger epidemic today is "more flamboyant, more self-righteous, and more theatrical than anger at other times in our history."**

When we stop thinking, others step in, manipulating and controlling our thoughts and emotions. Our minds become filled with a "continuous stream of … worries, fears and distorted perceptions, … which trigger degenerative processes in the mind and body."[45] These effects are now being seen in the elderly: people filled with cynical distrust and chronic anger are more likely to suffer stress-related illness, heart disease, and dementia in older age.[46]

In the Old Testament, people were warned against worshiping idols because they risked becoming like those idols—deaf, dumb, and blind to what was really important in life (see Psalm 135:15–18). In a similar way, an obsession with amusement can easily turn into a form of worship that makes us as thoughtless and angry as that which we spend our time pursuing. Worse, people that are thoughtless and angry are easy for counterfeit worldviews to manipulate, and today, as we will see, manipulation has become a finely-tuned art.

Manipulation may be the worst thing about the amusement culture. And today, counterfeit worldviews are doing a lot of manipulating through entertainment.

3. WORLDVIEWS AND ENTERTAINMENT

"I've always tried to be aware of what I say in my films, because all of us who make motion pictures are teachers," *Star Wars* producer George Lucas says, "—teachers with very loud voices."[47] Entertainers teach by telling stories that shape peoples' views of reality. Every one of these stories, Brian Godawa reminds us, "is informed by a worldview."[48] Many entertainers relish the power this gives them. Courtney Love, a singer who was married to the late Kurt Cobain, said, "I feel like I have a duty. I as an architect have a need to impose my worldview on the culture."[49]

> *Worldview:* a pattern of ideas, beliefs, convictions, and habits that help us make sense of God, the world, and our relationship to God and the world.

In fact, the entertainment culture itself has become so influential that in some ways it forms its own **worldview**, its own patterns of ideas, values, behaviors, and habits. Says movie critic Neal Gabler, "It is not any ism but entertainment that is arguably the most pervasive, powerful and ineluctable force of our time—a force so overwhelming that it has finally metastasized into life."[50] Whatever the case, there is a battle of worldviews in the entertainment culture, and it affects each of us every day.

The Battle for Hearts and Minds

The arts have long been noted for their mesmerizing power. Scottish writer Andrew Fletcher (1653–1716) said, "If a man were permitted to make all the ballads, he need not care who should make the laws of a nation."[51] Why? Because, as Plato explained in *The Republic*, "when the modes of music change, the fundamental laws of the State always change with them."[52]

Academic studies confirm this power. Eliana La Ferrara, a professor of economics at Bocconi University in Italy, studied the influence of Brazilian television soap operas, which include a significantly higher level of divorce and a significantly lower number of children per mother than the general population. After exposure to these programs, family size began to shift to reflect the size of families in the programs.[53]

Such influence can, of course, be positive. In India, producers of a wildly popular radio show *Tinka Tinka Sukh* ("Happiness Lies in Small Things") wrote a script in which a "beloved young girl dies in childbirth after being forced into an early marriage. After vicariously experiencing her death, audience members wrote over 150,000 letters in reaction."[54] The episode so affected India that for the first time, large segments of the population began questioning whether it was a good idea to marry off their daughters at a young age.

The larger question isn't whether the media is influential but what kind of influence it seeks to have. Leonard Goldberg, executive producer of some of television's top shows, admitted that Hollywood's agenda skews left in the political spectrum. Liberalism in the television industry, he confessed, is "100 percent dominant, and anyone who denies it is kidding or not telling the truth."[55]

> The larger question isn't whether the media is influential but what kind of influence it seeks to have.

Some people, based on a secular belief that God either doesn't exist or is irrelevant, overtly attempt to use entertainment to communicate their message. Philip Pullman's His Dark Materials series of books, and the movie *The Golden Compass*, were explicitly the anti–C. S. Lewis.[56] Other attempts are subtler. Walt Disney, for example, specifically excluded a church from Disney World's Main Street and even left churches out of the subdivision he was planning (though there are now several churches in the area).[57]

The growing acceptance of the homosexual lifestyle is a case in point. For most of history, homosexual behavior was considered a violation of God's created design for sexuality. The Gay and Lesbian Alliance Against Defamation (GLAAD) decided to harness the power of entertainment to change this, distributing a list of dos and don'ts to screenwriters, including, "*Do* use the term *sexual orientation* instead of *sexual choice*," and "*Do not* assume homosexuals are promiscuous."[58]

GLAAD also developed an awards show for gay-and-lesbian-friendly programs. A graduate student at Arizona State University, Erin Brownback, studied the GLAAD award–winning programs for the past thirteen years and found that all of them included activities wildly more outside the box than homosexual behavior, making gay and lesbian characters' behavior appear mild by comparison. In addition, nine of the thirteen programs featured interracial heterosexual couples to create a comparison frame in which gay relationships were seen as acceptable as interracial ones. The producers of these programs knew what they were doing, the researcher realized. They were, as phrased in a famous strategy paper in the homosexual movement, "overhauling … straight America."[59] It worked. People who watch programs in which homosexuality is normal are more likely to think of homosexuality as normal behavior.[60]

Some Christians, viewing such strategies, have wondered whether they might be able to employ similar ones to help biblical values flourish in entertainment. Many in Hollywood are trying, but the entertainment community is notoriously resistant. As Ted Baehr of Movieguide points out, "Imagine the church making similar demands [to those of GLAAD], such as 'Do not call all Christians fundamentalists,' or 'Do not call Christians right wing.' There would be a tremendous uproar as cries of censorship rang out across the land."[61] The late head of the Motion Picture Association

> Some Christians have wondered whether they might be able to employ strategies like those GLAAD has used to help biblical values flourish in entertainment.

of America (MPAA), Jack Valenti, confirmed Baehr's suspicions, thundering against conservative groups, "What we cannot do is allow zealots or self-anointed special groups who claim divine vision to intimidate us or coerce us or frighten us. Too many brave young men have died on battlefields, and are dying now, to protect, defend, and preserve our right of choice."[62] Whether any Americans have given their lives so people in Hollywood can say and do whatever they want is doubtful. But there undoubtedly is a battle going on for the hearts and minds of people, and the fighting is fierce in Hollywood.

How Different Worldviews Process the Entertainment Culture

Marxism: **an atheistic and materialistic worldview based on the ideas of Karl Marx that promotes the abolition of private property, the public ownership of the means of production (i.e., socialism), and the utopian dream of a future communistic state.**

Marxism. You can learn a lot about a worldview by the way it approaches entertainment. Some worldviews, such as **Marxism**, take a two-pronged approach. First, it critiques the arts as being like religion in keeping people from seeing the truth of their oppression and rising up. Art serves "the interests of the ruling class," as John Berger put it.[63] The self-proclaimed "cultural Marxist" professor Fredric Jameson, among others, has made it his lifework to "demystify" the culture so people can "envision an alternate society altogether" and work toward a utopian future he believes religion cannot deliver.[64] Second, Marxists manipulate entertainment to encourage audiences to rise up in revolution. Whether through fomenting class resentment, as in the classic movie *Salt of the Earth* and, more recently, *The Wolf of Wall Street*, or by blatantly glorifying Marxist revolution, as in *The Motorcycle Diaries*, Marxists have used entertainment to advance their aims.

Postmodernism. Marxism's close cousin **Postmodernism**, which my coauthor and I argued in *Understanding the Times* is a well-formed worldview in and of itself, is suspicious

Postmodernists believe that privileged people hijack art to create an idealistic view of reality.

of any story that proclaims truth. Postmodernists see their mission as critiquing the arts and entertainment to "disrupt bourgeois fantasies about art," as Glenn Ward phrased it, describing the way Postmodernists believe that privileged people hijack art to create an idealistic view of reality.[65]

But whereas Marxism critiques the arts for keeping people *from* reality, Postmodernism critiques the arts for assuming there is any such thing as reality to begin with. John Baudrillard's famous *Simulacra and Simulation* opens with a discussion of Jorge Luis Borges's allegory of a map so detailed as to be the exact scale of the empire it represented. In the end, people lost the ability to distinguish between the map and the reality, except in the outlying deserts of the realm, where they noticed the map fraying. Baudrillard said, "The territory no longer precedes the map, nor does it survive it. It is nevertheless the map that precedes the territory.... Today it is the territory whose shreds slowly rot across the extent of the map.... The desert of the real itself."[66] No one can say what is real, Postmodernists assert, and they've appointed themselves to make that "reality" clear.

Islam. The worldview of **Islam** forms an entirely different approach, criticizing the entertainment culture for keeping people from Allah. Surah 102:1 in the Quran says, "The mutual rivalry for piling up (the good things of this world) diverts you (from the more serious things)." Surah 47:36 observes, "[This] worldly life is only amusement and diversion." Surah 57:20 states, "Know that the life of this world is only play and amusement, pomp and mutual boasting among you, and rivalry in respect of wealth and children, as the likeness of vegetation after rain, thereof the growth is pleasing to the tiller; afterwards it dries up and you see it turning yellow; then it becomes straw." The Arabic word *dunya*, used throughout the Quran, is defined as "an ungodly focus on everyday concerns and earthly possessions."

> *Islam:* a theistic worldview centered on the life of the prophet Muhammad that derives its understanding of the world through the teachings of the Quran, Hadith, and *Sunnah.*

New Spirituality. While Muslims believe entertainment beguiles us into ignoring Allah, those of a New Spiritualist worldview think of it as keeping people from tapping into **higher consciousness**. In the Bhagavad Gita, Krishna said, "He who has let go of hatred, who treats all beings with kindness and compassion, who is always serene, unmoved by pain or pleasure, free of the 'I' and 'mine,' self-controlled, firm and patient, his whole mind is focused on me—that man is the one I love best."[67]

> *New Spirituality:* a pantheistic worldview that teaches that everyone and everything are connected through divine consciousness.

Filmmakers find the New Spiritualist story of the world a compelling "hero's journey" plotline in which we must rid ourselves of a sense of self to become enlightened.[68] Said George Lucas of his legendary *Star Wars* series, "With *Star Wars*, I consciously set about to re-create myths and the classic mythological motifs. I wanted to use those motifs to deal with issues that exist today.... I see *Star Wars* as taking all the issues that religion represents and trying to distill them down into a more modern and easily accessible construct.... I'm telling an old myth in a new way."[69] In describing the force to Luke Skywalker, Obi-Wan Kenobi said, "The Force is what gives a Jedi his power. It's an energy field created by all living things. It surrounds us and penetrates us; it binds the galaxy together."[70] This is very similar to the way New Spiritualists describe higher consciousness.

> *Higher Consciousness:* the state of awareness wherein individuals realize their divinity and the divine interconnectedness of all things.

We could examine more worldviews, but this brief sampling illustrates the split between the sacred and the secular. Islam and New Spirituality tend to be upper-story worldviews: this world is transitory; the otherworldly (Allah or higher consciousness) is real. Secular worldviews, such as Marxism and Postmodernism, form lower-story worldviews, distrusting any conception of a higher reality. Most worldviews tend to be one or the other.

So where does this leave the Christian worldview? Let's find out.

4. Why Should Christians Care?

In his letter to the fledgling church in Galatia (in modern-day Turkey), the apostle Paul contrasted the life of the "flesh"—living as if God doesn't exist—and the life of the "spirit"—living in full recognition of God's kingdom:

> Walk by the Spirit, and you will not gratify the desires of the flesh.… Now the works of the flesh are evident: sexual immorality, impurity, sensuality, idolatry, sorcery, enmity, strife, jealousy, fits of anger, rivalries, dissensions, divisions, envy, drunkenness, orgies, and things like these. I warn you, as I warned you before, that those who do such things will not inherit the kingdom of God. But the fruit of the Spirit is love, joy, peace, patience, kindness, goodness, faithfulness, gentleness, self-control; against such things there is no law. (Gal. 5:16, 19–22)

Clearly, Paul knew we can't make the fruit of the Spirit happen for ourselves. The Holy Spirit does it. But how can we know that the Holy Spirit is at work in our lives?

Some people say, "Paul was telling us that the things of this world are bad." This is an upper-story view of Christianity: what happens in creation is ultimately insignificant. But take a closer look. The fruit of the Spirit is borne *on this earth* for use *on this earth*. The Christian worldview isn't an upper-story or lower-story truth; it's a "whole-building" truth. The upper story and the lower story are resolved through the incarnation: God is with us in Jesus Christ.

> The Christian worldview is a "whole-building" truth. The upper story and the lower story are resolved through the incarnation: God is with us in Jesus Christ.

This is why Christians ought to care about the arts and entertainment: they are part of God's world and need to be redeemed. Rather than ignoring or trying to manipulate the arts and entertainment, Christians ought to ask how they might engage and transform them to the glory of Christ.

Movieguide reviewer Ted Baehr, whom we mentioned earlier, is also a professor of media studies, host of an awards show for family-friendly films, and a quiet presence inside the film business, encouraging movie studios to produce more family-friendly films. Baehr offers eight aspects of a Christian worldview of art and communication that dismantle the sacred-secular split:[71]

1. "God is the Author of creation and communication."

2. "God has given all authority in heaven and on earth to His Son, Jesus Christ."

3. "Art and communication are part of God's created order."

4. Art and communication work together.

5. Art and communication aren't just technical skills.

6. "Christ is the standard of excellence."

7. Art and communication are "worthy vocations" because they influence how people view reality.

8. "It is legitimate … to engage in art and communication without the need to include overt Christian symbolism or content."

If God is the creator and all authority has been given to Jesus, then through the Holy Spirit we have the power to bring the arts and entertainment under Christ's authority. Our goal isn't to hoodwink people but to bear God's image by producing creative, high-quality art that displays God's truth, beauty, and goodness to the whole world.

Does this grab your imagination? It does mine. But I still hesitate. How can I get involved without being overtaken by a decadent culture that appeals to my baser desires?

5. WHAT SHOULD CHRISTIANS DO?

Learn to Discern

As we discussed in chapter 4, living a redeemed life takes **discernment**, the "power to tell the good from the bad, the genuine from the counterfeit, and to prefer the good and the genuine to the bad and the counterfeit."[72] It takes training and thoughtfulness to prefer what is good. As John Stonestreet bluntly puts it, "What does it mean to find the truth in an entertainment driven society? If all you get out of life is what you see on TV, you will be dumb…. And it is a sin to be dumb."[73]

> *Discernment:* the ability to distinguish between truth and error, right and wrong, good and bad, and to prefer what is true, right, and good.

The world is full of false stories, stories that mislead people about what is actually true regarding God, the world, and our relationship to God and the world. Stripping false stories of bad language, violence, and sexuality doesn't render them true. Romance novels are a case in point. English professor Rosalie de Rosset thinks romance novels function as "porn for women," creating an unrealistic fantasy world in which men are strong and handsome and witty and would never think of watching football in their boxers while the dishes need to be done.

If the story of the world that romance novels tell is false, de Rosset wonders, does "Christianizing" them make it true? In the sense of avoiding degrading content, yes. But in the sense of moving readers deeper into real-world redemption, the answer is mixed. De Rosset says, "The difference between a good book and a bad book is that a good book takes you deeper into life and a bad book distracts you from life."[74] The same is true for movies and music. Christianity isn't sanitized Secularism. It's an entirely different story about why the world is the way it is and how we ought to live. Discerning people know this, and it changes their perspective in two significant ways.

1. Discerning people learn to see the worldviews behind the arts and entertainment. Dana Gioia, former chairman of the National Endowment for the Arts, said, "All art is a language—a language of color, sound, movement, or words When we immerse ourselves in a work of art, we enter into the artist's worldview. It can be an expansive and glorious worldview, or it can be a cramped, dehumanizing worldview."[75] Nancy Pearcey adds,

> T. S. Eliot once noted that the serious books we read do not influence us nearly as much as the books we read for fun (or the movies we watch for entertainment). Why? Because when we are relaxing, our guard is down and we engage in the "suspension of disbelief" that allows us to enter imaginatively into the story. As a result, the assumptions of the author or screenwriter may go unnoticed and seep all the more deeply into our consciousness.[76]

How do we discern whether a work of art or entertainment is expansive and glorious or cramped and dehumanizing? Pearcey suggests asking three questions in relation to the movies:[77]

- What worldview is the movie communicating?

- Are there elements that.are true?

- Are there elements that are false and destructive?

John Stonestreet offers the example of the *Ocean's Eleven* movies in which the audience was led to see a group of robbers as the "good guys."[78] Through humor and playing to the audience's desire to get back at mean bosses, the filmmakers left the impression that coveting, lying, and stealing are fine as long as they're done winsomely without hurting "innocent" people.

> Discerning people learn to see the worldviews behind the arts and entertainment.

But Pearcey's questions aren't just about moral plotlines. They get to the heart of how messages are *intentionally* crafted to elicit a certain response. Books like *Punk Marketing*, *Growth Hacker Marketing*, and *Social Media Marketing for Dummies* offer valuable insights into how to sell products, but they also reveal how marketers get us to buy things we don't want to fulfill needs we didn't realize we had to impress people we don't even like. If you find yourself easily swayed, start asking questions like these when you're presented with a person or company wanting you to do something:

- *What* do they want me to do?

- *Why* do they want me to do it?

- To what *motives* do they appeal?

- *How* do they make their case persuasive?

- Can they really *deliver* what they promise?

- What is *best*?

The last question is especially important. It's been said that the "good" is the enemy of the "best." Whether our actions hurt someone may be a good criteria for whether a law is needed against something, but it is an insufficient way to form a Christian worldview.

2. Discerning people choose their companions carefully. The people we hang out with shape our worldviews. Journalist Malcolm Gladwell warns, "We like to think of ourselves as autonomous and inner-directed, that who we are and how we act is something permanently set by our genes and our temperament.... We are actually powerfully influenced by our surroundings, our immediate context, and the personalities of those around us."[79] This is nowhere truer than in entertainment.

> "We are actually powerfully influenced by our surroundings, our immediate context, and the personalities of those around us."

In a recent webinar, I was asked, "If you could go back in time and give any advice to your sixteen-year-old self, what would it be?" I said I would tell my sixteen-year-old self to stop hanging out with bad influencers and instead seek wise mentors (not that my sixteen-year-old self would have listened to me). Here's why I would have given my younger self that advice: A study of young adults who stay involved in church revealed that they do so because of close relationships in which they learn to live thoughtfully, contribute meaningfully, succeed at work, and connect with Jesus in a deep and real way.[80] Their spiritual lives become more mature as they encounter caring people who act on their beliefs. These mentors, in turn, exert a profound influence in other areas, such as educational and career success.

On a surface level, we can know whether our companions are good or bad by whether they're influencing us to grow in God's image. Do they use language that brings life? Do they use their time as if their lives really matter?

At a deeper level, though, our companions influence us through their approaches to the world. Do they view the world with gratitude or resentment? Constant exposure to marketing can make us feel inadequate or dull or poor. We see how others live and feel shortchanged. Instead of being thankful for what we do have, we become bitter about what we lack.

> On a surface level, good companions influence us to grow in God's image. At a deeper level, though, our companions influence us through their approach to the world. Do they view the world with gratitude or resentment?

Gratitude—defined as "the capacity to feel the emotion of thankfulness on a regular and consistent basis, across situations and over time"—is one of life's most important character qualities.[81] Psychologists Robert Emmons and Cheryl Crumpler asked undergraduate students to complete a weekly log of their emotions, physical symptoms, and health behaviors. One-third were asked to record five major events or circumstances that affected them, one-third were asked to write down five hassles or minor stressors, and the remaining third were asked to write down five things for which they were grateful.

The study's results showed that those in the gratitude group felt better about their lives,

Gratitude: the quality or feeling of being thankful.

were more optimistic, reported fewer physical complaints, and spent more time exercising. Further, they were significantly more likely to report having made progress toward the goals they had written down at the beginning of the term.[82]

Gratitude is the wind in discernment's sails. Grateful people are higher in positive emotions and life satisfaction and lower in negative emotions, such as depression, anxiety, and envy. They're more focused on others, forgiving, agreeable, spiritually minded, and responsible.[83] Grateful people are full of hope, which inspires them to make wise decisions about where to direct their attention. This, as is turns out, is an often unnoticed key to thriving in an amusement-addicted world.

Work Hard at Something Valuable

Because entertainment ultimately fails to inject meaning into an otherwise empty life, we need a new approach. Mihaly Csikszentmihalyi suggests finding purposeful activities that produce a sense of well-being he calls "**flow**."[84] Purposeful

Flow: a state in which a person works intently on something fascinating and is able to work in a smooth rhythm, be creative, and recognize afterward that it was a pleasurable experience.

people are filled with joy, energy, satisfaction, and persistence in the face of obstacles.[85] Older adults who have purpose live longer.[86]

It takes hard work to achieve purpose. Good artists work hard. World-renowned pianist Van Cliburn practiced six hours a day, every day, including two hours of scales. Achieving purpose also takes dedication. Some say expertise is reached only after ten thousand hours of rigorous, focused practice.[87] Lots of people are talented, but talent isn't enough. The world of high performers is made up of thoughtful people who engage in "deliberate practice," getting continuous feedback so they can improve their performance.[88] "I'm a great believer in luck," Thomas Jefferson said, "and I find the harder I work, the more I have of it."

Aristotle said that virtues are "brought to completion through habit."[89] Working at developing good habits changes our wills. It also changes our bodies. Researchers found that through their rigorous training, London taxi drivers experienced a process in their brains called *myelination*, in which a substance called myelin built up around the nerve fibers and neurons in the part of their brains they were exercising (in this case, through spatial navigation). Myelination improves the speed at which connections happen in the brain. It happens in the brains of high performers, but only if the affected areas of their brains are stimulated millions of times through practice.[90] Life purpose isn't like winning the lottery. As the fiction writer Steven Pressfield says in *The War of Art*, "The Muse favors working stiffs. She hates prima donnas."[91]

Knowing all this, why do we still find life purpose so elusive? Mihaly Csikszentmihalyi's answer is simple: "Each of the flow-producing activities requires an initial investment of attention before it begins to be enjoyable."[92] Attention. We have to *stop* paying attention to meaningless pursuits and *start* paying attention to meaningful ones. Following are some thoughts about how to do that.

Discover your motivated abilities. Arthur F. Miller, who studied God's design for human beings, says we're all motivated to achieve certain outcomes, to fulfill specific purposes, as if pulled by a magnet.[93] As we exercise our motivations, patterns emerge that Miller calls "motivated abilities." He shows that motivated abilities are of supernatural design. Cultural circumstances cannot explain them, add to them, or take away from them. They exist even in hardship and tragedy. According to Miller, every invention, discovery, or creative act in all of human history goes back to the motivated abilities God has placed inside those inventors, explorers, and creators.[94]

People discover their motivated abilities as they try things and learn what returns energy to them and makes them feel more alive. Personally, I'm happiest when I'm teaching. When I see the "Aha!" look on the faces of my students, I know they're being changed.

> People discover their motivated abilities as they try things and learn what returns energy to them and makes them feel more alive.

My three siblings are all musicians, but with very different motivated abilities. My sister is a piano teacher. She loves seeing the joy others experience as they learn to play. One of my brothers is a worship leader, whose goal is to draw people closer to God and to one another. My other brother is an orchestra conductor, motivated to tackle complicated pieces of music and organize the efforts of very talented people to produce a result better than any of them could have imagined producing on their own.

It's not enough to just say, "I'm a musician." When you begin discovering what it is about music (or something else) that returns energy to you, you feel more alive. Be intentional to ask questions like these:

- What are some things that return energy to me and make me feel more alive?

- What am I learning from other people about how God made me?

- What do I long for?

- What truly makes me tick?

- What captivates my imagination?

Fight fragility. Nassim Nicholas Taleb is a pessimist. The thesis of his first book, *Black Swan*, is that major calamities in society are inevitable and unpredictable. In his second book,

AntiFragile, Taleb says we *can* do something about bad things happening, but it's not what people think. He notes that most people and organizations are fragile; that is, they crave stability and order, hate mistakes, and organize to avoid uncertainty. Some people and organizations move beyond fragility to become robust, creating their own sense of order and anticipating uncertainty. This is better but still not optimal, because in developing a hard shell that can't be crushed, robust people and organizations become slow and awkward. It's like driving a tank: you won't get hurt, but you also won't get around very well (and you'll never fit into a parking space).

But there is a third group of people, those Taleb calls the "antifragile." These are people who *grow* through instability, *thrive* in disorder, *love* mistakes, and *enjoy* uncertainty. Such people are resilient because rather than avoid risk, they embrace it. It's one of life's packages, says Taleb: "no stability without volatility."[95] This makes sense for Christians. God has created a dynamic world in which things change. He is in charge, but that doesn't mean we can control all our circumstances. Whether in war or in farming or in parenting or in business, the faster we can adapt to our circumstances, the more successful we'll be. Andrew Zolli, a business innovator and social-change theorist, calls this anti-fragile attitude *resilience*, defining it as "the capacity of a system, enterprise, or a person to maintain its core purpose and integrity in the face of dramatically changed circumstances."[96]

> God has created a dynamic world in which things change. The faster we can adapt to our circumstances, the more successful we'll be.

Resilient people know that the things we most often turn to for security cannot deliver it. As John Piper explains in *Don't Waste Your Life*, "The tragic hypocrisy is that the enchantment of security lets us take risks every day for ourselves but paralyzes us from taking risks for others on the Calvary road of love. We are deluded and think that it may jeopardize a security that in fact does not even exist."[97]

If you find yourself gravitating to the entertainment culture as a way of avoiding having to make risky decisions, ask yourself, *What am I afraid of? If I knew I could not fail, what would I attempt?* The goal isn't to avoid mistakes. "Forget mistakes," challenged British preacher F. W. Robertson. "[Retrieve] victory out of mistakes."[98]

> Escaping the world isn't the way to avoid Satan's tactics. Abiding in Christ is.

Jesus doesn't call us away from risk. Among his last words before going to the cross was a prayer for his disciples: "I do not ask that you take them out of the world, but that you keep them from the evil one" (John 17:15). Escaping the world isn't the way to avoid Satan's tactics. Abiding in Christ is.

Tackle bad habits. Researchers have found that of the actions people take every day, more than 40 percent are taken out of habit, not because people consciously choose them.[99] Just as a person experiencing electoral shock gets "stuck" to the thing shocking him or her, we get stuck to our habits and have to be "knocked away" to change our patterns.

Breaking habits requires willpower. Journalist Charles Duhigg describes a study in which people were asked to eat only the food assigned to them, either warm cookies or radishes, and then after several minutes, perform a problem-solving task. Those who were to eat only the radishes succeeded in avoiding the cookies, but they also gave up more easily on the assigned task. Once their willpower was depleted, they lost the ability to persevere.[100] Think of a bad habit you fall into. Is it easier to fall into that habit after you've exhausted your willpower by the end of the day? If you find yourself habitually going online at the end of the day, read a book instead. If you find yourself always looking at your phone, put it away and talk to someone instead.

Roy Baumeister and Julie Exline found that self-control operates like a strength: it's weaker after exertion, replenishes after rest, and becomes more durable with repeated exercise.[101] In one study, people who developed willpower muscles through a study-skills program not only improved their learning but also smoked and drank less, watched less television, got more exercise, and ate more healthful food.[102] It wasn't studying, per se, that gave them willpower but rather the fact they had done something intentional to gain control over an area of life that was out of control. Developing self-control in one area made it easier to be self-controlled overall.

> Self-control operates like a strength: it's weaker after exertion, replenishes after rest, and becomes more durable with repeated exercise.

Don't go it alone. As you might expect, the people who thrive most in adversity are those surrounded by a community, by mentors, and by those whose faith is robust enough to give meaning to otherwise inexplicable events and unendurable heartaches. These "high-functioning social networks" harness the strength of all the members to help each one of them bounce back.[103]

We see this in athletics. A track-and-field athlete will never run as fast as he otherwise could without a coach and teammates who challenge him to be his best. In a similar way, we need people—especially people who are older and have been where we would like to go—to walk with us. Rarely will we challenge ourselves as much as we need to be challenged to really grow. As Donald Miller says in his autobiography about making a movie, "Characters don't really choose to move. They have to be forced."[104]

Plus, we can really only pour into others if we're being poured into ourselves. As Howard Hendricks famously said, "We lead out of the overflow of a quality life." We have to be honest in asking questions like these:

- Where do I find myself struggling?

- What pain points do I feel in my faith journey?

- What kind of community do I have?

- What voices speak into my life and draw me deeper into my spiritual journey?

- What principles are my family, friends, and work centered on?

All of these steps—discovering our motivated abilities, fighting fragility, tackling our bad habits, and doing it all in the context of community—help put the entertainment culture in perspective. The bottom line is this: don't settle for bit parts in other stories; begin living the story God has given you.

6. Conclusion

Even secular researchers are now realizing that spiritually oriented lifestyles protect people from acting destructively.[105] Biblically speaking, we know life is tough, but God is always at work. As 2 Corinthians 4:16–18 says, "We do not lose heart.… For this light momentary affliction is preparing for us an eternal weight of glory beyond all comparison." Worship leader Matt Papa, echoing Saint Augustine, put it this way: "We were created by God and for God, and until we understand that, we are restless, brokenhearted glory chasers, always seeking something more."[106]

But the way of Christ isn't easy. There are no shortcuts. And even if there were, good stories aren't made by taking them. Donald Miller tells of attending a screenwriting workshop where the legendary Robert McKee described how characters in stories grow only by facing difficulties, and he observed that this is true in life as well as in the movies:

> "You have to go there. You have to take your character to the place where he just can't take it anymore." [McKee] looked at us with a tenderness we hadn't seen in him before. "You've been there, haven't you? You've been out on the ledge. The marriage is over now; the dream is over now; nothing good can come from this.… Joy is what you feel when the conflict is over. But it's conflict that changes a person." His voice was like thunder now. "You put your characters through hell. You put them through hell. That's the only way we change."[107]

> **We change through difficulty. God wants us to go deeper, to wait patiently through the silence, and to work hard while fully trusting him.**

We change through difficulty. Maybe this is why God often doesn't remove difficulties from us. He wants us to go deeper, to wait patiently through the silence, and to work hard while fully trusting him.

The relationship between difficulty and a beautiful life reminds me of Ed Catmull's story of how the emotionally complex animated feature *Up* was deepened into a story that meaningfully explored some of life's most tender themes. The movie tells the story of Carl Fredricksen, who copes with his wife's death by using helium balloons to turn their home into an airship and take the South American adventure they had long planned. As the house is hoisted aloft, Fredricksen finds himself accompanied by an insecure young Boy Scout, Russell, who is trapped on Fredricksen's porch.[108]

Catmull, president and cofounder of Pixar Animation Studios, says the story told in the film version looks nothing like the story as originally conceived. The original story featured a castle in the sky, two brothers quarreling over the throne, and a tall bird helping them understand each other. Only two elements of this original story survived: the title, *Up*, and the tall bird. If the original story had been carried through to the screen, it almost certainly would have been a failure. Few people are moved by castles in the sky and quarrels between spoiled rich kids. To arrive at a great story, the director, Pete Docter, had to go deep into his own pain and insecurities and ask, "What is this story *really* about?" He took a risk and dove deep. As a result, *Up* became a moving tale of finding significance, honor, caring, and hope.[109]

Sometimes our determination to settle for low-risk, small stories blinds us to what God is up to. Like Mia at the beginning of this chapter, will we continue to amuse ourselves with the fragments of other people's stories, or will we live God's bigger story?

ENDNOTES

1. Aldous Huxley, *Brave New World* (New York: Harper Perennial, 2006), 54.

2. Neil Postman, *Amusing Ourselves to Death: Public Discourse in the Age of Show Business* (New York: Penguin, 1986), vii–viii.

3. Michael Medved, *Hollywood vs. America: Popular Culture and the War on Traditional Values* (New York: HarperCollins, 1992), 11.

4. Nirvana, "Smells Like Teen Spirit," *Nevermind* © 1991, DGD.

5. John Piper, *Don't Waste Your Life* (Wheaton, IL: Crossway Books, 2003), 79.

6. If you're interested in exploring this subject further, check out the following passages: Genesis 4:21; 31:27; 1 Samuel 16:16, 23; 18:10; 1 Chronicles 16:5; 25:1–5; Psalms 33:2; 57:8; 81:2; 108:2; 144:9.

7. Plato, *The Republic*, vol. 2, *The Dialogues of Plato*, trans. B. Jowett (New York: Bigelow, Brown, 1914), 141.

8. Nancy Pearcey, *Saving Leonardo: A Call to Resist the Secular Assault on Mind, Morals, and Meaning* (Nashville: B&H, 2010), 26–27.

9. Pearcey, *Saving Leonardo*, chap. 4.

10. Pearcey, *Saving Leonardo*, 99–100.

11. Art critic Martha Bayles says, "Art became self-conscious when it began having radical doubts about its relationship with the truth." Martha Bayles, *Hole in Our Soul: The Loss of Beauty and Meaning in American Popular Music* (Chicago: University of Chicago Press, 1994), 33.

12. Brian Godawa, *Hollywood Worldviews: Watching Films with Wisdom and Discernment* (Downers Grove, IL: InterVarsity, 2002), 19–20.

13. Larry Norman, "Why Should the Devil Have All the Good Music?," *Only Visiting This Planet* © 1972, Verve.

14. Ravi Zacharias, "The Art of Losing One's Way," Ravi Zacharias International Ministries, April 1, 1998, http://rzim.org /just-thinking/the-art-of-losing-ones-way. Zacharias references Fyodor Dostoyevsky in making this statement. I haven't been able to find a reference from Dostoyevsky, but it's an interesting idea, and I'm comfortable attributing it to Zacharias.

15. Media Violence Commission, "Report of the Media Violence Commission," *Aggressive Behavior* 38 (2012): 335–41, www.israsociety.com/pdfs/Media%20Violence%20Commission%20final%20report.pdf.

16. Rollo May, *Love and Will* (New York: W. W. Norton, 1969), 14. See also Sigmund Freud's comments on how removing obstacles to sexual satisfaction lowers the libido and diminishes sex's psychical value (84).

17. Mina Cikara, Jennifer L. Eberhardt, and Susan T. Fiske, "From Agents to Objects: Sexual Attitudes and Neural Responses to Sexualized Targets," *Journal of Cognitive Neuroscience* 23, no. 3 (March 2011): 540–51, http://cnbc.cmu.edu/~cikaralab /Publications_files/Cikara%20et%20al.,%202011%20-%20JOCN_a.pdf, cited in Doug Eshleman, "Men View Half-Naked Women as Objects, Study Finds," *Daily Princetonian*, February 17, 2009, www.dailyprincetonian.com/2009/02/17/22773/.

18. C. S. Lewis, *Mere Christianity* (New York: HarperOne, 1980), 136–37.

19. Sherry Turkle, *Alone Together: Why We Expect More from Technology and Less from Each Other* (New York: Basic Books, 2011), 138.

20. C. S. Lewis, *The Weight of Glory: And Other Addresses* (New York: HarperCollins, 2001), 26.

21. Maggie Jackson, *Distracted: The Erosion of Attention and the Coming Dark Age* (Amherst, NY: Prometheus Books, 2008), 22.

22. Craig Gay, *The Way of the (Modern) World: Or, Why It Is Tempting to Live as If God Doesn't Exist* (Grand Rapids: Eerdmans, 1998), 201.

23. C. John Sommerville, *How the News Makes Us Dumb: The Death of Wisdom in an Information Society* (Downers Grove, IL: InterVarsity, 1999).

24. Sommerville, *How the News Makes Us Dumb*, chap. 3.

25. Anne-Marie Chang et al., "Evening Use of Light-Emitting eReaders Negatively Affects Sleep, Circadian Timing, and Next-Morning Alertness," *Proceedings of the National Academy of Sciences of the United States of America* 112, no. 4 (January 2015): 1233, www.pnas.org/content/112/4/1232.full.pdf.

26. John Stonestreet, "Amused to Death with Entertainment Culture" (lecture, Summit Ministries, Teach for Eternity Conference, October 2013).

27. Jeremy Begbie, "Sound Theology," *Christian Century*, November 13, 2007, 20, http://crcma.com /BegbieSoundTheologyChristianCentury%5B1%5D.pdf.

28. Begbie, "Sound Theology," 23.

29. Louis CK, interview by Conan O'Brien, *Late Night with Conan O'Brien*, 2013, quoted in Matt Papa, *Look and Live: Behold the Soul-Thrilling, Sin-Destroying Glory of Christ* (Bloomington, MN: Bethany House, 2014), 118.

30. Mihaly Csikszentmihalyi, *Finding Flow: The Psychology of Engagement with Everyday Life* (New York: Basic Books, 1997), 67.

31. Nielson, "An Era of Growth: Cross-platform Report Q4 2013," March 5, 2014, www.nielsen.com/us/en/insights /reports/2014/an-era-of-growth-the-cross-platform-report.html; Matt Petronzio, "U.S. Adults Spend 11 Hours per Day with Digital Media," Mashable, March 5, 2014, mashable.com/2014/03/05/american-digital-media-hours/.

32. Emily Adler, "Social Media Engagement: The Surprising Facts about How Much Time People Spend on the Major Social Networks," *Business Insider*, July 7, 2016, www.businessinsider.com/social-media-engagement-statistics-2013-12.

33. Eliana Dockterman, "Time Poll: What Makes Americans Happy?," *Time*, June 27, 2013, http://nation.time. com/2013/06/27/time-poll-what-makes-americans-happy/.

34. Stephen Marche, "Is Facebook Making Us Lonely?," *Atlantic*, May 2012, www.theatlantic.com/magazine/archive/2012 /05/is-facebook-making-us-lonely/308930/.

35. Begbie, "Sound Theology."

36. John Davies, "Nosce Teipsum" (Of Humane Knowledge), *The Complete Poems of Sir John Davies*, 2 vols., ed. Alexander B. Grosart (London: Chatto and Windus, 1876), 1:15–24. Posted online at "Sir John Davies: Nosce Teipsum," Luminarium: Anthropology of English Literature, www.luminarium.org/renlit/humane.htm.

37. Luton First, National Kids' Day survey, 2006, cited in "Being a Celebrity Is the 'Best Thing in the World' Say Children," *Daily Mail*, December 18, 2006. www.dailymail.co.uk/news/article-423273/Being-celebrity-best-thing-world-say-children .html.

38. Research cited in Brian Fung, "The Internet Isn't Making Us Dumb. It's Making Us Angry," *Washington Post*, September 16, 2013, www.washingtonpost.com/blogs/the-switch/wp/2013/09/16/the-internet-isnt-making-us-dumb-its -making-us-angry/.

39. Yalda T. Uhls et al., "Five Days at Outdoor Education Camp without Screens Improves Preteen Skills with Nonverbal Emotion Cues," *Computers in Human Behavior* 39 (October 2014): 387–92.

40. Peter Wood, *A Bee in the Mouth: Anger in America Now* (New York: Encounter Books, 2006), 2.

41. Wood, *Bee in the Mouth*, 4.

42. Stephen Galloway, "Steve Carell Says Comedy Has Become 'Uber-Cynical,' 'Borderline Mean,'" *Hollywood Reporter*, August 1, 2012, www.hollywoodreporter.com/news/steve-carell-emmy-nominee-not-driven-by-stardom-356375.

43. Daniel Johnson and Adam Pelser argue that ridicule and mockery of bad ideas have their place in apologetics. For example, the prophet Elijah mocked the prophets of Baal, wondering aloud whether Baal was busy or on vacation or going to the bathroom (see 1 Kings 18). John the Baptist and Jesus subtly mocked and even insulted those who were full of themselves. See Daniel M. Johnson and Adam C. Pelser, "Affective Apologetics: Communicating Truth through Humor, Ridicule, and Emotions," *Christian Research Journal* 35, no. 6 (2012): 44–48, www.equip.org/article /communicating-truth-through-humor-ridicule-and-emotions/.

44. Caroline Leaf, "You Are What You Think: 75–98% of Mental and Physical Illnesses Come from Our Thought Life!," *Dr. Leaf* (blog), November 30, 2011, http://drleaf.com/blog/you-are-what-you-think-75-98-of-mental-and-physical-illnesses -come-from-our-thought-life/.

45. Leaf, "You Are What You Think."

46. Elisa Neuvonen et al., "Late-Life Cynical Distrust, Risk of Incident Dementia, and Mortality in a Population-Based Cohort," *Neurology* 82, no. 24 (June 2014): 2205–12.

47. "George Lucas: Heroes, Myths, and Magic; About George Lucas," *American Masters*, January 13, 2004, www.pbs.org /wnet/americanmasters/database/lucas_g.html.

48. Godawa, *Hollywood Worldviews*, 25.

49. Courtney Love, quoted in Philip Weiss, "The Love Issue," *Spin* 14, no. 10 (October 1998): 100.

50. Neal Gabler, *Life the Movie: How Entertainment Conquered Reality* (New York: Vintage Books, 2000), 9.

51. Andrew Fletcher, *The Political Works of Andrew Fletcher, Esq.* (London: Bettesworth and Hitch, 1732), 372.

52. Plato, *Republic*, 140.54.

53. Eliana La Ferrara, Alberto Chong, and Suzanne Duryea, "Soap Operas and Fertility: Evidence from Brazil," *American Economic Journal: Applied Economics* 4, no. 4 (October 2012): 29.

54. Joseph Grenny et al., *Influencer: The New Science of Leading Change*, 2nd ed. (New York: McGraw-Hill, 2013), 168.

55. Leonard Goldberg, quoted in Ben Shapiro, *Primetime Propaganda: The True Hollywood Story of How the Left Took Over Your TV* (New York: Broadside Books, 2011), 63.

56. Stonestreet, "Amused to Death."

57. Ted Baehr, *The Media-Wise Family: A Christian Family Guide to Making Morally and Spiritually Responsible Decisions about Movies, TV, and Multimedia* (Colorado Springs, CO: Cook Communications, 1998), 204.

58. Baehr, *Media-Wise Family*, 195.

59. Marshall Kirk and Erastes Pill, "The Overhauling of Straight America," *Guide*, November 1978, http://library.gayhomeland.org/0018/EN/EN_Overhauling_Straight.htm; Erin Brownback, "Overhauling Straight America: A Guide for Gay Messaging" (paper, presented at Arizona State University, May 2015).

60. See the classic analysis of the show *Will and Grace*, which ran from 1998 to 2006, conducted by Edward Schiappa, Peter B. Gregg, and Dean E. Hewes, "Can One TV Show Make a Difference? *Will and Grace* and the Parasocial Contact Hypothesis," *Journal of Homosexuality* 51, no. 4 (2006): 15–37.

61. Baehr, *Media-Wise Family*, 196.

62. Jack Valenti, quoted in Medved, *Hollywood vs. America*, 22.

63. John Berger, *Ways of Seeing* (New York: Penguin, 1990), 86.

64. Fredric Jameson, "Interview with Xudong Zhang," in *Jameson on Jameson: Conversations on Cultural Marxism*, ed. Ian Buchanan (Durham, NC: Duke University Press, 2007), 191.

65. Glenn Ward, *Teach Yourself Postmodernism* (Chicago: McGraw-Hill, 2003), 51.

66. John Baudrillard, *Simulacra and Simulation: The Body, in Theory: Histories of Cultural Materialism*, trans. Sheila Faria Glaser (Ann Arbor: University of Michigan Press, 1994), 1. Fans of the movie *The Matrix* will remember the famous line where Morpheus says to Neo, "Welcome to the desert of the real" (*The Matrix*, directed by Lana Wachowski and Lilly Wachowski [Burbank, CA: Warner Brothers, 1999]). Now you know where the idea came from!

67. Stephen Mitchell, trans., *Bhagavad Gita* (New York: Three Rivers, 2002), 147.

68. Joseph Campbell, the celebrated author of *The Power of Myth* and *The Hero with a Thousand Faces*, believed that almost all hero myths—religious and secular, throughout history and across cultures—contain patterns of a hero's journey. Thus, all religions tell the same story. Campbell's conception of "god" is similar to the New Spiritualist view, as we saw in *Understanding the Times* in the chapter on the New Spiritualist worldview. See Joseph Campbell, *The Hero with a Thousand Faces*, 3rd ed. (Novato, CA: New World Library, 2008), 210.

69. Bill Moyers, "Of Myth and Men: A Conversation between Bill Moyers and George Lucas on the Meaning of the Force and the True Theology of *Star Wars*," *Time*, April 26, 1999, 92.

70. "Star Wars: Episode IV–A New Hope," *Star Wars*, directed by George Lucas (Lucasfilm/Twentieth Century Fox, 1977).

71. Ted Baehr, *How to Succeed in Hollywood (without Losing Your Soul)* (Washington, DC: WND Books, 2011), 13–14.

72. James Boswell, *Boswell's Life of Johnson*, ed. Charles Grosvenor Osgood (New York: Charles Scribner and Sons, 1917), xviii.

73. Stonestreet, "Amused to Death."

74. Rosalie de Rosset's chapel message at Bryan College in 2001, cited in Stonestreet, "Amused to Death."

75. Dana Gioia, quoted in Pearcey, *Saving Leonardo*, 76. Pearcey slightly condensed Gioia's remarks.

76. Pearcey, *Saving Leonardo*, 253–54.

77. Pearcey, *Saving Leonardo*, 253.

78. John Stonestreet, "Moving Worldviews to Living Well," presentation at Summit Ministries' Teach for Eternity conference, Orlando, Florida, October 2013.

79. Malcolm Gladwell, *The Tipping Point: How Little Things Can Make a Big Difference* (New York: Back Bay, 2002), 258–59.

80. Research for Faith That Lasts Project, 2007–2012, Barna Research Group, "5 Reasons Millennials Stay Connected to Church," Barna.org, September 17, 2013, www.barna.org/barna-update/millennials/635-5-reasons-millennials-stay-connected-to-church#.U5ImXPldWSo.

81. Robert A. Emmons and Cheryl A. Crumpler, "Gratitude as a Human Strength: Appraising the Evidence," *Journal of Social and Clinical Psychology* 19, no. 1 (2000): 56–69.

82. Emmons and Crumpler, "Gratitude as a Human Strength."

83. See Robert A. Emmons, *The Psychology of Ultimate Concerns: Motivation and Spirituality in Personality* (New York: Guilford, 1999), 167–73; Jeffrey J. Froh, William J. Sefick, and Robert A. Emmons, "Counting Blessings in Early Adolescents: An Experimental Study of Gratitude and Subjective Well-Being," *Journal of School Psychology* 46, no. 2 (April 2008): 213–33; Lynne M. Andersson, Robert A. Giacalone, and Carole L. Jurkiewicz, "On the Relationship of Hope and Gratitude to Corporate Social Responsibility," *Journal of Business Ethics* 70, no. 4 (February 2007): 401–9; Michael E. McCullough et al., "Is Gratitude a Moral Affect?," *Psychological Bulletin* 127, no. 2 (March 2001): 249–66.

84. Csikszentmihalyi, *Finding Flow*, 6.

85. William Damon, *The Path to Purpose: How Young People Find Their Calling in Life* (New York: Free Press, 2008).

86. Monika Ardelt, "Effects of Religion and Purpose in Life on Elders' Subjective Well-Being and Attitudes toward Death," *Journal of Religious Gerontology* 14, no. 4 (June 2003): 55–77.

87. For more information, see Malcolm Gladwell, *Outliers: The Story of Success* (New York: Little, Brown, 2008), 41.

88. Geoff Colvin, *Talent Is Overrated: What Really Separates World-Class Performers from Everybody Else* (New York:

Penguin, 2008), 66–72, 78.

89. Aristotle, *Nicomachean Ethics*, trans. C. D. C. Reeve (Indianapolis: Hackett, 2014), 21.

90. Colvin, *Talent Is Overrated*, 103–4.

91. Steven Pressfield, *The War of Art: Break through the Blocks and Win Your Inner Creative Battles* (New York: Black Irish Entertainment, 2002), 74.

92. Csikszentmihalyi, *Finding Flow*, 68.

93. Arthur F. Miller, *Designed for Life: Hard-Wired, Empowered, Purposed—the Birthright of Every Human Being* (Charlotte, NC: Life(n) Media, 2006), 42.

94. Miller, *Designed for Life*, 45.

95. Nassim Nicholas Taleb, *Antifragile: Things That Gain from Disorder* (New York: Random House, 2014), 107.

96. Andrew Zolli, with Ann Marie Healy, *Resilience: Why Things Bounce Back* (New York: Simon and Schuster, 2012), 7.

97. Piper, *Don't Waste Your Life*, 81.

98. F. W. Robertson, *F. W. Robertson's Sermons on Religion and Life*, vol. 1 (Whitefish, MT: Kessinger Publishing, 2007), 79.

99. Studies cited in Charles Duhigg, *The Power of Habit: Why We Do What We Do in Life and Business* (New York: Random House, 2014), xvi.

100. Study cited in Duhigg, *Power of Habit*, 135–37.

101. Roy F. Baumeister and Julie Juola Exline, "Self-Control, Morality, and Human Strength," *Journal of Social and Clinical Psychology* 19, no. 1 (2000): 29–42.

102. Duhigg, *Power of Habit*, 139.

103. Zolli, *Resilience*, 129.

104. Donald Miller, *A Million Miles in a Thousand Years: What I Learned While Editing My Life* (Nashville: Thomas Nelson, 2009), 101.

105. Emmons, *Psychology of Ultimate Concerns*, 171. Emmons's comments reference Raymond F. Paloutzian and Lee A. Kirkpatrick, "Introduction: The Scope of Religious Influences on Personal and Societal Well-Being," *Journal of Social Issues* 51, no. 2 (Summer 1995): 1–11.

106. Papa, *Look and Live*, 33.

107. Miller, *A Million Miles*, 180.

108. *Up*, directed by Pete Docter and Bob Peterson (Emeryville, CA: Walt Disney/Pixar, 2009).

109. Ed Catmull, *Creativity, Inc.: Overcoming the Unseen Forces That Stand in the Way of True Inspiration* (New York: Random House, 2014), 148–151; see also "*Up* (2009 Film): Production; Development," Wikipedia, accessed July 15, 2016, https://en.wikipedia.org/wiki/Up_(2009_film)#Development.

CHAPTER 8

8

THE VALUE OF HUMAN LIFE

1. A CULTURE OF DEATH

January 2011: Two undercover investigators disguised as a pimp and a prostitute walked into a Planned Parenthood clinic in Perth Amboy, New Jersey, claiming to operate a sex-trafficking ring of young teenage women who were in the country illegally. Shockingly, instead of acting out of concern for the would-be sex slaves, the clinic manager offered "business" advice to their captors.

Posted on YouTube, the video of the conversation exposed the seamy underside of the world's largest and most prestigious abortion business. What follows is a partial transcript of the conversation, edited with ellipses for the sake of space (the Planned Parenthood clinic manager's comments are marked as "PP"):[1]

Pimp: Um, this is all confidential ... alright?

PP: M'hm, yes.

Pimp: OK. Uhh so, we're involved in sex work, alright, and there are some girls that we manage.... Now the thing is, um, okay, so some of 'em are like, eh, some of 'em are young, they're kind of like, something like 15, 14, and then some of them don't speak any English.... You know, cause they're not even from here.... What if they need an abortion though?

PP: ...If they come in for pregnancy testing—um, s***, at that point it still needs to be, you never got this from me, just to make all of our lives easier [pulls out a piece of paper and circles an address].... They won't need ID ... their protocols aren't as strict as ours, and they don't get audited the same way that we do....

Pimp: Ok, take them to the Metropolitan Medical Associates? ... Is there any difference between the ones that are like 15 and 14? Will there be anything different that they need?

PP: No the only thing is the fees are cheaper....

Pimp: Ok.

PP: [Nineteen] and under, here's a thing too. If they're minors, just tell them to put down that they're students.

Pimp: Students?

PP: Yeah, just kind of play along ... that they're students. We want to make it look as legit as possible.... I'm assuming most of them are coming in illegally, right?

Pimp: Exactly, exactly ...

PP: Exactly, and you just kind of, so the whole thing is with me we already know, I see you, we already know we're gonna kind of alter the story and kinda see what we can do to kinda tweak information....

Pimp: Yeah, we don't want people getting all in our business and all of that ...

PP: Yeah, you know, just get exams, don't ask me a bunch of questions.... Worst ever comes to worst, you guys come see me. You get to this point, if I think there's gonna be

THE VALUE OF HUMAN LIFE

a massive bump in the road, I'll jump in, we'll see what I can do, with you know, nobody looking and s*** like that. But that's why you come in you ask for me only....

Pimp: We might just need to uh, is there any way we could stream line this? Like, holla at you, slide you a little, you know, and you can just get 'em streamlined—

PP: We can solve— Depending on what the situation is, we might be able to do that.

Pimp: We could slide you like a $100, to just like uh, help us.

PP: Exactly, and then, I'm sure you guys are going to have a decent amount of money.

It's stunning. The manager of this clinic worked for a company that receives more than half a billion dollars a year in federal funding, yet she not only failed to protect what are clearly being described as exploited young women, but she also conspired in a cover-up. It's horrific.

Of course, Planned Parenthood promptly fired the woman and claimed this was an isolated incident. However, the undercover investigators immediately released videos of three similar conversations in other clinics in which Planned Parenthood employees willingly aided the "pimp" to sexually traffic minors. Such gross misconduct indicates how the drive to sexual freedom creates a culture of exploitation and, in the case of **abortion**, death.

> *Abortion:* any medical procedure or medication that deliberately ends the life of an unborn human being.

Subsequent undercover stings have shown abortion providers willing to profit from the sale of body parts from aborted fetuses—something that is clearly illegal. One video showed an abortionist sifting through a tray of body parts. At one point she picked up a leg and exclaimed, "And another boy!"[2]

We live in a culture of death. The aim of this chapter is simple and straightforward. First, we'll outline how life is devalued today through abortion, euthanasia, and other biotechnologies. Second, we'll make a case for why Christians should defend the specialness of every human life. Finally, we'll suggest ways Christians can effectively do so.

> Undercover stings have shown abortion providers willing to profit from the sale of body parts from aborted fetuses.

2. ABORTION IN AMERICA

In January of 1973, thirty-eight years to the month before the Perth Amboy Planned Parenthood sting, the United States Supreme Court voted 7–2 to strike down a Texas law prohibiting abortion. The case, called *Roe v. Wade*, gave legal cover to abortion and immediately increased its occurrence. The Centers for Disease Control and Prevention (CDC) reported 615,831 legal abortions in 1973. Three years later, totals jumped to 988,267 abortions. By 1977, there were more than 1 million abortions a year, reaching a peak of over 1.4 million in 1990.

Though the number of reported abortions a year has declined slightly every year since then, the total is still between 800,000 and 900,000 per year.[3] These figures are so vast that many people have lost the ability to care. It reminds me of what Joseph Stalin reportedly told Winston Churchill: "When one man dies it is a tragedy. When thousands die it's statistics."[4]

In addition to the culture-wide acceptance of abortion on demand are such gruesome practices as **late-term abortion**, in which the unborn are partially birthed, their skulls are crushed, and their brains are sucked out to ensure they're born dead.[5] Once that sort of barbarism is tolerated, the lines between life and death get very murky indeed.

> *Late-Term Abortion:*
> **any abortion performed within the second or third trimester of a pregnancy.**

The trial of Kermit Gosnell, for example, exposed an abortionist who, on at least twenty-one occasions, killed infants beyond the twenty-four-week state ban by "snipping" the partially born infants' spinal cords with scissors. Gosnell operated under a valid medical license, but state officials had ignored him for three decades before he was finally brought to justice. In Pennsylvania, one cannot operate a food cart or nail salon without inspection, but the political pressure surrounding the abortion issue enabled state officials to ignore what one investigator coined Gosnell's "house of horrors."[6]

Those who assumed the *Roe v. Wade* decision would settle the abortion debate were wrong. A January 2013 Pew Research Center survey showed that 47 percent of Americans still think abortion is "morally wrong," compared to 13 percent who say it's "morally acceptable" and 27 percent who say it's "not a moral issue."[7] In the past few years, state legislatures have passed hundreds of bills aimed at reducing the frequency of abortion on demand.

In fact, proponents of legalized, elective abortion are growing alarmed. Forty years after the landmark *Roe v. Wade* decision, *Time* magazine's cover story read, "Abortion-rights activists won an epic victory in *Roe v. Wade*. They've been losing ever since."[8] While this certainly overstates the case, two trends are positive. First, pro-life students do seem better equipped to engage the issue than their abortion-choice counterparts. In a *Los Angeles Times* op-ed, abortion-choice advocates Frances Kissling and Kate Michelman lamented that a new generation of pro-life advocates present "a sophisticated philosophical and political challenge" to what once was considered a settled debate.[9]

Second, support for late-term abortion has slipped since the debates over **partial-birth abortion** in the 1990s.

> *Partial-Birth Abortion:*
> **a medical procedure in which a living fetus is partially extracted from the birth canal before being exterminated.**

Both trends are encouraging. But support for abortion in general seems to be growing. According to a UCLA study of incoming college freshmen, "nearly two-thirds of respondents (63.5%) believe that abortion should be legal." They also say they intend to engage politically to support causes they believe in.[10]

The value of human life is a worldview issue drawing on philosophy, science, and theology. Human rights and moral values are at stake. As we'll see in the next section, it's a problem sparked by the **sexual revolution** that involves how people see the value of persons, scientific issues in biotechnology, and even end-of-life issues.

3. What Is the Problem?

The Sexual Revolution and Its Consequences

That people want to end unwanted pregnancies, use technology to gain power over nature, and set aside those lives they see as lacking value is nothing new. What *is* new is the secular impulse driving the issues today. The word *secular* (based on the Latin word *saeculum*, meaning "to an age") implies that eternal considerations, such as what God thinks and what happens after death, are irrelevant to the way we ought to live.

The grip of **Secularism** on American culture has grown steadily since the 1930s, when a group of scholars drafted a document called the "**Humanist Manifesto**."[11] While it never garnered the attention *The Communist Manifesto* attracted, the "Humanist Manifesto" gave voice to a growing sentiment that the God-default switch should be turned off.

The signers of the "Humanist Manifesto" advocated **Secular Humanism** and rejected ethical codes like the Ten Commandments. Paul Kurtz, the late philosophy professor at the State University of New York (SUNY), contended that a code of ethics derived from a supernatural or religious base is repressive and immoral in that it "suppress[es] vital inclinations."[12]

Moral codes about sex were particularly offensive to Secular Humanists. To be clear, humanity has never needed encouragement to violate commands regarding fornication and adultery. Yet the Secular Humanists broke ground by advocating the abolition of traditional sexual mores. Lester Kirkendall, for instance, identified homosexuality, bisexuality, pre- and extramarital sexual relations, and "genital associations" (though no one is quite sure what the latter means) as behaviors that should no longer be subject to moral pressure.[13]

For some, like Margaret Sanger (1879–1966), sexual freedom brought up a practical concern: How can we encourage people to have sex without moral restraint and yet prevent "inferior" people from reproducing?[14] Most notoriously, Sanger's racist Negro Project encouraged birth control and even forced sterilization for blacks.[15] Out of Sanger's efforts, a new organization was born: Planned Parenthood. This new organization, according to Sanger, would provide birth control, help young people "obtain sex satisfaction before marriage," and "prevent fear and guilt."[16]

> *Humanist Manifesto:* the title of three manifestos laying out a Secular Humanist worldview: *Humanist Manifesto I* (1933), *Humanist Manifesto II* (1973), and *Humanist Manifesto 2000*. The central theme of all three is the elaboration of a philosophy and value system that do not include belief in God.

> *Secular Humanism:* a religious and philosophical worldview that makes humankind the ultimate norm by which truth and values are to be determined; a worldview that reveres human reason, evolution, naturalism, and secular theories of ethics while rejecting every form of supernatural religion.

With the aid of the media and popular culture, the sexual revolution largely achieved its aims, increasing sexual activity outside of marriage and redefining sexual norms within a generation.

Ideas have consequences, though, and overturning sexual morality also overturned long-established agreement about what makes human life valuable. Even with an increase in birth control (the most common forms of which have a failure rate of 9 to 28 percent),[17] the number of out-of-wedlock births rose sharply. All of a sudden there were lots more babies, but many were considered "unwanted" because they disrupted life plans and restricted freedom.

As the number of out-of-wedlock births rose, access to elective abortion rose as well.

> **Ideas have consequences, and overturning sexual morality also overturned long-established agreement about what makes human life valuable.**

According to the proabortion Guttmacher Institute, in spite of the widespread use of contraception, three out of ten women have had an abortion by age forty-five.[18] In fact, 51 percent of women who have abortions report using contraception in the month they conceived.[19]

As we'll see, nearly everyone—including those who support the availability of elective abortion—recognizes that abortion destroys a human life. By pressing forward anyway, sexual "revolutionaries" have dismantled a long-established understanding of human value, which has had startling effects, including tinkering with human life itself and a whole new approach to end-of-life issues, such as euthanasia and physician-assisted suicide.

The Dismantling of Human Value

No one doubts that a woman pregnant with a child is carrying a human being. Ultrasound technology allows mothers, grandparents, siblings, and everyone else to see a "**fetus**" as a

> *Fetus:* an unborn human being who is at least eight weeks from conception.

living, developing human being. More than three-fourths of women who visit a pro-life pregnancy center and see an ultrasound image of their child reject abortion. Former abortion doctor Joseph Randall admitted that in his clinic women were never allowed to look at the ultrasound "because we knew that if they so much as heard the heart beat, they wouldn't want to have an abortion."[20]

Here's what mothers see in an ultrasound:[21]

- Week four: "heart begins to beat"

- Week five: eyes, hands, and legs start developing

- Week six: "brain waves are detectible"

- Week seven: eyelids, toes, and nose forms; baby begins kicking and swimming

- Week eight: "every organ is in place; bones [and] fingerprints begin to form"

THE VALUE OF HUMAN LIFE

- Weeks nine and ten: "teeth begin to form, [and] fingernails develop"; babies use facial expressions

- Week eleven: babies can grasp objects placed in their hands, as discovered when surgeries have been performed on unborn children.

Keep in mind that most women don't even discover they're pregnant until weeks four to seven. By that time, the developing fetus is clearly a living human being.

But a fetus being a living human being does not, from the standpoint of a secular worldview, mean it has value. If nothing outside of the material world exists—if there is no God and no transcendent truth—then a human isn't valued as a person unless he or she operates at full human capacity or shows value to society. These beliefs are called the **performance view of human life** and the **utilitarian view of human life**.

> *Performance View of Human Life:* the belief that human beings have value only if they meet certain conditions (e.g., self-awareness, rationality, sentience, etc.).

The Performance View

Rather than seeing humans as being "endowed by their Creator with certain unalienable Rights," as the American Declaration of Independence states, the performance view says that humans have value only if they meet certain conditions. The **endowment view of human life** includes everyone, notes philosophy professor Christopher Kaczor, but the performance view *excludes* those who don't meet certain characteristics, which at various times could include "self-awareness, rationality, sentience, desirability, ethnicity, economic productivity, gender, nationality, native language, beauty, age, health, religion, race, ethnicity, fertility, birth, and national origin."[22] If you don't meet certain qualifications, the performance view says, you aren't deserving of respect and dignity.

The Utilitarian View

Utilitarianism can be traced back hundreds of years to a philosopher named John Stuart Mill. Today, though, a Princeton University philosopher named Peter Singer is perhaps the most well-known proponent of the utilitarian view. Utilitarianism is based on the principle of equal consideration of interests, which Singer defines as follows: "The essence of the principle of equal consideration of interests is that we give equal weight in our moral deliberations to the like interests of all those affected by our actions."[23] Simply put, if those around us stand to lose more than we stand to gain by our existence, then it's better for us not to exist.

Singer, to his credit, is consistent with the ugly implications of his philosophy. He advocates **infanticide**, or the killing of infants. Specifically, Singer advocates eliminating severely disabled infants but acknowledges that

> *Infanticide:* the deliberate killing of a human child within one year of birth.

his standard cannot distinguish between killing a disabled newborn and one born in perfect health:

> The difference between killing disabled and normal infants lies, not in any supposed right to life that the latter has and the former lacks, but in other considerations about killing. Most obviously, there is a difference that often exists in the attitudes of the parents.... They are likely to have planned for the child. The mother has carried it for nine months. From birth, a natural affection begins to bind the parents to it. So one important reason why it is normally a terrible thing to kill an infant is the effect the killing will have on its parents.[24]

So to Singer, it's wrong to kill an infant not because of the child's right to life but because the parents might have an emotionally negative response to the killing. Presumably, if the parents wouldn't have such a response, the killing wouldn't be wrong. Singer has proposed that parents be given twenty-eight days to decide whether an infant has a right to life.[25]

What the Performance and Utilitarian Views Have in Common

Both the performance view and the utilitarian view make human value a matter of degrees.

Both the performance view and the utilitarian view make human value a matter of degrees. For instance, if someone doesn't have the consciousness to express a basic desire to live, that person doesn't have a sufficient degree of humanity to warrant life. As Michael Tooley explains,

> First, I think that an entity cannot have a right to continued existence—or, indeed, any rights at all—unless it either has, or has had, conscious desires, since it seems to me both that something can have rights at a given time only if there can be things that are in its interest at that time, and that the morally relevant concept of interest presupposes the existence of desires.[26]

This reasoning leads straight to elective abortion. Unborn humans who are unwanted and cannot stand up for their own interests aren't valuable humans according to the performance and utilitarian views.

But as philosopher Francis Beckwith points out, "Intrinsic value is not a degreed property; you either have it or you don't."[27] If human value is based *in any way* on degree, then there is no solid basis for all people having equal worth.[28] Self-aware people might be seen as more valuable. Immature people might be seen as less valuable. People whose brains are still developing—that is, children—might be seen as less valuable than those whose brains have already developed. It's up to "society" to decide whether you pass muster or not.

Abandoning the idea that all humans are created equal leads to disturbing conclusions. Philosopher Jeff McMahan, who supports abortion on demand, argues that "the properties on which our moral status appears to supervene are all matters of degrees," but then he admits,

"It is hard to avoid the sense that our egalitarian commitments rest on distressingly insecure foundations.[29]

That McMahan would acknowledge the wrongness of the human-by-degrees view and still embrace it calls to mind the sinister story in George Orwell's book *Animal Farm*, in which the animals rebel against the farmer in a bid for equality, only to find that some animals (the pigs) see themselves as superior. The firm commandment "All animals are equal" soon gives way to an amendment: "All animals are equal, but some animals are more equal than others." Once equality was a matter of degrees in Orwell's story, "it did not seem strange when next day the pigs who were supervising the work of the farm all carried whips in their trotters."[30] Equality is impossible if people are human by degrees.

Technology makes it even easier to diminish the value of life. The clinical taking of human life seems less cruel. And if less cruel, it's easier to make it more clinical. This ever-accelerating process poses a serious threat to civilization, especially when we consider how easy technology makes it to create human life as well as destroy it.

Embryos and Technology: A Bioethics Problem

Through **contraception**, the sexual revolution sought to make it easy for people to have sex without becoming pregnant. Now, through technology, it has become possible to become pregnant without having sex. Scientific advances in the past thirty years have enabled technicians to combine human ovum and sperm to create embryos that can be implanted in a woman's uterus. Women who otherwise have difficulty conceiving have found this to be beautiful and life giving. Yet in the process, technicians often create excess embryos, all of whom are living human beings, and destroy or store the ones not "needed."

An **embryo** is tiny. Embryos aren't recognizable as human beings, but that is what they are. Indeed, that's why technicians "created" them in the first place. Because of this, many people have no problem destroying the ones they don't need. The destruction of human embryos has become a well-funded, scientifically respectable industry.[31]

The danger in producing more embryos than needed for implantation isn't primarily medical, though there are always medical risks with biotechnological experimentation. Nor is it a question of a woman's "right to privacy." Says ethicist Leon Kass, it is an issue of "trivializing the matter for the sake of rendering it manageable."[32] We may treat the destruction of human embryos as no big deal, but in the process we forfeit the very idea of what it means to be human.

Today, embryos are destroyed to harvest their stem cells. A **stem cell** is an undifferentiated cell that has the ability to develop into many kinds of cells, such as skin

> *Contraception:* any device, drug, procedure, or technique that is used to prevent pregnancy.

> *Embryo:* an unborn human being who is between four days and eight weeks from conception.

> *Stem Cell:* an undifferentiated cell that has the ability to replicate and develop into another kind of cell (e.g., skin cell, blood cell, or nerve cell).

cells, blood cells, and nerve cells. Stem cells are present in embryos as well as other sources in the human body. Because they're capable of renewing themselves and replenishing damaged or destroyed cells,[33] the healing potential of stem cells is tremendous, even for seemingly unhealable diseases and injuries such as multiple sclerosis, cerebral palsy, spinal-cord injuries, and sickle-cell anemia.

Embryonic Stem Cell: **a pluripotent stem cell harvested from human embryos.**

Unlike undifferentiated stem cells, an **embryonic stem cell** is harvested exclusively from a human embryo. Embryonic stem cells are thought to have greater potential than stem cells gathered from nonembryonic sources because they are "pluripotent" (they can "give rise to any type of cell in the body") and "immortal" (they can be "grown in cell culture for an extended period of time").[34] The ethical controversy surrounding the use of embryonic stem cells arose because initially it was thought impossible to obtain such cells without destroying young embryos.

In spite of this potential destruction, the great promise of embryonic stem cells once led many well-known people to advocate their use in treating Parkinson's disease (Michael J. Fox), severe spinal-cord injuries (the late Christopher Reeve), and Alzheimer's disease (Nancy Reagan, the late wife of president Ronald Reagan). Those who opposed such research were cast as villains who didn't care about people with serious illnesses.

But defenders of the intrinsic value of humans don't oppose stem-cell research. They *support* stem-cell research that doesn't destroy embryos, such as procedures that obtain stem cells from adults or harvest them from umbilical-cord blood, or what is called "induced pluripotent stem-cell research" (IPSC), which uses a process to induce mature cells to return to an immature stage, where they may be able to form any cell in the body. IPSC research is particularly promising because it violates no moral principles. Instead of destroying embryos to get cells, they can be obtained harmlessly from adult donors.[35] Research is developing so rapidly that by the time you read this, IPSC may have made embryonic-destructive research an irrelevant issue. Still, though, the issue of creating and destroying embryos will be with us as long as couples undergo in vitro fertilization to try to become pregnant and as long as research on therapeutic cloning continues.

The question of humanness is still the central issue. Do we believe it's legitimate to use and destroy one human life to service the needs of another? Yet it isn't just a beginning-of-life issue; it's an end-of-life issue too, which brings us to the issue of euthanasia.

Euthanasia

The word **euthanasia** comes from a Greek word that means "easy death." Also known as mercy killing, euthanasia has become an increasingly important issue as medical technology allows the prolonging of natural life.[36] Euthanasia brings up a whole host of questions: Should a life ever be taken? Does a patient have the right to decide when to end his or her life? Can another person *beside* the patient decide whether the patient's life ought to be ended? Whose life is

Euthanasia: **the practice whereby a physician intentionally aids in ending the life of a suffering patient.**

THE VALUE OF HUMAN LIFE

it anyway? How do we assess whether a person's quality of life makes him or her unworthy to be kept alive? When do we cross the line between deciding not to *prolong* life and deciding to actively *terminate* it?[37]

There are two kinds of euthanasia in question:[38]

1. Active euthanasia. Active euthanasia involves a physician taking terminal action against a patient—for example, ending the patient's life by administering a lethal dose of medicine or writing a prescription for lethal drugs the patient can self-administer. This latter practice is called **physician-assisted suicide**.

2. Passive euthanasia. Passive euthanasia involves withholding treatment with the intent of causing the patient's death—for example, withholding nutrition and hydration.

In both circumstances, the intent is for the patient to die. To some, this is hardly controversial: we put suffering pets to sleep out of mercy, so why would it be wrong to help terminally ill *people* die with dignity? Why should we treat Grandma any worse than we treat Grover?

The concern about ending life with mercy and dignity is legitimate. Our technology can extend our lives beyond when many would like them to end. Think, for example, of people with dementia who are radically dependent on others for their most basic needs and live lives governed by medical treatment. If you knew you'd be putting other people in that position, would you want your life to continue?

My friend Jay Watts, who helped substantially with the research for this chapter, faced this situation when his father died. Jay was forced to decide whether to cease certain medical measures that weren't helping his father recover or even stabilize but were merely artificially prolonging his life for a few hours.

Intent is the key. The traditional **Hippocratic oath** that doctors take includes the commitment to "do no harm." The proper intents of medicine are to heal and to comfort. But as Agneta Sutton points out, when we act on a so-called right to be killed, we're failing the patient.[39] By accepting killing as a legitimate medical treatment, we cross a line of intent. Once we've done so, the only remaining questions are who gets to decide and what constitutes a malady for which death is a proper "treatment."

> *Active Euthanasia:* the practice whereby a physician administers a lethal dose of medication with the intent of ending a suffering patient's life.

> *Physician-Assisted Suicide:* the practice whereby a physician writes a lethal prescription that is intended to end a suffering patient's life.

> *Passive Euthanasia:* the practice whereby a physician withholds treatment with the intent of ending a suffering patient's life.

> *Hippocratic Oath:* attributed to Hippocrates in the fourth or third century BC; the pledge taken by physicians outlining the obligations and proper ethical conduct of those who treat patients.

That line has definitely been crossed around the world. The Groningen protocol in the Netherlands tried to establish some guidelines by which infants can be euthanized.[40] Soon after, the *Journal of Medical Ethics* focused on the permissibility of "after-birth abortions" (infanticide).[41] Now doctors are actively euthanizing elderly patients outside of the accepted and legal protocol in both the Netherlands and Belgium.[42] Clearly, some doctors have decided that "right to die" means "right to kill."

Some of the pressure on ill patients to submit to death comes from the scarcity of medical resources. Many Western nations have highly regulated state-subsidized health-care systems in which doctors are pressured not to spend limited resources to prolong the lives of people they think are going to die soon anyway.

Obviously, though, saying to a patient, "You're going to die, so it might as well be sooner rather than later" is unacceptable. A cryptic kind of language has developed to make the decision to shorten life seem more acceptable to patients and their families. Instead of saying, "I think we should stop medical treatment," a doctor might say, "Wouldn't you like to go home to be with your family?" In a *New York Times* interview, Margaret Battin, a philosopher and medical professor, said that using language in this way can hide important information from patients: "If a doctor says, 'I can see you're in pain[;] let's start a morphine drip,' a patient may not realize that the pain medication will shorten his life.... The patient is being invited to make a choice without understanding what the stakes are."[43]

> Simply saying something in a merciful way doesn't make it an act of mercy. Indeed, it can have the unmerciful effect of justifying other acts of euthanasia.

Simply saying something in a merciful way doesn't make it an act of mercy. Indeed, it can have the unmerciful effect of justifying other acts of euthanasia, such as for people who suffer from depression and other medically treatable conditions from which they could recover, given time.

This doesn't mean patients in pain need to suffer. A patient in the final stages of terminal cancer may request increasingly large doses of morphine to control pain, even though the higher dose might (though not necessarily) hasten death. In this particular case, the intent of the physician is to relieve pain and provide the best care possible under the circumstances. Though death is foreseen, it isn't intended. In the end, the patient dies from her underlying illness, not because the doctor intentionally killed her.[44]

Adding "death" to the menu of treatment options makes it seem as if a person's current level of happiness or perceived quality of life or productivity are medical issues when, in fact, they're ethical ones. And once *quality* of life becomes the basis for *value* of life, we're right back to the performance or utilitarian view of human value. Wesley J. Smith notes that it has always been the case that people who aren't clear thinking, "able-bodied, productive, and generally pleasing to look" at are seen as a burden. "What has changed is that such beliefs have become respectable and mainstream," he says.[45]

Euthanasia isn't the proper way to care about suffering. With the improvement of end-of-life technologies, such as pain management and hospice care, people can be cared for and their dignity honored in their final days. People who understand the true value of human life ought to be involved in these discussions. Smith concludes, "When a value as fundamental as the equality-of-human-life ethic is weakened, it changes our attitudes toward each other, our behavior, our concept of what constitutes a human and compassionate society."[46]

Still, there are difficult issues to consider. When is it proper to withdraw treatment for a terminally ill patient? Ethicist Gilbert Meilaender notes the difficulty and says the attending physician ought to ask, "What, if anything, can we do that will benefit the life [this patient] has?" The goal is "not to judge the worth of this person's life relative to other possible or actual lives. Our task is to care for the life he has as best we can."[47] A medical decision—as opposed to a value decision—is to determine whether the *treatment* is valueless, not whether the *patient* no longer has value.[48]

4. Why Should Christians Care?

With each cultural issue we're tackling in this book, we need to ask, "Why should this matter to Christians more than anyone else?" Christians ought to care about the specialness of human life because humans are made in the **imago Dei**, the image of God. All humans possess what Nicholas Wolterstorff calls "bestowed worth."[49] As philosophers J. P. Moreland and Scott Rae put it, "There is something about the way God is that is like the way we are."[50]

From a secular viewpoint, humans claiming a special place is *speciesism*, in which one species views itself as better than another, in the same way that one race view-ing itself as better than another race is racism.[51] But Christians aren't saying that humans can do whatever they want to each other and to creation. Rather, the Christian claim that humans are made in God's image implies three things:

> *Imago Dei:* from the Latin for the "image of God"; the idea that human beings were created in God's likeness.

1. The *imago Dei* is the foundation for human value. As to what it means to be human, Genesis 1:26–27 says, "Then God said, 'Let us make man in our image, according to our likeness....' So God created man in his own image; in the image of God he created him; male and female he created them." Humans are bearers of God's image in their *created* state; being human is, in itself, image bearing.

The science of **embryology** affirms this. It teaches us that human life begins at fertilization. As Robert George and Christopher Tollefsen note, "There is widespread agreement among embryologists both that a new human individual comes into existence when there is a single, unified, and self-integrated biological system, and this happens no later than syngamy [the lining up of the twenty-three pairs of chromosomes]."[52]

> *Embryology:* the branch of biology that studies the early stages of human development.

Even among elective abortion's most sophisticated defenders, it's relatively uncontrover-sial to say that human life begins at conception.[53] Peter Singer, the philosopher we mentioned earlier, doesn't oppose elective abortion and yet admits, "There is no doubt that from the first moments of its existence, an embryo conceived from the human sperm and eggs is a human being; and the same is true of the most profoundly and irreparably intellectually disabled human being."[54]

Of course, by using the phrase "profoundly and irreparably intellectually disabled human being," Singer is taking back with his left hand what he gave with his right, implying that people with certain disabilities have less value. To Singer, the unborn, the severely handicapped, and the irreversibly disabled are all human. They just don't have inherent value.

If we're truly made in God's image, though, the ways people like Singer determine a human's value are a slippery slope. Scott Klusendorf from the Life Training Institute makes this point through his SLED acrostic defending the personhood of unborn babies. Here's my summary of his argument:[55]

- **S = Size.** Unborn babies are tiny. Does this mean they shouldn't be valued? Does the size of a person determine whether each is a person? Do we hold short people to be of less value than tall people?

- **L = Level of development.** Unborn babies are less developed than toddlers. But toddlers are less developed than grade schoolers, and grade schoolers are less developed than teenagers. Should rights be taken away from them because they're less developed?

- **E = Environment.** An unborn baby is inside the womb. But does a person's geographical location determine his or her value? If a premature baby is delivered and handed to the mother, no one questions whether the baby has value. So why should a baby of the same age just a few inches away be allowed to be killed?

- **D = Degree of dependence.** Without a doubt, an unborn baby is dependent on his or her mother to survive. But babies are dependent on their mothers after they're born too. Lots of people are dependent on others. People with pacemakers are dependent on a machine to keep their hearts beating. Sick people are dependent on medical personnel to get well. Does this take away their value as persons?

> When we go to sleep, we cease self-expressive activity, but this doesn't mean we lose our humanness. Nor do we lose it if we're somehow incapacitated.

What applies to the unborn applies to all humans. To say a person loses value because of size, level of development, environment, or degree of dependence is to say that those of us who are bigger, better developed, in a certain geographical location, and independent should have the right to determine the value of those who are less so. This isn't something a Christian worldview can affirm.

2. The *imago Dei* is the sure foundation for human dignity. *Inherent value*, *endowment*, and *substance view* are various terms philosophers use to describe the intrinsic value human beings enjoy just by virtue of being human. When we go to sleep, we cease self-expressive activity, but this doesn't mean we lose our humanness. Nor do we lose it if we're somehow incapacitated. The human being is a particular type of substance, says Francis Beckwith, "even if it is not presently exhibiting the functions, behaving in [certain] ways, or currently able to immediately exercise these activities that we typically attribute to active and mature rational moral agents."[56]

THE VALUE OF HUMAN LIFE

We all believe our identity remains the same through time and change. We don't allow a person to say, "Well, my cells have all been replaced since I committed that crime seven years ago, so *I am* not responsible for it." Beckwith sums it up nicely:

> Another way to put it is to say that organisms, including human beings, are onto-logically prior to their parts, which means that the organism as a whole maintains absolute identity through time while it grows, develops, and undergoes numerous changes, largely as a result of the organism's nature that directs and informs these changes and their limits.[57]

We are more than just the sum of our parts. We bear God's image. As Christian philosopher Mark Linville expresses it, "God and human persons share an overlap of … membership in personhood itself, and human dignity is found precisely in membership of that kind."[58]

3. The *imago Dei* is the foundation for loving our neighbors. Genesis 9:6 says, "Whoever sheds the blood of man, by man shall his blood be shed, for God made man in his image." We ought to never use our humanity to diminish the humanity of others. God commands us to love and honor our neighbors, even those who hate us or identify themselves as our enemies (Matt. 5:44).

When chimpanzees kill chimpanzees or dolphins kill dolphins, we don't apply the moral term *murder* to their behavior, though we all agree that chimpanzees and dolphins are uncommonly intelligent animals, and we may ourselves be sickened by the sight of such behavior. Rather, we reserve terms like *murder* for behaviors within the human family that violate the moral norms governing our behavior toward one another. From a biblical viewpoint, those norms aren't just for the sake of a social contract. They go back to our very purpose as humans: we're meant to love God and love those who bear his image.[59]

> From a biblical viewpoint, moral norms go back to our very purpose as humans: we're meant to love God and love those who bear his image.

In summary, Christians should care about the people around them for all the normal reasons—because we ought to treat people the way we want to be treated, because we want to be at peace with others, and because we want to do our part to create a safe community. But we recognize that these common human values have their source in the fact that we are created in the image of God and that this—not the fact that we contribute a lot to our communities—is what gives us intrinsic value.

5. What Should Christians Do?

If humans have intrinsic value, and the basis for this is God's nature and character as revealed in the Bible, what should Christians do?

Show how *imago Dei* is still true in a world that rejects God. When we say that humans bear God's image, we're making a *metaphysical* claim—a claim about what kind of beings we are. Even those who don't acknowledge God still experience the reality of the beingness derived from being his image bearers. But is it possible to establish common ground with nonbelievers over something so theological? Philosopher William Lane Craig believes it is, based on the fact that people, regardless of their belief in God, still share moral intuition, reflection, and the ability to discern right from wrong. We can also appeal to conscience, which enables people to not only discern but also discover for themselves what is right and wrong.[60]

Pointing out that God's law is written on our hearts (Rom. 2:14–15),[61] Craig says, "My argument is that theism is necessary for there to be moral goods and duties, not that it is necessary for us to discern the moral goods and duties that there are."[62] Regardless of their commitment to Christ, people have an internal sense of certain things we ought not to do to other human beings. It's a strong basis for dialoging about what constitutes the value of human life.

Respond logically to Secularist arguments. How do we respond to people who agree that we can discern and discover the difference between right and wrong but still believe elective abortion, destructive embryo research, and euthanasia are permissible? I've given a number of arguments throughout the chapter on each of these, but because the issue of elective abortion is front and center in the debate over the value of human life, I'd like to zero in on it specifically.

> Most arguments in favor of permitting elective abortion assume that unborn humans aren't valuable human beings in the sense that their right to life and dignity ought to be protected.

When responding to the arguments of abortion advocates, remember this: most arguments in favor of permitting elective abortion assume that unborn humans aren't valuable human beings in the sense that their right to life and dignity ought to be protected. If you keep this in mind, you'll be able to identify and respond to the most common objections to a pro-life stance. Here are a few examples:

"Abortion should be allowed to protect women from bad consequences." This argument is often stated in one of the following ways:

- "Abortion isn't to be preferred, but sometimes abortion is justified to protect the finances of families."

- "Women have the right to privacy regarding their medical decisions."

- "Abortion is needed to provide women equal footing with men in their professional lives."

Usually, people who say we have no moral duty to protect the unborn don't come right out and advocate killing. Rather, they assume that the unborn are *not* human to begin with. When people use this rationale, ask, "Would any of these arguments be used to defend the killing of a human toddler?" The answer is clearly no. So why should we assume that killing the unborn is different just because they're small, less developed, and not yet able to support themselves? And if the unborn are *not* persons, we shouldn't think anything more about killing them than we would about removing our wisdom teeth.

"If you can't trust me with a choice, how can you trust me with a child?" This slogan again assumes the unborn aren't human. Otherwise, it's absurd. It's like asking, "If you can't trust me to kill my child, how can you trust me to raise him?" At one of his talks, a woman confronted Jay Watts and offered this objection. He asked if she believed that she was free to choose to walk across the room and seize any possession she chose from one of her classmates. She answered no. Jay replied,

> Why should we assume that killing the unborn is different just because they're small, less developed, and not yet able to support themselves?

> We both agree that all women should be free to make the decisions that govern their lives. We also both agree that some choices are restricted and there are reasonable limits to how we can treat others or even use our own bodies. What we disagree on is whether or not ending the life of unborn human beings falls into the category of legitimate choice or the category of legitimately restricted choices, like stealing from your classmates. The real issue is not whether women's choices ought to be respected, but whether the unborn human is the kind of being who ought to be protected.[63]

"Making abortion illegal will force women into back-alley abortions and lead to their deaths." This is an appeal to pity that also assumes that the unborn aren't really human beings with value. If the unborn *are* valuable human beings, then this argument must be seen in a new light: Should we allow the killing of more than 1.2 million valuable human beings every year to protect a much smaller number of valuable human beings from the terrible consequences of their freely chosen immoral acts?[64] Abortion advocate Mary Anne Warren argued, "The fact that restricting access to abortion has tragic side effects does not, in itself, show that the restrictions are unjustified, since murder is wrong regardless of the consequences of prohibiting it."[65]

> Should we allow the killing of more than 1.2 million valuable human beings every year to protect a much smaller number of valuable human beings from the terrible consequences of their freely chosen immoral acts?

"My body, my choice." Some who favor permitting elective abortion will try to foreclose argument by saying that it isn't the business of anyone but the pregnant woman what she does with the baby she is carrying. Michael Tooley explains this view:

> The basic idea here is that someone who defends this … liberal view on abortion may grant that abortion is in itself a prima facie wrong—and perhaps even seriously so—but then go on to claim that all acts of abortion also have a serious right-making characteristic.… What might such a right-making property be? The usual answer is that it is a matter of a woman's right to determine what does and does not happen within her own body.[66]

This view is most famously represented by Judith Jarvis Thomson's violinist.[67] Thomson argues that a woman has no duty to allow a violinist with a serious kidney ailment to be connected to her body without permission and have the use of her kidneys. Further, she isn't responsible for the violinist's death if she decides to have him separated, even if waiting nine months would ensure that he would be cured. She may decide to keep the violinist attached out of niceness, as a "Good Samaritan," but she isn't *obligated* to do so as a moral duty. In the same way, Thomson says, a woman isn't obligated to allow an unborn human being the use of her organs even though its survival depends on her, and the unborn human in question is clearly a human being. If she decides based on a spirit of kindness to allow the child to use her organs, fine. If she decides not to allow it, she should not be held responsible for the child's neediness.

Francis Beckwith and Christopher Kaczor have both responded to Thomson's original article, as well as David Boonin's modified defense of it.[68] Their criticisms include the following observations of the violinist argument:

- It ignores the procreative nature of the sex act in denying the woman has any responsibility in the neediness of the child.

- It denies that pregnancy is a natural good and describes it in terms of a pathology or the child as an intruder.

- It denies the natural special responsibilities that one has to our offspring.

- It introduces a form of moral volunteerism without arguing for it by saying that women are responsible for only those duties they agree to accept.

- It confuses unplugging (where the violinist dies from his illness) with actively killing (where the fetus dies from being dismembered, chemically poisoned and burned, or sucked out of the mother's womb in pieces by a vacuum).

So what about rape? Some will say that there ought to be exceptions for rape because a woman is being forced against her will to bear a child she doesn't want. While only 1 percent of aborting women report that their pregnancy was due to rape,[69] the question of abortion in cases of rape is a deeply emotional issue that hits right at the heart of how we protect the powerless and vulnerable.

> The question of abortion in cases of rape is a deeply emotional issue that hits right at the heart of how we protect the powerless and vulnerable.

And yet if we consider the inherent value of the unborn human, the issue becomes more complex, not less. There are three people involved in the rape: the rapist, the woman, and the child. In most places in the world, convicted rapists are sent to prison but not killed. And no one would suggest that the woman ought to be killed for the rapist's crime. So why is it assumed that the only person who should be punished with death for the crime is the unborn child? Is that just?[70] Abortion advocates point

THE VALUE OF HUMAN LIFE

out that the trauma of bearing a rapist's child is simply too great a burden for women to bear. It *is* an unimaginably painful situation fraught with heartache. But as Amherst College political science professor Hadley Arkes asks, "Do you think she would have trauma in confronting the rapist, again, in a trial? Would you just order up the killing of the rapist, rather than have her go through that?"[71]

Without question, the gestation and birth of a human person is a ponderous issue. Having a baby changes a woman's life forever. The consequences flowing from the decision to have sexual intercourse can be life altering. But what does it say about a nation that refuses to grapple with it in any way except by allowing medical procedures that end a life? This goes beyond the way we view unborn children; it affects the way we as civilized people view the value of life. The abortion question is both personal and about the conscience of a whole nation.

Fight for the conscience of the nation. In his famous 1852 speech "What to the Slave Is the Fourth of July?," ex-slave and abolitionist Frederick Douglass insisted the slavery controversy was largely settled on the idea level. The slave was human, and everyone knew it. What people lacked was a properly formed conscience. "It is not light that is needed, but fire," said Douglass. "It is not the gentle shower, but thunder." The battle of ideas is ultimately a battle of conscience.

> The issue of abortion goes beyond the way we view unborn children; it affects the way we as civilized people view the value of life.

How might the conscience of the nation be awakened on the issue of life? First, people need to see the injustice of an anti-life stance in a way that changes how they feel about abortion and euthanasia. Second, people must be presented with facts and arguments to change how they think. Both are vital if people's behavior is to change.

Pictures are key. Daily we're confronted with pictures dramatizing child labor, starvation, war injustices, racial violence, and cruelty to animals. Pictures work in confronting people with the injustice of abortion too. During the 1990s, graphic illustrations of partial-birth abortion swayed public opinion toward the pro-life view, especially on late-term abortion.

If you show pictures of aborted babies, you can expect people who favor abortion to be outraged. Why? Because pictures seriously damage the proabortion argument. "One of the dirty secrets of abortion is it's really gruesome," admitted Cynthia Gorney, an abortion advocate. "With partial-birth, the right-to-life movement succeeded for the first time in forcing the country to really look at one awful abortion procedure."[72] Feminist Naomi Wolf writes, "When someone holds up a model of a six-month-old fetus and a pair of surgical scissors, we say 'choice' and we lose."[73] When abortion advocates like Gorney and Wolf concede such a critical point, perhaps we should listen.

> During the 1990s, graphic illustrations of partial-birth abortion swayed public opinion toward the pro-life view, especially on late-term abortion.

We must also make a good case. The flawed arguments we considered in the previous section attempt to justify not just the personal decisions of individual women but global policies that favor abortion. According to some estimates, there have been more than a billion abortions worldwide in the last half century.[74] If people gain value based on their performance or their utility to the group, then there simply is nothing wrong with abortion, even if the reasons for having it are trivial. If a woman aborts because she doesn't like morning sickness or doesn't want a baby bump during her upcoming vacation, who are we to say that's bad? And if abortion is okay because a child is likely to be mentally handicapped or unattractive, who's to say it's wrong to abort a girl when you wanted a boy?

On the other hand, if the unborn are human in the same way that you and I are, then the justifications given to support abortion rights are utterly insufficient.[75] We don't kill other human beings as a means of addressing poverty and anxiety over the future, or even to eliminate reminders of profoundly painful past events (rape). If unborn humans have inherent value, the appeal to the privacy or freedom of those around them can never excuse killing them any more than an abusive husband's freedoms should prevent authorities from intervening when he is beating his wife, even in the privacy of their home.

> **If the unborn are human in the same way that you and I are, then the justifications given to support abortion rights are utterly insufficient.**

If the unborn are human in the same way that you and I are, then the destruction of unborn human beings we're seeing in our time is unlike anything that has happened in human history. Entire nations of people quietly and efficiently wiped from the earth. Each day that passes with our silence deadens our consciences, making it harder to discern the value of any human life.

Learn to respond to fallacious attacks. As pro-life activists become more articulate at pointing out the inherent value of unborn humans, the elderly, and others whose existence is seen as inconvenient, their opponents often turn to fallacious attacks. Here are a couple of examples:

"You're biased." When confronting a man who opposes elective abortion, many abortion advocates decry, "But you're a man!" In what other areas of life would we accept this sort of reasoning? It's like saying that only people who support the right to slavery should have a voice in deciding whether it should be abolished.

"It's complicated." As a last resort, those who support elective abortion often claim that abortion and euthanasia are complicated issues and that families considering them should be left alone.

> **The fact that issues are complicated doesn't justify taking a life.**

Again, this kind of thinking assumes that a complicated decision justifies killing. Ask, "Would you be in favor of leaving a woman alone who wants to kill her three-year-old child because he is complicating her life?" The fact that issues are complicated doesn't justify taking a life.

Personally care. It's one thing to make intellectual arguments and another to come alongside to help people who are in difficult situations. Fortunately, movements promoting the value of human life have gone far beyond marching and waving signs. Today, women who find themselves with an unplanned pregnancy can find support at one of hundreds of pregnancy care centers that help with adoption connections, teach parenting skills, and acquire food, clothing, and supplies.

At the same time, activists like Lila Rose, whose organization Live Action sponsored the undercover investigators we met at the beginning of this chapter, have raised the alarm about the abortion business's seamy underside. Americans United for Life (AUL) has developed model legislation and seen it passed in state legislatures across the country. One AUL-designed bill, the Born-Alive Infants Protection Act of 2002, which requires legal protection for infants surviving abortion, has been passed in thirty states.

> Today, women who find themselves with an unplanned pregnancy can find support at one of hundreds of pregnancy care centers that help with adoption connections, teach parenting skills, and acquire food, clothing, and supplies.

Others have devised creative new methods for raising awareness. Students for Life of America (SFLA) has started student chapters on university campuses across the country that make the pro-life case to college students. Justice for All and Ratio Christi have done so as well. Scott Klusendorf and his team at Life Training Institute send speakers into Catholic and Protestant high schools nationwide and in Canada.

I highlighted another example, Joe Baker, in one of my blog posts.[76] Joe founded Save the Storks, "a pro-life organization aiming to convince mothers considering abortion to save their babies." Knowing that "abortion-minded women" are often persuaded to keep their babies after viewing an ultrasound and also recognizing that many are "unwilling to go to the trouble of cancelling their clinic appointment and scheduling an ultrasound at a cross-town location," Save the Storks' solution was to outfit a bus with the latest ultrasound equipment, hire a nurse, and park outside an abortion clinic.

In 2011, after one stork bus had toured the country, "Save the Storks then contracted with the Downtown Pregnancy Center in Dallas, Texas, which will permanently operate the bus around local abortion clinics." The success of the project inspired pregnancy centers around the country to order buses as well. Baker's goal is to have a bus in every major US city. "My wife and I are capable of building something that could make a lot of money," he told me. "Our desire, though, is really just to build the things we want to, like Save the Storks."

Along with Lila Rose and organizations such as Americans United for Life and Students for Life, Baker is helping not only to save babies but to restore a culture of life, persuading people at the level of both their minds and their hearts.

6. Conclusion: Human Life Is Special

As Christians, we understand that we're made in the image of God. We have inestimable value simply because we're human. We are to love and honor God as well as our fellow image bearers. Though many in our world reject grounding our value in God, they do recognize that there is a moral law and that humans have moral duties. These shared intuitions provide common ground on which we can dialogue about scientific and philosophical arguments supporting the intrinsic value of human beings.

Today, we live in a culture of death. Abortion, embryo-destructive technologies, and euthanasia represent a dereliction of our duties to the "least of these" (Matt. 25:40). Scripture makes our responsibility clear: be on the lookout for and take care of the most helpless in our communities (Matt. 25:40; Gal. 2:10; James 1:27).[77]

Sophisticated or tricky arguments to the contrary, human life is inherently valuable. Christopher Kaczor concludes,

> Do we really have reason to believe that for the very first time in human history we are justified in treating some human beings as less than fully persons? Or will we be judged by history as just one more episode in the long line of exploitation of the powerful over the weak?[78]

ENDNOTES

1. "Perth Amboy Planned Parenthood Transcript," Live Action, January 13, 2011, http://liveaction.org/files/transcripts/PerthAmboy%20Transcript.pdf.

2. Michael W. Chapman, "Planned Parenthood and Baby Body Parts Video: 'Was That Crack the Little Bits of the Skull?'—'Here's the Heart,'" CNSNews.com, July 30, 2015, www.cnsnews.com/news/article/michael-w-chapman/planned-parenthood-baby-body-parts-video-was-crack-little-bits-skull.

3. See "Table 2. Number, Ratio, and Rate of Legal Abortions and Source of Reporting for All Reporting Areas and for the 46 Areas That Reported in 1998–2005, by Year—United States, 1970–2005," in Sonya B. Gamble et al., "Abortion Surveillance—United States, 2005," National Center for Chronic Disease Prevention and Health Promotion, 2005, www.cdc.gov/mmwr/preview/mmwrhtml/ss5713a1.htm#fig1.

4. Joseph Stalin, quoted in Anton Antonov-Ovseenko, *The Time of Stalin: Portrait of Tyranny* (New York: Harper and Row, 1981), 278; see also David McCullough, *Truman* (New York: Simon and Schuster, 1992), 510. The attribution of this quote to Winston Churchill has been questioned; however, what is not in question is that Stalin was a mass murderer who expressed no remorse over his actions.

5. Warren M. Hern, *Abortion Practice* (Boulder, CO: Alpenglo Graphics, 1990), 151.

6. Sarah Hoye and Sunny Hostin, "Doctor Found Guilty of First-Degree Murder in Philadelphia Abortion Case," CNN, May 14, 2013, www.cnn.com/2013/05/13/justice/pennsylvania-abortion-doctor-trial/index.html.

7. Pew Research Center, survey conducted January 9–13, 2013, cited in "Roe v. Wade at 40: Most Oppose Overturning Abortion Decision," Pew Research Center, January 16, 2013, www.pewforum.org/2013/01/16/roe-v-wade-at-40/.

8. Kate Pickert, "What Choice? Abortion-Rights Activists Won an Epic Victory in Roe v. Wade. They've Been Losing Ever Since," *Time*, January 14, 2013, http://content.time.com/time/magazine/article/0,9171,2132761,00.html.

9. Kate Michelman and Frances Kissling, "Abortion's Battle of Messages," *Los Angeles Times*, January 22, 2008, http://articles.latimes.com/2008/jan/22/opinion/oe-kissling22.

10. Results of 2015 CIRP Freshman Survey monograph, cited in "The American Freshman: National Norms Fall 2015," Research Brief, Higher Education Research Institute at UCLA, February 2016, www.heri.ucla.edu/briefs/TheAmericanFreshman2015-Brief.pdf.

11. The authoritative history of the growth of Secularism is presented in Charles Taylor, *A Secular Age* (Cambridge, MA: Belknap, 2007). James K. A. Smith's book *How (Not) to Be Secular: Reading Charles Taylor* (Grand Rapids: Eerdmans, 2014) offers a popular explanation of Taylor's extensive and often complicated argument.

12. Paul Kurtz, ed., *The Humanist Alternative: Some Definitions of Humanism* (Buffalo: Prometheus Books, 1973), 50.

13. Lester Kirkendall, *A New Bill of Sexual Rights and Responsibilities* (Buffalo: Prometheus Books, 1976), 9.

14. See Edwin Black's *War against the Weak: Eugenics and America's Campaign to Create a Master Race* (Washington, DC: Dialog Press, 2012) for details regarding Sanger's eugenics connections. Also, see Jonah Goldberg, *Liberal Fascism: The Secret History of the American Left from Mussolini to the Politics of Meaning* (New York: Doubleday, 2007), 243–83. Three humanists of the year—Margaret Sanger, Mary Calderone, and Faye Wattleton—have held key positions in Planned Parenthood.

15. Linda Gordon, *The Moral Property of Women: A History of Birth Control Politics in America* (Chicago: University of Illinois Press, 2002), 235–36. For more information, visit the website Black Genocide, www.blackgenocide.org/sanger02.html.

16. Lena Levine, "Psycho-sexual Development," *Planned Parenthood News* (Summer 1953): 10.

17. According to the Centers for Disease Control (CDC), the most common contraceptive methods all have a failure rate of between 9 and 28 percent. See "Contraception: How Effective Are Birth Control Methods?," Centers for Disease Control and Prevention, May 25, 2016, www.cdc.gov/reproductivehealth/unintendedpregnancy/contraception.htm.

18. Rachel K. Jones and Megan L. Kavanaugh, "Changes in Abortion Rates between 2000 and 2008 and Lifetime Incidence of Abortion," *Obstetrics and Gynecology* 117, no. 6 (June 2011): 1358–66.

19. R. K. Jones, L. Frohwirth, and A. M. Moore, "More Than Poverty: Disruptive Events among Women Having Abortions in the USA," *Journal of Family Planning and Reproductive Health Care* 39, no. 1 (2012): 40, http://jfprhc.bmj.com/content /39/1/36.full.pdf+html.

20. Joseph Randall, quoted in David Kuperlain and Mark Masters, "Pro-Choice 1990: Skeletons in the Closet," *New Dimensions*, October 1990; Sarah Terzo, "78% of Pregnant Women Seeing an Ultrasound Reject Abortions," LifeNews.com, February 7, 2013, www.lifenews.com/2013/02/07/78-of-pregnant-women-seeing-an-ultrasound-reject-abortions/.

21. Various sources cited in "The Basics: Diary of an Unborn Baby," National Right to Life Educational Foundation, accessed July 16, 2016, www.nrlc.org/uploads/factsheets/FS02TheBasics.pdf.

22. Christopher Kaczor, *The Ethics of Abortion: Women's Rights, Human Life, and the Question of Justice* (New York: Routledge, 2011), 93.

23. Peter Singer, *Practical Ethics*, 3rd ed. (New York: Cambridge University Press 2011), 20.

24. Singer, *Practical Ethics*, 161.

25. Helga Kuhse and Peter Singer, *Should the Baby Live?* (Oxford, UK: Oxford University Press, 1985), 194–96, cited in Peter Singer, *Rethinking Life and Death: The Collapse of Our Traditional Ethics* (New York: St. Martin's Press, 1994), 217.

26. Michael Tooley, "Abortion: Why a Liberal View Is Correct," in Michael Tooley et al., eds., *Abortion: Three Perspectives* (New York: Oxford University Press, 2009), 10.

27. Francis J. Beckwith, *Defending Life: A Moral and Legal Case against Abortion Choice* (New York: Cambridge University Press, 2007), 139.

28. Beckwith, *Defending Life*.

29. Jeff McMahan, "Challenges to Human Equality," *Journal of Ethics* 12, no. 1 (2008): 104.

30. George Orwell, *Animal Farm/1984* (Orlando: Harcourt, 2003), 80.

31. President Obama swept away previous barriers to government funding of human embryonic stem-cell research by means of an executive order in 2009. National Institutes of Health (NIH) funding increased from $146 million in 2012 to $180 million in 2015. The projected increase in funding for 2016 and 2017 is $191 million. See "Executive Order 13505— Removing Barriers to Responsible Scientific Research Involving Human Stem Cells," March 9, 2009, www.whitehouse.gov /the-press-office/removing-barriers-responsible-scientific-research-involving-human-stem-cells; "Estimates of Funding for Various Research, Condition, and Disease Categories (RCDC)," Funding, NIH, February 10, 2016, https://report.nih.gov /categorical_spending.aspx. See also Robert P. George and Christopher Tollefsen, *Embryo: A Defense of Human Life* (New York: Doubleday, 2008), 4–5.

32. Leon R. Kass, *Life, Liberty, and the Defense of Dignity: The Challenge for Bioethics* (San Francisco: Encounter Books, 2002), 85.

33. David Prentice and Rosa Macrito, *Stem Cells, Cloning, and Human Embryos: Understanding the Ethics and Opportunity of Scientific Research* (Washington, DC: Family Research Council, 2013), 1–2, http://downloads.frc.org/EF/EF13E47.pdf.

34. Prentice and Macrito, *Stem Cells*, 3.

35. "Induced Pluripotent Stem Cells," Eli and Edythe Broad Center of Regenerative Medicine and Stem Cell Research, accessed June 28, 2016, www.stemcell.ucla.edu/induced-pluripotent-stem-cells. Scott Klusendorf, president of the Life Training Institute, says that caution must be taken with IPSC even though the research seems promising: "IPSC still results in tumor formation, rejection, etc. According to Dr. Maureen Condic, professor of neurobiology and anatomy at the University of Utah, despite the clear progress we have made, we are nowhere near the point of having a 'recipe book' for cooking up cellular repair kits to treat human disease and injury. Immune rejection, tumor formation, and embryonic development have proved themselves to be profoundly serious scientific challenges, and they are likely to remain so for decades into the future. Regarding IPSC in particular, Condic writes: 'Despite the astonishing scientific advance of direct reprogramming, it is important to remain realistic about the possibility of developing pluripotent stem-cell therapies. Direct reprogramming will not be a panacea for treatment of all human medical conditions. Because of problems with immune rejection, safety (cancer risk), and efficacy (ability to produce clinically useful cells), there are currently no medical treatments using pluripotent stem cells. Direct reprogramming resolves the significant problem of immune rejection by producing patient-matched cell lines. The serious issues of safety and efficacy, however, remain for IPSCs, just as they do for embryonic stem cells.' Indeed, the risks associated with IPSCs may be greater at this time because of the use of gene-therapy viruses for reprogramming, though the need for such viruses is likely to be eliminated as the technique is further refined. The risk of tumor formation, common to all pluripotent stem cells, can theoretically be addressed by converting stem cells into mature cells. Yet despite considerable effort, efficient conversion of pluripotent stem cells into clinically useful cells has not been accomplished. Because of these remaining hurdles, no immediate therapies should be expected from human pluripotent stem cells, whether they are derived from embryos or from direct reprogramming." Scott Klusendorf, remarks to author regarding his review of this chapter, February 22, 2016. See also Maureen L. Condic, "Getting Stem Cells Right," *First Things*, February 2008; and "What We Know about Embryonic Stem Cells," *First Things*, January 2007.

36. Agneta Sutton, *Christian Bioethics: A Guide for the Perplexed* (New York: T&T Clark, 2008), 48.

37. See chapter 5, "Euthanasia: Quality *versus* Sanctity of Life," in Sutton, *Christian Bioethics*, 48–58.

38. Sutton, *Christian Bioethics*, 48–49.

39. Sutton, *Christian Bioethics*, 55.

40. Wesley J. Smith, *Forced Exit: Euthanasia, Assisted Suicide, and the New Duty to Die* (New York: Encounter Books, 2006), 119–21.

41. See Alberto Giubilini and Francesca Minerva, "After-Birth Abortion: Why Should the Baby Live?," *Journal of Medical Ethics* 39, no. 5 (May 2013): 261–65, http://jme.bmj.com/content/early/2012/03/01/medethics-2011-100411.full.

42. Smith, *Forced Exit*, 116–28.

43. Margaret Battin, quoted in Gina Kolata, "'Passive Euthanasia' in Hospitals Is the Norm, Doctors Say," *New York Times*, June 28, 1997, www.nytimes.com/1997/06/28/us/passive-euthanasia-in-hospitals-is-the-norm-doctors-say.html?pagewanted=all.

44. Gilbert Meilaender, *Bioethics: A Primer for Christians* (Grand Rapids: Eerdmans, 2005), 66–69; Sutton, *Christian Bioethics*, 52–53.

45. Smith, *Forced Exit*, 42.

46. Smith, *Forced Exit*, 43.

47. Meilaender, *Bioethics*, 70–72.

48. Sutton, *Christian Bioethics*, 51–52.

49. Nicholas Wolterstorff, *Justice: Rights and Wrongs* (Princeton, NJ: Princeton University Press 2008), 352.

50. J. P. Moreland and Scott B. Rae, *Body and Soul: Human Nature and the Crisis in Ethics* (Downers Grove, IL: InterVarsity, 2000), 157.

51. *Speciesism* is a term that gained popularity through the work of Peter Singer, whose ideas we have already discussed in this chapter. See Peter Singer, *Animal Liberation: A New Ethics for Our Treatment of Animals* (New York: New York Review, 1975). Singer's claim is roughly that membership in a certain species has no moral significance.

52. George and Tollefsen, *Embryo*, 39.

53. Beckwith, *Defending Life*, 65.

54. Singer, *Practical Ethics*, 73.

55. SLED discussion based on Stephen Schwarz, *The Moral Question of Abortion* (Chicago: Loyola University Press, 1990), 18; and Scott Klusendorf, *The Case for Life: Equipping Christians to Engage the Culture* (Wheaton, IL: Crossway, 2009), 28.

56. Beckwith, *Defending Life*, 132.

57. Beckwith, *Defending Life*, 133.

58. Mark D. Linville, "The Moral Argument," in *The Blackwell Companion to Natural Theology*, eds. William Lane Craig and J. P. Moreland (Malden, MA: Wiley-Blackwell, 2012), 445.

59. Luke 10:27–28 records a conversation between Jesus and a lawyer. When Jesus asked him what he thought the basis of the law was, the lawyer replied, "You shall love the Lord your God with all your heart and with all your soul and with all your strength and with all your mind, and your neighbor as yourself." Jesus replied, "You have answered correctly; do this, and you will live."

60. William Lane Craig, "The Most Gruesome of Guests," in *Is Goodness without God Good Enough? A Debate on Faith, Secularism, and Ethics*, eds. Robert K. Garcia and Nathan L. King (Plymouth, UK: Rowman and Littlefield, 2009), 168.

61. Romans 2:14–15: "When Gentiles, who do not have the law, by nature do what the law requires, they are a law to themselves, even though they do not have the law. They show that the work of the law is written on their hearts, while their conscience also bears witness, and their conflicting thoughts accuse or even excuse them."

62. Craig, "Most Gruesome of Guests," 169.

63. Jay Watts told the story in research provided for this chapter. For more information about Jay Watts and the organization he represents, the Life Training Institute, see http://prolifetraining.com.

64. Beckwith, *Defending Life*, 95.

65. Mary Anne Warren, "On the Moral and Legal Status of Abortion," in *The Problem of Abortion*, 3rd ed., eds. Joel Feinberg and Susan Dwyer (Belmont, CA: Wadsworth, 1997), 59–60.

66. Tooley, "Abortion," 9.

67. Judith Jarvis Thomson, "A Defense of Abortion," *Philosophy and Public Affairs* 1, no. 1 (Fall 1971), http://spot.colorado.edu/~heathwoo/Phil160,Fall02/thomson.htm.

68. Beckwith, *Defending Life*, chap. 7; Kaczor, *Ethics of Abortion*, chap. 7; and David Boonin, *A Defense of Abortion*, Cambridge Studies in Politics and Public Policy (New York: Cambridge University Press, 2003), chap. 4.

69. Lawrence B. Finer et al., "Reasons U.S. Women Have Abortions: Quantitative and Qualitative Perspectives," *Perspectives on Sexual and Reproductive Health* 37, no. 3 (2005): 113, www.guttmacher.org/sites/default/files/pdfs/journals/3711005.pdf.

70. Scott Klusendorf taught me this approach.

71. Hadley Arkes, quoted in Marvin Olasky and Susan Olasky, "Doing Better on 'Hard Cases,'" *World*, January 11, 2013, 39, https://world.wng.org/2013/01/doing_better_on_hard_cases.

72. Cynthia Gorney, quoted in Larry Reibstein, "Arguing at a Fever Pitch," *Newsweek*, January 26, 1998.

73. Naomi Wolf, "Pro-Choice and Pro-Life," *New York Times*, April 3, 1997.

74. There have been more than 336 million abortions in China since 1971 and the enactment of the one-child policy, more than 55 million in the United States since 1973, and a conservative estimate of 40 million abortions per year worldwide in the past thirty years. This totals 1.2 billion abortions. Data gathered from the Guttmacher Institute (www.guttmacher.org) and China's health ministry.

75. See Klusendorf, *The Case for Life*; and Gregory Koukl, *Precious Unborn Human Persons* (San Pedro, CA: Stand to Reason, 1999).

76. Jeff Myers, "The Power of a Summit Story: Joe Baker," *The President's Desk* (blog), March 27, 2013, www.summit.org/blogs /the-presidents-desk/the-power-of-a-summit-story-joe-baker/.

77. Matthew 25:40: "The King will answer them, 'Truly, I say to you, as you did it to one of the least of these my brothers, you did it to me'"; Galatians 2:10: "They asked us to remember the poor, the very thing I was eager to do"; James 1:27: "Religion that is pure and undefiled before God, the Father, is this: to visit orphans and widows in their affliction, and to keep oneself unstained from the world."

78. Kaczor, *Ethics of Abortion*, 102.

CHAPTER 9

9

SEXUALITY

1. THE COST OF SEXUAL "FREEDOM"

The last few years of Christopher's life had been a disaster. Convinced he was gay, he immersed himself in the lifestyle: porn and parties. Disoriented from drugs, expelled from dental school, and tracked by the police as a drug dealer, Christopher was near the end when his parents showed up at his apartment, trying to help. Christopher shouted at them, "I don't want your religion. I don't want your Bible. I don't want you here. Just leave! Get out! And if you ever, ever bring up God or the Bible, you will never see me again!"[1]

Silently, Christopher's mom, Angela, asked God for the stamina to pray and work for Christopher's restoration. She fasted for 39 days.[2] It took a prison term and an HIV/AIDS diagnosis for Christopher, but her prayers were answered. Christopher came to faith in Christ and today teaches at a Bible college. He and his mother travel the country sharing the story of how God worked in their lives to draw them to Christ.

Still, Christopher admits, sexuality is a daily battle. "I had learned that I could live without sex," he says, "but what about my sexuality?" He wanted to change, but change is hard, and the culture says that homosexuals can't—and shouldn't—change. Christopher has concluded, "Change is not the absence of struggles; change is the freedom to choose holiness in the midst of our struggles. I realized that the ultimate issue has to be that I yearn after God in total surrender and complete obedience."[3]

Many today see their sexual orientation as the central aspect of their identity. Our bodies are all we have, and our sexual impulses are our strongest biochemical reactions. Therefore, sexual expression is the key to authenticity. Indeed, many think that securing sexual freedom for everyone is the pinnacle of liberty. Says commentator Rod Dreher, sexuality "is how the modern American claims his freedom."[4]

Sexual freedom has come at a high cost, though. One out of six people between the ages of 14 and 49 now have herpes, for which there is no known cure, and more than 1.2 million have HIV/AIDS.[5] About 20 million new sexually transmitted disease (STD) cases are diagnosed each year, and half are among those ages 15–24. This means that about twenty-five percent of teens will contract an STD.[6] But this is about more than STDs. At its heart, the **sexual revolution** is a struggle for culture itself. Said famed psychologist Philip Rieff, "The death of a culture begins when its normative institutions fail to communicate ideals in ways that remain inwardly compelling."[7] As we'll see in the next chapter, heterosexual, monogamous marriage has long been at the heart of Western civilization. But the modern age thought it had a better idea, one that would lead to blissful happiness. So why are we mired in confusion and despair?

> *Sexual Revolution:* a 1960s Western social movement that celebrated advances in contraception, encouraged sexual experimentation, and promoted sex outside of marriage.

> *Political Correctness:* the censoring of language, ideas, acts, and policies that are perceived to discriminate or alienate minority social groups.

There is a way out. The journey to sexual wholeness isn't an easy one, and it requires us to live out unpopular ideas that court mockery and spite. Much of what you'll read in this chapter ignores the rules of **political correctness**, but I hope that doesn't stop you from considering it. As the late Chuck Colson said, "Orthodoxy often requires us to be hard precisely where the world is soft, and soft where the world is hard.… In every way that matters, Christianity is an affront to the world; it is countercultural.[8]

What is countercultural about a biblical view of sexuality, however, may surprise you. God loves sex. In fact, he invented it. If we pay close attention to what he says in the Bible, we can learn to love sex too. *Real* sex. Sex that builds trust rather than destroying it. Sex that finds its highest fulfillment in a faithful marital relationship with the prospect of producing children rather than just being an outlet for physical urges.[9] Together we'll explore a call to a radical life, one of openness and honesty about our sexual feelings and failings. One of grace to those experiencing the consequences of sexual brokenness. And one in which we can experience intimacy with our creator in a way that transcends sexual brokenness and restores us as deeply loved image bearers of God.

2. What Is the Problem?

If sex was God's idea and he created it, why shouldn't we be free to express our sexuality any way we desire? Because God recognizes only one kind of legitimate sexual relationship. As professor Denny Burk puts it, "The only sex desire that glorifies God is that desire that is ordered to the covenant of marriage. When sexual desire/attraction fixes on any kind of non-marital erotic activity, it falls short of the glory of God and is by definition sinful."[10] The Bible begins sketching out its sexual ethic: "For this reason a man will leave his father and mother and be united to his wife, and they will become one flesh" (Gen. 2:24). As we will see in this chapter and also in chapter 10, the Christian worldview holds that this view alone ensures individual happiness as well as a healthy society. But for several generations now, there has been a revolt against the biblical view of sexuality. Where did it come from and where is it headed?

The History of the Sexual Revolution

A **revolution** is a rebellion against an established order. The seeds of the sexual revolution were planted during the **Age of Enlightenment**, when the church began to be viewed as a barrier to societal advancement. In the 1800s, **Darwinism** gave people room to believe that the universe wasn't the product of a loving creator and that humans were just complex animals for whom any constraint on sexual impulses was unnatural. But it wasn't until the 1900s that the sexual revolution truly took hold.

In 1905, Austrian psychoanalyst Sigmund Freud published a book called *Three Essays on the Theory of Sexuality*. Freud outlined what he saw as the stages of sexual development in humans and asserted that sex is basic to humanity's needs and desires. Following Freud, sexual-freedom advocates, such as Havelock Ellis and Bertrand Russell, began openly encouraging premarital intercourse and homosexuality. Russell, a philosopher and mathematician who enjoyed sharing his opinion on a variety of topics, argued that not having sex before marriage was "just as absurd as it would be if a man intending to buy a house were not allowed to view it until he had completed the purchase."[11] Margaret Sanger, the "mother of birth control" and the first president of Planned

Revolution: an overthrow of an established order, system, or state.

Age of Enlightenment: an eighteenth-century intellectual movement that emphasized reason, science, and individualism over tradition and religious authority.

Darwinism: the theory developed by Charles Darwin asserting that life arose and slowly evolved through the natural selection of favorable variations found within species.

Parenthood, shared this snide attitude. She advocated birth control and sterilization—both voluntary and involuntary (Sanger labeled minority groups as genetically inferior and called them "human weeds")—and said that the morality of those who refused to limit the number of children they bore was actually "moral imbecility."[12]

Unsurprisingly, these individuals lived out what they taught. Russell had several marriages and adulterous relationships. Sanger had several adulterous affairs, including one with Havelock Ellis. Ellis encouraged his wife to have lesbian relationships, which he then "researched."

Today, though, it is widely believed that suppressing sexual desire hurts people. This materialist, Darwinist view flowered most notoriously in the research of Alfred Kinsey, who issued two reports, *Sexual Behavior in the Human Male* (1948) and *Sexual Behavior in the Human Female* (1953), which challenged traditional views on sex and marriage. Kinsey's seemingly scientific reports, though now known to have been based on faulty and fraudulent research, had a tremendous impact.[13] To those convinced of Freud's and Kinsey's arguments, religious rules about sexuality make people unhealthy, unhappy, and mean.[14]

> To those convinced of Freud's and Kinsey's arguments, religious rules about sexuality make people unhealthy, unhappy, and mean.

The sexual revolution portrayed religious standards of sexuality as immoral and unhealthy because those promoting the sexual revolution were precommitted to **materialism**, which says that only the material world exists and that the supernatural world is an illusion. Yet while many sought to eliminate God from the sexual revolution, others sought to enlist his support for it. In language presaging modern efforts to deny the Bible's teachings on homosexuality, Rustum and Della Roy wrote in *Honest Sex* that premarital chastity and adultery weren't that important to God. "Infinitely better scholars than we have established that one cannot find any literal or simple connection in the Bible claiming that [monogamy, chastity, and the prohibition against adultery and masturbation] were God's law or will," they wrote.[15] Joseph Fletcher went even further, saying that so-called moral absolutes, such as prohibitions on lying, adultery, fornication, and theft, were sometimes permissible, depending on the situation. He suggested that each of the Ten Commandments be amended to add the word "ordinarily."[16]

> The absolute of complete individual autonomy has replaced the biblical absolute of sexuality inside of marriage.

These influences generated a tectonic shift in the West's moral core, and we're drowning in the resulting tsunami. Comprehensive sex education, now the norm even for young children, teaches a radical sexual libertinism. Few people blink when sexually explicit books, or those that normalize same-sex relationships, such as *Heather Has Two Mommies*, are featured in school libraries.[17]

The Consequences of the Sexual Revolution

The absolute of complete individual autonomy has replaced the biblical absolute of sexuality inside of marriage. And as the celebrated French sociologist Alexis de Tocqueville, who visited America in the 1830s, wrote, such individualism is selfish, and it tears at the fabric of society. According to de Tocqueville, "Selfishness blights the germ of all virtue; individualism, at first, only saps the virtues of public life; but, in the long run, it attacks and destroys all others, and is at length absorbed in downright selfishness."[18]

As it turns out, true freedom is one thing the sexual revolution failed to provide. Its handcuffs may be wrapped in velvet, but they are handcuffs nonetheless. As one blogger articulately noted, "We're told that we are sexually 'liberated' if we throw ourselves at strangers and give ourselves over to people who couldn't possibly care less about us.... If modern attitudes about sex have 'liberated' us, what, precisely, have we been freed from? Security? Commitment? Trust? ... Let freedom ring, right?"[19] John Stonestreet agrees: "Nothing is costing our society more, nothing is costing our churches and our homes [more], nothing is creating more human casualties than sexual brokenness masquerading as sexual freedom."[20]

> As it turns out, true freedom is one thing the sexual revolution failed to provide.

How is the sexual revolution hurting people? Let's look at both the personal and social consequences.

The Personal Consequences of the Sexual Revolution

Disordered sexuality. In *Mere Christianity*, C. S. Lewis illustrated disordered sexuality, imagining a country in which a full theater of people would watch as a covered plate was brought to the stage and a piece of meat was unveiled in the manner of a striptease act. Lewis asked, "Would you not think that in that country something had gone wrong with the appetite for food?"[21] In such a country, it isn't that people are starving, Lewis pointed out, but that their appetites cannot be satiated in the way they're attempting to fulfill them. Of course, to those selling sexuality, this is exactly the point. Somehow you have to fill them up but make them *feel* as if they're starving. That's what the sex industry does, and it is dehumanizing, Stonestreet explains, because it turns a beautiful, authentic part of God's creation into an impulse so base that it may be satisfied with virtual sex on a computer.[22]

Same-sex-attraction issues. The sexual revolution also legitimized same-sex sexual relationships. In recent times, same-sex marriage has gained significant momentum through the landmark US Supreme Court decision *Obergefell v. Hodges*. The court didn't just find that laws against same-sex marriage are unconstitutional. It found that the Constitution guarantees the right to **personal autonomy** and demanded removal of restrictions that prevent people from legally pursuing it. In this one decision, the court overthrew a millennia-old definition of marriage and established a precedent for overturning future laws seen as inhibiting sexual freedom.[23]

> *Personal Autonomy:* the belief that individuals should have the freedom to decide what is right for their own lives and live in whatever manner brings them the most happiness.

In many ways, popular-culture portrayals of homosexuality made this decision inevitable. Fewer than 4 percent of people are committed to the lesbian, gay, bisexual, or transgender (LGBT) lifestyle, but the overwhelmingly positive and constant portrayal of LGBT relationships in the media has led Americans to think that 25 percent of the population is LGBT.[24] Many self-proclaimed Christian writers have gotten on board, including psychologist David Myers and bloggers Rachel Held Evans and Matthew Vines. These writers argue that everyone has the right to sex and that the Bible is ambiguous about homosexual sex. Therefore, sexual relationships with those of the same sex aren't necessarily ungodly.[25]

To be fair, many Christians advocating same-sex sexual relations say homosexual sex must be monogamous to be godly. But this isn't a condition many same-sex activists are willing to accept. Liberal commentator Andrew Sullivan, a homosexual man, says, "There is something baleful about the attempt of some gay conservatives to educate homosexuals and lesbians into an uncritical acceptance of a stifling model of heterosexual normality."[26] Marvin Ellison, a Presbyterian Church (USA) pastor and retired professor of Christian ethics at Bangor Theological Seminary and a homosexual man, promotes a "liberating Christian ethic" called "erotic justice" that "goes beyond the prevailing patriarchal paradigm."[27] Ellison includes as ethical practices **sadomasochism** and **polyamory**, Greek for "many loves," which he justifies based on the model of the three persons of the Trinity.[28]

> *Sadomasochism:* the act of deriving pleasure from either inflicting (sadism) or receiving (masochism) pain during sex.

As we'll see later in this chapter, these authors don't have some source of new knowledge about sexual matters. They've just decided to depart from what the Bible says.

Pornography. Pornography means "the writings of a harlot." For men, pornography is usually visual. For women, it's often written, such as the book *50 Shades of Grey*. Pornography is seemingly ever present. Thirty-five percent of all web searches are now reportedly pornographic,[29] and of those who use the Internet—which is more than a third of the world's population—42.7 percent view porn.[30] And it's not just adults. According to some sources, up to 90 percent of eight- to sixteen-year-olds have viewed pornography online.[31]

> *Pornography:* any written or visual materials containing explicit sexual acts intended to elicit lustful desires in place of emotionally bonding with another human being.

Pornography changes how we view ourselves and how we treat others. As we saw in chapter 7, a Princeton University study showed that viewing pictures of scantily clad women activated the "tool-use part" of men's brains, causing them to view women as tools to be used.[32] At the very least, regular viewing of pornography seriously damages true intimacy by treating people as objects of lust rather than as human beings.

Frighteningly, pornography doesn't just change what people think *about*. It changes the anatomy and physiology of the brain itself. Citing the research of psychologist William Struthers, author Janice Crouse describes pornography as an addiction like crack cocaine that causes the brain to become "neurochemically dependent" on pornography viewing to "produce the surge of feelings" that can satisfy the brain's craving.[33] In fact, pornography *shrinks* the areas of the brain connecting the decision-making sector to the sector that links behaviors to outcomes. It also reduces brain activity in areas related to motivation. In plain English, a person who regularly looks at porn eventually loses the ability to consider the consequences of such behavior and ultimately the desire to do anything except look at porn.[34] Unfortunately, as we'll see next, these consequences aren't just personal. They affect all of society.

The Social Consequences of the Sexual Revolution

Confusion. The sexual revolution has led to society-wide confusion. In an interview with Lena Dunham, star of HBO's hit show *Girls*, television critic Tim Molloy asked about the artistic value of having so many characters naked for much of each episode. The show's producer, Judd Apatow, erupted, calling the question "sexist and offensive." Molloy asked why he saw it that way, but Apatow wouldn't answer.[35] Somewhere, in Apatow's view, Molloy crossed a line, but Apatow wasn't willing to say where the line was, or why it was drawn where it was. And if Molloy didn't understand why his question was out of line, then, as scholar William Voegeli puts it in his droll analysis of the situation, "his inability or refusal to recognize the boundaries of decent discourse [was] one more reason to condemn him."[36]

The rules have changed. Philosopher and pastor Dale Kuehne observes that one of society's biggest taboos is "One may not criticize someone else's life choices or behavior."[37] Questioning another's sexual choices simply isn't tolerated today. Those who violate this rule will be shunned.

> Questioning another's sexual choices simply isn't tolerated today. Those who violate this rule will be shunned.

Unfortunately, universities are making it even more confusing. Professors who trumpet aberrant sexuality are no longer viewed as "dirty old men" (and women). They're celebrated as cutting-edge scholars. A growing number of colleges and universities offer degrees in LGBT studies. The City College of San Francisco LGBT Studies major, for example, incorporates "queer theory" in its course offerings. Among the required courses are "Queer Creative Process" and "Queer Cinema in the 70's."[38] Not to be outdone, the University of Maryland offers a course on "The Queer Child."[39] Adding to these offerings, universities like Harvard University, the University of Southern California, and the University of Tennessee host "sex weeks" to screen pornographic films and hand out safe-sex kits.

But sex weeks and courses on queer theory seem tame compared to the offerings at the University of Waterloo in Ontario, Canada, where courses like "The Dark Side of Sexuality" and "Sexual Pleasure" involve "theoretical and empirical examination" of everything from pornography to paraphilia and sex toys to sexual role playing.[40]

Open, pornographic discussion of sexuality has the effect of taking something deeply personal and mysterious and making it political and mechanical. Postmodernist scholar Jean-Francois Lyotard saw open perversion as a delightful way to "gnaw away at the great institutionalized narrative apparatuses" defining what is normal.[41] Lyotard even defended the North American Man/Boy Love Association (NAMBLA), whose goal is to legalize men having "consensual" sex with underage boys.

When leading scholars openly defend a criminal inclination, such as **pedophilia**, sexual freedom has taken a dangerous turn. This is especially true with pornography. Regular users are more likely to believe that sexual-assault victims are to blame or that rape isn't a serious crime.[42] Forty-six percent of child molesters have said that pornography directly led to their molestations.[43] It is believed that thousands of children are exploited annually through child pornography and prostitution in the United States, and perhaps more than a million worldwide.[44] Ironically, if you ask people if they're against rape, molestation, and sex trafficking, they'll say yes. Yet an astounding number support these very things with every click of their mouses.

> *Pedophilia:* a psychiatric condition in which an adult has abnormal sexual desires for prepubescent children.

Worse, just like the cruel and arbitrary government that arose in the aftermath of the French Revolution, the sexual revolution's new rules are even more arbitrary and bizarre than the ones it overthrew. For example, in 2014, among the offenses considered to constitute sexual violence on a University of Michigan website was "withholding sex and affection."[45] From comments made in response to an online article about it, students were apparently brought up on charges of sexual violence for being reluctant to make sex a part of their relationships. This kind of thinking is to sexual health what an antibiotic-resistant superbug is to physical health. It's mutating and deadlier than ever.

Defiance. Admittedly, sexual politics would mean very little if humans weren't interested in sex. But we are. Historically, sexual relations have been tempered by *morality*, which isn't as much about rules as it is about forming character and minds.[46] Our sexual morality affects how we approach everything else, from the role of science and government to issues like adultery, gay marriage, and abortion.[47]

> Historically, sexual relations have been tempered by *morality*, which isn't as much about rules as it is about forming character and minds.

Take same-sex marriage, for example. Commenting on his own research, sociologist Mark Regnerus notes that "of the men who view pornographic material 'every day or almost every day,' 54 percent 'strongly agreed' that gay and lesbian marriage should be legal, compared with around 13 percent of those whose porn-use patterns were either monthly or less often than that."[48] In this study, porn use emerged as a significant variable even when a person's political views, marital status, age, religion, and sexual orientation were taken into account. Apparently, other researchers have speculated, pornography use "activates a sexually 'liberal' mindset" that "embraces non-judgment toward and even approval of nontraditional sexual behavior."[49] To theologian Albert Mohler, this is evidence that our worldviews "are not shaped only by arguments and cognitive engagements, but also by impressions and experiences."[50]

Even economics can't escape the sexual revolution. Marxists have employed the language of sexual revolution to insist that capitalism speaks primarily to heterosexual maleness and that it ought to give way to socialism, which speaks to the total "decentered subject[s]" of numerous genders that "may exhibit many different subjectivities simultaneously ..., none of which [are] given privilege as representing the [subjects'] real essence, whether natural or historical.... The processes of interpellation [are also] without a goal or end to which they are moving."[51] No one is sure where this kind of thinking will lead, but it's an odd fact of the sexual revolution that it has moved from parading down Pennsylvania Avenue in Washington, DC, in annual events like the Capital Pride Festival to marching on Wall Street.

When it comes to Main Street, the sexual revolution's target is the Christian faith. A study of Christian young men found that those who reported using pornography also reported lower levels of religious practice, lower self-worth, lower identity development regarding dating, and higher levels of depression.[52] Of course, people can return to their faith even after making a series of bad choices. But some choices—such as sex outside of marriage and living together outside of marriage—seem to have a long-term diminishing effect on faith.[53] How we relate to God affects our lifestyles, and our lifestyles in turn affect how we relate to God.

Despair. The shifting sexual landscape makes it harder for people to find the meaning and purpose the marriage culture once provided. Scholars Arthur Levine and Jeanette Cureton wrote about college students, "They are desperate to have only one marriage, and they want it to be happy. They don't know whether this is possible

> When it comes to Main Street, the sexual revolution's target is the Christian faith.

anymore."[54] Is it any wonder that such unfulfilled longings for marital bliss lead to despair? Mark Regnerus theorizes that sexual promiscuity and pornography have changed the relational calculus for young adults.[55] When sexuality was protected in marriage, women were also protected. If men wanted sex, they had to commit to marriage. As John Stonestreet puts it, "Women were able to keep the supply low through marriage, and men have a high demand."[56]

The sexual revolution, though, flooded the market. The price of sex went down, especially when men, through pornography, were "getting their demands met without even having another human being in the room. Suddenly the price-tag just bottoms out, sex becomes cheap, in the worst way possible."[57] When a man insists that a woman live with him before getting married, a woman who wants a stable relationship feels she must agree. As of 2012, 7.8 million couples were living together in the United States, a 900 percent increase in the past fifty years. That's two-thirds of couples. And only one in four Americans disapproves of the trend.[58]

Cohabitation doesn't lead to better marriages, though. Numerous studies have indicated that it often doesn't lead to marriage at all. Cohabiting couples are more likely to separate, less likely to reconcile, and more likely to be unfaithful than married couples.[59] Cohabiting before marriage has been associated with an increased divorce risk. Apologists for the living-together trend say

> *Cohabitation:* an arrangement whereby two people live together in a sexual relationship without being married.

the age at which a couple is married, not whether they live together, determines the likelihood of divorce.[60] A host of studies disagree, but even if it were true, it explains too little. Cohabiting couples report poorer relationship quality, accumulate less wealth, and are more likely to report depression and alcohol abuse.[61]

How the Church Contributes to the Sexual Revolution

The Bible considers sexual immorality to be sin, and yet it doesn't demean sexuality itself. Unfortunately, some of the church fathers, such as Chrysostom, Jerome, Origen, and Augustine, did. According to pastor Randy Alcorn, the church's approach to sexuality since that time has made things even worse: "In her zeal to hold the line against immorality, the church miserably failed to embrace or project a positive view of sex," he says. "The church's antisexual posture was ultimately anti-human, since people are sexual beings. That posture not only set the stage for the sexual revolution but caused the church to be caught flat-footed when the revolution came."[62]

Another reason the church's voice is muted on the topic of sexuality is that Christians themselves fall into sexual sin. Pornography is one clear example. My friend Josh McDowell believes that the issue of pornography is the greatest threat to the church in our time. Pastors and parishioners alike are addicted. Another example is hypocrisy. It has been said that **hypocrisy** is the tribute that vice pays to virtue. In other words, virtue is fake and hypocrisy is inevitable. It's deeply discouraging to those trapped in sexual brokenness to realize that the ones publicly holding up the standard of purity are privately committing mutiny against it. Indeed, as Dale Kuehne puts it, "There is good reason to believe the sexual revolution has more profoundly impacted the behavior of twenty-first-century Christians than has the Bible."[63]

> *Hypocrisy*: the practice of claiming to have moral standards that don't match a person's behavior; behaving in a manner contrary to how one believes people should behave.

Christians ought to be concerned—and not just for themselves. If we want to have a positive influence on the culture, we need to care.

3. WHY SHOULD CHRISTIANS CARE?

Summarizing the work of sociologist Philip Rieff, Rod Dreher points out that, historically, Christianity "did not merely renounce but redirected the erotic instinct."[64] It turned what can be a destructive impulse into something that stabilized society. It also gave men and women purpose and created a healthier environment in which to raise children. This all started with a biblical view of sexuality that informed views about health and wellness and promoted a reasonable understanding of gender differences.

Christians Should Care Because God Cares

A couple of years ago, I met a college student named Blake, who had shared his commitment to biblical teaching on homosexuality with his astronomy professor. The professor responded with a ten-page, single-spaced letter that not only claimed that the Bible doesn't speak against homosexuality but also veered into lengthy rants against the emperor Constantine's illegitimate "co-opting" of pagan holidays and accused the Bible of being pro-slavery and anti-science. The professor acknowledged having been a Pentecostal Christian in his youth and told Blake, "I am not trying to destroy your religious faith, but ... fundamentalism is intellectually, morally, and ethically bankrupt.... You owe yourself better than that."[65]

Contrary to what Blake's professor believes, the Bible is pro-love, not anti-sex. As pastor John MacArthur affirms, "God's love is the single central principle that defines the Christian's entire duty."[66] In both Romans 13:8–10 and Galatians 5:14,[67] the apostle Paul said that the commandments are summed up in the command to love our neighbors. This kind of love involves kindness, tenderheartedness, and forgiveness (Eph. 4:32).[68] As MacArthur emphasizes, "True love is always sacrificial, self-giving, merciful, compassionate, sympathetic, kind, generous, and patient."[69]

So what happened to love? Sin. Humanity departed from the way God says is best. In the fog of sin, sex and love parted ways too, and they still seem to be headed toward opposite poles. Without the guidance of God's love, we're left with a counterfeit sexuality based on immorality (from the Greek word **porneia**, "which includes every kind of sexual sin"), impurity (from the Greek word *akatharsia*, which refers to filth, crudeness, and perversion), and covetousness (self-gratification).[70] True love gives. Counterfeit love takes. True love builds up. Counterfeit love tears down. True love takes a long-term view. Counterfeit love focuses only on short-term pleasure. True love treats people as persons. Counterfeit love treats people as objects. True love is shapely and glorious. Counterfeit love is hideously distorted.

> *Porneia*: from the Greek for "sexually immoral acts," which include fornication, adultery, homosexuality, incest, and bestiality.

But all is not lost. The biblical account doesn't just condemn sin. It takes sin into account, focuses on protecting people from sexual harm, and anticipates redemption, starting in the Old Testament.

Sexuality in the Old Testament

The most quoted passage about sexuality in the Old Testament is probably Leviticus 18:6–23, which refers to "uncover[ing] nakedness," a euphemism for sexual relations, which literally means "dis-covering the sex of."[71] The passage prohibits people from having sexual relations with parents, with parents' spouses, with siblings or their spouses, with one's children or grandchildren or with their spouses, with close relatives, with married neighbors, with someone of the same sex, or with animals. God promised that if people did these things, the land itself would "vomit" them out (vv. 24–30).[72] Those who chose to be a part of the nation of Israel were to keep themselves from sexual impurity. Those who refused to pursue **sexual purity** or repent of their sexual sins were to be "cut off" or made to leave the community. In some cases, Levitical law called for the death penalty.

> *Sexual Purity*: the condition of being free from sexual immorality.

Due to the current cultural interest in sexual identity, particularly homosexual identity, passages that oppose such behavior are seen as de facto proof that the Bible is cruel and insensitive. Some just mock it, pointing to other passages in Leviticus that speak, for example, about keeping linen and wool separate in personal clothing (possibly a symbolic religious prohibition because these two fabrics were to be combined only in certain tabernacle cloths)[73] and saying, "See, we don't keep *those* rules. So why would we keep the rules about sexuality?"

Leviticus contains two kinds of laws: *ceremonial laws* and *civic laws*. It's pretty easy to tell the difference between the two, so you shouldn't be too concerned when people conflate them to create confusion. It's worth noting, though, that the civic laws in Leviticus are *not* about sexual attraction (i.e., our inward desires), nor do they single out one kind of sexual sin. All—including adultery, fornication, homosexual sex, incest, and bestiality—are treated as sinful. God views sexual sin as a tipping point toward idolatry and something that hurts the people themselves. Jeremiah 7:19 says, "'Is it I whom they provoke?' declares the LORD. 'Is it not themselves, to their own shame?'" Sexual sin produces shame among people in the community, breaks down relationships, and shatters trust. To violate the sexual commands of the community was to say, in effect, "I'm going to put my own interests above God and the needs of the community, and there is nothing you can do about it." Such impudence always hurt those most vulnerable—women and children. It has the same effect today.

> God views sexual sin as a tipping point toward idolatry and something that hurts the people themselves.

We must be careful how we apply Leviticus today. We don't live in a nation God chose in the same way he chose Israel. This doesn't mean that the sexual practices forbidden in Leviticus are okay, however. We're called to behave in a sexually pure way (1 Pet. 2:11)[74] and to show society how failing to heed God's principles breaks down relationships and communities.

Sexuality in the New Testament

In Matthew 19:4–6, Jesus affirmed the Old Testament teaching about marriage by saying,

> Have you not read that he who created [human beings] from the beginning made them male and female, and said, "Therefore a man shall leave his father and his mother and hold fast to his wife, and the two shall become one flesh"? So they are no longer two but one flesh. What therefore God has joined together, let not man separate.

Sexuality has a purpose. Marriage has a purpose. New Testament teaching on sexuality must be considered on this basis.

What constitutes sexual sin in the New Testament is clearly stated in Hebrews 13:4: "Let marriage be held in honor among all, and let the marriage bed be undefiled, for God will judge the sexually immoral and adulterous." Paul reiterated God's ideal for sexuality and added another motivation to remain sexually pure: we are part of Christ's body of believers. Paul wrote to the Corinthian believers, "Do you not know that your bodies are members of Christ? Shall I then take the members of Christ and make them members of a prostitute? Never! … Flee from sexual immorality. Every other sin a person commits is outside the body, but the sexually immoral person sins against his own body" (1 Cor. 6:13–18).[75] Paul didn't just condemn sin. He showed how it's possible to repent of all kinds of sins—sorcery, jealousy, anger, envy, and drunkenness as well as sexual sin—and to bear the fruit of the

Spirit: "love, joy, peace, patience, kindness, goodness, faithfulness, gentleness, [and] self-control" (Gal. 5:16–24).[76]

Some object to referencing Paul's words about sexual sin, especially about homosexuality. "*Jesus* didn't talk about it, so it's not important," they say. As Dale Kuehne notes, however, "The most plausible explanation for why Jesus didn't address the topic of homosexuality is that no one asked, and no one asked because no one imagined there was a need to ask."[77] Even if Jesus was silent about homosexuality, it means very little. He was also silent about sex between close relatives and sex between adults and children. This doesn't mean those practices are insignificant to God.

In fact, though, Jesus wasn't silent about sex. In Mark 7:21–23 he said, "From within, out of the heart of man, come evil thoughts, sexual immorality, theft, murder, adultery, coveting, wickedness, deceit, sensuality, envy, slander, pride, foolishness. All these evil things come from within, and they defile a person." The Greek word for "sexual immorality," *porneia*, was consistently used in early Judaism to refer to all manner of sexual sin, including same-sex intercourse, incest, adultery, and bestiality. Robert Gagnon summarizes the biblical passages about sexuality as follows: "As with the Old Testament, every New Testament text that treats sexual relations always presupposes a two-sex requirement."[78] Matthew Vines, a gay Christian author, disagrees. "My main argument is not that Paul is wrong," he asserts, "but that the very conception of what long-term, committed same-sex relationships are now did not exist in the ancient world."[79] But what Vines claims isn't true. Paul was a student of Greek philosophy. He would have been familiar with Greek writers like the philosopher Plato, the Spartan warrior Callicratidas, and the historian Plutarch, who filled their works with references to homosexual relationships. The relationships they described weren't based on promiscuity or violence, as Vines claims, but on tenderness.[80] Paul's goal wasn't to show how to engage in sin more tenderly but how to be set free through God's power.

> Paul's goal wasn't to show how to engage in sin more tenderly but how to be set free through God's power.

Some authors have accused conservative theologians of cherry-picking passages condemning homosexual sex and overlooking passages dealing with heterosexual sins, such as adultery. Personally, I don't see evidence that theologians are ignoring other sexual sins. But even if they are, does this make illicit sex a virtue and justify ignoring Jesus's teachings?[81] Clearly, given our human tendency to sin, we ought to be humble in interpreting Scripture. If our convictions run against Scripture, though, it is our convictions, not the text, that should change.[82] But Scripture's arc, which Jesus made clear, is that we are made male and female and that marriage is to be between one man and one woman.

Christians Should Care Because Sexual Brokenness Destroys Health and Wellness

In addition to caring about sexuality because God cares, Christians ought to care about sexual brokenness because it destroys human flourishing. Ideas have consequences, and the sexual revolution's path is a destructive one. On college campuses, 78 percent of undergrads have reported participating in hookups, with a third of the women reporting that they had engaged in sexual intercourse after hooking up.[83] More than 80 percent of hookups involve alcohol, which two-thirds of respondents said impaired their judgment and one-third said led to their being taken advantage of.[84] Twenty-three percent of college women in one survey reported a history of unwanted sexual intercourse (i.e., date rape).[85]

Promiscuity has led to the skyrocketing of STDs. In Alfred Kinsey's day, there were only two known STDs, both of which were treatable with penicillin. Now there are more than twenty-four, and more than half have no cure.[86] Of the STDs emerging since the 1950s, the most deadly is HIV/AIDS, which initially spread and continues to spread primarily through male homosexual sex. According to the Centers for Disease Control and Prevention (CDC), gay and bisexual men represented 83 percent of new HIV diagnoses in 2014, while heterosexuals represented 24 percent. The CDC also says that more than twenty thousand people in the United States become infected with HIV/AIDS each year. Around 36 percent of these new infections occur among young adults between the ages of twenty and twenty-nine.[87] Although deaths from HIV/AIDS have declined over the past decade, AIDS is still a killer. In 2013, approximately seven thousand deaths were attributed to HIV/AIDS, more than gun homicides during that same period.[88]

Even if a person doesn't acquire an STD, choosing to be involved in sexual activity outside of marriage affects the trajectory of a person's life. Those who have engaged in premarital sex fairly often are more likely to be unfaithful in marriage.[89] And women who are sexually active prior to marriage face a considerably higher risk of marital disruption (i.e., separation or divorce).[90] By contrast, lower sexual activity among adolescents is correlated with higher levels of well-being. Sexually active girls are more than three times as likely to report symptoms of depression as those who abstain, and sexually active boys are more than twice as likely to report symptoms of depression. In fact, these two groups report higher incidences of attempted suicide; the suicide risk for boys, in particular, is eight times higher if they're sexually active.[91]

> In Alfred Kinsey's day, there were only two known STDs, both of which were treatable with penicillin. Now there are more than twenty-four, and more than half have no cure.

Christians ought to discourage behaviors that have such a negative effect on health and wellness. And destruction and heartache are exactly what the sexual revolution has led to.

Christians Ought to Care Because the Sexual Revolution Has Redefined Gender Relationships

The biblical view of gender starts with the creation of male and female in Genesis 1:27.[92] Maleness and femaleness were portrayed as important even before Adam and Eve had sex.[93] But the modern view, which originated from the idea that each individual is his or her own authority, is that the body is irrelevant to a person's gender.

Interestingly, authors like Leonard Sax, a medical doctor and PhD psychologist who doesn't claim to be a Christian, have blown the whistle on the politically correct redefining of gender. Sax believes that the rise of neuroticism and anxiety among young adults is, at least in part, the result of our culture's mixed messages about gender.[94] Boys and girls are indeed different, he says, and ignoring the difference is a big mistake.

Among other things, Dr. Sax presents evidence from multiple studies that male and female brain tissue is "intrinsically different";[95] that girls hear better than boys;[96] that women are better than men at interpreting facial expressions;[97] that girls have more of the kinds of cells (cones) in their eyes that focus on color and texture, whereas boys have more cells (rods) that focus on location, direction, and speed;[98] that girls are better able to talk about their feelings;[99] that boys are more likely to enjoy risk taking for its own sake;[100] that boys and girls play differently;[101] and that boys and girls feel pain differently.[102]

These differences aren't just a matter of socialization. Male and female brains are wired differently. The wiring in a typical male brain runs between the front and back of either the left or right hemisphere, whereas in a typical female brain, it runs from side to side through both hemispheres. For women, there is a constant interplay between the left hemisphere, which is related to thinking tasks, and the right hemisphere, which is related to intuition.[103] It's different for men. Imagine the two sides of the brain being two banks of a river. Women build bridges between the two banks and move easily back and forth. Men race up and down one side of the river, crossing only to race up and down the other side. At the risk of oversimplifying brain function, a man either works with tools or relates to others. Women can work with tools and relate at the same time. That's a significant difference, and you can probably think of lots of examples from your own life.

Gender differences are present from birth and are most pronounced in childhood.[104] They affect how boys and girls live, learn, and make friends. And surprisingly, the differences persist even among boys who are more effeminate and girls who are more tomboyish. Says Dr. Sax, "Tomboys have more in common with very feminine girls than they have with boys, at least when it comes to how they see the world."[105] We'll all be better off, Sax believes, if we work *with* children's natures as boys and girls rather than minimizing them, because "human nature is gendered to the core."[106] Medical doctors Joe McIlhaney Jr. and Freda McKissic Bush agree: "We all lose when an entire generation grows up in a fictitious world where truth [about gender] is suppressed and health sacrificed."[107]

> **Gender differences aren't just a matter of socialization. Male and female brains are wired differently.**

Gender differences are especially pronounced when it comes to sexuality, and not just in the "liberated" West. An international consortium of psychologists surveyed sixteen thousand people from fifty-two countries in Europe, Asia, Africa, and the Americas. They found that men and women all over the world are different when it comes to sexual motivation and sexual interest.[108] In particular, females are more vulnerable in sexual relations. The institution of marriage balances this out, says researcher Janet Shaw Crouse.[109] When marriage disappears, everyone loses, particularly women.

"Men and women have inherent integrity in their respective sexes," Robert Gagnon says. "Men are wholly male and women are wholly female. They are not half-male and half-female, respectively."[110] Only in a man-woman union do the two make a sexual whole. Accepting the differences between men and women—rather than denying them—is the key to fulfilling relationships for both.

In their book *Every Young Man's Battle*, which encourages godly sexuality in young men, Steve Arterburn and Fred Stoeker bluntly state that "guys give emotions so they can get sex.

Girls give sex so they can get the emotions."[111] That's true, but it's more than that. It's about *honoring* the differences between men and women and seeing them as beautiful. Our failure to do that, Mary Eberstadt wistfully notes, has led not to a "sexual desert" but to a "sexual flood," a "torrent of poisonous imagery, beginning even in childhood, that has engulfed women and men, only to beach them eventually somewhere alone and apart, far from the reach of one another."[112]

> The sexual revolutionaries won sexual freedom at the expense of fulfilling relationships. And now we're all losing.

To summarize, the Bible speaks clearly about sexuality, but the rejection of Scripture has led to confusion about what is important in society and how to flourish in our complex times, and even about gender itself. The sexual revolutionaries won sexual freedom at the expense of fulfilling relationships. And now we're all losing. Is there anything Christians can do?

4. WHAT SHOULD CHRISTIANS DO?

Theologian D. A. Carson points out that "the plurality of errors and heresies that our generation confronts demands that lines be drawn—thoughtfully, carefully, humbly, corrigibly, but drawn nonetheless."[113] Somehow we need to draw the line without meanness or thoughtlessness, especially about an issue as close to the heart as sexuality.

John Stonestreet warns that when it comes to sexual brokenness, Christians tend to take one of three counterproductive approaches. First, they focus on fear: "Don't have sex because you'll get a disease or get pregnant or have your heart broken."[114] These are distinct possibilities, but love of the good, not fear of evil, should motivate us. Second, they focus on what Stonestreet calls "the princess approach": "If you abstain from sex outside of marriage you'll get a stunning, sexy wife or a handsome Prince Charming and life will be magical." But in life, we aren't guaranteed to win just because we play by the rules. Bad things happen, and it's self-centered to think our being good exempts us from that.[115] The third counterproductive approach, Stonestreet says, is giving in and viewing chastity as honorable but impractical. Jenell Paris, a professor at Messiah College, represents such a view with her call for a "sacred compromise," in which the church would encourage people to be chaste but also advise them to use contraception.[116] But contraception can't fix sexual brokenness. We need something more.

> Contraception can't fix sexual brokenness. We need something more.

So if these common approaches to sexual brokenness are inadequate, what ought we to do?

Elevate Intimacy

In *The World, the Flesh, and Father Smith*, Bruce Marshall's Father Smith character meets a famous author of erotica and counters her claim that religion is a substitute for sex. Father Smith says, "I still prefer to believe that sex is a substitute for religion and that the young man who rings the bell at the brothel is unconsciously looking for God."[117] It's a compelling point. What if obsession with sexual satisfaction is really a yearning for the kind of **intimacy** only

God can provide? If it is, then the way we satisfy our physical lusts may be preventing us from finding what we really seek. Only God can meet our deepest needs. As Douglas Wilson states it, "Lust demands from a finite thing … what only the Infinite can provide."[118]

Still, many have given up. God's design for intimacy isn't realistic, they say. Bestselling author Toni Bentley responded to an article on monogamy in *Time* magazine, saying, "Monogamy is … a charade we insist on, thus institutionalizing dishonesty."[119] But cynicism can't answer our deepest needs either. At a time in my life when I was wondering whether God could meet my need for intimacy, I happened across a book called *Passion and Purity* by Elisabeth Elliot. Elliot and her husband, Jim, courted chastely for seven years as they prepared to answer God's call to the mission field. At last they wed. Three years into their marriage, though, Jim and four other men were killed by the remote Ecuadoran tribe they were trying to reach. In a book about their courtship, Elliot said, "I am convinced that the human heart hungers for constancy.… There is dullness, monotony, sheer boredom in all of life when virginity and purity are no longer protected and prized. By trying to grab fulfillment everywhere, we find it nowhere."[120]

It's true. Saying we're just evolving animals doesn't answer the deepest question in our hearts: Am I loved? As pastor Andy Stanley says, "I've officiated my share of weddings and done my share of premarital counseling. I always ask couples why they are getting married. Survival

> "By trying to grab fulfillment everywhere, we find it nowhere."

of the species never makes the list.… We desire intimacy—to know and to be fully known without fear. Intimacy is fragile. Intimacy is powerful. And intimacy is fueled by exclusivity."[121]

Elevating intimacy means challenging the materialist assumption that the point of sex is to satisfy a physical urge. From a Christian viewpoint, the point of sex is to unite a man and a woman in a way that deepens them and protects them as it creates a context for procreation. In God's plan, sexuality isn't a give-and-take. It's all give. Theologian Albert Wolters points out that because of sin, the *good* structure of sex has been diverted to follow a destructive course. We ought "both to *affirm* human sexuality wholeheartedly and to *oppose* its perversions with equal conviction and vigor," he says.[122] As the late Lewis Smedes said, "Redemption does not turn us from sexuality; it illuminates the goodness of it."[123]

Apart from redemption, sex doesn't become bad, though it can be put to harmful—even violent—uses. Rather, it becomes wayward. The further we get from God's plan, the more lost we become, because his sexual standards are based on his image in us. In the end, we essentially say to our sexual partners, "By following my own rules rather than God's, I am making my desires my idol, and you must participate in the sacrifice by allowing me to use you as an object by which I can achieve satisfaction." The other person's willingness to be used doesn't make it any less selfish. In fact, two people using each other selfishly just multiplies selfishness.

Inside the marriage bond, though, two people can breathe life into each other. In the early Roman Church, it was said of Christians that they shared their table with strangers, not their spouses.[124] Before long, the whole culture began seeing the wisdom of Christian sexual morality. The Greek physician Galen said Christians had such an "intense desire to attain moral excellence that they are in no way inferior to true philosophers."[125] Ultimately, based on the example of Christians, Rome passed laws protecting marriage and prohibiting sexual exploitation.

Realize Our True Identity

> Placing our identity in Christ grounds our personhood in something eternal rather than merely physical urges.

People's sexuality is such a strong influence that they tend to see their identity as humans in its light. Many people see themselves as defined by their promiscuity or same-sex attractions, or even their gender ambiguity. Placing our identity in Christ grounds our personhood in something eternal rather than merely physical urges. But this understanding eludes the secular world. Let's consider why.

A secular understanding of identity. People with same-sex attractions often identify milestone events in their own experiences that serve as benchmarks for embracing a gay, lesbian, or bisexual identity. Such milestones include the "first experience of same-sex attraction, first experience of same-sex behavior to orgasm, labeling oneself as gay, lesbian, or bisexual, disclosure of identity to others, and first same-sex relationship."[126] But as has been well documented in extensive research, not everyone who experiences same-sex attraction develops a gay identity.[127] One interviewee said, "I refuse to identify as homosexual/gay because I find my identity in Christ and those are not Christ-like identities."[128]

The secular view says that such a person is in denial. "You won't be healthy or fulfilled until you admit you're gay," its followers say. But this is to focus on only one aspect of identity: the cues we take from our impulses. Mark Yarhouse, a professor at Regent University who has written extensively on Christianity and homosexuality and has conducted much social science research on the subject, points out that there is another kind of identity: "Just as we do not interpret the existence of predispositions toward depression or anxiety as God making a person depressed or anxious, we want to be cautious about jumping to the conclusion that the existence of an experience or condition reflects God's intention for that person."[129]

> We need to find a way to avoid two extremes: an *arrogant expectation* that people with same-sex attractions can miraculously change and *cynical pessimism* that says they can't change at all.

We have a choice to make. Will we insist that "God made me this way," or will we ask, "How does God want me to grow in Christ-likeness such that I display the fruit of the Spirit in my life and my relationships?"[130] People who make the second choice have often changed their sexual orientation. In fact, 38 percent in one study were able to either change their orientation or successfully live a chaste lifestyle. Only 12 percent failed to do so.[131] Somehow, in ministering to those experiencing same-sex attraction, we need to find a way to avoid two extremes: an *arrogant expectation* that people can miraculously change and *cynical pessimism* that says they can't change at all.

A biblical understanding of identity. We've been focusing on identity as it relates to same-sex attraction, but the same principles apply to heterosexual lust and promiscuity. The biblical understanding is this: our identity includes not only our urges but also what we hope to *become*. After listing many kinds of sinners, the apostle Paul said, "And such were some of you. But you were washed, you were sanctified, you were justified in the name of the Lord Jesus Christ and by the Spirit of our God" (1 Cor. 6:9–11). Paul wasn't necessarily describing a change in desire but rather a change in behavior to be consistent with a forward-looking design and purpose. We humans can set our sights on getting an education to enter a desirable vocation. We can set our sights on saving money in the hopes of starting a business. But most important, we can set our sights on becoming like Christ.

Christianity's attention to great evil is always nested in the context of how it constrains our pursuit of something of inestimably great value. Most people don't see this. I recently received a private note in one of my social-media accounts from someone who said, "I walked away from Christianity because of all the rules." I found it odd how quickly this person had given up. I've never heard someone say, "I had a million-dollar business idea, but I walked away from it because there were too many forms to fill out in getting a business license." That would be crazy. When people say they're tired of the rules, what they're really saying is they've lost hope that the pursuit of faith is a valuable one. Those who hang on are signaling that in spite of the difficulties they may face, they believe that disciplining their impulses will better meet their deepest needs for intimacy and true purpose.

> In spite of the difficulties we may face, disciplining our impulses will better meet our deepest needs for intimacy and true purpose.

Christianity sees sexuality as part of our identity but not as its "central or defining aspect."[132] When people say they have a "homosexual orientation" or even a "heterosexual orientation," they're using categories about identity that obscure God's redemptive work. Rosaria Butterfield, a lesbian, feminist professor who converted to Christianity, puts it this way:

> At its best, sexual orientation is a vestige of our flesh. The term itself cannot be labeled sin or grace.... One's sexual orientation—heterosexual or homosexual or bisexual or pansexual (and the list will not end here)—cannot be sanctified, because sanctification would indeed cause its eradication.... And while you must repent of sexual sin, you cannot repent of sexual orientation, since sexual orientation is an artificial category.[133]

In search of a more biblical idea of identity, some people who previously embraced a homosexual lifestyle now refer to themselves as "postgay." About this expression, Anglican priest Peter Ould says, "Post-gay ... is less about being straight or gay and rather about a choice of a journey."[134] The idea of a journey is a good metaphor. It takes the emphasis off of where our sexuality is right now and places it on what it means to steward it biblically.[135]

Pursue Purity

Many people ask, "How far can I go sexually without being impure?" The wrong assumption behind this question is this: **purity** is a *line*. But it's not. Rather, purity is something

> *Purity:* the condition of being free from immorality.

to be pursued. It's a *destination*. Two questions arise in this pursuit: first, whether we should apologize for pursuing purity; second, whether it's even possible to pursue it at all. Addressing the first question, professor J. Budziszewski says we shouldn't apologize. Rather, "what we should explain is that Christian morality is a prerequisite for happiness, and that it makes us more free, not less—free to do what is good rather than being jerked around by desires," he says. "People need to have the vision of the good that temptation is pulling them away from."[136]

Regarding the second question—whether the pursuit of purity is possible—the answer is yes. But it's not an easy yes, because it requires knowing where temptation lurks and running in the opposite direction. This, Steven Arterburn and Fred Stoeker say, requires building a "line of defense" with your *eyes*, with your *mind*, and with your *heart*.[137]

Building a line of defense with your eyes. What we pay attention to is a good indication of what we worship. And if we know people are watching, we pay attention differently. That's a good thing, from a biblical viewpoint. It's called **accountability**. Technology can help. Rather than filtering out bad Internet content, services like Covenant Eyes will arrange to send a report of your Internet activity to the person of your choice. Knowing that someone else is aware of your movements online is a great motivator for purity. Sin thrives in darkness. When light shines on it, temptation's stronghold is broken.

> *Accountability*: the act of accepting responsibility for one's actions.

Building a line of defense with your mind. Living a set-apart life requires mental alertness. First Peter 1:13–16 says, "Preparing your minds for action, and being sober-minded, set your hope fully on the grace that will be brought to you at the revelation of Jesus Christ." We have to choose to focus our minds on pursuing good goals. We must also focus on the reality behind the airbrushed images: the women and children who are victimized, the rape and molestation, the loneliness, and the fear of rejection. And we must set our minds on seeing others as God sees them.

Building a line of defense with your heart. As we have seen, biblical sexuality has more to do with what we pursue than what we seek to avoid. We must turn from what is bad but also do good (1 Pet. 3:11).[138] It's not just what we know; it's what's in our hearts. That's why Proverbs 4:23 says, "Keep your heart with all vigilance, for from it flow the springs of life." Professor Armand Nicholi has carefully watched his students at Harvard who reported experiencing a Christian conversion. Before their conversions, students described their sexual relationships as providing little of the emotional closeness they desired. After their conversions, they found that even though biblical standards seemed strict, they were less confusing and, in fact, *helpful* in relating to the opposite sex.[139] In turning their hearts toward purity, Nicholi's students found the emotional closeness and relational security that had eluded them.

Repentance and Reconciliation

God understands our weaknesses (Heb. 4:15–16).[140] Through Christ, we conquer them.[141] The Bible pictures God as loving us and wanting us to be restored to him. Psalm 103:8–14 says that in his love and compassion, God removes our sins from us "as far as the east is from the west."

What is required of us is **repentance**—turning from our present course toward Christ. Repentance is hard, but we must not think of it as a bad thing, or even a necessary evil. Repentance is proof of God's kindness. He invites us to repent and welcomes us to his forgiveness. When we acknowledge our wrongdoing and ask forgiveness, it strengthens our pursuit of what is good, true, and beautiful. As Sean McDowell and John Stonestreet put it, "By leading us to see our failures, God graciously leads us to restored lives. The call to repentance is a unique privilege that God's people should welcome."[142]

> *Repentance:* **the act of admitting our transgressions, seeking forgiveness, turning away from evil, and pursuing what is good.**

Repentance doesn't just mean saying we're sorry, though. It means we *stop* doing one thing and *start* doing something else. We *replace* one mind-set or behavior with another:[143]

- Put aside filthiness and instead be thankful (Eph. 5:4).

- Don't participate in the "works of darkness" but "expose them" (v. 11).

- Don't be treacherous, reckless, conceited, or a lover of pleasure, but instead be a lover of God (2 Tim. 3:4).

- Don't stumble around in lameness but "be healed" (Heb. 12:13).

- Don't live "for human passions but for the will of God" (1 Pet. 4:2).

Repentance helps us embrace God's plan for sexual wholeness. Repentance also helps us heal broken relationships. When we're reconciled to God, we become reconcilers ourselves (2 Cor. 5:18–19).[144] We are no longer slaves to sin, so we don't have to submit to its mastery any longer.

> *Chastity:* **the state of abstaining from fornication and adultery.**

Live Chastely

Singleness doesn't feel fair. As one young man said, "I feel like God made me a sexual being, but He's asking me to live as though I'm not."[145] But that mind-set isn't completely true. The Bible isn't just about abstaining from sexual relations outside of marriage. It's about pursuing the good, the true, and the beautiful. **Chastity** is about two things: (1) abstaining from **fornication** (sexual activity between the unmarried) and **adultery** (sexual activity by married people with those to whom they aren't

> *Fornication:* **any sexual activity between two people who are not married.**

> *Adultery:* **any sexual activity between a married person and someone who is not that individual's spouse.**

married); and (2) rightly relating to other sexual beings as a sexual being. Chastity is a good gift we give ourselves and others. It's a way of loving God and loving our neighbors. It's a spiritual practice as much as it is a physical one. And chastity isn't just something that singles should pursue. Married people must be chaste with those who aren't their spouses.

> Chastity is a good gift we give ourselves and others. It's a way of loving God and loving our neighbors.

Both nonmarital sex and chastity require "a kind of faith." Reporter Dawn Eden explains it this way in her advice book for women:

> Both experiences are centered on a kind of faith. One of them, sex before marriage, relies on faith that a man who has not shown faith in you—that is, not enough faith to commit himself to you for life—will come around through the persuasive force of your physical affection. It forces you to follow a set of Darwinian social rules—dressing and acting a certain way to outperform other women competing for mates.... The other experience, chastity, relies on faith that God, as you pursue a closer walk with Him, will lead you to a loving husband. Chastity opens up your world, enabling you to achieve your creative and spiritual potential without the pressure of having to play the dating game.[146]

Chastity involves a moment-by-moment recognition that only God can ultimately meet our need for intimacy. During a difficult time in my life, a counselor challenged me to search Scripture for evidence that God meets my need for intimacy. I was stunned to find dozens of promises of God's personal, devoted attention. God cares for us (1 Pet. 5:7).[147] God rejoices over us with singing (Zeph. 3:17).[148] God will never leave us (Heb. 13:5).[149] Nothing can separate us from God's love (Rom. 8:39).[150] Dale Kuehne observes that "because we are made in the image of God, we are made to be lovers, but for us to become the lovers we are meant to be, we need to dwell in the love of God."[151]

Some Secularists, recognizing the consequences of sexual freedom, are now opposing pornography and promoting virginity. But their reasons for doing so can never encompass all of God's design for us. For example, feminist Andrea Dworkin, based on the idea that any kind of a vulnerable relationship with a man violates a woman's wholeness, promotes a kind of radical virginity that militantly builds a wall around the heart and never lets anyone in.[152]

> Chastity involves a moment-by-moment recognition that only God can ultimately meet our need for intimacy.

The Bible's perspective on sexuality is much larger than this. As opposed to distrustful closed heartedness, chastity keeps an open heart to God and others, even while trusting God to meet our needs and maintaining boundaries around our purity. This gives great purpose to singleness, without denying the fact that single people are sexual beings. Yes, marriage makes some things possible, such as sexual relations, that aren't biblically permitted for singles. But singleness also makes some things possible that aren't part of marriage. As the apostle Paul said in 1 Corinthians 7:32–35,[153] single people have more freedom to minister without anxiety or restraint.

Persist in Selfless Grace

If the goal is to find our identity in Christ, then we need to be careful about dressing and acting in a way that turns others' attention to *us* rather than to *Christ*. Selfless grace replaces seduction with life-giving dignity. Even in areas of life as abstract as architecture, it turns out that there is a "fittingness" or "harmony" that is the essence of beauty.[154] Says Oxford philosopher Roger Scruton, beauty isn't merely an individual pursuit. It's about "fit[ting] appropriately together, creating a soothing … context" that tells a story about beauty itself.[155]

True beauty motivates us to appreciate and protect that which is beautiful. Lust, on the other hand, is focused on selfish possession. Be a person who insists on being appreciated and protected, and who is willing to appreciate and protect others. You may not have lovers throwing themselves at your feet, but your grace and calmness work both inside and out, creating true attractiveness.

> **True beauty motivates us to appreciate and protect that which is beautiful. Lust, on the other hand, is focused on selfish possession.**

Selfless grace is reflected in how we communicate with others, putting them first, listening, being sensitive to how they feel, and desiring them to become everything God has designed them to be. In a way, selfless grace is a more intimate act than sexuality. After all, a kiss is the outside of two bodies touching, but a conversation in which one feels known and desires to know the other person truly goes from the deepest interior of one person to the deepest interior of the other.

> **In a way, selfless grace is a more intimate act than sexuality.**

In his book *Eyes of Honor*, Jonathan Welton tells of overcoming lust to become a protector of beauty. Once when feeling lust for a young woman, Welton felt God saying to him,

> "Jonathan, you are called as a protector of beauty—whether in nature, infants, art, health, or this young lady—I have called you as a protector of beauty. I want you to begin to pray protection over her. Release the love of Father God over her and pray into her destiny." As I sat there praying for her in my heart, I began to feel God's love for her. In a matter of minutes, I had moved from a helpless victim with a mind full of temptation into a powerful man filled with the heart of God toward the woman.[156]

Trying to conquer lust solely in pursuit of our own freedom can also be selfish. The larger question is whether we'll fight against the way society exploits people. Says Welton, "If we are to truly align ourselves with the heart of God and live like Jesus, then whenever temptation rears its head, we will not simply try to avoid sin, but we will begin to cry out for our sisters in bondage."[157] Putting others first as we stand for truth and fight against evil and injustice is the very essence of selfless grace.

Friendship

Dale Kuehne's compelling book *Sex and the iWorld* contrasts two worlds: the "tWorld," based on tradition, and the "iWorld," based on individual autonomy. The tWorld, "constructed on relationships of *obligation*," fails to account for our experiences in a sexualized culture.[158] But so does the iWorld. Sex in the iWorld, Kuehne says, didn't fulfill the deepest longings of people's hearts, the desire to not be alone. In fact, individualism made both problems worse.

> **Sex by itself can never satisfy the deep longing of the soul to connect, to be known.**

"Two of the primary difficulties facing people in the iWorld are loneliness and insecurity," Kuehne observes. "These are inherent by-products of individualism."[159] Sex by itself can never satisfy the deep longing of the soul to connect, to be known. As the Epicurean poet Lucretius once lamented, "The tragedy of sexual intercourse is the perpetual virginity of the soul."[160]

Kuehne proposes replacing the tWorld and the iWorld with the "rWorld," a world of relationship made possible through reconciliation to God in Christ. The rWorld recognizes that sex doesn't satisfy the longing for intimacy because in and of itself, it cannot create a safe space in which to deal with the deeper issues of our hearts: control, envy, confusion, abandonment, abuse, and so forth. Relationships can create such a safe place, though it takes work. We have to commit to living in a Christ-like way. We must be safe to talk to, and we must be the kinds of friends who are open about our own struggles. This doesn't mean airing all of our dirty laundry with everyone; it means leading the way by expressing vulnerability and protecting the vulnerability of others when they share things close to their hearts. The rWorld goes far beyond mere respect. "Christ calls me not only to respect but to love," says Kuehne. "If I only respected, I could then choose to dismiss or ignore. Love means I must be willing to engage with, respect, dialogue with, and even die for [people]."[161]

Whereas the tWorld is ruled by rules, the iWorld is ruled by biochemistry. Having an orgasm is biochemically intense, so it seems it must be the way to pursue love and intimacy. This is why in iWorld movies and television programs, it is assumed that two people cannot fall in love *without* having had sexual relations. The rWorld is different, asserts Kuehne:

> The rWorld, however, has a very different definition of intimacy and love that is based on the idea that love is not merely the feeling produced by the biochemical reactions of a romantic or sexual relationship but a grace given to our souls. If this is true, our happiness and fulfillment would be ultimately rooted in developing our ability to relate to God and one another through our soul.[162]

When we experience intimacy with God, Kuehne explains, we learn to enjoy his love in a way that allows us to be more open with others. Our capacity for intimacy with God overflows into the ability to share love with others and to receive love from them.[163]

But we can't live in the iWorld and the rWorld at the same time. Insisting on individual freedom, by definition, shrinks our relational capacity. The first step out of the iWorld and into the rWorld is to make relationships, not the fulfillment of "I," our top priority.[164]

5. CONCLUSION

At the beginning of this chapter, we met Christopher, a man experiencing lifelong same-sex attraction. As a single man, Christopher has come to see his identity in Christ, not in his sexuality. "My sexual orientation didn't have to be the core of who I was. My primary identity didn't have to be defined by my feelings or sexual attractions. My identity was not 'gay' or 'homosexual,' or even 'heterosexual,' for that matter. But my identity as a child of the living God must be in Jesus Christ alone."[165] Meanwhile, Christopher waits. And his waiting isn't just abstaining from sex. It is rooted in love for God, for his family, and for others. He doesn't know how long the wait will be. But as the saying goes, love cannot be measured by how long you wait. It's about how well you understand why you're waiting.

Christopher's decision is a courageous one. He is often the target of vicious criticism for having made the choice to be chaste and to recommend this choice to others. You may face a similar situation. But like all the battles in life, we aren't running away from evil; we're running toward good. That is why we don't shrink back even when our culture—or our own flesh opposes us. Rather, we move forward into the Promised Land with God's words to Joshua echoing in our minds: "Have I not commanded you? Be strong and courageous. Do not be frightened, and do not be dismayed, for the LORD your God is with you wherever you go" (Josh. 1:9).

> Love cannot be measured by how long you wait. It's about how well you understand why you're waiting.

ENDNOTES

1. Christopher Yuan and Angela Yuan, *Out of a Far Country: A Gay Son's Journey to God; A Broken Mother's Search for Hope* (Colorado Springs, CO: WaterBrook, 2011), 109.

2. Yuan and Yuan, *Out of a Far Country*, 110.

3. Yuan and Yuan, *Out of a Far Country*, 188–89.

4. Rod Dreher, "Sex after Christianity: Gay Marriage Is Not Just a Social Revolution but a Cosmological One," *American Conservative*, April 11, 2013, www.theamericanconservative.com/articles/sex-after-christianity/.

5. See "Genital Herpes: CDC Fact Sheet (Detailed)," Division of STD Prevention, Centers for Disease Control and Prevention, January 23, 2014, www.cdc.gov/std/herpes/stdfact-herpes-detailed.htm; "HIV in the United States: At a Glance," Centers for Disease Control and Prevention, June 2016, www.cdc.gov/hiv/statistics/overview/ataglance.html.

6. Sexually Transmitted Disease Surveillance, 2014, cited in "CDC Fact Sheet: Reported STDs in the United States," Division of STD Prevention, Centers for Disease Control and Prevention, November 2015, www.cdc.gov/std/stats14/std-trends-508.pdf.

7. Philip Rieff, *The Triumph of the Therapeutic: Uses of Faith after Freud* (Chicago: University of Chicago Press, 1987), 18.

8. Charles Colson, *Against the Night: Living in the New Dark Ages* (Ann Arbor, MI: Servant, 1989), 151–52.

9. In a supreme irony for those seeking sexual satisfaction by bending or breaking the "rules" of Christianity, researchers have found that the greatest sexual satisfaction and pleasure are in the context of a monogamous, formal man-woman marriage. See Edward O. Laumann et al., *The Social Organization of Sexuality: Sexual Practices in the United States* (Chicago: University of Chicago Press, 2000), 364.

10. Denny Burk, "Is Homosexual Orientation Sinful?," *Journal of the Evangelical Theological Society* 58, no. 1 (2015): 102.

11. Bertrand Russell, *Marriage and Morals* (New York: Liveright, 1970), 166.

12. Margaret Sanger, "The Civilizing Force of Birth Control," 1929, www.nyu.edu/projects/sanger/webedition/app/documents/show.php?sangerDoc=320525.xml. Margaret Sanger said, "Birth Control is not contraception indiscriminately and thoughtlessly practiced. It means the release and cultivation of the better racial elements in our society, and the gradual suppression, elimination and eventual extirpation of defective stocks—those human weeds which threaten the blooming of the finest flowers of American civilization." Margaret Sanger, "Apostle of Birth Control Sees Cause Gaining Here," *New York Times*, April 8, 1923, 12, available at http://sangerpapers.org/sanger/app/documents/show.php?sangerDoc=320595.xml.

13. More than fifty years after Kinsey's published studies, evidence has emerged that Kinsey used faulty methods for gathering statistics, interviewing a disproportionate number of prisoners, pimps, prostitutes, pedophiles, and unmarried adults. The majority of those interviewed had *volunteered* to reveal their sexual histories to an interviewer, which biased the results toward the nonnormal end of the behavioral spectrum. Kinsey admitted that some of his statistics were taken from the personal diaries of pedophiles (although Kinsey didn't use that term). These revelations aren't surprising given the naturalistic foundation of Kinsey's research, which assumed that human behavior is no different in kind than animal behavior. Based

on this view, there is no moral value attached to the various kinds of sexual acts that are available to the human species. The most prolific critic of Kinsey is Dr. Judith Reisman, a research professor at Liberty University and author of many books about Kinsey's research. Reisman says that the Kinsey Institute has failed to repudiate any of her claims. Many of Reisman's books are available as free downloads from Dr. Reisman's website, www.drjudithreisman.com/the_kinsey_coverup.html.

14. C. S. Lewis called a lie the idea that "any sexual act to which you are tempted at the moment is also healthy and normal." C. S. Lewis, *Mere Christianity* (New York: HarperOne, 1980), 100; Armand M. Nicholi Jr., *The Question of God: C. S. Lewis and Sigmund Freud Debate God, Love, Sex, and the Meaning of Life* (New York: Free Press, 2002), 137.

15. Rustum Roy and Della Roy, *Honest Sex* (New York: Authors Choice, 2003), 56.

16. Joseph Fletcher, cited in Randy C. Alcorn, *Christians in the Wake of the Sexual Revolution: Recovering Our Sexual Sanity* (Portland: Multnomah, 1985), 55.

17. *Heather Has Two Mommies* attempts to show grade-school children that a lesbian couple can provide the same love and care as a heterosexual couple. "Safer" sex is now the term of choice when teaching teenagers the advantages of using a condom during intercourse, since this form of birth control and disease prevention was found *not* to be entirely "safe."

18. Alexis de Tocqueville, *Democracy in America*, 2nd ed., trans. Henry Reeve (Cambridge, UK: Sever and Francis, 1863), 2:119–20.

19. Matt Walsh, "Abstinence Is Unrealistic and Old Fashioned," *Matt Walsh Blog*, November 9, 2013, http://themattwalshblog.com/2013/11/09/abstinence-is-unrealistic-and-old-fashioned/.

20. John Stonestreet, "When Sex Got a Divorce," *Two Minute Warning*, July 12, 2012, www.colsoncenter.org/twominutewarning/entry/33/19793.

21. Lewis, *Mere Christianity*, 96.

22. Stonestreet, "When Sex Got a Divorce."

23. Obergefell v. Hodges, 576 U.S. ___ (2015).

24. That percentage of those identifying as LGBT is higher in larger cities, which might have to do with increased opportunities or, as some think, with whether they grew up in urban areas. Frank Newport, "Americans Greatly Overestimate Percent Gay, Lesbian in U.S.," Gallup, May 21, 2015, www.gallup.com/poll/183383/americans-greatly-overestimate-percent-gay-lesbian.aspx.

25. Dale Kuehne says, "Ironically, the rationalizations used by heterosexuals and homosexuals to justify breaking biblical sexual boundaries are identical: God wants me to be fulfilled; sex is an essential part of relational fulfillment; therefore, the Bible can't really mean what it says about sexual boundaries because that would rob me of fulfillment." Dale S. Kuehne, *Sex and the iWorld: Rethinking Relationship beyond an Age of Individualism* (Grand Rapids: Baker Academic, 2009), 160–61.

26. Andrew Sullivan, *Virtually Normal: An Argument about Homosexuality* (New York: Vintage Books, 1996), 203.

27. From book endorsement in Marvin M. Ellison, *Erotic Justice: A Liberating Ethic of Sexuality* (Louisville, KY: Westminster John Knox, 1996).

28. Robert A. J. Gagnon, "Why the Disagreement over the Biblical Witness on Homosexual Practice? A Response to Myers and Scanzoni, *What God Has Joined Together*?," *Reformed Review* 59, no. 1 (Autumn 2005): 37, www.davidmyers.org/davidmyers/assets/Gagnon-ReformedReview.pdf.

29. Study cited in Sean McDowell and John Stonestreet, *Same-Sex Marriage: A Thoughtful Approach to God's Design for Marriage* (Grand Rapids: Baker Books, 2014), 72.

30. See this statistic and many other statistics on pornography at "Pornography Statistics," Family Safe Media, accessed July 18, 2016, http://familysafemedia.com/pornography_statistics.html.

31. See "Pornography Statistics," Family Safe Media.

32. Mina Cikara, Jennifer L. Eberhardt, and Susan T. Fiske, "From Agents to Objects: Sexual Attitudes and Neural Responses to Sexualized Targets," *Journal of Cognitive Neuroscience* 23, no. 3 (March 2011): 540–51, http://cnbc.cmu.edu/~cikaralab/Publications_files/Cikara%20et%20al.,%202011%20-%20JOCN_a.pdf, cited in Doug Eshleman, "Men View Half-Naked Women as Objects, Study Finds," *Daily Princetonian*, February 17, 2009, www.dailyprincetonian.com/2009/02/17/22773/.

33. William M. Struthers, *Wired for Intimacy: How Pornography Hijacks the Male Brain* (Downers Grove, IL: InterVarsity, 2009), cited in Janice Shaw Crouse, *Marriage Matters: Perspectives on the Private and Public Importance of Marriage* (New Brunswick, NJ: Transaction Publishers, 2012), 71.

34. Simone Kühn and Jürgen Gallinat, "Brain Structure and Functional Connectivity Associated with Pornography Consumption: The Brain on Porn," *JAMA Psychiatry* 71, no. 7 (2014): 827–34.

35. Tim Molloy, "Judd Apatow and Lena Dunham Get Mad at Me for Asking Why She's Naked So Much on 'Girls,'" TheWrap, January 9, 2014, www.thewrap.com/judd-apatow-lena-dunham-get-mad-asking-shes-naked-much-girls/.

36. William Voegeli, "The Redskins and the Wrong Side of History," *Federalist*, June 20, 2014, http://thefederalist.com/2014/06/20/the-redskins-and-the-wrong-side-of-history/.

37. Kuehne, *Sex and the iWorld*, 71–72.

38. "Programs and Courses: Lesbian, Gay, Bisexual, Transgender Studies," *City College of San Francisco Catalog 2016–2017* (San Francisco: City College of San Francisco, 2016), 326, www.ccsf.edu/dam/ccsf/documents/OfficeOfInstruction/Catalog/Programs%20and%20Courses%202016-17.pdf.

39. University of Maryland, "LGBT Studies Course Descriptions," Lesbian, Gay, Bisexual, Transgender Studies Program, accessed September 21, 2016, www.lgbts.umd.edu/coursedescriptions.html.

40. University of Waterloo, "Sexuality, Marriage, and Family Studies: Course Descriptions—Undergraduate Calendar 2016–2017," accessed September 21, 2016, www.ucalendar.uwaterloo.ca/1617/COURSE/course-SMF.html.

41. Jean-Francois Lyotard, quoted in Glenn Ward, *Teach Yourself Postmodernism* (Chicago: McGraw-Hill, 2003), 176.

42. Mike Allen et al., "Exposure to Pornography and Acceptance of Rape Myths," *Journal of Communication* 45, no. 1 (March 1995): 5–26; Shawn Corne, John Briere, and Lillian M. Esses, "Women's Attitudes and Fantasies about Rape as a Function of Early Exposure to Pornography," *Journal of Interpersonal Violence* 7, no. 4 (December 1992): 454–61.

43. William L. Marshall, "Revisiting the Use of Pornography by Sexual Offenders: Implications for Theory and Practice," *Journal of Sexual Aggression* 6, nos. 1–2 (2000): 67–77. The latest statistics are available at http://en.wikipedia.org/wiki/Relationship_between_child_pornography_and_child_sexual_abuse.

44. See *Training Manual to Fight Trafficking in Children for Labour, Sexual and Other Forms of Exploitation: Understanding Child Trafficking; Textbook 1* (Geneva: International Labour Organization, 2009), 34, www.unicef.org/protection/Textbook_1.pdf.

45. Rod Dreher, "The Sexual Totalitarian Campus," *American Conservative*, September 26, 2014, www.theamericanconservative.com/dreher/the-sexual-totalitarian-campus/. The University of Michigan omitted this classification in its revised guidelines.

46. Steven Garber, *Fabric of Faithfulness: Weaving Together Belief and Behavior* (Downers Grove, IL: InterVarsity, 2007), 149.

47. See Paul Froese and Christopher Bader, *America's Four Gods: What We Say about God and What That Says about Us* (New York: Oxford University Press, 2010), 60, 66, 90–91, 104. Baylor University sociologists Froese and Bader found that there are four common views of God and that peoples' views of God affect everything else in their lives. For example, political conservatives are more likely to believe in an authoritative God, whereas liberals are more likely to believe in a distant God (60). Those who believe in an authoritative God are more likely to say that adultery, gay marriage, and abortion are always wrong, whereas those who believe in a distant God are more likely to say that such activities are only sometimes wrong or aren't wrong at all (66). People who believe that God is authoritative or benevolent are less likely to believe that science can solve human problems and less likely to believe that humans evolved from primates, but they're also more likely to view science as revealing God's glory (90–91, 104).

48. New Family Structures Study (NFSS) data, University of Texas, Austin, cited in Mark Regnerus, "Porn Use and Supporting Same-Sex Marriage," *Public Discourse*, December 20, 2012, www.thepublicdiscourse.com/2012/12/7048/.

49. Paul J. Wright and Ashley K. Randall, "Pornography Consumption, Education, and Support for Same-Sex Marriage among Adult U.S. Males," *Communication Research* 41, no. 5 (July 2014): 665–89.

50. Albert Mohler, "A Warped Worldview: Another Moral Effect of Pornography," AlbertMohler.com, March 4, 2013, www.albertmohler.com/2013/03/04/a-warped-worldview-another-moral-effect-of-pornography/.

51. David F. Ruccio and Jack Amariglio, *Postmodern Moments in Modern Economics* (Princeton, NJ: Princeton University Press, 2003), 249.

52. Larry J. Nelson, Laura M. Padilla-Walker, and Jason S. Carroll, "'I Believe It Is Wrong but I Still Do It': A Comparison of Religious Young Men Who Do versus Do Not Use Pornography," *Psychology of Religion and Spirituality* 2, no. 3 (July 2010): 136–47, www.researchgate.net/publication/232507019_I_Believe_It_Is_Wrong_But_I_Still_Do_It_A_Comparison_of_Religious_Young_Men_Who_Do_Versus_Do_Not_Use_Pornography.

53. Drug and alcohol use is also correlated with diminished religiosity. See Jeremy E. Uecker, Mark D. Regnerus, and Margaret L. Vaaler, "Losing My Religion: The Social Sources of Religious Decline in Early Adulthood," *Social Forces* 85, no. 4 (June 2007): 1667–92, www.geocities.ws/deeann_regnerus/LosingmyReligion.pdf.

54. Arthur Levine and Jeanette S. Cureton, *When Hope and Fear Collide: A Portrait of Today's College Student* (San Francisco: Jossey-Bass, 1998), 95.

55. Regnerus, "Porn Use and Supporting Same-Sex Marriage."

56. John Stonestreet, "How Sexual Brokenness Victimizes People," *Two Minute Warning*, July 16, 2012, www.colsoncenter.org/twominutewarning/entry/33/19837.

57. Stonestreet, "How Sexual Brokenness Victimizes People."

58. Arielle Kuperberg, "Does Premarital Cohabitation Raise Your Risk of Divorce?," Council on Contemporary Families, March 10, 2014, https://contemporaryfamilies.org/cohabitation-divorce-brief-report/; and Jonathan Vespa, Jamie M. Lewis, and Rose M. Kreider, *America's Families and Living Arrangements: 2012* (Washington, DC: US Census Bureau, 2013), www.census.gov/prod/2013pubs/p20-570.pdf, cited in Lauren Fox, "The Science of Cohabitation: A Step toward Marriage, Not a Rebellion," *Atlantic*, March 20, 2014, www.theatlantic.com/health/archive/2014/03/the-science-of-cohabitation-a-step-toward-marriage-not-a-rebellion/284512/.

59. Lynne M. Casper and Suzanne M. Bianchi, *Continuity and Change in the American Family* (Thousand Oaks, CA: Sage Publications, 2002), chap. 2, cited in Jason Dulle, "The Sociology of Cohabitation: 'Shacking Up' Isn't Such a Good Idea After All," *Theo-Sophical Ruminations* (blog), April 6, 2015, https://theosophical.wordpress.com/2015/04/06/the-sociology-of-cohabitation-shacking-up-isnt-such-a-good-idea-after-all/. See also "Cohabitation vs. Marriage: How Love's Choices

Shape Life Outcomes," FamilyFacts.org, 2016, www.familyfacts.org/briefs/9/cohabitation-vs-marriage-how-loves-choices-shape-life-outcomes.

60. Fox, "The Science of Cohabitation." See also "Cohabitation Doesn't Cause Divorce after All," Fox News Health, March 10, 2014, www.foxnews.com/health/2014/03/10/cohabitation-doesnt-cause-divorce-after-all.html.

61. "Cohabitation vs. Marriage," FamilyFacts.org.

62. Alcorn, *Christians in the Wake of the Sexual Revolution*, 35.

63. Kuehne, *Sex and the iWorld*, 23.

64. Dreher, "Sex after Christianity."

65. From correspondence provided by recipient of the letter. The student, whose name I changed to "Blake," withheld the name of the professor.

66. John MacArthur, "God's Word on Homosexuality: The Truth about Sin and the Reality of Forgiveness," *Master's Seminary Journal* 19, no. 2 (Fall 2008): 154, www.tms.edu/m/tmsj19f.pdf.

67. Romans 13:8–10: "Owe no one anything, except to love each other, for the one who loves another has fulfilled the law. For the commandments, 'You shall not commit adultery, You shall not murder, You shall not steal, You shall not covet,' and any other commandment, are summed up in this word: 'You shall love your neighbor as yourself.' Love does no wrong to a neighbor; therefore love is the fulfilling of the law"; Galatians 5:14: "The whole law is fulfilled in one word: 'You shall love your neighbor as yourself.'"

68. Ephesians 4:32: "Be kind to one another, tenderhearted, forgiving one another, as God in Christ forgave you."

69. MacArthur, "God's Word on Homosexuality," 154.

70. MacArthur, "God's Word on Homosexuality," 154–55.

71. For more on the Hebrew *erva galah*, see John S. Bergsma and Scott W. Hahn, "Noah's Nakedness and Curse on Canaan (Genesis 9:20–27)," *Journal of Biblical Literature* 124, no. 1 (2005): 25–40.

72. Leviticus 18:24–30: "Do not make yourselves unclean by any of these things, for by all these the nations I am driving out before you have become unclean, and the land became unclean, so that I punished its iniquity, and the land vomited out its inhabitants. But you shall keep my statutes and my rules and do none of these abominations, either the native or the stranger who sojourns among you (for the people of the land, who were before you, did all of these abominations, so that the land became unclean), lest the land vomit you out when you make it unclean, as it vomited out the nation that was before you. For everyone who does any of these abominations, the persons who do them shall be cut off from among their people. So keep my charge never to practice any of these abominable customs that were practiced before you, and never to make yourselves unclean by them: I am the Lord your God."

73. Gagnon, "Why the Disagreement?," 53.

74. First Peter 2:11: "Beloved, I urge you as sojourners and exiles to abstain from the passions of the flesh, which wage war against your soul."

75. First Corinthians 6:13–18: "'Food is meant for the stomach and the stomach for food'—and God will destroy both one and the other. The body is not meant for sexual immorality, but for the Lord, and the Lord for the body. And God raised the Lord and will also raise us up by his power. Do you not know that your bodies are members of Christ? Shall I then take the members of Christ and make them members of a prostitute? Never! Or do you not know that he who is joined to a prostitute becomes one body with her? For, as it is written, 'The two will become one flesh.' But he who is joined to the Lord becomes one spirit with him. Flee from sexual immorality. Every other sin a person commits is outside the body, but the sexually immoral person sins against his own body."

76. Galatians 5:16–24: "Walk by the Spirit, and you will not gratify the desires of the flesh. For the desires of the flesh are against the Spirit, and the desires of the Spirit are against the flesh, for these are opposed to each other, to keep you from doing the things you want to do. But if you are led by the Spirit, you are not under the law. Now the works of the flesh are evident: sexual immorality, impurity, sensuality, idolatry, sorcery, enmity, strife, jealousy, fits of anger, rivalries, dissensions, divisions, envy, drunkenness, orgies, and things like these. I warn you, as I warned you before, that those who do such things will not inherit the kingdom of God. But the fruit of the Spirit is love, joy, peace, patience, kindness, goodness, faithfulness, gentleness, self-control; against such things there is no law. And those who belong to Christ Jesus have crucified the flesh with its passions and desires."

77. Kuehne, *Sex and the iWorld*, 162.

78. Gagnon, "Why the Disagreement?," 55.

79. Matthew Vines, quoted in Greg Garrison, "'God and the Gay Christian' Author Says Apostle Paul Didn't Condemn Gay Marriage," *AL*, February 13, 2015, www.al.com/living/index.ssf/2015/02/god_and_the_gay_christian_auth.html.

80. Gagnon, "Why the Disagreement?," 73.

81. Gagnon, "Why the Disagreement?," 94. Gagnon also says, "What is problematic, however, is when the quality of the investigation suggests that one is going back to Scripture not so much to allow it the role of critic and ultimate authority as to neutralize it and thereby render it harmless to one's own newfound views" (103).

82. Gagnon, "Why the Disagreement?," 107–8.

83. Elizabeth L. Paul, Brian McManus, and Allison Hayes, "'Hookups': Characteristics and Correlates of College Students'

Spontaneous and Anonymous Sexual Experiences," *Journal of Sex Research* 37, no. 1 (February 2000): 81, www.tandfonline.com/doi/pdf/10.1080/00224490009552023?needAccess=true.

84. T. M. Downing-Matibag and B. Geisinger, "Hooking Up and Sexual Risk Taking among College Students: A Health Belief Model Perspective," *Qualitative Health Research* 19, no. 2 (September 2009): 1196–209; W. F. Flack et al., "Risk Factors and Consequences of Unwanted Sex among University Students: Hooking Up, Alcohol, and Stress Response," *Journal of Interpersonal Violence* 22, no. 2 (February 2007): 139–57, cited in McIlhaney, Bush, and Guthrie, *Girls Uncovered*, 30–32.

85. Flack et al., "Risk Factors and Consequences of Unwanted Sex," cited in McIlhaney, Bush, and Guthrie, *Girls Uncovered*.

86. For these and other statistics, see Meg Meeker, *Your Kids at Risk: How Teen Sex Threatens Our Sons and Daughters* (Washington, DC: Regnery, 2012), chap. 2.

87. "HIV in the United States: At a Glance," Centers for Disease Control and Prevention, June 2016, www.cdc.gov/hiv/statistics/overview/ataglance.html.

88. "HIV in the United States," Centers for Disease Control and Prevention.

89. Andrew M. Greeley, *Faithful Attraction: Discovering Intimacy, Love, and Fidelity in American Marriage* (New York: Thomas Doherty Associates, 1991), 201.

90. Joan R. Kahn and Kathryn A. London, "Premarital Sex and the Risk of Divorce," *Journal of Marriage and Family* 53, no. 4 (November 1991): 845–55.

91. National Longitudinal Survey of Adolescent Health, Wave 2, 1996, cited in Robert E. Rector, Kirk A. Johnson, and Lauren R. Noyes, "Sexually Active Teenagers Are More Likely to Be Depressed and to Attempt Suicide," Center for Data Analysis Report 3-04, Heritage Foundation, June 3, 2003, www.heritage.org/Research/Family/cda0304.cfm.

92. Genesis 1:27: "God created man in his own image, in the image of God he created him; male and female he created them."

93. Kuehne, *Sex and the iWorld*, 117–18.

94. Leonard Sax, *Why Gender Matters: What Parents and Teachers Need to Know about the Emerging Science of Sex Differences* (New York: Broadway Books, 2005), 236.

95. Cited in Sax, *Why Gender Matters*, 14.

96. Cited in Sax, *Why Gender Matters*, 17.

97. Cited in Sax, *Why Gender Matters*, 18.

98. Cited in Sax, *Why Gender Matters*, 22.

99. Cited in Sax, *Why Gender Matters*, 30.

100. Cited in Sax, *Why Gender Matters*, 41.

101. Cited in Sax, *Why Gender Matters*, 59.

102. Cited in Sax, *Why Gender Matters*, 66–67.

103. Madhura Ingalhalikar et al., "Sex Differences in the Structural Connectome of the Human Brain," *Proceedings of the National Academy of Sciences* 111, no. 2 (2013): 823–28, www.mit.edu/~6.s085/papers/sex-differences.pdf.

104. Cited in Sax, *Why Gender Matters*, 93.

105. Sax, *Why Gender Matters*, 35.

106. Sax, *Why Gender Matters*, 237.

107. McIlhaney and Bush, *Girls Uncovered*, 83.

108. Cited in Sax, *Why Gender Matters*, 37–38.

109. Crouse, *Marriage Matters*, 79.

110. Gagnon, "Why the Disagreement?," 40.

111. Stephen Arterburn and Fred Stoeker, with Mike Yorkey, *Every Young Man's Battle: Strategies for Victory in the Real World of Sexual Temptation* (Colorado Springs, CO: WaterBrook, 2002), 212.

112. Mary Eberstadt, "What Does Woman Want?: The War between the Sexless," *First Things*, October 2009, www.firstthings.com/article/2009/10/what-does-woman-want.

113. D. A. Carson, *The Gagging of God: Christianity Confronts Pluralism* (Grand Rapids: Zondervan, 1996), 365.

114. John Stonestreet, "How NOT to Respond to Sexual Brokenness," *Two Minute Warning*, July 25, 2012, www.colsoncenter.org/twominutewarning/entry/33/19903.

115. Stonestreet, "How NOT to Respond."

116. Jenell Paris, "Both Chastity and Contraception: A Sacred Compromise," *Christianity Today*, April 27, 2012, www.christianitytoday.com/ct/2012/aprilweb-only/chastity-contraception.html.

117. Bruce Marshall, *The World, the Flesh, and Father Smith* (Boston: Houghton Mifflin, 1945), 108, quoted in Glenn T. Stanton, *Loving My (LGBT) Neighbor: Being Friends in Grace and Truth* (Chicago: Moody, 2014), 71.

118. Douglas Wilson, *Fidelity: How to Be a One-Woman Man*, (Moscow, ID: Canon Press, 2012), 21.

119. Toni Bentley, "Monogamy Is a Charade," *Time*, September 11, 2015, http://time.com/4028153/toni-bentley-is-monogamy-over/.

120. Elisabeth Elliot, *Passion and Purity: Learning to Bring Your Love Life under Christ's Control* (Grand Rapids: Revell, 2002), 23.

121. Andy Stanley's response to David Barash's article "Is Monogamy Over? Monogamy Is Not Natural but It's Nice," *Time*,

September 10, 2015; Andy Stanley, "Is Monogamy Over? We Crave Something beyond Biology," *Time*, September 11, 2015, http://time.com/4028300/andy-stanley-is-monogamy-over/.

122. Albert M. Wolters, *Creation Regained: Biblical Basics for a Reformational Worldview* (Grand Rapids: Eerdmans, 2005), 107.

123. Lewis B. Smedes, *Sex for Christians: The Limits and Liberties of Sexual Living* (Grand Rapids: Eerdmans, 1994), 88.

124. See L. B. Radford, trans., *The Epistle to Diognetus* (London: Society for Promoting Christian Knowledge, 1908), 63.

125. Galen, quoted in Alvin J. Schmidt, *How Christianity Changed the World* (Grand Rapids: Zondervan, 2004), 83.

126. Mark A. Yarhouse, "A Christian Perspective on Sexual Identity," Carl F. H. Henry Center, January 1, 2010, 15, http://henrycenter.tiu.edu/wp-content/uploads/2013/11/Yarhouse-Homosexuality.pdf.

127. See research cited in Yarhouse, "A Christian Perspective on Sexual Identity," 18n52.

128. Quoted in Mark A. Yarhouse et al., "Project Inner Compass: Young Adults Experiencing Sexual Identity Confusions," *Journal of Psychology and Christianity* 24, no. 4 (2005): 352–60; Yarhouse, "A Christian Perspective on Sexual Identity," 19.

129. Yarhouse, "A Christian Perspective on Sexual Identity," 5.

130. Yarhouse, "A Christian Perspective on Sexual Identity."

131. Stanton L. Jones and Mark A. Yarhouse, *Ex-Gays?* (Downers Grove, IL: InterVarsity, 2007); Stanton L. Jones and Mark A. Yarhouse, "Ex-Gays?: An Extended Longitudinal Study of Attempted Religiously Mediated Change in Sexual Orientation" (paper, American Psychological Association annual conference, Toronto, Ontario, August 9, 2009), cited in Yarhouse, "A Christian Perspective on Sexual Identity," 9.

132. Yarhouse, "A Christian Perspective on Sexual Identity," 27.

133. Rosaria Champagne Butterfield, *Openness Unhindered: Further Thoughts of an Unlikely Convert on Sexual Identity and Union with Christ* (Pittsburgh: Crown and Covenant, 2015), 107.

134. Peter Ould, "You and Me Together," *An Exercise in the Fundamentals of Orthodoxy* (blog), April 19, 2007, www.peter-ould.net/2007/04/19/you-and-me-together/.

135. Yarhouse, "A Christian Perspective on Sexual Identity," 27.

136. J. Budziszewski, quoted in Marvin Olasky, "J. Budziszewski: Generation Disordered," *World*, August 21, 2015, https://world.wng.org/2015/08/j_budziszewski_generation_disordered.

137. Arterburn and Stoeker, *Every Young Man's Battle*, 140.

138. First Peter 3:11: "Turn away from evil and do good; … seek peace and pursue it."

139. Nicholi, *The Question of God*, 158.

140. Hebrews 4:15–16: "We do not have a high priest who is unable to sympathize with our weaknesses, but one who in every respect has been tempted as we are, yet without sin. Let us then with confidence draw near to the throne of grace, that we may receive mercy and find grace to help in time of need."

141. Romans 8:31–39: "What then shall we say …? If God is for us, who can be against us? He who did not spare his own Son but gave him up for us all, how will he not also with him graciously give us all things? Who shall bring any charge against God's elect? It is God who justifies. Who is to condemn? Christ Jesus is the one who died—more than that, who was raised—who is at the right hand of God, who indeed is interceding for us. Who shall separate us from the love of Christ? Shall tribulation, or distress, or persecution, or famine, or nakedness, or danger, or sword? As it is written, 'For your sake we are being killed all the day long; we are regarded as sheep to be slaughtered.' No, in all these things we are more than conquerors through him who loved us. For I am sure that neither death nor life, nor angels nor rulers, nor things present nor things to come, nor powers, nor height nor depth, nor anything else in all creation, will be able to separate us from the love of God in Christ Jesus our Lord."

142. McDowell and Stonestreet, *Same-Sex Marriage*, 88.

143. Thanks to Jonathan Welton for this insight. See Jonathan Welton, *Eyes of Honor: Training for Purity and Righteousness* (Shippensburg, PA: Destiny Image, 2012), 155–56.

144. Second Corinthians 5:18–19: "All this is from God, who through Christ reconciled us to himself and gave us the ministry of reconciliation; that is, in Christ God was reconciling the world to himself, not counting their trespasses against them, and entrusting to us the message of reconciliation."

145. Arterburn and Stoeker, *Every Young Man's Battle*, 26.

146. Dawn Eden, *The Thrill of the Chaste: Finding Fulfillment While Keeping Your Clothes On* (Nashville: Thomas Nelson, 2006), xi.

147. First Peter 5:7: "[Cast] all your anxieties on [God], because he cares for you."

148. Zephaniah 3:17: "The LORD your God is in your midst, a mighty one who will save; he will rejoice over you with gladness; he will quiet you by his love; he will exult over you with loud singing."

149. Hebrews 13:5: "Keep your life free from love of money, and be content with what you have, for [God] has said, 'I will never leave you nor forsake you.'"

150. Romans 8:39: "[Nothing] will be able to separate us from the love of God in Christ Jesus our Lord."

151. Kuehne, *Sex and the iWorld*, 143.

152. Andrea Dworkin, *Intercourse*, 2 vols. (Surrey Hills, Australia: Accessible Publishing Systems, 2008), 1:105–6. See also

the discussion in F. Carolyn Graglia *Domestic Tranquility: A Brief against Femininsm* (Dallas: Spence, 1998).

153. First Corinthians 7:32–35: "I want you to be free from anxieties. The unmarried man is anxious about the things of the Lord, how to please the Lord. But the married man is anxious about worldly things, how to please his wife, and his interests are divided. And the unmarried or betrothed woman is anxious about the things of the Lord, how to be holy in body and spirit. But the married woman is anxious about worldly things, how to please her husband. I say this for your own benefit, not to lay any restraint upon you, but to promote good order and to secure your undivided devotion to the Lord."

154. Roger Scruton, *Beauty: A Very Short Introduction* (Oxford: Oxford University Press, 2011), 10.

155. Scruton, *Beauty*, 10.

156. Welton, *Eyes of Honor*, 182.

157. Welton, *Eyes of Honor*, 184.

158. Kuehne, *Sex and the iWorld*, 35.

159. Kuehne, *Sex and the iWorld*, 77.

160. From John Dryden's translation of the poem "De Rerum Natura" ("On the Nature of Things"), by Epicurean poet Titus Lucretius Carus. See note in William Yeats, *A Vision* (New York: Scribner, 1965), 397n71.

161. Kuehne, *Sex and the iWorld*, 158.

162. Kuehne, *Sex and the iWorld*, 169.

163. Kuehne, *Sex and the iWorld*, 169.

164. Kuehne, *Sex and the iWorld*, 177.

165. Yuan and Yuan, *Out of a Far Country*, 187.

CHAPTER 10

10

MARRIAGE

1. MARRIAGE IS VERY GOOD

One key indicator of a society's state of health is the state of marriage in that society. Men and women who are married with children are a society's most basic stabilizing influence. But the landscape is changing. In a 2010 survey, 40 percent of Americans said they believe marriage is "becoming obsolete,"[1] and according to US Census data, the proportion of married adults has been steadily declining since the 1960s.[2]

Marriage matters for society in ways that go far beyond the love between two people. Judging by the books available on the topic, Christians have a lot of advice at their fingertips about *how* to date, *how* to have a good marriage, *how* to solve marital problems, *how* to understand the differences between men and women, *how* to love their spouses, *how* to have a better sex life, and *how* to recover from seemingly irreconcilable differences. It's all about the how.

But in most areas of life, understanding *how* without understanding *why* leads to trouble. If a military general understands *how* to attack the enemy but lacks an understanding of *why* the battle is being fought, the army is much less likely to achieve its objectives. Similarly, if two people in a marriage know *how* to keep their marriage together but have no compelling reason for *why* their marriage matters to themselves, their children, and society, they're on rocky ground.

We need to know the *why* if we're ever to make sense of the *how*.

Why Is Marriage Good?

Marriage: a lifelong, exclusive union between a man and a woman that involves the capacity to bear children and raise them in a stable environment.

Natural Law: the belief that morality can be seen in the natural order of creation and accessed through human reason; the belief that laws are rules based upon on an internal code of morality that all people possess.

In this chapter, we'll see that **marriage**, understood as the permanent and exclusive union of one man and one woman, is good for culture. It's about love, but not about how to improve your love life. It's about sex, but not about how to improve lovemaking. It's also about singleness, dating, kids, work, life purpose, politics, family relationships, and society.

God created marriage. It is theologically rich. It is spiritually significant. It is socially necessary. Marriage displays a common grace that benefits even those who don't understand it. From **natural law** alone, we could derive that the foundation of family is the permanent, exclusive, comprehensive bond of marriage between a man and a woman. We would also discern that such marriages form the foundation of a free society. As we'll see, though, the biblical idea of marriage adds enormous depth to what we naturally understand about such unions. Since the dawn of time, marriage has expressed God's very nature. Even if human beings hadn't sinned, marriage would still be good. It expresses real love—love that, as Tim and Kathy Keller put it, "instinctively desires permanence."[3]

"It Is Not Good That the Man Should Be Alone"

Throughout *Understanding the Culture*, we've seen that God made creation to be very good. The Hebrew phrase for "very good" is ***tob meod***, which means "the very best thing possible." It's splendid, abundant, rich, and happy. We ought to stand amazed by this. God created the planets and the stars and the fish and the animals and called them good. But when he created human beings and gave them dominion, he pronounced his plan "very good" (Gen. 1:31). The only thing about creation that was *not* good before the entrance of sin was the man's aloneness. Without marriage, man couldn't complete the task God had given him, which was to populate and fill the earth (v. 28).[4]

So to understand God's story, we need to understand marriage. In this chapter, we'll explore Scripture, starting at the very beginning, to see if we can figure out why God created it. As the puzzle pieces come together, they'll form a picture of beauty and magnificence, helping us grasp God's concept of marriage and how it is the basis for good in society. To put the puzzle together, though, we need to understand what marriage is, what various world-views say about it, why Christians should care, and how Christians—even those who aren't married—can support marriage as a path toward a better society.

2. WHAT IS THE PROBLEM?

Marriage as an Institution Is Dying

Traditional marriage, the idea of one man, one woman, faithful for life, and oriented toward having children, produces enormous benefits for individuals and society. Man-woman marriage is associated with better health, greater wealth, happiness, and better conditions for children.[5] This is part of what we mean when we say that marriage is a social good. What happens when we remove the stabilizing influence of man-woman marriage? No civilization has ever attempted such a thing and survived.[6]

> *Traditional Marriage:* the belief that society benefits most when marriage is defined as a monogamous and lifelong union between one man and one woman, oriented toward having children.

Yet marriage as an institution is in decline. More than 40 percent of children in the United States are born outside of marriage.[7] By 2023, the majority of American children will be born outside of wedlock if current trends continue.[8] Statistically, children born outside of wedlock are more likely to have mental, emotional, health, and educational problems and are four times more likely to live in poverty as children born to married parents.[9] Of course, many children born out of wedlock do just fine. Sadly, though, it's a much harder path than it ought to be.

Today more and more people are making a lifestyle choice to have children outside of marriage. It's a growing trend among middle-class and upper-middle-class professionals, not just among the poor. Increasingly, women are deciding they don't "need" men for anything except the procreative act. In fact, one study showed that rather than have a husband who is a breadwinner so the woman can focus on raising their kids, nearly 75 percent of women said they would rather get a divorce and raise their kids alone.[10] They insist on complete independence, even if it has the potential to destroy their children.

Every child deserves a mom and a dad. Approaches to relationships that ignore this, or give legal sanction to romantic relationships that prevent it, hurt the most vulnerable among us. Many people intuitively understand this. Others don't see how a marriage relationship would produce different results than any other committed relationship. To see why marriage is important, we need to define it clearly.

> Every child deserves a mom and a dad. Approaches to relationships that ignore this, or give legal sanction to romantic relationships that prevent it, hurt the most vulnerable among us.

What Is Marriage Anyway?

Princeton professor Robert George is an expert in both philosophy and law. He holds a doctor of philosophy degree from Oxford and a law degree from Harvard. In 2009, George and two research assistants, Sherif Girgis and Ryan Anderson, produced an important article for the *Harvard Journal of Law and Public Policy* in which the authors defined *marriage* and made the case for the state's interest in preserving man-woman marriage. They later wrote a book of such importance that I'll quote from it repeatedly in this chapter. Girgis, George, and Anderson's definition of *marriage* is as follows:

> Marriage is the union of a man and a woman who make a permanent and exclusive commitment to each other of the type that is naturally (inherently) fulfilled by bearing and rearing children together. The spouses seal (consummate) and renew their union by conjugal acts—acts that constitute the behavioral part of the process of reproduction, thus uniting them as a reproductive unit. Marriage is valuable in itself, but its inherent orientation to the bearing and rearing of children contributes to its distinctive structure, including norms of monogamy and fidelity. This link to the welfare of children also helps explain why marriage is important to the common good and why the state should recognize and regulate it.[11]

That's a mouthful. Let's break it down to understand it better.

Marriage is the union of a man and woman. Today, a "revisionist" definition of marriage is taking hold, as opposed to a "conjugal" view or what, for the sake of simplicity, we'll call *traditional marriage*. The revisionist view defines *marriage* as "the union of two people (whether of the same sex or of opposite sexes) who commit to romantically loving and caring for each other and to sharing the burdens and benefits of domestic life."[12]

> If God invented marriage, governmental attempts to redefine it are nonsensical.

But if God invented marriage, governmental attempts to redefine it are nonsensical. Even if 100 percent of the people insist that government define *marriage* as whatever they want it to mean, this doesn't change what marriage actually is any more than calling the number one a two means that one is now two, or that passing legislation that outdoor temperatures in the summertime are too hot will actually lower the temperatures.

Marriage is valuable in itself, but its inherent orientation to the bearing and rearing of children contributes to its distinctive structure. Children are naturally, or inherently, the product of marriage properly defined. If a couple is unable to have children, it doesn't make the marriage invalid. A relationship between two men or two women, on the other hand, cannot by its nature produce children. Such relationships aren't infertile, as some male-female marriages are, because infertility implies something that is supposed to be there but is broken. Same-sex marriages can't even in principle procreate and so are a different sort of relationship that doesn't sustain culture in the same way as man-woman marriage. When the definition of *marriage* changes, children are hurt. And a culture that fails to protect children is putting its own survival at risk.[13]

If what Girgis, Anderson, and George say is true, government has a vested interest in promoting the kinds of marriages that have a uniquely stabilizing influence on society. Man-woman marriage is of that sort. Other kinds of relationships can be stable, of course, such as mentoring relationships. But their impact is short term and localized. They don't create culture and sustain civilizations over time.

> Same-sex marriages can't even in principle procreate and so are a different sort of relationship that doesn't sustain culture in the same way as man-woman marriage.

The institution of marriage is under siege today. It's not just that it is wasting away of its own accord. Marriage is in the crosshairs in a worldview battle. Some want to destroy it altogether.

What Other Worldviews Say about Marriage

Secularism. Secularists—those who believe that God is irrelevant to what is important in society—seem far less likely than people of other religions to prioritize man-woman marriage and child rearing. Secularists are far more likely to support same-sex marriage.[14] One study of the Swiss population showed that the fewer religious services people attend, the fewer children they are likely to have.[15] In many cases, Secularists are strongly critical of the very idea of marriage. To Lawrence Casler, a psychology professor whose academic study included observing and interviewing nudists,

> marriage and family life have been largely responsible … for today's prevailing neurotic climate, with its pervasive insecurity, and it is precisely this climate that makes so difficult the acceptance of a different, healthier way of life.[16]

The late Syracuse University "sexologist" Sol Gordon maintained that marriage contributes nothing except turning women into breeders and slaves.[17]

Secularists, such as professor of sociology Robert Whitehurst, often advocate replacing the one-man-one-woman-for-life model with open marriage (i.e., open to adultery), triads, cooperatives, collectives, extended intimates, swinging and group marriage, and part-time marriage.[18]

Sexual experimentation may make Secularists feel free, but it victimizes everyone involved, especially children. A raft of research demonstrates that sexual experimentation on the part of parents strongly correlates with negative child outcomes, such as crime and substance abuse.[19] In the face of this evidence, why don't Secularists encourage people to enter traditional marriages, maintain them, and raise good kids? Because, as John Stonestreet commonly points out, every worldview is willing to sacrifice something on the altar of its convictions. If we're primarily animals, and if the sexual impulse is our strongest

> Sexual experimentation may make Secularists feel free, but it victimizes everyone involved, especially children.

impulse, then *everything* may be sacrificed on the altar of sexual freedom: innocence, protection of the unborn, and what it means to be human.[20]

Marxism. Marxists also consider the traditional model of the family to hinder progress, but not because it constrains individual expression. Rather, it's because families prop up **capitalism**, hoarding capital and wealth and presumably keeping it from the workers they believe deserve it. According to Marxist revolutionary and novelist Alexandra Kollontai, "The family stifle[s] the proletarian effort toward liberty [and] weaken[s] the revolutionary spirit of the working man and working woman" and must therefore be shunned.[21] In *The Communist Manifesto*, Karl Marx wrote, "The bourgeois family will vanish as a matter of course when its complement [capitalism] vanishes, and both will vanish with the vanishing of capital."[22] Once the **proletariat** is in power, Marxists believe, a new utopian society will develop a new form of family without sexual boundaries. Friedrich Engels seemed almost giddy about this:

> *Capitalism:* an economic system in which capital assets are privately owned and the prices, production, and distribution of goods and services are determined by competition within a free market.

> With the transfer of the means of production into common ownership, the single family ceases to be the economic unit of society. Private housekeeping is transformed into a social industry. The care and education of the children becomes a public affair.... Will not that suffice to bring about the gradual growth of unconstrained sexual intercourse and with it a more tolerant public opinion in regard to a maiden's honour and a woman's shame?[23]

> *Communist Manifesto:* a work commissioned by the Communist League and written by Karl Marx and Friedrich Engels, *The Communist Manifesto* is the 1848 political tract outlining the league's goal of and means for eliminating capitalism and achieving a communist society through a proletariat revolution.

In this brave new world, premarital and extramarital sex cease to be negative because, within the context of community, private property ceases to exist. Everyone belongs to everyone.

In *The Communist Manifesto*, Marx and Engels called this the "community of women": all women would be shared by all men.[24] When critics derided this as demeaning, Marx and Engels retorted that "bourgeois marriage" is really nothing more than a hypocritical system of wives in common anyway, and Marxists could hardly do worse.[25] By ending the institution of marriage and turning parenting over to schools, Marxists hope to retrain children not to develop an attachment to the old ways.[26]

Postmodernism. Postmodernists, those of a Secularist bent, also show contempt for Christian concepts of love, sex, and marriage. Postmodernist psychiatrist Adam Phillips is particularly harsh:

The only sane foregone conclusion about any relationship is that it is an experiment; and that exactly what it is an experiment in will never be clear to the participants. For the sane, so-called relationships could never be subject to contract.[27]

The very concept of a father, mother, and children protected by law and custom forms a "heterosexist norm" that enables society "to marginalize some sexual practices as 'against nature[,]' and thereby [attempt] to prove the naturalness of the heterosexual monogamy and family values upon which mainstream society bases itself."[28]

Many famous Postmodernists suggest ridding ourselves of this heterosexist norm by pushing the boundaries of sexual deviancy. Paraphrasing the personally troubled but brilliant Postmodernist philosopher Michel Foucault, who died of AIDS he caught through an anonymous homosexual encounter, Glenn Ward says,

[Talk about sex reveals] an ever expanding encyclopaedia of preferences, gratifications and perversions. It creates a realm of perversion by discovering, commenting on and exploring it. It brings it into being as an object of study and in doing so serves to categorize and objectify those who occupy what has been made into the secret underworld of "deviance."[29]

To Foucault, the problem wasn't perverted sex but guilt: "We must … ask why we burden ourselves today with so much guilt for having once made sex a sin."[30] Speaking for himself, Foucault admitted to being "a disciple of the Marquis de Sade."[31] This is, or ought to be, troubling. De Sade was a French aristocrat who sexually mistreated everyone around him and gleefully recorded his violent and criminal acts in books. The term **sadism**, the enjoyment of inflicting pain on others, is derived from his name. And yet Foucault is one of Postmodernism's great heroes. When Postmodernists critique institutions that "oppress" people, anything that limits sexual freedom, such as marriage, is in their crosshairs.

> *Sadism:* the condition, based on the work of the Marquis de Sade, whereby someone receives pleasure, especially sexual pleasure, by inflicting pain or humiliation on others.

New Spirituality. To those of a New Spiritualist (New Age) bent, social institutions like marriage are nothing more than a stage in the search for inner truth. Shakti Gawain enthuses, "People who divorce almost inevitably feel that they have failed, because they assume all marriages should last forever. In many cases, however, the marriage has actually been a success—it's helped each person to grow to the point where they no longer need the same form."[32]

What of those who may be hurt by the divorce—the children or a spouse who wants to stay married? Their pain simply shows how unenlightened they are. To Gawain, attempting to maintain traditional marriage and family is counter-evolutionary:

Relationships and families as we've known them seem to be falling apart at a rapid rate. Many people are panicky about this; some try to re-establish the old traditions and value systems in order to cling to a feeling of order and stability in their lives. It's useless to try to go backward, however, because our consciousness has already evolved beyond the level where we were willing to make the sacrifices necessary to live that way.[33]

According to new spiritualists, limits hamper growth, so we should do away with them. Kevin Ryerson, an acclaimed New Age author and "trance channeler," asserts that "an individual's sexual preference should be viewed as neither good nor evil—such preferences are but the functioning of the body's dialogue to and with another."[34]

Quran: the central holy book of Islam that Muslims believe to be the literal word of God, recited verbatim from God to Muhammad through the angel Gabriel.

Islam. Islam is similar to Christianity in that it affirms one God and even some aspects of the biblical creation account. The **Quran** says, "O mankind! Reverence your Guardian-Lord, who created you from a single Person, created, of like nature, his mate, and from them two of them scattered (like seeds) countless men and women" (surah 4:1). The Quran also declares that men and women are spiritual equals before God and will both receive God's forgiveness and reward if they are devout, true, humble, generous, and chaste.[35] Further, the Quran calls for men to protect women and for women to obey their husbands.[36]

Islam has opened itself to criticism, though, by teaching the inferiority of women and promoting men having multiple wives.[37] While most Muslim men have only one wife, the Quran permits men to have four (though Muhammad had at least nine, one of whom was six at the time of his marriage to her).[38] Muslim apologists point out that the Quran qualifies statements about multiple wives by saying that it requires Muslim men to treat each of their wives fairly, and

Hadith: the oral history of Muhammad's teachings and rulings, and the actions of his early companions.

since this is very difficult to do, having one wife is better.[39] But Islamic scriptures are hard to reconcile with the traditional view of marriage as one man, one woman, for life. In the **Hadith**, a record of Muhammad's conversations, Muhammad gave approval to Muslim men having sex with their slave girls.[40] These passages are significant given that devout Muslims revere and try to copy Muhammad's lifestyle, as well as obey his teachings. To be sure, most Muslims find rape repulsive. But radical Islamic groups, such as ISIS, have turned these passages into what the *New York Times* refers to as a "theology of rape," with ISIS fighters even quoting the Quran to their female captives before sexually abusing them.[41]

Polygamy: the practicing of having more than one spouse at the same time.

When confronted, Muslim apologists point out that many biblical heroes had multiple wives and say that Islam is superior because it at least limits the number of wives to four. While it's true that David, Solomon, and other biblical heroes engaged in **polygamy**, when we look closely, it's clear that they embraced this lifestyle contrary to God's design and commands. For instance, when God created the first humans, he created a normative

---

pattern of the family household consisting of one man and one woman (Gen. 2:21–25),[42] a biblical ideal that Jesus noted in his teaching (Matt. 19:4).[43] The first instance of polygamy in the Bible is that of arrogant and sinful Lamech (Gen. 4:19, 23).[44] The Bible clearly portrays the consequences of such a decision—*no instance in the Bible of a polygamous marriage turned out well!* God not only created our first parents as monogamous but also prohibited the kings of Israel from "multiplying wives" (Deut. 17:17),[45] though many of them did just that by marrying women from foreign nations and worshipping their false gods. This terrible compromise affected the entire nation. In view of this, the New Testament insists that leaders of the church are to be husbands "of one wife" (1 Tim. 3:2, 12).[46]

Though Islam doesn't oppose polygamy, it does stand strongly in opposition to homosexuality. Muslims are far less likely to support same-sex marriage than the general population in the United States,[47] and traditional Muslims consider homosexuality not only a sin but also a punishable crime in most Muslim countries.[48]

To summarize, Secularism, Marxism, Postmodernism, and New Spirituality all either ignore or oppose the idea of marriage as expressed in the·Bible, while Islam distorts it. How should Christians respond? Let's take a closer look to see what the Bible says about marriage and why Christians should care.

3. Why Should Christians Care?

What Does the Bible Teach about Marriage?

In many churches, the discussion about marriage often begins with the Love Chapter (1 Cor. 13) or the apostle Paul's direct instruction about marriage in Ephesians 5:22–33,[49] which implores wives to submit to husbands as the church submits to Christ, and husbands to love their wives as Christ loves the church. But unless we can glimpse marriage in the larger context of creation, fall, and redemption, we'll be trying to understand it with half our theology tied behind our backs.

God's design for marriage is evident in the very first chapter of the very first book of the Bible. Marriage is seen as good from the start, an integral part of God's plan for **human flourishing**. Marriage is good for adults, for children, and for society. God didn't wait until the New Testament to express what marriage is all about. If we really want to get at God's purposes, we have to go back to Genesis, where God revealed his plan. This is what Jesus himself did. In Matthew 19:3–6 and a parallel passage in Mark 10:2–9, Jesus quoted Genesis in his defense of man-woman marriage.[50]

> *Human Flourishing:* **the idea that true human fulfillment comes from the pursuit of truth, virtue, and beauty.**

When we begin with Genesis, we realize four things about marriage.

1. Marriage is based on God's image. Genesis 1:26 quotes God as saying, "Let us make man in our image, after our likeness."

While many religions denigrate women, and culture treats them harshly, the biblical account lifts up men and women as equally valuable image bearers of God. The word *image* appears 107 times in the Bible. Almost all the other occurrences refer to graven images—carved idols. Only 10 times does the term refer directly to the image of God or the image of Christ, and 3 of those occurrences are in this one passage. So what does *image* mean? Genesis 1 uses two mutually reinforcing Hebrew words to make God's perspective clear: *tselem*, which means "resemblance," and *demuth* (pronounced "demooth"), which means "likeness."[51]

Image was a very important concept in the ancient Near Eastern culture in which the Bible was written. Kings set up images of themselves in conquered cities to remind people who was in charge. An image symbolized authority over a certain domain. God's domain is the entire universe. When he created the earth, he didn't set up a statue of himself. He took the stuff of earth, breathed into it, and created a living, moving representation of his image. To realize we've been created in the image of almighty God is a fascinating, profound statement from God about what it means to be human in a world that says everything evolved from random processes. Everything else in our lives depends on this truth.

> To realize we've been created in the image of almighty God is a fascinating, profound statement about what it means to be human in a world that says everything evolved from random processes.

Let's look at the next verse: "And God blessed them" (v. 28). The creation of man and woman wasn't a curse but a blessing. "And God said to them, 'Be fruitful and multiply and fill the earth and subdue it, and have dominion'" (v. 28). The word *dominion* makes people nervous. It shouldn't. It simply means "having responsibility for a certain domain." If you have a family, you have responsibility in the family domain. If you have a job, you have responsibility in the vocational domain.

God gave humans domain over every living thing—over the fish of the sea, the birds, every plant, and every tree. All of creation. This vast domain covers the whole earth.[52]

2. Marriage creates oneness. Hebrew scholars say Adam's statement when he saw Woman, "This at last is bone of my bones and flesh of my flesh" (Gen. 2:23), is a poem, quite possibly even a song. It's remarkable that the first words in all of Scripture that a human being uttered were from a man singing a love song.[53] But the account of Woman's creation doesn't end there. Scripture says, "Therefore a man shall leave his father and his mother and hold fast to his wife, and they shall become one flesh" (v. 24). Why the mention of father and mother if Adam and Woman didn't have parents? It seems God was establishing a prototype. The creation of this man and this woman, the uniting of the two of them as one flesh, created a pattern for all subsequent human beings to adopt.

About this point, author and professor Sean McDowell says,

> The pattern is clear: *there is a one-flesh union, which consists of one man and one woman, and which is oriented towards procreation.* The man leaves his household (consisting of male and female), bonds to his wife, and then they will create their own household and also have kids in order to help fulfill the command to populate the earth (1:28). Such a union is only possible with complementary genders capable of procreation. Nevertheless, while the "one-flesh" union is much more than sexual complementarity, it is no less. Richard Davidson explains that "the 'one-flesh'

experience of husband and wife (2:24) involves not only the sex act but also a one-ness—a wholeness—in all the physical, sensual, social, intellectual, emotional, and spiritual dimensions of life."[54]

The story of creation thus begins not with a birth but with a wedding. The man and woman were together in a completely trusting relationship, made perfectly for each other, and engrossed in work so profoundly meaningful as to be worshipful. It's a picture of grace, enjoyment, pleasure, fulfillment, work, accomplishment, and satisfaction. All of these went together in creation.

3. Marriage pictures Christ and the church. In his letters to the fledgling churches after Jesus's resurrection and ascension into heaven, the apostle Paul revealed an additional significance to marriage: it pictures the relationship between Christ (the bride groom) and the church (the bride). Ephesians 5:31–32 says, "A man shall leave his father and mother and hold fast to his wife, and the two shall become one flesh.' This mystery is profound, and I am saying that it refers to Christ and the church." Marriage as a picture of Christ and the church is not just a mystery. It's a *profound* mystery. It's something deep that we can't quite put words to. As Timothy and Kathy Keller note,

> Marriage as a picture of Christ and the church is not just a mystery. It's a *profound* mystery. It's something deep that we can't quite put words to.

> In the Bible, [*mysterion*] is used to mean not some esoteric knowledge known only to insiders but rather some wondrous, unlooked-for truth that God is revealing through his Spirit. Elsewhere, Paul uses the term to refer to other revelations of God's saving purposes in the gospel. But in Ephesians 5 he applies this rich term, surprisingly, to marriage … [saying] that this is a *mega-mysterion* (verse 32)—an extraordinarily great, wonderful and profound truth that can be understood only with the help of God's Spirit.[55]

C. S. Lewis put it this way: "[In the imagery describing Christ and the church,] we are dealing with male and female not merely as facts of nature but as the live and awful shadows of realities utterly beyond our control and largely beyond our direct knowledge."[56]

Some revisionists, however, argue that this passage isn't about the genders involved in marriage but merely about the commitment to each other of those involved. Sean McDowell notes in response,

> While commitment is undoubtedly important for marriage, it is not the primary point of Ephesians 5:21–33.[57] Marriage is specifically portrayed as a *gendered* institution with husbands and wives, not merely "spouses." As with Romans 1:26–27,[58] Paul refers back to the creation account of male and female as the normative pattern for God's covenant with humanity ([Eph.] 5:31),[59] which is specifically about Christ as the groom and the church as the bride. To ignore the gender component of marriage is to violate the design of marriage in Genesis 1–2, which is the basis for Paul's analogy.[60]

This much is clear in the mystery of marriage as a picture of Christ and the church: the husband stands in relation to the wife as Christ stands in relation to the church. First Corinthians 11:3 says, "I want you to understand that the head of every man is Christ, the head of a wife is her husband, and the head of Christ is God." Some think this simply means that men are to lead and women are to follow. That's a shallow understanding. In proclaiming marriage as a picture of Christ and the church, the Bible fastens a silver cord between marriage and redemption. As Tim and Kathy Keller say, the secret of marriage is "that the gospel of Jesus and marriage explain one another. That when God invented marriage, he already had the saving work of Jesus in mind."[61]

> This much is clear in the mystery of marriage: the husband stands in relation to the wife as Christ stands in relation to the church.

4. Marriage pictures the relational nature of God. The Christian worldview says that God is a person, not a cosmic force. As theologian Millard Erickson phrases it, "God is personal. He is an individual being, with self-consciousness and will, capable of feeling, choosing, and having a reciprocal relationship with other personal and social beings."[62] Furthermore, Christianity teaches that God is Father, Son, and Holy Spirit: a trinity. One God, three persons, in communion with one another. As John Stonestreet phrases it, "Relationship is not something God *does*; it is something he *is*."[63] God, whose perfect expression of self-giving love isn't selfish, doesn't just "put up with" us; he really *relates* to us and seeks our highest good.

This relationship between the members of the Godhead establishes a pattern for the relationship between husbands and wives. Timothy and Kathy Keller explain:

> The Son submits to the Father's headship with free, voluntary, and joyful eagerness, not out of coercion or inferiority. The Father's headship is acknowledged in reciprocal delight, respect, and love. There is no inequality of ability or dignity. We are differently gendered to reflect this life within the Trinity. Male and female are invited to mirror and reflect the "dance" of the Trinity, loving, self-sacrificing authority and loving, courageous submission. The Son takes the subordinate role, and in that movement he shows not his weakness but his greatness. This is one of the reasons why Paul can say that the marriage "mystery" gives us insight into the very heart of God in the work of our salvation.[64]

Marriage is related to redemption. It's related to work and life purpose. It's based in relationship. Marriage isn't a concession to our sin nature. It's plan A, not plan B. Marriage was very good in the beginning, and it's very good now. So how should Christians—even singles—live in response to this truth?

4. WHAT SHOULD CHRISTIANS DO?

Recognize the Spiritual Battle Surrounding Marriage

As we've seen, Adam and Eve's marriage wasn't just about being two lovebirds in a fancy garden. Together, they could do far more than either of them could do separately. They were united in pursuing abundance and fruitfulness in a world teeming with life. But through an act of disobedience, the man and the woman spiraled downward in a cycle of irresponsibility, paranoia, and blame, touching off a spiritual war that continues to this day. Let's look at each aspect of it.

Irresponsibility. Responsibility was fundamental to God's design: our first parents were responsible to fill the earth, care for the animals and the garden, and care for each other. It would make sense that the enemy of the good would attack by getting them to neglect their responsibilities. And that's what happened.

In the dark turn from Genesis 2 to Genesis 3, the man and the woman acted irresponsibly and directly disobeyed God. Yes, they were tricked. Genesis 3:1 says, "The serpent was more crafty than any other beast of the field that the LORD God had made." Adam should have known that the serpent was crafty. After all, he had named it; he identified its characteristics and took responsibility for it. The serpent didn't try to deceive Adam but instead went after Eve, the newest of God's creations:

> [The serpent] said to the woman, "Did God actually say, 'You shall not eat of any tree in the garden'?" And the woman said to the serpent, "We may eat of the fruit of the trees in the garden, but God said, 'You shall not eat of the fruit of the tree that is in the midst of the garden, neither shall you touch it, lest you die.'" (vv. 1–3)

Had God said to the man, "You may not *touch* the tree"? No. He told the man not to *eat* of it, but he said nothing about not *touching* it.

Where did Eve get the idea that the tree was not to be touched? I'm only speculating here, but God had spoken to Adam about it before Eve was created, so possibly she learned that from Adam. Why would Adam add to God's commands in this way? Perhaps Adam was thinking, *If she doesn't touch it, she can't eat from it. I'm just helping protect her.* If true, Adam's strategy backfired. It made the woman more vulnerable because she wasn't quite sure what God had actually said or what her husband had claimed that God said.

Of course, we don't know whether this is what really happened. We know only what the text says. But adding to God's law is a serious offense. By saying, "*My* law is equivalent to *God's* law," or, even worse, "*My* law makes God's law *better*," we're engaging in **idolatry**. We're asking people to worship us on their pathway to worshipping God, and that's extremely dangerous. It is to say, like the serpent said, "Obey me rather than God."[65]

> *Idolatry:* the act of worshipping or valuing something above God; entertaining thoughts about God that are unworthy of him.

The way the narrative proceeds makes it clear that Eve found the serpent's argument persuasive. The tree was good for food; it was useful (a pragmatic argument about what is best), beautiful (an aesthetic argument about what is pleasing), and the key to knowledge (an epistemological argument based on what it means to know something). Interestingly, these are philosophical arguments people make to this day when explaining why they choose to live their lives apart from God.

Adam also exercised irresponsibility. Apparently, according to the text, he was a bystander to the conversation: "She took some of [the tree's] fruit and ate, and she also gave some to her husband who was with her, and he ate" (v. 6). As a man, it's painful for me to imagine the serpent and the woman talking. Based on the image I have of many men who fail to take responsibility when called on, I picture Adam slouching nearby, distracted and dumbfounded. This is especially the case if the man *knew* the serpent was crafty and if he had understood God's very clear command not to eat of the tree.

Paranoia. Next, irresponsibility spiraled downward to paranoia. The text says, "Then the eyes of both were opened, and they knew that they were naked. And they sewed fig leaves together and made themselves loincloths" (Gen. 3:7–8). The man and the woman must have already known they were naked. What changed wasn't the state of their nakedness but its implications.

In Scripture, we see over and over the idea of *investiture*. When somebody becomes a king or queen of a country, a robe is placed on him or her. Investiture is the formal cloaking of that person in the responsibility of the office. Today, when the chief justice of the United States Supreme Court swears in the president, he is cloaked in a robe signifying authority. Scripture talks about exchanging our rags with righteous robes and of covering our nakedness with God's holiness.[66]

As children of a heavenly king, Adam and Eve were, in essence, cloaked in God's glory.

> **As children of a heavenly king, Adam and Eve were, in essence, cloaked in God's glory. When they sinned, his glory was removed from them, and they saw their nakedness for what it really was.**

When they sinned, his glory was removed from them and they saw their nakedness for what it really was. Looking at this text so many millennia removed from the event, it seems an odd account. Who would *care* that the man and woman were naked? They were married to each other. No other people are mentioned—just animals. But in their paranoia, Adam and Eve hid from God: "They heard the sound of the Lord God walking in the garden in the cool of the day, and the man and his wife hid themselves from the presence of the Lord God among the trees of the garden" (v. 8). Even in the midst of their sin, the man and woman knew their fig-leaf loincloths were poor substitutes for God's glory.

Blame. The natural human response to being caught doing something we ought not to do is "It's not my fault." Adam and Eve were no different. Instead of retaking responsibility, Adam and the woman deepened their irresponsibility. The text says,

> The Lord God called to the man and said to him, "Where are you?" And he said, "I heard the sound of you in the garden, and I was afraid, because I was naked, and I hid myself." [God] said, "Who told you that you were naked? Have you eaten of the tree of which I commanded you not to eat?" (Gen. 3:9–11)

The man blamed the woman. In fact, he also blamed God for making the woman. The woman, in turn, blamed the serpent: "Then the Lord God said to the woman, 'What is this that you have done?' The woman said, 'The serpent deceived me, and I ate'" (v. 13).

Understanding this aspect of the creation narrative may help explain a passage in the New Testament that some feminists say proves the apostle Paul was anti-woman. In 1 Timothy 2:14, Paul said, "Adam was not deceived, but the woman was deceived." Rather than saying the woman was weaker because she was deceived, Paul may have been saying that the woman sinned because she opened herself up to deception, whereas the man sinned *on purpose*.

In this tragically dark situation, God pronounced a curse on the serpent. But something about his curse was, in fact, a blessing, and it sparked a war that rages to this day. We read about God's curse and blessing in Genesis 3:14–15:

> The LORD God said to the serpent, "Because you have done this, cursed are you above all livestock and above all beasts of the field; on your belly you shall go, and dust you shall eat all the days of your life. I will put enmity between you and the woman, and between your offspring and her offspring; he shall bruise your head, and you shall bruise his heel."

That phrase "I will put enmity between you and the woman, between your *offspring* and her *offspring*; he shall bruise your head, and you shall bruise his heel" calls for closer examination. The word *offspring* is the Hebrew word for "seed." It's a collective noun, both singular and plural. It's a word like *rice* which is flexible enough to refer to a single grain of rice, a bag of rice, or a truckload of rice. The word *seed* can refer to one of a thing but also to all of a thing.[67]

Theologians look at Genesis 3:15 as a prophecy of the coming Messiah—the one who will crush the head of the serpent. But it's also a reference to all the offspring as a group. The children of the woman are potential Satan crushers. Of course, it is God who does the crushing. But as Paul put it in Romans 16:20, "The God of peace will soon crush Satan under *your* feet."

Presumably, Satan doesn't want to be crushed. If you were he, what would you do? Let's conduct a thought exercise in the vein of C. S. Lewis's book *The Screwtape Letters*. How can you stop this crushing blow from falling on your head? There is only one way. Declare war on the family:

- Kill unborn babies.

- Make people fear, despise, or be ambivalent about marriage.

- Destroy existing marriages.

- Promote promiscuity.

- Promote alternatives to marriage.

- Promote homosexual behavior.

- Promote pornography.

- Trivialize sex.

- Create a wedge between parents and children.

- Get people to deceive themselves about what is true and important.

> **Jesus will ultimately and finally crush the work of Satan. Meanwhile, through God's power, we and our offspring can be little Satan crushers.**

It is precisely these things that are happening every day in our country. It's a spiritual battle, not just a physical one. Jesus will ultimately and finally crush the work of Satan. Meanwhile, through God's power, we and our offspring can be little Satan crushers. To be clear, we can't save ourselves from sin, but God has arranged things in this age of redemption such that our work has the effect of dismantling Satan's work. We can do the work God prepared in advance for us to do (Eph. 2:10).[68]

Make the Case for Marriage from Nature

While exclusive man-woman marriage is the kind of union the Bible describes, it is also possible to argue for such a view of marriage from nature without referring to the Bible. Here's how. As we saw earlier in our definition of marriage, there are three aspects that make marriage a social good: it is permanent, exclusive, and comprehensive.

1. Permanent. To realize the social, emotional, and familial good of marriage, a man and woman must make a permanent commitment to each other. Permanence is a *longitudinal* dimension. Without permanence, a marriage can be a mile deep and an inch wide. A promising marriage that doesn't last can never provide the stability society needs.

2. Exclusive. As with permanence, the societal good of marriage requires an exclusive commitment of one man and one woman. The organic union that defines marriage is possible between only two people. As Sherif Girgis, Ryan Anderson, and Robert George express it, "No act can organically unite three or more, or thus seal a comprehensive union of three or more lives."[69]

3. Comprehensive. Together, permanence and exclusivity constitute a comprehensive union. Girgis, Anderson, and George say, "[Marriage] unites two people in their most basic dimensions, in their minds *and* bodies; … it unites them with respect to procreation, family life, and its broad domestic sharing; and … it unites them permanently and exclusively."[70]

Bodily union is part of the one-flesh relationship of marriage. It expresses in the bodies of the man and woman what exists in the spirit. Marriage isn't just an "up there" kind of experience; it is embodied. We're physical beings as well as spiritual beings. And this physical relationship is complementary: the man and the woman fit together and do so in a way that brings life both to themselves and through the potential of having children.[71] The possibility of procreation is essential to marriage. Girgis, Anderson, and George state,

> The idea that we are trying to explain is not that the relationship of marriage and the comprehensive good of rearing children always go together. It is that, like a ball and

socket, they *fit* together: that family life specially enriches marriage; that marriage is especially apt for family life, which shapes its norms.[72]

In a relationship that's permanent, exclusive, and comprehensive and in which spouses make love in a way that may create new life, they seal the marriage covenant, which may lead the couple to prepare a new generation.[73] This is true regardless of the religious commitment of the couple. It is a natural law.

Recognize That Marriage Is a Public-Policy Matter

Marriage is in the state's interest. Unlike other intimate relationships that don't really warrant government attention, such as best friends or tennis partners, the marriage relationship affects the common good. Government protection of such relationships is part of the government's responsibility for securing justice and preserving public order. Marriage advocates John Corvino and Maggie Gallagher say,

> The critical public or "civil" task of marriage is to regulate sexual relationships between men and women in order to reduce the likelihood that children (and their mothers, and society) will face the burdens of fatherlessness, and increase the likelihood that there will be a next generation that will be raised by their mothers and fathers in one family, where both parents are committed to each other and to their children.[74]

Some think of public regulation as a bad thing, but as we'll see in the upcoming chapter on politics, government has a responsibility to promote good and punish evil. Public regulation gives structure to a fragile institution whose maintenance would be beyond the ability of individual couples to ensure.[75] As social theorist James Wilson frames it, "Marriage is a socially arranged solution for the problem of getting people to stay together and care for children that the mere desire for children, and the sex that makes children possible, does not solve."[76]

> Government has a responsibility to promote good and punish evil. Public regulation gives structure to a fragile institution whose maintenance would be beyond the ability of individual couples to ensure.

The revisionist definition of *marriage* sees it as being about any two people doing what makes them happy. According to this definition, it's hard to see why the state should care. After all, who needs a government stamp of approval on a couple's happiness? Girgis, Anderson, and George point out the absurdity of this view by asking, "Why involve the state in what amounts to the legal regulation of tenderness?"[77] After all, when you get a marriage license, the clerk doesn't ask if you truly love each other. They may ask if you're currently married, old enough to get married, or have been divorced. But the state isn't interested in love. That's not why it got involved in the marriage business in the first place.

But with the traditional definition of *marriage* as one man, one woman, for life, marriage as an institution is deeply related to good things the state should be interested in maintaining:[78]

- **Child well-being**: Children from intact homes perform the best on measurements of educational achievement, literacy, and graduation rates.

- **Emotional health:** Children from intact homes report lower rates of anxiety, depression, substance abuse, and suicide.

- **Familial and sexual development:** Children from intact homes display a strong sense of identity, normal onset of puberty (earlier onset may lead to sexual aggression and promiscuity), lower rates of teen and out-of-wedlock pregnancy, and lower rates of sexual abuse.

- **Child and adult behavior:** Children from intact homes have lower rates of aggression, attention deficit disorder, delinquency, and incarceration.

- **Spousal well-being:** "Marriage makes people better off." Wives have someone with whom to share the responsibility of caring for children and who will provide support and affirm their value. Husbands are better off as well: married men spend less time at bars and are a lot less likely to end up in jail. They also spend more time at religious gatherings and with their families. Everyone's better off when this happens.[79]

Marriage enables limited government. When marriages work well, the government has less to do. Stable families provide for their children and don't need government programs to avoid being swept out to sea by the current of short-term, if-it-feels-good-do-it lifestyles. Conversely, every negative thing that happens through the decline of marriage is one more issue government will be called upon to address. Heritage Foundation president and former senator Jim DeMint puts it like this:

> We cannot hope to limit government if we do not stand up for marriage. Marriage is the foundation of America's cultural stability and economic prosperity.… Without strong families grounded in marriage, we cannot hold back the ever-expanding power of government. As the marriage culture weakens, Big Government grows.[80]

Libertarianism: a political philosophy that upholds individual liberty as that highest good based upon the principle that people should be allowed to do whatever they want as along as they don't infringe upon the rights of others.

In addition to the increased costs and consequent need for greater governmental provision that would follow from an expanded definition of *marriage*, granting government the authority to redefine an institution as fundamental as marriage concedes to that government more power than it is due. It turns out that it's short sighted to argue, as **Libertarianism** does, that the interests of limited government require government to "get out of the marriage business." When families fail, the government steps in—and grows.

The costs of the marital breakdown are indeed enormous.[81] As of 2008, $112 billion in tax expenditures stemmed from divorce and children born out of wedlock.[82] The costs of divorce to governments at all levels (national, state, and municipal) are an estimated $33 billion each year.[83] The "collapse of marriage" indirectly erodes the work ethic as well, which is one of the "principal long-term causes of poverty."[84]

Marriage sustains civilization. Paul Popenoe, founder of the American Institute of Family Relations, was one of the first scholars to study marriage and family issues. He was also one of the first to sound the alarm and to be taken seriously at a national level. He said, "No society has ever survived after its family life deteriorated."[85] A major sociological study of marriage's economic effects concluded that "the wealth of nations depends in no small part on the health of the family."[86] Those who say that government has no interest in maintaining man-woman relationships ignore the fact that government, as well as churches and families, bears the responsibility of maintaining the stability of man-woman marriage so that society may remain cohesive, flourishing, and economically prosperous.

> Government, as well as churches and families, bears the responsibility of maintaining the stability of man-woman marriage so that society may remain cohesive, flourishing, and economically prosperous.

Respond to Anti-marriage Arguments

Some worldviews currently competing against Christianity have in mind the destruction of marriage. Consider the website SecularHumanism.org. The articles posted there cheer same-sex marriage except for one thing: they worry that when people think of marriage of any kind, they'll think of church, and when they think of church, they'll think of God. In one article, the authors come right out and admit that part of the motivation for getting rid of marriage is to stop people from thinking about God.[87]

How do Secularists propose to do this? By promoting such groups as the Alternatives to Marriage Project, which is now called Unmarried Equality. This organization's implied goal is **polyamory**, which means "many loves"—for example, a group of three or more adults who are monogamous within their group, or really any combination the participants agree to. Whatever else polyamory is, a move toward legitimizing it will dismantle any remaining concept of marriage.

> *Polyamory:* from the Greek for "many lovers"; the practice of having more than one lover at a time.

Even Marxists have joined in to do what they can to dismantle traditional marriage. On the website SocialistWorker.org, the sponsors say they think same-sex marriage is a good idea. Why? Because marriage is "part of the larger oppressive capitalist system."[88] If you want to overthrow capitalism, you must overthrow marriage.

Clearly, for worldviews like Secularism and Marxism, destroying marriage is like destroying an enemy fleet, clearing the way to advance their ideas on foreign shores. But all cheering aside, the dominant question remains: Should a revisionist view of marriage that sanctions marriage between same-sex partners ought be accepted by all? Proponents of same-sex marriage have attacked traditional marriage and the way families, the church, and government have handled it. When responding to arguments that same-sex marriage cannot be procreative, they point out the church's de-emphasis on procreation in traditional marriage. When responding to arguments that government shouldn't sanction any laws about marriage that could damage traditional marriage, they point out that the government has already loosened divorce laws and permitted unmarried people and same-sex couples to adopt children. When responding to the argument that same-sex marriage is unstable, they scoff and note that with today's divorce rate, traditional marriage isn't exactly a model of stability.

> **For worldviews like Secularism and Marxism, destroying marriage is like destroying an enemy fleet, clearing the way to advance their ideas on foreign shores.**

But to some same-sex marriage advocates, the inherent stability of marriage is what should make it attractive to same-sex couples. Author Jonathan Rauch plainly states, "Marriage stabilizes relationships."[89] He believes that his case should appeal to conservatives who are concerned about promiscuity, because it's like the town delinquent getting married. It would "help gay people settle down."[90] And because marriage promotes monogamy, allowing same-sex marriage would deflate the efforts of groups like Unmarried Equality.[91]

These are interesting points. But raising objections to the shortcomings of those involved in traditional marriages isn't the same as establishing the merits of same-sex marriage. Same-sex marriage isn't a default; if it is to prevail, it must stand on its own merits. Girgis, Anderson, and George state the point strongly:

> Whatever else is true, the revisionist view must be *false*: [it is] wrong about marriage. Its deep errors are often overlooked, on the implicit assumption that if the conjugal view is wrong, revisionism must be right. This is obviously mistaken logic[,] and, in fact, the revisionist view fails on its own terms: no coherent version of it can account for three points common to both sides of the debate: the state has an interest in regulating certain relationships; that interest exists only if the relationships are sexual; and it exists only if the relationships are monogamous.[92]

> **Saying same-sex marriage is valid because traditional marriage is in trouble is like saying that a stop sign should be removed because people have come to ignore it. They ought to instead ask, "Why was the sign there in the first place?"**

Saying same-sex marriage is valid because traditional marriage is in trouble is like saying that a stop sign should be removed because people have come to ignore it. They ought to instead ask, "Why was the sign there in the first place?"

And yet most arguments supporting same-sex marriage aren't so much *for* same-sex marriage as they are *against* traditional marriage. Here are some of the more prominent arguments:

"Traditional-marriage arguments are based in hate." It may be true that some traditional-marriage proponents have been motivated by hatred for homosexuals. In fact, we ought to each pause and examine our own hearts to be sure we're genuinely motivated by love for other people, keeping in mind that sometimes love involves taking a stand even if it's unpopular. That is what Jesus did. He never compromised the truth, and he was never unloving. That said, traditional-marriage arguments are fundamentally about marriage, not about homosexuality. Wise proponents of traditional marriage will avoid making the issue about same-sex *people* and instead focus on the institution of marriage itself.[93] This is important because "hate" has in no way been relevant in the development of traditional marriage. History proves it. Girgis, Anderson, and George put it this way:

> **Wise proponents of traditional marriage will avoid making the issue about same-sex *people* and instead focus on the institution of marriage itself.**

> History also shows that hostility to homosexually inclined people could not possibly have given rise to the conjugal view. The philosophical and legal principle that only coitus could consummate marriage arose centuries before the concept of gay identity, when the only other acts being considered were ones between a married man and woman. And even in cultures very favorable to homoerotic relationships (as in ancient Greece), something akin to the conjugal view has prevailed—and nothing like same-sex marriage was even imagined.[94]

Defenses of traditional marriage are intended to highlight the advantages of marriage for men, women, children, and society as a whole because of the way it creates a stable, free, and prosperous social and political order. Both heterosexuals and homosexuals benefit from this.

"Excluding same-sex couples from marriage led to inequality and unfairness." The flaw with this argument is that those who experience same-sex attraction were just as free to marry, under the traditional marriage view, as those who experience opposite-sex attraction. The only rule was that they must marry someone of the opposite sex. No law prevented homosexuals from doing this. What same-sex marriage advocates asked for is a *new* right, one far outside the historical and cultural norms. It's not logical to say, "Marriage benefits society"; therefore, "Marriage *in any way I define* it also benefits society." New research is being done all the time, but as of this writing, no data supports the idea that same-sex marriage offers society the same benefits as traditional marriage.

Turnabout is fair play: If recognizing only traditional marriage is discriminatory, is it not unfair to withhold the label *marriage* from any kind of relationship people want to call by that name? Now that the US Supreme Court has said that state laws prohibiting same-sex marriage violate the equal protection clause of the Constitution, experts are noting that all kinds of other relationships—including polyamorous ones and nonsexual ones—will also qualify as marriage.[95] Whether these sorts of relationships ever do become legal, there is no consistent, rational reason to deny them from being considered marriage.

Rewriting the definition of *marriage* has profound implications and carries us far beyond "just" same-sex marriage. In a dissent to the 5–4 majority decision of the Supreme Court in *Obergefell v. Hodges*, which allows same-sex marriages nationwide, justice Clarence Thomas ominously suggested—and in strong language that isn't his typical style—that religious liberty would come under attack as a result:

> Had the majority allowed the definition of marriage to be left to the political process—as the Constitution requires—the People could have considered the religious liberty implications of deviating from the traditional definition as part of their deliberative process. Instead, the majority's decision short-circuits that process, with potentially ruinous consequences for religious liberty.[96]

The changes that must be made to the institution of marriage to include same-sex relationships require us, as a matter of logic and "fairness" (as same-sex marriage advocates define it), to include relationships far beyond monogamous sexual unions. It also calls into question the right of people to speak freely about their opposition to same-sex marriage. Government policy has now hijacked constitutionally guaranteed rights.

> The changes that must be made to the institution of marriage to include same-sex relationships require us, as a matter of logic and "fairness" (as same-sex marriage advocates define it), to include relationships far beyond monogamous sexual unions.

> When the traditional definition of *marriage* is abandoned in favor of defining it as between persons who have a sexual bond, logic demands that all relationships fitting the new definition also be called "marriage."

"What's the harm in expanding the meaning and purpose of marriage?" "Traditional marriage doesn't seem to be working," say same-sex advocates. "Why not give same-sex marriage a shot?" There are two philosophical responses and one empirical response to this question.

Norms, law, and the common good. If law shapes belief and belief shapes behavior, then changing the law to recognize same-sex marriages will undoubtedly influence the beliefs and behavior of all who partake in the institution of marriage.[97] The focus on permanence and exclusivity gives way to the idea that marriage is whatever emotionally satisfies those who are involved. It "severs the ties" between marriage and children and makes it even harder to reverse the "damaging trends" we've seen that have already put the institution of marriage in jeopardy.[98]

The requirements of logic. When the conjugal or traditional definition of *marriage* as being one man, one woman, for life is abandoned in favor of defining it as between persons who have a sexual bond, logic demands that all relationships fitting the new definition also be called "marriage." And as Girgis, Anderson, and George argue, it moves the definition of *marriage* from "formlessness [to] pointlessness."[99]

The statistical reality about same-sex marriage. Social-science research has called into question the once prevailing belief that there is no difference between the life outcomes of children raised by heterosexual parents and those raised by homosexual parents.[100] The American

Psychological Association (APA) reviewed fifty-nine studies and arrived at the conclusion that there is no statistical difference between traditional marriage and same-sex marriage. However, Loren Marks from Louisiana State University reviewed these same fifty-nine studies and found that

> not one of the 59 studies referenced … compares a large, random, representative sample of lesbian or gay parents and their children with a large, random, representative sample of married parents and their children. The available data, which are drawn primarily from small convenience samples, are insufficient to support a strong generalizable claim either way.[101]

Studies that reveal what actually happens in the typical same-sex relationship are hard to come by. One study by Mark Regnerus from the University of Texas at Austin, though, reviewed a highly regarded nationwide database and found same-sex relationships to be inherently unstable. Over the course of the study, almost none of the same-sex relationships lasted more than five years. And compared with children who grew up in biologically intact mother-father families, children who lived with same-sex parents reported significantly lower levels of education and employment and significantly higher levels of sexual abuse and rape, depression, sexual promiscuity, and drug use.[102]

A word of caution: Regnerus's study, in particular, has drawn significant criticism from the scholarly community because of technical shortcomings and the way it defined terms, not just because its conclusions are politically incorrect.[103] This study and others like it, as well as research pointing in the opposite direction, are methodologically sophisticated, and we must be careful lest we misstate the conclusions the researchers were actually able to draw.

But we can at least say this: social-science data, whether in support of the traditional definition of *marriage* or otherwise, cannot *define* what marriage is. At best, such data can document the benefits that naturally follow from the traditional understanding of marriage, though the case for traditional marriage doesn't stand or fall on those benefits being realized.[104]

"If marriage is about procreation, shouldn't we also restrict marriage of heterosexual couples past child-bearing age?" No. Nor should we restrict marriage of heterosexual couples unable to procreate because of infertility, physical handicap, or other factors. The key question to be considered isn't one of fulfillment but one of design. A marriage that doesn't produce children is like a baseball team that doesn't win any games. We don't call such teams "lacrosse teams" or "hockey teams." We call them "baseball teams." Whether they win a single game, they're still playing the game of baseball.[105]

> We can at least say this: social-science data, whether in support of the traditional definition of *marriage* or otherwise, cannot *define* what marriage is.

Redeem Singleness

Many people think singleness is only a waiting room before being called to marriage. Certainly, singleness is a calling for many. But for all people who are single, even if they marry later in life, being single *with purpose* is part of God's design. Adam had purpose in the garden before God created Woman. He was single, yet he was busy taking responsibility.[106] When Genesis 2 zooms in on the single Adam, we see him being productive for God's purposes and for God's glory in this setting. The creation story is told in such a way that it demonstrates the significance of singleness in God's design.

> **For all people who are single, even if they marry later in life, being single *with purpose* is part of God's design.**

Some friends of mine, Brett Harris and Alex Harris, wrote a book as singles called *Do Hard Things* as part of a movement called the Rebelution. The book's subtitle, *A Teenage Rebellion against Low Expectations*, summarizes both our culture's expectations as well as the godly response to a culture of perpetual adolescence in which young adults aren't expected to grow up.[107] This is contrary to the biblical idea that singleness is a time to accomplish great deeds.

The ancient Hebrew culture had very high expectations of young people in education, commerce, and family relationships. Take Jesus's disciples, for example. Jesus was a rabbi (teacher). According to Hebrew historians, rabbis typically took on disciples who were between the ages of fourteen and sixteen.[108] If this astounds you, maybe you've seen too many movies with long-bearded disciples. But what if they weren't that old?[109]

Of the disciples, only Simon Peter was known to have been married at the time of Jesus's ministry. We know this because Peter had a mother-in-law (Matt. 8:14). But the marriageable age for Galilean boys at that time was eighteen.[110]

Another interesting clue about the disciples' ages was the story of the temple tax. All Hebrew males ages twenty and older were charged the temple tax (Exod. 30:11–16).[111] Those collecting the temple tax came to collect it from Jesus and his disciples. Jesus said to Peter, "What do you think? Should the king, who owns the temple, be paying the temple tax?" Peter said no. Then Jesus said, "Well, then, just so we can be a good witness, go and pay the temple tax. Go fishing and you will catch a fish, and in the mouth of the fish will be a coin that is enough to pay the temple tax for you and me" (Matt. 17:24–27).[112] Peter was originally asked whether Jesus *and his disciples* paid the temple tax. But Jesus offered it for only himself and Peter. Of the disciples, only Jesus and Peter seemed to have owed the temple tax. Of course, it's possible the other disciples just weren't around. But isn't it also possible they didn't have to pay the tax because they weren't yet twenty years of age and thus not old enough to owe it?

Though we can't really know the age of the disciples with any degree of certainty, these clues carry profound implications. If the disciples weren't married but were still given enormous responsibility, it could redefine our view of singleness today.

Value Children

> **If the disciples weren't married but were still given enormous responsibility, it could redefine our view of singleness today.**

Many students at our Summit twelve-day summer leadership courses tell me they don't want to raise a family. I tell them, "I'm going to pray that you will fall in love with kids."

At Summit, one way we love kids is by providing good benefits for our staff so our families can have as many babies as the Lord leads them to have. We don't want temporary economic concerns to stand in the way. For some families, it's meant helping them with housing. For others, it's meant giving them a vehicle to use. For all of our families, it has meant providing good insurance coverage to remove the perceived risk of having large families, should the Lord so lead.

We also invite staff families to partake of the meals we prepare for students studying with us during the summer. It's a great community-building time; it gives parents a break from meal preparation, and the Summit students love having all the little kids running around. It's like a family reunion. One by one, those in the rising generation are learning to love kids.

Years ago a student with a feminist mind-set came to study with us. She told me she resented my talks on family issues. One day after talking about loving kids, we took a break for lunch. My youngest son was in the lunchroom. He was a little bitty kid at the time, bare chested and eating chocolate cake. He had chocolate cake *everywhere*. I thought, *Oh no, that's going to be all over Facebook: "Look at the director's kid. Kids are such a mess!"*

At the end of the summer, though, this young woman wrote to say, "I resented what you said about family issues, but when I saw you with your kids, God turned my heart." Now is the time for Christians to set aside self-interest and renew our concern for children. We aren't to idolize them or entertain them or cater to their whims; we're to prepare them for godly, courageous leadership.

> Now is the time for Christians to set aside self-interest and renew our concern for children. We aren't to idolize them or entertain them or cater to their whims; we're to prepare them for godly, courageous leadership.

Be Reconciled

God puts us in families on purpose. We can choose our friends, but God chooses our families. And the strength of our families is in our relationships—husbands and wives, parents and children, brothers and sisters, aunts and uncles, and grandparents. If any of those relationships are strained, take the initiative to heal them. Scripture says, "Do not let the sun go down on your anger" (Eph. 4:26). Seek reconciliation.

The most important thing some people can do to be reconciled in family relationships is to ask forgiveness of someone with whom they have a strained relationship. I've seen the power of this in my own family. My father and my grandfather were in business together and experienced a lot of tension in their relationship. Both had a commitment to Christ, though, and I watched them work their way back into relationship with each other. When my grandfather passed away, I told my father, "I honor you for many reasons, but one of them is your desire to be an honoring son. I know your dad was proud of you."

Strengthening the traditional idea of marriage is something we can all do—by recognizing it's a spiritual

> The most important thing some people can do to be reconciled in family relationships is to ask forgiveness of someone with whom they have a strained relationship.

battle, by standing for marriage in public policy, by responding to attacks on marriage, by redeeming singleness, by valuing children, and by seeking reconciliation with the families we already have.

5. CONCLUSION

Measured against all of history, the years of our lives are very short. In this brief span of time, there is much to be done, and we must redouble our efforts to protect and build up the institution of marriage. The family was God's idea. And it's a very good idea. We have before us an opportunity to be restorers of the family as God designed it. It has everything to do with how we live as single people or married people. It affects home life, work, child rearing, and stewardship of our time and talents. It affects public policy and citizenship. And most important, it's our opportunity to glorify God through the way we live in these troubling days (Eph. 5:15–16).[113]

> We have before us an opportunity to be restorers of the family as God designed it.

ENDNOTES

1. Pew Research survey, 2010, cited in D'Vera Cohn et al., "Barely Half of U.S. Adults Are Married—A Record Low," Pew Research Center, December 14, 2011, www.pewsocialtrends.org/2011/12/14/barely-half-of-u-s-adults-are-married-a-record-low/.

2. Analysis of US Census Bureau data, American Community Survey (ACS), 2009, Mark Mather and Diana Lavery, "In U.S., Proportion Married at Lowest Recorded Levels," Population Reference Bureau, September 2010, www.prb.org/Articles/2010/usmarriagedecline.aspx. See also Richard Fry, "New Census Data Show More Americans Are Tying the Knot, but Mostly It's the College-Educated," FactTank, Pew Research Center, February 6, 2014, www.pewresearch.org/fact-tank/2014/02/06/new-census-data-show-more-americans-are-tying-the-knot-but-mostly-its-the-college-educated/.

3. Timothy Keller, with Kathy Keller, *The Meaning of Marriage: Facing the Complexities of Commitment with the Wisdom of God* (New York: Riverhead Books, 2011), 90.

4. Genesis 1:28: "God blessed [the man and woman]. And God said to them, 'Be fruitful and multiply and fill the earth and subdue it, and have dominion over the fish of the sea and over the birds of the heavens and over every living thing that moves on the earth.'"

5. For a brief review of the data, see FamilyFacts.org, which references credible, scholarly sources from well-respected secular publications. See also Linda J. Waite and Maggie Gallagher, *The Case for Marriage: Why Married People Are Happier, Healthier, and Better Off Financially* (New York: Doubleday, 2000). For a review that briefly summarizes Waite and Gallagher's book, see Richard Niolon, "*The Case for Marriage: Why Married People Are Happier, Healthier, and Better Off Financially,*" PsychPage, October 23, 2010, www.psychpage.com/family/brwaitgalligher.html.

6. See William Tucker, *Marriage and Civilization: How Monogamy Made Us Human* (Washington, DC: Regnery, 2014); Elizabeth Fox-Genovese, *Marriage: The Dream That Refuses to Die* (Wilmington, DE: Intercollegiate Studies Institute, 2008); and Carle C. Zimmerman, *Family and Civilization* (Wilmington, DE: Intercollegiate Studies Institute, 2008).

7. Brady E. Hamilton et al., "Births: Final Data for 2014," *National Vital Statistics Report* 64, no. 12 (December 2015): 2, www.cdc.gov/nchs/data/nvsr/nvsr64/nvsr64_12.pdf.

8. See "The Future of Nonmarital Childbearing in the U.S.," in W. Bradford Wilcox et al., *The Sustainable Demographic Dividend: What Do Marriage and Fertility Have to Do with the Economy?* (Charlottesville, VA: Social Trends Institute, 2011), 19, http://sustaindemographicdividend.org/wp-content/uploads/2012/07/SDD-2011-Final.pdf.

9. See, for example, the statistics cited in "The Consequences of Fatherlessness," National Center for Fathering, accessed July 20, 106, www.fathers.com/content/index.php?option=com_content&task=view&id=391.

10. Kathleen Gerson, *The Unfinished Revolution: Coming of Age in a New Era of Gender, Work, and Family* (Oxford, UK: Oxford University Press, 2010), cited in Madeleine Davies, "Most Women Would Rather Kick Their Husbands to the Curb Than Be a Housewife," *Jezebel*, February 4, 2013, http://jezebel.com/5981558/most-women-would-rather-kick-their-husbands-to-the-curb-than-be-a-housewife.

11. Sherif Girgis, Robert P. George, and Ryan T. Anderson, "What Is Marriage?," *Harvard Journal of Law and Public Policy* 34, no. 1 (Winter 2010): 246. Footnote to the definition also cites John M. Finnis, "Law, Morality, and 'Sexual Orientation,'"

Notre Dame Law Review 69 (1994): 1049, 1066; John Finnis, "Marriage: A Basic and Exigent Good," *Monist* (July–October 2008): 388–406; and Patrick Lee and Robert P. George, *Body-Self Dualism in Contemporary Ethics and Politics* (New York: Cambridge University Press, 2008), 176–97.

12. Girgis, George, and Anderson, "What Is Marriage?"; Stephen Macedo, "Homosexuality and the Conservative Mind," *Georgetown Law Journal* 84 (December 1995): 261, 259.

13. See Cardinal Dolan's speech accepting the 2013 Wilberforce Award, www.youtube.com/watch?v=nI2scvV5FUE&list =UUyyiGFXJkVuSWiXIaIJ7MaQ&index=5.

14. "Religion and Attitudes toward Same-Sex Marriage," Pew Research Center, February 7, 2012, www.pewforum.org /2012/02/07/religion-and-attitudes-toward-same-sex-marriage/.

15. Michael Blume, "The Reproductive Benefits of Religious Affiliation," in Eckart Voland and Wulf Schiefenhövel eds., *The Biological Evolution of Religious Mind and Behavior* (Berlin, Ger.: Springer, 2009), 119–20.

16. Lawrence Casler, *Is Marriage Necessary?* (New York: Human Sciences Press, 1974), 163.

17. Sol Gordon said, "The traditional family, with all its supposed attributes, enslaved woman; it reduced her to a breeder and caretaker of children, a servant to her spouse, a cleaning lady, and at times a victim of the labor market as well." Sol Gordon, "The Egalitarian Family Is Alive and Well," *Humanist* (May/June 1975): 18.

18. Robert N. Whitehurst, "Alternative Life-Styles," *Humanist* (May/June 1975): 24.

19. See, for example, Mark Regnerus, "How Different Are the Adult Children of Parents Who Have Same-Sex Relationships? Findings from the New Family Structures Study," *Social Science Research* 41 (2012): 752–70, www.markregnerus.com /uploads/4/0/6/5/4065759/regnerus_july_2012_ssr.pdf.

20. A particularly horrifying example of this way of thinking is Mary Elizabeth Williams's Salon.com article "So What If Abortion Ends a Life?" Williams concludes the article with this line: "I would put the life of a mother over the life of a fetus every single time—even if I still need to acknowledge my conviction that the fetus is indeed a life. A life worth sacrificing." Mary Elizabeth Williams, "So What If Abortion Ends a Life?," Salon.com, January 23, 2013, www.salon.com/2013/01/23 /so_what_if_abortion_ends_life/.

21. Alexandra M. Kollontai, *Communism and the Family* (New York: Contemporary Publishing Association, 1920), 17.

22. Karl Marx and Friedrich Engels, *The Communist Manifesto* (1848; Newark, NJ: Tribeca Books, 2011), 39.

23. Friedrich Engels, *The Origin of the Family, Private Property and the State* (New York: Penguin, 2010), 107.

24. Marx and Engels, *Communist Manifesto*, 40.

25. Marx and Engels, *Communist Manifesto*.

26. V. Yazykova, *Socialist Life Style and the Family* (Moscow, USSR: Progress Publishers, 1984), 7.

27. Adam Phillips, *Going Sane* (New York: Harper Perennial, 2005), 187.

28. Glenn Ward, *Teach Yourself Postmodernism* (Chicago: McGraw-Hill, 2003), 145.

29. Michel Foucault, paraphrased in Ward, *Teach Yourself Postmodernism*, 146.

30. Paul Rabinow, ed., *The Foucault Reader* (New York: Pantheon Books, 1984), 297.

31. Mark Lilla, *The Reckless Mind: Intellectuals in Politics* (New York: New York Review of Books, 2001), 142.

32. Shakti Gawain, *Living in the Light: Follow Your Inner Guidance to Create a New Life and a New World* (Novato, CA: New World Library, 2011), 133.

33. Gawain, *Living in the Light*, 123–24.

34. Kevin Ryerson, *Spirit Communication: The Soul's Path* (New York: Bantam Books, 1989), 172.

35. Abdullah Yusuf Ali, trans., *The Holy Qur'an* (Washington, DC: American International Printing, 1946), surah 33:35. Quotations from the Quran throughout this book are taken from Abdullah Yusuf Ali's translation. Different versions of the Quran may vary not only in translation but also in versification. We have updated punctuation and decreased the frequency of capital letters.

36. Quran, surah 4:34.

37. Islamic scriptures assume the inferiority of women in passages like the one indicating that the testimony of women is worth half that of a man (surah 2:282), and Muhammad's saying that women are more likely to go to hell and that they are ungrateful and unintelligent. The latter passage says, "Once Allah's Apostle went out to the Musalla (to offer the prayer) O 'Id-al-Adha or Al-Fitr prayer. Then he passed by the women and said, 'O women! Give alms, as I have seen that the majority of the dwellers of Hell-fire were you (women).' They asked, 'Why is it so, O Allah's Apostle?' He replied, 'You curse frequently and are ungrateful to your husbands. I have not seen anyone more deficient in intelligence and religion than you. A cautious sensible man could be led astray by some of you.' The women asked, 'O Allah's Apostle! What is deficient in our intelligence and religion?' He said, 'Is not the evidence of two women equal to the witness of one man?' They replied in the affirmative. He said, 'This is the deficiency in her intelligence. Isn't it true that a woman can neither pray nor fast during her menses?' The women replied in the affirmative. He said, 'This is the deficiency in her religion.'" Sahih al-Bukhari, vol. 1, bk. 6, hadith 301, http://hadithcollection.com/sahihbukhari/39-sahih-bukhari-book-06-menstrual-periods/883-sahih -bukhari-volume-001-book-006-hadith-number-301.html.

38. Muhammad's young wife Aisha was also his favored wife. "The Prophet [married her when] she was six years old, and he consummated his marriage [when] she was nine years old[,] and she remained with him for nine years (i.e. 'till his

death')." Bukhari, vol. 7, bk. 62, hadith 64. Muhammad's followers admired his legendary sexual strength. As recorded in one hadith, "'The Prophet used to visit all his wives in a round, during the day and night and they were eleven in number.' I asked Anas, 'Had the Prophet the strength for it?' Anas replied, 'We used to say that the Prophet was given the strength of thirty (men).' And Sa'id said on the authority of Qatada that Anas had told him about nine wives only (not eleven)." Bukhari, vol. 1, bk. 5, hadith 268.

39. "If ye fear that ye shall not be able to deal justly with the orphans, marry women of your choice, two or three or four; but if ye fear that ye shall not be able to deal justly (with them), then only one, or (a captive) that your right hands possess. That will be more suitable, to prevent you from doing injustice" (Quran, surah 4:3); "Ye are never able to be fair and just as between women, even if it is your ardent desire: but turn not away (from a woman) altogether, so as to leave her (as it were) hanging (in the air)" (surah 4:29). Ali notes, "Legally more than one wife (up to four) are permissible on the condition that a man can be perfectly fair and just to all. But this is a condition almost impossible to fulfill. If, in the hope that he might be able to fulfill it, a man puts himself in that impossible position, it is only right to insist that he should not discard one but at least fulfill all the outward duties that are incumbent on him in respect of her." Abdullah Yusuf Ali, *The Meaning of the Holy Qur'an* (Seattle: Pacific Publishing Studio, 2010), 2:129n639.

40. "Abu Sirma said to Abu Sa'id al Khadri (Allah be pleased with him): O Abu Sa'id, did you hear Allah's Messenger (May peace be upon him) mentioning al-'azl? He said: Yes, and added: We went out with Allah's Messenger (May peace be upon him) on the expedition to the Bi'l-Mustaliq and took captive some excellent Arab women; and we desired them, for we were suffering from the absence of our wives, (but at the same time) we also desired ransom for them. So we decided to have sexual intercourse with them but by observing 'azl (Withdrawing the male sexual organ before emission of semen to avoid conception). But we said: We are doing an act whereas Allah's Messenger is amongst us; why not ask him? So we asked Allah's Messenger (May peace be upon him), and he said: It does not matter if you do not do it, for every soul that is to be born up to the Day of Resurrection will be born. Bukhari, bk. 8, hadith 3371.

41. Rukmini Callimachi, "ISIS Enshrines a Theology of Rape," *New York Times*, August 13, 2015, www.nytimes.com/2015 /08/14/world/middleeast/isis-enshrines-a-theology-of-rape.html?_r=0.

42. Genesis 2:21–25: "The LORD God caused a deep sleep to fall upon the man, and while he slept took one of his ribs and closed up its place with flesh. And the rib that the LORD God had taken from the man he made into a woman and brought her to the man. Then the man said, 'This at last is bone of my bones and flesh of my flesh; she shall be called Woman, because she was taken out of Man.' Therefore a man shall leave his father and his mother and hold fast to his wife, and they shall become one flesh. And the man and his wife were both naked and were not ashamed."

43. Matthew 19:4: "Jesus answered, 'Have you not read that he who created them from the beginning made them male and female?'"

44. Genesis 4:19, 23: "Lamech took two wives. The name of the one was Adah, and the name of the other Zillah.… Lamech said to his wives: 'Adah and Zillah, hear my voice; you wives of Lamech, listen to what I say: I have killed a man for wounding me, a young man for striking me.'"

45. Deuteronomy 17:17: "He shall not acquire many wives for himself, lest his heart turn away, nor shall he acquire for himself excessive silver and gold."

46. First Timothy 3:2, 12: "An overseer must be above reproach, the husband of one wife, sober-minded, self-controlled, respectable, hospitable, able to teach.… Let deacons each be the husband of one wife, managing their children and their own households well."

47. Public Religion Research Institute, American Values Atlas, 2015, cited in Robert P. Jones, "Attitudes on Same-Sex Marriage by Religious Affiliation and Denominational Family," PPRI, April 22, 2015, www.prri.org/spotlight/attitudes -on-same-sex-marriage-by-religious-affiliation-and-denominational-family/#.VTetXy5Vikp.

48. "Islamic Views of Homosexuality," ReligionFacts.com, November 10, 2015, www.religionfacts.com/homosexuality /islam.

49. Ephesians 5:22–33: "Wives, submit to your own husbands, as to the Lord. For the husband is the head of the wife even as Christ is the head of the church, his body, and is himself its Savior. Now as the church submits to Christ, so also wives should submit in everything to their husbands. Husbands, love your wives, as Christ loved the church and gave himself up for her, that he might sanctify her, having cleansed her by the washing of water with the word, so that he might present the church to himself in splendor, without spot or wrinkle or any such thing, that she might be holy and without blemish. In the same way husbands should love their wives as their own bodies. He who loves his wife loves himself. For no one ever hated his own flesh, but nourishes and cherishes it, just as Christ does the church, because we are members of his body. 'Therefore a man shall leave his father and mother and hold fast to his wife, and the two shall become one flesh.' This mystery is profound, and I am saying that it refers to Christ and the church. However, let each one of you love his wife as himself, and let the wife see that she respects her husband."

50. Matthew 19:3–6: "Pharisees … tested [Jesus] by asking, 'Is it lawful to divorce one's wife for any cause?' He answered, 'Have you not read that he who created them from the beginning made them male and female, and said, "Therefore a man shall leave his father and his mother and hold fast to his wife, and the two shall become one flesh"? So they are no longer two but one flesh. What therefore God has joined together, let not man separate.'"

51. KJV Old Testament Hebrew Lexicon, Bible Study Tools, s.v. "*tselem*," Strong's no. 06754, *www.biblestudytools.com/lexicons/hebrew/kjv/tselem.html*; Bible Hub, s.v. "*demuth*," Strong's no. 1823, *http://biblehub.com/hebrew/1823.htm*.

52. Genesis 1:28–29 says that God gave man dominion "over the fish of the sea and over the birds of the heavens and over every living thing that moves on the earth. And God said, 'Behold, I have given you every plant yielding seed that is on the face of all the earth, and every tree with seed in its fruit. You shall have them for food. And to every beast of the earth and to every bird of the heavens and to everything that creeps on the earth, everything that has the breath of life, I have given every green plant for food.'"

53. Tim Keller emphasizes the significance of this occurrence, writing, "When Adam sees Eve, he breaks into poetry, a very striking move designed to signal the significance of the event and the power of Adam's inner response to Eve. His first words are hard to translate. Literally he says, 'This—this time!' The New International [Version] simply renders it, 'Now!' The New Revised Standard Version does a better job, translating it …, 'This *at last*—is bone of my bones and flesh of my flesh!'" Keller, *Meaning of Marriage*, 286n1.

54. Sean McDowell, personal correspondence to author (to be published in a forthcoming article), June 2, 2016; Richard M. Davidson, *Flame of Yahweh: Sexuality in the Old Testament* (Peabody, MA: Hendrickson, 2007), 37.

55. Keller, *Meaning of Marriage*, 41.

56. C. S. Lewis, *God in the Dock* (Grand Rapids: Eerdmans, 2014), 262. Originally published in "Notes on the Way," *Time and Tide* 29 (August 14, 1948).

57. Ephesians 5:21–33: "[Submit] to one another out of reverence for Christ. Wives, submit to your own husbands, as to the Lord. For the husband is the head of the wife even as Christ is the head of the church, his body, and is himself its Savior. Now as the church submits to Christ, so also wives should submit in everything to their husbands. Husbands, love your wives, as Christ loved the church and gave himself up for her, that he might sanctify her, having cleansed her by the washing of water with the word, so that he might present the church to himself in splendor, without spot or wrinkle or any such thing, that she might be holy and without blemish. In the same way husbands should love their wives as their own bodies. He who loves his wife loves himself. For no one ever hated his own flesh, but nourishes and cherishes it, just as Christ does the church, because we are members of his body. 'Therefore a man shall leave his father and mother and hold fast to his wife, and the two shall become one flesh.' This mystery is profound, and I am saying that it refers to Christ and the church. However, let each one of you love his wife as himself, and let the wife see that she respects her husband."

58. Romans 1:26–27: "For this reason God gave them up to dishonorable passions. For their women exchanged natural relations for those that are contrary to nature; and the men likewise gave up natural relations with women and were consumed with passion for one another, men committing shameless acts with men and receiving in themselves the due penalty for their error."

59. Ephesians 5:31: "Therefore a man shall leave his father and mother and hold fast to his wife, and the two shall become one flesh."

60. Sean McDowell, personal correspondence with the author, June 2, 2016. To be published in a forthcoming article.

61. Keller, *Meaning of Marriage*, 43.

62. Millard J. Erickson, *Introducing Christian Doctrine*, 3rd ed., ed. L. Arnold Hustad (Grand Rapids: Baker Academic, 2015), 89.

63. John Stonestreet, personal conversation with the author and lectures at Summit Ministries.

64. Keller, *Meaning of Marriage*, 198.

65. In Genesis 3:4–6, the serpent says, "'You will not surely die. For God knows that when you eat of [the tree] your eyes will be opened, and you will be like God, knowing good and evil.' So when the woman saw that the tree was good for food, and that it was a delight to the eyes, and that the tree was to be desired to make one wise, she took of its fruit and ate, and she also gave some to her husband who was with her, and he ate."

66. Scripture says our righteousness is as "filthy rags" (Isa. 64:6 KJV), that God has covered us with robes of righteousness (61:10), and that he covers us "with favor as with a shield" (Ps. 5:12). Lamentations 1:8 talks about Jerusalem becoming "filthy" through her sin and being despised by those who see her nakedness. Ezekiel 16:8 speaks of God spreading his garment over us to cover our nakedness. Revelation 3:18 says that God covers us with "white garments so that … the shame of [our] nakedness may not be seen." The idea of a covering of holiness is also referenced in 2 Corinthians 7:1; Ephesians 4:24; 1 Thessalonians 3:13 and 4:4, 7; and 2 Peter 3:11.

67. Walter C. Kaiser Jr., *Toward an Old Testament Theology* (Grand Rapids: Zondervan, 1991), 35–37.

68. Ephesians 2:10: "We are [God's] workmanship, created in Christ Jesus for good works, which God prepared beforehand, that we should walk in them."

69. Sherif Girgis, Ryan T. Anderson, and Robert P. George, *What Is Marriage? Man and Woman; A Defense* (New York: Encounter, Books, 2012), 33.

70. Girgis, Anderson, and George, *What Is Marriage?*, 23.

71. For elaboration on this topic, see "Appendix: Further Reflections on Bodily Union," Girgis, Anderson, and George, *What Is Marriage?*, 99–109.

72. Girgis, Anderson, and George, *What Is Marriage?*, 29.

73. Girgis, Anderson, and George, *What Is Marriage?*, 30.

74. John Corvino and Maggie Gallagher, *Debating Same-Sex Marriage* (New York: Oxford University Press, 2012), 96.

75. See Amy L. Wax, "Diverging Family Structure and 'Rational' Behavior: The Decline in Marriage as a Disorder of Choice," in *Research Handbook on the Economics of Family Law*, eds. Lloyd R. Cohen and Joshua D. Wright (Northampton, MA: Edward Elgar, 2011), 15–71.

76. James Q. Wilson, *The Marriage Problem: How Our Culture Has Weakened Families* (New York: HarperCollins, 2002), 41.

77. Girgis, Anderson, and George, *What Is Marriage?*, 16.

78. Findings from Witherspoon Institute, *Marriage and the Public Good*, http://winst.org/wp-content/uploads /WI_Marriage_and_the_Public_Good.pdf, cited in Girgis, Anderson, and George, *What Is Marriage?*, 42. For a review of empirical findings, see Witherspoon Institute, "Evidence from the Social and Biological Sciences," chap. 3 in *Marriage and the Public Good: Ten Principles* (Princeton, NJ: Witherspoon Institute, 2008). For an analysis of the consequences of a decline in marriage, particularly in the context of socioeconomic inequality, see Charles Murray, *Coming Apart: The State of White America, 1960–2010* (New York: Crown Forum, 2012), 149–67.

79. Findings of Steven L. Nock, *Marriage in Men's Lives* (New York: Oxford University Press, 1998) summarized in Girgis, Anderson, and George, *What Is Marriage?*, 44.

80. Jim DeMint, "Marriage Essential for Limited Government," *USA Today*, March 26, 2013, www.usatoday.com/story /opinion/2013/03/26/jim-demint-on-opposition-to-gay-marriage/2021867/.

81. See, generally, Witherspoon Institute, *Marriage and the Public Good*, 15.

82. Benjamin Scafidi, *The Taxpayer Costs of Divorce and Unwed Childbearing: First-Ever Estimates for the Nation and for All Fifty States* (New York: Institute for American Values, 2008), www.americanvalues.org/pdfs/coff-executive_summary.pdf.

83. Extrapolated estimate from David G. Schramm, "Individual and Social Costs of Divorce in Utah," *Journal of Family and Economic Issues* 27, no. 1 (January 2006): 133–51.

84. Robert Rector and Rachel Sheffield, "Executive Summary: Understanding Poverty in the United States; Surprising Facts about America's Poor," *Backgrounder* no. 2607 (September 2011), http://thf_media.s3.amazonaws.com/2011/pdf/bg2607.pdf.

85. Paul Popenoe, quoted in "Behavior: The American Family: Future Uncertain," *Time*, December 28, 1970, 34.

86. W. Bradford Wilcox et al., *The Sustainable Demographic Dividend: What Do Marriage and Fertility Have to Do with the Economy?* (Charlottesville, VA: Social Trends Institute, 2011), 3, http://sustaindemographicdividend.org/wp-content /uploads/2012/07/SDD-2011-Final.pdf.

87. See, for example, Tom Flynn, "Two Cheers for Same-Sex Marriage," *Free Inquiry* 29, no. 5 (July 2009), posted at Council for Secular Humanism, www.secularhumanism.org/index.php?section=library&page=flynn_oped_29_5.

88. Graham Shaw, "Good Reason to Be Wary of Marriage," SocialistWorker.org, May 28, 2008, http://socialistworker .org/2008/05/28/wary-of-marriage.

89. Jonathan Rauch, *Gay Marriage: Why It Is Good for Gays, Good for Straights, and Good for America* (New York: Henry Holt, 2004), 76–77.

90. Rauch, *Gay Marriage*, 77.

91. Rauch says, "Straight activists who want nonmarital options would no longer be able to piggyback on the movement to grant gay couples some form of legal recognition. They would have to live or die on the strength of the proposition that *heterosexuals* need alternatives to marriage. That does not mean the alternatives-to-marriage movement would pack its bags and move to Argentina. But the movement's legitimacy and appeal would be immensely diminished." Rauch, *Gay Marriage*, 89–90.

92. Girgis, Anderson, and George, *What Is Marriage?*, 14–15. See pages 15–19 for elaboration of this argument.

93. Girgis, Anderson, and George say, "Before we continue, we should clarify what our argument is *not*. First, it is in the end not about homosexuality. We do not address the morality of homosexual acts or their heterosexual counterparts. We will show that one can defend the conjugal view of marriage while bracketing this moral question and that the conjugal view can be wholeheartedly embraced without denigrating same-sex-attracted people, or ignoring their needs, or assuming that their desires could change. After all, the conjugal view is serenely embraced by many thoughtful people who are same-sex-attracted. Again, this is fundamentally a debate about what marriage is, not about homosexuality." Girgis, Anderson, and George, *What Is Marriage?*, 10.

94. Girgis, Anderson, and George, *What Is Marriage?*, 11.

95. Girgis, Anderson, and George write, "If you insist as a matter of *principle* that we should recognize same-sex relationships as marriages, the same principle will require you to accept (and favor legally recognizing) polyamorous—and … non-sexual— relationships as marriages. If you think conjugal marriage laws unjustly discriminate against same-sex relationships, you will have no way of showing why the same is not true of multiple-partner and nonsexual ones." Girgis, Anderson, and George, *What Is Marriage?*, 20.

96. Justice Clarence Thomas, dissenting opinion, Obergefell v. Hodges, 576 U.S.___(2015), quoted in Sarah Pulliam Bailey, "Here Are the Key Excerpts on Religious Liberty from the Supreme Court Decision on Gay Marriage," *Washington Post*, June 26, 2015, www.washingtonpost.com/news/acts-of-faith/wp/2015/06/26/here-are-the-key-excerpts-on-religious-liberty -from-the-supreme-courts-decision-on-gay-marriage/.

97. Girgis, Anderson, and George say, "Redefining civil marriage would change its meaning for everyone. Legally wedded opposite-sex unions would increasingly be defined by what they had in common with same-sex relationships," and "Underlying people's adherence to the marital norms already in decline, after all, are the deep (if implicit) connections in their minds between marriage, bodily union, and children. Redefining marriage as revisionists propose would not just wear down but sever these ties, making it immeasurably harder to reverse other damaging trends and restore the social benefits of a healthy marriage culture." Girgis, Anderson, and George, *What Is Marriage?*, 55, 58.

98. See Girgis, Anderson, and George, *What Is Marriage?*, 58.

99. Girgis, Anderson, and George, *What Is Marriage?*, 21.

100. For an accessible discussion of this research, see Ana Samuel, "The Kids Aren't All Right: New Family Structures and the 'No Differences' Claim," *Public Discourse*, June 14, 2012, www.thepublicdiscourse.com/2012/06/5640/.

101. Loren D. Marks, "Same-Sex Parenting and Children's Outcomes: A Closer Examination of the American Psychological Association's Brief on Lesbian and Gay Parenting," *Social Science Research* 41, no. 4 (July 2012): 748, www.baylorisr.org/wp-content/uploads/Marks.pdf.

102. Regnerus, "How Different Are the Adult Children?," 752–70.

103. Tom Bartlett, "Controversial Gay-Parenting Study Is Severely Flawed, Journal's Audit Finds," *Chronicle of Higher Education*, July 26, 2012, http://chronicle.com/blogs/percolator/controversial-gay-parenting-study-is-severely-flawed-journals-audit-finds/30255.

104. For example, the political scientist Charles Murray, once an opponent of same-sex marriage and parenting, announced in 2012 that empirical findings have convinced him otherwise, especially when considered in a relative context (i.e., outcomes of children with no parents versus children with same-sex parents). See Charles Murray, interview with Charlie Rose, *Charlie Rose* show, February 10, 2012, https://charlierose.com/videos/15096.

105. Girgis, Anderson, and George, *What Is Marriage?*, 30–31.

106. To some, this is a technical theological point based on the belief that there is no contradiction between Genesis 1, which describes the man and woman being created at the same time, and Genesis 2, which describes the man being created first, and then the woman. My approach, which I have explained in the book *Understanding the Faith*, is that there aren't two creation accounts but one presented as an overview followed by a close-up. The nature of the story, as well as the nature of the Hebrew mind-set, is that when you begin a story, you give the overview first. Describe the big picture first and then focus in on the key actors. Scholars call it *recapitulation*. It's a common technique in movies, showing the big story and then zooming in on the key individuals involved. Genesis 1 is the big picture of what God did. Genesis 2 focuses in on the man and the woman. See also Gleason Archer Jr., *A Survey of Old Testament: Introduction* (Chicago: Moody, 1994), 135.

107. See Alex Harris and Brett Harris, *Do Hard Things: A Teenage Rebellion against Low Expectations* (Colorado Springs, CO: Multnomah, 2013); Diana West, *The Death of the Grown-Up: How America's Arrested Development Is Bringing Down Western Civilization* (New York: St. Martin's Griffin, 2007); and Robert Epstein, *The Case against Adolescence: Rediscovering the Adult in Every Teen* (Sanger, CA: Quill Driver, 2007).

108. Young disciples, according to Ray Vander Laan, would enter Beth Midrash, the school of a rabbi, at the age thirteen or fourteen. See Ray Vander Laan, *In the Dust of the Rabbi: Learning to Live as Jesus Lived* (Grand Rapids: Zondervan, 2006), with companion DVD.

109. Günter Krallmann discusses much of the evidence for the young ages of Jesus's disciples in *Mentoring for Mission: A Handbook on Leadership Principles Exemplified by Jesus Christ* (Milton Keynes, UK: Authentic Media, 2003).

110. William Barclay, *The Ten Commandments* (Louisville, KY: Westminster John Knox, 1998), 90.

111. Exodus 30:11–16: "The LORD said to Moses, 'When you take the census of the people of Israel, then each shall give a ransom for his life to the LORD when you number them, that there be no plague among them when you number them. Each one who is numbered in the census shall give this: half a shekel according to the shekel of the sanctuary (the shekel is twenty gerahs), half a shekel as an offering to the LORD. Everyone who is numbered in the census, *from twenty years old and upward*, shall give the LORD's offering. The rich shall not give more, and the poor shall not give less, than the half shekel, when you give the LORD's offering to make atonement for your lives. You shall take the atonement money from the people of Israel and shall give it for the service of the tent of meeting, that it may bring the people of Israel to remembrance before the LORD, so as to make atonement for your lives.'"

112. Matthew 17:24–27: "When [Jesus and his disciples] came to Capernaum, the collectors of the two-drachma tax went up to Peter and said, 'Does your teacher not pay the tax?' He said, 'Yes.' And when he came into the house, Jesus spoke to him first, saying, 'What do you think, Simon? From whom do kings of the earth take toll or tax? From their sons or from others?' And when he said, 'From others,' Jesus said to him, 'Then the sons are free. However, not to give offense to them, go to the sea and cast a hook and take the first fish that comes up, and when you open its mouth you will find a shekel. Take that and give it to them for me and for yourself.'"

113. Ephesians 5:15–16 (NIV): "Be very careful, then, how you live—not as unwise but as wise, making the most of every opportunity, because the days are evil."

CHAPTER 11

CREATION CARE

1. THE TRAGEDY OF PREVENTABLE DEATH

Omari was just five years old when it happened. She never felt a thing. During the night a female anopheles mosquito came through an open window and drew blood, leaving behind a deadly parasite.[1] About ten days later, Omari complained of a fever and headache. Inside her tiny body, the parasite multiplied, invaded her red blood cells, and caused them to stick to the walls of her blood vessels. Blood flow to her brain was choked off. Omari fell into a coma and never recovered.

In 2015, an estimated 438,000 people like Omari died from the mosquito-borne disease called malaria, and nearly half the world's population is at risk.[2] Sadly, there is less hope of a solution now than fifty years ago. The approach once used to eradicate malaria has ground to a virtual halt through alarmist rhetoric and bureaucratic mismanagement. And it all started with a book. Here's the story.

As the United States entered the twentieth century, malaria was an "immense cause of human death, human illness, and economic loss," as entomologist Donald Roberts and anti-malaria activist Richard Tren describe it.[3]

In the 1940s, though, the United States found a way to beat mosquito-borne diseases using a pesticide called DDT. The state of Texas, for example, reduced incidents of typhus by 88 percent in just five years.[4] In Guyana, a South American country where a third of the population had been stricken with malaria and more than one of every ten infants died, incidents of malaria decreased by 99 percent in urban areas and 96 percent in rural areas in less than five years.[5] In Sri Lanka, infant mortality decreased by 62 percent, and within a few years, the rate of malaria infection plummeted from 413 per 1,000 people to 0.85.[6] The island of Taiwan eradicated malaria altogether.[7]

> As the United States entered the twentieth century, malaria was an "immense cause of human death, human illness, and economic loss."

Sprayed once or twice a year on the interior walls of homes, DDT repelled disease-bearing mosquitoes. No other solution even came close to DDT's effectiveness. DDT lasted twice as long as the next most effective pesticide, it cost one-fourth as much as the next cheapest alternative, and was repeatedly proved not only to repel malaria-spreading mosquitoes but also to kill them.[8]

But in 1962, marine biologist Rachel Carson penned an alarming book called *Silent Spring*, attacking the use of DDT and other pesticides. She challenged the world's fascination with chemicals (one chemical company proudly trumpeted the slogan "Better things for better living … through chemistry").[9] Carson warned that "death-dealing" chemicals were destroying animal habitats, causing disease-bearing pests to mutate, and putting the world on the brink of a cancer epidemic.[10] Looking back more than fifty years later, the "science" touted in *Silent Spring* turned out to be either overstated or false.[11] This makes what happened next seem all the more tragic.

Based largely on pressure *Silent Spring* generated, the US Environmental Protection Agency (EPA) held hearings on the potential harm of DDT.[12] The hearing examiner concluded that the data hadn't established DDT as a threat to humans or wildlife, but the EPA administrator overruled his findings and banned it anyway.[13] Manufacturing nearly ceased. The lack of supply, combined with environmentalist pressure, shut down DDT programs around the world. As of 2008, only twelve countries were still using it.[14]

> Looking back more than fifty years later, the "science" touted in *Silent Spring* turned out to be either overstated or false.

Meanwhile, malaria continues to kill hundreds of thousands each year, and perhaps as many as half a billion people suffer from its effects. Bowing to international pressure, the World Health Organization (WHO) finally released a directive in 2006 recommending that the chemical be used in countries with serious malaria problems.[15] It was too little too late. Poor countries rely heavily for their disease-prevention programs on money from donor organizations that refuse to endorse DDT. Without outside help, these countries find themselves incapable of organizing consistent malaria-control programs.[16]

The point of this story is not to promote chemical pesticides. Every solution has its drawbacks, including DDT. Government incompetence in ineffectively trying to coat vast swaths of nature with DDT was part of the problem that led to Carson's book in the first place. But the point is the tens of millions of preventable deaths that have resulted from the worldview battle over environmental issues and priorities. As we'll see in this chapter, many environmental efforts are dominated by special-interest groups whose ultimate goal is to displace Christianity. Many of these groups see humans as a rapacious, polluting, resource-depleting cancer on the planet. The death of millions isn't a tragedy; it's a necessity.

Those with a Christian worldview shouldn't be surprised. People have always tried to play God. And all radical rhetoric aside, it is no surprise that human fallenness has led to people abusing their God-given dominion over the earth.[17] When people rebel against God, Hosea 4:3 says, "the land mourns, and all who dwell in it languish, and also the beasts of the field and the birds of the heavens, and even the fish of the sea are taken away."

The consequences of poor **stewardship** are all around us. Hope College professor Steven Bouma-Prediger says, "The conclusion of many responsible earth-watchers is that the earth is not doing very well."[18] Hunger is a persistent problem. Natural habitats are being destroyed. Much of the world is lost in a fog of pollution. Clean drinking water is scarce, and many developed countries are very wasteful.[19] Other concerns include topsoil loss, water pollution, garbage disposal, and destruction of coral reefs and other habitats that cause unpredictable changes in the food chain.

> *Stewardship:* the process of managing something that has been entrusted to one's care.

People with a distinctly anti-Christian worldview are dominating the conversation about environmental issues, which many Christians shy away from. A few even justify inaction by saying, "It's all going to burn anyway. Just get people saved." Yet this is a false choice. God created the earth and called it good. As Leah Kostamo puts it, "Matter matters to God, who created the stuff and even became the stuff and calls us to steward the stuff on his behalf."[20] Creation matters. The worldview battle over creation matters. In this chapter, we'll discuss that battle, show why Christians should care, and explore what that caring might look like from a biblical worldview.

> *Conservationism:* a movement that supports the conservation of natural resources as a necessity for human thriving and survival.

2. WHAT IS THE PROBLEM?

The central problem is that our priorities about creation care have shifted as people's worldviews have become more secular. Whereas **conservationism**, going back to naturalist John Muir and president Theodore Roosevelt, seeks to understand and better steward natural resources *for* humans, **environmentalism**, defined as "advocacy for or work toward protecting the environment,"[21] focuses on protecting the environment *from*

> *Environmentalism:* a movement that seeks to protect the environment from a perceived threat of human beings.

humans. From the beginning, environmental advocates believed that scientific advances, despite their benefits, resulted in air and water pollution and other ills that affected the health of the planet itself. A new social movement was needed to fight back.

Ecology: the branch of biology that deals with how organisms relate to one another.

The philosophy of environmentalism found its scientific soul mate in the study of **ecology**, a branch of biology focusing on how organisms in nature relate to one another in a mutually supportive fashion. Several political movements have developed under environmentalism's banner as well, including **ecofeminism**, which says that male domination oppresses women and exploits the planet's resources, and **deep ecology**, which calls for a radical restructuring of society based on the idea that all living things, not just human beings, should have legal rights.[22]

Ecofeminism: a political philosophy that links the oppression of women and the exploitation of the environment with the values inherent in what advocates refer to as Western patriarchal society.

Today, two myths surrounding the environmental movement tend to keep Christians on the sidelines.

Myth No. 1: Environmental Issues Are Worldview Neutral

Deep ecology: an environmental philosophy based on the idea that all living beings form a spiritual and ecologically interconnected system, which is presently threatened by the harmful impact of human beings.

The first myth keeping Christians on the sidelines is the perception that environmentalism is an alternative religion. That's a valid concern. The late novelist Michael Crichton described environmentalism as "the religion of urban atheists"[23] in which "good" is that which is part of the natural world, and "evil" is that which is unnatural. Human actions are "outside nature," in this view, which places them in the category of evil.[24] The less human influence there is on the planet, the thinking goes, the better off the planet will be.

Environmentalism rose up to challenge another philosophy that people in the twentieth century held with religious fervor: progressivism. **Progressivism** is the idea that the story of humanity is one of steady progress from our prehuman ancestry to a society that uses scientific, technological, and economic insights to fulfill humanity's quest for perfection. Progressivism's mantra is, in short, "Every day, in every way, we're getting better." Historian J. B. Bury enthused that the idea of progress "belongs to the same order of ideas as Providence or personal immortality." It was a path to heaven on earth.[25]

Progressivism: the belief in human progress; the belief that political systems can be used to create economic prosperity, minimize risk, and advance society.

Environmentalism turned progressivism on its head by offering a new religious narrative. Carson's *Silent Spring* was one of its bibles, portraying nature as a lost paradise and progressivism as original sin. Progressivism had sold humanity's soul to the Devil, so to speak; efficiency, modern medicine, and economic growth were not our salvation but our downfall. Our only salvation was to retreat to the cathedral of nature.[26]

Some environmentalists even began to think of environmentalism in spiritual terms. In 1979, scientist James Lovelock wrote *Gaia: A New Look at Life on Earth*. Lovelock drew inspiration from an ancient goddess to portray the earth as "the superorganism composed of all life tightly coupled with the air, the oceans, and the surface rocks."[27] Lovelock sees no "who" behind the "what." Gaia just *is*. But his mystical descriptions of nature's inner-workings certainly seem spiritual to many people. It helped develop what my coauthor David Noebel and I call **New Spirituality** in our book *Understanding the Times*. It was love at first sight, and environmentalism and New Spirituality have been inseparable ever since.

So while secular environmentalists think the point is to stop stewarding nature and leave it alone, spiritual environmentalists see environmental damage as a spiritual offense. We must repent by listening to our mother—Mother Earth—and trying to achieve oneness with her. Both views are religious in that they propose answers to environmental problems based on a specific set of beliefs about the cause, nature, and purpose of the universe. Both views bother Christians, and rightly so. But if, out of concern over embracing a wrong worldview, we fail to involve ourselves in creation care, then we've fallen for myth number 2.

> While secular environmentalists think the point is to stop stewarding nature and leave it alone, spiritual environmentalists see environmental damage as a spiritual offense.

Myth No. 2: Only Radicals Care about the Environment

As noted earlier, environmentalism differs from conservationism. Conservationism was concerned with issues like sustainable farming, especially in the aftermath of the Dust Bowl in the 1930s when, during a drought, years of poor farming methods and soil depletion resulted in soil blowing away, uprooting millions of people and casting them into poverty.[28]

Environmentalist rhetoric took on a harder edge in the 1970s. With the help of Norwegian industrialist-turned-environmentalist Arne Naess, deep ecology emerged. Deep ecology, according to Steven Bouma-Prediger, says that "nonhuman organisms not only count morally but count equally."[29] Proponents of deep ecology see humans as no more valuable than other organisms. The idea that humans are specially made in God's image is not only wrong, deep ecologists say, but also dangerous.

> Proponents of deep ecology see humans as no more valuable than other organisms. The idea that humans are specially made in God's image is not only wrong, deep ecologists say, but dangerous.

As a Christian, it would be easy for me to write off the environmental movement as populated primarily by extremists. But as biologist Ray Bohlin reminds us, "We cannot allow the enemy to take over leadership in an area that is rightfully ours."[30] Bohlin is right. Christians might believe that humans living redemptively are the solution to the problem, but if they don't get involved, people who only see humans as the problem will dominate the environmental debate. In the Christian view, it would be better if humans prospered. In the view of environmental extremists, it would be better if humans disappeared. If the Christian viewpoint is to be represented, Christians have to show up and be part of the conversation. If your team shows up for the game, you might lose. But if you don't show up at all, your chance of losing by forfeit is 100 percent.

> Christians might believe that humans living redemptively are the solution to the problem, but if they don't get involved, people who only see humans as the problem will dominate the environmental debate.

There are radicals who care about the environment for the wrong reasons, but that doesn't mean Christians shouldn't care about the environment for the right ones. So what are those right reasons? To find out, we need to travel all the way back through history to the very beginning of creation, as described in the book of Genesis.

3. WHY SHOULD CHRISTIANS CARE?

Christians ought to care about creation. God commands it, and it's central to our understanding of the gospel. As Ray Bohlin points out,

> The Bible contains numerous examples of the care with which we are expected to treat the environment. Leviticus 25:1–12[31] speaks of the care Israel was to have for the land. Deuteronomy 25:4 and 22:6[32] indicate the proper care for domestic animals and a respect for wildlife. In Isaiah 5:8–10[33] the Lord judges those who have misused the land. Job 38:25–28[34] and Psalm 104:27–30[35] speak of God's nurture and care for His creation. And Jesus spoke on two occasions of how much the Father cared for even the smallest sparrow (Matt. 6:26[;] 10:29).[36, 37]

God made all things (John 1:1–18),[38] reigns over them (Ps. 103:19),[39] and sustains them (Heb. 1:1–3).[40] The earth is full of his glory (Isa. 6:3),[41] and he is reconciling it to himself (Col. 1:15–20).[42, 43] As Steven Bouma-Prediger says, "When we turn the attention of the church to a definition of the Christian relationship with the natural world, we are not stepping away from grave and proper theological ideas; we are stepping right into the middle of them."[44] We honor our Master, he says, by caring for his masterpieces.[45]

What the Bible Says about Creation

God created it. The Bible's doctrine of creation is central to understanding life in this world.[46] Genesis 1:1 says, "In the beginning, God created the heavens and the earth." The "universe had a beginning," and the Bible says God is the one who began it.[47] First, God created it ex nihilo—"out of nothing"—as a free, active expression of his nature. Creation is *contingent*; that is, it didn't *have* to come into being.[48] God relied on himself, and nothing else, to make something that didn't have to exist.

Second, creation is the work of the Trinity: Father, Son, and Holy Spirit.[49] Genesis 1:2 says the Spirit of God hovered over the waters. Throughout the Genesis creation account,

Scripture says, "And God said." God spoke creation into being. The gospel of John says that the word God spoke wasn't just phonated sound. It was *the Word (Logos)*: Jesus. John 1:2–3 says, "He was in the beginning with God. All things were made through him, and without him was not any thing made that was made." Not only did God bring creation into existence through Jesus but, according to Scripture, Jesus is the one sustaining creation. "In him all things hold together" (Col. 1:17). Theologian Jonathan Wilson emphasizes that

> we misuse creation as a noun denoting a collection of things rather than the continuing work of God as God keeps this world in existence and works for its redemption. In light of this, we do well to use occasionally, even frequently, the active form "creating." There is no creation apart from the continuing creating work of God.[50]

The act of creation was relational. The Father, Son, and Holy Spirit, in perfect communication, brought into physical form exactly what God wanted to have happen and actively sustained it.

Third, God is *other than* his creation. God made things, but he is not a thing. He transcends nature.[51] God doesn't depend on creation; creation depends on God.[52]

When we take these three insights together—that God created everything out of nothing as a free act of his will, that he created everything relationally through the Trinity, and that he is "other than" his creation—a picture emerges of a purposeful creation containing both structure and direction. It's going somewhere.[53] But where? Toward life.[54] Not just *supporting* life but *giving* life. In Hebrew, the idea of fullness of life is represented by the word **shalom**, which Old Testament professor Elmer Martens says "embraces concepts of harmony, security, serenity, right relationships, wholeness, health, prosperity, and even success."[55] The goal of creation is *shalom*.

That creation had a purpose and goal was a concept foreign to other ancient religions. The Greeks believed that nature was transient and therefore relatively unimportant. Other cultures embraced **animism**, the belief that spirits inhabit nature. The Bible rejects both of these beliefs. Creation is good, but it is not God. Scripture says that creation is designed to be understood. This is the basis not only of Christian belief but also of modern science. Even scientists who deny or ignore God conduct their experiments every day as if

Shalom: from the Hebrew for "peace, prosperity, and wellness"; a concept that implies harmony in creation and with one's neighbors as well as a right relationship with God.

Animism: the belief that various spirits inhabit plants, animals, and physical objects.

Deism: The belief that God exists and created the world but that he currently stands completely aloof from his creation; the belief that reason and nature sufficiently reveal the existence of God but that God has not revealed himself through any type of special revelation.

the world exists and can be understood in an orderly, predictable fashion. This is consistent with what Genesis reveals about creation.[56]

Unfortunately, beginning within the Age of Enlightenment, **deism**, the idea that God created the world but is no longer actively involved with it, has led to the dominance of

> *Materialism:* The belief that reality is composed solely of matter.

> *Dominion:* the power or right of an authority to rule over a territory or people.

materialism, which says that only nature exists and operates as an autonomous, self-sustaining machine. Some materialists see nature as an object of study—a specimen to be probed, experimented on, and cataloged. But others see it as an opportunity—a repository of raw materials to be exploited. If the physical world is all that exists, and there is no purpose or accountability to God, then why not? As Steven Bouma-Prediger says, "It is not difficult to see how such a materialistic worldview underwrites the pillage and plunder of the natural world."[57]

Worse, deism and materialism have poisoned the biblical understanding of what it means to have **dominion** over creation, exposing Christianity to the accusation that *dominion* and *pillage* are synonyms. We dealt with this issue briefly in the chapter on marriage, but it's important to look more in depth to see what biblical dominion really means.

We're to have dominion over creation. In Genesis 1:26, "God said, 'Let us make man in our image, after our likeness. And let them have dominion over the fish of the sea and over the birds of the heavens and over the livestock and over all the earth and over every creeping thing that creeps on the earth.'" The Hebrew words for "subdue" (*kabash*) and "rule" (*radah*) the earth are indeed strong words and are used elsewhere in the Bible to mean "to tread down," "to bring into bondage," and "to trample."[58] As Loren Wilkinson and his coauthors write in *Earthkeeping in the Nineties*, "There is no doubt at all that men and women are placed *over* the rest of creation. These verses express that superiority in the strongest possible terms."[59]

But "in chargeness" doesn't require brutality. You can know who your boss is without having to suffer daily beatings. Dominion is a call not to *meanness* but to *management*. John Mustol points out, "It is not up to dolphins, chimpanzees, wolves, or whales; it is up to us. We have to manage things."[60]

Dominion forsakes ruthlessness for caretaking, as is evident in Genesis 2, in which Adam and Eve were told to "till" and "keep" the garden. The Hebrew word for "till" (*abad*) also means "work" or "serve," and the word for "keep" (*shamar*) means "watch" or "preserve."[61] Both words imply coaxing something into fulfilling its design or bringing it to maturity. Loren Wilkinson and his colleagues explain:

> The original command to subdue and rule is not contradicted, but the *type* of ruling is explicitly directed. There is never any doubt that humans are masters; but the concept of mastery itself here begins to be clarified and reversed in a process which will culminate only in the crucifixion of Christ.[62]

We must bring Christ into our understanding of creation. Philippians 2 underscores that Christ's humility as a servant is part and parcel of his authority. *God superintends creation through Christ.* It's an ongoing act of servanthood that rejects the deist and materialist ideas of *domination* for a biblical idea of dominion that leads to *shalom*.[63] God was in essence saying, "See that peach tree? I want more peaches out of it. See that wheat field? I want a higher yield out of it. I want more of everything. I want more *quality* and I want more *quantity*." God was interested in abundance, not in having just enough to get by, or just making do.

God owns creation. We manage it under his authority. This is what dominion means. Philosopher E. Calvin Beisner puts it in balance: "It is not dominion per se but selfish or foolish dominion that leads to environmental abuse. Christians, who seek to be faithful to the Bible, cannot simply abandon its doctrine of dominion."[64]

> God was interested in abundance, not in having just enough to get by, or just making do.

We are stewards of creation. A steward is a caretaker who manages something on behalf of the owner. God owns it all. We're accountable to him for the flourishing of creation. Beisner says,

> As we think about creation stewardship, then, the first thing we must keep in mind is the doctrine of God—particularly, that an infinitely wise, infinitely powerful Creator made and sustains the universe and every part of it. This doctrine does not mean we have no responsibility for stewarding the creation. But it does mean that the design of all things reflects the wisdom of God, and the sustaining of all things reflects the power of God.[65]

Creation stewardship, then, is about God, not us. Some Christians have cultivated a belief that "the world isn't going to be around much longer anyway, so why protect it?" But creation isn't about us and our observations regarding what is possible or impossible. To be a steward, according to theologian Colin Gunton, is "a calling to be and to act in such a way as to enable the created order to be itself as a response of praise to its maker."[66] Moreover, as theologian Albert Wolters explains, because we steward the earth as God's image bearers, our obedience to him in this respect is what makes "free and healthy functioning" as human beings possible.[67]

> A steward is a caretaker who manages something on behalf of the owner. God owns it all. We're accountable to him for the flourishing of creation.

Sin affects creation, as well as our dominion and stewardship of it. Genesis 3 is a sad counterpoint to Genesis 1 and 2. In it, Adam and Eve succumb to the temptation of a serpent, later revealed to be Satan (Rev. 12:9; 20:2).[68] God pronounced a curse on the serpent, as well as on the productivity of the man and the woman. But this didn't end dominion and stewardship. Arguably, it intensified it. The curse didn't end Adam and Eve's work; it made it hard. Henceforth, the earth would rebel against humans because they had rebelled against God.

But creation itself remains *good*. "Sin has twisted creation," say Loren Wilkinson and his colleagues, "but [it] has not cancelled its fundamental goodness."[69] As humans, we're fallen. We are corrupt stewards. But just because a steward is corrupt doesn't mean his or her domain of stewardship is likewise corrupt. Certainly, creation can be damaged through mishandling. As Wolters notes, "Anything in creation can be directed either toward or away from God—that is, directed either in obedience or disobedience to his law."[70] Plus, Wolters explains, redemption changes everything: "Nothing in the world ought to be despaired of," he says. "Hope is grounded in the constant availability and the insistent presence of the good creation, even in those situations in which it is being terribly violated.[71]

> Redemption is meant to save us *for* life on this earth, not *from* it.

We have violated creation, but we haven't destroyed it. We have acted self-destructively, but this hasn't ruined our ability to bear God's image. Redemption restores to right what was made wrong. It also restores disobedient humanity so that we may pursue rightness.[72] The fall complicates our responsibility to creation, but it doesn't eliminate it.[73]

> *Gnosticism:* a second-century heretical Christian movement that taught that the material world was created and maintained by a lesser divine being, that matter and the physical body are inherently evil, and that salvation can be obtained only through an esoteric knowledge of divine reality and the self-denial of physical pleasures.

Put another way, redemption is meant to save us *for* life on this earth, not *from* it. As Jonathan Wilson argues, the earth isn't just a stage to be taken down once the play is over.[74] Rather, it is the very *substance* of redemption. "Creation is what God the Son redeems through his becoming flesh, bearing our sin, enduring death, and rising to life," he says.[75] Sin loses. Salvation wins. And it is in creation that the Spring of Living Water bubbles forth.

False doctrines about creation are on the loose. Environmental stewardship wasn't really even an issue until the Industrial Revolution. Thus, the early church fathers didn't say much about it.[76] But they *were* insistent in opposing **gnosticism**, a heresy that taught that a lesser god, known as the Demiurge, tragically was responsible for creating the material world, which is evil.[77] Consequently, as sociologist Rodney Stark points out, gnostics believed "the earth [was] held in thrall by an evil God."[78] Salvation, in turn, came through secret knowledge—*gnosis*—about how the spirit could escape the bondage of the physical body and the material world. To gnostics, the spirit was the true person. Bodies just slow us down.[79]

Irenaeus of Lyons (ca. AD 130–200) was an early critic of gnosticism. He "believed that the material creation was itself good," just as God had said in Genesis 1.[80] Irenaeus wrote a five-volume work *Against Heresies* or *On the Detection and Overthrow of the So-Called Gnosis*, stressing God's unity and "the goodness of the created world."[81] The Apostles' Creed, which focuses on God as creator and Christ as redeemer who entered into creation itself, was initially formulated as a line-by-line polemic against gnosticism.[82]

Needless to say, the gnostic view that the material world is evil (or "less than" the spiritual realm) isn't Christian. In their despair over the way things seem to be going, though, many Christians still fall into gnosticism when they think, *We suffer. The world must be meaningless. Just hang on until we get to heaven.*[83]

As opposed to gnosticism, orthodox Christianity affirms the material world and our bodies rather than denying them. And as Leah Kostamo points out, "God wouldn't have taken on a human body himself if flesh were inherently evil."[84] Our hope isn't in a disembodied existence, say Loren Wilkinson and his colleagues. "We *are* bodies: we were made for the earth."[85] Jonathan Wilson explains further:

> As opposed to gnosticism, orthodox Christianity affirms the material world and our bodies rather than denying them.

> First, … human embodiment is God's handiwork. Our bodies are part of the gift and blessing of God's creation. When we experience our bodies as burden and curse, that experience is part of the story of the fallen world. Second, humans have bodies from their beginning as humans. Therefore, there is no other way of being human apart from our bodies. If the salvation that Christ brings to us does not include our bodies, then our salvation is the process of becoming something other than fully human.[86]

The work of salvation is embedded in creation all the way to the very end, when God comes to make his home among his people. Revelation 21:2–4 says,

> I [John] saw the holy city, new Jerusalem, coming down out of heaven from God, prepared as a bride adorned for her husband. And I heard a loud voice from the throne saying, "Behold, the dwelling place of God is with man. He will dwell with them, and they will be his people, and God himself will be with them as their God. He will wipe away every tear from their eyes, and death shall be no more, neither shall there be mourning, nor crying, nor pain anymore, for the former things have passed away."

In the meantime, we have much to do in our bodies, such as producing the fruit of the Spirit: "love, joy, peace, patience, kindness, goodness, faithfulness, gentleness, [and] self-control" (Gal. 5:22–23). And it all happens in creation.[87]

To recap: God made creation good. We are to exercise dominion over it and be stewards of it. Sin damaged our ability to be stewards, but through Christ's redemption and his ongoing work in our lives, we're able to pursue rightness and faithful stewardship. Our bodies and the earth are integral, not incidental, to this. If what the Bible says is true, Christians ought to be the most enthusiastic people on Earth when it comes to caring for creation. But what specifically should we do?

> If what the Bible says is true, Christians ought to be the most enthusiastic people on Earth when it comes to caring for creation.

4. WHAT SHOULD CHRISTIANS DO?

Most people act as if the world revolves around them. But Psalm 24:1 says, "The earth is the LORD's, and everything in it" (NIV). As Sally Lloyd-Jones explains in *The Jesus Storybook*

Bible, "The Bible isn't mainly about you and what you should be doing. It's about God and what he has done."[88]

God is the owner. He is at the center, not us. God created the world, in love, for his own glory. Jesus Christ is the sole heir of all things (Heb. 1:2).[89] "Christ is the centre of Christianity," theologian John Stott wrote. "All else is circumference."[90] Starting here puts everything else in its proper perspective.

> Creation groans, but it isn't a groan of death. It's a groan of birth. Christ doesn't annihilate creation; he brings it to fruition.

In God's plan, creation is central. Romans 8:22 says that creation groans,[91] but it isn't a groan of death. It's a groan of birth. Christ doesn't annihilate creation; he brings it to fruition. It is with this in mind that we can put creation in perspective and figure out what stewardship of it means today, starting with loving people, loving creation, loving animals, loving productivity, loving innovation, and loving freedom.

Loving People

At the beginning of this chapter, we studied a disturbing example of how an irrational fear of DDT led to withholding a simple solution that might have prevented the deaths of millions. To some, especially those involved in deep ecology, this is a trade-off worth making.

> Christians see humans as made in God's image, and because of this, we should never support anti-human policies clothed in a proenvironment disguise.

Paul Watson, who founded the Sea Shepherd Institute to harass whaling vessels, calls for the human population to be reduced to one billion (from seven billion) and says, "Curing a body of cancer requires radical and invasive therapy, and therefore, curing the biosphere of the human virus will also require a radical and invasive approach."[92]

To Watson, being proenvironment means being anti-human. Conversely, Christians see humans as made in God's image, and because of this, we should never support anti-human policies clothed in a proenvironment disguise. Instead, we should ask, "Do the policies we support try to help people pull themselves up out of poverty, pollution, and illness?"

Here are some areas where the attack on humans is most severe.

Population. *The Golden Stamp Book of Earth and Ecology* intends to harness sympathy for an anti-human agenda among children at an early age. It reads, "If the population continues to explode, many people will starve. About half of the world's population is underfed now, with many approaching starvation.... All of the major environmental problems can be traced to people—more specifically, to too many people."[93]

The belief that population growth harms the planet and slows economic development has led to much inhumanity and the denial of personal freedom[94] in such places as China, whose one-child policy has led to horrifying consequences, including forced abortions. But the true impact is deeper. Celebrated science writer Mara Hvistendahl's research sheds light on the consequences of China's population policies. Though China relaxed its one-child policy in 2013, decades of social disapproval of large families still creates pressure to have fewer children,[95] and the overwhelming preference for boys (because they're seen as more likely to support their parents in old age, and because marriage arrangements for girls can lead to financial ruin) has driven parents to selectively abort baby girls. Now, according to Hvistendahl, there are significantly more men than women in China and in countries like India, resulting in dramatic increases in overall crime and specifically crimes like sex trafficking.[96]

But many people ask, "Isn't it true that having more babies leads to poverty?" No. Population expert and respected economist Julian Simon has flatly stated, "There is no evidence to prove that a large population *creates* poverty and underdevelopment."[97] True, some poor countries are crowded. But some of the most crowded places on the planet—cities like Hong Kong and Singapore—are also the most prosperous. Peter T. Bauer was made a member of the British House of Lords in recognition of his service as economic adviser to Margaret Thatcher, the prime minister. Speaking as an economist and one of the world's most influential theorists on economic development, Bauer stated that rapid population growth hasn't "inhibited economic progress in either the West or the contemporary Third World."[98] Perhaps it's not a population "bomb" but a population "bloom."

Prophecies of environmental disaster. Is the world on the brink of environmental disaster? Many alarming reports have surfaced making this claim, often citing "studies" like a World Bank report from the 1990s purportedly claiming that 40 percent of the world's population experiences chronic water shortages, endangering agriculture, people, and industry. If true, it justifies the call to reduce population: the more people we have, the thirstier we'll all be. But Danish environmentalist Bjorn Lomborg, an environmentalist who nonetheless thinks that proclamations of environmental disaster are overblown, found no study, just a World Bank press release that said the global water crisis affects 4 percent (not 40 percent) of the world's population.[99]

> True, some poor countries are crowded. But some of the most crowded places on the planet—cities like Hong Kong and Singapore—are also the most prosperous.

Of course, one misquoted reference doesn't mean all disaster reports are inflated. But it's easy to see how they might get that way. People find disaster and crisis exciting. This makes the media want to dish up more disaster through news alerts and dramatic headlines. "Consequently," Calvin Beisner says, "the public's perception of reality is skewed toward disaster and crisis."[100]

Some people think the climate-change crisis is one such example. The scientific basics are well known: an increased amount of carbon dioxide in the atmosphere bounces heat back to the earth's surface, raising temperatures. These increased temperatures affect climate and weather and are thought to change plant and animal habitats and shrink polar ice caps and glaciers, causing higher sea levels. Possible negative consequences of climate change ("global warming"), according to climate activists, include severe weather, droughts, floods, species extinction, and disease.[101]

Skeptics rarely challenge that the earth is in a long-term warming trend, though temperature data seems to indicate a cooling trend.[102] What the skeptics of climate change question isn't the existence of global warming or cooling but whether humans have caused it and whether dramatic action of the sort called for is financially and societally justified. Do we really need to give up internal combustion engines and grind our economy to a halt? And even if we did, would it actually make a difference?

> What the skeptics of climate change question isn't the existence of global warming or cooling but whether humans have caused it and whether dramatic action of the sort called for is financially and societally justified.

Developing countries are among the most skeptical. They see the whole climate-change issue as a cynical ploy on the part of developed countries to keep them down, a sort of "I've got mine; tough luck for you" strategy.[103] This seeming cynicism, along with reports over the unethical shading of scientific studies to support only politically correct conclusions, has led many to be suspicious.[104] This in turn is distressing to those who believe that people should be alarmed, such as former Democratic presidential nominee Al Gore, who has loudly labeled those who disagree with him climate-change deniers, saying that politicians should "pay a price for rejecting 'accepted science.'"[105]

Increasingly, climate-change experts and economists find themselves growing uncomfortable with Gore and others calling for extreme actions like punishing skeptics. Is dramatic restructuring of the world economy the best use of our resources? In the face of the sketchy evidence,[106] and in view of the potential loss of freedom and economic opportunity, the Copenhagen Consensus Center at the Copenhagen Business School commissioned papers from world-class experts on the ten greatest "challenges facing humanity." Eight "world-class economists, including four Nobel laureates" then reviewed these papers and ranked the "various opportunities for action." This panel of economists found that of the seventeen opportunities, the three worst, as far as return on investment, were those having to do with reducing "global warming by cutting carbon emissions."[107] If our goal is to help people, we'll get a far better return on our investment by helping solve problems like HIV/AIDS, hunger, and malaria.[108]

Resource depletion. The Center for Ecoliteracy, which develops resources for K–12 students on ecology, at one time posted this description on its website:

> Fossil fuels, groundwater, forests, minerals, cropland soils, marine fisheries, and other natural resources are being depleted much more quickly than they can be replenished.... We are living well beyond the Earth's carrying capacity.... Overconsumption—taking more than the Earth can provide—is threatening sustainability.[109]

Making the exact opposite point, economist and theologian Wayne Grudem says, "There is no good reason to think we'll ever run out of any essential natural resource."[110] This is because technological innovation, brought about by the opportunity for profit, is constantly changing the resource equation. The clearest example in our day is the use of fracking technologies to recover oil and natural gas that were once thought buried forever. Rather than running out of oil in a few years, as once predicted, geologists now believe the available supply may last hundreds of years, perhaps even a thousand.

How should we decide which claim to believe? Should we cut back on human activity, or should we encourage it, along with technological innovation, and trust that new resources will become available?

As we'll see, a review of the facts doesn't support the claim that we have too many humans and that this is leading to starvation and resource-depletion disasters. Thus, the answer to the previous question is that we should *encourage* human activity. Even though world population is growing, more people have access to drinking water and sanitation, housing, and more food calories. Life expectancy has risen dramatically and continues to rise, even in less-developed nations that are mired in extreme poverty.[111] In spite of claims about the destruction of South American rain forests, forests cover about one-third of the earth's surface, and this level "has remained relatively stable since World War II."[112] Pollution has decreased dramatically thanks to growing wealth, which has brought more affordable energy-saving devices to the market.

So what about species extinction? In 2011, news reports began warning that the "World's Sixth Mass Extinction May Be Underway" and prophesied that "the new threat is man-made, inflicted by habitation loss, over-hunting, over-fishing, the spread of germs and viruses and introduced species, and by climate change caused by fossil-fuel greenhouse gases."[113] But Patrick Moore, an ecologist and one of the founders of the environmentalist organization Greenpeace, who has now turned his back on some of the organization's initiatives, was among those who quickly condemned the study: "Since species extinction became a broad social concern, ... we have done a pretty good job of preventing species extinction."[114] The figures bear out Moore's point. An estimated 816 species have become extinct in the past five hundred years out of approximately 8.7 million,[115] and most of those extinctions took place long ago. Beware of claims of mass species extinction. They're overblown. For example, while acknowledging that around 1,000 species have become extinct in the past five hundred years, the Center for Biological Diversity claims that "literally dozens" are going extinct every day. This would equal more than 13,000 species a year, a figure that's utterly insupportable. In the same article, the center admits that "nobody really knows how many species are in danger of becoming extinct."[116]

> A review of the facts doesn't support the claim that we have too many humans and that this is leading to starvation and resource-depletion disasters.

But is our current level of growth sustainable? Roger Revelle, who used to direct Harvard University's Center for Population Studies, estimated in 1984 that two-thirds of the farmable land in the world wasn't being farmed, and if it had been, the world could have fed thirty-five billion people, even if it produced only half the crops of farm areas like the American Midwest.[117] This doesn't mean Revelle *wanted* thirty-five billion people on the planet. It just means that the carrying capacity of the earth is much higher than usually reported.

Based on a biblical worldview, we ought to care about the planet, but never at the expense of people. When those in developing countries see programs about the

> Based on a biblical worldview, we ought to care about the planet, but never at the expense of people.

environmental concerns of people in the West, they shake their heads. The issues poor countries face every day—respiratory illnesses caused from cooking fires, HIV/AIDS, infant death, diseases caused by waterborne parasites, malaria, and so forth—aren't even on the radar of people in wealthier countries.[118]

Loving Creation

If you've ever gazed at a beautiful sunset or landscape, you know the sense of awe that comes from recognizing creation's beauty. As Harvard professor Elaine Scarry puts it, "It is not that we cease to stand at the center of the world, for we never stood there. It is that we cease to stand even at the center of our own world. We willingly cede our ground to the thing that stands before us."[119]

> Creation's beauty arouses our protective instincts. But we need to realize that we aren't in charge. We're over creation as stewards, but we're also *in* it as created beings.

Creation's beauty arouses our protective instincts. But we need to realize that we aren't in charge. We are *part* of creation. We're over it as stewards, but we're also *in* it as created beings.[120] As creatures, we are physical beings embedded in creation and, as theologian and medical doctor John Mustol puts it, "subject to all the ecological principles, patterns, parameters, and limits that define and circumscribe the existence of all God's creatures on his earth."[121] Creation is the context in which we consider every other aspect of life. As Jonathan Wilson phrases it, "We are a part of the world, and the world is a part of us."[122]

Our care for creation means recognizing the intricate balance of plants and animals in creation.[123] John Muir, the conservationist who founded the Sierra Club and the National Audubon Society, said, "When we try to pick out anything by itself, we find it hitched to everything else in the Universe."[124] The misunderstanding and abuse of creation causes much suffering, especially among the poor.[125] And if we're too busy living in our man-made, electronic, plastic, steel, glass, and concrete world, we may fail to see what is most important. As Mustol aptly expresses it, "We have used our wealth and technology to exclude nature from our lives and from our consciousness and so have lost touch with it."[126]

In short, we need to get out more. Steven Bouma-Prediger observes,

> We care for only what we love. We love only what we know. We truly know only what we experience. If we do not know our place—know it in more than a passing, cursory way, know it intimately and personally—then we are destined to use and abuse it.[127]

> We need to be wondering onlookers, joyful appreciators, and astonished students of God's handiwork.

Start with where you live. Do you know its geography? Do you know its natural history? Do you know about its plants and animals? Do you know about the soil and the edible plants and the wilderness areas?[128]

But it's not just about knowing things. It's also about enjoying them. John Mustol says we need to be wondering onlookers, joyful appreciators, and astonished students of God's handiwork. Our amazement, he says, should inspire us to "be amateur biologists, geologists, botanists, zoologists, ecologists, astronomers—the ones, who like children, are forever pointing to the wonders around us, saying, 'Look there! Look here! Wow! Praise be to God!'"[129] It may even lead many believers to commit themselves to a lifetime of study as professional scientists who, out of love for God, want to delve into the mysteries of his creation.

Caring and enjoyment are part of living rightly—that is, "rightly aligned"—with creation.[130]

Loving Animals

Humans are more valuable to God than animals. This is clear in the teachings of Jesus.[131] And yet caring for animals is also a scriptural virtue. Proverbs 12:10 says, "The righteous care for the needs of their animals" (NIV). Deuteronomy 25:4 commands farmers not to muzzle their oxen while they're treading grain. Animals need to eat to be productive for their owners, and their owners

> Humans are more valuable to God than animals. And yet caring for animals is also a scriptural virtue.

ought to take care of them. As Abraham Lincoln so compellingly put it, "I care not for a man's religion whose dog and cat are not the better for it."

Care of animals began in Genesis 2:19: "Now out of the ground the LORD God had formed every beast of the field and every bird of the heavens and brought them to the man to see what he would call them. And whatever the man called every living creature, that was its name." Adam identified the animals and took responsibility for them.

It's not just about pets. Wild animals were part of God's covenant with Noah after the flood (Gen. 9:10).[132] Passages like Psalm 104:16–22[133] show that God cares for trees, birds, and wild animals.[134] Other passages, such as Job 38–39, show that God delights in stars, snowflakes, and wild animals, not just things for which we can find a use.[135] "An Evangelical Statement on Responsible Care for Animals" declares, "We understand from Scripture that God has given … all animals into our hand and for food as part of our responsible rule; but as we live in a fallen world and are prone to sin, we also have the capacity and inclination to cause suffering instead of care for animals and to act cruelly towards them."[136] It's a position affirmed throughout church history by the likes of Irenaeus of Lyons, Saint Augustine of Hippo, Saint Francis of Assisi, and Thomas Aquinas.

Scripture indicates that we're to care for animals, but we're also permitted to eat them (Gen. 9:3).[137] Some secular philosophers take issue with this. They don't believe that humans have been endowed by their creator with certain inalienable rights. What gives a creature rights, they say, is "sentience," the ability to feel pain and understand what is causing it. In taking this view, Peter Singer and others have provided a philosophical foundation for the animal-rights movement. Kenneth Feder and Michael Park write,

> Scripture shows that God delights in stars, snowflakes, and wild animals, not just things for which we can find a use.

> There is no objective rationale for elevating our species into a category separate from the rest of the animals with whom we share the presence of a nervous system, the

ability to feel pain, and behaviors aimed at avoiding pain. Thus, the fundamental rights we accord ourselves must be equally applicable to any other organism with these same characteristics.[138]

This leads to a lot of vibrant discussions on college campuses. Should we permit a lion to pursue happiness at the expense of an antelope, knowing we have the power to stop it? What about the antelope's feelings? And if humans are nothing special, shouldn't our aim be to *raise* the rights of animals and *lower* the rights of humans?

> One of our responsibilities as image bearers of God is to care for animals. Biblical teachings about this are reasonable, clear, sustainable, and humane.

In some ways, we already have lowered human rights and raised animal rights. Embryonic bald eagles already have more legal protection than unborn babies. If there is no God, then humans are not his image bearers, and what we call human rights are temporal, changeable, and, worst of all, subject to the whims of those in power. One of our responsibilities as image bearers of God is to care for animals. Biblical teachings about this are reasonable, clear, sustainable, and humane.

Loving Productivity

To materialists, everything that exists is a "thing." Animals are things. People are things. The goal of modern life, it seems, is to become hunter-gatherers who acquire more things to adorn our thingness. Living this way, says Jonathan Wilson, "our lives are becoming thinner, shallower, and less abundant as a result of the deeper truth that the things that we think we are consuming are actually consuming us."[139]

> "Our lives are becoming thinner, shallower, and less abundant as a result of the deeper truth that the things that we think we are consuming are actually consuming us."

Do you see yourself primarily as a consumer or a producer? People with a consumer mind-set consume not only products but also themselves—and others. The cheap goods we purchase are often manufactured in poor countries by people working in dangerous, polluted, even slave-like conditions. The Global Slavery Index says that nearly 3.4 million people are enslaved in China today, and 45.8 million live in slavery around the world.[140] According to Loren Wilkinson and his colleagues, "We need to ask ourselves, 'Is my comfort related (however distantly) to the discomfort of someone half a world away? If so (given the complexity of the systems by which we use and transfer the goods of creation), what do I do about it?'"[141]

As we've seen in our chapters on poverty care and justice, we must rescue those who are perishing. But as Leah Kostamo suggests, perhaps the most urgent question isn't what we should do but what should we "*stop* doing."[142] Loren and Mary Ruth Wilkinson put it this way: "Our fallenness is particularly evident in the habits by which we treat the rest of creation as an endless stock-pile—or an endless waste heap. We are all in a hurry to be about our own business, which traps us into ignoring the Creator's business—and the needs and health of creation."[143]

One thing we can stop doing is participating in a throw-away mentality. Dorothy L. Sayers said, "A society in which consumption has to be artificially stimulated in order to keep production going is a society founded on trash and waste, and such a society is a house built upon sand."[144] Though the original source of the claim is unknown, Kostamo notes that in America alone, we use "106,000 aluminum cans every thirty seconds, 15 million sheets of office paper every five minutes, 426,000 cell phones every day, [and] 3.6 million SUVs per year."[145] All of this comes from things that must be harvested from the earth.

It's good to live in a world with lots of choices, but that doesn't mean we need to be wasteful. We can learn to fix things instead of just throwing them away. We can focus on simplicity. We can learn to make food rather than always buying it prepackaged. Adding to this list, Kostamo says we can also be grateful for what we have instead of clamoring for more, we can be generous by spending more time giving than acquiring, and we can practice keeping the Sabbath, one day a week when we change pace and rest in God's provision.[146]

> It's good to live in a world with lots of choices, but that doesn't mean we need to be wasteful. We can learn to fix things instead of just throwing them away. We can focus on simplicity. We can also be grateful for what we have instead of clamoring for more.

Habits like repairing, refurbishing, and repurposing dovetail well with a mind-set of redemption. As John Stonestreet points out, God loves "re" words. He is at work restoring and renewing creation—including us. Loren and Mary Ruth Wilkinson suggest that "we work not to make 'all new things' but rather to make 'all things new.' And that work begins in our own backyard; in the kitchen, in the car, in using our repair skills and those of others."[147]

Loving Innovation

Fear and guilt sometimes drive our efforts at creation care. They shouldn't. We ought to be aware of the impact of our actions, but we also ought to remember that "everything created by God is good" (1 Tim. 4:4–5) and "provides us with everything to enjoy" (6:17). As Wayne Grudem reminds us, "God did not design the earth so that we would destroy it by obeying his commands."[148] God wants us to take initiative and be productive. Abundance is part of his redemptive work, as the prophet Amos so poetically expressed it:

> Fear and guilt shouldn't drive our efforts at creation care. We ought to be aware of the impact of our actions, but we also ought to remember that God created everything good for our enjoyment.

"Behold, the days are coming," declares the LORD,
   "when the plowman shall overtake the reaper
    and the treader of grapes him who sows the seed;
the mountains shall drip sweet wine,
   and all the hills shall flow with it.

I will restore the fortunes of my people Israel,
>   and they shall rebuild the ruined cities and inhabit them;
they shall plant vineyards and drink their wine,
>   and they shall make gardens and eat their fruit.
I will plant them on their land,
>   and they shall never again be uprooted
>   out of the land that I have given them,"
says the LORD your God. (Amos 9:13–15)

> *Malthusian Catastrophe:* **based on the work of Thomas Malthus; any disastrous event brought about by an increase in the human population (e.g., disease, famine, or war), which naturally returns the human population to a state of equilibrium.**

God is in the business of comforting waste places and turning wilderness into a garden (Isa. 51:3).[149]

But many environmental models predict scarcity, not abundance. These prediction models are often based on the thinking of Rev. Thomas Malthus (1766–1834), an English theologian who believed that while population increases geometrically, food and other resources increase only arithmetically. A **Malthusian catastrophe** suggests that as population grows, resources will run out, resulting in misery and mass starvation.

Such models fail to take one critical fact into account: we are image bearers of God. We're producers of creative ideas, not just consumers of scarce resources. In view of this, economist Julian Simon produced a different model, one that "treats people as people, who respond to their economic needs with physical and mental efforts up to and including the creative spark."[150] "In the long run," he said, "the contributions people make to knowledge are great enough to overcome all the costs of population growth."[151]

But aren't we running out of resources? As we discussed briefly earlier, many people believe so. It's hard to estimate how much of each natural resource we really have. Copper is more available today than thirty years ago, when fiber-optic cables replaced copper transmission wires. Fiber-optic cable is made from glass, and glass is made from sand—a resource that will never become scarce. Political interference, war, and natural disasters can lead to short-term shortages,[152] but according to Simon, "Over the course of history, up to this very moment, copper and other minerals have been becoming not more scarce but rather more abundant."[153] E. Calvin Beisner concurs: "Long-term inflation-adjusted price trends for extractive resources (mineral, plant, and animal) are downward both absolutely and, even more important, by comparison with wages.... As people apply their God-given and education-improved intelligence to the world around them, they multiply resources."[154]

While we certainly don't want to be wasteful, Beisner argues, the greatest threat to the environment is not resource use but poverty.[155] He observes that

> improvements in human well-being occur not only with rising wealth but also over time even for those whose wealth is not growing—so long as others around them are getting wealthier. Why? Because over time new technologies and the products they produce become more affordable, increasingly reaching the poor. Consequently,

from 1975 to 2002 people with under $1 (constant) daily income experienced large improvements in safe drinking water, food supply, infant mortality, life expectancy, the rate of child labor, and even college enrollment.[156]

The implications of this novel way of thinking are clear: we need to help people become more economically successful. As they become wealthier, they can afford more efficient technology. They have the time and energy and money to clean up past pollution.[157] Pollution as a by-product of increased economic activity may actually be an acceptable cost. Studies show that when economies grow, health and longevity improve, even though pollution may rise temporarily.[158]

Loving Freedom

This chapter opened with the story of the controversial banning of the pesticide DDT and the resulting negative effect on the health of millions of people. The DDT ban was based on the insights of Rachel Carson's book *Silent Spring*. One of the main points of Carson's book was to show how the government had contributed to the problem through a progressive view of improving society by "scientific management," doing things like spraying DDT over wide swaths of territory in a way that caused harm.[159] People in those days tended to trust the government. It must have been shocking to discover that sometimes government isn't the solution to the problem; sometimes government *is* the problem.

As we'll see in the following chapter on politics, God has ordained government to protect the innocent and punish the guilty. The government does have a role in protecting people from those who abuse the resources that belong to all of us. But the bias *for* government and *against* markets is a worldview bias.[160] As my coauthor David Noebel and I noted in *Understanding the Times*, some worldviews, such as Secularism and Marxism, seek government control to enforce their views. But when it comes to creation care, there is no good reason to assume that a governmental agency will manage environmental problems better than any other concern. Government agencies experience political infighting and high turnover and are prone to making decisions based on what maintains their budgets rather than what is in the public interest. And there's no guarantee that a government agency will do a better job *obeying* laws and regulations than anyone else who wants to maintain a good public reputation and long-term profitability.[161]

Consider the atrocious environmental record of the Soviet Union, long considered the model socialist state, where centralized government controlled every aspect of life. For example, the Aral Sea in Kazakhstan and Uzbekistan used to be the planet's fourth-largest body of freshwater, in addition to the Caspian Sea, Lake Superior in North America, and Lake Victoria in Africa. As a result of Soviet policies, the Aral Sea is half its original size and reeks of chemicals. The fish are gone. Decades of dumping poison in the form of fertilizers, pesticides, and herbicides in the lake has led to astronomical levels of infant deaths.[162]

Economists call this the "**tragedy of the commons**."[163] When everyone owns it, no one takes responsibility for it. Please understand: there is no question that a productive society must preserve the environment from destruction,

> *Tragedy of the Commons:* a situation in which a natural resource becomes exploited because it is collectively shared by individuals seeking their own self-interest.

and government does have a proper role in this. But government at the state and federal levels has repeatedly bungled environmental concerns. This has prompted economists to rethink ways to address environmental issues. They want to do this without increasing the size of government bureaucracy or veering away from the benefits of a **free-market economy**. It's a very different strategy than we're used to, but it's probably appropriate to at least outline what it might look like.

Free-Market Economy: an economy in which economic decisions are freely made by individuals, households, and firms instead of being regulated by the government.

In their new book *Free Market Environmentalism for the Next Generation*, economists Terry Anderson and Donald Leal explain that two things are necessary for a proper balance in changing human activity: incentives and information.[164]

1. Incentives. When the government controls incentives (such as rewarding actions it supports or punishing those it doesn't), good behavior usually lasts as long as people perceive the government to have power over them. Issuing these incentives often involves a lot of backroom deals, special treatment, and even corruption—what the news media calls **crony capitalism**. On the other hand, when prices control incentives—such as when the scarcity of water drives up prices to the point where manufacturers are motivated to be more efficient—the distribution of resources in many cases becomes self-regulating. For more information on how this works, see the "Economics" chapter in *Understanding the Times* and the sources quoted there.

Crony Capitalism: an economic system in which businesses that have close relationships with government officials are given unfair economic advantages through some kind of special treatment (e.g., incentives, grants, and tax breaks).

2. Information. When the cost of information is high—when people don't have the ability to get the knowledge they need to make good decisions—the economic system becomes sluggish. Power struggles break out over who gets to control the decision-making process. When information is widely available, such as clear, rationally derived estimates of the amount of oil available on the market this week, people can make better decisions about how to price the oil they have to sell or how to buy the oil they wish to purchase. As with all resources, when the price of gasoline goes up, demand goes down. The sooner people can access information about the actual price (assuming the government doesn't act to control prices), the sooner they can make a decision to either cope with rising prices by carpooling or getting a more fuel-efficient car or celebrate dropping prices by scheduling a family vacation by car.

Economic Interventionism: an economic system in which the government influences aspects of a market economy in an attempt to improve the public good.

Letting prices rather than government-sponsored **economic interventionism** influence the ebb and flow of economic activity internalizes information and drives the cost of information down. This can even help in areas like conserving natural habitats for animals, as Anderson and Leal explain:

If a private resource owner believes that grizzly bear habitat is more valuable and can capitalize on that value, then politics will not matter. Moreover, if those who demand grizzly habitat are willing to pay more than those who demand campsites, then incentives and information reinforce one another. Management simply cannot be adequately analyzed without careful attention to the information and incentives that actors [e.g. those demanding more habitat or campers] face under alternative institutional arrangements.[165]

Clamping down with too much government regulation can dry up these resources, as in the case of the government's denial of drilling in certain parts of the United States, or international agreements about things like global warming that hurt the ability of developing countries to raise their standards of living, something developed nations take for granted.[166]

But can a free-market approach help preserve nature and protect animals where there is no obvious economic benefit to doing so? More and more economists think the answer is yes. Wayne Grudem and economist Barry Asmus say,

The correct approach is to weigh the costs and benefits of a development project. If it will help human beings but harm some part of nature, some value must be assigned to both the benefit and the cost, and then a decision can be made. Often a market-based approach is helpful, asking both those who want to preserve an untouched area and those who want to develop it how much they are willing to pay for their preference to be enacted. It is not a proper approach to simply say we should *never* interfere with some animal or plant. God deems us to be much more valuable than they are, and has given us "dominion" (Gen. 1:26; Ps. 8:6) over all the earth, both to preserve it and to use its resources wisely.[167]

Some of this information is rather technical, but the point is clear: there are those who use the threats of environmental disaster to call for dramatic changes in society, usually including a dramatically expanded role for government. Christians ought to be aware of this ploy.

Christians can—and should—care for creation. We ought to reconsider our consumptive habits. We ought to spend more time appreciating God's creation. Yet at the same time, we must also recognize that God has designed the world to produce abundance. And when we reduce people's freedom to grow in wealth or make vast administrative laws that don't take into account the needs of real people, we can actually hurt the environment we want to help. We need to focus on innovating and increasing freedom if our caring is to have any effect beyond our own personal spheres.

> **We need to focus on innovating and increasing freedom if our caring is to have any effect beyond our own personal spheres.**

5. CONCLUSION

God made creation. The earth is his. It expresses his glory. Our role is to have dominion over creation and be stewards of our environment. How good we are as stewards affects the ability of those who are alive now, as well as those yet to be born, to flourish. As Steven Bouma-Prediger puts it, "Care for the earth is integral to what it means to be a Christian—it is an important part of our piety, our spirituality, our collective way of being authentically Christian."[168]

We've also seen in this chapter that to the degree people are free to achieve their potential as image bearers of God, the world prospers. And as poverty goes down, so does damage to the environment. If we want to help nature, we have to help people.

> **If we want to help nature, we have to help people.**

Creation care may involve making life changes, including being more thoughtful about our habits, being more attentive to the world around us, volunteering, gardening, hiking, sharing stuff, cooking real food, fixing things, and finding joy in simple pleasures rather than in acquiring more stuff. People rarely get medals for this kind of thing. As novelist and cultural critic Wendell Berry puts it, "The real work of planet-saving will be small, humble, and humbling, and (insofar as it involves love) pleasing and rewarding. Its jobs will be too many to count, too many to report, too many to be publicly noticed or rewarded, too small to make anyone rich or famous."[169]

Yet faith in our creator and king compels us. In J. R. R. Tolkien's *Return of the King*, Denethor, the steward of Gondor, despairs of the king ever returning. Gandalf wisely replies,

> The rule of no realm is mine, neither of Gondor nor any other, great or small. But all worthy things that are in peril as the world now stands, those are my care. And for my part, I shall not wholly fail of my task, though Gondor should perish, if anything passes through this night that can still grow fair or bear fruit and flower again in days to come. For I also am a steward.[170]

This is precisely our position. Darkness often seems to be falling over the earth, but it is precisely at these times that we can enjoy living minute by minute in the hope of redemption, knowing that the King has come to make all things new.

ENDNOTES

1. There are around one hundred different malaria-inducing parasites, but *Plasmodium falciparum* is the most deadly and also the most common in Africa, where it affects millions of children, represented in Omari's fictional example. For a quick explanation, see "What Is Malaria?," Malaria No More, accessed July 22, 2016, www.malarianomore.org/pages /what-is-malaria. For a lengthier explanation, see the World Health Organization's "Fact Sheet: Malaria," April 2016, www.who.int/mediacentre/factsheets/fs094/en/.

2. Global Health Observatory (GHO) data for 2015, cited in "Number of Malaria Deaths: Estimated Deaths 2000–2015," World Health Organization, accessed July 22, 2016, www.who.int/gho/malaria/epidemic/deaths/en/; "10 Facts on Malaria," November 2015, World Health Organization, accessed July 22, 2016, www.who.int/features/factfiles/malaria/en/.

3. Donald R. Roberts and Richard Tren, "Did Rachel Carson Understand the Importance of DDT in Global Public Health Programs?," in Roger Meiners, Pierre Desrochers, and Andrew Morriss, eds., *Silent Spring at 50: The False Crises of Rachel Carson* (Washington, DC: Cato Institute, 2012), 173.

4. Data cited by Roberts and Tren, "Did Rachel Carson Understand?," in Meiners, Desrochers, and Morriss, *Silent Spring at 50*, 181.

5. Data cited by Roberts and Tren, "Did Rachel Carson Understand?," in Meiners, Desrochers, and Morriss, *Silent Spring at 50*, 183.

6. Data cited by Roberts and Tren, "Did Rachel Carson Understand?," in Meiners, Desrochers, and Morriss, *Silent Spring at 50*, 184.

7. Cited by Roberts and Tren, "Did Rachel Carson Understand?," in Meiners, Desrochers, and Morriss, *Silent Spring at 50*, 185.

8. Tina Rosenberg, "What the World Needs Now Is DDT," *New York Times Magazine*, April 11, 2004, www.nytimes.com /2004/04/11/magazine/what-the-world-needs-now-is-ddt.html.

9. The DuPont chemical company featured this slogan beginning in 1935 and kept it more than fifty years, finally replacing it with "The miracles of science." See "Innovation Starts Here: 1939 Better Things" and "Innovation Starts Here: 1999 The Miracles of Science," DuPont, www.dupont.com/corporate-functions/our-company/dupont-history.html.

10. Carson's claims about overuse weren't without merit. Based on a near-worship of science, the government had indiscriminately sprayed DDT over vast swaths of land. Its efforts were ineffective at best, and possibly counterproductive. See especially chapter 4, "Surface Waters and Underground Seas," and chapter 10, "Indiscriminately from the Skies," in Rachel Carson, *Silent Spring* (Boston: Houghton Mifflin, 1994).

11. Nelson, "*Silent Spring* as Secular Religion," in Meiners, Desrochers, and Morriss, *Silent Spring at 50*, 90.

12. Roberts and Tren, "Did Rachel Carson Understand?," in Meiners, Desrochers, and Morriss, *Silent Spring at 50*, 187.

13. Jonathan H. Adler, "The False Promise of Federalization," in Meiners, Desrochers, and Morriss, *Silent Spring at 50*, 240.

14. World Health Organization, *World Malaria Report 2009* (Geneva: World Health Organization, 2009), 9, http://whqlibdoc.who.int/publications/2009/9789241563901_eng.pdf.

15. David Brown, "WHO Urges Use of DDT in Africa," *Washington Post*, September 16, 2006, www.washingtonpost.com /wp-dyn/content/article/2006/09/15/AR2006091501012.html.

16. Rosenberg, "What the World Needs Now Is DDT."

17. See Ray Bohlin, "Christian Environmentalism," Probe Ministries International, 1992, www.leaderu.com/orgs/probe /docs/ecology.html.

18. Steven Bouma-Prediger, *For the Beauty of the Earth: A Christian Vision for Creation Care* (Grand Rapids: Baker Academic, 2010), xiii.

19. Bouma-Prediger, *For the Beauty of the Earth*, 36.

20. Leah Kostamo, *Planted: A Story of Creation, Calling, and Community* (Eugene, OR: Cascade Books, 2013), 8.

21. *The Free Dictionary*, s.v. "Environmentalism," accessed July 22, 2016, www.thefreedictionary.com/environmentalism.

22. For more information, see E. Calvin Beisner, "The Competing Worldviews of Environmentalism and Christianity," Cornwall Alliance for the Stewardship of Creation, accessed July 22, 2016, www.cornwallalliance.org/docs/THECOM~1.PDF.

23. Michael Crichton, quoted in Nelson, "*Silent Spring* as Secular Religion," in Meiners, Desrochers, and Morriss, *Silent Spring at 50*, 94.

24. Nelson, "*Silent Spring* as Secular Religion," in Meiners, Desrochers, and Morriss, *Silent Spring at 50*.

25. J. B. Bury, *The Idea of Progress: An Inquiry into Its Origen and Growth* (London: Macmillan, 1921), 4, quoted in Nelson, "*Silent Spring* as Secular Religion," in Meiners, Desrochers, and Morriss, *Silent Spring at 50*, 70.

26. Nelson, "*Silent Spring* as Secular Religion," in Meiners, Desrochers, and Morriss, *Silent Spring at 50*, 79.

27. James Lovelock, *Gaia: A New Look at Life on Earth* (Oxford, UK: Oxford University Press, 1995), xii. The term "Gaia," named after the Greek goddess of the earth, was suggested by Lovelock's friend, the novelist William Golding (see p. vii, same volume).

28. Loren Wilkinson et al., *Earthkeeping in the Nineties: Stewardship of Creation*, rev. ed. (Grand Rapids: Eerdmans, 1991), 176–77.

29. Bouma-Prediger, *For the Beauty of the Earth*, 125.

30. Bohlin, "Christian Environmentalism."

31. Leviticus 25:1–12: "The LORD spoke to Moses on Mount Sinai, saying, 'Speak to the people of Israel and say to them, When you come into the land that I give you, the land shall keep a Sabbath to the LORD. For six years you shall sow your field, and for six years you shall prune your vineyard and gather in its fruits, but in the seventh year there shall be a Sabbath of solemn rest for the land, a Sabbath to the LORD. You shall not sow your field or prune your vineyard. You shall not reap what grows of itself in your harvest, or gather the grapes of your undressed vine. It shall be a year of solemn rest for the land. The Sabbath of the land shall provide food for you, for yourself and for your male and female slaves and for your hired servant and the sojourner who lives with you, and for your cattle and for the wild animals that are in your land: all its yield shall be for food. You shall count seven weeks of years, seven times seven years, so that the time of the seven weeks of years shall give you forty-nine years. Then you shall sound the loud trumpet on the tenth day of the seventh month. On the Day of Atonement you shall sound the trumpet throughout all your land. And you shall consecrate the fiftieth year, and proclaim liberty throughout the land to all its inhabitants. It shall be a jubilee for you, when each of you shall return to his property and each of you shall return to his clan. That fiftieth year shall be a jubilee for you; in it you shall neither sow nor reap what grows of itself nor gather the grapes from the undressed vines. For it is a jubilee. It shall be holy to you. You may eat the produce of the field.'"

32. Deuteronomy 25:4: "You shall not muzzle an ox when it is treading out the grain"; Deuteronomy 22:6: "If you come across a bird's nest in any tree or on the ground, with young ones or eggs and the mother sitting on the young or on the eggs, you shall not take the mother with the young."

33. Isaiah 5:8–10: "Woe to those who join house to house, who add field to field, until there is no more room, and you are made to dwell alone in the midst of the land. The LORD of hosts has sworn in my hearing: 'Surely many houses shall be

desolate, large and beautiful houses, without inhabitant. For ten acres of vineyard shall yield but one bath, and a homer of seed shall yield but an ephah.'"

34. Job 38:25–28: "Who has cleft a channel for the torrents of rain and a way for the thunderbolt, to bring rain on a land where no man is, on the desert in which there is no man, to satisfy the waste and desolate land, and to make the ground sprout with grass? Has the rain a father, or who has begotten the drops of dew?"

35. Psalm 104:27–30: "[All creatures] look to you, to give them their food in due season. When you give it to them, they gather it up; when you open your hand, they are filled with good things. When you hide your face, they are dismayed; when you take away their breath, they die and return to their dust. When you send forth your Spirit, they are created, and you renew the face of the ground."

36. Matthew 6:26: "Look at the birds of the air: they neither sow nor reap nor gather into barns, and yet your heavenly Father feeds them. Are you not of more value than they?"; Matthew 10:29: "Are not two sparrows sold for a penny? And not one of them will fall to the ground apart from your Father."

37. Bohlin, "Christian Environmentalism."

38. John 1:1–18: "In the beginning was the Word, and the Word was with God, and the Word was God. He was in the beginning with God. All things were made through him, and without him was not any thing made that was made. In him was life, and the life was the light of men. The light shines in the darkness, and the darkness has not overcome it. There was a man sent from God, whose name was John. He came as a witness, to bear witness about the light, that all might believe through him. He was not the light, but came to bear witness about the light. The true light, which gives light to everyone, was coming into the world. He was in the world, and the world was made through him, yet the world did not know him. He came to his own, and his own people did not receive him. But to all who did receive him, who believed in his name, he gave the right to become children of God, who were born, not of blood nor of the will of the flesh nor of the will of man, but of God. And the Word became flesh and dwelt among us, and we have seen his glory, glory as of the only Son from the Father, full of grace and truth. (John bore witness about him, and cried out, 'This was he of whom I said, "He who comes after me ranks before me, because he was before me."') For from his fullness we have all received, grace upon grace. For the law was given through Moses; grace and truth came through Jesus Christ. No one has ever seen God; the only God, who is at the Father's side, he has made him known."

39. Psalm 103:19: "The LORD has established his throne in the heavens, and his kingdom rules over all."

40. Hebrews 1:1–3: "Long ago, at many times and in many ways, God spoke to our fathers by the prophets, but in these last days he has spoken to us by his Son, whom he appointed the heir of all things, through whom also he created the world. He is the radiance of the glory of God and the exact imprint of his nature, and he upholds the universe by the word of his power. After making purification for sins, he sat down at the right hand of the Majesty on high."

41. Isaiah 6:3: "One [seraph] called to another and said: 'Holy, holy, holy is the LORD of hosts; the whole earth is full of his glory!'"

42. Colossians 1:15–20: "[Jesus Christ] is the image of the invisible God, the firstborn of all creation. For by him all things were created, in heaven and on earth, visible and invisible, whether thrones or dominions or rulers or authorities—all things were created through him and for him. And he is before all things, and in him all things hold together. And he is the head of the body, the church. He is the beginning, the firstborn from the dead, that in everything he might be preeminent. For in him all the fullness of God was pleased to dwell, and through him to reconcile to himself all things, whether on earth or in heaven, making peace by the blood of his cross."

43. For more of an exegesis on many of these passages, see Jonathan R. Wilson, *God's Good World: Reclaiming the Doctrine of Creation* (Grand Rapids: Baker Academic, 2013), 133–64.

44. Bouma-Prediger, *For the Beauty of the Earth*, xvi.

45. Bouma-Prediger, *For the Beauty of the Earth*, 129.

46. Wilson, *God's Good World*, 10.

47. Colin E. Gunton, *The Triune Creator: A Historical and Systematic Study*, Edinburgh Studies in Constructive Theology (Grand Rapids: Eerdmans, 1998), 9–10.

48. Gunton, *The Triune Creator*.

49. Gunton, *The Triune Creator*, 9.

50. Wilson, *God's Good World*, 64.

51. For some of the many passages emphasizing that God transcends nature, Ray Bohlin suggests exploring Genesis 1–2; Job 38–41; Psalms 19; 24; 104; Romans 1:18–20; and Colossians 1:16–17. See Bohlin, "Christian Environmentalism."

52. Wilkinson et al., *Earthkeeping in the Nineties*, 278.

53. Gunton, *The Triune Creator*, 9–10.

54. Wilson, *God's Good World*, 117.

55. Elmer A. Martens, *Jeremiah*, Believers Church Bible Commentary (Scottdale, PA: Herald Press, 1986), 308.

56. Nancy Pearcey and Charles Thaxton argue in their book *The Soul of Science* that the founders of modern science—who were almost all Christians—based their insights on a uniquely biblical view of the world. For a wonderfully illustrated and footnoted explanation, see Nancy R. Pearcey and Charles B. Thaxton, *The Soul of Science: Christian Faith and Natural Philosophy* (Wheaton, IL: Crossway Books, 1994), 21–37.

57. Bouma-Prediger, *For the Beauty of the Earth*, 77.

58. Wilkinson et al., *Earthkeeping in the Nineties*, 286.

59. Wilkinson et al., *Earthkeeping in the Nineties*, 287.

60. John Mustol, *Dusty Earthlings: Living as Eco-Physical Beings in God's Eco-Physical World* (Eugene, OR: Resource Publications, 2012), 135.

61. Robert L. Thomas, ed., *New American Standard Exhaustive Concordance of the Bible; Hebrew-Aramaic and Greek Dictionaries* (Nashville: Holman Bible Publishers, 1981), s.v. "*abad*" (Strong's no. 5646) and "*shamar*" (Strong's no. 8104).

62. Wilkinson et al., *Earthkeeping in the Nineties*, 287.

63. Bouma-Prediger, *For the Beauty of the Earth*, 64.

64. E. Calvin Beisner, "What Is the Most Important Environmental Task Facing American Christians Today?," *Mount Nebo Papers*, no. 1 (November 2007): 5, www.ecalvinbeisner.com/freearticles/MtNebo.pdf.

65. Beisner, "What Is the Most Important Environmental Task?," 3.

66. Gunton, *The Triune Creator*, 12.

67. Albert M. Wolters, *Creation Regained: Biblical Basics for a Reformational Worldview* (Grand Rapids: Eerdmans, 2005), 50.

68. Revelation 12:9: "The great dragon was thrown down, that ancient serpent, who is called the devil and Satan, the deceiver of the whole world—he was thrown down to the earth, and his angels were thrown down with him"; Revelation 20:2: "[An angel] seized the dragon, that ancient serpent, who is the devil and Satan, and bound him for a thousand years."

69. Wilkinson et al., *Earthkeeping in the Nineties*, 237.

70. Wolters, *Creation Regained*, 59.

71. Wolters, *Creation Regained*, 62.

72. The constant theme of righteousness in the Bible is a vitally important topic for Christian disciples to understand, though it isn't the purpose of this particular chapter. Scripture makes it clear that we aren't righteous in and of ourselves (Eccles. 7:20; Rom. 3:10), and that God's favor toward us isn't because of our righteousness (Deut. 9:6; Titus 3:5). Yet we're called to pursue righteousness (1 Tim. 6:11; 2 Tim. 2:22), which assumes we have the ability to do so, even though we're deeply affected by our fallenness.

73. Beisner, "What Is the Most Important Environmental Task?," 1.

74. Wilson, *God's Good World*, 60.

75. Wilson, *God's Good World*, 12.

76. Beisner, "What Is the Most Important Environmental Task?," 8.

77. Michael Allen Williams, *Rethinking "Gnosticism": An Argument for Dismantling a Dubious Category* (Princeton, N.J: Princeton University Press, 1996), 4–5, 51–52.

78. Rodney Stark, *Cities of God: The Real Story of How Christianity Became an Urban Movement and Conquered Rome* (New York: HarperCollins, 2007), 148.

79. According to Irenaeus of Lyons, "Adam and Eve had had the bodies that were light and shining, as if they were spiritual, just as they had been modeled; but when they came Here [to the material world], they changed into something darker, heavier, and more sluggish." Irenaeus of Lyons, *Against Heresies*, 1.30.9, quoted in Williams, *Rethinking "Gnosticism,"* 121.

80. Beisner, "What Is the Most Important Environmental Task?," 6.

81. Jonathan Hill, *The History of Christian Thought* (Oxford, UK: Lion, 2003), 24–25.

82. Justo L. González, *A History of Christian Thought*, vol. 1, *From the Beginnings to the Council of Chalcedon* (Nashville: Abingdon, 1970), 154–56. The Apostles' Creed reads as follows: "I believe in God the Father Almighty, Maker of heaven and earth. And in Jesus Christ his only Son our Lord; who was conceived by the Holy Ghost, born of the Virgin Mary, suffered under Pontius Pilate, was crucified, dead, and buried; he descended into hell; the third day he rose again from the dead; he ascended into heaven, and sitteth on the right hand of God the Father Almighty; from thence he shall come to judge the quick and the dead. I believe in the Holy Ghost; the holy catholic Church; the communion of saints; the forgiveness of sins; the resurrection of the body; and the life everlasting. Amen." See "The Apostles' Creed: Traditional English Version," About.com, accessed July 23, 2016, http://christianity.about.com/od/christiandoctrines/qt/thenicenecreed.htm.

83. M. Elizabeth Lewis Hall and Erik Thoennes, "At Home in Our Bodies: Implications of the Incarnation for Embodiment and Christian Higher Education," *Christian Scholar's Review* 36, no. 1 (Fall 2006): 34.

84. Kostamo, *Planted*, 26.

85. Wilkinson et al., *Earthkeeping in the Nineties*, 315.

86. Wilson, *God's Good World*, 244.

87. Wilson, *God's Good World*, 246.

88. Sally Lloyd-Jones, *The Jesus Storybook Bible: Every Story Whispers His Name* (Grand Rapids: Zonderkidz, 2007), 14.

89. Hebrews 1:2: "In these last days [God] has spoken to us by his Son, whom he appointed the heir of all things, through whom also he created the world."

90. John R. W. Stott, *Basic Christianity* (Grand Rapids: Eerdmans, 1971), 21.

91. Romans 8:22: "We know that the whole creation has been groaning together in the pains of childbirth until now."

92. Paul Watson, "The Beginning of the End for Life as We Know It on Planet Earth?," Sea Shepherd Conservation Society, May 4, 2007, www.seashepherd.org/commentary-and-editorials/2008/10/30/the-beginning-of-the-end-for-life-as-we-know-it-on-planet-earth-340.

93. *The Golden Stamp Book of Earth and Ecology* (New York: Golden Press, 1972), quoted in Julian L. Simon, *Population Matters: People, Resources, Environment, and Immigration* (New Brunswick, NJ: Transaction Publishers, 1996), 162.

94. Simon, *Population Matters*, 174–75.

95. Christina Larson, "Why China's Second-Baby Boom Might Not Happen," Bloomberg.com, August 1, 2014, www.bloomberg.com/news/articles/2014-08-01/with-end-of-chinas-one-child-policy-there-hasnt-been-a-baby-boom.

96. Mara Hvistendahl, *Unnatural Selection: Choosing Boys over Girls, and the Consequences of a World Full of Men* (New York: Public Affairs, 2011), 22–23.

97. Simon, *Population Matters*, 169.

98. Peter T. Bauer, quoted in Simon, *Population Matters*, 177.

99. Bjorn Lomborg, *The Skeptical Environmentalist: Measuring the Real State of the World*, trans. Hugh Matthews (Cambridge, UK: Cambridge University Press, 2001), 20.

100. Beisner, "What Is the Most Important Environmental Task?," 15.

101. Beisner, "What Is the Most Important Environmental Task?," 16.

102. NOAA temperature data, cited in James Taylor, "Government Data Show U.S. in Decade-Long Cooling Trend," "Opinion," *Forbes*, June 25, 2014, www.forbes.com/sites/jamestaylor/2014/06/25/government-data-show-u-s-in-decade-long-cooling/#36b7c1d97894.

103. The point of this chapter isn't to make an exhaustive study of the issue of global warming, or climate change. But here is some brief background on the issue. Greenhouse gases (mostly water vapor and warming clouds) absorb heat from the sun and bounce it back into space. There are also cooling effects, such as evaporation, wind, and rain, all of which cool the earth. This affects weather patterns, leading to slight changes in the average temperature of the earth. The issue of global warming is the concern that excessive carbon dioxide in the atmosphere will trap more greenhouse gases, leading to a dramatic increase in the earth's surface temperature, which could cause negative climate change. Theories about what will happen with climate change are based on computer models. For these models to work, scientists must feed into them certain assumptions about what might happen. Predictions about global warming are based on hypotheses scientists make rather than actual measurements and observations. The models currently in use predict that the increase of carbon dioxide in the atmosphere, caused by human activity, will increase the earth's temperatures by 3.5 degrees Fahrenheit to 7 degrees Fahrenheit. (These figures are cited in Wayne Grudem, *Politics according to the Bible: A Comprehensive Resource for Understanding Modern Political Issues in Light of Scripture* [Grand Rapids: Zondervan, 2010], 365.) But the science of prediction is a tricky one. Many credible scientists have questioned the models used to predict future global warming. Often these scientists are pressured to abandon their skepticism of human-caused global warming because their results contradict a political agenda popular in Western nations. That political agenda uses governmental power to shape the world according to non-Christian worldviews. Actual observations show that the earth's temperature has remained steady or even fallen for the last decade and a half (cited in Grudem, *Politics according to the Bible*, 372). More than thirty-one thousand degreed scientists have gone on record saying that there is "no convincing scientific evidence that human release of carbon dioxide, methane, or other greenhouse gases is causing or will, in the foreseeable future, cause catastrophic heating of the Earth's atmosphere and disruption of the Earth's climate" ("Global Warming Petition Project," Oregon Institute of Science and Medicine, accessed July 23, 2016, www.petitionproject.org/). It's not just the overall numbers but the fact that all of the listed signers have received formal education in areas relevant to the global-warming debate, with more than nine thousand of them having earned PhD degrees in relevant fields.

104. Two examples: (1) Al Gore repeatedly quoted in his famous documentary *An Inconvenient Truth* a review of many global-warming studies by Harvard historian Naomi Oreskes, which Klaus-Martin Schulte reviewed. According to Schulte's findings, while Oreskes claimed that 75 percent of the papers she reviewed agreed with the consensus that global warming is human caused, only 7 percent *explicitly* stated this, and only one mentioned "'catastrophic' climate change" but offered no evidence. (See Klaus-Martin Schulte, "Scientific Consensus on Climate Change?," *Energy and Environment* 19, no. 2 [2008]: 281.) (2) The United Nations' Intergovernmental Panel on Climate Change (IPCC) was scandalized in 2009 and 2010 when it was discovered that key scientists were, among other "misdeeds," fabricating data, developing computer models that exaggerated warming trends to make it appear to be human caused, and suppressing studies that didn't reach their predetermined conclusions. As Wayne Grudem notes, "This is simply not the way researchers act when they are confident that the actual facts are overwhelmingly on their side." Grudem, *Politics according to the Bible*, 375.

105. Al Gore, speech at SXSW festival, Austin, Texas, March 2015, quoted in John Carpenter, "SXSW: Gore Says Climate-Change Deniers Should Pay Political Price," *Chicago Tribune*, March 13, 2015, www.chicagotribune.com/bluesky/originals/chi-sxsw-al-gore-penny-pritzker-bsi-20150313-story.html.

106. Grudem, *Politics according to the Bible*, 376–78.

107. Beisner, "What Is the Most Important Environmental Task?," 21–22.

108. Grudem, *Politics according to the Bible*, 382.

109. "Resource Depletion," Center for Ecoliteracy, www.ecoliteracy.org/issues/resource-depletion#issue-expanded. (Information no longer posted on site as of July 23, 2016.)

110. Grudem, *Politics according to the Bible*, 329. See, in particular, the evidence Grudem offers on pages 329–53.

111. Grudem, *Politics according to the Bible*, 352–53.

112. Grudem, *Politics according to the Bible*, 348.

113. Anthony D. Barnosky et al., "Has the Earth's Sixth Mass Extinction Already Arrived?," *Nature* 471 (March 2011): 51–57, cited in "World's Sixth Mass Extinction May Be Underway," Seeker, March 3, 2011, http://news.discovery.com /earth/weather-extreme-events/mass-extinction-humans-animals-110303.htm.

114. Patrick Moore, interview by Climate Depot, in Marc Morano, "Greenpeace Co-Founder Slams Species Extinction Scare Study as Proof of How 'Peer-Review Process Has Become Corrupted'—Study 'Greatly Underestimate the Rate New Species Can Evolve,'" Climate Depot, March 4, 2011, www.climatedepot.com/2011/03/04/greenpeace-cofounder-slams-species -extinction-scare-study-as-proof-of-how-peerreview-process-has-become-corrupted-ndash-study-greatly-underestimate -the-rate-new-species-can-evolve/#ixzz3gmDj7O2G.

115. "Status and Trends of Global Biodiversity," chap. 1 in *Global Biodiversity Outlook 1* (Quebec: Convention on Biological Diversity, 2001), Census of Marine Life, cited in "How Many Species on Earth? 8.7 Million New Estimate Says," ScienceDaily, August 24, 2011, www.sciencedaily.com/releases/2011/08/110823180459.htm.

116. "The Extinction Crisis," Center for Biological Diversity, accessed September 22, 2016, www.biologicaldiversity.org /programs/biodiversity/elements_of_biodiversity/extinction_crisis/.

117. Roger Revelle, "The World Supply of Agricultural Land," in *The Resourceful Earth: A Response to Global 2000*, eds. Julian L. Simon and Herman Kahn (New York: Basil Blackwell, 1984), 184–85, quoted in Grudem, *Politics according to the Bible*, 336–37.

118. Beisner, "What Is the Most Important Environmental Task?," 23.

119. Elaine Scarry, *On Beauty and Being Just* (Princeton, NJ: Princeton University Press, 1999), 112.

120. Wilkinson et al., *Earthkeeping in the Nineties*, 286.

121. Mustol, *Dusty Earthlings*, 4.

122. Wilson, *God's Good World*, 23–24.

123. Wilkinson et al., *Earthkeeping in the Nineties*, 216.

124. John Muir, *My First Summer in the Sierra* (Boston: Houghton Mifflin, 1911), 211.

125. Kostamo, *Planted*, 108–9.

126. Mustol, *Dusty Earthlings*, 6.

127. Bouma-Prediger, *For the Beauty of the Earth*, 21.

128. See Loren Wilkinson and Mary Ruth Wilkinson, *Caring for Creation in Your Own Backyard* (Vancouver: Regent College Publishing, 1997), 214.

129. Mustol, *Dusty Earthlings*, 221–22.

130. Wilson, *God's Good World*, 125.

131. Matthew 6:26: "Look at the birds of the air: they neither sow nor reap nor gather into barns, and yet your heavenly Father feeds them. Are you not of more value than they?"; Matthew 10:31: "Fear not … you are of more value than many sparrows"; Matthew 12:12: "Of how much more value is a man than a sheep!"

132. Genesis 9:10: "With every living creature that is with you, the birds, the livestock, and every beast of the earth with you, as many as came out of the ark; it is for every beast of the earth."

133. Psalm 104:16–22: "The trees of the LORD are watered abundantly, the cedars of Lebanon that he planted. In them the birds build their nests; the stork has her home in the fir trees. The high mountains are for the wild goats; the rocks are a refuge for the rock badgers. [God] made the moon to mark the seasons; the sun knows its time for setting. You make darkness, and it is night, when all the beasts of the forest creep about. The young lions roar for their prey, seeking their food from God. When the sun rises, they steal away and lie down in their dens."

134. Wilkinson et al., *Earthkeeping in the Nineties*, 283.

135. Bouma-Prediger, *For the Beauty of the Earth*, 152.

136. "Every Living Thing: An Evangelical Statement on Responsible Care for Animals," Every Living Thing, 2016, www.everylivingthing.com/sign-the-statement/.

137. Genesis 9:3: "Every moving thing that lives shall be food for you. And as I gave you the green plants, I give you everything."

138. Kenneth L. Feder and Michael Alan Park, "Animal Rights: An Evolutionary Perspective," *Humanist* (July/August 1990): 44.

139. Wilson, *God's Good World*, 207.

140. 2016 statistics from Global Slavery Index, www.globalslaveryindex.org/. An Australian organization called the Walk Free Foundation produces the Global Slavery Index (GSI). It defines slavery as being forced to work without wages and also includes such practices as debt bondage, forced marriage, and the sale and exploitation of children.

141. Wilkinson et al., *Earthkeeping in the Nineties*, 330.

142. Kostamo, *Planted*, 110.

143. Wilkinson and Wilkinson, *Caring for Creation in Your Own Backyard*, 26.

144. Dorothy Sayers, *Letters to a Diminished Church: Passionate Arguments for the Relevance of Christian Doctrine* (Nashville: W Publishing Group, 2004), 119.

145. Statistics cited in Kostamo, *Planted*, 128.

146. Kostamo, *Planted*, 129–33.

147. Wilkinson and Wilkinson, *Caring for Creation in Your Own Backyard*, 111.

148. Grudem, *Politics according to the Bible*, 369.

149. Isaiah 51:3: "The LORD comforts Zion; he comforts all her waste places and makes her wilderness like Eden, her desert like the garden of the LORD; joy and gladness will be found in her, thanksgiving and the voice of song."

150. Simon, *Population Matters*, 171.

151. Simon, *Population Matters*, 168.

152. "If the price of a raw material is deliberately held down, there may be waiting lines or rationing, and these may also be taken as signs of scarcity," says Julian Simon, but this isn't a good indicator of actual scarcity. Simon, *Population Matters*, 69.

153. Simon, *Population Matters*, 67–68.

154. Indur M. Goklany, *The Improving State of the World: Why We're Living Longer, Healthier, More Comfortable Lives on a Cleaner Planet* (Washington: Cato Institute, 2007), 99, cited in Beisner, "What Is the Most Important Environmental Task?," 12.

155. Beisner, "What Is the Most Important Environmental Task?," 23.

156. Goklany, *Improving State of the World*, 81, cited in Beisner, "What Is the Most Important Environmental Task?," 11.

157. Beisner, "What Is the Most Important Environmental Task?," 12–13.

158. Beisner, "What Is the Most Important Environmental Task?," 14.

159. Nelson, "*Silent Spring* as Secular Religion," in Meiners, Desrochers, and Morriss, *Silent Spring at 50*, 71.

160. Terry L. Anderson and Donald R. Leal, *Free Market Environmentalism* (San Francisco: Pacific Research Institute for Public Policy, 1991), 10–11.

161. Anderson and Leal, *Free Market Environmentalism*, 7.

162. David S. Landes, *The Wealth and Poverty of Nations: Why Some Are So Rich and Some So Poor* (New York: W. W. Norton, 1999), 497, cited in Wayne Grudem and Barry Asmus, *The Poverty of Nations: A Sustainable Solution* (Wheaton, IL: Crossway, 2013), 251.

163. Grudem and Asmus, *Poverty of Nations*, 252.

164. Terry L. Anderson and Donald R. Leal, *Free Market Environmentalism for the Next Generation* (New York: Palgrave Macmillan, 2015), 8.

165. Anderson and Leal, *Free Market Environmentalism*, 11.

166. Wayne Grudem and Barry Asmus focus particularly on energy resources: "Energy resources enable human beings to do immensely greater amounts of work than they can do if they use only their own power or animal power. A man driving a diesel-powered tractor can plow dozens of acres in the time it would take a man guiding a horse to plow only part of one acre. A man driving a semitrailer or locomotive can haul many thousands of times the weight of goods that can be hauled by a man with a wheelbarrow, a bicycle, or a horse-drawn wagon, and can travel hundreds of miles more safely and in far less time. Oil-based gasoline or diesel power enables all of these tasks." Grudem and Asmus, *Poverty of Nations*, 281.

167. Grudem and Asmus, *Poverty of Nations*, 335.

168. Bouma-Prediger, *For the Beauty of the Earth*, 173.

169. Wendell Berry, "Out of Your Car, Off Your Horse: Twenty-Seven Propositions about Global Thinking and the Sustainability of Cities," *Atlantic* (February 1991), www.theatlantic.com/magazine/archive/1991/02/out-your-car-your-horse/309159/.

170. J. R. R. Tolkien, *The Return of the King* (New York: Del Ray, 2012), 16.

CHAPTER

12

12

POLITICS

1. STANDING TALL WHEN EVERYONE ELSE IS ON THEIR KNEES IN WORSHIP

The year was 1933. Germany was desperate. In the aftermath of their defeat in the Great War, high unemployment, suffocating debt, and an out-of-control currency had left peoples' life savings in shatters. In the midst of the chaos, one candidate's frightening vision stood out, overshadowing his political party's shady past. When the votes were counted, the National Socialist Party had won 33 percent, enough to make Adolf Hitler reich chancellor.

It was a disaster wearing the mask of triumph. The Nazis were thugs. As bestselling author Eric Metaxas ominously phrased it, "In the babble of their clamoring, they had summoned the devil himself, for there now rose up from the deep wound in the national psyche something strange and terrible and compelling."[1]

Hitler's title, *führer*, simply means "leader" in German. But it signifies so much more. Channeling the ancient spirit of German nationalism, Hitler was essentially saying to the nation, "I am your father. I am your god. I am all-powerful and, indeed, the very source of all power."

According to Metaxas, Hitler was "a symbol who symbolized himself."[2] For the next five years, he grew in power. Having invested him with supreme authority, the German people expected miraculous results. And Hitler seemed to deliver sensationally, restoring the economy and renewing German confidence.

> **A bad seed produces bad fruit, and those who plant it reap the harvest they deserve.**

But a bad seed produces bad fruit, and those who plant it reap the harvest they deserve. So it was with Germany and, ultimately, all of Europe. Looking back, it seems self-evident that Hitler was beastly. But could anyone have known this five years before he ignited war and exterminated millions?

Who Will Stand?

Dietrich Bonhoeffer was one who saw the writing on the wall. Though he was a pastor, not a political leader, Bonhoeffer knew the Führer Principle would be catastrophic. He had to speak out. But what can one pastor do? Hitler had taught that religion should be kept out of politics, and the people believed him. Any words Bonhoeffer spoke would merely condemn him as out of touch.

In spite of his reservations, Bonhoeffer voiced his concerns in a 1933 radio address, warning that "the image of the Leader [führer] will [gradually become] the image of the mis-leader [*verführer*]." He stated that

> the true Leader must always be able to disillusion. It is just this that is his responsibility and his real object. He must lead his following away from the authority of his person to the recognition of the real authority of orders and offices.[3]

> **A true leader doesn't gather power and lord it over others. He serves. All other paths lead to perdition.**

A true leader doesn't gather power and lord it over others. He serves. All other paths lead to perdition. Mysteriously, Bonhoeffer's microphone was shut off during the broadcast. He was now on Hitler's radar. He would be watched.

Offered safety in America, Bonhoeffer traveled to New York. But after a short time, he regretted his decision. "I have come to the conclusion that I have made a mistake in coming to America," he wrote. "I must live through this difficult period of our national history with the Christian people of Germany."[4]

Returning home, Bonhoeffer crossed the line, joining the Abwehr (the German military intelligence organization) as a double agent who intended to conspire against Hitler. On the outside he played a fawning and naive pastor, convincing people he was loyal to "his" führer. Behind the scenes, though, Bonhoeffer was helping plan the führer's assassination.[5] The attempt failed. Bonhoeffer was caught, sentenced to prison, and executed on April 9, 1945, just days before the Allies defeated Germany.

Though Bonhoeffer was widely admired as a martyr, his approach still raises questions. What role ought Christians to have in resisting political leaders they believe are engaged in evil? And, in view of our own times, could we muster the will to stand against powerful and popular political leaders? Beneath these questions is a more basic one: Should Christians even bother with politics in the first place, and if so, how do they remain faithful to Christ in the process?

Can the Church Still Stand?

While the church is growing in Africa and South America, it's losing influence in the United States.[6] More and more people think the church should mind its own business and leave politics alone. Indeed, many people increasingly support punishing the church for not conforming to current notions about issues like same-sex marriage.[7]

The question of Christianity and politics has always been hard. It's harder now, with a growing paganism and a state that demands ever more in taxes and obedience to politically correct demands. Will the church bow too? Or will we be like Shadrach, Meshach, and Abednego, who, when King Nebuchadnezzar commanded them to bow to his image, replied, "Be it known to you, O king, that we will not serve your gods or worship the golden image that you have set up" (Dan. 3:18).

As Eric Metaxas notes, the church is the institution that asks of the state whether its actions tend toward law and order or lawlessness and disorder. "It is the church's role to help the state be the state," he says.[8] If the church steps away from this role, who will stand against the gods of power and their tyrannical ambitions? To answer these perplexing questions, we'll look at the nature of politics (what politics is) as well as the accusations other worldviews make to keep Christians on the sidelines. We'll also explore whether there is even such a thing as a coherent Christian worldview of political involvement and how Christians ought to act differently if there is.

2. What Is the Problem?

What Is Politics?

Polis is the Greek word for city (or community), and *politikos* means "of, or relating to, the citizens within a community." **Politics**, then, seeks to answer the question, "What is the best way to use power to organize community for the citizens?"

The United States, as you may know from government class in school, is organized as a constitutional republic. It's a **democracy** (from the Greek for "rule of the people"), but not in the sense that everyone decides everything. Rather, it's a **republic** (from the Latin for

Democracy: a system of government in which citizens vote directly for or against particular laws, officials, measures, and so on.

Republic: a system of government in which citizens elect agents to represent the interests of those who elected them.

"the state is the public's interest"). Citizens elect representatives. These representatives are to follow the US Constitution in establishing and enforcing laws that promote orderly and just governance. In fact, the Latin word for law, *legum*, is where we get our words *legislate* and *legislature*.

In a constitutional republic, citizens willingly constrain their own freedom for the greater good. As the Roman statesman Cicero claimed, *"Legum ... servi sumus ut liberi esse possimus"* ("We are slaves of the law so that we may be free").[9] It seems paradoxical to use freedom to constrain freedom, but long experience has shown that unless we exercise discipline individually and as communities, tyranny will be our lot. As Edmund Burke said,

> Society cannot exist unless a controlling power upon will and appetite be placed somewhere, and the less of it there is within, the more there must be without. It is ordained in the eternal constitution of things, that men of intemperate minds cannot be free. Their passions forge their fetters.[10]

Upon a firm foundation of self-discipline, citizens willingly give up some of their freedom and choose representatives to ensure that the Constitution is followed. Although it's less than perfect, in America that's what government and politics have been all about.

How Government Works

People form civil governments at the federal, state, and local levels to establish order and justice. Each governmental unit operates inside certain boundaries. Using the authority the people have given them, lawmakers—legislators—establish administrative bureaus to carry out the laws they pass. Usually these bureaus have clear jurisdictions (from the Latin for "law" and "say") that "speak the law" to maintain order and justice. Every time you get a drink of water or flush the toilet or turn on the lights or drive down the street, you're using services these administrative bureaus provide, funded with agreed-upon taxes and fees. People who operate these bureaus are called bureaucrats (from the French for "the power of the desk").

You've probably heard the term *bureaucrat* used derisively. That's because administrative bureaus often create so many rules and regulations that order and justice get bogged down in "red tape," a term harkening back to a custom of bundling government documents with red ribbon. It's an ever-present problem. How do we set up enough rules to keep things from getting out of control without setting up so many that people just start ignoring them? One of the ironies of modern government is that attempts to secure order and justice, when bungled, can result in greater disorder and injustice.

> One of the ironies of modern government is that attempts to secure order and justice, when bungled, can result in greater disorder and injustice.

Laws securing the power of various government agencies are taken very seriously. I learned this as a teenager when I got pulled over by someone I thought was a police officer. The man wasn't wearing a uniform, and when he walked up and pulled out a badge, I sensed something was wrong.

"Where's your uniform?" I asked.

"I'm undercover," he replied.

After a brief conversation, I realized something was amiss and drove away. The next day I filed a complaint. The police investigated and found that the person who had pulled me over was a prankster impersonating a police officer. He may have thought it was funny, but the police weren't amused, and they charged him with very serious crimes. I now understand why: if someone illegitimately claims power, it compromises the power of governmental units to enforce the law.

When government is working properly, legislators stay attuned to the will of the people and establish orderly and just laws. Administrative bureaus carry out these laws respectfully and efficiently, within clear boundaries, recognizing that government exists to serve citizens, not the other way around.

But as we all know, reality often doesn't turn out this way. If you've ever tried to get a driver's license, you've probably encountered bureaucrats who seemed overwhelmed, resigned to inefficiency, and grumpy. But public servants aren't excused for acting this way. People are policy. If government doesn't work the way it's supposed to, it is a worldview problem: either people have the wrong worldview or they lack the will or ability to practice the right one. *Someone's* worldview assumptions will govern. If these assumptions aren't biblically based, they will be based on some other source of authority. As we'll see, these other sources of authority form into worldviews that, while very different from one another, have a common thread: they are organized to push Christianity out of the public square. Following is a brief analysis of what some of those worldviews are and why they so stridently oppose Christian involvement in politics.

> If government doesn't work the way it's supposed to, it is a worldview problem: either people have the wrong worldview or they lack the will or ability to practice the right one.

What Do Other Worldviews Say?

Politics is one issue every worldview takes into account. Christianity is a dominant worldview, but in our volume *Understanding the Times*, David Noebel and I examined five others: Secularism, Marxism, Postmodernism, New Spirituality, and Islam. Each of these worldviews plants certain seeds in hopes of harvesting certain kinds of fruit. Secularism produces government that ignores God, Marxism produces government that is hostile to God and confiscates goods from the wealthy and redistributes them to workers, and so forth. You can temporarily decorate these worldviews with other kinds of fruit, but if you want different fruit, you must plant different seeds. Before we explore the kind of fruit a Christian worldview of politics ought to produce, let's dig into each of the other five worldviews to see what they've planted and what they hope to harvest.

Secularism. In the words of philosopher Paul Kurtz, "No deity will save us[;] we must save ourselves."[11] We need saving, Secularism says, but religion can't do it, because faith and facts are two different worlds, and those who try to mix them do harm. Hunter Baker says in his critique of Secularism,

Although the U.S. is one of the most religious of the developed nations, there is still an expectation among those who define public reality in the media, academy, and government that appeals to God should be saved for one's private life.... To swim against the tide of secular modernity indicates one may be uncivil, unbalanced, and possibly even dangerous.[12]

Secularists don't mind if people are religious on their own time, but they think it's alarming when people bring God into the public sphere. Such people, Secularists believe, must be strongly opposed.

But if God is irrelevant, what are ethics and laws based on? Secularists say that human thinking and consensus are what make social progress possible.[13] Secularists often draw on the philosophy of **legal positivism**, which says that what ought to be done in society is what people in authority think is best, rather than what is based on moral rules derived from nature or God's revelation.

Not everyone thinks legal positivism is a good idea. Christian attorney and author John Whitehead observes, "If there is no fixity in law and no reference point, then law can be what a judge says it is. If, however, there is a fixity to law, there is some absolute basis upon which judgment can be made."[14] Without a fixed standard for what is right and wrong, Secularists tend to look to outcomes rather than inputs to decide what to do. Take, for example, the Declaration of Independence's focus on the pursuit of happiness as an unalienable right. A government holding that laws are derived from nature and God's revelation will ask, "Is the government being restrained from infringing on the pursuit of happiness?" A Secularist who embraces legal positivism, though, asks, "Are people actually *experiencing* happiness?" If not, it's up to the government to guarantee that people are happy. Secularist professor Mark Reader wrote, "In the end politics is the place of public happiness."[15] But as another Secularist, Morris Storer, admits, it's not easy because "the 'good life' or 'quality of life' is relative to each individual's preferences, desires, and needs."[16]

> Without a fixed standard for what is right and wrong, Secularists tend to look to outcomes rather than inputs to decide what to do.

There are two ironies here. First, trying to guarantee outcomes practically guarantees that the government will grow larger and more powerful, drawing resources out of economically productive pursuits to feed itself. We've seen this happen in the federal government, which has spent $22 trillion in the past fifty years to conquer poverty, only to find that poverty is at the same level as before and that the bureaucracy is many hundreds of times larger. Second, it's an impossible aim. No matter how big government becomes, it can never take care of everyone and make them all happy. We might have done well to heed the words of Thomas Jefferson (and Secularists' hero) that good government is one "which shall restrain men from injuring one another, shall leave them otherwise free to regulate their own pursuits of industry and improvement, and shall not take from the mouth of labor the bread it has earned."[17]

Secularists remain undeterred by reality, however. Believing government is the solution, they long to unite the nations to create "a new world order."[18] Paul Kurtz advocated a "World Parliament" to enact legislative policies on behalf of global citizens, rather than their governments, as the current United Nations is tasked to do.[19] Advocating a Secularist approach, Julian Huxley thought humanity's evolution demanded this new approach: "Major steps in the human phase of evolution are achieved by breakthroughs to new dominant patterns of mental organization, of knowledge, ideas and beliefs—ideological instead of physiological or biological organization."[20] Kurtz agreed, noting, "There are powerful forces moving us toward a new ethical global consciousness."[21] Secularist philosopher Timothy Madigan says world government is simply acknowledging a reality: "It is no longer feasible to arbitrarily divide it into separate states and hope that each one can satisfactorily manage itself."[22]

In sum, Secularists don't really care whether you believe in God, as long as you keep it to yourself. Religion is based on opinions, Secularists say, whereas good government is based on how well we can measure whether it's meeting people's felt needs. Even political philosophy, the college major designed to train people to be politically astute citizens, is now called *political science*. The assumption is that good government is a scientific pursuit rather than a thoughtful debate about what is right and wrong. This is a massive worldview shift. As journalist Christopher Caldwell says, "Political philosophy asks which government is best for man. Political science asks which government is best for government."[23]

Marxism. Many of America's founding fathers saw government as a concession to humanity's sin nature. "If men were angels," said James Madison, "no government would be necessary."[24] Karl Marx and his followers, though, believed that men—those in the working class, at least—*were* angels. Once the workers revolted, they would set the world on the path to a communist utopia, and government would disappear.[25]

Marxists believe this revolution has already begun. Georgi Shakhnazarov, a top aide to former Soviet president Mikhail Gorbachev, believed the Russian Revolution of October 1917 will continue until the means of production are in the hands of the people. This is the defining trend of our time: "Our epoch is the epoch of the revolutionary transformation of capitalist society into communist."[26] According to Marxists, when the **proletariat** rules, economic classes and governments will be abolished, and the world will experience cooperation and consensus. The church would also have to be abolished in this process, because it is, as Clemens Dutt put it, "diverting [workers] from the struggle against capitalism."[27]

On the surface, Marxists claim to support democracy, but they define the word in a different way. To the Marxist, democracy is simply the means to an end, a necessary tool for moving toward **socialism** and, ultimately, **communism**. Marxists feel safe with their version of democracy because they believe it will take power away from the elites and give it to the working class, which will then abolish democracy and establish the "dictatorship of the proletariat"[28] (the people's dictatorship). The people's dictatorship will redefine everything, including the very definition of right and

> *Socialism:* an economic system based on governmental or communal ownership of the means of production and distribution of goods and services.

> *Communism:* the Marxist ideal of a classless and stateless utopian society in which all property is commonly owned and each person is paid according to his or her abilities and needs.

wrong. "Right" becomes whatever benefits the workers, and "wrong" becomes whatever harms their interests. Howard Selsam explained:

> Marxism, which has been so often accused of seeking to eliminate moral considerations from human life and history emphasizes rather the moral issues involved in every situation. It does so, however, not by standing on a false platform of absolute right, but by identifying itself with the real needs and interests of the workers and farmers.[29]

Because the needs of workers and farmers change over time, what is right and wrong will also need adjustments. Morality is relative to what those in power think is "best" for workers and farmers. E. B. Pashukanis wrote, "We require that our legislation possess maximum elasticity. We cannot fetter ourselves by any sort of system."[30] To Pashukanis, it wasn't about the equal application of law; it was about doing whatever is needed to get the results Marxist leaders want to achieve.

Marxism teaches that the transformation to a people's dictatorship will be accomplished through a worker's revolution. Purified by their suffering, workers will have gained the moral authority to lead. Vladimir Lenin was clear that this kind of leadership would be a dictatorship, and that it would be forceful. "Whoever expects that socialism will be achieved without social revolution and a dictatorship of the proletariat is not a socialist. Dictatorship is state power, based directly upon force."[31]

Historically, what happened is this: people didn't become saintly and wise just because they were poor and their jobs were hard. So, on their behalf, communist leaders formed a communist political party to make all the decisions for the working class. According to the authors of *Socialism as a Social System*, "Marxist-Leninist theory and the experience of history show conclusively that the working class can carry out its historic mission only if led by a strong, well-organised party."[32] But this is simply a cynical way for power-hungry rulers to seize control and justify it as a benefit to the people. Joseph Stalin wrote,

> Our Party guides the government. The Party supervises the work of the administration … and tries to secure for them the support of the masses, since there is not any important decision taken by them without the direction of the Party.[33]

Totalinarianism: **a highly centralized system of government in which the state retains and exerts complete authority over its citizens and seeks to regulate every aspect of people's lives.**

Inside the gift-wrapped package of the people's dictatorship was plain, old-fashioned tyranny, and of the most brutal sort. Tens of millions of people perished, and Marxism now stands as the most brutal form of **totalitarianism** in all of human history, more brutal than all other forms combined.[34]

Secularism and Marxism are the most prevalent worldviews competing against the influence of Christians in government, but other worldviews do have something to say about politics. Let's take a brief look at Postmodernism, New Spirituality, and Islam.

Postmodernism. An offshoot of Marxism, Postmodernism developed as a means of "deconstructing" political and religious metanarratives to expose the ways they persuade others to unthinkingly turn over the reins of power. Simply put, a **metanarrative** is single, overarching interpretation of reality. To Postmodernists, politics is bad, but religion is worse. Politics and religion together are intolerable. "Religion is unobjectionable," said pragmatist, philosopher, and hero-to-Postmodernists Richard Rorty, "as long as it is privatized."[35] During his lifetime, Rorty felt this so strongly that he regularly quoted the French revolutionary Denis Diderot: "Man will never be free until the last king is strangled with the entrails of the last priest."[36]

> *Metanarrative:* A single, overarching interpretation, or grand story, of reality.

Postmodernism has been influential in causing people to be cynical about the motives of those in power. But it hasn't generated a better form of government, because Postmodernism is primarily about critique rather than constructive change. Postmodernists are like armchair quarterbacks who yell at the television screen but wouldn't have the first idea of what to do if they were actually responsible for real results.

New Spirituality. Another worldview that is quite unlike the others, and not as influential in the Western world as Secularism and Marxism, is New Spirituality. *New Spirituality* is a blanket term describing any view that applies Eastern religion to Western life. It says the universe is a living organism connected by "higher consciousness," or what some people call "God" or the "divine." Consciousness is seen as a unified field of energy that is self-contained, self-knowing, and self-sustaining. According to Robert Oates, it "contains within it the seeds of all the force and matter fields in nature."[37]

To New Spiritualists, the good life comes from tapping into higher consciousness through meditation. Some New Spiritualists, including Transcendental Meditation (TM) advocate John Hagelin, believe that getting enough people to meditate on the same thing creates the Maharishi Effect (named after TM's founder, the Maharishi Mahesh Yogi). The Maharishi is quoted as saying, "It is not the system of government that is important. Every system can rise to fulfillment, every system can bring satisfaction to the aspirations of all the people."[38] The Maharishi Effect, say its advocates, will generate the ideal society. It makes children smarter, lowers crime, and ends wars.[39]

What might stop us from harnessing higher consciousness in this way? According to New Spiritualist teacher Eckhart Tolle, it's our individual egos. Ego, Tolle says, is what sunk the Communist Revolution. Because communism didn't put any emphasis on changing peoples' inner realities, it couldn't overcome the dysfunction that egoistic people have brought into society.[40] New Spiritualists have similar doubts about Secularism and Islam and to some extent historical Christianity (at least in its formal high-church sense).

Even though many sympathize with its aims, New Spirituality simply doesn't have enough dedicated adherents to have much impact—directly, at least. Indirectly, New Spirituality has influenced popular culture a great deal, as Philip Goldberg demonstrates in his book *American Veda*.[41] Yoga studios are everywhere. People talk about karma. Meditation is a common practice. Teaching about the science of consciousness, which originated with Indian gurus, fills the airwaves on programs like *The Oprah Winfrey Show* and in bestselling books like *The Secret* by

Rhonda Byrne. A new paganism is emerging to convince people that everything is "one" and that all distinctions must be eliminated.[42] This means eliminating the distinction between ourselves and God. But it could also mean that the distinctions between male and female are artificial, as well as the distinctions between good and bad, between nations based on geographic boundaries, and so forth. This new paganism touches everything, including politics.

Islam. The final worldview we'll look at in our discussion of politics is Islam, a rapidly growing force in the Western world. *Islam* means "submission," and adherents are called *Muslims*, which means "those who submit." Islam is a comprehensive reality, a form of government as well as a religion that's governed by sharia law. Sharia prescribes harsh punishments for what Islam considers crimes, including stealing and murder, as well as religious conversion from Islam and homosexual behavior. Yet the Muslim world is divided about how far to go in applying sharia. Some Muslims favor nation-states (with laws, constitutions, and boundaries distinct from other nations), and others promote **pan-Islam**, a view that the Muslim community should unite and establish a global Islamic state. Those favoring the nation-state view sometimes produce nations where sharia law dominates, but others, such as Turkey, are Muslim nations with a constitution not based solely on Islamic principles, though this is shifting as the character of national leadership changes.

> Islam is a comprehensive reality, a form of government as well as a religion that's governed by sharia law.

> *Pan-Islam:* The belief that all Muslims should be united under a single Islamic state; the belief that the world should be united under a global Islamic state.

In these more moderate countries, though, are many who favor a pan-Islamic community and actively work to establish sharia through reform, denouncement, protest, and even terrorism. In the last several decades, such groups have shaken many nations to their core, calling Secularism into question and, in many cases, brutally asserting what they see as Allah's will over nations.

One thing all non-Christian worldviews have in common. Though these worldview perspectives are very different, they all share the belief that Christianity has no place in the public realm. To Secularism, Christianity is an outmoded way of thinking that prevents people from ordering society according to nonreligious principles. To Marxism, Christianity is dangerous because it props up capitalism and prevents revolution. To Postmodernism, Christianity is a false story of life that oppresses people. New Spirituality disagrees with Christianity about who God is, and it asserts that changing peoples' inner realities—not bringing biblical principles to bear in society—is what improves government. To Islam, Christians are infidels who must cease their rebellion against Allah and hand the keys of power over to followers of the prophet Muhammad.

In short, other worldviews see Christianity as an artifact of a bygone era, and perhaps one that has done more harm than good. Proponents of these other worldviews say it's time for Christians to mind their own business and stop meddling in politics. Deceived by these arguments, some Christians timidly step aside. But that's not the right thing to do. Instead of shrinking into the shadows, believers ought to do the hard work of discerning a biblical basis for political involvement and then become more involved, not less. Caring, not capitulation, is the answer.

3. WHY SHOULD CHRISTIANS CARE?

Politics is often a touchy subject among Christians, but it shouldn't be. Christians played a formative role in developing ideas of good government, particularly representative democracy, the rule of law, and limited government. Interestingly, Christianity's concept of original sin also made a difference. Lord Acton coined the now famous phrase "Power tends to corrupt; absolute power corrupts absolutely,"[43] but it wasn't a new thought. Nearly two thousand years before Lord Acton made his statement, the apostle Paul wrote that *no one* is righteous (see Romans 3). Humans cannot be trusted with too much power. Those who *want* power are especially suspect. Realizing this, America's founders divided power among three branches of government: the executive, the legislative, and the judicial. This division balances power and checks its abuse.

> Christians played a formative role in developing ideas of good government, particularly representative democracy, the rule of law, and limited government.

As Christians, we should welcome opportunities to participate in government. Our goal ought to be influencing the state to protect the innocent and punish the guilty, according to what is actually true in reality, not what political pundits say to sound clever. Proverbs 11:11 states, "By the blessing of the upright a city is exalted, but by the mouth of the wicked it is overthrown."

The Bible talks about government from cover to cover. Many theologians say government began in Genesis 9:5–6,[44] just after the account of Noah and the flood. God told Noah that if a man sheds the blood of another man, his punishment is to forfeit his own life. The particular point was about murder, but it implies law enforcement and a judicial system capable of judging guilt and innocence.

My own view is that government began before that, in Genesis 2:15,[45] when the Lord God took the man and put him in the garden of Eden to work it and keep it. The man was responsible for organizing his surroundings. That's government. If it's just one person, it's self-government. If it's a group, it might be one of three kinds of government we'll consider in this chapter: civil government, family government, and church government, which is a unique form of government organized around religious worship and practice. The church's responsibility, as we saw earlier, is to help the state be the state. We could also say that it helps the family be the family. The church is—or ought to be—the conscience of society.

It may seem like a technical point, but if government began before Adam and Eve fell into sin, then it's part of God's creation, not just a response to sin. We need government not to keep everyone in line but to free them to flourish. Even if humans hadn't fallen, we'd still have government to serve human society in the way that a traffic cop is needed to help regulate the flow of traffic even when all the drivers are well meaning and polite. God is truth. Justice is truth in relationships. Government is truth applied to community.

The **Mosaic law** (also called the Torah) is one of the earliest sources of written rules about government. It was a set of laws God gave the Israelites, newly freed from slavery, to govern themselves while surrounded by hostile nations and possessing no natural source of food and water. Survival was at stake.

Mosaic Law: the set of laws God gave Moses and the Hebrews following their exodus from Egypt.

Reading this ancient law can be confusing, though. Civil laws about crime and punishment are mixed in with ceremonial laws about personal hygiene. It takes a great deal of discernment to understand how these laws apply to us, but the Christian tradition is that we may not simply ignore them because salvation comes through faith in Christ, not by obedience to the Law (Eph. 2:8–9).[46] Jesus himself said, "I have not come to abolish [the Law and the Prophets] but to fulfill them (Matt. 5:17).

Treating Old Testament law as if it's still relevant is odd to us. We can't imagine government regulations on the kinds of fabrics we can wear, the length of beards, and so forth. But as Jonathan Burnside, a professor at the University of Bristol, England, points out, the Torah tells a story about how life ought to be lived. Reading through the biblical texts as a legal scholar, Burnside asked what they contribute to our understanding of law and found that the Torah has profoundly helpful insights into justice, taking care of the earth, property, welfare, criminal law, marriage and divorce, and sex.[47]

If we recognize the Bible as revealing something about God and what he wants, we can see three clear ways it can inform our own political involvement today.

God's Image: Equality

The first way God's nature informs politics is that as his image bearers, we're all equally valuable in God's sight. This idea forms the basis for the Christian approach to democracy. Most people think democracy originated in ancient Athens, but what the Athenians called democracy would hardly be recognized as such today. Only adult males with a certain status were permitted to vote. And these voters often acted as a mob, voting to execute generals who lost battles, passing laws one day and reversing them the next, and looting the public treasury for their own benefit. Philosophers like Plato and Aristotle saw this and concluded that democracy was degenerate.

America's founders emphasized more of a biblical approach. The Declaration of Independence proclaims, "All men are created equal ... [and] are endowed by their Creator with certain unalienable rights." We don't just exist for ourselves; we have a higher purpose that is God given. If our rights aren't tied inextricably to God's character, they can be arbitrarily changed according to the whims of each passing generation or political party. An antidote to the undisciplined rule by the majority is the fact that "unalienable" rights are based on God's unchanging character.

We're all equally valuable in God's sight. This idea forms the basis for the Christian approach to democracy.

Christianity says all people are God's image bearers. This is a far different vision of society than other worldviews promote. As C. S. Lewis put it, "Individuals are more important, for they live eternally; and races, civilizations, and the like, are in comparison the creatures of a day."[48]

Christians throughout history have understood the relationship between bearing God's image and political equality. The first communities in history that allowed every member an equal vote were Christian monasteries. One of the most important principles of medieval law (known as *quod omnes tanget*) says that everyone affected by a law must have the right to a say about it. This is why legislators must meet in public and offer the opportunity for people to comment. It's also why America's founders insisted that tax bills must originate in the House of Representatives, the legislative body closest to the people. Such laws promote equality based on the belief that we're all equal as God's image bearers.

God's Character: Justice

The second way God's nature informs politics is through his character quality of **justice**. Justice is truth applied to relationships. As we've already seen, God's relationship as Father, Son, and Holy Spirit isn't something *he does*; it's something he *is*. He made humans to be relational creatures as well. Genesis 2:18 says, "It is not good that the man should be alone." Sociologist S. D. Gaede observes that

> *Justice:* the moral principle of equally observing the rights of everyone and treating them fairly.

> God designed the human being to be a relational creature. Note this point well. Humankind was created to relate to other beings. It was not an accident. It was not the result of sin. It was an intentional, creational given.[49]

Relationship calls for justice. Put two people together and you'll need a clear understanding of the rights and obligations of each person. From a biblical viewpoint, we cannot make up rights for ourselves or deprive others of their rights just because we think we're better. This is what happened in Greece and Rome.[50] Jesus taught that relationships are based on serving rather than demanding to be served. He told his disciples that the "last will be first and the first will be last" (Matt. 20:16; Mark 10:43; Luke 22:27).[51]

Servanthood changes how we treat people. It's no coincidence that Christians elevated the status of women, built hospitals and schools, and instituted ministries to the poor. In fact, as sociologist Rodney Stark points out, effective moral opposition to slavery arose *only* because of Christian theology.[52] Various cultures have opposed slavery in certain circumstances or for themselves, but opposing slavery in all its forms because it's sinful is a Christian impulse unique in the world to this very day. Servanthood also changes government's focus. We aren't *followers* of our political leaders but *constituents*. We aren't *subjects*. Rather, we are *customers*. Government is to serve justly.

> From a biblical viewpoint, we cannot make up rights for ourselves or deprive others of their rights just because we think we're better.

America's founders implanted this understanding of justice in the Declaration of Independence, which speaks of *securing* the rights to "life, liberty, and the pursuit of happiness," not *granting* them. The goal of justice is to remove barriers to liberty, not so people can do whatever they *want* but so they have the freedom to do what they *ought*. For example, a just government establishes courts not to *create* justice but to *serve* justice.[53] Similarly, government exists not to *make* people happy but to create space for living virtuously.[54] True justice isn't based on whim. It is part of God's unchangeable nature.

God's Law: Rights

The third way God's nature informs politics is through his divinely revealed law. The revered legal scholar William Blackstone, whose work explored and systematized common law and was copiously referred to by America's founders, recognized that law comes from two places: **natural law** (laws that all humans who aren't biased by preexisting commitments will recognize) and *Scripture*. Blackstone wrote, "Upon these two foundations, the law of nature and the law of revelation [the Bible], depend all human laws; that is to say, no human laws should be suffered to contradict these."[55]

> *Natural Law:* the belief that morality can be seen in the natural order of creation and accessed through human reason; the belief that laws are rules based upon an internal code of morality that all people possess.

Grounding our legal system in the law of nature and revelation gives law a fixed foundation. John Whitehead explains: "Law has content in the eternal sense. It has a reference point. Like a ship that is anchored, law cannot stray far from its mooring."[56] If those in power wish it to be based on their own image instead of God's, too bad. Earthly legislators don't *make* laws; they respond to God's law. Theologian Carl F. H. Henry wrote, "God is the only Legislator. Earthly rulers and legislative bodies alike are accountable to Him from whom stems all obligation—religious, ethical and civil."[57]

Dietrich Bonhoeffer put it this way:

> It is God's will that there shall be labour, marriage, government and church in the world; and it is His will that all these, each in its own way, shall be through Christ, directed towards Christ, and in Christ.… This means that there can be no retreating from a "secular" into a "spiritual" sphere.[58]

Nothing lies outside Christ's influence. All of life is bound inextricably with Christ's authority (Matt. 28:18–20).[59] In Bonhoeffer's view, "the world is relative to Christ."[60] Whitehead argues that the very term *legislator* doesn't mean "one who makes laws but one who moves them—from the divine law written in nature or in the Bible into the statutes and law codes of a particular society."[61] Thus, governments exist not so much to *create* law as to *secure* law—to apply divine law to general and specific situations and to act as impartial enforcers of such laws.

It may seem unusual to us today to consider God and Christ as the basis of law, but it was a natural conclusion to America's founders, even to those who didn't believe in Christ's divinity. John Adams, in a letter to Thomas Jefferson in 1813, wrote,

The general Principles, on which the Fathers [achieved] Independence, were the only Principles in which that beautiful Assembly of young Gentlemen could Unite.... And what were these general Principles? I answer, the general Principles of Christianity, in which all those Sects were United.... Now I will avow, that I then believed, and now believe, that those general Principles of Christianity, are as eternal and immutable, as the Existence and Attributes of God.[62]

John Witherspoon said that the best friend of liberty is one who is

most sincere and active in promoting true and undefiled religion, and who sets him-self with the greatest firmness to bear down on profanity and immorality of every kind. Whoever is an avowed enemy of God, I scruple not to call him an enemy to his country.[63]

Noah Webster concurred: "The moral principles and precepts found in the scriptures ought to form the basis of all our civil constitutions and laws. These principles and precepts have truth, immutable truth, for their foundation."[64]

George Washington, in his inaugural address as the first president of the United States, referred to "the propitious smiles of Heaven" that fall only on that nation that does not "[disregard] the eternal rules of order and right which Heaven itself has ordained."[65] The understanding of men like Adams, Witherspoon, and Washington was so evident in early America that French sociologist Alexis de Tocqueville said after his visit in the 1830s,

There is no country in the world where the Christian religion retains a greater influ-ence over the souls of men than in America; and there can be no greater proof of its utility and of its conformity to human nature than that its influence is powerfully felt over the most enlightened and free nation of the earth.[66]

God exists. He communicates. We can know him well enough to make good laws. This is the basis of our whole understanding of rights.

But doesn't the fact that we humans are fallen and in rebellion against God mean that we cannot accu-rately craft laws that reflect his nature and character? Interestingly, America's founders actually believed the opposite: that recognizing humanity's sinfulness actually helps us create *better* laws. Let's look next at how this is so.

> God exists. He communicates. We can know him well enough to make good laws. This is the basis of our whole understanding of rights.

The Reality of Sin

Adam's and Eve's failure to obey God in the garden of Eden resulted not only in their expulsion from their garden paradise but also in a cycle of paranoia, blame, and harmful actions. Scripture assumes they were capable of acting differently than they did and thus were responsible. William Stanmeyer explains:

If man's behavior were somehow conditioned by genetic code or social externals then no just judge could blame him for the evil he commits. But the scripture teaches unequivocally that God blamed Adam and Eve for succumbing to the temptation to disobedience and punished them accordingly.[67]

> Though we're not able to make ourselves righteous, we are nonetheless able to choose right over wrong and good over evil.

Because we're made in God's image, we each bear responsibility for our actions. Right and wrong and good and evil actually exist, and though we're not able to make ourselves righteous, we are nonetheless able to choose right over wrong and good over evil. We can take responsibility, and this makes society better.

As sons and daughters of Adam and Eve, we're all in sin's grip. This is why no one person or group is to be trusted with government. From the Middle Ages on, nearly all Western governments have had a system of checks and balances in place to mitigate the effects of corruption. The US Constitution manifests this through a system of separating powers, actually *encouraging* each branch of government to jealously guard its own boundaries and keep a watchful, even distrustful, eye on the other branches so they don't exceed their authority.

Government is biblical. It is rooted in God's nature as creator, upholder of justice, and giver of law. In turn, we're able to govern because we bear God's image equally and are able to discern what is just and lawful. God cares about government. He cares about politics. So should we.

4. What Should Christians Do?

It's one thing to know that God cares about politics and that we should care too, since we're made in his image. It's another thing entirely to know what Christian involvement ought to look like. Some think Christians ought to take over government to make everyone comply with God's law. Within this view, some advocate confiscating wealth (because God cares about the poor). Others suggest slashing government's size (because God cares about freedom and stewardship). Sandwiched between self-righteousness and political opportunism are thick layers of questionable Bible interpretation. Political parties love this. Take a few Bible verses out of context, and voilà, voters flock to your "righteous" candidate or viewpoint.

> When it comes to involvement in politics, Christians should be wise and morally centered rather than gullible.

Christians should be wise and morally centered rather than gullible. But power is alluring. How can we avoid being seduced by it? First, we must be clear about what forms us, our culture or our community, and courageously stand for truth. Second, we must identify the proper boundaries of society's spheres and protect the proper domain of each. Third, we must be good citizens. And fourth, in all things, we must be prepared to obey God rather than people. Let's examine each in turn.

Be Clear about What Forms Us: The Principle of Subsidiarity

What shapes us more: the culture or our communities? It's an important question. People in our own communities know more about the problems we face than people working in offices in far-off capital cities. Many fail to consider that our greatest influence might not be in grabbing the reins of power at the highest level but in mobilizing people to seek solutions at the lowest levels. This is called subsidiarity, and it goes back to medieval theologian and philosopher Thomas Aquinas.[68] Subsidiarity claims that it's wrong for a "larger or higher association" to step in and try to fix a problem when an institution closer to the issue can act.[69] So, for example, when a young family finds itself in trouble, it's inappropriate—even unjust—for the state or federal government to provide aid when extended family members, a local church, or neighbors can help the family in need.

> Subsidiarity claims that it's wrong for a "larger or higher association" to step in and try to fix a problem when an institution closer to the issue can act.

Economist Samuel Gregg thinks subsidiarity is consistent with biblical thought and suggests five biblical values to apply in our world today:[70]

1. **Wealth creation over wealth redistribution.** History shows that people benefit when they can work to improve their lots themselves. We're made to be producers, not merely consumers. It's not okay to force other people to hand over what they've worked to earn. And it doesn't suddenly become right if we can persuade the government to do it for us.

2. **Accountability and transparency: Truth over falsehood.** In a true market economy, people are held accountable for poor economic decisions by the outcomes of those decisions. A culture of bailouts and corporate welfare undermines this value. It's not fair to ask government to force taxpayers to make sacrifices for the risky decisions of the elites.

3. **Justice: The rule of law over the rule of people.** None of these values will amount to much if the government fails to enforce just laws. In addition to protecting the innocent and punishing wrongdoers, securing justice provides a climate of stability in which wealth creators can reap the rewards of their risk and create greater abundance.

> *Dirigisme:* an economic system in which the government exerts control over the private sector and directly manages its investments.

4. **Property rights over *dirigisme*.** Dirigisme (pronounced deer-a-GEEsm) is simply the government stepping into the private sector to directly manage wealth. Leaders who regularly threaten to diminish private-property rights create uncertainty, diminish investment, and generate a climate of fear.

5. **Hope over fear: Openness versus defensiveness.** We shouldn't be fearful of a market economy. We shouldn't have a bias against business. Productive people aren't the bad guys, and our society ought to stop portraying them as such.

These points make subsidiarity practical. They break the spell of power and emphasize servanthood instead. They direct our thinking to living wisely in community.

We must abide by a clear understanding of justice, accountability, and rights, lest we become corrupted by seeking the power we think we need to do good. Power is enticing. The more we have, the more successful we think we are. Power makes us feel important. It offers the illusion of earthly security. As the Colson Center's John Stonestreet warns, "It is nearly impossible not to confuse power with success." Complicating the problem is the practice of political parties viewing Christians as an interest group whose loyalty may be bought. People who advocate government intervention, for instance, appeal to Christians' concern for the downtrodden to justify power-expanding government programs. People who worship money, on the other hand, may appeal to Christians' appreciation of hard work to justify policies that help large corporations secure an unfair advantage.

Charles Colson is an example of a believer who transcended political partisanship. First known as a Republican firebrand who proudly proclaimed his ruthlessness in achieving the Nixon administration's goals, Colson later served a term in prison and became a born-again Christian. Based on his prison experience, Colson emerged as what journalist David Plotz called "the nation's greatest prison reformer" who started Bible studies to transform prisoners.[71] *New York Times* columnist Ross Douthat says, "Colson's prison work served as a kind of countersign—a public reminder that his belief in the gospel of Jesus Christ shaped his public commitments rather than the other way around."[72]

Another example of a believer who seems to be transcending political partisanship is Princeton professor Robert George. George is a committed conservative. An article in the Catholic magazine *Crisis* a few years ago stated that "if there really is a vast right-wing conspiracy, its leaders probably meet in George's kitchen."[73] But George's scholarly work has earned such respect that he now occupies a prestigious academic position Woodrow Wilson once held. And yet George doesn't hesitate to admonish leaders to stand for what is right. For example, he urged Republican president George W. Bush to restrict embryonic stem-cell research and challenged Democratic president Barack Obama to actively protect religious freedom.

Christians may be partial to one political party or another for various reasons. This is fine in and of itself. But if Christians find themselves overly fascinated by power, it's time to go back to the basics and seek to be informed by what God says rather than what the popular culture says.

> *Sphere Sovereignty:* the belief formulated by Abraham Kuyper asserting that God ordained certain spheres of society, such as family, church, and state, and that society functions best when each sphere is properly managing its own area of responsibility.

Help Protect the Spheres

As God's image bearers, we're caretakers of our families, the church, and the government. But how do we manage the boundaries between these three spheres?[74] In the late 1800s and early 1900s, Dutch theologian and statesman Abraham Kuyper, who for a time was the prime minister of the Netherlands, called for a view of **sphere sovereignty**, in which each sphere has a proper domain, balancing each other and managing its own areas of responsibility.[75]

When one sphere abandons its responsibility or steps into another sphere, it can cause oppression and misery. Imagine three balloons in a box just big enough to fit them all. If one balloon is blown up bigger, the other two get squeezed. Sphere sovereignty says the balance between the institutions in society is like that. If the church sphere gets too big, as often happened in the Middle Ages, families and the government will get squeezed. If the family sphere gets too big—as happened in Italy in the 1400s, when a handful of powerful families, such as the Medici family, controlled everything—the church and the government will find it difficult to operate properly. Today the rapid expansion of government can hurt families and churches. But what is the proper boundary of each sphere? Let's have a look.

Family. The family sphere is responsible for forming stable marriages and providing for and educating children. Other worldviews focus on logic, economic structures, spoken language, higher consciousness, or sharia law, but Christianity says the family is the glue of society. A society can survive the miseries of corruption, violence, and crime, but if the family falls apart, societal collapse is inevitable.[76]

From a Christian worldview, God ordained the family (Gen. 2:23–25).[77] It was the first social institution. Man-woman marriage is at its core. Scripture teaches in Ephesians 5:25 that husbands should love their wives just "as Christ loved the church." This radically departs from the ways of ancient Greece and Rome, in which sexual perversion, especially homosexual pedophilia, was common. Christianity taught that sexuality was meant to be experienced only within marriage, to bond a man and woman together and to produce children. Only in Christianity, said Will Durant, did sexual fidelity become a virtue.[78]

> A society can survive the miseries of corruption, violence, and crime, but if the family falls apart, societal collapse is inevitable.

But families today are unraveling at an alarming rate. Fatherlessness has reached epidemic proportions. Young men and women between the ages of seventeen and twenty-four are far more likely to abuse drugs or commit crimes if they come from fatherless homes. Legalized abortion has led to a devaluing of children, and child-abuse rates have risen in tandem with abortion rates. Being raised by parents who have been involved in same-sex relationships is correlated with several negative social outcomes, including crime, substance abuse, and forced sexual encounters.[79]

According to the biblical view, the correction for these ills is a disciplined commitment to marriage between one man and one woman, for life.[80] This, not bigotry, explains why Christians call for a return to traditional marriage and traditional values, such as love, fidelity, and respect.

Church. The church sphere is responsible for interpreting God's Word and discipling people to obey it in every area in which Jesus Christ has authority, which is every area of life (Matt. 28:18–20).[81] The Greek word for "church" used in the New Testament is *ekklēsia*, a community united by God's Spirit and charged with proclaiming the reality of Christ's kingdom to the whole world. The church was a new, unfamiliar idea in New Testament times, and Scripture writers employed many metaphors to describe it, such as bride, army, nation, body, family, team, temple, flock, feast, and hospital. The church is the very model of what the good life is about.

Churches are to proclaim the truth regarding sin, repentance, and salvation, but the church sphere involves much more. Churches invite individuals into communities to work together to nurture one another and serve the larger society. The church can model true community by demonstrating what it means to "love your neighbor as yourself."[82] Theologian and social thinker Francis Schaeffer thought the twin roles of proclaiming truth and fostering community were the basis of the church's credibility: "I am convinced that in the twentieth century people all over the world will not listen if we have the right doctrine, the right polity, but are not exhibiting community."[83]

> The church can model true community by demonstrating what it means to "love your neighbor as yourself."

The church isn't merely a place to listen to sermons. It's where God's people gather to learn how to minister to the world (Eph. 4:14–15).[84] As pastor Tony Evans puts it, "To be a part of the church of Jesus Christ, as Jesus defined it, is to be a part of a spiritual legislative body tasked to enact heaven's viewpoint in hell's society."[85]

Government. The government sphere has two God-ordained tasks: protect the innocent and punish the guilty (Rom. 13:3–4).[86] By administering justice and defending against attack, governments play a key role in society. In an age of ever-expanding government, it is up to the family sphere and church sphere to keep watch on government so it doesn't overstep its bounds or fail to fulfill its responsibilities.

In most nations with a functioning government, a written constitution restricts government's activity. As society becomes more secularized, though, the demand for larger government pushes against these boundaries. When we say things like, "Government ought to take care of this," or "There ought to be a law about this," we risk idolizing government. Recognizing the sovereignty of each sphere helps us avoid this. It helps keep government from becoming alluring as a means by which to gain power and prestige and puts power in the hands of people who truly want to serve rather than be served.

Still, in spite of the best efforts of good people, government often fails. But this shouldn't cause us to be pessimistic. Government helps secure freedom and enable responsibility, which enables us to better bear God's image with dignity and significance. This, in turn, empowers us to get involved and make sure government does its job in protecting the innocent and maintaining justice.

Because of the human sin nature, though, it's wise to keep government's powers in perspective. Government isn't God. It secures rights but doesn't invent them. It acknowledges human value but doesn't grant it. Government may not be the source of most of our problems, but it often makes them worse when it tries to solve them, as we'll see in the chapter on poverty.

> Government may not be the source of most of our problems, but it often makes them worse when it tries to solve them.

Here's an example of how a proper balance between the spheres can help everyone live better lives. Imagine a city finding it has a high number of children whose parents have abandoned them. Would it be wise for government to take matters into its own hands and house the children in city-run orphanages, compelling taxpayers to fund the effort? Well, the government *is* supposed to protect the innocent, but taking on the responsibility that families are to bear and that the church can greatly help with risks harming children rather than helping them. Also, the government isn't equipped, like the family or the church, to offer the kind of precise solutions required when dealing with individual lives.

If, on the other hand, the city government asks churches for help, churches can recruit and support families willing to take in foster children. The government can exercise its proper role as a clearinghouse for identifying children in need of help. Families, in turn, can give unwanted children a loving environment in which to grow and flourish.

When faced with a decision about which sphere ought to act and in what ways, we need to grapple with three questions:

1. Is this the proper domain of this sphere?

2. What is the effect on the other spheres?

3. How can this problem be solved in a way that strengthens each sphere?

God cares about the spheres of family, church, and state. Indeed, he cares about everything. As Abraham Kuyper expressed it, "There is not one square inch of the entire creation about which Jesus Christ does not cry out, 'This is mine! This belongs to me!'"[87]

Ensuring a proper balance between the spheres isn't just something family, church, and government leaders are to do. It's our individual responsibility as well. Both individuals and societal groups are accountable to God (2 Kings 17:7–23; Acts 17:31).[88] The role of people in ensuring the proper functioning of society is called *citizenship*. What it involves is what we'll explore next.

> Ensuring a proper balance between the spheres isn't just something family, church, and government leaders are to do. It's our individual responsibility as well.

Be Good Citizens

In an earlier chapter, I quoted theologian A. W. Tozer, who noted that what you think about when you think about God is the most important thing about you. It's true for nations as well as people, he says: "The history of mankind will probably show that no people has ever risen above its religion, and man's spiritual history will positively demonstrate that no religion has ever been greater than its idea of God."[89]

If people have a big view of God, society thrives. If they have a small view of God, society withers. This doesn't mean Christians should step in and take over government. Rather, it means we should be good citizens in balancing family, church, and state. We can do this by being interested, being involved, and being informed.

Be interested. As servant leaders, Christians are to take others into account and think about others' needs, not just their own. At a basic level, this means taking care that the pursuit of our interests doesn't injure other people. Take, for example, the Mosaic command in Exodus 21:33–34:

> When a man opens a pit, or when a man digs a pit and does not cover it, and an ox or a donkey falls into it, the owner of the pit shall make restoration. He shall give money to its owner, and the dead beast shall be his.

Tort law: the area of law governing remedies for those wronged by others, such as through negligence.

Such laws about neighborliness evolved into what we call **tort law**: we're obligated to act in a way that won't harm our neighbors' interests.[90]

Just as we must avoid negligently harming others, we must also take an interest in helping others flourish. Are our communities flourishing because we're there? Are we and those around us reflecting the image of God? Are the people in our realm of influence becoming more mature?

Expressing interest also means voting. For many years I taught political communication at a Christian college in which students complained incessantly about their elected officials. Yet the day after the election, I discovered that only two of my students had voted. Most weren't even *registered* to vote! I told them, "For the rest of the semester, if you didn't vote, you have lost your right to complain." For probably a decade after that, one student called me every election season to let me know she voted. Let's face it: voting is the most basic act a citizen can take. In a government where the authority rests with the people, failing to vote is disobeying the biblical command to submit to "the governing authorities" (Rom. 13:1).[91]

Be involved. Get to know your elected officials and their office staff personally. Find ways to help them in areas of agreement. Not only will this promote the common good, but it will give you credibility in persuading them in areas where you disagree. Political figures are real people struggling with real issues. The people who work in their offices aren't just faceless, nameless bureaucrats. They are real people who have families, hopes, dreams, and frustrations. Get to know them. Express concern for them. Be the kind of person they want to take seriously when they get a telephone call from you about a pressing issue.

Being involved in politics at a grassroots level is easier than it sounds. Every elected

Political figures are real people struggling with real issues. Get to know them. Express concern for them.

official has a website with an email address and telephone number. Just Google it. Find out when they're having an open meeting and go. Make it a point to introduce yourself to the elected official and his or her staff members and key supporters. Perhaps volunteer for that person's campaign or offer to help in the office. Study the job responsibilities this official has been given by law—they'll be posted on their website and perhaps on city, county, state, and federal government websites as well. Making a difference doesn't begin with a dreamy, feel-good state. It begins with showing up. It ends with showing up. Those who show up will make a difference. Those who don't, won't.

Be informed. At Summit Ministries one of our themes is "If you want to be a leader, you've got to be a reader." You can't truly understand political issues merely by reading Internet snippets and watching obnoxious sound-bite debates. If you want to do everything you can to exercise your rights and privileges as a citizen, you've got to develop a clear and purposeful reading strategy. Read Christian publications like *World* magazine, a local newspaper, and at least one substantial book a month.

But don't just passively absorb information. Read legislative bills. Follow the blogs of people who are putting in the time to study issues. Examine founding documents, such as the Federalist papers and anti-Federalist papers, as well as classic political texts by authors like John Locke and Samuel Rutherford. When political candidates speak, show up. In my personal experience, this takes no more than four or five hours a month. Could you devote an hour a week to making your community, state, and nation a better place? If you don't act to secure God-given rights, why would anyone take you seriously when those rights are in jeopardy?

Obey God Rather Than People

We opened this chapter with an example from Dietrich Bonhoeffer, who, out of concern over Hitler's evil activities, chose the course of **civil disobedience**. It seems like a fairly straightforward choice given the difficulties of the times, but controversy rages about it to this day. Are Christians ever justified in breaking laws they're convinced are unjust?

> *Civil Disobedience:* the practice of resisting a government's unjust laws.

If we can't discern God's law, it's almost impossible to object when human laws contradict it. In his letter from the Birmingham jail, Martin Luther King Jr. wrote,

> I would agree with St. Augustine that "an unjust law is no law at all." Now, what is the difference between the two? How does one determine whether a law is just or unjust? A just law is a man-made code that squares with the moral law or the law of God. An unjust law is a code that is out of harmony with the moral law.[92]

If it's true that all just human laws are based on God's law, then when human laws come into conflict with God's laws, we must choose to obey God. We must say, as Peter and the other apostles did in Acts 5:29, "We must obey God rather than men."

Often the issue is more complex than a simple choice between obeying God's law and obeying human law. Sometimes it involves *ignoring* human laws that don't please God. This was the conclusion Andrew van der Bijl reached. Van der Bijl became famous as Brother Andrew for smuggling Bibles into communist countries against the will of those country's leaders. His moment of decision came as he watched a socialist parade in one of the countries he was hoping to influence:

> If it's true that all just human laws are based on God's law, then when human laws come into conflict with God's laws, we must choose to obey God.

Not for a moment did I believe [the young socialists] were there under coercion. They marched because they believed. They marched eight abreast: healthy, vital, clean-cut. They marched singing, and their voices were like shouts. On and on they came for ten minutes, fifteen minutes, rank after rank of young men and young women. The effect was overwhelming. These were the evangelists of the twentieth century. These were the people who went about shouting their good news. And part of the news was that the old shackles and superstitions of religion, the old inhibiting ideas about God, no longer held. Man was his own master: The future was his to take.[93]

What should be done? wondered Van der Bijl. Should anti-God forces be allowed to win by default? In his personal Bible study, he came across this passage from Revelation 3:2: "Awake, and strengthen what remains and is on the point of death" (RSV).[94] Van der Bijl realized he was responsible not for overthrowing governments but for strengthening the hand of those who were committed to obeying God first and foremost. Thus began a smuggling operation that brought Bibles into countries that were openly promoting atheism and trying to destroy Christianity's influence.

But how is Bible smuggling any different from evading arrest or refusing to pay taxes? It certainly appears rebellious. Aren't Christians supposed to "be subject to the governing authorities" (Rom. 13:1)[95] and live at peace with everyone (12:18)?[96] Van der Bijl said those who oppose God's law are enemies. We're to love them (Matt. 5:44),[97] but we're not to let them win. We're not to be conquered by evil (Rom. 12:21).[98]

Van der Bijl used the following example: Imagine you're a soldier reporting to your commanding officer that you can't capture the position you've been ordered to take because the enemy won't let you. This is unacceptable. It is your *duty* to capture the position *in spite of* opposition. "Yet," said Van der Bijl, "a lot of Christian soldiers seem to be saying to their Commander, 'We can't advance because the enemy disapproves of our objectives and is not willing to let us succeed.'"[99]

> In the end, we may have to choose between obeying God and obeying people, and we must be prepared to make that choice regardless of the possibility of punishment.

In future chapters, we'll look at difficult questions regarding justice, the use of force, and defending religious freedom and try to gain insight into how to wisely obey God even when it means disobeying people. This isn't a light decision. We need the counsel of wise people in the church, the *ekklēsia*. We need to be certain there is no recourse available through existing laws. But in the end, we may have to choose between obeying God and obeying people, and we must be prepared to make that choice regardless of the possibility of punishment.

5. CONCLUSION

As God's image bearers, we each take responsibility before God to discern his will through natural law and revelation and then take action to ensure that government does its job to protect the innocent and establish justice. This is what politics is all about. The family, in educating and nurturing the rising generation, is involved in politics. The church, in discipling all people to obey God, is involved in politics too.

The alternative to being interested, involved, and informed is unthinkable. President Abraham Lincoln once mused about how we are our own worst enemy:

> At what point then is the approach of danger to be expected? I answer, If it ever reach us it must spring up amongst us; it cannot come from abroad. If destruction be our lot we must ourselves be its author and finisher. As a nation of freemen we must live through all time or die by suicide.[100]

We are image bearers of God. We are citizens. Politics is our opportunity and also our responsibility.

ENDNOTES

1. Eric Metaxas, *Bonhoeffer: Pastor, Martyr, Prophet, Spy* (Nashville: Thomas Nelson, 2010), 144.

2. Metaxas, *Bonhoeffer*.

3. Dietrich Bonhoeffer, *No Rusty Swords: Letters, Lectures and Notes 1928–1936; From the Collected Works of Dietrich Bonhoeffer*, ed. Edwin H. Robertson, trans. Edwin H. Robertson and John Bowden (New York: Harper and Row, 1965), 1:202.

4. Dietrich Bonhoeffer, to Reinhold Niebuhr, July 1939, quoted in Metaxas, *Bonhoeffer*, 321.

5. Metaxas, *Bonhoeffer*, 361–71.

6. Gallup telephone survey, June 2–7, 2015, cited in Lydia Saad, "Confidence in Religion at New Low, but Not among Catholics," Gallup, June 17, 2015, www.gallup.com/poll/183674/confidence-religion-new-low-not-among-catholics.aspx.

7. See Jeff Myers, "The Fix Is in on Traditional Marriage," *Summit Journal* 15, no. 4 (May 2015): 2–3, www.summit.org/media/journal/2015-5_Summit_Journal_Full_1.pdf.

8. Metaxas, *Bonhoeffer*, 153.

9. M. Tullii Ciceronis, *Orationes*, eds. George Long and A. J. Macleane (London: Whittaker, 1855), 2:353.

10. Edmund Burke, "Letter to François-Louis-Thibault de Menonville," 1791, published as "Letter to a Member of the National Assembly," in Edmund Burke, *Reflections on the Revolution in France*, ed. L. G. Mitchell (Oxford, UK: Oxford University Press, 1999), 289.

11. Paul Kurtz, *Humanist Manifestos I and II* (Amherst, NY: Prometheus Books, 1973), 4.

12. Hunter Baker, *The End of Secularism* (Wheaton, IL: Crossway Books, 2009), 25.

13. See Jeff Myers and David A. Noebel, *Understanding the Times: A Survey of Competing Worldviews* (Colorado Springs, CO: David C Cook, 2015), chap. 14.

14. John W. Whitehead, *The Second American Revolution* (Westchester, IL: Crossway Books, 1982), 21.

15. Mark Reader, "Humanism and Politics," *Humanist* (November/December 1975): 38.

16. Morris B. Storer, ed., *Humanist Ethics: Dialogue on Basics* (Buffalo: Prometheus Books, 1980), 130.

17. Thomas Jefferson, "Inaugural Address," March 4, 1801, in Gerhard Peters and John T. Woolley, American Presidency Project, www.presidency.ucsb.edu/ws/index.php?pid=25803.

18. See Georgi Shakhnazarov, *The Coming World Order* (Moscow, USSR: Progress Publishers, 1984), 9.

19. Paul Kurtz, *Humanist Manifesto 2000: A Call for a New Planetary Humanism* (Amherst, NY: Prometheus Books, 2000), 57.

20. Julian Huxley, *The Humanist Frame* (London: Allen and Unwin, 1961), 16. Julian Huxley served as the first director general of the United Nations Educational, Scientific, and Cultural Organization (UNESCO).

21. Paul Kurtz, *Forbidden Fruit: The Ethics of Secularism* (Amherst, NY: Prometheus Books, 2008), 192.

22. Timothy J. Madigan, "Humanism and the Need for a Global Consciousness," *Humanist* (March/April 1986): 17–18.

23. Review of Francis Fukuyama's book *Political Order and Political Decay*, Christopher Caldwell, "Twilight of Democracy," *Claremont Review of Books* 14, no. 4 (Fall 2014): 38, www.claremont.org/download_pdf.php?file_name=9904Caldwell.pdf.

24. This quotation is popularly attributed to James Madison, but Alexander Hamilton may have been the author of the essay in which it appears. See James Madison, "Federalist No. 51: The Structure of the Government Must Furnish the Proper Checks and Balances between the Different Departments," *The Federalist Papers*, New York Packet, February 8, 1788, www.congress.gov/resources/display/content/The+Federalist+Papers#TheFederalistPapers-51.

25. V. I. Lenin said, "Only in Communist society, when the resistance of the capitalists has been completely broken, when the capitalists have disappeared, when there are no classes … only then 'the state ceases to exist.'" V. I. Lenin, *State and Revolution* (New York: International Publishers, 1932), 73.

26. Shakhnazarov, *Coming World Order*, 18.

27. Clemens Dutt, ed., *Fundamentals of Marxism-Leninism* (Moscow, USSR: Progress Publishers, 1959), 310.

28. Karl Marx, *The Class Struggles in France (1848–1850)*, ed. Clemens P. Dutt (London: Martin Lawrence, 1895), 126.

29. Howard Selsam, *Socialism and Ethics* (New York: International Publishers, 1943), 13.

30. E. B. Pashukanis, in *Soviet Legal Philosophy* (Boston: Harvard University Press, 1951), 279.

31. V. I. Lenin, "*O Lozunge Razoruzheniia*," October 1916, quoted in Elliot R. Goodman, *The Soviet Design for a World State* (New York: Columbia University Press, 1968), 287.

32. T. M. Jaroszewski and P. A. Ignatovskii, *Socialism as a Social System* (Moscow, USSR: Progress Publishers, 1981), 185.

33. Joseph Stalin, "*Beseda S Pervoi Amerikanskoi Rabochei Delegatsiei*," September 9, 1927, quoted in Goodman, *Soviet Design for a World State*, 191.

34. R. J. Rummel demonstrated that more human beings in the twentieth century died at the hands of their governments, committed to Marxist or fascist ideology, than in all previous centuries combined. See R. J. Rummel, *Death by Government* (New Brunswick, NJ: Transaction Publishers, 1994).

35. Richard Rorty and Gianni Vattimo, *The Future of Religion*, ed. Santiago Zabala (New York: Columbia University Press, 2005), 33.

36. Denis Diderot, quoted in Ronald Hamowy, ed., *The Encyclopedia of Libertarianism* (Thousand Oaks, CA: Sage, 2008), 125.

37. Robert M. Oates, *Permanent Peace: How to Stop Terrorism and War—Now and Forever* (Fairfield, IA: Institute of Science, Technology, and Public Policy, 2002), 108.

38. Maharishi Mahesh Yogi, quoted in Oates, *Permanent Peace*, 199.

39. John Hagelin makes these claims, and many others, in *Manual for a Perfect Government* (Fairfield, IA: Maharishi University of Management, 1998).

40. Eckhart Tolle, *A New Earth: Awakening to Your Life's Purpose* (New York: Plume, 2005), 13.

41. Philip Goldberg, *American Veda: From Emerson and the Beatles to Yoga and Meditation; How Indian Spirituality Changed the West* (New York: Harmony, 2010).

42. See Peter Jones, *One or Two: Seeing a World of Difference* (Escondido, CA: Main Entry Editions, 2010).

43. Lord Acton, letter to Bishop Creighton, April 5, 1887. See John Bartlett, *Bartlett's Familiar Quotations*, 18th ed. (Boston: Little, Brown, 2012), 518. Lord Acton's English name was Sir John Dalberg-Acton (John Emerich Edward Dalberg-Acton, 1st Baron Acton, KCVO, DL). He was not only the deputy lieutenant to the queen (DL) but also a knight of the Royal Victorian Order (KCVO).

44. Genesis 9:5–6: "For your lifeblood I will require a reckoning: from every beast I will require it and from man. From his fellow man I will require a reckoning for the life of man. 'Whoever sheds the blood of man, by man shall his blood be shed, for God made man in his own image.'"

45. Genesis 2:15: "The LORD God took the man and put him in the garden of Eden to work it and keep it."

46. Ephesians 2:8–9: "By grace you have been saved through faith. And this is not your own doing; it is the gift of God, not a result of works, so that no one may boast." For further study, see Romans 5–8 and Galatians 2:11–3:25.

47. See Jonathan Burnside, *God, Justice, and Society: Aspects of Law and Legality in the Bible* (New York: Oxford University Press, 2011).

48. C. S. Lewis, *God in the Dock* (Grand Rapids: Eerdmans, 1970), 110.

49. S. D. Gaede, *Where Gods May Dwell: Understanding the Human Condition* (Grand Rapids: Zondervan, 1985), 75–76.

50. For more information, see "What If Jesus Had Never Been Born?," *Summit Journal* 11, no. 12 (December 2011), www.summit.org/media/journal/2011-12-Summit-Journal.pdf.

51. Matthew 20:16: "The last will be first, and the first last"; Mark 10:43: "It shall not be so among you. But whoever would be great among you must be your servant"; Luke 22:27: "Who is the greater, one who reclines at table or one who serves? Is it not the one who reclines at table? But I am among you as the one who serves."

52. Rodney Stark, *For the Glory of God* (Princeton, NJ: Princeton University Press, 2003), 291. All Christians should carefully study the entirety of chapter 4, "God's Justice: The Sin of Slavery."

53. Whitehead, *Second American Revolution*, 89.

54. See Nicholas Wolterstorff, "Why Eudaimonism Cannot Serve as a Framework for a Theory of Rights," chap. 7 in *Justice: Rights and Wrongs* (Princeton, NJ: Princeton University Press, 2008).

55. Marshall Davis Ewell, ed., *Essentials of the Law*, vol. 1, *A Review of Blackstone's Commentaries with Explanatory Notes for the Use of Students at Law*, 2nd ed. (Albany, NY: Matthew Bender, 1915), 3.

56. Whitehead, *Second American Revolution*, 73.

57. Carl F. H. Henry, *Twilight of a Great Civilization: The Drift toward Neo-Paganism* (Westchester, IL: Crossway Books, 1988), 147.

58. Dietrich Bonhoeffer, *Ethics* (New York: Simon and Schuster, 1995), 204.

59. Matthew 28:18–20: "Jesus came and said to [his disciples], 'All authority in heaven and on earth has been given to me. Go therefore and make disciples of all nations, baptizing them in the name of the Father and of the Son and of the Holy Spirit, teaching them to observe all that I have commanded you. And behold, I am with you always, to the end of the age.'"

60. Bonhoeffer, *Ethics*, 204.

61. Whitehead, *Second American Revolution*, 76.

62. Lester J. Cappon, ed., *The Adams-Jefferson Letters: The Complete Correspondence between Thomas Jefferson and Abigail and John Adams* (Chapel Hill, NC: University of North Carolina Press, 1987), 339–40.

63. John Witherspoon, quoted in Buckner F. Melton Jr., ed., *The Quotable Founding Fathers: A Treasury of 2,500 Wise and Witty Quotations from the Men and Women Who Created America* (Washington, DC: Brassey's, 2004), 249.

64. Noah Webster, "Advice to the Young," in *History of the United States* (New Haven: Durrie and Peck, 1832), 339.

65. George Washington, "Inaugural Address," April 30, 1789, in Gerhard Peters and John T. Woolley, American Presidency Project, www.presidency.ucsb.edu/ws/index.php?pid=25800.

66. Alexis de Tocqueville, *Democracy in America* (New York: Vintage Books, 1990), 303–4.

67. William A. Stanmeyer, *Clear and Present Danger: Church and State in Post-Christian America* (Ann Arbor: Servant Books, 1983), 42.

68. For more information on subsidiarity, read "Do You Know Why Economics Is a Moral Issue?," *Summit Announcements* (blog), August 7, 2013, www.summit.org/blogs/summit-announcements/do-you-know-why-economics-is-a-moral-issue/.

69. Jay W. Richards, *Money, Greed, and God: Why Capitalism Is the Solution and Not the Problem* (New York: HarperOne, 2009), 51.

70. Commentary and illustrations based on Samuel Gregg, "How America Can Have a Non-European Future," chap. 9 in *Becoming Europe: Economic Decline, Culture, and How America Can Avoid a European Future* (New York: Encounter Books, 2013), 280–303.

71. David Plotz, "Charles Colson: How a Watergate Crook Became America's Greatest Christian Conservative," *Slate*, March 10, 2000, www.slate.com/articles/news_and_politics/assessment/2000/03/charles_colson.html.

72. Ross Douthat, "Charles Colson, R.I.P.," *New York Times*, April 23, 2012, http://douthat.blogs.nytimes.com/2012/04/23/charles-colson-r i-p/?_r=0.

73. Anne Morse, "Conservative Heavyweight: The Remarkable Mind of Professor Robert P. George," *Crisis Magazine*, September 1, 2003, www.crisismagazine.com/2003/conservative-heavyweight-the-remarkable-mind-of-professor-robert-p-george.

74. As a historical note, some think the idea of three spheres of society originated with the Puritan theologian and Cambridge professor William Perkins. Perkins studied biblical texts and concluded, "Now all societies of men are bodies; a family is a body; so is every particular Church a body; and the commonwealth also. And in these bodies there are several members, which are men walking in several callings and offices, the execution of which must tend to the happy and good estate of the rest—indeed, the good of all men everywhere, as much as possible." See William Perkins with C. Matthew McMahon, *Glorifying God in Our Jobs* (Crossville, TN: Puritan Publications, 2015), 26–27.

75. Abraham Kuyper, *Lectures on Calvinism* (1898; New York: Cosimo Classics, 2009).

76. For a helpful essay on this subject, see Kerby Anderson, "The Decline of a Nation," Probe Ministries International, 1991, accessed March 27, 2014, www.leaderu.com/orgs/probe/docs/decline.html.

77. Genesis 2:23–25: "The man said, 'This at last is bone of my bones and flesh of my flesh; she shall be called Woman, because she was taken out of Man.' Therefore a man shall leave his father and his mother and hold fast to his wife, and they shall become one flesh. And the man and his wife were both naked and were not ashamed."

78. Will Durant, *The Story of Civilization*, vol. 3, *Caesar and Christ* (New York: Simon and Schuster, 1944), 598.

79. See, for example, Mark Regnerus, "How Different Are the Adult Children of Parents Who Have Same-Sex Relationships: Findings from the New Family Structures Study," *Social Science Research* 41, no. 4 (July 2012): 752–70, www.markregnerus.com/uploads/4/0/6/5/4065759/regnerus_july_2012_ssr.pdf.

80. Mark 10:6–9 records Jesus saying, "From the beginning of creation, 'God made them male and female.' 'Therefore a man shall leave his father and mother and hold fast to his wife, and the two shall become one flesh.' So they are no longer two but one flesh. What therefore God has joined together, let not man separate."

81. Matthew 28:18–20: "Jesus came and said to [his disciples], 'All authority in heaven and on earth has been given to me. Go therefore and make disciples of all nations, baptizing them in the name of the Father and of the Son and of the Holy Spirit, teaching them to observe all that I have commanded you. And behold, I am with you always, to the end of the age.'"

82. Matthew 22:39–40: "A second [commandment] is like [the first]: You shall love your neighbor as yourself. On these two commandments depend all the Law and the Prophets."

83. Francis A. Schaeffer, *The Church at the End of the Twentieth Century* (Wheaton, IL: Crossway, 1994), 72.

84. Ephesians 4:14–15: "[We are being built up in Christ] so that we may no longer be children, tossed to and fro by the waves and carried about by every wind of doctrine, by human cunning, by craftiness in deceitful schemes. Rather, speaking the truth in love, we are to grow up in every way into him who is the head, into Christ."

85. Tony Evans, *Oneness Embraced: Through the Eyes of Tony Evans* (Chicago: Moody, 2011), 251.

86. Romans 13:3–4: "Rulers are not a terror to good conduct, but to bad. Would you have no fear of the one who is in authority? Then do what is good, and you will receive his approval, for he is God's servant for your good. But if you do wrong, be afraid, for he does not bear the sword in vain. For he is the servant of God, an avenger who carries out God's wrath on the wrongdoer."

87. Abraham Kuyper, *Near unto God: Daily Meditations Adapted for Contemporary Christians*, ed. James C. Schaap (Grand Rapids: CRC Publications, 1997), 7.

88. Second Kings 17:7–8: "This [exile] occurred because the people of Israel had sinned against the LORD their God, who had brought them up out of the land of Egypt from under the hand of Pharaoh king of Egypt, and had feared other gods and walked in the customs of the nations whom the LORD drove out before the people of Israel, and in the customs that the kings of Israel had practiced"; Acts 17:31: "[God] has fixed a day on which he will judge the world in righteousness by a man whom he has appointed; and of this he has given assurance to all by raising him from the dead."

89. A. W. Tozer, *The Knowledge of the Holy* (New York: HarperOne, 1978), 1.

90. The nineteenth-century baron Lord Atkin said, "The rule that you are to love your neighbour becomes in law: You must not injure your neighbour, and the lawyer's question: Who is my neighbour? receives a restricted reply. You must take reasonable care to avoid acts or omissions which you can reasonably foresee would be likely to injure your neighbour. Who then, in law, is my neighbour? The answer seems to be persons who are so closely and directly affected by my act that I ought reasonably to have them in contemplation as being so affected when I am directing my mind to the acts or omissions which are called in question." James Richard Atkin, quoted in Carol Harlow, *Understanding Tort Law*, 3rd ed. (London: Sweet and Maxwell, 2005), 47–48.

91. Romans 13:1: "Let every person be subject to the governing authorities. For there is no authority except from God, and those that exist have been instituted by God."

92. Martin Luther King Jr., "Letter from a Birmingham Jail," Birmingham, Alabama, April 16, 1963, in Martin Luther King Jr., *Why We Can't Wait* (Boston: Beacon, 1986), 93.

93. Brother Andrew, with John Sherrill and Elizabeth Sherrill, *God's Smuggler* (Bloomington, MN: Chosen Books, 2015), 90–91.

94. Quoted in Brother Andrew, *God's Smuggler*, 91.

95. Romans 13:1: "Let every person be subject to the governing authorities. For there is no authority except from God, and those that exist have been instituted by God."

96. Romans 12:18: "If possible, so far as it depends on you, live peaceably with all."

97. Matthew 5:44: "I say to you, Love your enemies and pray for those who persecute you."

98. Romans 12:21: "Do not be overcome by evil, but overcome evil with good."

99. Brother Andrew, *Is Life So Dear? When Being Wrong Is Right* (Nashville: Thomas Nelson, 1985), 11.

100. Abraham Lincoln, "The Perpetuation of Our Political Institutions" (address, Young Men's Lyceum, Springfield, Illinois, January 27, 1837), quoted in Marion Mills Miller, ed., *Life and Works of Abraham Lincoln*, vol. 2, *Early Speeches: 1832–1856* (New York: Current Literature, 1907), 15.

CHAPTER 13

RELIGIOUS FREEDOM AND PERSECUTION

1. RELIGIOUS FREEDOM IS UNDER ATTACK

In Iran, converting to Christianity is a potentially deadly decision. It was especially so for Saeed Abedini because he wanted to tell people about it. Wherever he went, he talked about Jesus. Iranian authorities were so angry that even after

Saeed married and moved to America to raise a family, they didn't forget. They banned him from publicly evangelizing in Iran.

For Saeed, life in America was safe. Too easy, even. He remembered the faces of the young Iranians so eager to hear about Christ. They were fed up with Islamic radicalism. They hungered for truth.

While Saeed was forbidden from publicly evangelizing, authorities there did agree to let him start an orphanage. Leaving Idaho in the summer of 2012, Saeed flew back to Iran. At home with their two young children, Saeed's wife, Naghmeh, anticipated his phone call in the following weeks sharing what God had been doing. Instead, in September she received horrifying news: in spite of the Iranian government's promise, Saeed was placed under house arrest. Subsequently, he was sentenced to eight years in one of Iran's most notorious prisons for sharing his Christian faith. Saeed suffered immensely in prison. He was tortured and denied medical treatment because the doctors and nurses considered him an unclean "infidel." Other prisoners began asking about his devotion to Christ, and some of them even had dreams in which Jesus appeared. Even though prison officials beat Saeed for sharing his faith, he continued to do so, and many people, from fellow prisoners to hospital workers, came to Christ.

While explaining why the Iranians were reluctant to release Saeed, a US government official told Naghmeh, "He's making it hard! He just keeps sharing Christ wherever. And the Iranian government is just pretty frustrated about that."

Naghmeh replied, "Well, he's not doing it out of defiance[;] he's doing it out of his passion for Christ." She then shared with the government official how Jesus Christ had changed Saeed's life and told the official that "the Iranian government could always kick him out of the country!"[1]

After three years of wrangling and an unbearably high cost to his family, Saeed Abedini was finally released from prison in January of 2016. Unfortunately, Saeed's case isn't unique. The respected Pew Forum on Religion and Public Life says that more than 70 percent of the world's population lives under regimes that severely restrict religious freedom.[2] And in countries around the world, Christians suffer government harassment more than any other religious group.[3]

Sadly, attacks on religious freedom are accelerating even in Western countries, including the United States. Over the past decade, US federal and state government actions have established a dangerous trend of intentionally restricting religious freedom. Christian groups on college campuses have been forced to either accept people as leaders who may not support the group's Christian mission or leave campus. Pharmacists who object to pills that lead to chemical abortions have been forced to stock them anyway. Religious foster-care programs that object to placing children with same-sex couples or unmarried opposite-sex couples have had their charities' licenses and contracts revoked. Business owners, such as bakers, florists, and wedding photographers, have been sued, fined, and even driven out of business for declining to provide services to same-sex marriage ceremonies because this would violate their Christian beliefs (the business owners in question all provided services

> More than 70 percent of the world's population lives under regimes that severely restrict religious freedom.

to same-sex attracted people as individuals, without discrimination, but saw the support of same-sex weddings as a separate issue and a violation of their consciences). New York City has banned religious groups from renting public-school auditoriums. Anti-religious groups are taking down crosses erected as memorials to the war dead in places like Camp Pendleton in Southern California. The US Air Force has stopped providing Bibles at its lodging facilities, has removed the word *God* from its logos, and has withdrawn its support of the Operation Christmas Child charity at the Air Force Academy.

While these attacks on religious expression haven't yet led to physical violence or overt persecution, they point to a potentially dangerous—and growing—intolerance of religion. Sociologists Brian Grim and Roger Finke have demonstrated a direct link between governmental and social restrictions on religion and religious persecution and conflict.[4] When governments restrict religion, anti-religious groups become bolder at opposing and even attacking those with whom they disagree.

Leaders who ignore the issue of religious liberty are playing with fire. They are unraveling a basic freedom that has led to unprecedented liberty and prosperity around the world.

While a lot of Christians are concerned about fellow believers being harassed and tortured and killed for their faith, most don't see how they can make a difference. As conflicts accelerate, Christians need to understand the problem and act on behalf of our suffering brothers and sisters around the world, as well as prepare to defend freedom in our own nation.

As we'll see in this chapter, religious freedom is the first domino. If it falls, so will other freedoms. It is imperative to grasp what religious freedom is, what constitutes the scourge of persecution, and what Christians can do to make a difference.

2. Defining the Problem

What Is Religious Freedom?

Religious freedom is "the right of all human beings to think as they please, believe or not believe as their conscience leads, and live out their beliefs openly, peacefully, and without fear."[5]

Article 18 of the 1948 Universal Declaration of Human Rights says, "Everyone has the right to freedom of thought, conscience and religion; this right includes freedom to change his religion or belief, and freedom, either alone or in community with others and in public or private, to manifest his religion or belief in teaching, practice, worship and observance."[6]

> *Religious Freedom:* the universal right of human beings to think, live, and worship as they feel convicted by their religious beliefs, without fear of persecution.

To live in dignity, people must be able to follow the leading of their consciences. If we're coerced into saying we believe something we don't, our integrity is violated because we're being forced to lie. If we're compelled to refrain from acting on what we do believe, we can't live authentically. In either case, truth, honesty, trust, creativity, and thought all suffer. Rights that protect the body but not the mind fail to account for what it means to be human.[7] We must be free in our minds in order to be truly free. In this sense, the right to religious freedom is the most basic right of all.

Of course, governments may restrict rights when it's necessary to protect public safety, order, and health. To use the classic example from Oliver Wendell Holmes Jr., having the freedom of speech doesn't mean you have the right to falsely shout "Fire!" in a crowded theater, because such a lie can hurt people as they try to escape. Similarly, you don't have a right to exercise the freedom of religion in a way that restricts the religious freedom of others, for example, by bringing blasphemy charges against someone whose view of God differs from your own.

Restriction of religious freedom leads to persecution. According to the US International Religious Freedom Act of 1998 (IRFA), religious persecution occurs when a nation arbitrarily prohibits, restricts, or punishes people for

- "assembling for peaceful activities such as worship, preaching, and prayer …;

- speaking freely about one's religious beliefs;

- changing one's religious beliefs and affiliation;

- [possessing or distributing] religious literature, including Bibles; or

- raising one's children in the religious teachings and practices of one's choice."[8]

Religious freedom requires tolerance, a word that needs to be carefully defined. Today, **tolerance** is often used to imply that everyone is right, or that no one is wrong. A better definition of *tolerance* is "respecting the dignity of all people, including those we think are wrong." If we want the freedom to practice our religion free from persecution, then we must protect those freedoms for others.

> *Tolerance:* the willingness to recognize and respect the dignity of those with whom one disagrees.

The right to religious freedom has often not been protected in history. Religious persecution has been common. And even though we've made many advances in the world, religious persecution is still growing today. We need to understand what caused persecution in the past and what is causing it today in order to know how to stand up for the oppressed and safeguard our own freedoms.

> *Religious Persecution:* the restriction or punishment of any religious group or individual due to that group's or individual's religious beliefs and practices.

What Causes Religious Persecution

Religious persecution doesn't just happen. It occurs when people are antagonistic toward one or more religious groups because they believe that people shouldn't be allowed to disagree with the dominant religion.[9] According to sociologist Rodney Stark, if lots of religious groups are accepted in a culture, religious conflicts rarely move beyond debate or name-calling. When one religion

RELIGIOUS FREEDOM AND PERSECUTION

monopolizes power and insists on obedience, though, it begins to challenge the political power of the state. That religion then begins to force itself on the nation, and as Stark puts it, "*heresy* inevitably becomes *treason*."[10]

What caused religious persecution in the past? It's happened often in history, such as with Donatism,[11] Albigensianism,[12] and the wars of religion in Europe between the early 1500s and the mid-1600s. According to historian Thomas Kidd, "In the medieval period, Europeans had simply assumed that a union between church and state, and the persecution of those who challenged it, was a natural, even God-sanctioned state of affairs."[13]

The tension between church and state, for instance, led to "inquisitions" in which church and government leaders put people on trial for heresy and punished them if they weren't judged to be sufficiently devout. There have been several inquisitions in history that involved widespread abuses, even torture. The **medieval inquisition**, for example, was established in the late twelfth century in response to the Albigensians (also called the Cathari), a group the religious authorities of the day deemed heretical. Pope Innocent III sent a representative to restore the Albigensians to the good graces of the church, but the representative was assassinated. In response, the pope raised an army and conquered the Albigensians; then he set up an inquisition to deal with the remaining heretics. This particular inquisition also caught in its net a group called the Waldensians, another Christian sect the pope deemed heretical. Eventually the medieval inquisition expanded even further, targeting the Knights Templar[14] and the Beguines, a women's lay religious group thought to be tied to heretical groups.

> *Medieval inquisition:* a series of Catholic courts formed to prosecute and punish perceived heretics in the twelfth and thirteenth centuries in France and Italy.

Today, critics of Christianity point to historical inquisitions as proof that Christians hypocritically insist on religious freedom for themselves but deny it for those with whom they disagree. It's not a Christian problem, though. It happens when any religion—including Islam, Hinduism, and Buddhism—becomes dominant enough to use the state's power to enforce religious decrees. When this occurs, what is central to that religion's teaching often becomes irrelevant, and brute government force takes over.

Ironically, when the government gets involved in religion, the church has often had to rescue people from the events it set in motion. For example, historian Thomas Madden says that one of the purposes of the inquisition was to rehabilitate those accused of heresy so they wouldn't be executed for treason. Madden notes that

> heresy was a crime against the state. Roman law in the Code of Justinian made it a capital offense.… When someone was accused of heresy in the early Middle Ages, they were brought to the local lord for judgment, just as if they had stolen a pig or damaged shrubbery (really, it was a serious crime in England). Yet in contrast to those crimes, it was not so easy to discern whether the accused was really a heretic. For starters, one needed some basic theological training—something most medieval lords sorely lacked. The result is that uncounted thousands across Europe were

executed by secular authorities without fair trials or a competent assessment of the validity of the charge.[15]

Madden also notes that mobs sometimes killed people accused of heresy. During the **Spanish Inquisition**, some of the accused were so afraid of what the government or mobs would do to them that they purposefully blasphemed so they could be transferred to the church courts, which seemed more fair and humane.[16]

> *Spanish Inquisition:*
> a series of Spanish courts formed to preserve Catholic orthodoxy against perceived heresies in the fifteenth century.

Something similar happened in the witch trials. For most of the Middle Ages, there was very little belief in witches. The witch trials only got going in the 1400s, when government authorities began identifying witchcraft with magic, magic with devil worship, devil worship with heresy, and heresy as a type of treason.[17] Some have claimed that 9 million witches were executed in witch trials between the 1400s and 1600s. The actual total is probably closer to 60,000, or between 150 and 300 a year during the time the fervor lasted. Such witch trials ended in the aftermath of the execution of 19 accused witches during the **Salem witch trials** in Massachusetts. Horrified, respected ministers Deodat Lawson, Increase Mather, and Samuel Willard joined with the governor Sir William Phips to bring the trials to an end.[18]

> *Salem Witch Trials:*
> a series of trials that led to the execution of nineteen individuals accused of witchcraft in late seventeenth-century colonial Massachusetts.

It seems, though, that the world has learned very little from history. Religious persecution not only still exists but is growing. And most of its victims are Christians.

What causes religious persecution today? When a few powerful religious organizations exist and are fighting for political power, it's usually small, nonthreatening religious groups that are hurt most.[19] This is what happened with Jews in Europe in the eleventh century, who were victims of a low tolerance for all non-Christian groups during the conflict between Christianity and Islam. Sometimes so-called Christians participated in the violence, even though it was at odds with everything their savior taught. Other Christians, though, worked to stem violence directed against Jews, for example, during the First Crusade and the Black Death.

> When a few powerful religious organizations exist and are fighting for political power, it's usually small, nonthreatening religious groups that are hurt most.

Today, Christians of all denominations are on the receiving end of religious intolerance, largely at the hands of Islamic governments and "secular religions," such as Marxism. Islam and Marxism are totalistic viewpoints, which means they see no separation between the church and the state and are thus comfortable demanding strict adherence to their religious worldviews as part of the cost of citizenship.

Either way, Christians are in the crosshairs. Michael Horowitz says that historically Jews were the "canaries in the coal mine"—if a nation persecuted Jews, it was more likely to deny freedoms to others as well. But now, Horowitz says, the canaries are Christians.[20] Let's see how this is so around the world and even in the United States.

Where Religious Persecution Takes Place in the World Today

Three-fourths of the world's population lives in countries with severe religious restrictions, according to the Pew Research Center.[21] These countries regularly persecute Christians. In places like Burma and Eritrea, which are some of the worst persecutors of Christians, the government brutally cracks down on all those they view as a threat to their power.[22] Because the allegiance of Christians to God is higher than their allegiance to the state, they often find themselves victimized. In 2015, says the watchdog group Open Doors, more than seven thousand Christians were killed for "faith-related reasons."[23]

Christians, Buddhists, and Hindu nationalists have all been persecutors. But because Christians have experienced the worst persecution in the past hundred years at the hands of Muslims and Marxists, that's where we'll focus in the following discussion.

Marxism. Marxism is based on the "dictatorship of the proletariat." Marxist dictators justify their despotism by claiming to represent the interests of the workers (the **proletariat**) against those of the property owners (the **bourgeoisie**). Whatever helps the proletariat is right; whatever helps the bourgeoisie is wrong (**proletariat morality**). Religion helps the bourgeoisie, Marxists think, in that priests convince the oppressed that their reward is in heaven to keep them from revolting against their oppressors in this life. Marxists, consequently, don't feel bad about stripping people of religious freedom.

It's been this way from Marxism's beginnings. In the former Soviet Union (USSR), Marxists aggressively sought to eliminate the influence of the church. In the days following the October Revolution of 1917, Marxists discriminated against priests and tried to wipe out religion through state controls. On April 8, 1929, for example, the USSR enacted a law forbidding religious organizations from carrying out charitable activities or meeting at any time other than for religious services. In effect, Marxist sociologists declared war against the church, a conflict that continues to the present day wherever communists are in power.[24]

> *Proletariat:* a term used in Marxist theory to describe the working-class wage earners who do not own the means of production.

> *Bourgeoisie:* a term used in Marxist theory to describe those who own the means of production.

> *Proletariat Morality:* the belief that whatever advances the proletariat and communism is morally good and that whatever hinders them is morally evil.

The 1936 Soviet Constitution affirmed that all citizens were granted certain rights "in conformity with the interests of the working people, and in order to strengthen the socialist system."[25] Citizens whose actions Marxist-Leninist leaders deemed unacceptable found themselves without any rights. Aleksandr Solzhenitsyn in *The Gulag Archipelago*[26] and Stephane

Courtois and colleagues in *The Black Book of Communism: Crimes, Terror, Repression*[27] documented the loss of rights of those deemed enemies of the state. Religious people were among the most mistreated.

In 1955, Soviet premier Nikita Khrushchev said, "Communism has not changed its attitude of opposition to religion. We are doing everything we can to eliminate the bewitching power of the opium of religion."[28] *The Atheist's Handbook* was published in conjunction with Khrushchev's campaign to eliminate religion and used "science" to attack figures like Jesus and the apostle Paul as mythical.[29]

All of this discrimination had a common source: **atheism**. From Marx's time to the present, communists everywhere have vehemently denied the existence of God. *The Great Soviet Encyclopedia*, published in Moscow in 1950, called on the Communist Party to oppose religion and "to fight for the 'full victory' of atheism."[30] The Young Communist League's "Ten Commandments" contained the declaration "If you are not a convinced atheist, you cannot be a good Communist.... Atheism is indissolubly bound to Communism."[31]

> *Atheism:* the belief that God does not exist.

Because it's based on a form of **materialism**, a belief that only the material world exists, a hatred of anything supernatural—especially of a Christian variety—comes easily to Marxists. Although the July 10, 1918, constitution of the former USSR recognized freedom of both "religious and anti-religious propaganda" as the right of every citizen,[32] the Soviet state constantly worked to suppress theistic religion. Article 4 of the 1918 constitution declared "monks and clergy of all denominations" to be among those prohibited from voting or holding government office.[33] Ultimately, they were denied ration cards, and their children were barred from attending school above the elementary grades.[34] Church after church was declared counterrevolutionary and shut down, and church buildings were turned into cinemas, radio stations, granaries, museums, and machine repair shops.[35]

> From Marx's time to the present, communists everywhere have vehemently denied the existence of God.

The 1936 Soviet Constitution also guaranteed freedom of religious worship, but Marxist attacks on religious people continued. Some Christians, attempting to conform to the law, registered with the government. In turn, they were required to collect fifty signatures of friends and neighbors who sympathized with them. When they presented the signatures, the government declared the signatories conspirators and counter-revolutionaries. Those who could be found were subsequently arrested.[36]

Similar persecution continues today in "formerly Marxist" countries that many in the West mistakenly assume have been reformed. Turkmenistan, Uzbekistan, Armenia, and Georgia all restrict religious freedom, grinding down believers and eroding the free expression of their faith.[37] Belarus, a Soviet-like state, prevents Christians from worshipping freely because it damages "traditional" Belarus.[38]

The communist governments of Vietnam and Laos also brutally oppress Christians, especially those who insist on meeting together in groups.[39] Cuba is no better. Dr. Oscar Elias Biscet, a Christian human-rights activist, was sentenced to twenty-five years in a

Cuban prison for his opposition to abortion. He spent ten years in solitary confinement, was denied access to a Bible, and was deprived of medical treatment. Pressure from the Catholic Church led to his release from prison, and he chose to stay in Cuba to continue the fight for human rights.[40] Biscet says,

> My country continues to be run by a brutal regime that oppresses the people, systematically violating our basic freedoms.... Government agents ... beat and imprison anyone seeking peaceful political change. They arbitrarily arrest and detain Cubans for Orwellian infractions like "disrespecting patriotic symbols" and "insulting symbols of the fatherland." Cuban state security closely monitors citizens' daily life, including all of our incoming mail, telephone calls and emails.[41]

Biscet says Cuba restricts the press and sends journalists to jail who cross the party line. Having spent more than twelve years in Cuban jails himself, Biscet describes them as "living hells" that flagrantly violate human dignity.[42]

For sheer evil, though, none of these regimes reaches the brutality of persecution found in the communist regime of North Korea. Respected journalist Melanie Kirkpatrick has written extensively of the plight of North Koreans, who daily face nightmarish fear and hardship. Nearly one of every hundred North Koreans is locked in a prison camp for offenses that include "disrespecting" a photo of the supreme leader. Up to a million people have died in these hellish conditions.[43] But these haven't been the only casualties. In a real-life example of *Hunger Games* brutality, North Korea's inept economic policies led to a man-made famine in the 1990s that killed up to 2.5 million people.[44] Those who try to escape are virtually guaranteed death. In 2011, North Korea's young dictator, Kim Jong-Eun, issued a "shoot-to-kill order" to border guards if anyone tried to flee the country.[45]

Christians are especially singled out for persecution, which is particularly startling given that until the mid-1900s, North Korea was a very Christian country. In the 1940s, so many Christians lived in Pyongyang (now the capital of North Korea) that it was nicknamed the "Jerusalem of the East." As a teen, Kim Il Sung, the founder of North Korea's dictatorship, attended worship services with his parents, where he played the organ.[46] When he came to power, however, he began an intensive program of repressing Christians, killing them, jailing them, or banishing them to remote areas of the country.[47] Entire families have been put to death if a single family member possesses a Bible.[48]

Because China engages in so much international trade, many assume that it has been reformed from the blood lust and terror that characterized the regime of Mao Tse-tung. Certainly, things have improved. But the scale of persecution is still breathtaking. Christians who run afoul of laws restricting religion can be sent to prison or to *laogai*, "reeducation through labor" camps, and they're often brutally detained without a trial or hearing.[49] People who try to enter China to escape North Korean

> Cuba "continues to be run by a brutal regime that oppresses the people, systematically violating ... basic freedoms."

> Christians who run afoul of Chinese laws restricting religion can be sent to "reeducation through labor" camps, and they're often brutally detained without a trial or hearing.

persecution are coldheartedly returned to the North Koreans, which all but guarantees their torture and execution.[50]

China's one-child policy has also led to persecution. The government bans the church from teaching that an unborn child has a right to life.[51] Even though China made a show of loosening the policy in 2013, people who desire to have more than one child are denied education, health care, and even marriage for their "illegal" children. Such families can face fines ten times the average household income. Families who cannot or will not pay the fines can have their homes vandalized, and their young child might even be killed.[52]

Marxist countries brutally persecute Christians, but when all countries are taken together, the evidence is that the worst persecution of Christians in the world is in Muslim countries.

Islam. Muslim apologists often portray Islam as a peaceful, tolerant religion. One Islamic scholar stated that "humanity is one single family of God and there can be no sanction for … barriers.… Islam gives the revolutionary concept of the unity of mankind."[53] The Quran supports religious freedom, says Abdullah Saeed, professor of Islamic studies at the University of Melbourne in Australia, quoting such passages as "There shall be no coercion in matters of faith" (Quran, surah 2:256). Professor Saeed says that belief is a choice, "forced conversions" are against Islam, and those who use force are disobeying the Quran.[54]

Most Islamic regimes act differently, however. In their comprehensive study of global persecution, Paul Marshall, Lela Gilbert, and Nina Shea state, "The most widespread persecution of Christians today takes place in the Muslim world, and it is … intensifying."[55] Radical Islam's ultimate goal is a global Islamic state (**pan-Islam**) in which religious leaders rule (an **Islamic theocracy**) according to the principles of **sharia law**.[56] Sharia requires all Muslims to engage in **jihad**, which means resisting anything hindering the advance of Islam.[57] Christians and Jews ("people of the Book") are called *dhimmis*. A **dhimmi** is expected to express submission to Muslim rulers by paying a tax called the **jizya**.[58]

Theoretically, as long as Christians and Jews pay the *jizya* and keep their views to themselves, they're granted what eighth-century Islamic legal scholar Abdullah Yusuf Ali called their "personal liberty of conscience."[59] As we'll

Islamic Theocracy: a state ruled by Islam and Islamic religious leaders.

Sharia Law: the moral and legal code derived primarily from the Quran and the *Sunnah* that governs the lives of Muslims. Sharia addresses a wide variety of subjects such as diet, hygiene, prayer, contracts, business, crime, and punishment.

Jihad: from the Arabic word translated as "struggle," signifies both the inner spiritual battle of every Muslim to fulfill his or her religious duties and the outer, physical struggle against the enemies of Islam.

Dhimmi: a non-Muslim living in an Islamic state.

Jizya: a tax imposed on dhimmis (i.e., non-Muslims) living in Islamic states.

see shortly, the reality is very different. Violence against Christians and Jews is commonplace and even widely accepted in predominantly Muslim countries, and it's especially severe against Muslims who convert to Christianity.

Uncomfortably for those who wish to view Islam as a religion of peace and for many Muslims themselves who honestly desire to live in harmony with their neighbors, Islam has historically treated Christians as second-class citizens and, at its worst, has enslaved and slaughtered Christians and sought to destroy Christianity's holy sites.[60] The persecution continues today. Here are some examples:

> Islam has historically treated Christians as second-class citizens and, at its worst, has enslaved and slaughtered Christians.

- In **Saudi Arabia**, state schools teach students to "hate" Christians and view them as "enemies."[61] Christian prayers are forbidden, even in private.[62]

- In **Iran**, arrests of Christians are accelerating, and the regime considers them "conspirators" and "parasites."[63]

- In **Egypt**, the Coptic Christians, an ancient community the apostle Mark established nearly two thousand years ago, are attacked for "insulting Islam." Its priests endure death threats. Coptic Christian homes have been tagged with crosses to make their inhabitants easier to harass.[64] Even today they are massacred.[65] Converts to Christianity are threatened with jail time, marriage annulment, and having their children forcibly reregistered as Muslim.[66]

- **Pakistan** forbids "blasphemy" against Islam but doesn't spell out what counts as blasphemy. Christians have little defense against frequent false accusations based on business rivalry, property disputes, and grudges. Thugs and mobs, and even the police, have killed hundreds of people.[67] Paul Marshall notes that "Christians cannot effectively counter such charges against them because their testimony is of less legal worth than a Muslim's in sharia courts. The testimony of a Christian woman is worth [even] less."[68]

- **Jordan**, while not banning conversion to Christianity or evangelizing Muslims, puts all laws concerning religion, marriage, divorce, child custody, and inheritance under the jurisdiction of sharia courts, in which Christians are denied full legal representation.[69]

- In **Afghanistan**, according to a US Department of State report, "male citizens over age 18 or female citizens over age 16 of sound mind who converted from Islam had three days to recant their conversion or be subject to death by stoning, deprivation of all property and possessions, and the invalidation of their marriage."[70]

- **Iraq** is such a hotbed of religious persecution that "the country has now been included as one of the world's worst places for religious persecution on a recommended short list of 'Countries of Particular Concern' by the United States Commission on International Religious Freedom (USCIRF)."[71]

- In **Turkey**, a supposedly secular state, national security agencies have reportedly spied on Christians. They've also been "threatened, attacked, hauled into court on bogus charges, and even brutally murdered by ultra-nationalists" seeking to destabilize the government.[72]

- **Algeria**, **Yemen**, the **Palestinian Territories**, and even the island nation of **Indonesia**, which styles itself as a democracy, have been known to turn a blind eye when Muslim mobs target Christians. Christians in Pakistan, Afghanistan, Iraq, Nigeria, Turkey, and Somalia have all died for their faith.[73] Sometimes Muslims themselves are persecuted for blasphemy when expressing dissenting political or religious views.[74]

In 2014 a new form of Islamic persecution arose at the hands of a group called the Islamic State in Iran and Syria (ISIS), a terrorist organization with a growing army of "fighters" numbering in the tens of thousands.[75] ISIS zealously pursues a radical Islamist agenda with hundreds of millions of dollars in funding from oil revenue.[76] Its fighters routinely enslave and gang-rape women as young as nine years of age and publicly torture and execute those ISIS believes are its enemies. Posted on the Internet, these executions often have the perverse effect of encouraging Western young people to sympathize with the group's bloodthirsty aims.

Frighteningly, many Western leaders have failed to grapple with the threat ISIS presents. They find it hard to acknowledge that ISIS is an explicitly religious group aiming to

> Frighteningly, many Western leaders have failed to grapple with the threat ISIS presents.

take over the world, even though the leader of ISIS, Abu Bakr al-Baghdadi, declared a global caliphate (Islamic government) in 2014, with himself as its leader.[77] In just a one-year period following al-Baghdadi's announcement, more than ten thousand people were beheaded, shot, drowned, stoned, or thrown off buildings at the hands of ISIS fighters. Thousands more were killed in war actions and suicide bombings.[78]

Christians, especially, are the targets of ISIS, which has destroyed ancient Christian communities and forced Christians to either convert to Islam or die. In Syria, more than six hundred thousand Christians have been displaced, leading the *New York Times* to ask, "Is This the End of Christianity in the Middle East?"[79]

Given the brutality we've just discussed, it seems juvenile to complain about relatively minor instances of religious persecution occurring in the United States. But America's unique and strong foundation of religious freedom is increasingly under attack. Historically speaking, when a society begins restricting religious freedom, coercive restrictions on other liberties follow. Historian Will Durant warned in another context, "From barbarism to civilization requires a century; from civilization to barbarism needs but a day."[80] It's like a dam that gives way little by little, until it collapses entirely with catastrophic results. Attacks on religious freedom, even small ones, need to be taken seriously.

Attacks on Religious Freedom in America

America's tradition of religious freedom. Religious freedom has long been considered America's first freedom. America's founders prominently enshrined it in the First Amendment to the US Constitution. In its infancy, however, the United States consisted of colonies committed to certain Christian denominations, such as Congregational, Presbyterian, Baptist, or Anglican. Religious freedom was extended only as far as each colony's established denomination would allow. Each denomination lobbied to be the officially recognized religion, and some colonies made the relationship with the colonial government official. In Virginia, for example, Anglicans paid their priests with tax dollars, and Dissenters were often persecuted.

All of this changed in the course of just a few years. The Baptist evangelist John Leland was instrumental in making it happen. He influenced Thomas Jefferson and James Madison, who in turn advocated strongly for religious freedom at the First Congress. Together, they "[had] it in [their] power to begin the world over again," as Thomas Paine so eloquently expressed it in *Common Sense*.[81]

Fanning the religious freedom spark into a fire, the British Parliament sought to increase the Anglican Communion's influence in the American colonies. Many founders were alarmed: if Parliament was willing to diminish religious freedom, then all freedom was at risk. John Adams said this apprehension contributed "as much as any cause" to the corroding of America's loyalty to Britain, leading directly to the American Revolution.[82]

To secure religious freedom, our founders refused to establish a national church and instead constitutionally guaranteed a free market of religion, which led to both greater freedom and also greater devotion. According to Brian Grim and Roger Finke, "The rate of church adherence increased from 17 percent of the population in 1776 to 51 percent by 1890."[83]

> To secure religious freedom, our founders refused to establish a national church and instead constitutionally guaranteed a free market of religion.

Behind the founders' actions was a belief that restrictions on religious freedom would lead to restrictions on other freedoms.[84] Even while recognizing that nations around the world had official state churches and still protected religious freedom, American Deists and Christians united on these five points in establishing the United States of America:[85]

1. State-sanctioned churches should be disestablished.

2. A creator-God was the "guarantor of fundamental human rights."

3. Human sinfulness posed a threat to polity (especially via the power of the state).

4. A republic needed to be sustained by virtue on the part of ordinary citizens.

5. God/Providence moved in and through the work of particular nations.

Nowhere else in the world was the effort to secure religious freedom so robust.

America's founders intentionally limited government's power in religious matters. They heeded the words of British political leader Lord Acton that "power tends to corrupt; absolute power corrupts absolutely."[86] Just as freedom of the press entails the state respecting the press's sphere of authority, religious freedom entails the state respecting the church's sphere of authority.[87]

> Heeding the words of Lord Acton that "power tends to corrupt [and] absolute power corrupts absolutely," America's founders intentionally limited government's power in religious matters.

Interestingly, the founders based their convictions about religious freedom on principles that were aligned with the Bible, were derived only from the Bible, or were self-evident but justified only by the Bible: the soul's immortality, divine judgment, providential acts, the sin nature, moral absolutes, the human capacity to bear God's image, order in the universe, public virtue, and the general teachings of the Bible. America's founders had little doubt that these beliefs formed the link between public virtue and national success. This in turn grounded their belief in limited government, just war, and the importance of Christian influence in national life.

> America's founders had little doubt that biblical beliefs formed the link between public virtue and national success.

Now a growing divide on these principles is making it easier for the government to begin choking out religious freedom not by threatening physical safety but through bureaucracy.[88]

Government attacks on religious freedom in America. In early 2012, when the Obama administration first announced that the Department of Health and Human Services (DHS)—as part of the Patient Protection and Affordable Care Act (Obamacare)—would force employers to provide contraceptive and abortion drugs to employees at no cost, alarm bells rightly went off among both Catholics and Protestants.

The Christian owners of Hobby Lobby—a private, for-profit business—successfully challenged the government's mandate. But nonprofits still face heavy fines if they refuse to pay for abortion drugs for their employees as part of their insurance coverage. These fines of up to $36,500 per person per year are monstrous compared to the $2,000-a-year fine *for not providing health insurance at all.*[89] In essence, organizations face ruin if they fail to comply with the administration's proabortion stance. For instance, in the year the mandate was pronounced, the organization I lead had thirty-six employees. We would have faced fines of more than 1.3 million dollars per year. The ministry would have been shut down.

Is it really so burdensome for people to buy their own contraceptives that businesses and ministries must be forced to pay for them? Yet these mandates have reached absurd lengths. The Little Sisters of the Poor, a group of elderly Catholic nuns who take a vow of poverty to serve the elderly poor, were told that they must provide contraceptives to their members as part of their health-care plan.[90] The court said they must sign a waiver to be exempted, but this waiver would instruct a third-party provider to provide the services they object to. This is like forcing a pacifist who objects to war to pay for someone to go to war in his place. It violates the very principle the freedom is intended to protect.

I once asked Eric Metaxas why religious liberty was a big deal. Eric, whose book *Bonhoeffer* is the source for the story told in the politics chapter of this book about the minister martyred for standing against Hitler's tyranny, explained that in Nazi Germany, the abuses against the Jews started out as small bureaucratic rule changes. When no one objected, the Nazis pushed harder, destroying more freedoms. Eric ended by saying, "You can't sit this one out. This is where you have to draw the line."[91]

Meanwhile, the rise of the same-sex marriage issue will continue putting private citizens in an untenable position. Politicians promise to protect religious rights of clergy (promises that in a similar situation in Canada have proved empty), but nonclergy Christians are being sued for choosing not to provide services that run counter to their religious convictions. For example, Catholic Charities in Massachusetts had to close its doors because it wouldn't facilitate adoptions by same-sex couples, even though other adoption agencies in Massachusetts would facilitate them.[92]

> "You can't sit this one out. This is where you have to draw the line."

In this vein, Focus on the Family president Jim Daly relates a disturbing conversation he had with Chai Feldblum, one of three commissioners for the Equal Employment Opportunity Commission (EEOC), which regulates employment practices and thus has an enormous influence in both business and government. Daly asked, "Chai, tell me what a perfect world for you would look like." Feldblum replied,

> Well, if I wanted to get married to my partner and a Christian person was working at the county courthouse, if they refused to do it—even politely and had somebody else come over to do it—she shouldn't work or he shouldn't work in the county courthouse. What about a doctor that wouldn't do in vitro fertilization for a lesbian couple? Well, they should never be licensed by the state because they would be violating my rights.[93]

When Daly questioned whether this would violate religious liberty, Feldblum told him that her sexual rights trump religious freedom.

Feldblum represents the crowning triumph of Secularism in the public sphere. As David Noebel and I demonstrate in *Understanding the Times*, Secularism isn't just a political viewpoint; it's a religion that denies God's relevance to life.[94] In essence, a new religion of self-worship has seized the helm and is steering the ship of state into the uncharted waters of total liberation, even if it requires plowing through a few vital but fragile freedoms along the way.

The trend toward elected officials and unelected bureaucrats ignoring constitutional boundaries continues. In a 2012 interview, Chick-fil-A CEO Dan Cathy affirmed his support for the biblical view of marriage. Within days of Cathy's interview, Boston mayor Thomas Menino vowed to block any efforts by the fast-food chain to move into his city (but later backtracked). Chicago

> In essence, a new religion of self-worship has seized the helm and is steering the ship of state into the uncharted waters of total liberation, even if it requires plowing through a few vital but fragile freedoms along the way.

alderman Joe Moreno, with an attitude worthy of the Chicago bosses of old, also promised to do everything in his power to stop a Chick-fil-A from opening in his ward, even as one was in the licensing process to do that very thing.[95] (He later backtracked as well). In 2015, based on Cathy's stance on marriage, Denver city councilman Paul Lopez opposed allowing Chick-fil-A to open a restaurant at Denver International Airport (DIA), calling it a "moral issue."[96] In the end, the council approved the license, but only after a nationwide outcry from free-speech advocates.[97]

Nongovernment attacks on religious freedom in America. Archbishop Charles Chaput of Philadelphia says that "compared to almost anywhere else in the world, our religious freedom situation is good." But "the situation is changing," Chaput notes, because people "use words like justice, rights, freedom and dignity without any commonly shared meaning to their content. As a result, our most important debates boil [down] to who can deploy the best words in the best way to get power."[98]

> At the time of this writing, the greatest threats to religious freedom in America come from activists who think sexual expression, particularly acceptance of same-sex marriage, should trump all other freedoms and rights.

At the time of this writing, the greatest threats to religious freedom in America come from activists who think sexual expression, particularly acceptance of same-sex marriage, should trump all other freedoms and rights. Princeton professor Robert George writes that activists are "giddy with success and … urged on by a compliant and even gleeful media."[99] Eric Metaxas says, "The message is clear: not only should Christians remain silent about gay marriage if we know what's good for us, but we must be made to agree with and even celebrate what Scripture calls sin."[100] Case in point: in a rambling burst of newspeak, *New York Times* columnist Frank Bruni informed Christians that it's time to bow to "the enlightenments of modernity" and, in the words of gay philanthropist Mitchell Gold, "take homosexuality off of the sin list."[101]

Backing these activists are major foundations—funded with business profits—pouring millions of dollars into efforts to reframe the issue of religious liberty as *one* right among many and not necessarily as the first freedom America's founders envisioned it to be. One such project is called the Public Rights/Private Conscience Project, hosted by the Columbia University Law School.[102]

Then there is the tyranny of the majority. Thanks to social media, negative stories planted in the press have accused Christians standing for religious liberty of being anti-gay bigots. As a result, support for religious freedom has dipped. A study undertaken by the First Amendment Center in 2000 found nearly 73 percent of Americans agreeing that "the freedom to worship as one chooses … applies to all religious groups, regardless of how extreme their beliefs are." Just seven years later, that number dropped to 56 percent.[103] Even if these dips are temporary, they give political cover to those who oppose religious freedom.

Businesses have become ground zero for such religious-freedom conflicts. In early 2015, the Indiana legislature passed a state version of the federal Religious Freedom Restoration Act (RFRA), which Congress passed decades ago and president Bill Clinton signed into law. A coordinated effort by same-sex marriage advocates painted the decision as bigotry and a religious "right to discriminate."[104] Buoyed by a social-media campaign, businesses like Apple, Wal-Mart, Eli Lilly, Angie's List, and others put immense pressure on lawmakers, who subsequently caved in to activists' demands. It was a cynical move. After all, companies like Apple do business in such countries as Uganda, Saudi Arabia, Qatar, and Nigeria, where homosexuals receive the death penalty. Political science professor Patrick Deneen wrote, "The decision to #BoycottIndiana was not made because it was the politically courageous thing to do; it was made because it was the profitable thing to do." Deneen concluded by saying that this "libertarian indifference," left unchecked, will ultimately give wealthy companies the power to set the national agenda without respect to culture, place, or morality.[105]

The mix of homosexual activism, profit, and government pressure, whipped up through a carefully designed social-media campaign, shows how easily citizens can be swept up into a technological version of a torchlight mob, complete with self-righteous social-media posts serving as digital pitchforks. In such a world, we should worry not about middle-of-the-night secret-police raids but about the middle-of-the-day click-clack of the power-drunk bloggers' and bureaucrats' keyboards.

> Citizens can easily be swept up into a technological version of a torchlight mob, complete with self-righteous social-media posts serving as digital pitchforks.

Christians need to care. And act. Let's discuss two reasons why and four things Christians can do.

3. Why Should Christians Care?

God Cares about the Oppressed

Jesus sets spiritual captives free with real-world effects. In fact, Jesus began his public ministry reading the following passage in a synagogue: "The Spirit of the Lord is upon me, because he has anointed me to proclaim good news to the poor. He has sent me to proclaim liberty to the captives and recovering of sight to the blind, to set at liberty those who are oppressed" (Luke 4:18). Jesus was quoting Isaiah 61:1–2,[106] which seems to deal with literal captives, not just spiritual captives. Thus, he connected humanity's spiritual condition and physical condition in a new way. No longer helplessly bound to sin, individual lives begin to change. Society changes too. As Jesus put it in John 8:32, "You will know the truth, and the truth will set you free."

The Jewish people would have been well aware of how Jesus's words dovetailed with their rich tradition of being set free. The prophet Isaiah said,

> Jesus sets spiritual captives free with real-world effects.

> Is not this the fast that I choose: to loose the bonds of wickedness, to undo the straps of the yoke, to let the oppressed go free, and to break every yoke? Is it not to share your bread with the hungry and bring the homeless poor into your house; when you see the naked, to cover him, and not to hide yourself from your own flesh? (Isa. 58:6–7)

Indeed, the story of the Hebrew nation began with a quest for religious freedom. The book of Exodus opens with Egypt's new king deciding to oppress God's chosen people: "Come, let us deal shrewdly with them, lest they multiply, and, if war breaks out, they join our enemies and fight against us and escape from the land" (1:10). In response, God sent Moses to liberate them: "Behold, the cry of the people of Israel has come to me, and I have also seen the oppression with which the Egyptians oppress them. Come, I will send you to Pharaoh that you may bring my people, the children of Israel, out of Egypt" (3:9–10).

Moses's initial appeal to Pharaoh was for freedom of worship: "The God of the Hebrews has met with us. Please let us go a three days' journey into the wilderness that we may sacrifice to the LORD our God, lest he fall upon us with pestilence or with the sword" (5:3). Pharaoh's growing resistance to Hebrew freedom was eventually broken through an increasingly severe cycle of plagues. Exodus tells a thrilling story of God rescuing the Hebrews from one disaster after another, leading them to freedom and flourishing.

> **Why does God care so much about the oppressed? Because every person bears his image.**

Why does God care so much about the oppressed? Because every person bears his image (Gen. 1:26–27).[107] Even slaves. We see this in the book of Job, where Job recognized that his bondservants were just as much image bearers of God as he was and that he would have to answer to God if he mistreated them (31:13–14).[108] The Old Testament law makes provisions for the care and protection of slaves in Exodus 11, 12, 21; Leviticus 19, 22, 25; and Deuteronomy 5, 15, 16, and 21.

As the Bible's story unfolds, it becomes clear that *all* are one through faith in Christ Jesus, no matter their role in life (1 Cor. 12:13; Gal. 3:28; Col. 3:11).[109] The apostle Paul appealed to Philemon to treat the slave Onesimus as a brother (Philem. v. 16).[110] Revelation 18:10–13[111] condemns trading humans as "cargo," echoing Ezekiel 27:13.[112] First Timothy 1:9–10[113] condemns enslavers, people who force humans into slavery. Throughout history, Christians, inspired by Jesus's focus on setting captives free, have provided the basis for anti-slavery movements, human rights, and the protection of the vulnerable.[114]

Religious Freedom Is Essential for Sustaining a Free and Virtuous Society

Brian Grim and Roger Finke found that religious freedom is inextricably linked with the overall well-being of a society. The decline of religious freedom is correlated with a decline of gross domestic product (GDP) and foreign investment, an increase in inflation, and an erosion of democracy.[115] The American founders' hypothesis appears to be right: apart from its inherent value, religious freedom secures other liberties and, by checking the powers of the state, enables **human flourishing**.

> **Apart from its inherent value, religious freedom secures other liberties and, by checking the powers of the state, enables human flourishing.**

These freedoms are being eroded today. According to Grim and Finke, clues of growing government restriction include the requirement that particular religious groups register with the government limits on the freedom to worship, restrictions on foreign missionaries, and regulations against proselytizing.[116] Much of this is happening right now. But restrictions on religious freedom don't have to stand. There are things we can do to make a difference.

4. What Should Christians Do?

Forsake a Gospel of Abandonment

Many Christians believe that their faith is a matter of personal preference and has nothing to do with what is going on in the world. They would agree with the description of faith provided by historian Theodore Roszak as "socially irrelevant, even if privately engaging."[117] Christianity became this way because many church leaders in the past taught that it deals with the inner, personal world, not the external, public world. As historian Richard Pierard observed, the external world was often seen as irrelevant to Christianity belief because it operated on "nature, scientific knowledge, [and] statecraft" and "operated on the basis of its own internal logic and discernable laws."[118] As one nineteenth-century theologian put it, "The Gospel has absolutely nothing to do with outward existence but only with eternal life, not with external orders and institutions which could come in conflict with the secular orders but only with the heart and its relationship with God."[119]

> Many Christians believe that their faith is a matter of personal preference and has nothing to do with what is going on in the world.

This is a counterfeit Christianity. Those who wonder how so many "Christian" people could blindly follow Adolf Hitler need look no further than a theology that groomed an entire generation of Christians to be weak minded and easily fooled. Christians today are often similarly disengaged. In the last few presidential elections, approximately 40 percent of evangelical Christians didn't vote.[120] They chose comfort over liberty, unaware that such a choice spells death for both.

Historian Gary DeMar warns that the church's refusal to be the conscience of the nation makes it a poor refuge when persecution strikes. "The day may come when the State starts attacking you and me. While our churches might speak out against the action of the State," he says, "they might not intervene to save us."[121]

As we saw in chapter 12, without accountability, the state tends toward lawlessness and disorder. The church's job is to help the state remember to protect the innocent and punish evil. As Eric Metaxas puts it, "It is the church's role to help the state be the state."[122] To preserve religious freedom, the church will need to reassert this role.

> The church's refusal to be the conscience of the nation makes it a poor refuge when persecution strikes.

In the past, Christians willingly did so. In fact, when missionaries went to spread the gospel, they brought freedom with them. Sociologist Robert Woodberry has found that the single most important determining factor for whether an emerging country had a functioning, modern, liberal democracy, a working education system, and economic stability was the presence of "conversionary Protestant" missionaries in the nineteenth century. Controlling for all other variables, this was the overwhelmingly important factor that led to stable states rather than dictatorships or theocracies.[123] And many clergy played a key role in defending the rights of native people. Historian Kenneth Stewart says that while not all clergy supported the rights of native people, no one *other than* the clergy defended their human rights.[124]

In many ways, the development of what we call international law today began with the work of two Spanish theologians, Francisco de Vitoria (1486–1546) and Domingo de Soto (1494–1560).[125] Another strong advocate for native rights was Bartolomé de Las Casas (1484–1556). As a young man, Las Casas came to the New World and participated in abuses and atrocities against the Native Americans. Challenged by Dominican friars about this, he eventually concluded that the Spanish treatment of the natives was deeply wrong, and he dedicated his life to fighting for their rights. Las Casas lobbied the royal court of Spain to end enslavement of natives, the central cruelty and abuse inflicted on them. Initially, he advocated for the use of African slaves, though he later changed course and worked to protect them as well. Las Casas was motivated by his faith. Along with everything else, he was concerned about evangelizing the natives and knew they would be receptive only if they were freed from coercion and abuse. The gospel should be freely preached and freely accepted or rejected.[126]

> The single most important determining factor for whether an emerging country had a functioning, modern, liberal democracy, a working education system, and economic stability was the presence of "conversionary Protestant" missionaries in the nineteenth century.

Defend Religious Freedom

Politicians who refuse to grant business licenses because they don't like the political or religious beliefs of the business owner need to be held accountable. It's the very violation of freedom of conscience that America's founders sought to avoid. Fortunately, many legal organizations have now organized to fight back. These include Alliance Defending Freedom (ADF) and the Becket Fund for Religious Liberty. ADF has defended hundreds of businesses and ministries. The Becket Fund played a key role in the 9–0 Supreme Court decision in Hosanna-Tabor Evangelical Lutheran Church and School v. Equal Employment Opportunity Commission, which recognized for the first time that religious organizations have the constitutional right to choose their own ministers "free from government interference or manipulation."[127]

> Politicians who refuse to grant business licenses because they don't like the political or religious beliefs of the business owner need to be held accountable.

ADF and the Becket Fund are good organizations to watch because they know not only how to fight hard but also how to fight fair. Coercion and religiously motivated violence aren't valid options according to the teachings of Jesus, nor is using the coercive powers of the state to promote or defend the church or to attack dissenters. The state may and must respond to violence, but it should not use force against ideas. Jesus tells us that we're to give to Caesar what is rightfully his, but we must reserve for God the things that belong to him, which includes our consciences (Luke 20:25).[128]

In standing for their own religious liberty, Catholics and Protestants also must not fail to stand for the religious freedom of Muslims, Jews, Latter-day Saints, and other religious groups. As Robert George puts it,

> The first (and more important) reason is simply that it is the right thing to do. Faith and reason bear common witness to the profound truth that religious liberty is a right held equally by all. The second reason is that the denial of religious liberty for any one group erodes the foundations of religious liberty for everyone.[129]

Christians can also advocate for religious freedom in other countries. It starts by knowing what violations are occurring. One organization calling attention to religious persecution around the world is the Voice of the Martyrs, founded by Richard Wurmbrand, a Romanian pastor imprisoned for fourteen years and tortured for preaching the gospel.

Americans can hold their government accountable to advocate for the persecuted in other nations as well. One avenue is the United States Commission on International Religious Freedom (USCIRF). This commission regularly reviews "Countries of Particular Concern" that discriminate based on religion.[130] The federal government has the power to warn and even impose economic sanctions on countries that do this. But whether they do depends on the priorities of those in charge. For example, Saudi Arabia, which blatantly violates principles of religious freedom, has been given a waiver based on its promise to reform, a promise it hasn't yet carried out. The United States gains a lot trading economically with Saudi Arabia. Are we willing to overlook blatant persecution to keep the money flowing? As long as those who care about religious freedom are silent, nothing will change.

Christians can play a particularly important role by impressing the importance of religion when communicating with government officials. Eighty-four percent of the people in the world are religious;[131] to overlook the role of religion is to remain purposefully ignorant about what is really going on. In their ignorance, US officials in a position to help the persecuted have often looked away. When speaking of Nigeria's brutal, anti-Christian Boko Haram organization, whose name means "Western education is a sin" and whose fighters have killed more than thirteen thousand civilians, Johnnie Carson, US State Department assistant secretary of state for African affairs, asserted, "Religion is not driving extremist violence in ... northern Nigeria."[132]

> **As long as those who care about religious freedom are silent, nothing will change.**

Stay Clear about What the Real Issue Is

Denver cake-shop owner Jack Phillips, Masterpiece Cakeshop, refused a gay couple when they asked him to make a wedding cake for their upcoming same-sex wedding. Judge Robert N. Spencer said that under Colorado's public-accommodation law, Phillips did not have the right to refuse the couple service.[133] This is so even though same-sex marriage wasn't legal in Colorado at the time of the refusal.

The case generated strong opinions on both sides. The media largely portrayed the baker as an anti-gay person. But the point was missed in all the furor. It wasn't about whether Phillips would serve gay customers, which he had always done. Rather, it was about being asked to participate in a ceremony honoring a particular kind of *relationship* he deemed immoral. Many homosexual activists cheered the decision to punish Phillips. But prohomosexual advocate Andrew Sullivan wasn't among them:

> I would never want to coerce any fundamentalist to provide services for my wedding—or anything else for that matter—if it made them in any way uncomfortable. The idea of suing these businesses to force them to provide services they are clearly uncomfortable providing is anathema to me. I think it should be repellent to the gay rights movement as well.[134]

It's not just that Christians want the right to *believe* that man-woman marriage is biblical. It's that they defend the very *idea* of man-woman marriage. As we saw in our chapter on marriage, the biblical worldview is that, as English professor Mark Bauerlein explains, "some souls in the world are caught in troubled, disordered desires, and … if we accept those desires we allow disorder in family and society, and we act contrary to God's will."[135]

The issue isn't just the freedom to assemble for worship. It's the right to advocate ideas that might even be politically unpopular, and to do so with like-minded people. When this kind of freedom is abridged, freedom itself is in jeopardy.

5. Conclusion

In a scene from J. R. R. Tolkien's *The Two Towers*, Pippin and Merry entreat the peace-loving Ents (ancient trees that walk and talk) to join the battle against the evil Sauron. When the trees refuse, Pippin comforts Merry by saying, "Maybe Treebeard's right. We don't belong here, Merry. It's too big for us. What can we do in the end? We've got the Shire. Maybe we should go home."

Merry replies with desperation in his voice, "The fires of Isengard will spread, and the woods of Tuckborough and Buckland will burn. And all that was once great and good in this world will be gone."[136]

Merry's understanding should resonate with contemporary Christians. It may seem as if freedom will inevitably fail. If we refuse to act while we still have the freedom to speak our minds, there may come a day when the power plays of political correctness will eliminate our liberties, and all that was once "great and good" about the land of the free will cease to exist.

Feeling helpless isn't a good excuse for doing nothing, though. As Dutch theologian and statesman Abraham Kuyper once said, "As soon as principles gain ground that are contrary to your deepest convictions, then resistance is your duty and acquiescence [is] a sin."[137]

> **In the coming years, it may be costly to follow Christ, even in America. But those who love freedom must stand.**

Of course, in many cases persecution nurtures the spread of the gospel. While imprisoned in Iran, American Christian Saeed Abedini continued sharing his faith. Thousands of young Iranians have come to Christ in the past decade and are starting churches. It isn't without cost, however. Naghmeh and Saeed paid the cost. Their children suffered. Their marriage suffered. But as Saeed wrote to his eight-year-old daughter, "People die and suffer for their Christian faith all over the world, and some may wonder why. But you should know the answer of WHY is WHO. It is for Jesus. He is worth the price."[138]

In the coming years, it may be costly to follow Christ, even in America. But those who love freedom must stand. As the nineteenth-century abolitionist Wendell Phillips is thought to have written, "Eternal vigilance is the price of liberty." The light of freedom must remain lit. Often throughout history, it has been lit by the sacrifice of those who have gone to their deaths out of love for their savior. Before the Catholic queen Mary I of England commanded that bishop Hugh Latimer be burned at the stake, he was said to have proclaimed to his fellow sufferer, bishop Nicholas Ridley, "Be of good cheer, master Ridley, and play the man; we shall this day light such a candle in England as I hope, by God's grace, shall never be put out."[139] May we have the courage to keep the flame of religious liberty lit throughout the world.

ENDNOTES

1. Naghmeh Abedini, interview by Jeff Myers, Summit Adult Conference 2015, in "Summit Adult Conference 2015: Full Interview with Naghmeh Abedini," *Summit Announcements* (blog), April 14, 2015, www.summit.org/blogs/summit-announcements/summit-adult-conference-2015-interview-with-naghmeh-abedini/.

2. Brian J. Grim et al., *Rising Tide of Restrictions on Religion* (Washington, DC: Pew Research Center, 2012), www.pewforum.org/files/2012/09/RisingTideofRestrictions-fullreport.pdf. According to the Pew Research Center, the percentage of the world's population living in severely restricted countries dropped from 77 percent in 2013 to 74 percent in 2014. See "Trends in Global Restrictions on Religion," Pew Research Center, June 23, 2016, www.pewforum.org/2016/06/23/trends-in-global-restrictions-on-religion/.

3. Grim et al., "Harassment of Specific Groups," in *Rising Tide of Restrictions on Religion*, 22.

4. Brian J. Grim and Roger Finke, *The Price of Freedom Denied: Religious Persecution and Conflict in the Twenty-First Century* (New York: Cambridge University Press, 2011), 79, 219.

5. Robert P. George et al., *Annual Report of the US Commission on International Religious Freedom* (Washington, DC: US Commission on International Religious Freedom, 2014), 1.

6. United Nations, "The Universal Declaration of Human Rights," December 10, 1948, www.un.org/en/universal-declaration-human-rights/.

7. See George et al., *Annual Report of the US Commission on International Religious Freedom*, especially pages 2–3.

8. International Religious Freedom Act of 1998, H.R. 2431, 105th Cong. 105, January 27, 1998, www.state.gov/documents/organization/2297.pdf.

9. Rodney Stark, *One True God: Historical Consequences of Monotheism* (Princeton, NJ: Princeton University Press, 2001), 117. Rodney Stark says, "It is among those committed to the particularistic principle—that there is only one authoritative belief system—that truly dangerous religious antagonisms arise. Moreover, where particularism rules, bitter antagonism is inevitable because *theological disagreement is inevitable....* These disputes are the normal consequences of theological study, for heresy is inherent in the act of seeking to fully understand and to reconcile the deeper meanings of scriptures and revelations within any context wherein there can be only one correct answer." Stark, *One True God*, 118.

10. Stark, *One True God*, 120.

11. Donatism was a Christian sect that arose in what are now Algeria and Tunisia in response to the persecution of Christians in Rome under the emperor Diocletian. Donatism flourished in the fourth and fifth centuries but was wiped out during the Arab conquest of Africa in the seventh and eighth centuries.

12. The Albigensian Crusade was a twenty-year war (1209–1229) launched by Pope Innocent III to fight against the Cathari in southern France. The Cathari were a Christian sect that departed from the Roman Catholic teaching and raised the pope's ire by assassinating one of his representatives. The Cathari became known as Albigensians because many of them were from the region surrounding the town of Albi. A peace treaty ended the war ended in 1229, but the destabilizing influence of the crusade led to continued religious and political strife.

13. Thomas S. Kidd, *God of Liberty: A Religious History of the American Revolution* (New York: Basic Books, 2010), 39.

14. Historians think that King Philip IV of France instigated the inquisition against the Knights Templar because he wanted their wealth.

15. Thomas F. Madden, "The Real Inquisition: Investigating the Popular Myth," *National Review*, June 18, 2004, www.nationalreview.com/article/211193/real-inquisition-thomas-f-madden.

16. Madden, "Real Inquisition."

17. See Brian P. Levack, *The Witch-Hunt in Early Modern Europe*, 2nd ed. (London: Longman, 1995), chap. 2.

18. The full account of the Salem witch trials is complex and at times baffling, involving a perfect storm of war, economic uncertainty, disease, paranoia, and political calculation. What seems undisputed now is that witch trials came to an end after the people of Salem awakened to the evil they had carried out. See the account by Emerson W. Baker, a history professor at Salem State University, in *A Storm of Witchcraft: The Salem Trials and the American Experience* (New York: Oxford University Press, 2015), chap. 7.

19. Rodney Stark says, "The first [principle explaining religious conflict] notes that religious conflict will be maximized where, other things being equal, a few powerful and particularistic religious organizations coexist.... Moreover, such conflicts will tend not to be restricted to the main contenders but will generate a climate of general religious intolerance extending to minor religious groups that would ordinarily tend to be tolerated. Hence the second major principle: ... toleration will be withheld or withdrawn from nonthreatening but nonconforming religious groups." Stark, *One True God*, 122–23.

20. Michael Horowitz, quoted in Grim and Finke, *Price of Freedom Denied*, 202.

21. "Trends on Global Restrictions on Religion," Pew Research Center.

22. Paul Marshall, Lela Gilbert, and Nina Shea, *Persecuted: The Global Assault on Christians* (Nashville: Thomas Nelson, 2013), 259.

23. "The Year of Fear: Persecution Trends in 2016," Open Doors, accessed September 23, 2016, www.opendoorsuk.org /persecution/trends.php.

24. Anne Applebaum documents the way this happened in Eastern Europe as well. The communist parties identified popular priests, developed charges against them, and had them arrested as a matter of course. See Anne Applebaum, *Iron Curtain: The Crushing of Eastern Europe, 1944–1956* (New York: Doubleday, 2012).

25. "1936 Constitution of the USSR," adopted December 1936, chap. 10, art. 125, posted by Robert Beard, Bucknell University, accessed July 27, 2016, www.departments.bucknell.edu/russian/const/36cons04.html.

26. Aleksandr I. Solzhenitsyn, *The Gulag Archipelago*, 3 vols. (New York: Harper and Row, 1973–1978).

27. Stephane Courtois et al., *The Black Book of Communism: Crimes, Terror, Repression*, trans. Jonathan Murphy and Mark Kramer (Cambridge, MA: Harvard University Press, 1999). See also R. J. Rummel, *Death by Government* (New Brunswick, NJ: Transaction Publishers, 1994).

28. Nikita Khrushchev (speech, Moscow, USSR, September 22, 1955), quoted in *A Primer on Communism: 200 Questions and Answers* (Washington, DC: US Information Agency, 1956), 39.

29. *The Atheist's Handbook* (Washington, DC: US Joint Publications Research Service, 1961), 69, 117; originally published as *Sputnik Ateista* (Moscow, USSR: Gos. Izd. Politicheskoi Literatury, 1961).

30. *The Great Soviet Encyclopedia* (Moscow, USSR: 1950), quoted in James D. Bales, *Communism: Its Faith and Fallacies* (Grand Rapids: Baker Books, 1962), 37.

31. Young Communist League's "Ten Commandments of Communism," quoted in *Executive Schedule for War 1955: Executive Hearings before the Committee on Un-American Activities, House of Representatives, Eighty-Third Congress, First Session* (Washington, DC: Government Printing Office, 1953), 2072–73.

32. "1918 Constitution of the Russian Soviet Federated Socialist Republic," Fifth All-Russian Congress of Soviets, July 10, 1918, art. 2, chap. 5, sec. 13, accessed September 23, 2016, www.marxists.org/history/ussr/government/constitution/1918 /article2.htm.

33. "1918 Constitution," art. 4, chap. 13, sec. 65, www.marxists.org/history/ussr/government/constitution/1918 /article4.htm.

34. Paul Kurtz, the late Secularist and atheist philosopher, is one of those who acknowledged the anti-religious crimes of the USSR: "From 1918 to 1921," he wrote, "religious persecution continued unabated.... All church property was nationalized, and it is estimated that tens of thousands of bishops, clerics, and laymen were killed or imprisoned." Paul Kurtz, *Toward a New Enlightenment: The Philosophy of Paul Kurtz*, eds. Vern L. Bullough and Timothy J. Madigan (New Brunswick, NJ: Transaction Publishers, 1994), 178.

35. See Courtois, *Black Book of Communism*; see also Rummel, "61,911,000 Murdered: The Soviet Gulag State," chap. 4 in *Death by Government*.

36. Alexander Weissberg, *The Accused* (New York: Simon and Schuster, 1951), 461, cited in Robert Conquest, *The Harvest of Sorrow: Soviet Collectivization and the Terror-Famine* (New York: Oxford University Press, 1986), 209. Many of the facts concerning the church closings are found in chapter 10, "The Churches and the People."

37. Marshall, Gilbert, and Shea, *Persecuted*, 65.

38. Marshall, Gilbert, and Shea, *Persecuted*, 81.

39. Persecution reports for Vietnam, Laos, and other countries can be found at the Open Doors USA website, www.opendoorsusa.org/christian-persecution/world-watch-list/.

40. Marshall, Gilbert, and Shea, *Persecuted*, 51.

41. Oscar Biscet, "A Cuban's Prayer for Pope Benedict: What Will the Castro Brothers Hear during the First Papal Visit in over a Decade?," *Wall Street Journal*, March 20, 2012, www.wsj.com/articles/SB10001424052702304636404577293681582 420986.

42. Biscet, "Cuban's Prayer."

43. Statistics from South Korea's National Human Rights Commission and Christian Solidarity Worldwide, cited in Melanie Kirkpatrick, *Escape from North Korea: The Untold Story of Asia's Underground Railroad* (New York: Encounter Books, 2014), 6.

44. United Nations Human Rights Council, *Report of the Commission of Inquiry on Human Rights in the Democratic People's Republic of Korea* (Geneva, Switz.: United Nations, 2014), cited in Joshua Stanton and Sung-Yoon Lee, "Pyongyang's Hunger Games," *New York Times*, March 7, 2014, www.nytimes.com/2014/03/08/opinion/pyongyangs-hunger-games.html.

45. Kirkpatrick, *Escape from North Korea*, viii.

46. Cited in Bradley K. Martin, *Under the Loving Care of the Fatherly Leader: North Korea and the Kim Dynasty* (New York: Thomas Dunne, 2004), 12.

47. Kirkpatrick, *Escape from North Korea*, 44.

48. Marshall, Gilbert, and Shea, *Persecuted*, 60–61.

49. Marshall, Gilbert, and Shea, *Persecuted*, 30.

50. See Roberta Cohen, "China's Forced Repatriation of North Korean Refugees Incurs United Nations Censure," *The Brookings Institution*, July 7, 2014, www.brookings.edu/opinions/chinas-forced-repatriation-of-north-korean-refugees -incurs-united-nations-censure.

51. Marshall, Gilbert, and Shea, *Persecuted*, 31.

52. Cited in Marshall, Gilbert, and Shea, *Persecuted*, 34.

53. Ebrahim Ahmed Bawany, comp. and ed., *Islam: Our Choice* (Riyadh, Saudi Arabia: Ministry of Islamic Affairs Endowment, 1992), 4–5.

54. Abdullah Saeed, "The Islamic Case for Religious Liberty," *First Things*, November 2011, www.firstthings.com/article /2011/11/the-islamic-case-for-religious-liberty.

55. Marshall, Gilbert, and Shea, *Persecuted*, 123.

56. The late Zaki Badawi commented on the inability of Islam to develop a theology or political system that doesn't involve being in control: "As we know, the history of Islam as a faith is also the history of a state and a community of believers living by Divine law. The Muslims, jurists and theologians, have always expounded Islam as both a Government and a faith. This reflects the historical fact that Muslims, from the start, lived under their own law. Muslim theologians naturally produced a theology with this in view—it is a theology of the majority. Being a minority was not seriously considered or even contemplated. The theologians were divided in their attitude to the question of minority status. Some declared that it should not take place; that is to say that a Muslim is forbidden to live for any lengthy period under non-Muslim rule. Others suggested that a Muslim living under non-Muslim rule is under no obligation to follow the law of Islam in matters of public law. Neither of these two extremes is satisfactory. Throughout the history of Islam some pockets of Muslims lived under the sway of non-Muslim rulers, often without an alternative. They nonetheless felt sufficiently committed to their faith to attempt to regulate their lives in accordance with its rules and regulations in so far as their circumstances permitted. In other words, the practice of the community rather than the theories of the theologians provided a solution. Nevertheless Muslim theology offers, up to the present, no systematic formulation of the status of being a minority. The question is being examined. It is hoped that the matter will be brought to focus and that Muslim theologians from all over the Muslim world will delve into this thorny subject and allay the conscience of the many Muslims living in the West and also to chart a course for Islamic survival, even revival, in a secular society." Zaki Badawi, quoted in Colin Chapman, *Cross and Crescent: Responding to the Challenge of Islam* (Downers Grove, IL: InterVarsity, 2007), 150–51.

57. Islamic scholar Khurshid Ahmad says, "*Jihad* has been made obligatory, which means that the individual should, when the occasion arises, offer even his life for the defense and protection of Islam and the Islamic state." Khurshid Ahmad, *Islam: Its Meaning and Message*, 3rd ed. (Leicester, UK: Islamic Foundation, 1999), 39.

58. The Quran says, "Fight those who believe not in God nor the Last Day, nor hold that forbidden which has been forbidden by God and His Apostle, nor acknowledge the Religion of Truth, (even if they are) of the People of the Book, until they pay the *jizya* with willing submission, and feel themselves subdued" (surah 9:29).

59. Abdullah Yusuf Ali, trans., *The Holy Qur'an* (Washington, DC: American International Printing, 1946), 447.

60. Those who visit the revered city of Jerusalem today can see clear evidence of this. In AD 1009, the caliph al-Hakim actually leveled the Church of the Holy Sepulchre in Jerusalem, which was believed to be the burial place of Jesus, and destroyed the tomb itself, cutting away the rock so no trace of it remained. His successors did allow the Byzantines to rebuild the church, but visitors today see nothing but a bare rock.

61. U.S. Department of State, "Saudi Arabia," *2009 Report on International Religious Freedom*, October 26, 2009, www.state.gov /j/drl/rls/irf/2009/127357.htm. The report says, "Textbooks continued to contain some overtly intolerant statements against Jews and Christians and subtly intolerant statements against Shi'a and other religious groups, notwithstanding Government

efforts to review educational materials to remove or revise such statements."

62. Marshall, Gilbert, and Shea, *Persecuted*, 284.

63. Marshall, Gilbert, and Shea, *Persecuted*, 173.

64. Marshall, Gilbert, and Shea, *Persecuted*, 187.

65. In October of 2011, Egyptian forces massacred two dozen Coptic Christians during a peaceful protest in Cairo in which the protestors were standing against religious violence and the failure of Egyptian forces to protect them. Marshall, Gilbert, and Shea, *Persecuted*, 298.

66. Marshall, Gilbert, and Shea, *Persecuted*, 190.

67. Marshall, Gilbert, and Shea, *Persecuted*, 200.

68. Marshall, Gilbert, and Shea, *Persecuted*, 287.

69. Marshall, Gilbert, and Shea, *Persecuted*, 147.

70. "Afghanistan," in *July–December, 2010 International Religious Freedom Report* (Washington, DC: US Department of State/Bureau of Democracy, Human Rights, and Labor, 2011), www.state.gov/j/drl/rls/irf/2010_5/.

71. Marshall, Gilbert, and Shea, *Persecuted*, 229.

72. Marshall, Gilbert, and Shea, *Persecuted*, 287.

73. Marshall, Gilbert, and Shea, *Persecuted*, 288.

74. Marshall, Gilbert, and Shea, *Persecuted*, 291.

75. Estimates vary, but most reports in 2014 ranged between 20,000 and 31,500 fighters. See, for example, Robert Windrem, "ISIS by the Numbers: Foreign Fighter Total Keeps Growing," February 28, 2015, www.nbcnews.com/storyline/isis-terror/isis-numbers-foreign-fighter-total-keeps-growing-n314731.

76. Janine di Giovanni, Leah McGrath Goodman, and Damien Sharkov, "How Does ISIS Fund Its Reign of Terror?," *Newsweek*, November 6, 2014, www.newsweek.com/2014/11/14/how-does-isis-fund-its-reign-terror-282607.html.

77. Graeme Wood, "What ISIS Really Wants," *Atlantic*, March 2015, www.theatlantic.com/magazine/archive/2015/03/what-isis-really-wants/384980/.

78. Jay Akbar, "Revealed: ISIS Has Executed More Than 10,000 Men, Women and Children ...," DailyMail.com, September 24, 2015, www.dailymail.co.uk/news/article-3244641/Revealed-ISIS-executed-10-000-men-women-children-Iraq-Syria-year-doesn-t-include-thousands-killed-battles-suicide-bombings-cut-fled.html.

79. Eliza Griswold, "Is This the End of Christianity in the Middle East?," *New York Times Magazine*, July 22, 2015, www.nytimes.com/2015/07/26/magazine/is-this-the-end-of-christianity-in-the-middle-east.html?_r=0.

80. Will Durant, *The Story of Civilization*, vol. 6, *The Reformation* (New York: Simon and Schuster, 1957), 190.

81. Thomas Paine, *Common Sense*, ed. Isaac Kramnick (New York: Penguin Books, 1976), 120.

82. John Adams, quoted in Kidd, *God of Liberty*, 59.

83. Roger Finke and Rodney Stark, *The Churching of America, 1776–2005: Winners and Losers in Our Religious Economy* (New Brunswick, NJ: Rutgers University Press, 2005), 22, cited in Grim and Finke, *Price of Freedom Denied*, 7.

84. One main reason: if governments tolerated using religion as a means by which the state would control people, they would almost certainly resort to other means of control as well. Kidd, *God of Liberty*, 51.

85. Kidd, *God of Liberty*, 6–8.

86. Lord Acton, letter to bishop Mandell Creighton, April 5, 1887. Also see Bartlett, *Bartlett's Familiar Quotations*, 518.

87. Correspondence between Lord Acton and Richard Simpson, October 6, 1862, cited in Lord Acton, *Essays in Religion, Politics, and Morality: Selected Writings of Lord Acton*, ed. J. Rufus Fears (Indianapolis: Liberty Fund, 1988), 611.

88. Grim and Finke, *Price of Freedom Denied*, 33.

89. The Patient Protection and Affordable Care Act of 2010, H.R. 3590, 111th Cong. (2010), www.gpo.gov/fdsys/pkg/BILLS-111hr3590enr/pdf/BILLS-111hr3590enr.pdf.

90. Nigel Duara, "Court Rules against Little Sisters of the Poor in Contraceptive Coverage Case," *Los Angeles Times*, July 14, 2015, www.latimes.com/nation/la-na-ff-little-sisters-of-the-poor-20150714-story.html.

91. Eric Metaxas, quoted in Jeff Myers, "From the President's Desk," *Summit Journal* 12, no. 8 (August 2012), www.summit.org/media/journal/2012-08_Summit_Journal-WEB.pdf.

92. Michael Terheyden, "Catholic Charities Forced to Shut Down Services around the Country," Catholic Online, June 7, 2011, www.catholic.org/news/national/story.php?id=41680.

93. Chai Feldblum, conversation with Jim Daly, quoted in Rachel Martin, "For Evangelical Leader, Gay Marriage 'Outside of God's Design,'" National Public Radio, March 25, 2013, www.npr.org/2013/03/24/175173113/for-evangelical-leader-gay-marriage-outside-of-gods-design.

94. The case David Noebel and I make in *Understanding the Times* is simple and clear. A religion is a system of belief that attempts to define the nature of God and how human beings can understand and interact with the divine. Secularists have a clearly articulated set of beliefs about these matters. Therefore, Secularism is a religious impulse.

95. "Mayor Rahm Emanuel Wants to Block Chick-fil-A from Building in Chicago after Gay Marriage Scandal," DailyMail.com, July 27, 2012, www.dailymail.co.uk/news/article-2179620/Chick-fil-A-anti-gay-controversy-Company-denounced-Chicago-Mayor-Rahm-Emanuel-gay-marriage-scandal.html.

96. *Denver Post* Editorial Board, "Denver City Council Clucking about Chick-fil-A at DIA," *Denver Post*, August 20, 2015, www.denverpost.com/editorials/ci_28675353/denver-city-council-clucking-about-chick-fil-at-dia/.

97. Carla Caldwell, "Chick-fil-A Cleared to Land at Denver International Airport after Bumpy Approach," *Atlanta Business Chronicle*, September 23, 2015, www.bizjournals.com/atlanta/morning_call/2015/09/chick-fil-a-cleared-to-land-at-denver-airport.html.

98. Archbishop Charles Chaput (speech to archdioses seminarians, Philadelphia, March 2015), quoted in Eric Metaxas, "Religious Freedom: The New Un-American Activity?," Breakpoint Commentaries, April 1, 2015, www.breakpoint.org/bpcommentaries/entry/13/27124.

99. Robert George, "Who Will Stand?," *First Things*, April 5, 2015, www.firstthings.com/blogs/firstthoughts/2015/04/who-will-stand.

100. Eric Metaxas, "The Shifting Definition of Religious Freedom," Breakpoint Commentaries, April 13, 2015, www.breakpoint.org/bpcommentaries/entry/13/27177.

101. Frank Bruni, "Bigotry, the Bible and the Lessons of Indiana," *New York Times*, April 3, 2015, www.nytimes.com/2015/04/05/opinion/sunday/frank-bruni-same-sex-sinners.html?_r=0.

102. "Public Rights/Private Conscience Project (PRPCP)," Columbia Law School, accessed September 23, 2016, http://web.law.columbia.edu/gender-sexuality/public-rights-private-conscience-project.

103. "State of the First Amendment 2007: Final Annotated Survey," First Amendment Center, 2007, accessed July 28, 2016, www.firstamendmentcenter.org/madison/wp-content/uploads/2011/03/SOFA2007results.pdf.

104. See, for example, *Boston Globe* Editorial Board, "Indiana's 'Religious Freedom' Law Should Be Repealed," *Boston Globe*, March 31, 2015, www.bostonglobe.com/opinion/editorials/2015/03/31/indiana-religious-freedom-law-should-repealed/LmM9y4Iru36zg63u41UVL/story.html.

105. Patrick J. Deneen, "The Power Elite," *First Things*, June 2015, www.firstthings.com/article/2015/06/the-power-elite.

106. Isaiah 61:1–2: "The Spirit of the Lord GOD is upon me, because the LORD has anointed me to bring good news to the poor; he has sent me to bind up the brokenhearted, to proclaim liberty to the captives, and the opening of the prison to those who are bound; to proclaim the year of the LORD's favor, and the day of vengeance of our God; to comfort all who mourn."

107. Genesis 1:26–27: "God said, 'Let us make man in our image, after our likeness. And let them have dominion over the fish of the sea and over the birds of the heavens and over the livestock and over all the earth and over every creeping thing that creeps on the earth.' So God created man in his own image, in the image of God he created him; male and female he created them."

108. Job 31:13–14: "If I have rejected the cause of my manservant or my maidservant, when they brought a complaint against me, what then shall I do when God rises up? When he makes inquiry, what shall I answer him?"

109. First Corinthians 12:13: "In one Spirit we were all baptized into one body—Jews or Greeks, slaves or free—and all were made to drink of one Spirit"; Galatians 3:28: "There is neither Jew nor Greek, there is neither slave nor free, there is no male and female, for you are all one in Christ Jesus"; Colossians 3:11: "There is not Greek and Jew, circumcised and uncircumcised, barbarian, Scythian, slave, free; but Christ is call, and in all."

110. Philemon verse 16: "[Treat Onesimus] no longer as a bondservant but more than a bondservant, as a beloved brother—especially to me, but how much more to you, both in the flesh and in the Lord."

111. Revelation 18:10–13: "'Alas! Alas! You great city, you mighty city, Babylon! For in a single hour your judgment has come.' And the merchants of the earth weep and mourn for her, since no one buys their cargo anymore, cargo of gold, silver, jewels, pearls, fine linen, purple cloth, silk, scarlet cloth, all kinds of scented wood, all kinds of articles of ivory, all kinds of articles of costly wood, bronze, iron and marble, cinnamon, spice, incense, myrrh, frankincense, wine, oil, fine flour, wheat, cattle and sheep, horses and chariots, and slaves, that is, human souls."

112. Ezekiel 27:13: "Javan, Tubal, and Meshech traded with you; they exchanged human beings and vessels of bronze for your merchandise."

113. First Timothy 1:9–10: "Understanding this, that the law is not laid down for the just but for the lawless and disobedi-ent, for the ungodly and sinners, for the unholy and profane, for those who strike their fathers and mothers, for murderers, the sexually immoral, men who practice homosexuality, enslavers, liars, perjurers, and whatever else is contrary to sound doctrine."

114. See Rodney Stark, *For the Glory of God: How Monotheism Led to Reformations, Science, Witch-Hunts, and the End of Slavery* (Princeton, NJ: Princeton University Press, 2003), chap. 4.

115. Grim and Finke, *Price of Freedom Denied*, 207.

116. Grim and Finke, *Price of Freedom Denied*, 36, 39.

117. Theodore Roszak, *Where the Wasteland Ends* (New York: Doubleday, 1972), 449.

118. Richard V. Pierard, "Why Did Protestants Welcome Hitler?," *Fides et Historia* 10, no. 2 (Spring 1978): 13.

119. Richard V. Pierard quoting Christian Ernst Luthardt (1867) in Karl H. Hertz, *Two Kingdoms and One World: A Sourcebook in Christian Ethics* (Minneapolis: Augsburg, 1976), 83.

120. Philip Bump, "Ted Cruz Undersells Evangelical Turnout. But He Has a Good Reason," Washington Post, March 23, 2015,

www.washingtonpost.com/news/the-fix/wp/2015/03/23/ted-cruz-undersells-evangelical-turnout-but-he-has-a-good-reason/.

121. Gary DeMar, "Two Big-Name Evangelical Pastors Do Not Endorse Minnesota Marriage Amendment," *Godfather of Politics*, June 23, 2012, http://godfatherpolitics.com/5826/two-big-name-evangelical-pastors-do-not-endorse-minnesota-marriage-amendment/.

122. Eric Metaxas, *Bonhoeffer: Pastor, Martyr, Prophet, Spy* (Nashville: Thomas Nelson, 2010), 153.

123. Robert D. Woodberry, "The Missionary Roots of Liberal Democracy," *American Political Science Review* 106, no. 2 (May 2012), www.academia.edu/2128659/The_Missionary_Roots_of_Liberal_Democracy. It's important to note that some missionaries did participate in mistreatment of natives by doing things like forcing native children into mission schools, forbidding them to use their native language in favor of English, requiring them to wear European-style clothing, and prohibiting many of their culture's rituals and practices. Such practices, though, stemmed from some missionaries' stubborn insistence on conforming to Anglo cultural norms, not out of an adherence to biblical truth. Today most missionary organizations are very sensitive about maintaining a focus on spreading the gospel rather than spreading the cultural norms of Western civilization.

124. See Kenneth J. Stewart, "Calvinism and Missions: The Contested Relationship Revisited," *Themelios* 34, no. 1 (April 2009), http://themelios.thegospelcoalition.org/article/calvinism-and-missions-the-contested-relationship-revisited.

125. See Rámon Hernández, "The Internationalization of Francisco de Vitoria and Domingo de Soto," *Fordham International Law Journal* 15, no. 4 (1991): 1031–59, http://ir.lawnet.fordham.edu/cgi/viewcontent.cgi?article=1325&context=ilj.

126. See Paul S. Vickery, *Bartolomé de Las Casas: Great Prophet of the Americas* (Mahwah, NJ: Paulist Press, 2006).

127. Michael Sean Winters, "Hosanna-Tabor v. EEOC," *National Catholic Reporter*, January 12, 2012, www.ncronline.org/blogs/distinctly-catholic/hosanna-tabor-v-eeoc.

128. Luke 20:25: "[Jesus] said to them, 'Then render to Caesar the things that are Caesar's, and to God the things that are God's.'"

129. Robert P. George, "Defend Religious Liberty for Muslims," *First Things*, June 5, 2012, www.firstthings.com/blogs/firstthoughts/2012/06/defend-religious-liberty-for-muslims.

130. United States Commission on International Religious Freedom, "About USCIRF: Who We Are/What We Do," accessed July 28, 2016, www.uscirf.gov/about-uscirf/who-we-arewhat-we-do.

131. Jennifer Harper, "84 Percent of the World Population Has Faith; A Third Are Christian," *Washington Times*, December 23, 2012, www.washingtontimes.com/blog/watercooler/2012/dec/23/84-percent-world-population-has-faith-third-are-ch.

132. Johnnie Carson, "Promise and Peril in Nigeria: Implications for U.S. Engagement" (presentation, Center for Strategic and International Studies, Washington, DC, April 9, 2012), quoted in Marshall, Gilbert, and Shea, *Persecuted*, 299.

133. *Denver Post* Editorial Board, "No Right to Refuse Gay Couple's Wedding Cake," *Denver Post*, December 9, 2013, www.denverpost.com/editorials/ci_24687970/no-right-refuse-gay-couples-wedding-cake.

134. Andrew Sullivan, "Erick Erickson Has a Point," *The Dish* (blog), February 24, 2014, http://dish.andrewsullivan.com/2014/02/24/erick-erickson-has-a-point/.

135. Mark Bauerlein, "Religious Liberty Is a Rearguard Position," *First Things*, April 8, 2015, www.firstthings.com/blogs/firstthoughts/2015/04/religious-liberty-is-a-rearguard-position.

136. *The Lord of the Rings: The Two Towers*, directed by Peter Jackson (Los Angeles: New Line Cinema, 2002).

137. Abraham Kuyper, "Modernism: A *Fata Morgana* in the Christian Domain," *Abraham Kuyper: A Centennial Reader*, ed. James D. Bratt (Grand Rapids: Eerdmans, 1998), 89.

138. Jeff Myers, "An Amazing Story of Hope," *Summit Journal* 15, no. 3 (April 2015): 2, www.summit.org/media/journal/Summit_Journal_-_April_2015.pdf.

139. Bishop Hugh Latimer, quoted in *The Revivalist* (London: Thomas Ward, 1843), 267.

CHAPTER 14

14

POVERTY CARE, POVERTY CURE

1. STEWARDSHIP, COMMUNITY, AND CREATIVITY

If you met Muhammad Yunus, you might never guess that he is listed in *Financial Times* alongside American billionaire Warren Buffett as one of the six greatest financial pioneers of all time.[1] As a young man, Yunus came to the United States to earn a doctorate in economics and then returned to his native Bangladesh to be a professor. To his horror, he found that thousands of people were dying of starvation just outside the university gates. What caused that starvation was the most horrifying thing of all.

People were starving, Yunus discovered, not because they were dumb or lazy but because they lacked the few cents they needed to take their ideas and turn them into businesses that could help their families survive. As Joseph Grenny and his colleagues tell it, "Yunus was dumbfounded when he discovered that a woman who made beautiful handcrafted stools was held in poverty because she lacked the 5 cents she would need to buy supplies each day. Five cents!"[2]

How is it possible to lack *five cents*? It turns out this woman had taken money from a loan shark in a desperate bid to buy the materials she needed to make her products. Charged a level of interest many times the total amount of profit she received, this woman found herself in an economic black hole from which she would never be able to emerge without help from someone.

Captivated, Yunus studied forty-two people and discovered that the total amount of money they needed to finance their businesses was twenty-seven dollars.[3] Inspired to act, Yunus started Grameen Bank, which is now a multi-billion-dollar banking and business operation. Grameen Bank provides loans to help more than one hundred million people out of poverty. In the process, Yunus has pioneered a whole new industry to help the poor, called **microfinance**, in which investors give small loans to people in developing countries to begin or grow their businesses.[4] Recipients have proved themselves to be enormously responsible, with a repayment rate of around 98 percent. For his efforts, Yunus was awarded a Nobel Prize.[5]

> *Microfinance:* any venture in which investors give small loans to low-income individuals for the purpose of helping them start a self-sustaining business.

One of Yunus's unique contributions was recognizing that business success is usually not an individual pursuit. To receive loans from Grameen bank, recipients found four friends, each of whom submitted a business plan and held the other members of the team accountable for establishing their business and repaying the loan. It was just such accountability that inspired Tanika, a woman in India. Tanika moved from being a wig maker to collecting hair to sell to a company that extracts oil from hair follicles to make health products. This allows hundreds of women to earn money from helping Tanika collect the hair. Lots of families have moved beyond avoiding starvation to actually running a thriving enterprise.

> Stewardship. Community. Creativity. These are solidly biblical principles.

Stewardship. Community. Creativity. These are solidly biblical principles. As we've seen throughout this book, the key to human flourishing is recognizing our value as image bearers of a loving creator-God. In this chapter, we'll learn how it's also the answer to understanding poverty's causes and effects and audaciously moving beyond poverty *care* to poverty *cure*.

It is in this hope that we'll look at some of the causes of poverty, ask why Christians should care, explore why other worldviews fail to cure poverty, and look at three things Christians ought to do to lift individual people—indeed, entire societies—out of poverty.

POVERTY CARE, POVERTY CURE

2. What Is the Problem?

What Is Poverty?

Poverty is defined in absolute terms as "the state or condition of having little or no money, goods, or means of support."[6] Some governmental organizations define *poverty* in relative terms as referring to people whose income falls below a certain level relative to others in their society.[7] This has led to the demand for **government redistribution** of economic wealth to meet the social and cultural "needs" of the poor and reduce inequality, rather than helping them survive and make it on their own. It's a good example of how the way we define terms determines our actions and the outcomes we expect.

In the United States, the federal government defines the *poverty threshold* as an income that is less than "three times the cost of a minimum food diet."[8] As of 2015, this was around $12,000 for a single person (assuming that person doesn't have additional means of support) or just over $24,000 for a family of four.[9] The federal government also uses a supplemental measure (SPM) that includes clothing, shelter, and utilities sufficient to meet basic needs.[10] By either standard, a surprisingly high number of people in America are poor. During a three-year period from 2009 to 2011, approximately one-third of the US population had "at least one spell of poverty lasting 2 or more months."[11]

> *Poverty:* the state of not having the money or resources to regularly meet one's basic needs (e.g., water, food, clothing, and shelter).

> *Government Redistribution:* a state-controlled economic policy that taxes the wealthy at a higher rate than others and then reallocates those assets to the poor either through direct subsidies or government-sponsored social programs.

But even the poor in America appear wealthy by the world's standards. For example, Africa expert Martin Meredith has estimated that more than two-thirds of the population lives in extreme poverty.[12] In the 1990s, Meredith reported that the economic output of the entire continent of Africa was less than Mexico and was falling—its share of world trade was half of what it was in the 1980s. Meredith noted that the twenty-five countries with the lowest human-development scores were African. In fact, Africa was the only region in the world where investment, savings, school enrollment, and life expectancy had fallen since 1970. Africa was also the only region of the world in which illiteracy was commonplace.

By 2004, twenty million Africans had died from AIDS, and the infection rates were unthinkably high. In Botswana, one of the more well-developed countries in Africa, 37 percent of the population was infected.[13]

In spite of these staggering challenges, there are signs of hope. A 2013 report in the *Economist* noted that as country after country rejects socialism and embraces economic freedom, the African economic situation is improving.[14] According to the World Bank, extreme poverty has dropped by half in just the last generation, from 36 percent of the world's population to 18 percent.[15] *Time* magazine reports,

Africa's progress is real, dramatic and, by now, well established. The International Monetary Fund says that since 2003, GDP across sub-Saharan Africa's 48 countries has risen an average of 5% to 7% per year. In the past decade, six of the 10 fastest-growing countries in the world were African, and this year five African countries will outgrow China, [and] 21 will beat India.[16]

Progress, though, is still tenuous. Africa's material improvement hasn't yet led to political stability. African leaders are notorious for raiding their nations' treasuries of billions of dollars. Election-related violence, including murder, is common.[17] Clearly, short-term prosperity isn't the same thing as long-term economic growth. If Africa uses up its resources in a reckless way, we could see a temporary improvement followed by a long-term setback. Still, says analyst Oliver August, Africa's retreat "from socialist economic models has generally made everyone better off."[18]

> As counterintuitive as it may seem, the root of the poverty problem may not be economic at all.

All the talk about economic poverty misses a significant point, though. As counterintuitive as it may seem, the root of the poverty problem may not be economic at all.

Not All Poverty Is Economic

Philosopher Ronald Nash pointed out that while poverty is sometimes the result of oppression and exploitation, there are also times when it's the result of misfortune—such as accidents, injuries, and illness—or laziness.[19] Proverbs 6:10–11 says, "A little sleep, a little slumber, a little folding of the hands to rest, and poverty will come upon you like a robber, and want like an armed man."[20] Poverty is a worldview problem. For example, Theodore Dalrymple, a physician and psychiatrist in the poorest areas of London, contends that "most of the social pathology exhibited by the underclass has its origin in ideas that have filtered down from the intelligentsia." It was intellectuals, he says, who championed sexual promiscuity, which led to illegitimate births in his hospital totaling 70 percent. "[Intellectual elites] considered the purity of their ideas to be more important than the actual consequences of their ideas," he says. "I know of no egotism more profound."[21]

> Bad thinking about poverty has led to bad solutions that may have actually worsened the plight of the poor.

The poor bought into this pack of lies and have suffered accordingly. It's a worldview problem.

As you might expect, bad thinking about poverty has led to bad solutions that may have actually worsened the plight of the poor. It's painful to acknowledge, but we're unlikely to find the right way to help the poor without first understanding how the solutions previous generations implemented went wrong.

Modern Society's War on Poverty Fails

Before the Protestant Reformation in the 1500s, all the nations of the world were poor, much like the continent of Africa today. In fact, throughout most of history, even the wealthy were poor by today's standards. According to economist Angus Maddison, the average person two thousand years ago made about a dollar a day, in today's dollars. Until 2008, a dollar a day was the World Bank definition of *extreme poverty*.[22]

After the Reformation, literacy flourished, economic principles were articulated, and entire nations rose out of poverty. This produced a thriving middle class for the first time in human history. Social equality grew. As we saw in chapter 3, biblical thinking about government led to the birth of political freedom and more just systems of law. In spite of dramatic change, though, widespread poverty reigned well into the eighteenth century. Working conditions were deplorable. Starvation was common. In places like Russia, even into the early 1900s, four out of five people were peasants with very little property who were always on the brink of starvation.[23] Then something changed, and quickly. In *The Grand Pursuit*, a sweeping look at the history of economics, Sylvia Nasar reports,

> A mere fifty years after [Jane Austen's] death, [the] world was altered beyond recognition. It was not only the "extraordinary advance in wealth, luxury and refinement of taste" [or] the unprecedented improvement in the circumstances of those whose condition was assumed to be irremediable.... It was the sense that the changes were not accidental or a matter of luck, but the result of human intention, will, and knowledge.[24]

As I noted earlier, economist Cleon Skousen called it a "5,000-year leap."[25] Economies grew by leaps and bounds. Because of **free-market economy** innovations, poverty was being eradicated. In their enthusiasm to finish the job, though, intellectuals and political Progressives decided to give it a little push. The result was disaster, and the story of how it happened serves as a cautionary tale for us today.

> After the Reformation, literacy flourished, economic principles were articulated, and entire nations rose out of poverty. This produced a thriving middle class for the first time in human history.

Can Government Management of the Economy Ensure Prosperity?

Economic growth is always a bumpy ride. Fortunes can be won and lost overnight. Catastrophic lows follow euphoric highs. In the twentieth century, a British economist named John Maynard Keynes noticed how self-regulating markets can leave people vulnerable to wild swings and wondered whether the government could intervene to make things smoother and more predictable. He concluded that "depressions could be cured by encouraging spending and discouraging saving."[26] According to journalist Nicholas Wapshott, Keynes gained followers during the Great Depression in the United States by persuading members of the Franklin D. Roosevelt administration to embrace this view.[27] Roosevelt himself embraced Keynes's ideas enthusiastically. In a radio address, FDR said,

> We suffer primarily from a failure of consumer demand because of lack of buying power. It is up to us to create an economic upturn.... Not only our future economic

soundness but the very soundness of our democratic institutions depends on the determination of our Government to give employment to idle men.[28]

With this, Roosevelt embarked on a massive program of government spending and market regulation.

> **Roosevelt embraced Keynes's ideas enthusiastically, embarking on a massive program of government spending and market regulation. And for a while it worked.**

For a while it worked. In post–World War II America between 1947 and 1952, every dollar of debt in the economy yielded $4.61 in value. But according to Summit lecturer and private-equity-fund manager Toby Neugebauer, today it yields only eight cents.[29] If you borrowed a dollar, invested it, and got your dollar back plus $3.61, you'd be pretty happy. But if you borrowed a dollar, invested it, and lost $0.92, you'd be wise to give up the investment. If you're foolish, you'd still have to give up the investment but probably wouldn't until the coffers were empty.

If you got to print money, though, you might never quit your bad habits at all. Probably not even Keynes's cheerleaders could foresee that the federal government could borrow, print, and take so much money out of productive use in the economy that it would drag an entire nation into a more or less permanent recession with more or less permanent unemployment, low tax revenue, and a staggering level of debt that could never be repaid. And much of the borrowing habit began in the aftermath of the Great Depression.

Can Government Programs Ensure Prosperity?

One example of the Roosevelt administration's Keynesian schemes was the National Recovery Administration (NRA). The NRA, headed by General Hugh S. Johnson, operated in a military style. It developed a symbol (a blue eagle) and held marches, rallies, and parades. NRA codes were put into effect for everything imaginable, and industries were pressured to follow them. General Johnson overlooked nothing in his zeal. Here are some of the more odd examples: Code 450 regulating the dog-food industry, Code 427 regulating the curled-hair manufacturing industry and the horse-hair dressing industry, Code 262 regulating the shoulder-pad manufacturing industry, and even Code 348 regulating strippers in the burlesque theatrical industry.[30]

Looking back, many Progressives who champion government intervention are uncomfortable with all the hoopla. It looks like something out of Adolf Hitler's propaganda machine. But at the time, before the world learned how propaganda facilitated the murder of millions, people thought it was a good idea. Those desperate for relief didn't just accept government intervention as a fact of life. They became cheerleaders for it.

> **During the Depression, those desperate for relief didn't just accept government intervention as a fact of life. They became cheerleaders for it.**

Was it a winning strategy, though? Not really. It seems that the effect of the NRA was negative even in areas where it was trying to help. For example, the auto industry was forced to raise the wage of factory workers from thirty-five cents an hour to forty cents, but those same workers had their workweeks reduced from sixty to forty hours, which reduced their weekly pay from twenty-one dollars to sixteen dollars.[31]

Roosevelt tried funding his programs by dramatically increasing taxes. President Hoover had already raised the top federal income tax rate from 25 percent to 63 percent. Roosevelt raised it to an unthinkable 79 percent, assuming that this would bring in the revenue he needed.[32] What actually happened is that people with the highest salaries just quit working so hard. It's easy to see why. If you left your house and knew for a fact that a robber would stick a gun in your ribs and take ninety-four of the hundred dollars in your wallet, you either wouldn't leave home or would leave the money behind. Roosevelt nearly destroyed the recovery with these maneuvers just at the time it was beginning.

Of course, governments need tax revenue to operate. But political leaders have learned the hard way (though some haven't yet learned) that tax policy is very difficult to get right. If you tax goods people need, such as food (an **inelastic good**), you end up hurting those with the least ability to pay. If you tax goods people don't need but like to have, such as a luxury item (**elastic good**), people who can afford those goods will just buy something else.

Can Government Win the War on Poverty?

In the 1960s, president Lyndon Johnson declared a "war on poverty" and committed billions of tax dollars to develop welfare programs, build housing, and buy food for poor people. Most Americans like the idea of a **social safety net** and agree we should help people get back on their feet. But how much did the kind of intervention represented by the **War on Poverty** actually help? In the six years before the War on Poverty began, poverty had dropped to 15 percent. After the federal government spent more than twenty trillion dollars to eradicate poverty, the poverty rate today remains between 12 and 15 percent. Jay Richards says somberly, "The statistics hide the full cost: not only did the War on Poverty fail; it created economic and social problems worse than those it was meant to solve."[33]

Sometimes intervention on behalf of those needing help can actually hurt them. For example, the federal government gives several billion dollars in aid to countries in Africa. It

Inelastic Good: any good whose demand is affected very little by price increases and decreases (e.g., food and gasoline).

Elastic Goods: any good whose demand is highly correlated with price increases and decreases (i.e., as the price increases or decreases, consumer demand responds conversely).

Social Safety Net: any collection of government programs intended to assist individuals who fall on hard times and keep them out of poverty (e.g., welfare, unemployment insurance, and universal health care).

War on Poverty: the set of government programs initiated by president Lyndon Johnson to reduce poverty in the United States.

also gives several billion dollars a year to American cotton farmers so they can sell their cotton at about 25 percent below the price on the world market. This **government subsidy** makes it hard for African countries to sell their cotton profitably.[34] Martin Meredith notes that "the trade losses associated with U.S. farm subsidies that West Africa's eight main cotton exporters suffered outweighed the benefits they received from U.S. aid."[35] These interventions cost taxpayers billions of dollars and simultaneously hurt the world's poor. How can this possibly be justified? Good question.

> *Government Subsidy:* any financial benefit that the government gives to an individual or group of people.

Granted, politicians and bureaucrats have their work cut out for them trying to balance the need for tax revenue while having minimal impact on free trade between households and firms. Tax too little and you may not have enough money to provide government services people want. Tax too much and you hurt the ability of people to grow the economy. George Gilder explains: "There is a paradox of redistribution. Beyond a certain point already reached in most modern democracies, raising the taxes on high incomes leads to more, not less, luxurious living by the rich, and to less, not more, support and opportunity for the poor."[36]

The failure to cure poverty is a worldview problem. When you embrace wrong assumptions about God, the world, and humanity, failure is not only likely; it's practically guaranteed.

3. WHY COUNTERFEIT WORLDVIEWS FAIL TO CURE POVERTY

Throughout *Understanding the Culture*, we've looked at how six different worldviews approach life's most complex problems based on what each holds to be true about God, the world, and our relationship to God and the world. Here's how each of these worldviews attempts to solve the poverty problem.

Secularism. If the material world is all there is, there really is no fundamental reason to fight poverty. Only the fittest survive. If people can't figure out how to survive on their own, too bad. In their desire to live long, healthy lives, though, Secularists recognize that when some humans struggle to survive, it threatens the survival of us all. We're on a rock hurtling through space; we live and die together. Because Secularists either don't believe in or don't care about the afterlife, their goal boils down to to helping others live as long as possible. Feed them and give them medicine so they can live a greater number of disease-free days.

There's another implication of the notion that the material world is all there is: the belief that economic resources are finite. We can't make more oil or minerals, for example. So if someone is hoarding, they should be punished before their greed harms the rest of us. If some people or groups have more, Secularists reason, it can actually be an ethical good to take it from them.

But who gets to decide what is fair to take, and from whom? As economist E. Calvin Beisner states,

> When people speak of "the fair distribution of advantages, assets, and benefits among all members of a society," they tacitly assume that some identifiable person

or persons, other than God, do the distributing. But no such moral actors exist with regard to the most important advantages, assets, and benefits.[37]

Typically, government is granted the power to do the taking because it can enforce its decisions through law.[38]

In essence, whoever decides to do the taking is claiming to know better than the rest what ought to be done. These individuals seek power not to set people free from the constraints that keep them from flourishing but to gain the ability to enforce their decisions. For one group of Secularists, those who embrace the teachings of Karl Marx, this is the whole point.

Marxism. Marxists believe this world's ills come from powerful people taking wealth away from others. The good life, to the Marxist, isn't one of creativity and hard work fostered by free enterprise but of fomenting revolution to seize economic power by force. The end result of this process, the workers' paradise, is called **communism**. The path to communism is **socialism**, which Marx defined as the "abolition of private property."[39]

By taking away private property, socialists aim to move power from the market to the government. Undoubtedly, many companies have abused their responsibilities in a craven drive for higher profits. Examples include pollution, unsafe work conditions, and price manipulation. Is turning power over to the government the best way to solve these problems, though? Critics of the Marxist approach point out that at least in a free market, people must serve in order to succeed. Natural resources or raw materials, in and of themselves, aren't productive. They require human thought, ingenuity, and energy to become useful. Land by itself produces only weeds. With people's hard work and creativity, land can produce enough fruits and vegetables to feed far more people than just the producer.

> By taking away private property, socialists aim to move power from the market to the government.

Concentrating power in the government seems not to have this effect. Socialism requires a planned economy and state control of pricing, production, and distribution of goods and services. It relies on increased political power and a highly involved central government to achieve the goals of economic equality and a planned economy. Calvin Beisner says, "The only way to arrive at equal fruits is to equalize behavior, and that requires robbing men of liberty, making them slaves."[40]

The thousands of years of experiments with socialist economic systems, mixed with Darwinian ideas of survival of the fittest, made a toxic brew out of which some of the world's most infamous tyrants conjured up fascism, Nazism, and communism.[41] And in a great historic irony, the response to the failures of government-sponsored socialism led not to a return to biblical ideas of stewardship but to a cynical giving up of meaning altogether. It's called *Postmodernism*.

Postmodernism. Like Marxism, the postmodern worldview says that the stories we accept about how the world works are cynical ploys designed to keep us in power by marginalizing others—the poor, the unemployed, migrants, and minorities.[42] Unlike Marxism, Postmodernism has no hope that revolution will solve the problem.

Still, Postmodernists think highly of socialism's promise to reverse the plight of the marginalized. As Stephen Hicks phrases it,

> Postmodern thinkers inherit an intellectual tradition that has seen the defeat of all of its major hopes, but there was always socialism. As bad as the philosophical universe became in metaphysics, epistemology, and the study of human nature, there was still the vision of an ethical and political order that would transcend everything and create the beautiful collectivist society.[43]

Some Postmodernists prefer to replace the term *socialism* with *everyday economics*.[44] An older term is *collectivism*. Whatever name is used, there is a consistent denunciation of **capitalism** because it is said to prioritize profits over people, subject workers to grueling stress, and fleece consumers.[45] Yet Postmodernism solves little, seeming to content itself with critiquing modern systems. Critiquing modern ways of doing things, as we'll see, is also characteristic of the Islamic worldview.

Islam. On the surface, Islam has much in common with Christianity's concern for the poor. In fact, the giving of alms (***zakat***) is one of the five clear requirements of being Muslim.

> *Zakat:* the third pillar of Islam establishing a mandatory donation of 2.5 percent of a Muslim's annual net income.

Every Muslim is required to give 2.5 percent (one-fortieth) of his or her annual net income (income after expenses, taxes, etc.)[46] to the poor, either directly or through charities. This enables the poor, widows, orphans, the sick, and the unfortunate to survive.[47] In some Muslim countries, the *zakat* is enforced by law, while it remains voluntary and unaccounted for in others.[48] Nevertheless, it's a duty Allah prescribed in the Quran, and Muslims believe that everyone will be held accountable in the final judgment.

Below the surface, though, there are many differences between Islam and the Christian tradition. Whereas the Judeo-Christian ethic requires justice and charity to *all*, Muslims aren't mandated to help needy non-Muslims with their alms. Hammudah Abdalati listed eight groups worthy of receiving help from the *zakat*: poor Muslims, needy Muslims, new Muslim converts, Muslim prisoners of war, Muslims in debt, Muslim employees whose wages are to be paid through the *zakat,* Muslims serving the cause of Allah, and Muslim wayfarers.[49]

Muslim scholars and apologists speak of the practice of *zakat* in grand terms. Abdalati said,

> Zakat does not only purify the property of the contributor but also purifies his heart from selfishness and greed for wealth. In return, it purifies the heart of the recipient from envy and jealousy, from hatred and uneasiness; and it fosters in his heart, instead, good will and warm wishes for the contributor. As a result, the society at large will purify and free itself from class warfare and suspicion, from ill feelings and distrust, from corruption and disintegration, and from all such evils.[50]

To this way of thinking, *zakat* is a form of worship, not a mere tax. That helping the poor is somehow a spiritual issue isn't just the view of Muslims. New Spiritualists also frame economic issues in spiritual—rather than material—terms.

New Spirituality. New Spirituality describes those in the Western world who draw on Eastern principles of tapping into a **higher consciousness** as the basis of the good life. By higher consciousness, New Spiritualists mean a sort of force, like light and sound, that created the universe and may be tapped into to help us reach our dreams and make the world a better place. Sometimes "higher consciousness" is called *god* or *Gaia*, or simply *consciousness*.

New Spiritualists believe that as we evolve toward higher states of consciousness, we'll overcome our need for structures like capitalism and socialism. Marilyn Ferguson claimed, "Both capitalism and socialism, as we know them, pivot on material values. They are inadequate philosophies for a transformed society."[51] Economic problems such as greed, theft, and covetousness are, according to actress and New Spiritualist advocate Shirley MacLaine, "a manifestation of the need for human love."[52]

In one way, New Spiritualists agree with Christians that creativity, power, love, and joy are spiritual, not material, values and thus are not limited. Michael Bernard Beckwith says,

> The truth is that there's more than enough good to go around. There's more than enough creative ideas. There's more than enough power. There's more than enough love. There's more than enough joy. All of this begins to come through a mind that is aware of its own infinite nature.[53]

So how do we get abundance? By overcoming our false sense that we are deprived, and starting to give generously. Eckhart Tolle put it this way: "You don't have it? Just act as if you had it, and it will come. Then, soon after you start giving, you will start receiving. You cannot receive what you don't give. Outflow determines inflow."[54] This sounds like a biblical servanthood ethic, but the writings of most New Spiritualists show that it isn't as much a desire to see God glorified as it is to derive a personal sense of satisfaction in life. As Marianne Williamson says, "Our purpose on this earth is to be happy."[55] It's about "me." This is why personal prosperity (**universal enlightened production**) is at the heart of New Spiritualist economics. Poverty comes from being unenlightened. When people achieve higher consciousness, they'll see their own true power and make economic choices that bring prosperity. Then poverty will disappear. Economic theorizing will be irrelevant.

> *Universal Enlightened Production:* the belief that an individual's financial success is directly proportional to his or her level of enlightenment; the belief that positive thought creates wealth.

None of these views—Secularism, Marxism, Postmodernism, Islam, or New Spirituality—offers a vision of human flourishing in quite the same way Christianity does. Let's take a look at that next.

4. Why Should Christians Care?

One doesn't need to read very far in the Bible to see that God cares very much about the poor and helpless. The ancient Israelites were commanded to care for their poor neighbors and were given very specific ways of doing so. Curses were pronounced on those who harmed widows and the fatherless. Why Christians should care about the poor can be summed up in Jesus's command to love God and love our neighbors. We love God by bearing his image well and recognizing that all human beings are made in his image. We love our neighbors by showing justice, kindness, and humility. Here's a brief review of what the Old and New Testaments say about poverty and the poor.

What the Bible Says about Poverty

> **Why Christians should care about the poor can be summed up in Jesus's command to love God and love our neighbors.**

Most references to the word *poverty* are in the book of Proverbs and serve as a warning against laziness and idle talk. But throughout both the Old and New Testaments, believers are admonished to provide for the poor. Leviticus 23:22, for example, instructs harvesters to leave the edges of their fields unharvested so the poor will be able to come out and work to glean food for their families.

And while private property is assumed throughout the Bible—especially in the commandments not to bear false witness, covet, or steal—Leviticus 25 outlines a system by which people could "rent" property to increase their stewardship opportunities, with the property being returned after seven years. This enabled the poor to earn money by letting others use their property, and it protected them from being taken advantage of. When it comes to financial aid, God instructed the people, in Deuteronomy 26:12, to set aside a tithe to give to the church as well as to foreigners, the fatherless, and widows.

It seems, though, that God intended to bring the children of Israel to the Promised Land so they would no longer experience poverty. Deuteronomy 15:4 says, "There will be no poor among you; for the LORD will bless you in the land that the LORD your God is giving you for an inheritance to possess." In the Old Testament, God instructed the people to set aside a tithe to give to the church as well as to foreigners, the fatherless, and widows.

> **It seems that God intended to bring the children of Israel into the Promised Land so they would no longer experience poverty.**

In the New Testament, Jesus spoke regularly about the poor. He even claimed a prophecy from Isaiah for himself, saying, "The spirit of the Lord is upon me … to proclaim good news to the poor" (Luke 4:18). In his most well-known sermon, Jesus said, "Blessed are you who are poor, for yours is the kingdom of God. Blessed are you who are hungry now, for you shall be satisfied. Blessed are you who weep now, for you shall laugh" (6:20–21).

Many times Jesus's words about the poor were illustrations rather than principles for how to treat the poor. For example, in Matthew 5:6, Jesus said, "Blessed are those who hunger and thirst for righteousness, for they shall be satisfied." In verse 3, he said, "Blessed are the poor in spirit, for theirs is the kingdom of heaven." These verses apply people's understanding of hunger, thirst, and poverty to their spiritual condition.

In other passages, though, Jesus clearly commanded providing for the poor. In Luke 14:13, Jesus told his hearers, "When you give a feast, invite the poor, the crippled, the lame, the blind." And in Matthew 25, Jesus offered a narrative about the coming judgment in which the king (referring to himself) tells his hearers that their good deeds toward the poor are a reflection of their love for him: "Truly, I say to you, as you did it to one of the least of these my brothers, you did it to me" (v. 40).

Some people think Jesus taught that poverty would never end because of an incident in which a woman in the town of Bethany anointed him with an expensive perfume. To the ensuing criticism, Jesus replied, "You always have the poor with you, but you will not always have me" (26:11). Some people fatalistically assume this means poverty will never end. But the context indicates that Jesus was alerting his disciples to how little time remained before his crucifixion. Presumably, there would be many opportunities to provide for the poor, but the days when they could walk with Jesus were coming to an end.[56]

Taken together, these passages reveal something about who God is, who we are as his image bearers, and how we ought to act toward our neighbors. Being image bearers of God is such a critical aspect of living out a biblical worldview that we'll now take a look at *how* bearing God's image affects our relationship with the poor.

Loving God: How a Biblical Cure for Poverty Is Rooted in Bearing God's Image

What it means to be human is at the root of how we relate to the poor. Are we merely animals to be fed, or are we something more? Are we fated merely to consume resources in our struggle for survival, or are we able to create value? Are resources finite materials in the ground, or are they virtually unlimited products of human imagination?

Secularists say that God is irrelevant to our life decisions. When they scan the horizon, they fail to see the outworking of God's creativity. Rather, they see a *closed system*, with nothing existing outside the universe to bring meaning into it. Humans are moist bags of bones held together by skin, helplessly spinning on a remote planet in a huge, impersonal universe. If there is to be any meaning in life, we must make it for ourselves.

> **What it means to be human is at the root of how we relate to the poor.**

When Secularists apply this thinking to resources, they see mainly physical things in the ground. Resources are limited by definition because the universe is a closed system. If one person consumes more, there is less left for everyone else. This is why they see a growing human population as a threat. As British cleric and demographic theorist Thomas Malthus (1766–1834) articulated it, our ability to find and use resources does grow, but the number of mouths to feed grows much faster. Eventually we'll run out of resources, and everyone on the planet will die.

But we aren't helpless against this, Secularists say. We can postpone our demise by redistributing scarce resources so no one person or group has an advantage in the struggle for life. We can take from the haves and distribute our takings to those have-nots through welfare programs and aid.

Of course, there is another possible solution. We could voluntarily extinguish ourselves. Margaret Sanger, founder of Planned Parenthood International, advocated this second solution. Sanger's approach to the poor was to "clear the way for a better world" by weeding them out as you would a garden:

> Birth Control is not merely an individual problem; it is not merely a national question, it concerns the whole wide world, the ultimate destiny of the human race. In his last book, Mr. [H.G.] Wells speaks of the meaningless, aimless lives which cram this world of ours, hordes of people who are born, who live, yet who have done absolutely nothing to advance the race one iota. Their lives are hopeless repetitions. All that they have said has been said before; all that they have done has been done better before. Such human weeds clog up the path, drain up the energies and the resources of this little earth. We must clear the way for a better world; we must cultivate our garden.[57]

These two solutions represent the thinking of secular worldviews. Either redistribute scarce resources from the haves to the have-nots or prevent more have-nots from being born in the first place.

The Judeo-Christian framework is radically different. Its first principle is that God existed in three persons before the universe began. The universe isn't meaningless; God has filled it with personality and relationship. Humans are, according to Genesis 1:26–28,[58] image bearers of God. We aren't simply mouths to be fed but are endowed with minds to think and hearts to imagine, create, and discover the resources God has hidden in the creation. Darrow Miller expresses it this way: "God spoke and created the universe; his image bearers speak and shape the universe and create culture."[59]

> We aren't simply mouths to be fed but are endowed with minds to think and hearts to imagine, create, and discover the resources God has hidden in the creation.

If God exists and humans bear his image, our primary resource isn't what's in the ground. It's what's in our minds. Imagination and moral stewardship of creation *creates* the resources we need to make life better for everyone.

> If God exists and humans bear his image, our primary resource isn't what's in the ground. It's what's in our minds.

Consider as an example the wealthy nation of Singapore, where five million people inhabit an island of 274 square miles. Nearly twenty thousand people live in each square mile. Contrast that with neighboring Malaysia, a country rich in natural resources, in which fewer than one hundred people per square mile compete for that abundance. And yet Malaysia is quite poor. Singapore, on the other hand, has no natural resources at all. Even her drinking water must be imported. However, she is vastly wealthy because of her enterprising population.

When you think about it, our favorite companies demonstrate the power of imagination and hard work too. As of 2015, the Apple corporation was valued at more than $700 billion, an amount greater than the total production of all but about eighteen of the world's nations.[60] It's perhaps the most valued brand in the world. Apple says it has created nearly two million jobs in the United States alone and many tens of thousands more in other countries.[61] And yet Apple wasn't destined to be created. No one dug around in the ground and discovered it. All of its value represents *new wealth* created when two men, Steve Jobs and Steve Wozniak, brought it forth from their minds just four decades ago. Imagine that. All this wealth birthed from nothing but the imagination and hard work of two men.

You're probably familiar with the ancient Chinese proverb "If you *give* a man a fish, you feed him for a day. If you *teach* a man to fish, you feed him for a lifetime." Certainly, the first priority when it comes to helping the poor is to provide emergency relief from life-threatening conditions. But from a biblical viewpoint, true help involves much more. It includes helping the poor break down the governmental, personal, and cultural barriers that keep them poor, so they can use their imaginations and hard work to provide for themselves.

Humans made in God's image need more than a safety net and the ability to care for themselves. As Darrow Miller suggests, we should add a third line to the fish proverb: "*Empower* a man *to think* about fishing and his life will be changed forever."[62] Helping people bear God's image more fully brings transformation and enables them to truly flourish. Not only that, they become capable of helping others in turn.

> The biblical solution to poverty is helping the poor break down the governmental, personal, and cultural barriers that keep them poor, so they can use their imaginations and hard work to provide for themselves.

Working toward human flourishing requires a biblical motivation and a biblical mind-set. We have to see people differently, as image bearers of God who are held captive by some stronghold, whether government corruption, self-doubt, or cultural barriers that tell them they'll always be poor. The poor need a paradigm shift to see reality as God sees it. This freedom clears the way for flourishing.

How can we help create this paradigm shift? The Bible calls us to three specific actions. Let's take a look at each for clues as to how we can love our neighbors who are poor.

> Helping people bear God's image more fully brings transformation and enables them to truly flourish and help others in turn.

Loving Our Neighbors: How a Biblical Cure for Poverty Is Rooted in How We Live as Image Bearers

I've used the phrase **human flourishing** many times in this book. It's a vital concept. Our goal is to help the poor not just survive but really come alive. But how? Micah 6:8 says, "[God] has told you, O man, what is good; and what does the Lord require of you but to do justice, and to love kindness, and to walk humbly with your God?" Doing justly, loving kindness, and walking humbly with God provide the framework we need to help the poor come alive.

Do justly. God cares about justice. According to Calvin Beisner, the Bible outlines four criteria for justice:[63]

- **Impartiality.** Impartiality means applying all the relevant rules to everyone in every relevant situation (see Exod. 23:3; Deut. 1:16–17).[64] The Bible recognizes that while the poor are most vulnerable to injustice, this doesn't mean that justice should be partial to them.

- **Rendering to each his or her due.** Justice demands that "something about the person being judged merits ... the judgment" (see Prov. 24:12; Matt. 16:27; Rom. 2:6; 13:7; 1 Cor. 3:8; and Gal. 6:7–8).[65] Justice punishes evil and rewards good.

- **Proportionality.** The Bible distinguishes between intentional harm, accidental harm, and harm from negligence. When harm comes from an accident, justice demands that the loss be evened up (see Exod. 21:35).[66] In negligence, the person responsible must "bear the full loss" and "restore the full value" (see 22:6).[67] If harm is done intentionally, the person at fault must restore to the harmed person what is taken, plus a multiple of the item's value (v. 1).[68]

- **Conformity to the standard set forth in God's law.** An example of this kind of justice is the demand for honesty. For example, in Leviticus 19:35–36,[69] Scripture commands the use of just weights and measures. Honesty is the bedrock of trust, on which economic prosperity can grow.

Love kindness. First John 4:19 says that "we love because [God] first loved us." Our good works should display *his* greatness, not *our* well-meaningness. Truth be told, we're helpless before the rightness and justice of God. Only when we realize our lostness and embrace *his* kindness do *we* become capable of kindness. In this way, kindness proceeds from brokenness. Psalm 51:17 says, "The sacrifices of God are a broken spirit; a broken and contrite heart, O God, you will not despise."

Contrary to worldviews that express confidence in human ability to solve every problem, Christianity is based on a belief that seems pessimistic at first. The belief is that we're full of sin and capable only of making things worse than they are, apart from God's grace. To help the poor, we must be broken by our own poverty of spirit. Steve Corbett and Brian Fikkert put it this way: "Until we embrace our mutual brokenness, our work with low-income people is likely to do far more harm than good."[70] Contrary to worldviews that express confidence in human ability to solve every problem, Christianity teaches that to help the poor, we must be broken by our own poverty of spirit.

> Our good works should display *God's* greatness, not *our* well-meaningness.

Sometimes religious people are the worst because they think their obedience to God will automatically cause them to do the right thing. The prophet Isaiah condemned those who think this way:

Is not this the kind of fasting I have chosen:
to loose the chains of injustice
    and untie the cords of the yoke,
to set the oppressed free
    and break every yoke?
Is it not to share your food with the hungry
    and to provide the poor wanderer with shelter—
when you see the naked, to clothe them,
    and not to turn away from your own flesh and blood?
Then your light will break forth like the dawn,
    and your healing will quickly appear;
then your righteousness will go before you,
    and the glory of the Lord will be your rear guard.
Then you will call, and the Lord will answer;
    you will cry for help, and he will say: Here am I. (Isa. 58:6–9 NIV)

We do good to others not because we're better but because we, too, are broken. As it's been said, we're beggars telling other beggars where to find bread. Perhaps this is why Jesus warns us to "Take care, and be on your guard against all covetousness, for one's life does not consist in the abundance of his possessions" (Luke 12:15). And we're to give "in secret," anticipating God's reward, not the acclaim of others (Matt. 6:3–4).

The point Jesus made in both passages is straightforward. Good intentions aren't enough. We can't assume that because our motives are good, we'll produce good results. We help others out of a recognition that we're all broken. In the end, the most important thing we can do is show up and walk alongside.[71]

Steve Corbett and Brian Fikkert emphasize that if we fail to understand our brokenness, we'll just march in and try to play god in the lives of the poor, reinforcing the feelings of inferiority and shame that already plague them.[72] There are literally thousands of examples of projects people have engaged in under the guise of showing compassion to the poor, when in fact they were feeding their own vanity and possibly making the problem worse.

One company, for example, commits to give away one pair of shoes to the poor for every pair of shoes a customer purchases. It's a noble intention, but the company has been forced to change some of its practices in response to criticism that theirs was a "vanity project" designed to enrich the company while making customers feel good about doing something that didn't really help the poor. While perhaps too harsh, these critics had two valid points: first, what people in poverty-stricken countries need isn't shoes but jobs. Why not help them *make* shoes and earn a living instead of dropping off free shoes that will last only a short time? Second, shoe giveaways create a new problem: they destroy the livelihood of those selling shoes, deepening a community's dependence on aid.[73]

Walk humbly with God. Jesus taught in Mark 9:35 that "if anyone would be first, he must be last of all and servant of all." The apostle Paul explained in Philippians 2:4–8 how Jesus did this, and how it should change the way we live:

Let each of you look not only to his own interests, but also to the interests of others. Have this mind among yourselves, which is yours in Christ Jesus, who, though he was in the form of God, did not count equality with God a thing to be grasped, but emptied himself, by taking the form of a servant, being born in the likeness of men. And being found in human form, he humbled himself by becoming obedient to the point of death, even death on a cross.

> **Arrogance shows up as a smug do-gooder focused on getting attention. Humility shows up as a servant emptying him- or herself in pursuit of others' interests.**

Arrogance shows up as a smug do-gooder focused on getting attention. Humility shows up as a servant emptying himself or herself in pursuit of others' interests.

Thinking that wealthy, educated nations know "better" has led to a lot of heartache. This assumption has brought entire regions of the world to the brink of disaster. For example, European countries claimed territory across the African continent in the 1800s and 1900s. Plainly, some of these countries were just interested in taking resources and cared very little about how the people native to those countries fared. Other countries brought economic prosperity, peace, and order, along with their rulership. Over time, though, the arrogance of the colonizers stirred up a noxious brew of dependence and resentment—and, ultimately, civil war. Unfortunately, postcolonial rulers, corrupt and dedicated to socialist aims, left things worse than before. Fifty years after the colonial era ended in Africa, not one nation on the continent was better off than before European rule, and most countries were worse off.[74]

Without a clear sense of God's image and our own brokenness, we humans tend to take with one hand while we give with the other, grasping power in exchange for what we give in sustenance, doling out short-term benefit but demanding long-term fealty.

A biblical mind-set, on the other hand, opens our eyes to genuine abundance. Give—clear eyed, lovingly, and extravagantly; there's plenty more where that came from.[75]

> **We should care about the poor because we're made in the image of an almighty God for whom there are no limitations on imagination and love. Therefore, love: love justly, kindly, and humbly.**

So why should Christians care about the poor? Not just because we can find a Bible verse saying so. Not just because we feel guilty. We should care about the poor because we're made in the image of an almighty God for whom there are no limitations on imagination and love. Therefore, love: love justly, kindly, and humbly.

Such love isn't merely a feeling; it's a set of actions. What specifically can we do differently to help the poor truly flourish? Here are three ideas, from the personal to the global, that seem consistent with the Scripture passages we looked at earlier.

5. WHAT SHOULD CHRISTIANS DO?

Can poverty be cured? Yes. Maybe not all at once. And certainly not without bumps in the road. If it is to happen, though, each one of us must be part of the solution. Here's how.

Start Local and Give Generously (and Not Just Money)

Nearly everyone reading this chapter is rich by the world's standards. You may not feel advantaged, but think of all the things you've experienced without a second thought. As Harvard professor Robert Putnam bluntly states it, "Every summer camp you went to or every piano lesson you got or every time you went to soccer club, you were getting some advantage."[76] Kids growing up in poverty don't have these experiences. The adults in their lives are more likely to be irresponsible or preoccupied, often leaving them alone for long periods of time and not even feeding them. Consequently, they lose their trust in adults. Over time these disadvantages add up, perpetuating a generational cycle of poverty.[77]

Thinking from this perspective, it seems that the needs are almost overwhelming. The first step is to take care of emergencies by giving financially to private charities that know the people they're serving and how best to help them. Because they work with individuals, not just "the poor," private charities tend to run much more efficiently than even well-meaning, tax-funded, government programs. Economist John Lott notes that when private charities distribute aid, 80 to 90 percent of people's donations to charity actually reach the needy. By contrast, 70 cents of every dollar of federal government aid to the poor goes to government bureaucracy and others who serve the poor, not the poor themselves.[78] Ministries like Compassion International serve as a positive example of the private approach. Donors give thirty-eight dollars a month (at the time of this writing) to sponsor a child's meals, education, health care, and spiritual nurturing. More than one million children are currently being supported in this way.[79]

But it's easy to look at poverty around the world and miss opportunities in our own communities. Start with your church. If everyone who goes to church on Sunday gave a 10 percent tithe, churches would have more than enough money to solve the poverty problem.[80] It's sad that we would rather pay 25 to 50 percent of our incomes to the government than 10 percent to the church. Yet according to Patrick Johnson with GenerousChurch, a financial ministry that equips church leaders, "The average Christian gives about 2.4 to 3% of their income during good times and bad times. It doesn't really change dramatically depending on what the economy is doing."[81]

> If everyone who goes to church on Sunday gave a 10 percent tithe, churches would have more than enough money to solve the poverty problem.

Keep in mind, though, it isn't just about money. We each have lots of "currencies" we can give to help others: friendship, caring, creative ideas, encouragement, time, joy, persistence, possessions, spiritual gifts, networking, mentoring, persuasion, tutoring, cheering, insight, talents, skills, persuasion, hugs, smiles, words of blessing, and so much more.

One sixteen-year-old I know had very little money but loved to design clothes. She came up with some designs and got a chain of stores to carry them, raising hundreds of thousands of dollars for scholarships to send inner-city youth to a sports camp. Another young woman taught sewing skills to young women who had been sex-trafficking victims. Others tutor struggling children. One young man I know organized and led a soccer program for disadvantaged youth, using the experience to help his players gain social skills and learn good character. Older adults can have a significant influence as well. Robert Putnam documents how older adults who just sit and listen to children read can help them increase reading scores by a full grade level.[82]

The problem isn't just "out there" in the world somewhere. It's next door. Start where you are and give as generously as you can.

Move beyond Aid to Asset Development

In economics, as in life, it's better to give than to receive. This is true for the poor as well as for the wealthy. Joseph Remenyi is a professor at Deakin University in Australia who closely examines income levels for the poor and publishes regular reports on his findings. Discussing Remenyi's research, Herbert Schlossberg makes a startling claim:

> Remenyi makes a statement that will appear to some readers to be a quiet truism, but in the context of the actual debates is a blockbuster. He says that projects that actually alleviate poverty do so by "seeking to improve output per person." What's this—the *output* of poor people is to be increased? This will flummox many people associated with the redistribution mentality or with any relief and development program with a "helping-the-poor mentality." It will do so because it is a reversal of the common assumption that you help people by giving *to* them. It says that we help people by getting more *from* them.[83]

This sounds almost impossibly naive. How can people who have almost nothing produce anything at all? From a secular viewpoint, which says that people are just matter in motion, they probably cannot. Just give them aid.

But merely giving money to people doesn't solve the problem. It could make it worse. Jay Richards references a study from the National Bureau of Economic Research (NBER) showing "*no* correlation between the amount of aid a country receives and its economic growth, even when you account for the fact that it's the poorer countries that normally receive aid."[84]

The executive director of the Acton Institute, Kris Alan Mauren, states it even more strongly, with respect to the Africa example:

> Floods of Western aid serve not to lift developing countries out of poverty, but only to poison their homegrown industries, to promote unrest within their borders, and ultimately, to strip away the dignity of their people. At the risk of sounding trite, the solution to Africa's problems is Africa; its people—not neocolonialist U.N. bureaucrats—are best equipped to solve the crises of hunger and disease the continent faces.[85]

While we're presented with tantalizing figures of how much money could "end hunger forever," and while in our hearts we want to help make it happen, Mauren warns, "Feelings don't alleviate poverty, and neither do the hefty but seemingly blank checks we've been writing for years."[86]

Still, there will always be those who, in hopes of achieving some sort of socialist utopia, believe that the rich got their wealth by taking it from the poor and that it must be taken back. They sell their approach to the public by inciting envy, making people feel greedy for that to which they think they're entitled. But as syndicated columnist Cal Thomas notes, "Envy, greed, and entitlement never created a job or a small business or improved a single life."[87]

Not only does redistributed wealth hurt as much as it helps, but the attempts to redistribute it through tax policy usually end up hurting the most those who were intended to benefit from it in the first place. We might feel envious watching the rich lounge about on their yachts, but taxing doesn't hurt rich people—they'd just buy a vacation house instead. Tax vacation houses, and they'll just rent a hotel room in a nice spot. Those who are hurt the most when luxuries are taxed are the people trying to work their way out of poverty by building yachts or vacation houses. The history of tax policy shows that using taxes to punish the rich hurts the middle class the most.[88]

So if redistribution and aid don't work, what will? Is it actually possible for the poor to help themselves? As we've seen, the goal of poverty care is poverty *cure*. To do this, we need to go beyond the "give a man a fish" mind-set (emergency aid) and even beyond the "teach a man to fish" mind-set (sustainability). Destroying the stronghold of poverty requires us to "teach a man to think about fishing." This requires understanding the larger context of fishing—the ethic of work, stewardship of the land, smart use of water, and so forth.

What I'm describing here is the difference between **need-based community development** and **asset-based community development**. Need-based community development (NBCD) enters a community and asks, "What do you need?" After determining what is lacking, it then provides for that need. This is the tendency of secular models of understanding poverty. Such an approach is driven by the belief that people who are poor cannot help themselves; the outsider must send money. This paradigm tends to increase dependency and, ultimately, poverty.

The Judeo-Christian paradigm envisions a plethora of resources "inside" the community—asset-based community development (ABCD). This position argues that God has provided each community and nation the assets they need to flourish. It asks the community, "What assets do you have that you can use to solve your problem?" Helping poor communities, from this perspective, involves identifying the dynamic, life-enhancing assets people in the community already possess. These assets include skills like artistic ability or coaching or neighborhood watch, structures like churches or parks or libraries, services like child care or music lessons or recycling, and businesses that supply jobs and needed services. These assets are both natural and supernatural and lie both within and outside the individuals in the community.

> *Need-based community development:* **the process of trying to improve the economic conditions of a community by giving outside resources, such as money, goods, and aid.**

> *Asset-based community development:* **the process of trying to improve the economic conditions of a community by developing inside resources, such as people's talents and skills.**

Everyone can bring something to the table. Yet this is only the beginning. To cure poverty forever, we have to begin thinking big.

Move beyond Subsistence

As we saw earlier, aid doesn't build wealth. If anything, it encourages corruption by tempting those who control governmental power to take a greater share for themselves. Many of these efforts, while well intentioned, serve mainly to employ lots of people in the aid business.[89] In the developing world, the fight to control the aid money ends up destabilizing countries, leading even to civil war.[90]

Many ministries and entrepreneurs have moved beyond aid to helping people set up roadside businesses and family enterprises. This is a crucial next step to providing emergency relief. And yet it isn't the final step. Subsistence efforts cannot lead to long-term stability, regardless of the pure hearts and hard work that motivate them. Even if they were entirely successful, they could raise out of poverty only "a small portion of the world's 7 billion people."[91] Paying more for coffee to provide a living wage for coffee producers won't raise the global price of coffee. As soon as the subsidies go away or the subsidizers lose interest and move on to their next cause, the coffee farmers will be right back where they were before.

> Subsistence efforts to alleviate poverty cannot lead to long-term stability, regardless of the pure hearts and hard work that motivate them.

This brings up an uncomfortable reality. We've already seen how destructive the we-know-better mind-set can be as Western nations patronize developing ones. But there's another aspect to this mind-set: telling ourselves that some people are just destined to subsist and that they're better off or even happier the way they are. This attitude is just as patronizing. As Wayne Grudem and Barry Asmus write in *The Poverty of Nations*,

We simply do not know that people living by means of subsistence farming were happier. We tend to paint an idealized picture in our minds, forgetting the short life spans (often under thirty years), the crippling diseases and frequent deaths, the anxiety of never knowing whether there would be enough to eat next month, the weariness of dawn-to-dusk manual labor for one's entire lifetime, the unfulfilled longing of parents for better lives for their children, the yearning after the option of choosing another way of life, and so on.[92]

We cannot assume that poor people are better off or happier the way they are. Nor can we assume that traditional tribal policies of holding resources or forcing those who have experienced an economic windfall to provide for everyone else. As Grudem and Asmus state,

The results are inefficient exhaustion of the resources, deterioration of the environment, and social conflict among those who compete for resource use. While it may seem emotionally pleasing to believe that land, oceans, and wildlife belong to everyone as a common heritage, the economic consequences are typically tragic.[93]

So is there a middle ground between controlling the poor and just leaving them to muddle through on their own? The answer is yes. We can help the poor learn to use their natural resources efficiently and their talent to develop large-scale economic enterprises that can serve the world's needs. It may seem to us that less developed nations can't progress to develop products that world markets demand, but it has happened many times in history. Britain wasn't a traditional cloth-producing country, but it embraced machines that revolutionized the textile industry. Japan wasn't a traditional auto-producing nation, but now cars produced there are in demand in virtually every nation of the world. What can be done to promote creative ingenuity in countries that today are very poor? "The correct answer," as Grudem and Asmus point out, "is not 'Nothing.'"[94]

This last point seems overwhelmingly large, but to those gifted in invention, engineering, architecture, construction, supply-chain management, business development, banking, transportation, and so many other pursuits, it is proof that God's call in life goes far beyond serving as missionaries and pastors, as valuable as those vocations are. Everyone is called. All of our gifts are needed. And this should fill us with joyful enthusiasm, not fear. "For God gave us a spirit not of fear but of power and love and self-control" (2 Tim. 1:7).

> We can help the poor learn to use their natural resources efficiently and their talent to develop large-scale economic enterprises that can serve the world's needs.

6. CONCLUSION

The Paradigm Project makes stoves. They're nothing fancy. Just low-tech cooking devices that burn wood or coal much more efficiently than open fires. They're designed for use in developing countries where millions of people die every year from respiratory illnesses caused by inefficient cooking methods. The stoves are sold—not given away—because the company's founders have discovered that people are much more likely to care for their stoves and use them if they have money invested in them.

Those who buy the stoves find that for their small financial investment, they not only can save 70 to 80 percent of their fuel costs, as well as the grueling labor of spending hours every day searching for wood to burn, but they can improve their family's health at the same time. The environmental effect is also notable. Carbon emissions are reduced. Trees are saved. Fewer people die of respiratory illnesses caused by smoke. On top of all this, investors in the company make a high rate of return by selling carbon credits to companies that want to make up for their use of carbon-based fuels. This isn't just a win-win. It's a win-win-win-win-win-win-win.

The Paradigm Project is a small company, but it represents awesome potential by embracing a biblical worldview of human nature and economics, living fully inside the circle of reality and taking into account the order of the created world.[95] It's a fascinating example of poverty *cure*, not just poverty *care*, and it leads to a question with which we'll end our discussion: What is *your* project?

ENDNOTES

1. James Mackintosh, "Business Pioneers in Finance," *Financial Times*, March 31, 2015, https://next.ft.com/content/7a1a9882-cc9d-11e4-b5a5-00144feab7de. See also Muhammad Yunus, Yunus Centre, www.muhammadyunus.org/.

2. Joseph Grenny et al., *Influencer: The New Science of Leading Change*, 2nd ed. (New York: McGraw-Hill, 2013), 190.

3. Grenny et al., *Influencer*, 191.

4. For more about microloans and how you can get involved in this simple way of helping people out of poverty, take a look at Kiva, www.kiva.org/.

5. Mackintosh, "Business Pioneers in Finance." See also www.muhammadyunus.org/.

6. Dictionary.com, s.v. "poverty," http://dictionary.com/browse/poverty.

7. "Learning to Live Together: Poverty," United Nations Educational, Scientific and Cultural Organization (UNESCO), accessed July 29, 2016, www.unesco.org/new/en/social-and-human-sciences/themes/international-migration/glossary/poverty/.

8. Kathleen Short, *The Research Supplemental Poverty Measure: 2011; Current Population Reports* (Washington, DC: US Census Bureau, 2011): 3, www.census.gov/hhes/povmeas/methodology/supplemental/research/Short_ResearchSPM2011 .pdf. See also US Census Bureau, "Measuring America: How Census Measures Poverty," January 2014, www.census.gov /library/visualizations/2014/demo/poverty_measure-how.html.

9. US Census Bureau, "Data: Poverty Thresholds," 2015, www.census.gov/data/tables/time-series/demo/income-poverty /historical-poverty-thresholds.html.

10. US Census Bureau, "Measuring America: How Census Measures Poverty."

11. Carmen DeNavas-Walt and Bernadette D. Proctor, *Income and Poverty in the United States: 2013; Current Population Reports* (Washington, DC: US Census Bureau, 2014), 4, www.census.gov/content/dam/Census/library/publications/2014 /demo/p60-249.pdf. In the United States, to live below the "poverty threshold" means to have an income that is less than three times the cost of a minimum food diet, as determined in 1963 and updated annually for inflation. The federal government now also uses a supplemental measure (SPM) that includes clothing, housing, and utilities. (See US Census Bureau, "Measuring America: How Census Measures Poverty.") Statistics are updated annually by two government agencies, the Economics and Statistics Administration and the US Census Bureau, both of which are part of the US Department of Commerce.

12. Martin Meredith, *The Fate of Africa: A History of Fifty Years of Independence* (New York: Public Affairs, 2005), 292.

13. Cited in Meredith, *Fate of Africa*, 682.

14. "Africa Rising: A Hopeful Continent," *Economist*, March 2, 2013, www.economist.com/news/special-report /21572377-african-lives-have-already-greatly-improved-over-past-decade-says-oliver-august.

15. Poverty statistics for 1990 and 2010, respectively. See World Bank Group, *Prosperity for All: Ending Extreme Poverty* (Washington, DC: World Bank, 2014), 1, http://siteresources.worldbank.org/INTPROSPECTS/Resources /334934-1327948020811/8401693-1397074077765/Prosperity_for_All_Final_2014.pdf.

16. Alex Perry, "Africa Rising," *Time*, December 3, 2012, 50, http://content.time.com/time/magazine/article/0,9171,2129831,00 .html.

17. The Mo Ibrahim Foundation, founded by Sudanese businessman Mo Ibrahim, tracks Africa's progress in governance and leadership (www.moibrahimfoundation.org). Ibrahim's Index of African Governance seeks to use accountability and education to improve governance in African countries. See also the research of Human Rights Watch, particularly the report *High Stakes: Political Violence and the 2013 Elections in Kenya* (Washington, DC: Human Rights Watch, 2013), www.hrw.org/sites/default/files/reports/kenya0213webwcover.pdf.

18. Oliver August, "Africa Rising: A Hopeful Continent," *Economist*, March 2, 2016, www.economist.com/news/special -report/21572377-african-lives-have-already-greatly-improved-over-past-decade-says-oliver-august.

19. Ronald H. Nash, *Poverty and Wealth: The Christian Debate over Capitalism* (Westchester, IL: Crossway Books, 1987), 71.

20. See also Proverbs 13:4: "The soul of the sluggard craves and gets nothing, while the soul of the diligent is richly supplied"; Proverbs 24:30–34: "I passed by the field of a sluggard, by the vineyard of a man lacking sense, and behold, it was all overgrown with thorns; the ground was covered with nettles, and its stone wall was broken down. Then I saw and considered it; I looked and received instruction. A little sleep, a little slumber, a little folding of the hands to rest, and poverty will come upon you like a robber, and want like an armed man"; Proverbs 28:19: "Whoever works his land will have plenty of bread, but he who follows worthless pursuits will have plenty of poverty."

21. Theodore Dalrymple, *Life at the Bottom: The Worldview That Makes the Underclass* (Chicago: Ivan R. Dee, 2002), x, xv.

22. Angus Maddison, *The World Economy: A Millennial Perspective* (Paris: Development Centre of the Organisation for Economic Co-operation and Development, 2001), cited in Partha Dasgupta, *Economics: A Very Short Introduction* (New York: Oxford University Press, 2007), 16. As of October 2015, the World Bank raised its defining line of extreme poverty to $1.90 per day from its 2008 level of $1.25 per day (see "FAQs: Global Poverty Line Update," World Bank, September 30, 2015, www.worldbank.org/en/topic/poverty/brief/global-poverty-line-faq).

23. A picture of life for Russian peasants in the early 1900s can be found in Candace Fleming, *The Family Romanov: Murder, Rebellion, and the Fall of Imperial Russia* (New York: Schwartz and Wade Books, 2014), 5–7.

24. Sylvia Nasar, *The Grand Pursuit: The Story of Economic Genius* (New York: Simon and Schuster, 2011), xiii. The internal citation is to James Edward Austen Leigh, *A Memoir of Jane Austen* (London: Richard Bentley & Son, 1871), 13.

25. For more information, see W. Cleon Skousen, *The Five Thousand Year Leap* (Franklin, TN: American Documents Publishing, 2009), 4.

26. See Nasar, *Grand Pursuit*, 310.

27. Nicholas Wapshott, *Keynes Hayek: The Clash That Defined Modern Economics* (New York: W. W. Norton, 2011), 169–70.

28. Franklin D. Roosevelt, "Fireside Chat," April 14, 1938, cited in Gerhard Peters and John T. Woolley, American Presidency Project, www.presidency.ucsb.edu/ws/?pid=15628. See also Wapshott, *Keynes Hayek*, 189.

29. Cited in Toby Neugebauer, "A Borrowed Prosperity" (presentation at Summit Ministries, Manitou Springs, Colorado, August 20, 2011). See http://vimeo.com/29115347.

30. Clarence B. Carson, *The Welfare State, 1929–1985* (Wadley, AL: American Textbook Committee, 1985), 52. For a full list of codes, see "NRA Codes of Fair Competition," HD3616, U452, A19, Library of Congress, www.loc.gov/rr/business /nra/NRA%20intern%20project_test.html.

31. Carson, *The Welfare State*, 54–55.

32. Veronique de Rugy, "High Taxes and High Budget Deficits: The Hoover-Roosevelt Tax Increases of the 1930s," *Tax and Budget Bulletin*, no. 14 (March 2003), http://object.cato.org/sites/cato.org/files/pubs/pdf/tbb-0508-25.pdf.

33. Carmen DeNavas-Walt, Bernadette D. Proctor, and Cheryl Hill Lee, *Income, Poverty, and Health Insurance Coverage in the United States: 2005* (Washington, DC: Government Printing Office, 2006), 13, www.census.gov/prod/2006pubs /p60-231.pdf. Data cited in Jay Richards, *Money, Greed, and God: Why Capitalism Is the Solution and Not the Problem* (New York: HarperOne, 2009), 47.

34. Meredith, *Fate of Africa*, 684.

35. Oxfam data, cited in Meredith, *Fate of Africa*, 684. The study being referred to is Kevin Watkins, *Cultivating Poverty: The Impact of US Cotton Subsidies on Africa* (Washington, DC: Oxfam International, 2002), http://policy-practice.oxfam.org .uk/publications/cultivating-poverty-the-impact-of-us-cotton-subsidies-on-africa-114111. Elimination of US subsidies would not only save US taxpayers billions of dollars, but it could more than double income of cotton producers in developing countries, which would have a significant effect on the poverty level in cotton-producing nations. See Julian M. Alston, Daniel A. Sumner, and Henrich Brunke, *Impacts of Reductions in US Cotton Subsidies on West African Cotton Producers* (Boston: Oxfam America, 2007), www.oxfamamerica.org/static/oa3/files/paying-the-price.pdf.

36. George Gilder, *Wealth and Poverty: A New Edition for the Twenty-First Century* (Washington, DC: Regnery, 2012), 236.

37. E. Calvin Beisner, *Social Justice: How Good Intentions Undermine Justice and Gospel* (Washington, DC: Family Research Council, 2013), 22, http://downloads.frc.org/EF/EF13E133.pdf.

38. Knowing what happened to America during the Great Depression should make us wary of the notion that government necessarily makes smarter decisions about how much wealth to confiscate and how to redistribute it. About Roosevelt's New Deal, critic Clarence Carson said, "The New Deal gave the impression that much was going on and something was being done, especially in the early months. It was the responsibility of government to set things right, so its programs said, to rescue the banks, manage the money, organize and rehabilitate industry, put people to work, provide emergency relief, save the farmers, and put everything on an even keel. The New Deal was part bread and part circus; it was scurry, experiment, legislate, create agencies, and spend money. The motif of the New Deal was to do something even if it was wrong, but do something." Carson, *The Welfare State, 1929–1985*, 50. Anti-government libertarians, but few others, widely study Carson's book. Newer books, however, have made a credible case for his main points through widely respected publishing channels. Examples include Amity Shlaes, *The Forgotten Man: A New History of the Great Depression* (New York: Harper Perennial, 2008), which explores the New Deal in searing detail. Several books also challenge conventional wisdom that federal government intervention was necessary to "save" the economy in the wake of the 2008 recession. See former FDIC chairwoman Sheila Bair's book *Bull by the Horns: Fighting to Save Main Street from Wall Street and Wall Street from Itself* (New York: Simon and Schuster, 2012); and David A. Stockman, *The Great Deformation: The Corruption of Capitalism in America* (New York: Public Affairs, 2013).

39. Karl Marx and Friedrich Engels, *The Communist Manifesto* (New York: Bantam, 2004), 27. Marxists think of socialism as the first phase of communism. The underlying principle, according to Marx, is that each person gives according to his abilities and receives according to his needs. All must work, but the results of the labor are equally shared. See V. I. Lenin, "The Economic Basis of the Withering Away of the State," sec. 3 in *The State and Revolution* (New York: Penguin, 1992), chap. 1, www.marxists.org/archive/lenin/works/1917/staterev/ch05.htm#s3.

40. E. Calvin Beisner, *Prosperity and Poverty: The Compassionate Use of Resources in a World of Scarcity* (Eugene, OR: Wipf and Stock, 2001), 54.

41. The catastrophic failings of these ideologies are documented in many works, such as Igor Shafarevich, *The Socialist Phenomenon* (New York: Harper and Row, 1980); Ludwig von Mises, *Socialism: An Economic and Sociological Analysis* (Indianapolis: Liberty Classics, 1981); and Joshua Muravchik, *Heaven on Earth: The Rise and Fall of Socialism* (San Francisco: Encounter Books, 2002).

42. Women's studies, black studies, gay/queer studies, and the like are taught from the Postmodernist point of view. For example, see F. Carolyn Graglia, *Domestic Tranquility: A Brief against Feminism* (Dallas: Spence Publishing, 1998).

43. Stephen R. C. Hicks, *Explaining Postmodernism: Skepticism and Socialism from Rousseau to Foucault* (Tempe, AZ: Scholargy Publishing, 2004), 197.

44. David F. Ruccio and Jack Amariglio, *Postmodern Moments in Modern Economics* (Princeton, NJ: Princeton University Press, 2003), 270.

45. Ruccio and Amariglio, *Postmodern Moments*, 269.

46. Hammudah Abdalati wrote, "[A Muslim's] personal expenses, his family allowances, his necessary expenditures, his due credits—all are paid first, and [zakat] is for the net balance." Hammudah Abdalati, *Islam in Focus* (Indianapolis: American Trust Publications, 1975), 97.

47. See Abdalati, *Islam in Focus*.

48. George W. Braswell Jr., *Islam: Its Prophet, Peoples, Politics, and Power* (Nashville: Broadman and Holman, 1996), 65.

49. Abdalati, *Islam in Focus*, 97–98. According to the *Sahih Muslim*, "alms are only for the poor, the needy, the officials charged with the duty of collection, those whose hearts are inclined to truth [i.e., Muslims], the ransoming of captives,

those in debt, in the way of Allah, and the wayfarer [i.e., a traveling Muslim, especially one on pilgrimage]." Quran, surah 9:60, cited in Abdul Hamid Siddiqui, trans., "The Book of Zakat," bk. 5 in *Sahih Muslim*.

50. Abdalati, *Islam in Focus*, 95–96.

51. Marilyn Ferguson, *The Aquarian Conspiracy: Personal and Social Transformation in the 1980s* (Los Angeles: J. P. Tarcher, 1980), 326–27.

52. Shirley MacLaine, *Out on a Limb* (New York: Bantam Books, 1983), 291.

53. Michael Bernard Beckwith, quoted in Rhonda Byrne, *The Secret* (New York: Atria Books, 2006), 147.

54. Eckhart Tolle, *A New Earth: Awakening to Your Life's Purpose* (New York: Dutton, 2005), 191.

55. Marianne Williamson, *A Return to Love: Reflections on the Principles of "A Course in Miracles"* (London: Aquarian, 1992), 170.

56. Scott Todd, "The Poor Will Not Always Be with You," *Compassion Blog*, October 4, 2010, Compassion International, http://blog.compassion.com/the-poor-will-not-always-be-with-you/#ixzz3XR1tPwuv.

57. Margaret Sanger, in Adolf Meyer, ed., *Birth Control: Facts and Responsibilities—A Symposium Dealing with This Important Subject from a Number of Angles* (Baltimore: Williams and Wilkins, 1925), 15.

58. Genesis 1:26–28: "God said, 'Let us make man in our image, after our likeness. And let them have dominion over the fish of the sea and over the birds of the heavens and over the livestock and over all the earth and over every creeping thing that creeps on the earth.' So God created man in his own image, in the image of God he created him; male and female he created them. And God blessed them. And God said to them, 'Be fruitful and multiply and fill the earth and subdue it, and have dominion over the fish of the sea and over the birds of the heavens and over every living thing that moves on the earth.'"

59. From Darrow L. Miller's research for this chapter. You can discover more of Miller's breakthrough work on his website Disciple Nations Alliance, www.disciplenations.org/.

60. Patrick Gillespie, "Apple: First U.S. Company Worth $700 Billion," CNN Money, February 10, 2015, http://money.cnn.com/2015/02/10/investing/apple-stock-high-700-billion/.

61. Updated estimate in "Creating Jobs through Innovation," Apple.com, accessed September 24, 2016, www.apple.com/about/job-creation/.

62. From Miller's research for this chapter.

63. Beisner, *Social Justice*, 11–14.

64. Exodus 23:3 "Nor shall you be partial to a poor man in his lawsuit"; Deuteronomy 1:16–17: "I charged your judges at that time, 'Hear the cases between your brothers, and judge righteously between a man and his brother or the alien who is with him. You shall not be partial in judgment. You shall hear the small and the great alike. You shall not be intimidated by anyone, for the judgment is God's. And the case that is too hard for you, you shall bring to me, and I will hear it.'"

65. Proverbs 24:12: "If you say, 'Behold, we did not know this,' does not he who weighs the heart perceive it? Does not he who keeps watch over your soul know it, and will he not repay man according to his work?"; Matthew 16:27: "The Son of Man is going to come with his angels in the glory of his Father, and then he will repay each person according to what he has done"; Romans 2:6 "[God] will render to each one according to his works"; Romans 13:7: "Pay to all what is owed to them: taxes to whom taxes are owed, revenue to whom revenue is owed, respect to whom respect is owed, honor to whom honor is owed"; 1 Corinthians 3:8: "He who plants and he who waters are one, and each will receive his wages according to his labor"; Galatians 6:7–8: "Do not be deceived: God is not mocked, for whatever one sows, that will he also reap. For the one who sows to his own flesh will from the flesh reap corruption, but the one who sows to the Spirit will from the Spirit reap eternal life."

66. Exodus 21:35: "When one man's ox butts another's, so that it dies, then they shall sell the live ox and share its price, and the dead beast also they shall share."

67. Exodus 22:6: "If fire breaks out and catches in thorns so that the stacked grain or the standing grain or the field is consumed, he who started the fire shall make full restitution."

68. Exodus 22:1: "If a man steals an ox or a sheep, and kills it or sells it, he shall repay five oxen for an ox, and four sheep for a sheep."

69. Leviticus 19:35–36: "You shall do no wrong in judgment, in measures of length or weight or quantity. You shall have just balances, just weights, a just ephah, and a just hin: I am the LORD your God, who brought you out of the land of Egypt.

70. Steve Corbett and Brian Fikkert, *When Helping Hurts: How to Alleviate Poverty without Hurting the Poor … and Yourself* (Chicago: Moody, 2009), 64.

71. Corbett and Fikkert, *When Helping Hurts*, 147.

72. Corbett and Fikkert, *When Helping Hurts*, 65.

73. James Poulos, "Toms Shoes: A Doomed Vanity Project?," *Forbes*, April 11, 2012, www.forbes.com/sites/jamespoulos/2012/04/11/toms-shoes-a-doomed-vanity-project/.

74. For a thorough analysis, see Martin Meredith's highly regarded book *The Fate of Africa: A History of Fifty Years of Independence*. For a travel narrative from someone who crossed the entire African continent over land, see Paul Theroux, *Dark Star Safari: Overland from Cairo to Cape Town* (New York: Mariner, 2003).

75. Contrary to what many say about capitalism being greedy and self-serving, economist George Gilder identifies

socialism with selfishness and capitalism with servanthood: "Capitalism begins with giving. Not from greed, avarice, or even self-love can one expect the rewards of commerce, but from a spirit closely akin to altruism, a regard for the needs of others, a benevolent, outgoing, and courageous temper of mind." Gilder, *Wealth and Poverty*, 27.

76. Emily Badger, "The Terrible Loneliness of Growing Up Poor in Robert Putnam's America," *Wonkblog*, March 6, 2015, *Washington Post*, www.washingtonpost.com/blogs/wonkblog/wp/2015/03/06/the-terrible-loneliness-of-growing-up-poor -in-robert-putnams-america/.

77. Badger, "Terrible Loneliness."

78. Michael Tanner, Congressional Testimony before the Finance Committee, U.S. Senate, March 9, 1995, www.cato.org /publications/congressional-testimony/welfare-reform. Cited in John R. Lott, *Freedomnomics: Why the Free Market Works and Other Half-Baked Theories Don't* (Washington, DC: Regnery, 2007), 93.

79. "Sponsor a Child Today," Compassion International, accessed July 29, 2016, www.compassion.com/sponsor_a_child /default.htm.

80. My calculations, which I did in 2015, work out as follows: Fiscal year 2015 federal, state, and local welfare spending in the United States was estimated to be $454.3 billion (see www.usgovernmentspending.com/us_welfare_spending_40.html). Approximately 40 percent of Americans claim to attend church, which translates to 127.6 million people, of which I estimate that half are potential wage earners. If each person tithed 10 percent of the average income of wage earners ($50,500), the total raised would be $319.3 billion. If we assume that this money would be distributed through private charity, which Lott has demonstrated is three times as efficient as government programs at channeling aid to those in need (see Lott, *Freedomnomics*, 93) and could presumably accomplish the same goals as government programs with much greater efficiency, it's conceivable that following the biblical idea of a 10 percent tithe, America's churches could solve the poverty problem. (For example, urban charter schools achieve higher academic results for about one-quarter the money as urban public schools; see Marcus A. Winters, "Better Schools, Fewer Dollars," *Wall Street Journal*, June 21, 2012, www.wsj.com/articles/SB100014240527023038 22204577468783242379036.) This assumes, of course, that people who attend church get involved personally and don't just throw money at the problems they identify, as impersonal governments are often wont to do.

81. Patrick Johnson, quoted in Stacy Long, "Generous Church," *AFA Journal*, January 2013, www.afajournal.org/2013 /January/012013generous.html.

82. The program Putnam explores is called Experience Corps. Its goal is "to improve the literacy rates of children, enrich the lives of our volunteers and strengthen schools in the communities we serve." See Robert D. Putnam and Lewis M. Feldstein, "Experience Corps: Bringing 'Old Heads' to the Schools," chap. 9 in *Better Together: Restoring the American Community* (New York: Simon and Schuster, 2004). See also "AARP Foundation Experience Corps," AARP Foundation, accessed September 24, 2016, www.aarp.org/experience-corps/.

83. Joe Remenyi, *Where Credit Is Due: Income Generating Programs for the Poor in Developing Countries* (London: Intermediate Technology, 1990), 35, cited in Herbert Schlossberg, "Destroying Poverty without Destroying Poor People," in *Christianity and Economics in the Post–Cold War Era: The Oxford Declaration and Beyond*, eds. Herbert Schlossberg, Vinay Samuel, and Ronald J. Sider (Grand Rapids: Eerdmans, 1994), 119.

84. Raghuram G. Rajan and Arvind Subramanian, "Aid and Growth: What Does the Cross-Country Evidence Really Show?" (working paper no. 11513, National Bureau of Economic Research, Cambridge, Massachusetts, 2005), www.nber. org/papers/w11513.pdf, cited in Richards, *Money, Greed, and God*, 46.

85. Kris Alan Mauren, "What's behind PovertyCure?," *Religion and Liberty* 21, no. 4 (Summer 2006), www.acton.org/pub /religion-liberty/volume-21-number-4/whats-behind-povertycure.

86. Mauren, "What's behind PovertyCure?"

87. Cal Thomas, "Waking Up Washington to What Works," *Centennial Review* 7, no. 2 (February 2015): 2.

88. N. Gregory Mankiw, *Principles of Economics*, 5th ed. (Mason, OH: South-Western, 2007), 131.

89. In her book *Dead Aid*, Dambisa Moyo controversially suggests that the aid business continues because half a million people work for aid organizations, and their livelihood depends on giving money away without regard to whether it helps or hurts. See Dambisa Moyo, *Dead Aid: Why Aid Is Not Working and How There Is a Better Way for Africa* (New York: Farrar, Straus and Giroux, 2010), 54.

90. Rwandan president Paul Kagame said, "Much of this aid was spent on creating and sustaining client regimes of one type or another, with minimal regard to developmental outcomes on our continent." H. E. Paul Kagame, "Making Aid Work for Africa" (Brenthurst Discussion Paper, Brenthurst Foundation, Johannesburg, South Africa, July 2007), 2, www.thebrenthurstfoundation.org/Files/Brenthurst_Commisioned_Reports/BD0707_HE_Paul_Kagame_Making_Aid _Work_Better.pdf.

91. Wayne Grudem and Barry Asmus, *The Poverty of Nations: A Sustainable Solution* (Wheaton, IL: Crossway, 2013), 111.

92. Grudem and Asmus, *Poverty of Nations*.

93. Grudem and Asmus, *Poverty of Nations*, 116.

94. These examples come from Grudem and Asmus, *Poverty of Nations*, 62–63.

95. "Why Stoves?," Paradigm Project, accessed July 30, 2016, www.theparadigmproject.org/why-stoves-/#why-stoves-intro.

CHAPTER 15

┌─────────────┐
│   │
│   *15*   │
│   │
└─────────────┘

THE USE OF
FORCE

1. CAN CHRISTIANITY AND THE USE OF FORCE BE RECONCILED?

There were many places in the world Henry Gerecke could have imagined being, but the city of Nuremberg, Germany, wasn't one of them. The once beautiful city was reduced to rubble and would now be forever known as home to the Nuremberg trials, in which Nazi leaders faced public reckoning for their crimes.

When he signed up to be a US Army chaplain, Gerecke (rhymes with "Cherokee") could never have foreseen that his

Lutheran training and knowledge of the German language would land him there, as the chaplain to some of history's most vicious mass murderers.

Footsteps echoing off the bare walls, Gerecke hurried to keep up with the guard who would be introducing him to his new flock. They arrived at the first door. After two quick knocks from the guard and a key in the lock, the rusty hinges of the door groaned.

Suddenly Gerecke was face-to-face with one of the most infamous men alive, Hitler's deputy führer, Rudolf Hess.

He looks like any other man, thought Gerecke, extending his hand to the prisoner. Hess took his hand and shook it. Instantly, Gerecke knew the next day's headline would read, "Army Chaplain Shakes War Criminal's Hand!" But he didn't care. *Nothing can be allowed to hinder the work of the gospel in the lives of these men*, he reminded himself. *If a small gesture of friendship helps me break through, then forget what the world thinks. If anyone needs the gospel right now, it is these men, on trial for their lives.*

But Gerecke's spontaneous handshake with an infamous Nazi war criminal served as more than a gesture of friendship. It reminded the world of the difference between the church's priorities and the state's. Governments would host the trial to restore justice, but the gospel's importance was supreme. Without it, justice had no meaning; nor did repentance, healing, or truth.

Gerecke had agonized over the decision to serve as the Protestant chaplain to these men. Homesick after years overseas, exhausted at the war's end, and anxious to be reunited with his family, Gerecke found himself on a park bench wrestling in prayer. His biographer perfectly captured the struggle: "If, as never before, he could hate the sin but love the sinner, he thought, now was the time."[1]

So Gerecke said yes to the assignment. Judging by the body count of their victims, his little flock was one of the most sinful ever assembled. Yet Gerecke treated his charges humanely, walking the halls, praying with and counseling the men, communicating with family members, and leading the prisoners in worship. When the verdicts were announced, thirteen of his parishioners had received the death sentence. Twelve were hanged, and one, Hermann Göring, committed suicide. Before their deaths, by Gerecke's account, many had repented of their sins and trusted Jesus Christ as their savior.

> When asked how he could pastor such a blood-soaked congregation, Gerecke replied that it was the *court's* job to decide whether these men were guilty before the law, and it was the *chaplain's* job to restore their humanity and prepare them for eternity.

When asked how he could pastor such a blood-soaked congregation, Gerecke replied that it was the *court's* job to decide whether these men were guilty before the law, and it was the *chaplain's* job to restore their humanity and prepare them for eternity. Gerecke's biographer wrote that the chaplains were "attempting to give Hitler's henchmen new standing as human beings before their impending executions."[2]

The fight against the Nazis was just. No one seriously doubts that. Led by the madman Hitler, the men on trial at Nuremberg had sparked a war that cost millions of lives. They had also systematically murdered millions more. But what role should Christians play, even in such a clear-cut case? Knowing that souls are eternal, are Christians ever justified in taking life? And what about the church? Does it—or should it—have anything to say about war and peace?

For Gerecke, these weren't theoretical questions. Of all the issues being settled at Nuremberg, Gerecke's was ultimate. His war was for men's souls.

Questions of war and peace aren't theoretical for you or me, either. Earthly warfare rarely ceases. Whether we should serve in the armed forces and how we should support friends and loved ones who do serve are always in the front of our minds. Many believers live in countries that require military service. How to reconcile Christianity and the use of force is a question they cannot wish away.

The Bible was written against the backdrop of warfare, so by studying God's revelation in its pages, we can learn how to live in a world in which peace is as fleeting as ever. Over time, four distinct Christian views of warfare, military service, and peace have emerged: pacifism, nonresistance, just-war theory, and crusade/prevention. Our goal in this chapter is to explore what the Bible says about war and peace and then study each of these views to see if we can arrive at a consistent, livable perspective on the use of force.

> The Bible was written against the backdrop of warfare, so by studying God's revelation in its pages, we can learn how to live in a world in which peace is as fleeting as ever.

2. What Is the Problem?

War Is Violent

The history of humanity is that of near-constant war, punctuated by brief periods of peace. War correspondent Chris Hedges observes that "of the past 3,400 years, humans have been entirely at peace for 268 of them, or just 8 percent of recorded history."[3] The human cost has been enormous. In the twentieth century alone, more than 38 million people died in wars, including civil wars, and over 169 million people died as a result of their own governments using force against them.[4]

> The history of humanity is that of near-constant war, punctuated by brief periods of peace.

These figures are so large, we can hardly get our minds around them. But the cost of war is personal, even for the warriors who survive it. Tim Khan, a summer staffer at Summit, joined the Marine Corps at age eighteen and served five years on active duty, including deployment to the war in Afghanistan. Tim appreciates the marines' core values of honor, courage, and commitment. But during his deployment in Afghanistan, his job involved watching video feeds of drone strikes. The regular viewing of insurgents burning to death changed him. After spending entire shifts watching the enemy die violently, Tim would often attend funerals for coalition personnel. Everywhere he turned, it seemed, he was surrounded by death—the death of enemies, the death of friends.

Over time this exposure to the horrors on the battlefield, combined with the constant tension, pounded away at Tim. Disillusioned, he stopped caring about life. A relationship with Christ became his only salvation, physically as well as spiritually.

Like Tim, we all must be transformed by the renewing of our minds (Rom. 12:2).[5] Through Christ our hearts are "sprinkled clean from an evil conscience" (Heb. 10:22).[6] This changes how we see the value of everyone else. If the enormous tragedy of war doesn't move us, we ought to engage in some serious soul-searching. Every life lost is the life of someone with a soul, someone made in God's image, someone others cared for, someone who had thoughts and ideas and will be missed. We are never to take this lightly, because at the heart of Christianity is a God-initiated, unconditional, sacrificial love.

Christianity Is about Love

Jesus said to "love one another" (John 13:34–35),[7] and not just those we like. We are to love our enemies as well (Matt. 5:44).[8] Theologian George Kalantzis says,

> At the core of the Christian message is love. This is not an ordinary kind of love, as one has for one's kin. It is God's love for God's enemies. It is this love of God for the world, expressed in the divine self-giving through the incarnation of the Son that reconciles God's enemies with the Triune God, Father, Son, and Holy Spirit.[9]

Shalom: from the Hebrew for "peace, prosperity, and wellness"; a concept that implies harmony in creation and with one's neighbors as well as a right relationship with God.

The end of this love is peace—peace with God and peace with our neighbors (Mark 12:31).[10] And, as Jesus made clear, everyone is our neighbor. In chapter 1, we noted Scripture's repeated emphasis on the tie between our neighbors' well-being and our love for God. It pleases God when we pursue **shalom**, which means "peace, wellness, prosperity, tranquility, and contentment," both for ourselves and for others. God promised the Israelites, even in their captivity, that their *shalom* would be secured as they worked to secure *shalom* for those around them, including their captors (Jer. 29:7).[11]

At the heart of *shalom* is reconciliation with the One who made us in his own image. The first kind of peace we need is peace with God. As Kalantzis puts it, this is "a peace not based simply on the absence of conflict, but on the proactive love of one's enemies as a first principle for the community that claims to have been born of this Gospel of Peace."[12]

Few Christians would disagree with this assessment. What does give rise to disagreement, though, is whether, as individuals, we should use force for our personal protection, to protect our loved ones, or in defense of the state. Does the government have the right to *make* us personally participate in war? And more to the point, is it even *possible* to be a Christian and a warrior at the same time?

Warfare and the Early Church

Roland Bainton, a Quaker pacifist and church historian, gave the impression in his writings that early Christians were pacifists who refused to practice violence in any form. This changed, Bainton argued, during the time of Constantine's rule, when Christianity became the state religion. Bainton's position is that early Christians compromised the purity of their pacifist stance to maintain their power in the secular realm.[13]

Bainton's reading of the early church fathers has caused a great deal of controversy, leading other scholars, such as James Turner Johnson, to carefully reread those early writings. The evidence is more mixed than Bainton portrayed.[14] While some church fathers clearly did oppose military service, many of them did not. Scripture itself doesn't prohibit military service. In fact, many scriptural heroes were warriors, even in the time of Jesus and the apostles. Jesus called the Roman centurion near his hometown a man of great faith (Matt. 8:5–13).[15] The apostle Peter converted another centurion, Cornelius, to Christianity (Acts 10:1, 30–35).[16] In neither case does Scripture record these men being told to give up their military service.

Bainton's picture of early Christians' attitude toward government isn't accurate either. Rather than being uncritically accepting of Roman rule, early Christian leaders, such as Augustine, consistently called civic authorities to account and insisted that Christians needed to be prepared to speak the truth even when it was unpopular. Augustine wrote an entire book about this, titled *City of God*.[17]

The apostles don't clarify for us how Jesus's commands to love one another relate to military service. And in view of the fact that the early church fathers were divided over the issue, perhaps it would be best to begin our analysis by looking back over the words of the Bible itself. Then we'll examine each of the four common Christian views to ask:

- Is a Christian's use of force permissible or required?

- Under what circumstances, if any, should a Christian serve in the military?

- What are the prospects for peace?

- Indeed, what do we mean by peace?

Most of our discussion will be related to war and military service. Police authority is important too, but we'll deal with it in the next chapter, which is on justice. In this chapter, the outstanding research of Rouven Steeves, a graduate of Summit and now a professor at the US Air Force Academy, will guide a great deal of our discussion. One might think that a professor at a service academy would be biased in favor of war, but Dr. Steeves's approach is balanced and generous to various points of view, a spirit I hope carries over into this text. There is plenty of room inside a Christian worldview for wise and thoughtful people to diverge on questions of war and peace.

3. Why Should Christians Care?

It seems that an enduring feature of life in this world is, as Jesus phrased it, "wars and rumors of wars" (Matt. 24:6; Mark 13:7).[18] Questions of how to avoid war and how to conduct it, how to pursue peace and how to enforce it will be with us all through our lives.

As we consider these questions, let's first define **force** as "the strength or power used to influence others." People talk about those who have forceful personalities, those whose persuasive force moves people to action, and those who force others to do things against their will. All of these have to do with compelling other people to do things.

From a secular viewpoint, all force is ultimately physical. Do you have the ability in the physical world to *make* people do what you want? If so, you possess force. But the Bible tells us that the physical world isn't all there is. A spiritual world exists, and the writers of Scripture were clear that principles of warfare apply in the spiritual realm as well as in the physical. The apostle Paul said, "The weapons of our warfare are not of the flesh but have divine power to destroy strongholds" (2 Cor. 10:4).

> *Force:* strength or power used to influence or oppress others.

To understand force from a biblical perspective, then, we need to understand both spiritual and physical force.

Spiritual Force

Our primary battles are spiritual, not physical. "We do not wrestle against flesh and blood, but against the rulers, against the authorities, against the cosmic powers over this present darkness, against the spiritual forces of evil in the heavenly places," wrote the apostle Paul in Ephesians 6:12. The story of the world, according to the Bible, is that sin is a parasite on God's creation, turning us into unwise, self-obsessed people who think we know better than God what the good life is. Ephesians 2:1–5 says,

> You were dead in the trespasses and sins in which you once walked, following the course of this world, following the prince of the power of the air, the spirit that is now at work in the sons of disobedience—among whom we all once lived in the passions of our flesh, carrying out the desires of the body and the mind, and were by nature children of wrath, like the rest of mankind. But God, being rich in mercy, because of the great love with which he loved us, even when we were dead in our trespasses, made us alive together with Christ—by grace you have been saved.

Through God's mercy, we're rescued from our own self-destruction and are able, as God's image bearers, to love others more every day. Every waking moment, we testify to God's perspective on truth, goodness, and beauty, in the way we live and by what we say.

The enemies of the redeemed life are the flesh, the world, and the Devil. The word *flesh* is used in many ways in the Bible, but in the context of temptation to sin, it refers to decisions we make in our bodies that are apart from faith. Romans 6:12–13 says,

> Let not sin therefore reign in your mortal body, to make you obey its passions. Do not present your members to sin as instruments for unrighteousness, but present yourselves to God as those who have been brought from death to life, and your members to God as instruments for righteousness.

The world also tempts us to sin. Creation is subject to futility, which causes it to decay (Rom. 8:20-21).[19] The temptation of the world is very hard to resist because it seems so normal. Jesus said, "Woe to the world [*kosmos*—the whole world, the affairs of the world] for temptations to sin! For it is necessary that temptations come, but woe to the one by whom the temptation comes!" (Matt. 18:7).

The Devil is the "the god of this world" (2 Cor. 4:4), "the tempter" (1 Thess. 3:5), and "the accuser of [the] brothers" (Rev. 12:10). He is also "an angel of light," deceiving humankind by appearing to be full of light (2 Cor. 11:14) when he is actually "full of darkness" (Matt. 6:23). The apostle Peter exhorted, "Be sober-minded; be watchful. Your adversary the devil prowls around like a roaring lion, seeking someone to devour. Resist him, firm in your faith, knowing that the same kinds of suffering are being experienced by your brotherhood throughout the world" (1 Pet. 5:8–9).

To fight the battle against the world, the flesh, and the Devil, we must put on God's armor: truth, righteousness, the gospel of peace, faith, salvation, God's Word, and prayer (Eph. 6:14–18).[20] With this armor we can stand alert against the weapons Satan would use against us. In the end he will fail. As the great preacher Charles Spurgeon said,

> To fight the battle against the world, the flesh, and the Devil, we must put on God's armor: truth, righteousness, the gospel of peace, faith, salvation, God's Word, and prayer.

> Be not afraid. The lion may howl, but rend you in pieces he never can. The enemy may rush in upon you with hideous noise and terrible alarms, but there is no real cause for fear. Stand fast in the Lord. Ye war against a king who hath lost his crown; ye fight against an enemy whose cheek-bones have been smitten, and the joints of whose loins have been loosed. Rejoice, rejoice ye in the day of battle, for it is for you but the beginning of an eternity of triumph.[21]

When it comes to spiritual force, we face lifelong battles against sin. But Christ's death and resurrection secure our triumph. Physical war begins with spiritual war. In our fallenness, we humans demand power, recognition, respect, security, safety, and conquest. And we believe that physical force will help us secure these aims.

Physical Force

As mentioned earlier, physical warfare is the Bible's backdrop. We have to distinguish between the use of force *described* in the Bible and the use of force *prescribed* by God as we grapple with how to deal with force both personally and as citizens of nations that must "bear the sword," to use the biblical terminology (Rom. 13:4).

The Use of Force in the Old Testament

Israel as a nation. Wars in the Old Testament were, as theologian Loraine Boettner put it, "sanctioned as a means of gaining righteous ends."[22] God allowed Israel to conquer the nations around it that threatened their survival, and permitted other nations, such as the Midianites, the Philistines, and the Assyrians, to attack and even conquer the Israelites when they rebelled against him (Judg. 6:1; 13:1; Isa. 10:5–14).[23]

Battle narratives in the Bible tell us a lot about God. "In such events God is revealed as Creator, Lawgiver, Father, and Judge, and also as the Lord God of battle," said Boettner.

> He commands Israel to go to war, and goes before her, but (and this is the important point) Israel must not go before God. When Israel was so presumptuous as to go to war after God had forbidden it, she was disastrously defeated [cf. Num. 14:39–45; 1 Sam. 28:15–19; Josh. 7:1–8:29].[24]

Yet according to Israel's prophets, God's aim was peace. Isaiah said, "[The Lord] shall judge between the nations, and shall decide disputes for many peoples; and they shall beat their swords into plowshares, and their spears into pruning hooks; nation shall not lift up sword against nation, neither shall they learn war anymore" (Isa. 2:4).

> *Lex Talionis:* the principle that a wrong should be righted with a retributive act equal in degree and kind.

Individual members of the community. Of the Ten Commandments given to Moses on Mount Sinai, the sixth was, "You shall not murder" (Exod. 20:13). And yet in Leviticus 24, Moses pronounced the principle of **lex talionis** (the law of retaliation):

> Whoever takes a human life shall surely be put to death. Whoever takes an animal's life shall make it good, life for life. If anyone injures his neighbor, as he has done it shall be done to him, fracture for fracture, eye for eye, tooth for tooth; whatever injury he has given a person shall be given to him. Whoever kills an animal shall make it good, and whoever kills a person shall be put to death. You shall have the same rule for the sojourner and for the native, for I am the LORD your God. (vv. 17–22)[25]

But aren't murder and the death sentence inconsistent? Boettner thought they weren't, because the first is directed to individuals, and the second to the nation as a matter of official policy. He noted,

> Sometimes we hear the sixth commandment quoted to prove that all war is wrong. But the same God who in the twentieth chapter of Exodus said, "Thou shalt not kill," which literally means, "Thou shalt not commit murder," says in the twenty-first chapter, "He that smiteth a man so that he dieth, shall surely be put to death." And centuries before that, the commandment had been given, "Whoso sheddeth man's blood, by man shall his blood be shed" (Gen. 9:6). The command against wilful murder is to be made effective by the sentence of capital punishment against the offender. The judge who sentences the criminal to death is no more guilty of murder than he would be guilty of robbery were he to sentence him to pay a fine.[26]

In war, and regrettably in public safety, soldiers and officers are called upon to make decisions about ending the lives of others. A retired soldier or an off-duty police officer has no more right to take a life than anyone else. But in their positions as soldiers or as officers of the law, they act on behalf of the state and not as individuals. They may use force to move others into compliance with the law.

In Bible times, it seemed common that people were permitted to carry weapons. In Nehemiah 4:18, for example, the people carried weapons to defend themselves while rebuilding Jerusalem's wall.[27] Even Jesus's own disciples were armed (Luke 22:49).[28] Everyday people were capable of wielding lethal force. Yet Scripture is clear that God's people aren't to admire men of violence (Prov. 3:31–32)[29] and are to put their trust in God, not in their weapons (Ps. 44:6–7).[30]

> Scripture is clear that God's people aren't to admire men of violence and are to put their trust in God, not in their weapons.

So what about self-defense? The laws relating to self-defense in ancient Israel seem to have been similar to our own. Indeed, many modern laws are based on those timeless biblical principles. For example, in Exodus 22, the Mosaic law said the Israelites were permitted to defend their families against thieves during the nighttime and were guiltless if they struck an intruder and he died. But if it was daytime, the law assumed they could discern through common sense whether the person was there to steal or to cause physical harm. If the person was a thief, lethal force wasn't justified. The assumption seems to have been that if a man firmly believed his life and the lives of his family members were in mortal danger, he had the right to act with lethal force.

The New Testament has a very different focus on questions of war and peace. What changed wasn't God but the circumstances in which God's people found themselves.

The Use of Force in the New Testament

The use of force by the state. Great changes occurred in the period between the Old and New Testaments. The nation of Israel was subjugated, first by the Babylonians, then by Greece, and then by Rome. In the time of Jesus and the apostles, the Roman Empire ruled the nation of Israel. God was as present as ever, but other nations now ruled over Israel. While Jesus and the apostles might have been citizens concerned with governmental issues, most of the New Testament's teachings dealt with the church as spiritual Israel, not as a form of government. We don't have the right to rule in God's name simply because we are Christians.

Theologian Albertus Pieters explained that now "there are two independent sovereignties both ordained of God: Church and State." According to Pieters, the difference between them is this:

> The State is as truly a divine institution as is the Church. The State is the trustee of the law, the Church of the Gospel; the former bears the sword for forcible restraint of sin, the latter holds the secret of the only remedy for sin. The former (state) compels men to abstain from the grosser forms of open sin; the latter (church) inspires them with a hatred of secret sin and a love for holiness. Both are necessary, and neither has the right to interfere with the other.[31]

The apostle Paul called believers to obey the governing authorities, insofar as they are properly within the bounds of their sovereign authority, "for rulers are not a terror to good conduct, but to bad" (Rom. 13:3).

This doesn't mean the church must roll over and let the state do whatever it wants. As we saw in chapter 12 on politics, Dietrich Bonhoeffer, a German theologian who stood against Adolf Hitler, wrestled with this question. As his biographer Eric Metaxas said, "It is the church's role to help the state be the state."[32] In other words, the church must always ask whether the state's actions are legitimate or lawless. Sometimes the church must stand up against the state when it oversteps its lawful authority. Bonhoeffer maintained that one of the responsibilities of the church "is not just to bandage the victims under the wheel, but to put a spoke in the wheel itself."[33] By this he meant that when the state's evil actions crush the innocent, the church must take steps to stop it.[34]

> The church must always ask whether the state's actions are legitimate or lawless. When the state's evil actions crush the innocent, the church must take steps to stop it.

The use of force by individuals. Jesus specifically addressed the legal principle of *lex talionis* in Matthew 5:38–44 and explained that it wasn't a justification for personal retribution:

> You have heard that it was said, "An eye for an eye and a tooth for a tooth." But I say to you, Do not resist the one who is evil. But if anyone slaps you on the right cheek, turn to him the other also. And if anyone would sue you and take your tunic, let him have your cloak as well. And if anyone forces you to go one mile, go with him two miles.… You have heard that it was said, "You shall love your neighbor and hate your enemy." But I say to you, Love your enemies and pray for those who persecute you.

The New Testament writers believed Jesus was the incarnate Son of God. Thus, his words express God's true intent behind the Law given to Moses. Jesus summarized the Old Testament Law as follows:

> You shall love the Lord your God with all your heart and with all your soul and with all your mind. This is the great and first commandment. And a second is like it: You shall love your neighbor as yourself. On these two commandments depend all the Law and the Prophets. (Matt. 22:37–40)

> We aren't to take our own revenge. But to say that certain scriptures prohibit protecting one's family against physical harm is to stretch them far beyond their context.

So as individuals, our love for God is to overflow to our neighbors. We might even say that the love we show for our neighbors is a thermometer registering whether our hearts are warm or cold toward God.

But what does loving our neighbors mean if a neighbor intends physical harm? May force be used against that person in that situation? It depends. Personal insults don't justify physically harming another person. This much is clear from Jesus's teachings. Other passages seem to touch on these principles as well. We aren't to take our own revenge (Rom. 12:19) or be quick tempered (Titus 1:7).[35] But to apply these verses by saying that they prohibit protecting one's family against physical harm is to stretch them far beyond their context.

Scripture is clear that we must resist evil. But what form ought this resistance take? Do Jesus's teachings apply when it comes to taking up arms in the legitimate defense of the state's God-given authority? Through time, four viewpoints have emerged. Let's take a look at each one.

4. What Should Christians Do?

So far we've seen that the history of fallen humanity is one of warfare. God's revelation in the Old and New Testaments took place against the backdrop of warring nations, and Scripture offers six principles with which most Christians can agree:

War is an unfortunate evil in a fallen world.

The church is not the state.

The state is ordained by God, and Christians ought to submit to its authority, but only insofar as it doesn't clearly violate God's law.

The state, not the church, may use force to punish evil and those who commit it.

The church, not the state, is entrusted with the gospel, which is the remedy for sin and the motivation for holy living.

Individual believers—in the Old and New Testaments—are called to love God and their neighbors, even those who are enemies.

Even given these six principles, though, different Christian traditions arrive at divergent understandings of war, military service, and peace. Robert Clouse's book *War: Four Christian Views* introduces each of these traditions and allows their representatives to have their say, while also allowing representatives of the other traditions to respond to their claims. The four views Clouse presents are (1) nonresistance (Herman A. Hoyt), (2) Christian pacifism (Myron S. Augsburger), (3) the just war (Arthur F. Holmes), and (4) the crusade or preventive war (Harold O. J. Brown).[36]

It may be worth noting that other people have defined these four positions differently. John Howard Yoder, for example, defined the four positions as holy war, justifiable war, pacifism, and "*raison d'état*" (also called *realpolitik*), which is a secular view that decisions about war and peace must be made based on power, diplomacy, and other practical considerations, not on moral or theological principles.[37] For the sake of our

> Although Christians agree on certain principles, different Christian traditions arrive at divergent understandings of war, military service, and peace.

discussion, we'll restrict ourselves to examining the Christian viewpoints, not the secular ones, which would involve discussions of international law, natural law versus legal positivism, and so forth. The book *Understanding the Times* examines many of these issues in depth in the chapters on politics, ethics, and law. This volume has examined a Christian view of politics, tolerance, and religious freedom and will look at a Christian view of justice in the next chapter.[38]

Some readers may find it interesting to examine the views of Christian thinkers of the distant past, such as Augustine, Aquinas, Luther, Vitoria, and Calvin, and the more recent past, such as Stanley Hauerwas, John Yoder, and George Weigel. It's a good idea to study their work if you're interested in how the various Christian viewpoints developed. (Some of their works are referenced in the endnotes for those who may want to pursue the subject further.)[39] But to keep our discussion focused, I'll only briefly mention how each of the four views came about and which Christian traditions tend to hold to each view.

Pacifism

Pacifism asserts that neither the state nor the church should take up arms. Pacifism traces its tradition back to early church fathers, such as Tertullian and Gregory of Nyssa,

> *Pacifism:* the belief that violence and war are always unjust and that conflicts should be settled by peaceful means.

and through certain sects, such as the Quakers, the Brethren, and the Mennonites. Seventh-Day Adventists have also held a pacifist approach. As Myron Augsburger states, "The Old Testament prophet said, 'They will beat their swords into plowshares and their spears into pruning hooks' (Mic. 4:3 NIV), a prophecy fulfilled where the people take the way of Christ and his Spirit seriously."[40] Augsburger acknowledges that there are other viewpoints, and there appear to be times when war is unavoidable, or the lesser of two evils. But, he concludes, "from my perspective the issue is not answered by any of these, rather it is to be faced by the people of God on the basis of the character of his kingdom."[41]

Augsburger believes that the apostle Paul's teachings are clear when he admonished believers to "owe no one anything, except to love each other, for the one who loves another has fulfilled the law" (Rom. 13:8), and to "repay no one evil for evil" (12:17). In Matthew 22:21, Jesus said to "render to Caesar the things that are Caesar's, and to God the things that are God's." In that context, Augsburger says, we must read these passages as a mission for "discipling people to become members of the kingdom of Christ, not helping to justify participation in war."[42]

Harold O. J. Brown, another respected theologian, points out what he believes to be a fatal flaw in Augsburger's approach. It is this: unless pacifism is accepted by everyone, evil governments will use it as a way to grow in the wrong use of power. Brown says pacifism is a nice idea, but it's utopian, not biblical.[43]

What the pacifism view says about military service. According to Augsburger, when a Christian participates in war, he is doing so at the expense of missions and evangelism.

"The way for Christians to change the world is by sharing the love of Christ and the good news of the gospel rather than to think we can stop anti-God movements by force."[44]

Furthermore, given the international character of Christianity, there is a good chance that fighting against other nations would require us to fight against those who are fellow believers, which directly violates the command to love one another, says Augsburger.[45]

So what should Christians do? Augsburger contends that they must practice a "consistent, conscientious objection" that avoids any support—direct or indirect—of military service. Serving as noncombatant members of the military is insufficient because, Augsburger argues, this "still supports the function of war and at best only releases the individual from directly taking life, a legalistic distinction which misses the spirit of separation and discipleship."[46]

> Augsburger contends that Christians must practice a "consistent, conscientious objection" that avoids any support—direct or indirect—of military service.

It may be ideal to avoid war completely, responds theologian Herman Hoyt, but it isn't realistic. There is no way for Christians to be completely separated from war, "except by departure from the world."[47] That may be what is necessary, Augsburger frankly admits: "As Christians, our answer to the violence in the world is simply that we don't have to live; we can die. This is the ultimate testimony of our belief in the kingdom of Christ and the resurrection."[48] For many pacifists, pacifism extends to other involvements with the government, such as voting, running for political office, or suing another person in the courts.

What the pacifism view says about peace. Pacifists recognize that peace *making* is something more than peace *keeping*. We must have a holistic understanding of peace that is positive and active, says Augsburger.[49]

Pacifism says both the state and the church should pursue peace and limit or eliminate the use of force, even in the face of overt aggression. If the state must be involved, Christians must separate themselves entirely from its efforts. Christians should then,

> counteract violence by positive actions of love and thereby to promote peace in our society and in the world. Such activity is not a neutralizing of relationships, but an active expression of the love of Christ which treats every person as having ultimate worth.[50]

Ethicist Arthur Holmes thought that in proclaiming that every person has "ultimate worth," Myron Augsburger was going beyond scriptural teaching. "Perhaps the human person with his eternal destiny is utterly sacrosanct, but not physical, biological existence," he said. "Yet even there I hesitate, for theism insists that only God is of infinite worth. Every creature has worth that is limited by God's infinite worth and is as contingent on God as is one's very existence."[51]

Furthermore, Holmes thought Augsburger's view of love moved beyond what is biblical: "The call to love one's enemies does not change the picture for ... the law of love embraces rather than excludes retributive justice."[52]

Nonresistance

Nonresistance means not resisting those who are trying to harm you. Applied to warfare, the nonresistance position says that while the state may, and ought to, take up arms, the church must not do so. Nonresistance traces its history in parallel to pacifism, using as its starting point what it believes to be the Bible's teaching on "separation from the world."[53] We live in an evil age, Herman Hoyt explains, and "one of those evils is the exercise of physical force to accomplish the purposes of life. This includes the use of force in times of peace and also in times of war." The church and the state are separate realms, and their methods ought to be different too. Christian conduct "should be conditioned by the pattern of the kingdom of the heavens." In this, "physical violence is forbidden to believers as a method of accomplishing a purpose."[54]

> *Nonresistance*: the belief that individuals shouldn't resist those who seek to do them harm.

Jesus telling his followers to "render to Caesar the things that are Caesar's, and to God the things that are God's" (Matt. 22:21); Paul reminding believers to "be subject to the governing authorities" (Rom. 13:1); and Peter admonishing fellow Christians to honor God, other believers, and the emperor (1 Pet. 2:13–17)[55] indicate to Hoyt that "nonresistance is a spiritual principle intended for individual believers under any form of government."[56]

But the state is permitted to take up arms. Hoyt believes "the obligations of nonresistance are laid upon believers only."[57] Harold Brown, however, finds this position "inconsistent. How can a person who wants his nation to be preserved refuse to defend it—or permit other Christians to do so?[58]

What the nonresistance view says about military service. When it comes to whether Christians should serve in the military, Herman Hoyt draws the line at combat roles. Christians do have a responsibility to be good citizens, pay taxes, pray for those in authority, and submit to laws that don't contradict God's law. But, as he interprets God's commandments, the taking of human life is prohibited (Exod. 20:13).[59] Because believers must not take life "in times of peace, they are under the same obligation during war."[60]

So when it comes to military service, "believers must respectfully refuse to comply with the regulations of military operation," Hoyt says. As noncombatants, though, "believers can serve in the medical corps and as chaplains, to encourage the sick and dying and bear a personal witness to the saving grace of our blessed Lord. In this way they can serve their country and at the same time faithfully discharge their responsibilities as Christians in everything that pertains to life and [godliness]."[61]

> Hoyt asserts that "believers [as noncombatants] can serve in the medical corps and as chaplains, to encourage the sick and dying and bear a personal witness to the saving grace of our blessed Lord."

What the nonresistance view says about peace. People who hold to the nonresistance view see peace as something the church must constantly pursue, even when the state must resist evil through force. Those in the church, Herman Hoyt says, while forbidden to use physical force, "are still obligated to exercise spiritual means to do good and to bring blessing to others."[62] Christians may participate in government, short of armed conflict. They "let war take its course knowing that shortly Christ will come and usher in the age of peace."[63] Hoyt imagines a time when everyone in a nation might be Christian and practicing non-resistance. This, he says, is the kingdom of God established on earth, and it will happen only "when Christ has returned and by his almighty power set up his kingdom and purged all those unfit for it."[64] He bases this on Jesus's parable of separating the wheat from the weeds (Matt. 13:24–30, 36–43)[65] and the sheep from the goats (25:31–46).[66]

Just War

The just-war view says the state should take up arms only when a war has been judged as just by the just-war criteria, which early church fathers advanced and are now enshrined in much of international law. Articulated by Augustine and Aquinas, the just-war view is the view the Catholic Church holds. It's also common in many different Protestant traditions. The just-war view recognizes that evil isn't just a personal problem; it is, as Arthur Holmes stated, "a pervasive condition of fallen human existence that riddles the political and social reality with which we are forced to contend."[67]

The question, to Holmes, wasn't whether war is evil. "To call war anything less than evil would be self-deception," he said. "The Christian conscience has throughout history recognized the tragic character of war." Rather, the issue is whether war is avoidable in all cases.[68]

> The just-war view says the state should take up arms only when a war has been judged as just by the just-war criteria the early church fathers advanced.

Holmes wrote that for its part, the church should resist evil not through violence but "by its preaching and teaching, by ministering to the needs of those who might be tempted to erupt violently against society, by supporting just and compassionate government, [and] by protesting today's social evils, injustices and violence."[69]

Individual Christians should also resist evil not only by participating with the church but also by participating in the government's resistance. In addition, they can resist evil by individual efforts through legal means, community building, and more.

So how does the idea that Christians may participate in just war square with, say, Matthew 5:39, where Jesus said that if someone slaps you on the cheek, you should "turn to him the other also"? Holmes said the answer is in the context, which refers to individuals, not to governments or churches.[70] "It means that as an individual I do not take the law into my own hands," he noted.

> Instead of carrying out my own private scheme of retributive justice (*lex talionis*), I turn the cheek and go a second mile. It does not mean that justice no longer matters, that we have no stake and no part in law enforcement.[71]

Nor does it mean that while turning our own cheeks, we may not protect the cheeks of our loved ones. Vengeance, though, Holmes believed, isn't allowed:

(1) The use of force in resisting and punishing violence is entrusted to governments. (2) Believers in both Old and New Testaments are involved in governmental uses of force. (3) Such uses of force are to be drastically limited to what is necessary in securing peace and justice. (4) Vengeance is thereby ruled out, along with all aggression; love and mercy must temper justice.[72]

Jus ad bellum: in just-war theory, a concept dealing with the requirements that constitute a just cause for fighting a war.

From the government's standpoint, what constitutes a just war, both in going to war (**jus ad bellum**) and proper conduct during a war (**jus in bello**), is derived from natural law and biblical revelation. They are found in both pagan and Christian sources. Typically, **just-war theory** comprises seven required criteria:[73]

Just cause. Only defensive war is permitted; wars of aggression are condemned.

Jus in bello: in just-war theory, a concept dealing with what constitutes ethical behavior in the act of fighting a war.

Just intention. The goal is to secure a just peace. This is the *only* legitimate goal. It's never right to wage war to secure revenge or to conquer for the purpose of economic gain or to prove that your side is superior.

Last resort. War may be waged only when every other path—such as negotiation and compromise—has failed.

Just-War Theory: the belief that war is justifiable only if a certain set of criteria are met.

Formal declaration. War may be waged only by government, not private individuals, and the government's highest authorities must officially declare their government's intentions.

Limited objectives. The purpose of war is to win peace. It is never right to destroy the enemy's economic or political institutions.

Proportionate means. The kinds of weapons used and the level of force employed should be restricted to what is needed to fend off an attack and prevent future attacks.

Noncombatant immunity. Only those who act in an official government capacity may fight. Those who aren't contributing to or directly engaged in the conflict (i.e., innocent civilians and prisoners of war) should not be attacked.

These seven criteria are key to a *just* war, but they don't *justify* war. Their goal is to cause both the church and the government to deliberate carefully about waging war so as to secure justice. One important question would be, "If these principles were consistently practiced by all of the parties, would it eliminate war altogether?" The answer ought to be yes.[74]

What the just-war view says about military service. The just-war standard isn't intended only for Christians. It is consistent with God's law, Arthur Holmes observed, and therefore applies to everyone, everywhere. "The question, then, is not whether a Christian may fight, but whether anybody at all may fight," he noted.[75] Of those who say the Christian calling is different when it comes to politics and the military, Holmes said it must be clear that this "is a vocational claim not an ethical one, and the person called thereby to nonviolence cannot label all soldiering as ethically wrong."[76] If Christians may legitimately participate in other activities related to government, and if the government itself is committed to justice, then Christians are permitted to participate in using force as long as it is as representatives of a government, not as individuals, and the goal is to preserve peace and maintain a just order.[77] Said Holmes, "Inasmuch as Christians participate in government and serve as government's official agents, then, they may—however regretfully and with however much moral caution—fight."[78]

What the just-war view says about peace. Based on God's revelation in Scripture and the teachings of Jesus, the church desires peace. It ought to "help the state be the state" by encouraging it to pursue peace while resisting evil.[79] The just-war theory takes human nature into account. There will be wars. The question is whether the church can offer clear criteria for when it's legitimate to wage war and figure out how to restore peace once the objectives have been reached (*jus post bellum*).[80]

Like pacifists and those who embrace nonresistance, just-war advocates want peace. The disagreement is over how to reach that objective. Do we achieve peace by doing nothing to oppose war, or by seeking to limit it? Just-war advocates point out that "peace at any price" isn't wise in a world where our hearts are desperately wicked. Said Arthur Holmes,

> In a limited war with limited ends, forced on us by violent aggression, when the alternatives are either to let unjust violence rampage unchecked against innocent populations or else to let others without our aid attempt to check the assault, can a Christian fight?[81]

His answer was yes.

Crusade or Preventive War

A fourth view not often advocated today, but one that has been a part of church history, is that the state may go to war with the support of the church when a threat is imminent. According to Harold Brown, "By preventive war we mean a war that is begun not in response to an act of aggression, but in anticipation of it. A preventive war intends to forestall an evil that has not yet occurred."[82] Often used as well is the term **preemptive war**, which means attacking an enemy whose aggression is imminent but has not yet occurred. Today it happens when governments "preempt" acts of war, for example, by killing or capturing people planning a terrorist attack.

> *Preemptive War:* attacking an enemy whose aggression is imminent but has not yet occurred.

Brown says that we must allow for **preventive war** in our day. Just-war criteria, he notes, is a good start, but waiting until one is attacked, or defending one's government only when there is a chance of succeeding, and when the means are proportionate, as just-war theory prescribes, is a very difficult thing to discern. "Unfortunately, many of the actual war situations that arise in history will not fit precisely into any category," he says[83] and asserts that war "is a primary reality and cannot be submitted totally to a theory."[84]

> *Preventive War:*
> **a war started to prevent another state from acquiring the capabilities to attack.**

A crusade is a different sort of war. Says Brown, "Perhaps we can define a crusade as a war that is begun not in response to a present act of aggression, but as the attempt to set right a past act. A crusade is essentially an act not of conquest but of reconquest."[85]

Obviously, this is controversial with pacifists, nonresistance advocates, and just-war theorists alike. Myron Augsburger, representing the pacifist view, says Brown doesn't "adequately deal with the theological question of the separation of church and state," by which he means that it runs the risk of the church being complicit in unjust actions on the part of the state.[86] Arthur Holmes agreed: "In terms of ethics, Brown's case is at best incomplete."[87]

What the crusade/preventive-war view says about military service. The crusade/preventive-war view obviously accepts the idea that Christians can legitimately be involved in military service. Harold Brown says,

> Some Christians hold that it is always better to endure violence than to perpetrate it. But if we do not agree with that, then there is no good reason to deny ourselves as Christians the same right to intervene against gross injustice that we give to others.[88]

Brown imagines a scale with complete pacifism on one end and unquestioning obedience to one's superiors on the other. Both, he says, "represent an abdication of moral responsibility."[89] Pacifists focus on not *committing* evil, but part of making peace is refusing to *endure* or *resist* evil. This, to Brown, justifies taking action when there is a good chance the action will prevent evil in the first place.[90] We can imagine a police officer, acting on a tip, stopping a car full of people on their way to commit a crime. Surely this is more moral, the crusade/preventive-war view argues, than allowing the crime to take place and then apprehending the suspects. Similarly, we might imagine that if a legitimate government had been able to apprehend Adolf Hitler before his evil plans had fully taken effect, it would have been doing something moral. In the same way, according to the crusade/preventive-war view, the state has the power to stop people from committing evil and, if it is doing this in a way that doesn't violate God's law, Christians may ethically participate in its efforts.

> **Pacifists focus on not *committing* evil, but part of making peace is refusing to *endure* or *resist* evil.**

What the crusade/preventive-war view says about peace. The crusade/preventive-war view is similar to the just-war theory, but more expansive. It encourages active involvement in politics, for example, as a way of ensuring that bad leaders—who would likely make unethical decisions—either don't get elected in the first place or are voted out of office when they transgress the law. Preserving the ethical integrity of government, then, is a key means of preventing immoral things from happening.[91]

Another application of the crusade/preventive-war view is in how to extract ourselves from military commitments made to others. In the Iraq War, for example, officials in the Obama administration described the situation on the ground as a civil war between Iraqis and indicated that the presence of American troops made the situation worse. In the drawdown of troops, though, it was discovered that there was *not* a civil war but an insurgent group trying to start one. Thousands of Iraqis died as this insurgent group, commonly referred to as ISIS (Islamic State of Iraq and Syria) overwhelmed Iraqi Security Forces, terrorizing the local population. Men, women, and children failing to pledge allegiance to this group were beheaded. Thousands died.

One could argue that Americans should never have been in Iraq in the first place, but at the moment these events took place, it was beside the point. The question was, "What is the best way to respond in a no-win situation?" Perhaps the moral thing to do at that point of the conflict isn't to withdraw but to commit more troops, establish order, and then work toward a more enduring peace.

Admittedly, this is an aggressive interpretation of the just-war doctrine because it argues that *greater* military commitment would forestall a more disastrous outcome. In a world of sin, no choices are easy. This much is clear from our discussion, though. Trying to paint a thin layer of solution over a thick problem through the selective application of a handful of Bible verses can be an immoral thing to do.[92] Examples of a dangerous application of the Bible could include quoting passages about peace to justify doing nothing when something needs to be done, or quoting verses about God telling people to go to war in justifying force as a response to a particular situation we're facing today.

> In a world of sin, no choices are easy. Trying to paint a thin layer of solution over a thick problem through the selective application of a handful of Bible verses can be an immoral thing to do.

5. How to Live Christianly in the Battles We Face

Jesus was for peace. "Blessed are the peacemakers," he said (Matt. 5:9). But as the prophet Jeremiah warned, saying "'Peace, peace,' when there is no peace" is to heal a wound lightly (Jer. 6:14). When evil reigns, peace dies.

Myron Augsburger says,

> War is the problem of man's sinfulness writ large. Confronted with the fact that we cannot escape all evil, the basic question for us is what is the most effective way of changing human lives and altering society for the good?[93]

We may not agree with his response to the question, but the way he frames it can help us all. As Rouven Steeves puts it,

> Given the sinfulness of this present age, nothing will succeed in creating world peace short of the Second Coming. The question then is not of absolute success but relative success—what can we do to mitigate the effects of sin in a fallen world.[94]

As Christians, we are citizens of the kingdom of God. As such, we ought to be the best citizens of the kingdom of humanity as well, since we recognize a higher authority than the state and can thus hold government accountable to do nothing more or less than fulfill all its responsibilities to punish evil and restore justice.

Most of all, we need believers who are willing to think through all the issues surrounding war and peace and, with a grounding in God's revelation in nature and in Scripture, to help both the church and the state fulfill their respective responsibilities. Steeves thinks scholars like Daniel Bell, who thinks of just war as a form of Christian discipleship, might be making headway in resolving the differences between the just-war tradition and the pacifist tradition.[95] Specifically, Bell references the trend of "**just peacemaking**," which focuses on identifying practices that can reduce injustice and make conflict less likely in the first place. Some examples include fostering economic development and developing organizations that promote human rights. Examples might also include training in nonviolence and conflict resolution and reducing the arms trade.[96]

> *Just Peacemaking:* a movement in Christendom that seeks to identify and encourage practices that can reduce injustice and make conflict less likely.

Other believers working in this area include Eric Patterson, from the Berkley Center for Religion, Peace, and World Affairs at Georgetown University. Patterson focuses on how to apply just-war principles in a modern era of rogue states, insurgents, trade in weapons of mass destruction, and violent factions that use the chaos of war to advance their own aims. Ending war well includes bringing perpetrators to justice, reintegrating troops into society, destroying weapons stockpiles, and restoring services to communities. For some communities, the most urgent need is ensuring access to clean water. In others, it's removing land mines. In yet others, it involves hosting reconciliation efforts to allow opposing sides to establish peace with one another.[97]

The church is responsible to spread *shalom*, and yet it must restrain itself from taking over government. The state has the power of force and must restrain itself so as not to create injustice by using what God has given for just purposes. Given the limitations of both the church and the state, bringing to life the principles of just war may be the best we can do to, as Harold Brown memorably phrased it, "muddle through in as Christian a fashion as possible."[98]

> The church is responsible to spread *shalom*, and yet it must restrain itself from taking over government.

Such an approach takes tremendous courage. It requires us to stand against acts of injustice committed in the name of justice, just as it requires us to stand bravely for justice in the first place. As I consider this double responsibility, I think of a letter from Marc, writing home from the war in Iraq.

Marc had seen it all, from service members giving their food to hungry children to helping coalition forces set up hospitals and provide security so people could be safely treated. But he had also seen American troops do things that were uncalled for. He had witnessed hateful attitudes. Marc wrote, "My question is, when does glory fade away and become a wrongful crusade, or an unjustified means [to an end that] consumes one completely?"

Marc wondered whether he was doing enough. "My point … is how can we come over here and help a less than fortunate country without holding contempt or hate towards them if we can't [even] do [that] in our [own] country?"[99] When he was home, Marc admitted, he was more likely to be a taker than a giver.

These aren't the thoughts of a reluctant warrior. Marc Alan Lee was a Navy SEAL, a member of an elite military unit tasked with extremely difficult missions in Ramadi, Iraq, a hellhole in the middle of what seemed like hell itself. Based on his Christian faith, he decided to show his love through self-sacrificing courage. Shortly after writing the letter from which I've quoted, Marc found himself pinned down on a rooftop with an injured comrade, with no way for the medic to get onto the roof to evaluate the man's condition. Rather than hiding behind the cement wall forming the border of the rooftop, Marc stood up in the middle of the roof and fired at insurgents, exposing himself to great danger but giving the medic time to reach the injured man. And when it was determined that the man would need immediate treatment to survive, Marc once again stood up, drawing fire long enough for the injured man to be evacuated.

Two weeks later, Marc's commander announced that thirty of the insurgents they had been fighting that day had survived and needed to be rooted out.

> Based on his Christian faith, Marc decided to show his love through self-sacrificing courage.

"Roger that[,] let's go get 'em," said Marc in spite of the fact that daytime temperatures were reaching 115 to 120 degrees and the team had just been in an intense two-hour firefight.

The team went back to Ramadi. They had just cleared the lower floor of the target building when Marc led his team upstairs. They received fire. To protect his men, Marc turned into the fire and in so doing gave his own life.[100]

It turns out that Marc's letter was the last he would ever write. His concluding paragraph is a fitting conclusion to our discussion about Christianity and the use of force:

> What I do over here is only a small percent of what keeps our country great. I think the truth [of] our greatness is each other. Purity, morals and kindness, passed down to each generation through example. So to all my family and friends, do me a favor and pass on the kindness, the love, the precious gift of human life to each other so that when your children come in contact with a great conflict [like the one] we are now faced with here in Iraq, … they [will be] people of humanity, of pure motives, of compassion.[101]

I didn't know Marc very well, but I remember meeting him as he sat through two of our Summit courses in Colorado. He was every bit the warrior and every bit the Christian, a loving man committed to justice. Will we accept his challenge to humanity, pure motives, and compassion, whether our fight is in the spiritual realm, the physical realm, or both?

ENDNOTES

1. Tim Townsend, *Mission at Nuremberg: An American Army Chaplain and the Trial of the Nazis* (New York: William Morrow, 2014), 105.

2. Townsend, *Mission at Nuremberg*, 251.

3. Chris Hedges, "What Every Person Should Know about War," *New York Times*, July 6, 2003, www.nytimes.com/2003/07/06 /books/chapters/0713-1st-hedges.html?pagewanted=all.

4. See R. J. Rummel, *Death by Government* (Piscataway, NJ: Transaction Publishers, 1994), chap. 1.

5. Romans 12:2: "Do not be conformed to this world, but be transformed by the renewal of your mind, that by testing you may discern what is the will of God, what is good and acceptable and perfect."

6. Hebrews 10:22: "Let us draw near [to God] with a true heart in full assurance of faith, with our hearts sprinkled clean from an evil conscience and our bodies washed with pure water."

7. John 13:34–35: "A new commandment I give to you, that you love one another: just as I have loved you, you also are to love one another. By this all people will know that you are my disciples, if you have love for one another."

8. Matthew 5:44: "Love your enemies and pray for those who persecute you."

9. George Kalantzis, *Caesar and the Lamb: Early Christian Attitudes on War and Military Service* (Eugene, OR: Cascade Books, 2012), 8.

10. Mark 12:31: "The second [commandment] is this: 'You shall love your neighbor as yourself.' There is no other commandment greater than these."

11. Jeremiah 29:7: "Seek the welfare of the city where I have sent you into exile, and pray to the LORD on its behalf, for in its welfare you will find your welfare."

12. Kalantzis, *Caesar and the Lamb*, 9.

13. Roland Bainton, *Christian Attitudes toward War and Peace* (New York: Abingdon, 1960), 66, 81, cited in J. Daryl Charles, *Between Pacifism and Jihad: Just War and Christian Tradition* (Downers Grove, IL: InterVarsity Press, 2005), 37. See also Charles's discussion of Bainton's position in J. Daryl Charles, "Pacifists, Patriots, or Both?: Second Thoughts on Pre-Constantinian Early-Church Attitudes toward Soldiering and War," *Logos: A Journal of Catholic Thought and Culture* 13, no. 2 (Spring 2010).

14. James Turner Johnson, *The Quest for Peace* (Princeton, NJ: Princeton University Press, 1987), chap. 1, cited in Charles, *Between Pacifism and Jihad*. Johnson's moderate and moderating conclusion is likely the most correct and does justice to the full range of biblical and historic theology. That having been said, there is much dissent. George Kalantzis, for instance, arrives at a different conclusion: "I argue that the literary evidence confirms the very strong internal coherence of the Church's non-violent stance for the first three centuries." Kalantzis, *Caesar and the Lamb*, 7. Johnson's and Bainton's works are referenced herein.

15. Matthew 8:5–13: "When [Jesus] had entered Capernaum, a centurion came forward to him, appealing to him, 'Lord, my servant is lying paralyzed at home, suffering terribly.' And he said to him, 'I will come and heal him.' But the centurion replied, 'Lord, I am not worthy to have you come under my roof, but only say the word, and my servant will be healed. For I too am a man under authority, with soldiers under me. And I say to one, "Go," and he goes, and to another, "Come," and he comes, and to my servant, "Do this," and he does it.' When Jesus heard this, he marveled and said to those who followed him, 'Truly, I tell you, with no one in Israel have I found such faith. I tell you, many will come from east and west and recline at table with Abraham, Isaac, and Jacob in the kingdom of heaven, while the sons of the kingdom will be thrown into the outer darkness. In that place there will be weeping and gnashing of teeth.' And to the centurion Jesus said, 'Go; let it be done for you as you have believed.' And the servant was healed at that very moment."

16. Acts 10:1: "At Caesarea there was a man named Cornelius, a centurion of what was known as the Italian Cohort"; Acts 10:30–35: "And Cornelius said, 'Four days ago, about this hour, I was praying in my house at the ninth hour, and behold, a man stood before me in bright clothing and said, "Cornelius, your prayer has been heard and your alms have been remembered before God. Send therefore to Joppa and ask for Simon who is called Peter. He is lodging in the house of Simon, a tanner, by the sea." So I sent for you at once, and you have been kind enough to come. Now therefore we are all here in the presence of God to hear all that you have been commanded by the Lord.' So Peter opened his mouth and said: 'Truly I understand that God shows no partiality, but in every nation anyone who fears him and does what is right is acceptable to him.'"

17. See Augustine, *The City of God against the Pagans*, ed. and trans. R. W. Dyson (Cambridge, UK: Cambridge University Press, 1998).

18. Matthew 24:6: "You will hear of wars and rumors of wars. See that you are not alarmed, for this must take place, but the end is not yet"; Mark 13:7: "When you hear of wars and rumors of wars, do not be alarmed. This must take place, but the end is not yet."

19. Romans 8:20–21: "For the creation was subjected to futility, not willingly, but because of him who subjected it, in hope that the creation itself will be set free from its bondage to corruption and obtain the freedom of the glory of the children of God."

20. Ephesians 6:14–18: "Stand therefore, having fastened on the belt of truth, and having put on the breastplate of righteousness, and, as shoes for your feet, having put on the readiness given by the gospel of peace. In all circumstances take up the shield of faith, with which you can extinguish all the flaming darts of the evil one; and take the helmet of salvation, and the sword of the Spirit, which is the word of God, praying at all times in the Spirit, with all prayer and supplication."

21. Charles H. Spurgeon, "Christ Triumphant," in *The New Park Street Pulpit* (London: Passmore and Alabaster, 1894), 5:389.

22. Loraine Boettner, *The Christian Attitude toward War* (Phillipsburg, NJ: Presbyterian and Reformed Publishing, 1985), 16.

23. Judges 6:1: "The people of Israel did what was evil in the sight of the LORD, and the LORD gave them into the hand of Midian seven years"; Judges 13:1: "The people of Israel again did what was evil in the sight of the LORD, so the LORD gave them into the hand of the Philistines for forty years"; Isaiah 10:5–14: "Ah, Assyria, the rod of my anger; the staff in their hands is my fury! Against a godless nation I send him, and against the people of my wrath I command him, to take spoil and seize plunder, and to tread them down like the mire of the streets. But he does not so intend, and his heart does not so think; but it is in his heart to destroy, and to cut off nations not a few; for he says: 'Are not my commanders all kings? Is not Calno like Carchemish? Is not Hamath like Arpad? Is not Samaria like Damascus? As my hand has reached to the kingdoms of the idols, whose carved images were greater than those of Jerusalem and Samaria, shall I not do to Jerusalem and her idols as I have done to Samaria and her images?' When the Lord has finished all his work on Mount Zion and on Jerusalem, he will punish the speech of the arrogant heart of the king of Assyria and the boastful look in his eyes. For he says: 'By the strength of my hand I have done it, and by my wisdom, for I have understanding; I remove the boundaries of peoples, and plunder their treasures; like a bull I bring down those who sit on thrones. My hand has found like a nest the wealth of the peoples; and as one gathers eggs that have been forsaken, so I have gathered all the earth; and there was none that moved a wing or opened the mouth or chirped.'"

24. Boettner, *Christian Attitude toward War*, 16.

25. See also Exodus 21:23–25: "But if there is harm, then you shall pay life for life, eye for eye, tooth for tooth, hand for hand, foot for foot, burn for burn, wound for wound, stripe for stripe." The formulation of an "eye for an eye" is commonly referred to as the *lex talionis*.

26. Boettner, *Christian Attitude toward War*, 16–17.

27. Nehemiah 4:18: "Each of the builders had his sword strapped at his side while he built. The man who sounded the trumpet was beside me."

28. Luke 22:49: "When those who were around [Jesus] saw what would follow, they said, 'Lord, shall we strike with the sword?'"

29. Proverbs 3:31–32: "Do not envy a man of violence and do not choose any of his ways, for the devious person is an abomination to the LORD, but the upright are in his confidence."

30. Psalm 44:6–7: "Not in my bow do I trust, nor can my sword save me. But you have saved us from our foes and have put to shame those who hate us."

31. Albertus Pieters, quoted in Boettner, *Christian Attitude toward War*, 27.

32. Eric Metaxas, *Bonhoeffer: Pastor, Martyr, Prophet, Spy* (Nashville: Thomas Nelson, 2010), 153.

33. Dietrich Bonhoeffer, quoted in Metaxas, *Bonhoeffer*, 154.

34. Metaxas, *Bonhoeffer*.

35. Romans 12:19: "Beloved, never avenge yourselves, but leave it to the wrath of God, for it is written, 'Vengeance is mine, I will repay, says the Lord'"; Titus 1:7: "An overseer, as God's steward, must be above reproach. He must not be arrogant or quick-tempered or a drunkard or violent or greedy for gain."

36. Robert G. Clouse, ed., *War: Four Christian Views* (Downers Grove, IL: InterVarsity, 1991).

37. John Howard Yoder, *Christian Attitudes to War, Peace, and Revolution*, eds. Theodore J. Koontz and Andy Alexis-Baker (Grand Rapids: Brazos, 2009), 28–30.

38. For a thorough overview of the secular approach to just war, see political philosopher Michael Walzer's *Just and Unjust Wars: A Moral Argument with Historical Illustrations*, 4th ed. (New York: Basic Books 2006).

39. John Yoder's *Christian Attitudes to War, Peace, and Revolution* (Grand Rapids: Brazos, 2009) offers a balanced treatment of the various views as they developed over time. In addition, Roland H. Bainton's classic *Christian Attitudes toward War and Peace: A Historical Survey and Critical Re-evaluation* (Nashville: Abingdon Press, 1979) is a chronologically ordered study, though with limitations as we saw earlier in the chapter. Similarly, James Turner Johnson's *Just War Tradition and the Restraint of War: A Moral and Historical Inquiry* (Princeton, NJ: Princeton University Press, 2014)—which ideally should be read as the sequel to his study *Ideology, Reason, and the Limitation of War: Religious and Secular Concepts, 1200–1740* (Princeton, NJ: Princeton University Press, 2015)—covers similar terrain but with a focus on just war. As already mentioned, Michael Walzer's secularly rooted *Just and Unjust Wars: A Moral Argument with Historical Illustrations* (New York: Basic Books, 2006) is still a classic deserving attention. Both George Kalantzis' *Caesar and the Lamb: Early Christian Attitudes on War and Military Service* (Eugene, OR: Cascade Books, 2012) and Arthur F. Holmes's *War and Christian Ethics: Classic and Contemporary Readings on the Morality of War* (Grand Rapids: Baker Academic, 2005) provide insight into

primary sources in the early church and among early philosophers and political thinkers.

40. Myron Augsburger, quoted in Clouse, *War*, 81.

41. Augsburger, quoted in Clouse, *War*, 97.

42. Augsburger, quoted in Clouse, *War*, 95.

43. Harold O. J. Brown, referenced in Clouse, *War*, 111.

44. Augsburger, quoted in Clouse, *War*, 92.

45. Clouse, *War*, 90.

46. Augsburger, quoted in Clouse, *War*, 63.

47. Herman Hoyt, quoted in Clouse, *War*, 104.

48. Augsburger, quoted in Clouse, *War*, 92.

49. Clouse, *War*, 86–87.

50. Clouse, *War*, 97.

51. Arthur Holmes, quoted in Clouse, *War*, 108.

52. Holmes, quoted in Clouse, *War*, 109.

53. Clouse, *War*, 32.

54. Hoyt, quoted in Clouse, *War*, 32–33.

55. First Peter 2:13–17: "Be subject for the Lord's sake to every human institution, whether it be to the emperor as supreme, or to governors as sent by him to punish those who do evil and to praise those who do good. For this is the will of God, that by doing good you should put to silence the ignorance of foolish people. Live as people who are free, not using your freedom as a cover-up for evil, but living as servants of God. Honor everyone. Love the brotherhood. Fear God. Honor the emperor."

56. Hoyt, quoted in Clouse, *War*, 38.

57. Hoyt, quoted in Clouse, *War*, 37.

58. Harold Brown, quoted in Clouse, *War*, 76.

59. Exodus 20:13: "You shall not murder."

60. Clouse, *War*, 57.

61. Hoyt, quoted in Clouse, *War*, 48–49.

62. Hoyt, quoted in Clouse, *War*, 34.

63. Hoyt, quoted in Clouse, *War*, 47.

64. Hoyt, quoted in Clouse, *War*, 39.

65. Matthew 13:24–30, 36–43: "[Jesus] put another parable before them, saying, 'The kingdom of heaven may be compared to a man who sowed good seed in his field, but while his men were sleeping, his enemy came and sowed weeds among the wheat and went away. So when the plants came up and bore grain, then the weeds appeared also. And the servants of the master of the house came and said to him, "Master, did you not sow good seed in your field? How then does it have weeds?" He said to them, "An enemy has done this." So the servants said to him, "Then do you want us to go and gather them?" But he said, "No, lest in gathering the weeds you root up the wheat along with them. Let both grow together until the harvest, and at harvest time I will tell the reapers, Gather the weeds first and bind them in bundles to be burned, but gather the wheat into my barn."' … Then he left the crowds and went into the house. And his disciples came to him, saying, 'Explain to us the parable of the weeds of the field.' He answered, 'The one who sows the good seed is the Son of Man. The field is the world, and the good seed is the sons of the kingdom. The weeds are the sons of the evil one, and the enemy who sowed them is the devil. The harvest is the end of the age, and the reapers are angels. Just as the weeds are gathered and burned with fire, so will it be at the end of the age. The Son of Man will send his angels, and they will gather out of his kingdom all causes of sin and all law-breakers, and throw them into the fiery furnace. In that place there will be weeping and gnashing of teeth. Then the righteous will shine like the sun in the kingdom of their Father. He who has ears, let him hear.'"

66. Matthew 25:31–46: "When the Son of Man comes in his glory, and all the angels with him, then he will sit on his glorious throne. Before him will be gathered all the nations, and he will separate people one from another as a shepherd separates the sheep from the goats. And he will place the sheep on his right, but the goats on the left. Then the King will say to those on his right, 'Come, you who are blessed by my Father, inherit the kingdom prepared for you from the foundation of the world. For I was hungry and you gave me food, I was thirsty and you gave me drink, I was a stranger and you welcomed me, I was naked and you clothed me, I was sick and you visited me, I was in prison and you came to me.' Then the righteous will answer him, saying, 'Lord, when did we see you hungry and feed you, or thirsty and give you drink? And when did we see you a stranger and welcome you, or naked and clothe you? And when did we see you sick or in prison and visit you?' And the King will answer them, 'Truly, I say to you, as you did it to one of the least of these my brothers, you did it to me.' Then he will say to those on his left, 'Depart from me, you cursed, into the eternal fire prepared for the devil and his angels. For I was hungry and you gave me no food, I was thirsty and you gave me no drink, I was a stranger and you did not welcome me, naked and you did not clothe me, sick and in prison and you did not visit me.' Then they also will answer, saying, 'Lord, when did we see you hungry or thirsty or a stranger or naked or sick or in prison, and did not minister to you?' Then he will answer them, saying, 'Truly, I say to you, as you did not do

it to one of the least of these, you did not do it to me.' And these will go away into eternal punishment, but the righteous into eternal life."

67. Holmes, quoted in Clouse, *War*, 118.

68. Holmes, quoted in Clouse, *War*, 117.

69. Holmes, quoted in Clouse, *War*, 71.

70. Clouse, *War*, 123.

71. Holmes, quoted in Clouse, *War*, 71.

72. Holmes, quoted in Clouse, *War*, 123.

73. Summary of just-war criteria in Clouse, *War*, 120–21. For further discussion of these criteria and how they developed over time, in addition to many of the sources already mentioned and cited, I recommend David D. Corey and J. Daryl Charles, *The Just War Tradition: An Introduction* (Wilmington, DE: ISI Books, 2012). Furthermore, the following work is a classic in the field, though less than sanguine about the possibilities of waging a just war: Paul Ramsey, *The Just War: Force and Political Responsibility* (Lanham, MD: Rowman and Littlefield Publishers, 1983). Arthur Holmes also offered a brief historical overview in his section "Just War" in Clouse, *War*, 122–30.

74. Clouse, *War*, 119–20. Just-war criteria shouldn't be seen as a checklist to be pulled out to justify a war. Rather, they should be employed as an integral part of the discussions contemplating war. For a thoughtful treatment of just war rightly construed, see Daniel M. Bell Jr., *Just War as Christian Discipleship: Recentering the Tradition in the Church Rather Than the State* (Grand Rapids: Brazos, 2009). Paul Ramsey makes a similar point in *The Just War: Force and Political Responsibility*. It is telling that the pacifist Stanley Hauerwas found this approach so compelling that he wrote a foreword to Ramsey's book and endorsed Bell's.

75. Holmes, quoted in Clouse, *War*, 142.

76. Holmes, quoted in Clouse, *War*, 119.

77. Clouse, *War*, 120.

78. Holmes, quoted in Clouse, *War*, 130.

79. Metaxas, *Bonhoeffer*, 153.

80. With respect to *jus post bellum* considerations, see Eric D. Patterson, *Ending Wars Well: Order, Justice, and Conciliation in Contemporary Post-Conflict* (New Haven, CT: Yale University Press, 2012). See also Larry May and Andrew T. Forcehimes, eds., *Morality, Jus Post Bellum, and International Law* (New York: Cambridge University Press, 2012).

81. Holmes, quoted in Clouse, *War*, 135.

82. Brown, quoted in Clouse, *War*, 155.

83. Brown, quoted in Clouse, *War*, 153.

84. Brown, quoted in Clouse, *War*, 164.

85. Brown, quoted in Clouse, *War*, 155.

86. Augsburger, quoted in Clouse, *War*, 177.

87. Holmes, quoted in Clouse, *War*, 187.

88. Brown, quoted in Clouse, *War*, 159.

89. Brown, quoted in Clouse, *War*, 166.

90. Clouse, *War*.

91. Clouse, *War*, 177.

92. For more on this point as well as the example illustrating it, see Jean Bethke Elshtain, "Just War and an Ethic of Responsibility," in Eric Patterson, ed., *Ethics: Beyond War's End* (Washington, DC: Georgetown University Press, 2012), 126.

93. Augsburger, quoted in Clouse, *War*, 145.

94. Rouven Steeves, research report submitted in preparation for this chapter.

95. Bell, *Just War as Christian Discipleship*.

96. Bell, *Just War as Christian Discipleship*, 194.

97. See Patterson, *Ending Wars Well*.

98. Brown, quoted in Clouse, *War*, 149.

99. Marc Alan Lee, "Marc's Last Letter Home," July 2006, quoted in America's Mighty Warriors, accessed July 31, 2016, http://americasmightywarriors.org/marcs-last-letter-home/.

100. Details of Marc Alan Lee's story taken from "First Navy SEAL Killed in Iraq," 2006, America's Mighty Warriors, accessed July 31, 2016, http://americasmightywarriors.org/about-marc/.

101. Lee, "Marc's Last Letter Home."

CHAPTER 16

JUSTICE

1. "When the Cup of Endurance Runs Over"

In 1963, Birmingham, Alabama, was known as America's most segregated city. Eugene "Bull" Connor, Birmingham's commissioner of public safety, made sure of it. "You can never whip these birds if you don't keep you and them separate," he told one audience. "You've got to keep your white and the black separate."[1] Later, when asked whether he thought he could keep Birmingham in its present segregated condition, he said, "I may not be able to do it, but I'll die trying."[2]

In his eagerness, Connor had Martin Luther King Jr. arrested for illegal assembly as King led a children's march on April 12, 1963. King's arrest caused an uproar. Attempting to calm the community, a group of Jewish, Catholic, and Protestant ministers wrote "A Call for Unity." Their statement expressed sympathy for desegregation but condemned "outsiders" (meaning King) for creating unrest.

King, serving his eleven-day sentence, penned a response to the ministers' statement. In "Letter from a Birmingham Jail," King made historical, religious, and personal arguments to give moral force to the protests. This helped spark a situation in which children marching peacefully in the Children's Crusade were confronted with police dogs and sprayed with fire hoses. As soon as pictures hit national newspapers, segregation began losing its force. President John F. Kennedy had previously been reluctant to become involved, but now he addressed the nation to propose what would ultimately become the Civil Rights Act of 1964.

One phrase in particular leaps out of King's nearly seven-thousand-word letter: "Injustice anywhere is a threat to justice everywhere."[3] In other words, ending racial segregation was about justice, not about power (as the Black Panther Party would later claim) or white people being devils (as Malcolm X stated). Justice wasn't just an issue of public order. It was deeply personal for King:

> As you seek to explain to your six-year-old daughter why she can't go to the public amusement park that has just been advertised on television, and see tears welling up in her eyes when she is told that Funtown is closed to colored children, and see ominous clouds of inferiority beginning to form in her little mental sky … then you will understand why we find it difficult to wait. There comes a time when the cup of endurance runs over, and men are no longer willing to be plunged into the abyss of despair.[4]

"Injustice anywhere is a threat to justice everywhere."

Interestingly, King's sharpest words were reserved not for segregationists but for "moderates," such as the ministers to whom King's rebuke was addressed. They were, King argued, denying God-given rights by focusing on the smooth functioning of society. If King's appeal was radical, it was radical in the most basic sense of the term—"back to the roots":

> One day the South will know that when these disinherited children of God sat down at lunch counters, they were in reality standing up for what is best in the American dream and for the most sacred values in our Judeo-Christian heritage, thereby bringing our nation back to those great wells of democracy which were dug deep by the founding fathers in their formulation of the Constitution and the Declaration of Independence.[5]

To King, justice should be grounded in the permanent rights of each person rather than on doing whatever it takes to keep order in society. It's a very different focus than is common today, when the longing for justice seems to revolve around vague, aspirational concepts, such as social justice. There's never been a better time to think through what the Bible says about justice and its role in expressing Christ's redemption in culture.

That's what this chapter is about. To make sense of such a broad topic, we'll ask questions like these: What is justice? Of the competing ideas of justice, which ones are true? What is government's role in securing justice? Is a view of justice based on what the Bible says about God, humanity, and the world superior to other views? Finally we'll ask, "What should Christians, in particular, do in response?"

2. What Is the Problem?

Lots of things about our society work very well, at least on the surface. But you needn't dig far below the surface to uncover serious problems. *Poverty* is a serious problem. In spite of an investment of around $22 trillion dollars of tax money, the United States poverty level remains about the same as it was in the 1960s.[6] *Crime* and *society's response* to it are also serious problems. The United States has lowered its crime rate by putting more people behind bars. Yet the prison population has outpaced the increase in crime. Between 1972 and 2008, the incarceration rate grew by more than 700 percent.[7] The public expense has been enormous, and former prisoners rarely integrate well into society once their punishments are served.

Research has shown that poverty and crime often go hand in hand.[8] Politicians and sociologists believe that if they could solve one of these problems, they could solve the other. But how? Clearly, government plays a role, but can its power be deployed without eroding liberty? To answer this question, we need to grapple with other fundamental questions, such as these:

> **Research has shown that poverty and crime often go hand in hand.**

- *What is the basis of justice?* Is justice based on the rights every person has as a human being, or is it based on what society needs to be well ordered?

- *What is the government's role?* Should government's role in securing liberty be primarily negative (removing the restraints to liberty) or positive (helping people fulfill their full potential)?

We'll start our discussion of justice looking at what justice is and then move on to what justice is based on and how it is accomplished.

What Is Justice?

Justice is the moral principle of equally observing the rights of all people and treating them fairly. Nicholas Wolterstorff says, "A society is just insofar as its members enjoy the goods to which they have a right."[9] By goods, Wolterstorff doesn't mean just physical possessions. He also means things like equal access to the judicial system.

What Is the Basis of Justice?

Our understanding of what is just depends on how we understand liberty and law. Let's look at liberty first.

Liberty. There are two dominant, competing views of **liberty**: negative liberty and positive liberty.

> *Liberty:* **freedom from undue restraint.**

1. Negative liberty. Many of America's founders feared the growing power of government more than criminal activity or even foreign invasion. They thought liberty was something the Creator gave. Government shouldn't be allowed to take it away without due process of law. People's rights under the law are spelled out in the Bill of Rights of the US Constitution. Among them are the right to free speech and the right to a fair trial. The Bill of Rights compels the federal government to use its power to protect people from itself so they may be free. This is **negative liberty** because it focuses on how government secures liberty by negating restraints against it.

> *Negative Liberty:* the belief that liberty is secured when the government removes unwarranted constraints (e.g., ensuring a right to assembly or guaranteeing free speech).

Negative liberty must be secured by both forms of government mentioned in the Constitution: federal and state. The framers structured the document to ensure state power and to limit the power of the federal government to mediating disputes between the states, forming alliances with foreign governments, and ensuring a strong defense. After more than two centuries of lawmaking, court decisions, and amendments passed to curb state abuses (such as slavery), the role of the federal government has expanded dramatically. Still, states are mostly responsible for criminal-law creation and enforcement.[10]

In theory, when state governments secure negative liberty by helping protect people's safety and property, and the federal government protects negative liberty by defending the states and settling disputes among them, people are free to establish businesses, raise families, be good neighbors, and live peaceful lives. Justice should reign. Unfortunately, it often doesn't because of the wrong worldview assumptions people have embraced and the effects of human fallenness.

> *Positive Liberty:* the belief that liberty is secured when the government acts to remove inequality between people or people groups (e.g., enforcing affirmative action or passing minimum-wage laws).

2. Positive liberty. In recent decades, the idea of liberty as freedom from restraint has diminished. Now governments focus on expanding benefits for those they believe have been unable to enjoy the fruits of liberty as much as those around them. Usually the focus is on "oppressed" groups of people, such as racial minorities, women, illegal immigrants, and homosexuals. Negative liberty asks, "What are the external restraints that make it hard for people to fulfill their potential, and how might we remove them?" In contrast, **positive liberty** asks, "What are the internal conditions that make it hard for people to fulfill their potential, and how can government remedy them?"[11]

Negative liberty focuses on making sure barriers to fulfillment are *absent*. Positive liberty focuses on making sure conditions for people's fulfillment are *present* by using government power to remedy perceived injustices. A few examples of positive-liberty programs the government has enacted include mandates for colleges to accept a certain percentage of minorities (affirmative action), rent control, and giving money to the poor.

The differences between negative liberty and positive liberty matter greatly. In fact, many of today's political debates are between these two conceptions. Some believe government has grown to the point where it hurts liberty. Others believe government needs to intervene to help people fulfill their potential.

Because government's only real power is the power of coercion, though, it can exercise positive liberty only by coercing some people to give of their resources to provide for those who are judged to have been historically disadvantaged or who have fallen into misfortune. This is called *redistribution* because the government must take from the haves to distribute to the have-nots.

Law. There are two competing conceptions of **law**: natural law and legal positivism.

> *Law:* the study of ordinances designed to help citizens coexist peacefully.

1. Natural law. In the aftermath of World War II, the victorious nations wrestled with how to prosecute Nazis accused of war crimes, igniting a debate over the source of law. One side said law was based on something everyone would know to be true about the world if they weren't swayed by previous commitments or views of law. This idea is called **natural law**, which goes back to the Christian theology of Thomas Aquinas, as well as various secular thinkers. Natural law says that people's rights are "inherent," meaning everyone has them without having to prove they are worthy of them. Such rights may not be taken away without due process of law. That each person has inherent rights is why, when someone is charged with a crime, the legal elements must be proved beyond a reasonable doubt before that individual's rights and freedoms can be taken away. The US Declaration of Indepence affirms that the rights to life, liberty, and the pursuit of happiness were endowed by the Creator. Government doesn't *grant* these rights; it *secures* them.

> *Natural Law:* the belief that morality can be seen in the natural order of creation and accessed through human reason; the belief that laws are rules based upon an internal code of morality that all people possess.

To be just according to the natural-law view, laws must be clearly spelled out, free of contradiction, well publicized, fairly applied, and consistently enforced.[12] These common-sense principles, constantly referred to in debates about whether certain laws are appropriate, provide the basis for legal standards to this day.

2. Legal positivism. Not everyone agrees with a natural-law approach. Some say that people's needs change as society advances and that law shouldn't be tied to unchanging absolutes. People taking this view advocate **legal positivism**. Legal positivism says that the law is whatever those in authority agree to do.

The Nazis on trial took full advantage of the disagreement between these two camps. When confronted with evidence of their mass murder of millions of people,

> *Legal Positivism:* the belief that laws are rules created by human authorities and that there is no inherent or necessary connection between law and morality.

they said, "You have no right to judge us. We acted legally, based on the laws we were ordered to follow." Legal-positivism advocates were in a quandary. If they argued that law was based on what those in authority decided, they would be granting that they had the right to judge the Nazis because the Nazis lost, and the new authorities had the right to judge them. This implies that, had the Nazis won, the Nazi cause would have to be acknowledged as just, and they would have, in turn, had the moral authority to judge their opponents.

Natural-law advocates face no such quandary. They argue that every human being knows it's wrong to kill people en masse just because their leader tells them to. The Nazi leaders should have known better, regardless of what the Nazi government's laws said. In the end, many Nazi leaders were condemned to long prison sentences or death by hanging.

Whether someone accepts a natural-law view or a legal-positivism view depends largely on what justice is supposed to accomplish. Here, too, there are significant disagreements that affect the way the whole justice system operates.

What Is Justice Supposed to Accomplish?

While the struggle rages over whether negative or positive liberty ought to be embraced, there is also a conflict over what outcomes justice ought to lead to. Two views have emerged: the inherent-rights view of justice and the right-ordering-of-society view of justice.

1. The inherent-rights view of justice. The **inherent-rights view of justice** says that a just society ought to secure the permanent rights of every person. In America these rights are threefold: "life, liberty, and property." No person may be separated from these rights without due process of law, as spelled out in the US Constitution. The Constitution's preamble makes clear the founders' conviction that government didn't *grant* the blessings of liberty but merely *secured* them. As the Declaration of Independence put it, those rights came from "Nature and Nature's God."

Inherent-Rights View of Justice: the belief that justice involves the government seeking to protect the inherent rights of its citizens.

Mosaic Law: the set of laws God gave Moses and the Hebrews following their exodus from Egypt.

Right-Ordering View of Justice: the belief that justice involves the government seeking to preserve social order.

The inherent-rights view is often thought to be an Enlightenment invention from the 1700s, but ethicists like Nicholas Wolterstorff say its lineage goes back much further, to the **Mosaic law**, and even to the idea of humans as God's image bearers. Wolterstorff says that when the inherent-rights view falls out of favor, we become worse off: "Hitler's Germany was extraordinarily orderly; the trains ran on time. It was a profoundly wrong order, however."[13]

2. The right-ordering view of justice. Not everyone agrees with the inherent-rights view. Those advocating a **right-ordering view of justice** say that justice is whatever helps a society function smoothly for as many people as possible. Often those holding this view treat justice as if it is not about the treatment of individual people but about how groups of people relate in a well-ordered society. It is why governments increasingly express a willingness to *remove* rights from one group in order to *reward* them to another group, in the interests of having an orderly society. Because this view is growing, we'll address it in more detail in the following discussion of retributive and distributive justice.

To recap, justice is about liberty and law. There are two views of liberty: negative (removing the restraints to liberty) and positive (helping people fulfill their full potential). There are also two views of law: natural law (law is discovered in nature) and legal positivism (law is what those in authority decide to do). How people view liberty and law affects the outcomes they hope justice will achieve. Some focus on the inherent-rights view of justice (expecting government to secure the rights of every person); others focus on the right-ordering view (expecting government to preserve societal order).

But before we move on, one more distinction needs to be made. People who believe in the right-ordering view of justice typically align with one of two camps: *retributive* justice or *distributive* justice. When people advocate a law-and-order approach and say things like "Lock them up and throw away the key," they're talking about *retributive* justice. When people say, "People commit crimes because they're uneducated and poor, and it's the government's responsibility to fix this," they're talking about *distributive* justice. We'll examine retributive justice first.

Retributive justice. Retributive justice says that society is better off when the state focuses only on punishing those who commit crimes rather than trying to identify the underlying causes of crime and fix them. People in prison cannot disrupt the order of society; after all, if someone steals your car, wrecks it, and then goes to prison, that person won't be stealing any more cars while he or she is locked away.

> *Retributive Justice:* the belief that a just society should focus on punishing criminals rather than rehabilitating them or removing the root causes of crime.

Yet if the thief who steals your car is caught and goes to prison, you still have a problem. Your car is ruined. Even if the judge orders the thief to pay you back, is that even possible if the person is in jail? This brings up an important question. It seems that the crime was against *you* because your car is the one that was stolen. But the retributive-justice view treats the crime as if it were against the *state*. Yes, the state suffers when crimes like theft are committed. But aren't the primary victims the *people* who were harmed?

According to Heather Rice-Minus, director of government affairs for the Justice Fellowship, a division of Prison Fellowship Ministries, the right-ordering view of justice diminishes both victims and perpetrators.[14] This is true whether it is distributive or retributive because neither has in mind making things right for those individuals who were harmed. Victims have their fundamental dignity and property taken away, with no means by which to regain it. And because perpetrators never have to confront how people were affected by their wrongdoing, they seldom learn from what they've done wrong and may even develop a spirit of resentment rather than repentance.

In the long term, the retributive view of justice can reduce crime. But it does so by expanding the category of those who have a criminal record. A study by scholars at Princeton University in 2010 found that approximately twenty million Americans have a felony criminal record and thus face significant obstacles when it comes to getting a job or even volunteering in church.[15] The figure is likely even higher today. At the same time, victims of crime seldom gain a hearing for how they've lost loved ones in senseless acts of violence or had their property or livelihood destroyed by crime.

> Being tough on crime can create a more orderly society, but at what cost?

Being tough on crime can create a more orderly society, but at what cost? Richard Viguerie, founder of a direct-mail advertising firm that helped Ronald Reagan become president in 1980, is among those asking this question. He says he was a law-and-order guy until he began studying the criminal-justice system and realized that punishments often don't fit the associated crimes. Furthermore, the rights and needs of the victims are ignored. Viguerie states,

> As Christians we should be offended, and as conservatives we should be outraged. The prison system is the largest government program in the country. If you are a small-government conservative, the size of the prison system in this country should be appalling to you.[16]

What can we do? After all, the inner workings of the justice system seem overwhelming. Such inner workings include

- the daily grind of small-claims court, where customers bicker with business owners they believe have defrauded them;

- civil courts in which victims sue to recover damages for harms they allege were done to them;

- family courts, where people sue their spouses for divorce and try to establish custody arrangements for bewildered children;

- juvenile courts, where exasperated public defenders try to reason with sullen teenagers whose misbehavior has caught the attention of the police;

- law-enforcement activity in which accused criminals are arrested, brought to police stations, and held in jails while the system chugs slowly along; and

- criminal courts, where prisoners shuffle in and plead guilty or not guilty to having broken certain laws.

On top of this we have the prison system, which costs states approximately $50 billion a year.[17] All the while, judges and attorneys come and go, and citizens called for jury duty wait impatiently to be interviewed and selected to make a judgment in one trial or another. It's a complicated and messy system.

Reform is needed. But if these reforms occur *inside* a right-ordering-view-of-justice framework, they'll fail to take into account the way people bear God's image and the way God has organized society to function best.

Many crack-down-on-crime reforms, based on retributive justice, have been tried. Success has been limited. For instance, states like Alaska and Washington passed laws banning plea bargaining and mandating minimum sentences to keep judges from going easy on criminals.[18] Politically, it has been a popular solution because both liberals and conservatives dislike plea bargaining, in spite of the fact that 95 percent of all criminal cases are resolved that way.[19] Liberals dislike **plea bargaining** because they feel it coerces defendants into abdicating their procedural protections. Conservatives dislike it because they feel it enables criminals to avoid the full punishment they deserve.[20] Abolishing plea bargaining, though, throws hundreds of thousands of cases into trial courts, utterly overwhelming them. And it isn't clear from the research that abolishing plea bargaining actually reduces crime anyway.

> *Plea Bargaining:* an arrangement between a criminal and the courts whereby a defendant pleads guilty in exchange for a lesser punishment.

Another example of a tough-on-crime reform that may not be working as promised is **minimum mandatory sentencing**. In the past, sentences were usually determined by an informal "courtroom workgroup" made up of the judge, the prosecutor, and the defense attorney.[21] Because these three interact with each other so frequently, they learn to cooperate with one another and make decisions based on local mores. Mandatory sentencing limits this discretion, often removing the ability of judges to use punishments that don't involve incarceration. Judges work around this, however, by offering punishments that have nothing to do with the crime committed, which makes a mockery of criminal law.[22]

> *Minimum Mandatory Sentencing:* a legal requirement that sets minimum standards of punishment for particular crimes.

Everyone is frustrated. The state doesn't seem to be achieving its goal of a rightly ordered society. Criminals feel mistreated. Victims feel mistreated. And communities are unraveling. We can hardly lose by asking the obvious question: Would shifting our perspective back to the inherent-rights view of justice—rather than the right-ordering view of justice—make a difference, where reforms tinkering with the right-ordering view haven't worked? We'll look at some promising reforms in the following pages.

Rather than move outside the right-ordering-view framework, though, policy makers are constantly tempted to make a pendulum swing *within* it to a view that is nearly the opposite of the retributive-justice view. It's called *distributive* justice.

Distributive justice. As the 2015 Baltimore riots raged, mayor Stephanie Rawlings-Blake expressed her response as "giving those who wished to destroy space to do that."[23] From her perspective, the rioters were just getting even for what they perceived to be a pattern of injustice. Forces beyond the rioters' control were to blame, she implied, and government's job was to restore order and then find ways to redistribute society's resources to remedy those injustices. While Mayor Rawlings-Blake didn't explicitly say so, her assumptions were clear: people were rioting because they were poor and mistreated. The government can fix this through a twin focus on equality of outcomes and redistribution of resources.

> **Distributive Justice:** the belief that a just society should seek to redistribute its citizens' resources equally among everyone.

Distributive justice is about equality of outcomes. Remember our definition of *justice*: the moral principle of equally observing the rights of all people and treating them fairly. **Distributive justice** doesn't ask whether the *process* of justice is occurring but whether the end result of that process is *equality*.[24] If not, they say, justice has been denied.

Political scientists mostly use the term *distributive justice*. The term sociologists and social workers use has caught on much more: *social justice*.

The National Association of Social Workers (NASW) defines *social justice* as "the view that everyone deserves equal economic, political and social rights and opportunities."[25] How is social justice secured? The NASW says, "Peace is not possible where there are gross inequalities of money and power, whether between workers and managers, nations and nations or men and women."[26] In other words, social injustice comes through inequality and can be restored only by equalizing the distribution of society's goods. That this is the common usage is clear in the *Oxford English Dictionary* definition of *social justice*: "Justice in terms of the distribution of wealth, opportunities, and privileges within a society."[27] Social justice is simply distributive justice by another, less politically charged, name.

> **Social-justice advocates believe that social injustice comes through inequality and can be restored only by equalizing the distribution of society's goods.**

In the past, the focus of justice was usually on the civil or criminal courts: a person accused of wrongdoing would have been treated justly if given a fair trial with fair rules and an impartial judge and jury. When this occurs, we can say "justice [has been] done."[28] As economist Thomas Sowell points out, though, social justice defines *fairness* as eliminating "undeserved disadvantages for selected groups."[29] It's not about the rules of the game; it's about deciding what the final score ought to be.

Here's the problem: Who decides what equality is and how to secure it?[30] Every individual has advantages and disadvantages. Some people have beauty but lack intelligence; others are born into wealth but lack emotional stability; still others have athletic ability but are crippled by a quick temper. Who could possibly know enough to judge which advantages and disadvantages should be taken into account or disregarded?

Such a judgment is not only impossible but also dangerous. Liberty is the ultimate victim when we try to control for the billions of variables involved in forcing equality. Recognizing this, the onetime 1960s radical David Horowitz warned, "The regime of social justice, of which the Left dreams, is a regime that by its very nature must crush individual freedom."[31]

Social justice also requires mandating *injustice* for some to achieve its aims for others. Sowell says that social justice "disregards the interests of others who are not the immediate focus of discussion, but who nevertheless pay the price of the decisions made."[32] Forcing equality might begin with noble aims, but good intentions don't necessarily make good public policy. Still, many policy makers are so convinced that uneven outcomes are unfair that they work hard to quantify, control, and redistribute whichever societal resources they think are unevenly distributed. This is called *redistribution*.

Distributive justice is about redistribution. Imagine that Harvard University reviewed its scholarship policy, only to find that it was giving most of its scholarship money to students who achieved high test scores and were from largely intact middle-class families with many social advantages. Furthermore, let's say they decided that such a policy was unjust and that instead they ought to give most of the money to low-scoring students. What would happen? The answer, uncomfortably, is that Harvard would then become a remedial institution trying to help unqualified students achieve a basic level of success. This might be a worthy mission, but it's far different from Harvard's current mission of producing the best scholars and best scholarship possible. Among the many effects of this policy shift would likely be that its professors and best students would go elsewhere. Its alumni would feel that the value of their education had been eroded. And it would ruin the university's reputation as one of the world's top institutions of higher learning.

Maybe, considering all these factors, redistributing "scholarship wealth" is still called for. Perhaps low-achieving students are doing poorly because they are victims of social conditions that are no fault of their own. Harvard is a private institution. It can choose to admit as many low-performing students as it wants. It wouldn't be illegal or unethical or immoral. But what if the *government* forced Harvard to change its standards under the penalty of law? What began as perhaps an unwise decision would now be a tyrannical one.

This is what redistribution does. It assumes that every resource in society actually belongs to all of us, and thus the government must control these resources so they can be parceled out in a "fairer" manner until the desired outcome is achieved: making everyone equal and ensuring that no one has more resources than anyone else. But even if equality of outcomes was a good idea, is it even possible for government to achieve it?

> Redistribution assumes that every resource in society actually belongs to all of us, and the government must control these resources so they can be parceled out in a "fairer" manner.

> Justice is fairness, Rawls thought, and the way to remove unfairness is to remove inequality by distributing "social goods" equally.

How does redistribution work? Philosopher John Rawls thought he knew the answer to this question. Justice is fairness, he thought, and society is kept from being fair because of fear, self-interest, and a judgmental attitude. The way to remove this unfairness is to remove inequality.[33] This would be done by equally distributing "social goods," which Rawls defined as "income and wealth," as well as liberty, opportunity, and self-respect. All of these must be distributed equally, he said, unless it is to everyone's advantage to have them not so distributed.[34]

To show how redistribution might work, Rawls proposed a thought experiment. Imagine that each person serves as a representative for an unknown person hiding behind a "veil of ignorance."[35] The representative doesn't know the race of the person, whether the person is creative or smart, or whether this person has been successful in business or is struggling to find employment. The job of the representative is to advocate for the interests of this unknown person in dividing up social goods.

Because the representatives would be completely unbiased, in theory, Rawls thought we should consider the results of their decisions to be the "original position" from which decisions could be made about whether social goods were distributed unfairly in the past.[36] The goal is to make the judgments fall as close to the original position as possible.

A generation of political-science students studied John Rawls's ideas. One of them, presidential candidate Barack Obama, told a potential voter, "I think when you spread the wealth around, it's good for everybody."[37] This is a Rawlsian idea. And to those who think society lacks compassion and that some people don't get a fair shake, it sounds like a loving thing to do. As we saw in the chapter on politics, though, government can't show compassion. It can use its power only to coerce people to do things that appear compassionate.

> **Rawls assumed that it's fair and morally right to redistribute resources by taking them from those who have them and giving them to those who wish they had them.**

Plus, Rawls's ideas work only if "social goods" can be quantified. We know how to count money and assess the value of wealth, but how do we quantify liberty, opportunity, and self-respect? Rawls also assumed that it's fair and morally right to redistribute resources by taking them from those who have them and giving them to those who wish they had them.[38]

To redistributionists, equality is more important than liberty. Certainly, society can be harmed if rich people benefit economically by exploiting poor people, or companies harm their workers by treating them unfairly. But as we saw in the chapter on poverty, this problem is most acute when societies aren't economically free. Take the example of restaurant workers. If there is only one restaurant in town, no other job possibilities, and no possibility of the workers moving elsewhere, they're stuck with whatever work conditions exist and the pay they receive. However, if new restaurants are opening, or if schools exist where workers can be trained for higher-paying jobs, or if workers are free to move to another place, then they're really stuck only if government policy somehow discourages new businesses from starting up or formally restricts citizens' movements.[39]

A distributive-justice agenda, though, looks at these restaurant workers differently. It requires the government to set the work conditions and pay levels and to tax wealthier people so wage earners like those who work in restaurants may be given more benefits. This is often done under the guise of helping the poor, but as the atheistic and pragmatist philosopher Richard Rorty admitted, the goal is putting "shared utopian dreams—dreams of an ideally decent and civilized society—in the place of knowledge of God's Will, Moral Law, the Laws of History, or the Facts of Science."[40] To Rorty, such an agenda is more important than individual freedom.[41]

As you can see, there is much at stake in the current debates about what justice is and how it ought to be secured. In addition to the question of whether it's okay to diminish liberty in the pursuit of equality, there are serious justice problems in the United States, and many attempts to solve them have failed. Is justice about inherent rights or about the right ordering of society? Should we solve the crime problem by tough retributive measures or by redistributing resources in the hope that people won't feel the need to commit crime to get ahead?

Here's another pressing question related to the overall purpose of this book: Is the issue of justice something Christians, in particular, should be concerned with, and if so, why?

3. WHY SHOULD CHRISTIANS CARE?

What the Bible Says about Justice

A biblical worldview shows support for governmental authority. Governments are to respond to God's revelation in nature by punishing wrongdoers and protecting those who live in accordance with God's laws (Rom. 13:3–4).[42] Government is needed not just because we haven't yet reached utopia. Government is an institution God designed to secure justice. It is right and proper and good. Let's examine three aspects of justice that emerge from the biblical text.

1. God loves justice. Justice is one of God's attributes. Jeremiah 9:24 says, "I am the LORD who practices steadfast love, justice, and righteousness in the earth. For in these things I delight." We ought to care about justice, and not just because there is sin in the world. Justice is important, period. God delights in it. We might even go so far as to say that because God acts justly and delights in justice, it would have been an important thing for us to pursue even if we weren't fallen creatures.

But in a world of sin, the cause of justice takes on great urgency. The **doctrine of original sin** says that humans are so *thoroughly* fallen that nothing remains unaffected by our fallenness. Bad people aren't the only ones who do very bad things and make life miserable for the rest; *each of us* falls short of God's glory (Rom. 3:23).[43]

When we're gathered together in community, our individual sin natures can morph into "structural" evil, in which historical and cultural patterns, expectations, and habits are established that perpetuate sin from one generation to another.[44] We might be tempted to excuse ourselves from our part in structural sin. For example, we may reason that if someone grew up as a racist because he or she lived in a racist culture and didn't know any better, that person wouldn't be responsible for the sin of racism and would therefore not be obligated to do anything about it. But the biblical approach is that although we humans are stuck in a web of social evil we didn't create, we ought to act intentionally against such evil. As theologian Cornelius Plantinga Jr. points out, to not act intentionally against sin is to perpetuate it.[45]

> *Doctrine of Original Sin:* the orthodox Christian belief that Adam's first sin corrupted the nature of his descendents, leading to humanity's present propensity toward committing sin.

2. Justice isn't just avoiding what's wrong; it's pursuing what's right. That justice is something we ought to *pursue* rather than just fall in line with is the underlying assumption of Scripture. The Hebrew word *tzedek*, which means "justice or righteousness," implies that God's people are to purposely seek to do what is *right*, not just avoid doing what is *wrong*. The call to be just, pursue justice, and act justly occurs over and over again in Scripture.[46] The psalmist declared, "The LORD loves righteousness and justice; the earth is full of his unfailing love" (Ps. 33:5 NIV).

To be clear, the Bible isn't a book about how to set up legal statutes. But we can learn a great deal about what good law is by examining the advanced legal system God gave to Moses for the nation of Israel. When Moses led the children of Israel out of Egypt, it was critical that they have a clear system of laws. These were former slaves who presumably had little idea of how to govern themselves. A lot was at stake for this fledgling nation surrounded by hostile, wicked forces and with no natural sources of food and water. Even small mistakes could doom the community.

Within this context, we can gain many insights into how God's revelation of himself translated into rules by which his chosen people were to live every day. Further, these laws were written down so that leaders couldn't change them, make up new rules, or enforce rules that didn't exist. This protected the people from injustice.

> We can learn a great deal about what good law is by examining the advanced legal system God gave to Moses for the nation of Israel.

Many of the laws recorded in the Old Testament, in what the Jewish people called the Torah, seem confusing to us today. Administrative laws about zoning are mixed in with ceremonial laws and laws about personal hygiene, diet, and disease prevention, which are mixed in with criminal laws. Considering how long ago these laws were written, it makes sense they would be somewhat jumbled. If people several thousand years in the future found fragments of our laws, some of the laws would probably make no sense. What do our traffic signs mean, for example? Those in a future society who make snap judgments about what our culture meant might very well misunderstand it entirely.

3. Structures of justice are important to remedy structural evil. Given the passage of time and cultural differences, it's astounding how sensible and forward looking Israel's laws were. From them, we can gain insight into what an ordered system ought to look like. Here are just a few examples:

The responsibility of the community. Exodus 21:33–34 says, "When a man opens a pit, or when a man digs a pit and does not cover it, and an ox or a donkey falls into it, the owner of the pit shall make restoration. He shall give money to its owner, and the dead beast shall be his." This law established relationships between neighbors. As Lord Atkin said in the nineteenth century,

> The rule that you are to love your neighbour becomes in law: You must not injure your neighbour.… Who then, in law, is my neighbour? … Persons who are so closely and directly affected by my act that I ought reasonably to have them in contemplation as being so affected when I am directing my mind to the acts or omissions that are called in question.[47]

The biblical principles regarding neighbors' obligations to one another form the basis of **tort law** (from the Latin word *torquere*, which refers to laws governing what happens when things get twisted out of shape).

> *Tort Law:* the area of law governing remedies for those wronged by others, such as through negligence.

Honest government. Judges in the Old Testament were appointed to decide disagreements between people according to God's laws and teachings (e.g., Exod. 18:13–16; Deut. 1:16–17; 19:15–21).[48] These judges were commanded to be honest and not take bribes or show favoritism (Exod. 23:1–8).[49] Looking at how God instructed the ancient nation of Israel to operate, it's clear that he wants the process of justice to be equitable. Each person has the right to be judged by the same standard. Deuteronomy 1:17 (NIV) says, "Do not show partiality in judging; hear both small and great alike."

The dignity of the accused. We also see the care with which the Mosaic code treated those accused of a crime and how important it is to avoid hasty condemnation. Simon Greenleaf explains:

> The importance of extreme care in ascertaining the truth of every criminal charge, especially where life is involved, may be regarded as a rule of law. It … does not inflict the penalty of death until the crime "be told thee" (viz., in a formal accusation), "and thou hast heard of it" (upon a legal trial), "and inquired diligently, and behold it be true" (satisfactorily proved), "and the thing certain" (beyond all reasonable doubt).[50]

Because of our fallen nature, our reason and will are corrupted. Human error is likely, not just possible. God instructed the Israelites to err in favor of the defendant rather than punish an innocent person.

The dignity of the victim. The Old Testament law also focused on restitution. If someone stole an animal, he was to repay four or five times the value (Exod. 22:1).[51] If a person lied on a contract or profited by deceiving his neighbor, he was to repay what was taken and add a fifth to it to compensate for the victim's inability to use in a profitable way what was stolen (Lev. 6:2–5).[52] In Luke 19, Jesus befriended a tax collector who was known as a cheater. This man, named Zacchaeus, repented of his sins, offered half of his possessions to the poor, and committed to repay four times what he had taken. In this, Zacchaeus was showing his willingness to obey the Old Testament law as part of his repentance. Jesus affirmed this, saying, "Today salvation has come to this house" (v. 9).

> Due to our fallen nature, human error is likely, not just possible. God instructed the Israelites to err in favor of the defendant rather than punish an innocent person.

We have enough of Israel's legal code to know that God cares about the rights of each person, that justice requires being careful about applying the rules, and that the overall focus of the law is restoring God's order in the midst of a sinful world. To quote C. S. Lewis, what we know about God is this: "[Christianity] thinks that a great many things have gone wrong with the world that God made and that God insists, and insists very loudly, on our putting them right again."[53]

What should this lead us to do? Next, we'll look at restorative justice and prison reform.

4. What Should Christians Do?

Pursuing justice isn't easy. It's complicated to figure out what, if any, principles from the Bible apply to our current situation. After all, we're not trying to establish a new Israel. Rather, we're seeking to understand who God is, what justice looks like from his perspective, and where injustice reigns because of sin. We also want to know how to live as if justice actually exists—even when it's hard to understand or define—and to treat people as image bearers of God who have inherent rights.

> Pursuing justice isn't easy. It's complicated to figure out what, if any, principles from the Bible apply to our current situation.

One Christian who grasps this is Bruce Strom, who founded Administer Justice (AJ), a nonprofit organization that offers free or low-cost legal services to Chicago's poor and elderly, as well as immigrants who don't understand the legal system. One of his first clients was a Brazilian woman trying to get her son back from her fiancé's family after her fiancé died in a car accident. The family had placed a voodoo curse on her, and she was terrified. When Strom explained that the voodoo curse was powerless because of the work of Christ on the cross, the woman trusted Christ as her savior. And with one phone call, she was able to get her son back. Since then, more than forty thousand people have come to AJ and its network of 250 attorneys, seeking help on everything from tax problems to custody agreements.[54]

Other initiatives focus on caring for the children of prisoners. In 1991, Loren Miller founded a Mennonite mission, New Horizons Ministries, to care for the babies of incarcerated women. The ministry is based in Fremont County, Colorado, which is home to nine state and four federal penal institutions, including the notorious supermax prison that houses some of the worst criminals alive. New Horizons host families and nannies have cared for more than 142 children. The babies are taken to visit their mothers, who also receive mentoring and parental training to ease the transition back into family life upon their release. One former prisoner, Sherelle Brown, gave birth to her son, Macaiah, in prison. A New Horizon nanny cared for Macaiah, and the ministry helped Sherelle—and continues to help her now that she has been released. "[Without New Horizons] I'd probably be back in prison. I didn't have to walk all by myself," Brown says. Now Brown is taking classes at a technical school and preparing for her future.[55]

> Ultimately, restoring justice means taking a hard look at serious problems in the system itself and seeing if biblical principles can make a difference in bringing about reform.

These are astounding initiatives. But working outside the justice system can accomplish only so much. Ultimately, restoring justice means taking a hard look at serious problems in the system itself and seeing if biblical principles can make a difference in bringing about reform.

Restoring Justice

In today's system, criminal justice focuses on the government versus the defendant. The person who was wronged and the community stand almost helplessly on the sidelines. **Restorative justice** changes this. Instead of the government playing the victim, restorative justice encourages the government to pursue justice between the victim and the perpetrator. Restorative justice "prioritizes participation of those who are harmed by crime, promotes accountability of those who are responsible, and cultivates community engagement," says Heather Rice-Minus.[56]

> *Restorative Justice:* the practice of pursuing justice between a victim and a perpetrator.

There are five goals of restorative justice:[57]

To attend fully to victims' needs—material, financial, emotional, and social.

To prevent reoffending by reintegrating offenders into the community.

To enable offenders to assume active responsibility for their actions.

To re-create a working community that supports the rehabilitation of offenders and victims and is active in preventing crime.

To provide a means of avoiding the escalation of legal justice and the associated costs and delays.

Restorative justice works by enabling the victm and perpetrator to see each other as human beings. For instance, if a rioter destroying a car had to face the single mom who had worked for years to earn money to buy it, and had to hear her story of how she's now unable to get to work or to take her child to school, he would probably have an entirely different attitude toward his actions. In this way, restorative justice restores the humanity of both the victim and the perpetrator.

> Restorative justice works by enabling the victm and perpetrator to see each other as human beings.

Here are five examples of restorative justice at work:

1. Diversions. In the United States, the court system itself needs reform. The Constitution guarantees the right to a speedy trial, but "speedy" is a relative term in places like the New York City borough of the Bronx, where it takes an average of 988 days for the case of an accused felon to be brought to trial.[58] Some defendants are left in jail for up to five years before getting their day in court. This is wrong. To quote a common legal maxim, "Justice too long delayed is justice denied." Inefficient courts delay justice for both the accused and the victim. People become discouraged when it takes a long time to receive justice. As Proverbs 13:12 says, "Hope deferred makes the heart sick, but a desire fulfilled is a tree of life." Plus, delayed justice destroys justice's deterrent effect. Would-be criminals stop fearing the consequences of their actions. As Ecclesiastes 8:11 warns, "Because the sentence against an evil deed is not executed speedily, the heart of the children of man is fully set to do evil."

One solution to this problem is diverting offenders from standard justice-system processing. Diversions, such as mediation, allow the offender to avoid the negative elements of formal case processing and work toward repairing the damage done to the victim.

Mediation and sentencing circles are other forms of diversion. In mediation, a mediator brokers an agreement to help restore what was lost. Typically employed in lieu of formal probation or prison, mediation usually applies to property offenders or low-level assault cases. In a sentencing circle, members of the community reach a consensus on the sentence in a discussion with the victim and the offender. In both cases, the victim and offender must choose this option over the right to a trial. Examples of agreements reached include apologies, restitution, and, in some cases, community service. There are some parallels between the use of restorative justice in individual cases and its broader use in society. For example, a program in Fresno, California, that mediates thousands of individual cases also successfully mediated a conflict between two rival youth gangs.

> In mediation, a mediator brokers an agreement to help restore what was lost.

Mediation also shows promise at an international level. Prominent restorative-justice scholar Mark Umbreit, who heads the University of Minnesota's Center for Restorative Justice and Peacemaking, has been called on to help mediate conflicts between Israelis and Palestinians. In South Africa, bishop Desmond Tutu and the Truth and Reconciliation Commission (TRC) created a national postliberation, public tribunal in which twenty-two thousand victims and seven thousand offenders from the apartheid era shared their stories and explained their actions to one another in a safe space.

2. Victim-impact panels. In 1980, officer Pat Todd was shot five times by a man who became angry when she issued him a parking ticket. As of 2008, Pat had undergone forty-one reconstructive surgeries and lives with chronic pain. As a volunteer for the innovative Bridges to Life program, she hosts victim-impact panels that help those who have committed crimes understand the full impact of what they've done. One inmate, Bryan, whose brother had committed suicide, said that he was determined to do the same. But then he thought of Pat and how she could endure so much and still allow God to use her. As a former police officer, Pat helps put a human face to the "enemy," softening hearts and helping offenders see their victims as brothers and sisters, moms and dads, and sons and daughters.[59]

3. Victim-offender mediation. John Sage founded Bridges to Life after the brutal murder of his sister, Marilyn. The program takes crime victims into the prison system for a several-week-long program that empowers them to tell their stories. Inmates are rehabilitated by educating them about what their crimes have done to the victims, their families and friends, and the community.[60] One of the volunteers had a nineteen-year-old brother who was killed while serving as a security guard. Through a victim-offender mediation program, she was able to meet with her brother's killer and express forgiveness to him, as well as receive forgiveness from God for her anger and bitterness.[61]

Research has shown that such programs satisfy the victims' need for justice.[62] They also increase the collection of restitution and reduce recidivism as many offenders come to realize that their actions haven't just violated the text of a law but have harmed another person. Programs such as victim-offender mediation are the default option in places like New Zealand, and there are now three hundred such programs in the United States.[63]

4. Prioritizing restitution to victims. One key way restorative justice can make a difference is by prioritizing restitution to the victim over the payment of fines and fees to the courts. That can mean reducing or eliminating actual prison or jail time in favor of allowing a perpetrator to work and pay restitution to the victims. Heather Rice-Minus says that restitution isn't always monetary and tells the story of the mother of a murdered son who asked the murderer to send a card each year on her deceased son's birthday signed "I remember him." "Allowing for individualized restitution personalizes the harm and illuminates human dignity and value," Rice-Minus says.[64] Making amends for the harm caused by wrongdoing involves purposeful ways to set things right, such as apology, service, and payment.

5. Creating safety for victims. One very sad type of crime that often flies below the radar is **human trafficking**. The United Nations defines *human trafficking* as "a process by which people are recruited in their community and exploited by traffickers using deception and/or some form of coercion to lure and control them."[65] **Sex trafficking**, the practice of forcing people against their will to be put in a situation where they are sexually exploited, is particularly heartbreaking. While women and girls are by far the most common victims of trafficking, it isn't unheard of for men and boys to be victims as well.[66] Sex trafficking makes up roughly 58 percent of all trafficking cases globally.[67] Efforts to stop it have been limited; however, one area of focus is to ensure that a greater percentage of such cases are reported. Public appeals from law enforcement in a variety of languages assures victims that they'll receive protection if they come forward.

> *Human Trafficking:* the illegal trade and movement of human beings who are bought and sold for some type of coerced labor.

> *Sex Trafficking:* a form of human trafficking that uses violence, debt, abduction, and fraud to coerce human beings to work in the sex trade.

But many people are as afraid of law enforcement as they are of lawbreakers. Until people are convinced that law enforcement has their best interests at heart and can adequately protect them, they will often risk being victimized. Bringing injustice to light and creating safety for victims is of paramount importance.

In addition to restorative justice, prison reform is also an essential key to restoring justice.

Prison Reform

The prison population is skyrocketing. For most of US history, the prison population has been relatively stable. Prior to 1980, the incarceration rate remained below 125 prisoners for every 100,000 people.[68] Deviations occurred with certain events (such as prohibition), but the United States remained at or below this level during this time period.[69] Then in the early 1980s, incarceration rates began skyrocketing.[70] They continued doing so until 2009, when the overall prison population declined for the first time in thirty-eight years.[71] While the United States comprises only 5 percent of the global population, since 2008, it imprisons nearly 25 percent of the world's inmates.[72]

There is no universal consensus as to why the US prison population is so large, but theories abound. Here are a few:

The crime rate. The United States has a high crime rate, so it makes sense that our prison rates would be high as well. While property crimes are higher in some nations, such as Canada and England, the rate of violent crimes (murder, robbery, and assault) are many times greater in America than in those nations.[73] Violent crime is also more likely to be punished with incarceration than are property or so-called victimless crimes.

Drugs. America's drug problem and the government's means of dealing with it have contributed substantially to the number of offenders behind bars.[74] Often blamed for this are harsh sentences for offenders, preference for punishment over treatment, and a lucrative black market kept afloat by the risk premium paid to criminal traffickers. With the rapid growth of the black market in drug trafficking, ancillary violence erupts. Drug dealers would rather take care of the problem on their own than go to the police, which increases the amount of violent crime.

> Minimum mandatory sentences, both for drug-related crime and nondrug-related crime, have contributed substantially to the growth in the prison population.

Minimum mandatory sentences. As noted earlier, a minimum mandatory sentence is a provision whereby a predetermined sentence is issued once a person is found guilty of a crime. The politics surrounding the criminal justice system, often undergirded by tough-on-crime rhetoric, has led policy makers to impose minimum sentences of increasing length lest they be seen as being soft on crime.[75] Minimum mandatory sentences, both for drug-related crime and nondrug-related crime, have contributed substantially to the growth in the prison population. Laws that take away the discretion of judges and prosecutors, though, have tied the hands of courtroom officials when it comes to the length of sentences, even when mercy is warranted.[76]

Statutory changes can help solve the prison overpopulation problem. One method of dealing with swelling prison numbers would be to eliminate ineffective, overly broad, and pernicious laws. A law may be deemed ineffective if it fails to achieve its desired end. For example, drug laws in many states seek to lessen the usage of illegal drugs by issuing harsh punishments. However, drug use has remained relatively stable over the past several decades.[77] New approaches are needed.

Overly broad laws, while perhaps well intentioned, tend to punish those who aren't the original target of the legislation. Take gun laws, for example. By supporting government bans on certain types of guns or cosmetic features, gun-control advocates feel they can suppress gun crime. However, such legislation tends to make criminals out of individuals who legally own those weapons and are unlikely to use them for criminal ends in the first place. Such laws haven't been demonstrated to lower gun crime.[78]

Pernicious laws are those that serve the interests of one group to the detriment of many others. Licensure laws are a good example. While most would agree that it's important for doctors and lawyers to maintain professional licenses, there is little reason to license, as various states do, private investigators, bloggers, monks, tour guides, pumpkin and Christmas-tree sellers, and interior designers.[79] In several states, cutting hair without the appropriate license is a jailable offense in the name of upholding professional standards. Perhaps we should leave well enough alone. In the words of Sir Edward Coke, "Ignorance is a sufficient punishment" for the unskilled who would violate these standards.[80]

> The best way to reduce prison populations is to prevent people from going to prison in the first place.

Structural changes can help solve the prison overpopulation problem. The best way to reduce prison populations is to prevent people from going to prison in the first place. There are a number of creative ways to do this.

Community corrections. Offenders who pose little risk to public safety can be kept out of prison entirely. Offenders who are sentenced to probation or a halfway house or issued some other community-based sanction can be monitored by law-enforcement professionals, maintain gainful employment, pay taxes, and keep their families intact. Community sanctions also cost taxpayers far less than incarceration.[81] In the past several years, many jurisdictions, such as Texas, have been able to reduce crime and incarceration simply by using funds to make community corrections more available. These funds have been used in the past to build prisons.

> Through timely intervention, many people who commit crimes might be persuaded to change their ways.

Persuasion. As image bearers of God, people can change. Through timely intervention, many people who commit crimes might be persuaded to change their ways. Indeed, some of our greatest Bible heroes were murderers, including Moses and David (see Exod. 2:12 and 2 Sam. 11:15, respectively).[82] The apostle Paul was at the very least an accessory to murder and was probably a conspirator in the stoning of Stephen (Acts 8:1, 2–3).[83] God changed these men, and they in turn changed the world.

In one state, law-enforcement officers host meetings with people who have compelling videotaped evidence against them for such crimes as drug dealing. The district attorney promises they won't be arrested during the ninety-minute meeting, but if they refuse to attend, they'll be arrested immediately and prosecuted for their crimes. Officers show the offenders the evidence and explain what will happen to them if they don't turn from their lives of crime and seek normal employment. Family and friends are invited to plead with the accused as well. Finally, authorities tell the offenders that they've been put on a "special list" and will be aggressively prosecuted if they're caught again.

In certain neighborhoods where this strategy has been employed, small crimes have dropped by 35 percent. Joseph Grenny and his colleagues state,

> Those who go through the program and don't stay with their new job training or do commit a crime are also immediately arrested. Soon word gets out that the authorities are serious about what they say.[84]

This way, says Grenny, the accused, "enjoy the benefit of the threat without having to actually suffer its consequences."[85]

Community pressure. Civil rights activist Robert Woodson, the founder and president of the Center for Neighborhood Enterprise in Washington, DC, offers an effective example of how to bring community relationships to bear in cutting down crime. Woodson established the Violence-Free Zone program that crafts peace agreements between warring youth factions and creates life-skills programs as well as job-training and job-placement services. The program looks for young leaders who are using their influence negatively and helps them transform it for the good.[86]

> **Some community programs craft peace agreements between warring youth factions and create life-skills programs.**

Youth advocacy. Linda White, whose daughter was killed by two fifteen-year-old boys, knows the grief of losing a child to violence. But White has become an advocate for youth offenders. "I believe children are more than the worst thing they have ever done," she says. The change came for Linda when she was able to meet with one of her daughter's murderers in a mediated dialogue. The young man was deeply remorseful and didn't excuse his behavior as he described a life of abuse and neglect. Ultimately, he was released and is living a reformed life today.[87]

Mental-health advocacy. Paton Blough, who struggles with bipolar disorder, trains police officers how to deal with people experiencing psychotic episodes. He describes his disorder as follows:

> One minute I'm so high that my mind and body enter a nirvana-like state with feelings of ultimate power and supreme authority. And then in the next minute I feel so paranoid and scared that I think my heart will thump out of my chest.... When I [give my presentations], I want the officers to understand how bizarre psychosis can be.... I want the officers to have this insight into psychosis so they can keep themselves safe, but keep people like me safe too.[88]

Miami judge Steven Leifman estimates that in Miami-Dade County twenty thousand people are arrested each year and housed at a cost of $80 million, when they actually need some form of mental-health treatment. The jail system is overwhelmed. But under the judge's direction, the Criminal Mental Health Project helps those with mental-health issues—who have committed "low-level offenses"—receive treatment and community-based care rather than incarceration.[89] As a result, the county was able to close a jail, which has saved taxpayers $12 million a year.[90]

Susan Pamerleau, sheriff of San Antonio, Texas, and Lt. Lionel Garcia (ret.) from the Los Angeles Police Department initiated similar programs.[91] San Antonio officers, who are trained to handle mental-health crisis situations, have been able to reduce the use of physical force in making an arrest from fifty times a year to only twice in the past five years. A Misdemeanor Mental Health Court has helped as well, reducing the level of recidivism to 17 percent for those offenders with mental-health issues.[92]

Rehabilitation. Simply put, **rehabilitation** is the attempt to change specific behaviors of those who commit crimes in order to make them less likely to break laws in the future. It aims to reduce prison populations by helping ensure that people who leave don't come back. Rehabilitation began in the early twentieth century as a way to improve the "stability of American society" by altering the way it handled offenders.[93] The overarching ethos was "an individual approach" in the belief that "ameliorative action had to be fitted specifically to each individual's special needs."[94] To administer individualized justice, a greater degree of discretionary latitude was given to justice officials to mete out the most rehabilitative punishment they deemed appropriate for the individual offender.

> *Rehabilitation:* any attempt to change a criminal's tendency to commit crimes so that the individual will be less likely to reoffend when he or she is reintroduced into society.

However, in the 1960s and 1970s, powerful sociopolitical movements focused on the rights of particular groups, mainly racial minorities and women. The criminal-justice system began to shift away from a case-by-case rehabilitation system and instead laid the blame for crime at the feet of "social causes." Each violent crime led to a mini social crisis. Conservatives wondered whether judges would be soft on crime by trying to use short sentences and reform, while liberals wondered whether judges would perpetuate what they saw as structural injustice by failing to do just that.[95]

So when Robert Martinson published a seminal treatise in 1974 on the state of rehabilitation at the time and found that roughly half of the rehabilitation programs studied failed to decrease recidivism, rearrests, and reoffending in the treated population compared to a sample of similar offenders, it was the final nail in the coffin for rehabilitation programs.[96]

Or so it seemed. In the early 1990s, under the strain of swelling prison populations, a renewed interest in rehabilitation emerged. New programs—based on the idea that even prisoners have inherent value as image bearers of God—are now turning the tide. One program, the Prison Entrepreneurship Program (PEP), helps prisoners produce a business plan and get excited about becoming economically productive. Over the course of five years, PEP is estimated to have produced economic savings and gains of more than $5 million in prison costs and government assistance, tax revenues, and child-support payments from newly employed prisoners.[97]

PEP saves money. It also restores hope. One PEP participant said,

> I had spent over 14 years of my life in prison by the time I came to PEP. The program helped me to take a closer look at myself and make a lot of the internal changes … that needed to happen for me to be ready to face the reality of life out here in the free world. Within four years, I am now managing not one but two companies. PEP helped me in ways that I can't even explain.[98]

Prison Fellowship's InnerChange Freedom Initiative (IFI) is highly effective: only 8 percent of those who complete the program end up back behind bars.

The participant noted that some of the benefits of the program also included a network of people who wanted to help him succeed, people who believed in him, opportunities to succeed, and hope.[99]

Prison Fellowship, founded by Watergate felon-turned-Christian-activist Chuck Colson, has developed a program called the InnerChange Freedom Initiative (IFI), which offers vocational training, values and life-skills training, mentoring, and aftercare. Prisoners begin the IFI program up to eighteen months before release from prison and continue for a year after release. The initiative is highly effective: only 8 percent of those who complete the program end up back behind bars.[100] Interestingly, even in the midst of antitheist opposition, IFI leaders don't hide their faith. In fact, everything they do is based on it. The results speak for themselves.

Initiatives that focus on specific communities and needs of victims as well as offenders and that operate on the principle that humans are made in God's image have shown tremendous promise in helping restore dignity and property to victims. These initiatives also help offenders successfully transition back into society. Perhaps there is a chance for justice after all.

5. Conclusion

It isn't surprising that biblically informed justice initiatives are proving effective in restoring justice. For believers who care deeply about injustice, there are many opportunities to dive into the nitty-gritty work of criminal justice. Christians are very much needed in law, criminal justice, and social work. Volunteers are essential too. Given the number of opportunities, there's no reason for Christians to fall for politically motivated redistribution schemes in the name of helping the less fortunate.

The reason the Christian worldview makes such a difference, though, is because it's rooted in the original idea that justice involves pursuing righteousness, not just avoiding wrongdoing. To put it another way, the Christian worldview goes beyond rehabilitation to focus on transformation. Says Robert Woodson,

> If I'm killing myself, I do not need to be rehabilitated. I need to be transformed. I need to become a new person. Therapy does not make you another person.

Rehabilitation rarely removes bad stuff. Transformation, on the other hand, replaces the bad stuff with good stuff. That is the difference.[101]

Why does a focus on transformation work so well? Sociologist Byron Johnson spent six years studying the answer to that question. Through observation and interviews, Johnson found that participants grew spiritually over the course of their IFI experience, and their comments attest to that transformation:[102]

> The Christian worldview goes beyond rehabilitation to focus on transformation.

1. "I'm not who I used to be." Participants see themselves as genuinely loved by God and others and as having been forgiven and given another chance.

2. "I'm growing spiritually." Participants recognize the need to develop a strong trust in God through Scripture reading and prayer to successfully complete their journeys.

3. "God is bigger than the prison code." The prison code promotes antisocial behavior and blame. IFI helps prisoners become transparent, accountable, and compassionate.

4. "I have a positive outlook." Participants get excited about who they've become and are focused on finding meaning and purpose rather than being gloomy about their hardships.

5. "I'm ready to give back." As opposed to prisoners who cultivate resentment against the state, IFI participants "express an unusual sense of gratitude for this new life."

Through these five pronouncements, we see transformation taking place, from tough to transparent, from taker to giver. It looks a lot like what the apostle Paul, the evangelist who was once an accessory to murder, described in 2 Corinthians 5:17: "If anyone is in Christ, he is a new creation. The old has passed away; behold, the new has come." Through Christ we have hope of seeing Amos's prophecy fulfilled for justice to "roll down like waters" (Amos 5:24). It's not just about rightly ordered communities. It's about the heart of God himself. God delights in justice. We should too.

ENDNOTES

1. Eugene Connor, quoted in "Alabama Divided as Court Prepares to Hear Voting Rights Challenge," NPR.org, February 21, 2013, www.npr.org/2013/02/25/172603328/alabama-divided-as-court-prepares-to-hear-voting-rights-challenge.
2. Eugene Connor, quoted in "The Sixties: The Long March to Freedom," June 26, 2014, CNN, www.cnn.com/TRANSCRIPTS /1406/26/tsix.01.html.
3. Martin Luther King Jr., "Letter from a Birmingham Jail," Birmingham, Alabama, April 16, 1963, in Martin Luther King Jr., *Why We Can't Wait* (Boston: Beacon, 1986), chap. 5.
4. King, *Why We Can't Wait*.
5. King, *Why We Can't Wait*.
6. Data cited in Michael A. Needham et al., *Opportunity for All: Favoritism to None, 2015* (Washington, DC: Heritage Foundation and Heritage Action for America, 2015), 125, 127, http://thf_media.s3.amazonaws.com/2015/pdf /OpportunityForAll.pdf.

7. Patrick A. Langan et al., "Historic Statistics on Prisoners in State and Federal Institutions, Yearend 1925–86," US Department of Justice and Bureau of Labor Statistics, NCJ-111098, May 1988, www.ncjrs.gov/pdffiles1/digitization /111098ncjrs.pdf.

8. In the 1990s, crime dropped significantly. This drop coincided with massive federal welfare reform. Many think this is more than coincidental, though. See the 1995 testimony of Michael Tanner, director of health and welfare studies at the Cato Institute, a libertarian think tank in which Tanner cites research and argues in favor of welfare reform because of the likely effect on decreasing crime; see Michael D. Tanner, "Relationship between the Welfare State and Crime" (testimony before the Subcommittee on Youth Violence, Committee on the Judiciary, US Senate, Washington, DC, June 7, 1995), available at www.cato.org/publications/congressional-testimony/relationship-between-welfare-state-crime-0.

9. Nicholas Wolterstorff, *Justice: Rights and Wrongs* (Princeton, NJ: Princeton University Press, 2008), 35.

10. Prior to 1925 and the landmark US Supreme Court decision in *Gitlow v. New York*, procedural standards for how states handled criminal matters were wholly spelled out and enforced under state law. While *Gitlow* didn't concern itself with criminal procedure, it was the first case in which states were compelled to protect a federally guaranteed right, the right to freedom of speech. Subsequently, other criminal-justice-related amendments (notably the Fourth, Fifth, Sixth, and Eighth Amendments) were selectively incorporated to the states. Even with the court's rulings post-*Gitlow*, a great deal of criminal procedure is established through state law. States may establish procedural protections beyond that which is guaranteed by the Constitution but may not provide any less. See v. New York, 268 U.S. 652 (1925).

11. For a helpful article on the difference between negative liberty and positive liberty, see *Stanford Encyclopedia of Philosophy*, s.v. "Positive and Negative Liberty," 2015, http://plato.stanford.edu/entries/liberty-positive-negative/.

12. Lon L. Fuller, *The Morality of Law* (New Haven, CT: Yale University Press, 1964), 33–38.

13. Wolterstorff, *Justice*, 29.

14. Heather Rice-Minus, cited in Warren Cole Smith and John Stonestreet, *Restoring All Things: God's Audacious Plan to Change the World through Everyday People* (Grand Rapids: Baker Books, 2015), 103.

15. Sarah Shannon et al., "Growth in the U.S. Ex-Felon and Ex-Prisoner Population, 1948–2010" (paper, presented at the annual meeting of the Population Association of America, Washington, DC, April 2011), http://paa2011.princeton.edu /papers/111687.

16. Richard Viguerie, quoted in Smith and Stonestreet, *Restoring All Things*, 104. From an interview with Warren Cole Smith, February 8, 2014. Aired as an episode of the WORLD News Group radio program *Listening In*, February 15, 2014. Available online at www.wng.org/ListeningIn.

17. Data from US Census Bureau's "Annual Survey of State Government Finances, 1982–2010," cited in Tracey Kyckelhahn, "State Corrections Expenditures, FY 1982–2010," Bureau of Justice Statistics, Bulletin NCJ 239672, April 30, 2014 revision, www.bjs.gov/content/pub/pdf/scefy8210.pdf.

18. Michael L. Rubenstein, Stevens H. Clarke, and Teresa J. White, *Alaska Bans Plea Bargaining* (Washington, DC: US Department of Justice, 1980); Deidre M. Bowen, "Calling Your Bluff: How Prosecutors and Defense Attorneys Adapt Plea Bargaining Strategies to Increased Formalization," *Justice Quarterly* 26, no. 1 (March 2009): 2–29.

19. Data from 2006, cited in Samuel Walker, *Sense and Nonsense about Crime, Drugs, and Communities*, 8th ed. (Stamford, CT: Cengage Learning, 2015), 207.

20. Walker, *Sense and Nonsense*.

21. James Eisenstein and Herbert Jacob, *Felony Justice: An Organizational Analysis of Criminal Courts* (Boston: Little, Brown, 1977), 10, 63.

22. For example, in 1977 Michigan enacted a law mandating a minimum two-year sentence for those who used a gun to commit a crime. A study of the law in its first six months of implementation found that the law didn't significantly alter the outcome of the sentencing process. Prosecutors circumvented the law by charging defendants under different laws than they would otherwise have charged them. See Milton Heumann and Colin Loftin, "Mandatory Sentencing and the Abolition of Plea Bargaining: The Michigan Felony Firearm Statute," *Law and Society Review* 13, no. 2 (Winter 1979): 393–430.

23. Stephanie Rawlings-Blake, quoted in Josh Sanburn, "Mayor under Fire: 'Do I Look Like I'm Having an Easy Time?,'" *Time*, April 30, 2015, 37.

24. Thomas Sowell, *The Quest for Cosmic Justice* (New York: Free Press, 1999), 8–9.

25. "Social Justice," National Association of Social Workers, accessed August 2, 2016, www.socialworkers.org/pressroom /features/issue/peace.asp.

26. "Social Justice," National Association of Social Workers.

27. OxfordDictionaries.com, s.v. "social justice," www.oxforddictionaries.com/us/definition/american_english/social -justice.

28. Sowell, *Quest for Cosmic Justice*, 9.

29. Sowell, *Quest for Cosmic Justice*.

30. Sowell, *Quest for Cosmic Justice*, 12.

31. David Horowitz, *The Politics of Bad Faith: The Radical Assault on America's Future* (New York: Touchstone, 1998), 183.

32. Sowell, *Quest for Cosmic Justice*, 13.

33. John Rawls, *A Theory of Justice* (Cambridge, MA: Belknap, 2005), 62.

34. Rawls, *Theory of Justice*, 62, 79.

35. See Rawls, *Theory of Justice*, 118–22.

36. Rawls, *Theory of Justice*. In a concession to those who say people cannot be completely free from judgment in the real world, Rawls calls for a "reflective equilibrium" between the principles that are ideal and people's considered judgments—those in which their moral capacities are most likely to be displayed without distortion. See Rawls, *Theory of Justice*, 42–44.

37. Barack Obama, quoted in "Questions over Obama's Off-the-Cuff Remarks," FoxNews.com, October 14, 2008, www.foxnews.com/story/2008/10/15/questions-over-obama-off-cuff-remark.html.

38. Robert Nozick pointed out some of the shortcomings of distributive justice in *Anarchy, State, and Utopia*, a book written in response to Rawls from a libertarian viewpoint. Nozick argues that people are better off when they have the freedom to choose their course rather than when they get a share of forcefully divided resources. Nozick also understands that in a state of complete freedom, some people are going to get hurt, but his solution is very different from Rawls's. Whereas Rawls's ideal world was one of perfect equality, Nozick's is one of maximal freedom without harm. He suggests that if we thought of each person as a miniature business and made sure they had the freedom to exchange the goods and services they produced according to clearly articulated, fair rules, we would actually achieve a more just outcome than trying to control that outcome to begin with. Robert Nozick, *Anarchy, State, and Utopia* (New York: Basic Books, 1974), 186.

39. When the government props up some businesses to ensure their success, it ends up hurting the economy as a whole. In the United States, the federal government regularly props up airlines, auto companies, banks, and agricultural businesses, arguing that their failure would be devastating to the security of the country. See David Brodwin, "The Double-Edged Subsidy Sword," *U.S. News and World Report*, September 5, 2013, www.usnews.com/opinion/blogs/economic-intelligence/2013/09/05/how-government-subsidies-both-help-and-hurt-taxpayers.

40. These comments are in the context of Rorty's discussion of the works of poet Walt Whitman and educational theorist John Dewey. See Richard Rorty, *Achieving Our Country: Leftist Thought in Twentieth-Century America* (Cambridge, MA: Harvard University Press, 1999), 106–7.

41. Rorty, *Achieving Our Country*, 101.

42. Romans 13:3–4: "Rulers are not a terror to good conduct, but to bad. Would you have no fear of the one who is in authority? Then do what is good, and you will receive his approval, for he is God's servant for your good. But if you do wrong, be afraid, for he does not bear the sword in vain. For he is the servant of God, an avenger who carries out God's wrath on the wrongdoer."

43. Roman 3:23: "All have sinned and fall short of the glory of God."

44. Cornelius Plantinga Jr., *Not the Way It's Supposed to Be: A Breviary of Sin* (Grand Rapids: Eerdmans, 1995), 25.

45. Plantinga, *Not the Way It's Supposed to Be*, 24–27.

46. See, for example, Leviticus 19:15; Deuteronomy 16:20; Psalm 106:3; Proverbs 29:7; Isaiah 51:4–5; Micah 6:8; and Zechariah 7:9.

47. James Richard Atkin, quoted in Carol Harlow, *Understanding Tort Law*, 3rd ed. (London: Sweet and Maxwell, 2005), 47–48.

48. Exodus 18:13–16: "The next day Moses sat to judge the people, and the people stood around Moses from morning till evening. When Moses' father-in-law saw all that he was doing for the people, he said, 'What is this that you are doing for the people? Why do you sit alone, and all the people stand around you from morning till evening?' And Moses said to his father-in-law, 'Because the people come to me to inquire of God; when they have a dispute, they come to me and I decide between one person and another, and I make them know the statutes of God and his laws'"; Deuteronomy 1:16–17: "I charged your judges at that time, 'Hear the cases between your brothers, and judge righteously between a man and his brother or the alien who is with him. You shall not be partial in judgment. You shall hear the small and the great alike. You shall not be intimidated by anyone, for the judgment is God's. And the case that is too hard for you, you shall bring to me, and I will hear it'"; Deuteronomy 19:15–21: "A single witness shall not suffice against a person for any crime or for any wrong in connection with any offense that he has committed. Only on the evidence of two witnesses or of three witnesses shall a charge be established. If a malicious witness arises to accuse a person of wrongdoing, then both parties to the dispute shall appear before the LORD, before the priests and the judges who are in office in those days. The judges shall inquire diligently, and if the witness is a false witness and has accused his brother falsely, then you shall do to him as he had meant to do to his brother. So you shall purge the evil from your midst. And the rest shall hear and fear, and shall never again commit any such evil among you. Your eye shall not pity. It shall be life for life, eye for eye, tooth for tooth, hand for hand, foot for foot."

49. Exodus 23:1–3, 6–8: "You shall not spread a false report. You shall not join hands with a wicked man to be a malicious witness. You shall not fall in with the many to do evil, nor shall you bear witness in a lawsuit, siding with the many, so as to pervert justice, nor shall you be partial to a poor man in his lawsuit.... You shall not pervert the justice due to your poor in his lawsuit. Keep far from a false charge, and do not kill the innocent and righteous, for I will not acquit the wicked. And you shall take no bribe, for a bribe blinds the clear-sighted and subverts the cause of those who are in the right." See also

John Eidsmoe, *God and Caesar: Biblical Faith and Political Action* (Westchester, IL: Crossway, 1985), 197.

50. Simon Greenleaf, *A Treatise on the Law of Evidence,* 16th ed., ed. Edward Avery Harriman (Boston: Little, Brown, 1899), 3:35n4. In this note, Greenleaf was citing the reasoning of Lord Matthew Hale in the British record.

51. Exodus 22:1: "If a man steals an ox or a sheep, and kills it or sells it, he shall repay five oxen for an ox, and four sheep for a sheep."

52. Leviticus 6:2–5: "If anyone sins and commits a breach of faith against the LORD by deceiving his neighbor in a matter of deposit or security, or through robbery, or if he has oppressed his neighbor or has found something lost and lied about it, swearing falsely—in any of all the things that people do and sin thereby—if he has sinned and has realized his guilt and will restore what he took by robbery or what he got by oppression or the deposit that was committed to him or the lost thing that he found or anything about which he has sworn falsely, he shall restore it in full and shall add a fifth to it, and give it to him to whom it belongs on the day he realizes his guilt."

53. C. S. Lewis, *Mere Christianity* (New York: HarperOne, 1980), 38.

54. Bruce D. Strom, *Gospel Justice: Joining Together to Provide Help and Hope for Those Oppressed by Legal Injustice* (Chicago: Moody, 2013).

55. Smith and Stonestreet, *Restoring All Things,* 109.

56. Heather Rice-Minus, quoted in Smith and Stonestreet, *Restoring All Things,* 102.

57. Primary restorative-justice objectives from Tony Marshall, in Andrew Ashworth, "Is Restorative Justice the Way Forward for Criminal Justice?," *Restorative Justice: Critical Issues,* eds. Eugene McLaughlin et al. (Thousand Oaks, CA: Sage, 2003), 164.

58. New York Office of Court Administration data, cited in Alice Brennan, "How Long Does It Take for a Criminal Case to Go to Trial?," *New York World,* February 27, 2012, www.thenewyorkworld.com/2012/02/27/the-daily-q-how-long-criminal-cas/.

59. Deborah Hartman, "Pat Todd Receives 2008 'Carol S. Vance' Volunteer of the Year Award," Bridges to Life, accessed August 2, 2016, www.bridgestolife.org/index.php?option=com_content&view=article&id=59&Itemid=82.

60. "History and Mission," Bridges to Life, accessed August 2, 2016, www.bridgestolife.org/index.php?option=com_content &view=article&id=3&Itemid=62.

61. "The Wards," Bridges to Life, accessed September 24, 2016, www.bridgestolife.org/index.php%3Foption%3Dcom _content%26view%3Darticle%26id%3D1%26Itemid%3D76.

62. Ilyssa Wellikoff, "Victim-Offender Mediation and Violent Crimes: On the Way to Justice," *Journal of Conflict Resolution* 5 (no. 1), http://cardozojcr.com/issues/volume-5-1/note-1/.

63. "Introduction," National Survey of Victim-Offender Mediation Programs in the United States, Office for Victims of Crime, April 2000, www.ncjrs.gov/ovc_archives/reports/national_survey/natsurv3.html.

64. Rice-Minus, quoted in Smith and Stonestreet, *Restoring All Things,* 105.

65. Sandeep Chawla et al., *Global Report on Trafficking in Persons, 2012* (New York: United Nations, 2012), 16, www.unodc.org /documents/data-and-analysis/glotip/Trafficking_in_Persons_2012_web.pdf.

66. Chawla, *Global Report on Trafficking,* 9–10.

67. Chawla, *Global Report on Trafficking,* 1.

68. See table 3.3 in Margaret Werner Calahan, *Historical Corrections Statistics in the United States, 1850–1984* (Washington, DC: US Department of Justice, 1986), 30, http://www.bjs.gov/content/pub/pdf/hcsus5084.pdf.

69. Langan et al., "Historic Statistics on Prisoners."

70. Langan et al., "Historic Statistics on Prisoners."

71. *Prison Count 2010: State Population Declines for the First Time in 38 Years* (Washington, DC: Pew Center on the States, 2010), 1, www.pewtrusts.org/uploadedFiles/wwwpewtrustsorg/Reports/sentencing_and_corrections/Prison_Count _2010.pdf.

72. Data cited in Adam Liptak, "U.S. Prison Population Dwarfs That of Other Nations," *New York Times,* April 23, 2008, www.nytimes.com/2008/04/23/world/americas/23iht-23prison.12253738.html?pagewanted=all&_r=0.

73. Walker, *Sense and Nonsense,* 5.

74. Alfred Blumstein and Allen J. Beck, "Population Growth in U.S. Prisons, 1980–1996," *Crime and Justice* 26 (1999): 17–61.

75. Stuart A. Scheingold, *The Politics of Law and Order: Street Crime and Public Policy* (New York: Longman, 1984), 153. See chap. 6, "Equity in the Criminal Courts," 145–170.

76. Walker, *Sense and Nonsense,* 180–81.

77. "Drug Facts: Nationwide Trends," National Institute on Drug Abuse, June 2015, www.drugabuse.gov/publications /drugfacts/nationwide-trends.

78. Gary Kleck and Don B. Kates, *Armed: New Perspectives on Gun Control* (Amherst, NY: Prometheus Books, 2001), 337.

79. These are some of the examples of licenses required in various states. See Michael Snyder, "12 Ridiculous Government Regulations That Are Almost Too Bizarre to Believe," *Business Insider,* November 12, 2010, www.businessinsider.com /ridiculous-regulations-big-government-2010-11.

80. Edward Coke, *The Reports of Sir Edward Coke,* vol. 6, *The Eleventh Part of the Reports of Sir Edward Coke,* trans. George

Wilson (London: J. Rivington and Sons), 53–54.

81. See "Community Corrections Programs," in American Bar Association, "State Policy Implementation Project," accessed September 24, 2016, www.americanbar.org/content/dam/aba/administrative/criminal_justice/spip_communitycorrections .authcheckdam.pdf. See also "Supervision Costs Significantly Less Than Incarceration in Federal System," United States Courts, July 18, 2013, www.uscourts.gov/news/2013/07/18/supervision-costs-significantly-less-incarceration-federal-system.

82. Exodus 2:12: "[Moses] looked this way and that, and seeing no one, he struck down the Egyptian and hid him in the sand"; 2 Samuel 11:15: "In the letter [David] wrote, 'Set Uriah in the forefront of the hardest fighting, and then draw back from him, that he may be struck down, and die.'"

83. Acts 8:1, 2–3: "Saul approved of [Stephen's] execution.... Devout men buried Stephen and made great lamentation over him. But Saul was ravaging the church, and entering house after house, he dragged off men and women and committed them to prison."

84. Joseph Grenny et al., *Influencer: The New Science of Leading Change*, 2nd ed. (New York: McGraw-Hill, 2013), 239.

85. Grenny et al., *Influencer*.

86. "Reducing Youth Violence: The Violence-Free Zone," Center for Neighborhood Enterprise, 2016, www.cneonline.org /reducing-youth-violence-the-violence-free-zone/; see also Byron R. Johnson, *More God, Less Crime: Why Faith Matters and How It Could Matter More* (West Conshohocken, PA: Templeton, 2011), 47.

87. Linda White, "Texas Needs Alternatives to Prison Terms for Kids," *Houston Chronicle*, June 19, 2013, www.chron.com /opinion/outlook/article/White-Texas-needs-alternatives-to-prison-terms-4610470.php.

88. "Personal Stories: Paton Blough," National Alliance on Mental Illness, April 30, 2015, www.nami.org/Personal -Stories/31-Stories,-31-Days-Paton-Blough.

89. "Steve Leifman: A Judge on the Mental Health Frontlines in Miami," Stepping Up Initiative, Council of State Governments Justice Initiative, https://stepuptogether.org/people/steve-leifman.

90. "Patrick Kennedy: Focusing on Treatment Will Make Our Communities Safer," Stepping Up Initiative, Council of State Governments Justice Initiative, 2015, https://stepuptogether.org/people/patrick-kennedy.

91. Lt. Lionel Garcia developed a triage program for the Los Angeles Police Department (LAPD) to help officers handle mental-health crisis situations. Officers calling the "triage desk" receive immediate advice on how to approach a person in crisis. In 2015, the department received more than fourteen thousand mental-health crisis calls. Only 2.8 percent of those situations required the use of force to protect the person and the public, compared to other police forces where force is used 50 percent of the time. See "Lt. Lionel Garcia: Lion Exits after Making LAPD Unit Model for Nation," Stepping Up Initiative, Council of State Governments Justice Initiative, 2015, https://stepuptogether.org/people/lt-lionel-garcia.

92. "Susan Pamerleau: San Antonio Sheriff's Personal Fight to Fix Broken System," Stepping Up Initiative, Council of State Governments Justice Initiative, 2015, https://stepuptogether.org/people/susan-pamerleau.

93. David J. Rothman, "Individualized Justice: The Progressive Design," in *Conscience and Convenience: The Asylum and Its Alternatives in Progressive America* (New Brunswick, NJ: AldineTransaction, 2002), 49.

94. Rothman, "Individualized Justice," in *Conscience and Convenience*, 50.

95. Francis T. Cullen and Karen E. Gilbert, eds., "Attacking Rehabilitation," chap. 4 in *Reaffirming Rehabilitation* (Cincinnati: Anderson, 1982).

96. Robert Martinson, "What Works?—Questions and Answers about Prison Reform," *Public Interest*, no. 35 (Spring 1974): 25, www.nationalaffairs.com/doclib/20080527_197403502whatworksquestionsandanswersaboutprisonreformrobertmartinson.pdf.

97. Byron Johnson, William Wubbenhorst, and Curtis Schroeder, *Recidivism Reduction and Return on Investment: An Empirical Assessment of the Prison Entrepreneurship Program* (Waco, TX: Baylor Institute for Studies of Religion, 2013), 28, www.pep.org/wp-content/uploads/2015/12/2013BaylorStudy.pdf.

98. Johnson, Wubbenhorst, and Schroeder, *Recidivism Reduction*, 22.

99. Johnson, Wubbenhorst, and Schroeder, *Recidivism Reduction*.

100. "InnerChange Freedom Initiative," Prison Fellowship, accessed August 3, 2016, www.prisonfellowship.org/about/reentry -support/innerchange-freedom-initiative/.

101. Robert Woodson, quoted in Johnson, *More God, Less Crime*, 45.

102. Adapted from Johnson, *More God, Less Crime*, 122–30.

CHAPTER 17

17

COMMUNITY RENEWAL

1. HOW ONE SMALL GROUP CAN CHANGE THE WORLD

The Clapham Sect just might be the most influential group of people you've never heard of. A network allied with William Wilberforce at the turn of the century, the Clapham Sect led British efforts to end the slave trade. Its members showed how God can use a group of believers committed to working together, giving generously, and persisting in the face of intimidating odds.

Meeting in the Clapham-village home of banker Henry Thornton, the group included influential evangelical pastors, politicians, scholars, and businesspeople operating with clear goals to

- abolish slavery,

- reform the prison system,

- transform society's morals, and

- protect animals.

Clapham members fought for child-labor laws and better working conditions in factories. They helped establish Christian schools and founded several missionary-sending organizations, including the Baptist Missionary Society that sent to the mission field the "father of modern missions," William Carey (1761–1834). Carey, in turn, helped transform India.

Realizing that both public persuasion and political action were important, the Clapham Sect sought to change people's minds, not just government policy. They published a journal called *The Christian Observer*; wrote letters, tracts, and pamphlets; and spearheaded petition drives. Its members took every opportunity to deliver public addresses and gave generously to achieve their aims. They also worked within Parliament to initiate measures designed to end the slave trade. Year after year Wilberforce fought for legislation to end Britain's hideous trafficking practices. He never quit.

> Realizing that both public persuasion and political action were important, the Clapham Sect sought to change people's minds, not just government policy.

But the Clapham Sect experienced hardship as well. Many in high society opposed its members and ridiculed them as "the Saints." Their zeal often led to personal hardship. Zachary Macaulay booked passage on an African slave ship to witness firsthand the horrors of the slave trade. He subsequently worked without sleep, neglected his business, and lost much of his fortune to secure the abolition of slavery.

Proslavery forces hounded James Ramsay with malicious accusations against his character. Falsely accused of seditious preaching and immorality, he died brokenhearted at age fifty-five. Wilberforce suffered a nervous breakdown, and his life was often threatened.

Yet despite these difficulties, the Clapham Sect succeeded in profound ways. Its actions led to the end of the slave trade and, after another twenty-six years of persistent action, the emancipation of slaves throughout the British Empire. The sect also advanced criminal justice and labor reforms and pressured the British East India Company to allow missionaries to work in India. This last feat was a major contributing factor to the growth of the modern missions movement, which, as we saw in chapter 3, has been a significant force for good in the world.

We can learn a lot from the Clapham Sect about how to transform our own communities. Its members set clear and specific goals, compiled research to provide irrefutable evidence for their claims, appealed to the conscience of their nation regarding the rightness of their causes, and built a loyal community of support. They persevered through decades of setbacks, but they also regularly celebrated small victories that moved them toward their goals.

The Clapham Sect stayed focused in spite of their opponents' vicious attacks. Perhaps most important was their decision to embrace the name by which they were derisively called: "the Saints." They pressed in, empathizing with their opponents' positions and dialoging with them. They didn't resort to hostility, name-calling, gossip, shady tactics, or violence.

> *Grassroots Movement:* an approach to change that mobilizes people in local communities in an effort to bring about positive social transformation.

In this book, we've learned of dozens of ways our culture needs transformation. The question now is how. Some say we ought to go straight to the top of society and seize the reins of power so as to make dramatic changes in the way our nation operates. Others say true change comes through the **grassroots movement**, which is ignited by ordinary people and grows until it possesses undeniable power forcing leaders to change.

But the Clapham Sect illustrated a third way, a "**grasstops movement**."[1] They took a both-and, not an either-or, approach. As a result, they changed their own communities, then England, and then much of the British Empire. They didn't fret about things they couldn't change; rather, they set about changing the things they could.

> *Grasstops Movement:* an approach to change that mobilizes people in local communities (bottom up) and seeks to influence government policy (top down) in an effort to bring about positive social transformation.

Today many effective movements begin at the community level. That's where most of society's problems are birthed, so it makes sense that it's also the level at which they may be best understood and solved. It's called **community renewal**. In this chapter, we'll look at all kinds of communities experiencing transformation. We'll also explore why Christians should care and examine specific ways they can act on their concerns.

> *Community Renewal:* any effort taken to restore and rebuild a community so that its people can thrive and prosper.

2. Where Should We Begin?

Community renewal revolves around cities. There are many reasons to care about cities, but I think two are the most important. First, more and more people are moving to cities. Urbanization seems to be the world's future. Second, communities are deeply affected by— and in turn affect—the brokenness of sin.

The Future Is Cities

Like it or not, cities are the future. In 1800, only 3 percent of the world's population lived in cities. As of 2014, more than half the world's population was living in settlements of five hundred thousand people or more.[2] Imagine six billion people packed together with others of different racial groups, religious affiliations, and political opinions. Think of the daily challenges of protecting our families from crime, making a living and getting food, and even providing basic health care and sanitation.

I was born in Detroit, Michigan. During its heyday in the 1950s, Detroit was one of the best cities in the world. It became the fifth-largest city in America, with a population of 1.8 million people, featuring beautiful art-deco architecture and neatly kept neighborhoods. In 1967, though, racial tensions boiled over, and Detroit experienced devastating race riots. Forty-three people died, more than one thousand were injured, and two thousand buildings were destroyed. It was as if the city had gone insane. People were angry and afraid. They felt unsafe, and I understand why. I was offered hard drugs for the first time at age seven, and I remember watching police remove the body of our neighbor after he died from a drug overdose. I vividly recall diving under my bed in panic at the sound of a gunshot in the street.

My parents left Detroit just before I turned ten, joining a mass exodus that saw more than a million people leave over the course of thirty years. To this day, much of Detroit lies in ruins. In 2011, nearly half the owners of the city's 305,000 properties failed to pay their property taxes.[3] In addition to property decay, Detroit has one of the highest crime rates of any city in the United States.[4]

> When cities unravel, everyone with the means to do so leaves. Yet God doesn't abandon cities just because they're broken. Those are the kind of cities he cares about the most.

The rioters in Detroit—as well as those in Newark, New Jersey; Los Angeles; and Ferguson, Missouri; and other places—were reacting to decades of race-based injustice. Instead of remedying injustice, however, they terrified people, destroyed property, and severed the already-hemorrhaging artery of trust that makes community possible. When cities unravel, everyone with the means to do so leaves. Only the poorest and most vulnerable remain. Yet God doesn't abandon cities just because they're broken. In fact, those are the kind of cities he cares about the most.

Communities as Well as People Are Broken

How the people around us are doing affects how well we're doing. A sixty-five-year longitudinal study of heart disease in Framingham, Massachusetts, demonstrated the role of relationships in building a healthy community. It found that for every content person someone knows, the propbability of being content increases by two percent. For every discontent person someone knows, the probability of being discontent increases by four percent. In other words, unhappy people are twice as damaging to your state of mind as happy people are good for it.[5] If this study is true, being surrounded by discontent people practically guarantees that you'll be discontent yourself. Your neighbors' struggles and your own struggles are related. If your neighbors are doing well, their attitude affects lots of things, including your physical and emotional health.

> If your neighbors are doing well, their attitude affects lots of things, including your physical and emotional health.

A community isn't just a place we live. It's a way of life, with neighbors who look out for one another, seek each other's best interests, and become friends. Yet today this is becoming rarer. A 2006 study showed that the number of Americans who said they have no one with whom to discuss important matters has "nearly tripled" since 1985.[6] More and more of our communication is mediated by technology—social-media apps and texting—often at the expense of face-to-face interactions.

Meanwhile, city governments face perpetual shortages of funds for dealing with crime, congestion, waste, ineffective schools, dilapidated housing, pollution, poor health care, lack of adequate services, homelessness, and corruption. Each year city governments become less able to solve significant community problems. We cannot assume government can fix everything. And as we saw in chapter 10 on marriage, the collapsing family structure is eroding a key source of society's stability. Abortion on demand, dignity-stripping overdependence on welfare, and fatherlessness plague the urban poor, especially racial minorities. As of 2015, only 17 percent of African American youth reached the age of seventeen in a home with both of their married biological or adoptive parents.[7]

Realizing that government is failing to solve problems like these, churches are beginning to step in, showing that God is the "Father of the fatherless" (Ps. 68:5) and seeking to provide strong, wise, and compassionate guidance. Church involvement can be the glue that helps people in a community stick together. In Detroit, one church that is stepping up is Evangel Ministries, a congregation of more than 1,600 people. Pastor Chris Brooks, an African American with training in apologetics and finance, understands how urban problems morph into big government, and not always in a helpful way.[8] Says Brooks, "Think about this for a moment. You're an African American child growing up in a single-parent, female-led home. Your mom is struggling to meet the bills. Who makes up for housing and food and all those things? The government does. Government becomes a quasi-father."[9] Evangel and other like-minded churches welcome broken families, provide health care in the community, and assist hurting families when they have emergencies.

> Evangel Ministries and other like-minded churches welcome broken families, provide health care in the community, and assist hurting families when they have emergencies.

Often, hope is birthed through the pain of honest reflection. As community leaders grapple truthfully with their problems, hope is rising in and around Detroit. Ministries like Grace Centers of Hope take in the homeless, drug addicts, and those being released from prison and not only shelter them but also get them involved in caring churches and teach them job skills. Almost every graduate of the centers' one-year rehabilitation program enters the workforce. Of those who stick with the program for four months, 87 percent finish and graduate sober. They can even become homeowners, thanks to a unique program that sells homes for very little money to those willing to do the remodeling work themselves.[10]

In communities across the nation, programs like Grace Centers of Hope are springing up, showing God's kindness and inspiring hope. They're the "grasstops" efforts of churches, concerned citizens, and leaders whose vision is for people, not for an ever-more-expansive government or for dismantling capitalism. Commenting on such programs, the late Catholic priest and scholar Richard John Neuhaus said, "In cities across the country, and generally under conservative auspices, such street-level programs of personal and community renewal are rapidly multiplying. Nothing comparable is happening on the left."[11] In communities overrun with difficult problems, Christians are largely the ones who are stepping up.

But we need to do more to our help our neighbors. Even though the world's Christian population is higher than ever, far too many privatize their faith, seeking to escape from the world rather than minister to it.

> The tipping point for community change is somewhere between 5 percent and 15 percent of the population. There are enough Christians in almost every community to bring transformation many times over if they'll choose to care.

Christian faith is about more than personal solace or individual salvation. The church exists to disciple nations to obey God in every area in which Jesus Christ has authority. This is the Great Commission (Matt. 28:18–20).[12] We need revival. But we also need reformation that renews our communities.

As we'll see, engaging culture based on a biblical worldview makes a bigger difference than we may realize. In a *Leadership Journal* article titled "To Transform a City," Timothy Keller, who pastors a church in New York City, wrote that the tipping point for community change is somewhere between 5 percent and 15 percent of the population.[13] There are enough Christians in almost every community to bring transformation many times over if they'll choose to care.

3. WHY SHOULD CHRISTIANS CARE?

Scripture makes it clear that God loves people. And cities are where people are. "If you love what God loves, you will love the city," says Timothy Keller.[14] To understand how cities fit into God's plan, let's look at how God forms redemption in general, what he thinks about cities, and how the church is the agency through which he re-forms that which is broken.

God's Forming Process

In the beginning, the earth was without form (Gen. 1:2).[15] God, the original sculptor, took the unformed mass and shaped it into a pattern. He gave design to the formless. The word *form* can be helpful in understanding not only creation but also the fall, redemption, and consummation of history. As community-development specialist Darrow Miller points out, a whole family of words surrounds the Latin root *forma*:[16]

- **Un-formed.** In the beginning, the universe was without form. It wasn't *de-formed*; it just had no design at all.

- **Formed.** God formed creation (Gen. 1:1),[17] and at each step along the way, he declared that what he had made was good. When creation was complete, he pronounced it "very good" (v. 31).[18] The creation was made to flourish, not languish. The idea of flourishing comes from the Hebrew word *parah*, which means "to sprout, bloom," or "blossom."[19] Flourishing things grow luxuriantly, toward their God-designed potential. God intends this for all living things.

- **De-formed.** With humanity's rebellion against God, things were de-formed (Gen. 3; Rom. 1:28–31).[20] As Webster's 1828 dictionary defines it, *deformed* means "injured in the form; disfigured; distorted; ugly; wanting natural beauty, or symmetry."[21] Whole things become fractured; holy things become unrighteous; the beautiful becomes hideous. De-formed things wither and perish and spiral downward to death.

- **Trans-formed.** Romans 12:1–2 says we need to be *trans-formed* through the renewing of our minds.[22] The word *transform* is based on the Greek verb *metamorphoō*, meaning to "to change inwardly in fundamental character or condition."[23] This begins with the renewing of our minds so that we may understand what God's will is. It's a *metamorphosis*, a word we use to denote a complete and permanent change into something we were designed to be all along, like a caterpillar turning into a butterfly.

- **Con-formed.** Trans-formation brings us to the state where we are con-formed to the image of Christ rather than to the image of the world (Phil. 2:1–8; James 1:2–4).[24] As we grow to be like Christ, we'll be "perfect and complete, lacking in nothing" (James 1:4).[25]

- **Re-formed.** When we re-form things, we participate in God's plan for the nations (Matt. 28:18–20; Rom. 16:25–27).[26] When we come to Christ, we're to become re-forming agents who teach people to obey all that he has commanded.

Because the Reformation was a famous movement in Christian history, we ought to pause here to examine the idea of reforming in more detail. During the Reformation, one of the Reformers, John Calvin (1509–1564), focused his efforts in part on reforming Geneva, Switzerland, turning it from a depraved, dysfunctional city to a moral, well-ordered community. Known as "the Protestant Rome" and "the City on the Hill," Geneva became a "light to the nations."[27]

Calvin and his fellow Swiss Reformers had a threefold strategy for renewing the city: *preaching* the gospel, *educating* the citizens, and *applying* the Bible's teachings to individuals and institutions. Calvin and his fellow Reformers studied how the Scriptures applied to all areas of life. Geneva became a laboratory. Pastors and civic leaders came from all over Europe to see what was happening in Geneva. What happened there spread to John Knox in Scotland (1505–1572), to Puritan England (1600s), across the Atlantic to Puritan New England (1630–1680), and finally to Jonathan Edwards and the First Great Awakening (1734–1750), which influenced America's founding.

Calvin's noble effort wasn't without failures or excesses. Yet it set the stage for substantial and much-needed reforms throughout the Western world.

The Reformation was a form of **community discipleship** involving prayer, Bible reading, evangelism, and worship. Community discipleship may be unfamiliar to

> *Community Discipleship*: the idea that God called his followers not just to save souls but also to transform communities.

people today, but it's an example of what American cultural critic Ken Myers calls "alternative enculturation."[28] It forms a new way of understanding what is real. And what is real is this: God's plan doesn't just save individuals; it transforms communities.

How Cities Are Central to God's Plan

As Father, Son, and Holy Spirit, God is in relationship with himself. Relationship isn't merely something God *does*; it's something he *is*. Even before creation, there was community. Genesis 1:26 says, "Then God said, 'Let us make mankind in our image, after our likeness.'" When the text says "let *us*," we get a sense of this divine community speaking together about the created purpose of human beings. We see this again in John 17:24, where Jesus said that the Father loved the Son "before the creation of the world" (NIV). God is community, and we too are made for relationship.

God wants his image bearers to rule on his behalf. Adam and Eve were to create culture and fill the earth with their heirs, fellow bearers of the **imago Dei**. By having families and developing communities, they would fill the earth with the knowledge of God.

While the centerpiece of creation was a garden, the centerpiece of redemption is a city. At the end of all things, we don't go to God; God's city comes down to us. Revelation 21:2–3 says, "I [John] saw the holy city, new Jerusalem, coming down out of heaven from God.... And I heard a loud voice from the throne saying, 'Behold, the dwelling place of God is with man. He will dwell with them, and they will be his people, and God himself will be with them as their God.'"

In the Old Testament, even when God's people were taken captive, they were told to care for the cities in which they lived. The prophet Jeremiah wrote a letter to the Babylonian exiles that said,

> Build houses and live in them; plant gardens and eat their produce. Take wives and have sons and daughters; take wives for your sons, and give your daughters in marriage, that they may bear sons and daughters; multiply there, and do not decrease. But seek the welfare of the city where I have sent you into exile, and pray to the LORD on its behalf, for in its welfare you will find your welfare. (Jer. 29:5–7)

Shalom: from the Hebrew for "peace, prosperity, and wellness"; a concept that implies harmony in creation and with one's neighbors as well as a right relationship with God.

The word translated "welfare" is **shalom**, a word that, as we've seen throughout this text, means "peace, prosperity, completeness, safeness, salvation, health, satisfaction, contentment, and blessing."[29] *Shalom* involves the good of every person in every relationship. A person experiencing *shalom* moves from deformation to reformation, from wasting away to flourishing, from poverty to prosperity, from disorder to order, from injustice to justice, from ignorance to knowledge, and from sickness to health.

In short, *shalom* is the very best thing that can happen to a person or community. It is what God wants to see happen, even when we're in "exile."

The Agency through Which God Brings Reform: The Church

The church represents the kingdom of God on the earth. It is to teach the nations and to be their conscience. The whole earth is to be filled with the knowledge of God until everyone has the opportunity to understand the implications of God's truth in every area of life and work.[30]

The church is called to reform society. Some Christians today believe that because things will only get worse until Christ returns, the church's job is to hold tight as things fall apart. This isn't an accurate picture of reality. The ultimate outcome of history is in God's sovereign hands. His plan cannot be thwarted. Meanwhile, his people are called to both share the good news of salvation through Jesus's death and resurrection and engage the culture compassionately and generously, putting flesh on Christ's redemptive work.

> God's people are called to both share the good news of salvation and engage the culture compassionately and generously, putting flesh on Christ's redemptive work.

Christ won the battle of the cross (Col. 2:15).[31] As his body (Rom. 12:4–5; 1 Cor. 12:27),[32] the church is God's key agent for advancing his kingdom (Eph. 3:10–11).[33] As Darrow Miller puts it, "The church gathers on Sunday for equipping and corporate worship and scatters on Monday to engage society, to bring the culture of the kingdom (Truth, Beauty and Goodness) into every sector of society."[34]

This means that all of us are commissioned agents of the King, leaders whose message inspires hope of an abundant life. Every believer is therefore a leader. Some leaders *of* the church—the clergy, vocational ministers, and pastors—are called to equip the church for works of service (Eph. 4:11–13).[35] Others are leaders *in* the church, comprising what has come to be known as the "laity," men and women who lead in such spheres of society as the family, the arts, business, education, and science. *All of them are full-time Christian leaders.*

And by "the church" I mean not *a* church *in* the city but *the* church *of* the city. The church is individual congregations working together to discover what aspects of the city need Christ's touch—whether it is people who are hurting or structures that need to be transformed—and meet those needs with the aim of reforming communities and nations.[36] God works in every generation to extend his kingdom. As the church, we participate with him in this. To the children of Israel he said,

> If my people who are called by my name humble themselves, and pray and seek my face and turn from their wicked ways, then will I hear from heaven and will forgive their sin and heal their land. (2 Chron. 7:14)

The church and Israel are distinct, but both comprise God's people. In his letter to what he called the *elect*, or the chosen, the apostle Peter said, "You are a chosen race, a royal priesthood, a holy nation, a people for [God's] own possession" (1 Pet. 2:9). As God's people, we do the repenting; God does the healing where and how he chooses.

The church shapes the destiny of nations only within the framework of God's providence. We make plans, and God guides our steps (Prov. 16:9).[37]

True change happens from the inside out. Many worldviews assert that nothing inside us can change unless everything "out there" changes first. Over time this view has morphed into an alternative form of salvation, suggesting that all of society's structures must be destroyed and reformed or else things will never get better. What exactly needs to be overthrown depends on the worldview of those who've appointed themselves as change agents. Some want to overthrow the church. Others want to overthrow the government. Still others want to overthrow economic structures. This follows from **materialism**, the belief that we are really nothing more than matter in motion, neurons and receptors. We are animals essentially. If we aren't trained properly, then it's someone else's fault. Until they change, we can't change.

The biblical view is that change comes from the inside out. Changed individuals spread change outward, through their families, churchs, and communities, and into sectors of society like the arts, education, science, government, and business. Transformation begins with the renewing of our minds (Rom. 12:2).[38] Christ lives in us (Gal. 2:20).[39] Small seeds grow into tall trees, and a pinch of yeast permeates the whole loaf (Matt. 13:31–33).[40]

> Many worldviews assert that all of society's structures must be destroyed and reformed or else things will never get better.

If we want the church to be relevant to our communities, it must be more than just a building. As the church, we need to remember our uniqueness as a living organism, joined to the head of the church, Jesus Christ himself. It's a body, not a business. The question "How can we extend the kingdom of God?" comes before questions like "How can we raise attendance?" and "How can we expand our campus?" Next, we'll examine a few ways we can bring about the change our communities desperately need.

4. What Should Christians Do?

As we're conformed to Christ's image and bonded together as a body, we'll see real change take place in our communities. Here's how …

> To help people flourish, we must identify and remove the barriers that prevent them from living out their full potential as image bearers of God. Many of the cultural battles of our day are being forfeited because Christians have lost sight of this focus.

Focus on Human Flourishing

Remember, change usually happens from the inside out. To help people flourish, we must identify and remove the barriers that prevent them from living out their full potential as image bearers of God. Many of the cultural battles of our day are being forfeited because Christians have lost sight of this focus. From a biblical viewpoint, winning isn't about seizing the reins of power as much as it is about creating a robust vision of a flourishing society.

Aristotle is often thought to have coined the term **human flourishing**. Some people think it means to chase after happiness, which in our time conjures thoughts of extended enjoyment uninterrupted by pain or loss. Aristotle thought of flourishing as pursuing virtue and building value, not merely pursuing personal pleasure. According to Michael Miller, research fellow at the Acton Institute, human flourishing is "a life well lived according to our nature made in the image of God; it seeks the good, the true, and the beautiful."[41]

Shalom is the way the Bible describes human flourishing. As theologian Cornelius Plantinga Jr. puts it,

> Shalom means universal flourishing, wholeness, and delight—a rich state of affairs in which natural needs are satisfied and natural gifts fruitfully employed, a state of affairs that inspires joyful wonder as its Creator and Savior opens doors and welcomes the creatures in whom he delights.[42]

Journalist Andy Crouch agrees: the *shalom* of creation is "designed for the flourishing of exquisitely relational creatures, male and female, who themselves are very good because they bear the image of a relational God."[43]

But when Adam and Eve sinned, that *shalom*, or ability to flourish, was broken. Christ's life, death, and resurrection not only restores our standing before a holy God but also gives Christians the opportunity to seek the *shalom* we were meant to enjoy before the fall, though we know we'll never realize it fully this side of eternity. Christ's sacrifice doesn't just bandage up creation. It restores its fullness and wholeness.[44]

> **When Adam and Eve sinned, *shalom*, or their ability to flourish, was broken. Christ's sacrifice restores fullness and wholeness.**

Shalom changes everything for us personally, for humanity and for institutions, such as marriage and the family:

- ***Shalom* says that each of us is gifted with a vocation—a calling.** We each are blessed with specific callings we can exercise for God's glory and in the service of others.

- ***Shalom* says that we humans aren't mere consumers.** We aren't meant to be kept fed, literally and emotionally, by the bread and circuses of condescending secular elites. We are producers whose work increases the total economic value in the world, benefiting everyone.

- ***Shalom* says that through marriage and families, we learn virtues and behaviors central to community.** Societies that prize these institutions produce people who flourish.[45]

As is often the case, asking questions helps us get to the root issues. To help us think better about flourishing in our communities, think through these four questions:[46]

1. Is cultural power growing in my community? For example, by keeping unemployed citizens dependent on handouts, government grows, siphoning power away from those it's supposed to empower. But when people become self-sufficient, they affirm their God-given dignity and are empowered to help their families and communities flourish.

2. Does my community prize charity or merely "humanitarianism"? Humanitarianism is the habit of providing people with handout after handout. But this diminishes cultural power and drains away people's desire to be productive and self-sufficient. Charity is different. It seeks the good of others, empowering them rather than merely meeting their needs.

3. Are people around me reflecting the nature of God? Our most basic calling as humans is to demonstrate characteristics of the *imago Dei*: creativity, order, responsibility, kindness, generosity, and reconciliation.

4. Who in my community is flourishing? How can they help others who aren't? Through discipleship groups and mentoring, churches can get people together to learn what creates flourishing and facilitate more of it.

As a real-life example, recall the story of William Carey from chapter 3. After teaching himself multiple European languages and overcoming his church's objections, Carey traveled to India to evangelize and work for social reform. He helped end **suttee** (or sati), a religious practice of burning widows to death on their husbands' funeral pyres. He also ended distinctions in the **caste system** among Christian converts and achieved breakthroughs in education, economic development, agriculture, forestry, banking, printing, and industry. Together with his coworkers, Carey developed local dialects into written languages that he then used to produce Bibles. Modern written Indian languages got their start with William Carey. Today, Indians acknowledge Carey for setting the stage for the Bengali renaissance in the nineteenth century.

> *Caste System:* **the Hindu practice of assigning individuals to various static social classes based on one's birth.**

Carey experienced a lot of opposition, and not just from traditional Hindus. His fiercest opponents were secular governments and businesses, such as the British East India Company, that essentially controlled India and had little regard for whether Indians became educated and capable of managing their own affairs. Carey and his colleagues, along with the Clapham Sect, helped bring that control to an end.[47]

Love Your Neighbor

Luke 10 records an exchange in which a lawyer asked Jesus how one could inherit eternal life. When Jesus asked the man what the **Mosaic law** said, he answered, "You shall love the Lord your God with all your heart and with all your soul and with all your strength and with all your mind, and your neighbor as yourself."

"Do this, and you will live," Jesus said.

But the lawyer wasn't satisfied. "And who is my neighbor?" he asked (vv. 27–29).

That's when Jesus told of the Good Samaritan, a man from an ethnicity the Jews considered inferior, who personally cared for a robbery victim when a priest and a Levite—men supposedly close followers of the Law—did nothing.

Mosaic Law: the set of laws God gave Moses and the Hebrews following their exodus from Egypt.

This part of the message, at least, is clear: if you want to renew your community, start by being present in its pain. It's part of a long Christian tradition. Jesuit priests in South America, in the region that would become Paraguay, were engaged in missionary activity intended to convert the indigenous peoples to Christianity while maintaining their culture. Called *reductions* because of the intent of consolidating the population from scattered villages, these communities brought agricultural innovation, manufacturing, and education to the residents. When the Spaniards attacked and tried to enslave the natives, the Jesuit priests themselves entered into the natives' pain, risking their own lives to fight back (and together they won).[48]

If you want to renew your community, start by being present in its pain. It's part of a long Christian tradition.

Throughout history, Christians have asked, "What are the pain points in our community, and how can we help?" Sometimes the answer is really simple. Jim Liske, the CEO of Prison Fellowship Ministries, tells of a visit to the ancient city of Ephesus, which at the time of the apostles was controlled by priests of the temple of Artemis. The priests sought to be the sole source of fire for the community. If someone's fire went out, he had to go to the temple and pay the priests to get hot coals. The priests told the people that getting fire from any other source would make the gods angry.

Christians responded by keeping their own fire bowls to replenish the coals of neighbors whose fires had gone out. According to Warren Smith and John Stonestreet, this not only provided lifesaving fire for people who might have been too poor to pay a temple tribute but also deprived the temple of the financial support by which it exercised such control. Most important, though, it proclaimed that the Christians weren't afraid of pagan gods or the pagan priests. Liske asks, "What does it mean to be a firebearer today?"[49] In other words, how can we display God's truth and diminish evil's influence in loving our neighbors?

Prison Fellowship, which Chuck Colson established in 1976, now operates in more than one hundred countries. One of its "fire-bearer" programs is called Angel Tree, an outreach to children who have at least one parent in prison.[50] Every year, Angel Tree volunteers provide 350,000 Christmas gifts to these children. The gifts are given on behalf of the incarcerated parents, whose children are thrilled their parents have remembered them. Smith and Stonestreet tell one story of this program's impact:

> By age sixteen, Chris was kicked out of school. His parents divorced, his mom died of cancer, and, as Chris says, he "shook his fist" at God. And before he landed in prison with sixty-nine felony charges, he'd fathered a son, Christopher.

Although Chris gave his life to Christ in prison, he fretted about his son. Chris says, "He knew his dad had to be a real scoundrel." Chris had no way to show his boy that Jesus had changed him.

Until, that is, someone slid an Angel Tree pamphlet through Chris's cell door.

Chris signed up Christopher for Angel Tree, and by Christmas, Christopher had a brand-new basketball. An excited Christopher called his dad, and all he could talk about was his basketball. The wounds began to heal.[51]

After being released from prison, Chris won custody of Christopher and started a transitional home for ex-prisoners. Christopher is now growing in Christ and apprenticing at a local church.

Another ministry showing love for neighbors is Focused Community Strategies (FCS) Urban Ministries in Atlanta, Georgia. FCS's projects include inviting families to move in among the urban poor to be good neighbors and opening a healthful-food grocery store in an underserved neighborhood. One of its most visible projects is transforming the old Atlanta Stockade, a fearsome former prison in a blighted neighborhood, into tasteful and safe apartments for the urban poor.[52]

> One of FCS's projects included transforming the old Atlanta Stockade, a fearsome former prison in a blighted neighborhood, into tasteful and safe apartments for the urban poor.

Victory Trade School (VTS) of Springfield, Missouri, is another example. Young men come to VTS from around the country to learn culinary arts. Students learn the basics of the restaurant trade and get on-the-job training at one of two local eateries. VTS boasts an 89.5 percent graduation rate as students learn not only to cook but to discern a calling as well. They participate in Bible studies, worship, and gospel preaching, and they earn their GEDs. The program is tough and features a zero-tolerance policy for drinking and drug use. VTS provides Christian community and helps people get back on track with their lives.[53]

Some of the challenges causing pain for communities are racial ones. After a series of shootings by police and the deaths of African Americans in police custody, angry rioters confronted police and destroyed property in communities across America in recent years. In the midst of the chaos, churches have awakened. Pastor Rodrick Burton from New Northside Missionary Baptist Church, near Ferguson, Missouri, helped lead cleanup efforts in the aftermath of a riot sparked by anger over a grand jury's decision not to indict white police officer Darren Wilson for the 2014 shooting death of an African American teenager, Michael Brown.[54]

> Some of the challenges causing pain for communities are racial ones.

Burton, an African American pastor, was distressed at how many pastors engaged in angry rhetoric over the perceived injustice of an unarmed teenager being killed in a struggle with a police officer. He understands. Government sins against people. But retribution is also a sin. Burton says, "I do know that Christ is consistent in that we are supposed to pray for our enemy and we are supposed to forgive."[55]

Like Burton, Michelle Higgins is another Christian who focused on being present during the dark days of the Ferguson riots. As outreach coordinator for South City Church, she stocked the church with medicine, sleeping bags, and food to help believers who came to minister to protesters as well as police officers. To her, it's about displaying the hope of Christ in what seems like a hopeless situation. Higgins notes that "when we clothe ourselves in the gospel and we walk into the midst of blocked highways and deep pain and heavy tragedy, just by being there we can communicate this profound theology that is the answer to all of their problems."[56]

Start with the Community's Assets

Everyone can contribute. As we discussed in an earlier chapter, many efforts to renew communities begin with **need-based community development** (NBCD). Eager to help, many go into poor communities and ask, "What is the *need*?" Then they design their programs to meet that need. Often this leads to dependency and greater poverty. A better approach is to ask communities, "What do you *have* that can be used for transformation?" This is **asset-based community development** (ABCD).

ABCD is a natural extension of the idea that God supplies each of us with talents to extend his kingdom (Matt. 25:14–15).[57] His grace overflows into everything (Matt. 5:45).[58] Because communities are made of people, we know that each community has resources it can use to solve its own problems—resources such as intellect, skills, relationships, employers, and experiences. The community itself and the part of creation it inhabits are full of unidentified resources. The Bible says that God uses the foolish and weak things of this world to shame the wise and powerful (1 Cor. 1:26–29; 2 Cor. 12:9–10).[59] When these resources are deployed and multiplied by God's miraculous intervention, amazing things happen.

As we saw in the chapter on poverty, materialistic worldviews tend to regard poverty as a material problem requiring a material solution. If people are poor because they lack money, the thinking goes, then take money from the wealthy and redistribute it to the poor. Much international aid is based on this model. But redistribution of wealth doesn't lead to long-term change.

From a biblical viewpoint, individuals aren't born empty. They are filled with potential. Bearing God's image is the source of our value; the abilities he gives us—intelligence, health, opportunity, and so forth—enable us, as stewards, to add value to our culture. If you buy a trinket for your shelf, it usually doesn't increase in value. But if you buy a lawn mower, you can use it to earn money. Things we possess that grow value are called *capital assets*. Each of us has five different kinds of **capital**:

> *Capital:* any asset that has monetary value.

- **Physical capital.** Our *bodies* enable us to see, hear, and touch so we can build things, assemble things, play games, speak the truth, help kids, and assist the elderly.

- **Emotional capital.** Our *hearts* enable us to feel and experience, dream of unexplored worlds, initiate good activities, intervene when wrong is taking place, and create art and thus bring beauty into our world.

- **Intellectual capital.** Our *minds* enable us to reason and analyze, explore the universe, think about what God thinks about, and use our knowledge to solve problems.

- **Moral capital.** Our *consciences* enable us to distinguish right from wrong, truth from falsehood, and the beautiful from the hideous. Conscience enables us to identify wrongs and clear the path for human flourishing.

- **Volitional capital.** Our *wills* enable us to make real moral choices, choose good goals and bring them about, and shape history.

It's up to each of us to steward these five capital assets and grow them in value. If those around us don't know how to do it, we need to help them learn.

ABCD also focuses on *community* capital, not just *individual* capital. This could be

- **Natural capital** (such as water, soil, and natural resources);

- **Social capital** (such as community closeness and friendship);

- **Physical capital** (such as road systems, parks, and utilities); and

- **Institutional capital** (such as churches, libraries, and courts).

Darrow Miller calls these forms of social capital "seeds" because they're resources that, when invested, can grow into healthy communities.[60] For example, an entrepreneur can start a business and employ others to provide goods and services. Neighbors can come together to fight sex trafficking, repair storm-damaged homes, or build and maintain a soccer field. Using their resources, communities can make life better for everyone.

> Let's not discount the *spiritual* resources God gives us. God is rich in mercy and grace and has provided Christians with giftings and insight as part of our God-given design.

And let's not discount the *spiritual* resources God gives us. God is rich in mercy and grace and has provided Christians with giftings and insight as part of our God-given design. We have salvation and the power of the Holy Spirit that bears fruit, such as love, joy, peace, longsuffering, and goodness (Gal. 5:22–23).[61] We have God's Word and spiritual disciplines like prayer, fellowship, and worship. We have the Lord's Supper and baptism. And while many people tend to discount them, we have miracles God performs in answer to prayer. He heals. He brings revival. He guides nations. And he promises a coming kingdom.

Don't Forget the Power of the Market

No one has a right to someone else's stuff. From a materialist view, power is a zero-sum game in which one person's gain is another person's loss. Materialists believe that resources are limited; the economic pie cannot expand but can only be redivided—or redistributed. If that's true, our best shot at bringing people out of poverty is to take from the haves and give to the have-nots. But much of this chapter is built around challenging this assumption.

In his book *Playing God*, Andy Crouch illustrates the zero-sum principle using the example of his cello lessons. When he goes to his teacher's house for the lesson, he has $50 in his pocket. When he leaves, the teacher has the $50. It looks like a zero-sum game. But in truth, it isn't that way. The teacher doesn't know *less* about playing the cello just because Andy knows more. Arguably, he knows *more* about playing the cello because he's helped Andy in learning to play, and he now plays better too. So as a result of the exchange, the total amount of cello-playing power in the world has increased. The only way such an exchange would be seen as a bad thing is if money is all that matters or if either Andy or the teacher is forced against his or her will to participate in the lessons.[62] Additionally, as Andy gains expertise in playing the cello, he develops the capacity to bring enjoyment to others through his playing and, if he so chooses, earn income by playing for events. This is a created benefit that previously didn't exist. It demonstrates the falsity of the **zero-sum game**.

> ***Zero-Sum Game:*** any situation in which one participant's gain (or loss) is proportionally offset by another participant's loss (or gain).

We must get away from the idea that we have a **right** to anything other than the natural and spiritual endowments God has given us. As E. Calvin Beisner expresses it, "Properly understood, rights are not guarantees that something will be *provided for us* but guarantees that what is ours will not be unjustly *taken from us.*"[63]

> ***Right:*** a guarantee that what belongs to someone will not be unjustly taken.

This runs counter to the secular inclination to define the possession of economic and social goods as a "right." Humanist "chaplain" (his self-described term) Corliss Lamont defined *economic democracy* as "the right of every adult to a useful job at a decent wage or salary, to general economic security and opportunity, to an equitable share in the material goods of this life, and to a proportionate voice in the conduct of economic affairs."[64] This is redistribution.

Often, tax policy is used to force those who are better off to pay higher taxes, thereby fulfilling their "moral obligation" to give back some of what they have "taken" from others. Wealth redistribution substitutes for wealth creation.[65] But this short-term fix can make the problem worse because it can slow the growth necessary to conquer poverty. When job creators have fewer resources because those resources are coercively redistributed, they can't create as many jobs. Economic slowdown follows as inevitably as night follows day.

When economies are shrinking or growing slowly, it's easy to get the impression that the rich are prospering at the expense of the poor. Why? Because while the rich are able to maintain their lifestyles through investing, the poor are dependent on jobs, and a slow-growing economy provides fewer of them, and at lower wages.

Low taxes are a critical part of the solution. Economist Alvin Rabushka studied tax and growth rates for fifty-four developing countries over a thirty-year period. He found that the growth rates of high-tax countries were less than one-fifth of the growth rates of low-tax countries.[66]

Economic growth helps poor people in ways higher taxes never can. Community renewal happens when everyone does better, and in a growing economy, one person's gain doesn't necessarily mean another person's loss. As William Voegeli puts it, "Even if [your income] grows more rapidly than mine, mine still grows. A smaller slice of a bigger pie could leave more on my plate than I formerly had with a bigger slice of a smaller pie."[67]

Raising taxes also decreases people's incentive to work. In the mid-1990s, for example, France had a tax rate of almost 60 percent. As people realized it was unproductive to work more, the average workweek shrank to just 17.5 hours.[68] With a shrinking workforce, though, taxes increased for the remaining workers, which in turn decreased their incentive to work.

Rather than tinker with the tax structure, many Christian ministries have come up with ingenious solutions to help the poor meet their needs in a dignified fashion by equipping them to help others. Friends Ministry in Lake City, Michigan, for example, features a community garden that grows berries, tomatoes, peppers, herbs, and an assortment of other produce on its sixty-one-acre property. The ministry also maintains a well-stocked thrift store.

Friends Ministry is a unique model that began as an outreach to the poor. Rather than giving away fruits and vegetables and clothing, the program inspires a work ethic by employing people as laborers. In exchange, they help those workers pay off their bills. When laborers reach 37.5 hours of work, Friends Ministry will directly pay off one of their bills, up to $300. This enables workers to regain financial stability by paying rent, utilities, and repair bills they otherwise wouldn't be able to pay. When people come for help, the ministry's executive director shows them how to make a budget and prays with them about surrendering their difficulties to God. As director Mark Mortenson puts it, "People respond when you love them enough to give 'em a little push."[69]

Remember that self-interest isn't all bad. Stewardship works. Even for children. Katherine Hussman Klemp found that if she assigned clear ownership to each new toy she brought into the house, her children squabbled less. They also shared more, knowing the toys they shared were their own and would be returned.[70] When people are stewards, they take responsibility as if they were owners and seek to increase the value of what they're stewarding.

> *Greed:* the selfish desire for excessive wealth or power.

> *Self-Interest:* the desire to make sure one's own needs are met.

Doesn't self-interest make people greedier, though? Theologian Wayne Grudem and economist Barry Asmus say no, pointing out the difference between **greed** and **self-interest**:

Self-interest is unavoidable. Self-interest might even lead someone to give generously to the needs of others because giving carries its own rewards—Jesus said, "It is more blessed to give than to receive" (Acts 20:35). Greed, on the other hand, is excessive self-interest. It is wanting more than you rightfully deserve or failing to care for the needs of others as well as yourself.[71]

No economic system has ever eliminated greed, but a **free-market economy** takes into account the fact that people will operate out of a healthy self-interest and, frankly, will even operate out of their greed to best serve the needs of others. For instance, if a restaurant offers bad service, bad food, and high prices, it will lose customers. In a free-market system, if you want to succeed in the restaurant business, you have to serve well. You have to be a good steward.

Start successful businesses. Some people are called to love their neighbors and build their communities by coming up with great ideas and taking risks to turn them into profitable businesses. Communities that help people take these risks do better. As economist George Gilder observes,

> A successful economy depends on the proliferation of the rich, on creating a large class of risk-taking men who are willing to shun the easy channels of a comfortable life in order to create new enterprise, win huge profits, and invest them again.[72]

Of course, some people think that business is the problem, not the solution. Many are taught that unless government heavily regulates businesses and taxes them at high rates, the owners of those businesses become "robber barons." Historian Burton Folsom strongly objects to this characterization and says that critics' concerns are misplaced. Rather than distrust businesspeople, they should distrust those who try to secure their own economic prosperity through government enforcement.

For example, Folsom notes an ironic reference to Cornelius Vanderbilt that Thomas Bailey made in his history text *The American Pageant*: "Though ill-educated, ungrammatical, coarse, and ruthless, he was clear-visioned. Offering superior railway service at lower rates, he amassed a fortune of $100 million."[73]

Folsom asks, "To whom was Vanderbilt ruthless?" Not to consumers—according to Bailey, they received "superior railway service at lower rates." If Vanderbilt was ruthless at all, it was toward his competitors, such as Edward Collins, who used the state to "extort subsidies and impose high rates on consumers."[74]

Folsom also points out the benefits of the competitive practices of the industrialist John D. Rockefeller in relation to his battle to open up markets in Europe for American oil products:

> Three facts show the importance of Rockefeller's battle with the Russians. First, about two-thirds of the oil refined in America in the late 1800s was exported. Second, Russia was closer than the U.S. to all European and Asian markets. Third, Russian oil was more centralized, more plentiful, and more viscous than American oil. If Rockefeller had not overcome Russia's natural advantages, no one else could have. America would have lost millions of dollars in exports and might have even had to import oil from Russia. The spoils of victory—jobs, technology, cheap kerosene, cheap by-products, and cheap gas to spur the auto industry—all of this might have been lost had it not been for Rockefeller's ability to sell oil profitably at six cents a gallon.[75]

> For many Christians, their work and their worship are separate. The biblical worldview integrates all of life. God uses our work *and* our worship to advance his kingdom.

What some interpreted as ruthless, men like Vanderbilt and Rockefeller saw as increasing efficiency to meet competitive challenges.

This isn't to say that all business owners do the right thing. Many do cut corners. Many don't have a proper concern for their employees' safety and well-being. In this situation, community is even more important. Citizens, working through their local governments, can put in place reasonable and prudent regulations that maintain public safety and allow citizens to focus on things other than whether their water is contaminated and whether they'll be protected from injury at work. Customers, too, have enormous power in admonishing business owners to do the right thing. This is especially true in a free market, where customers can spend their money elsewhere.

Think Biblically about Vocation

Most people have two buckets into which they place their life activities: a sacred bucket for life's most meaningful, worshipful activities, and a secular bucket for everything else.[76] For many Christians, how they vote has little to do with where they go to church on Sunday, or if they go at all. Their work and their worship are separate. The biblical worldview integrates all of life. We see this in the Hebrew word *abad*, which means "serve" and is translated as both "work" and "worship."[77] Scripture doesn't separate these. Our work is worship, and our worship is work. God uses our work *and* our worship to advance his kingdom.

> *Abad:* from the Hebrew for "to serve"; the term also means "to work and worship."

This is true even in areas as seemingly unspiritual as city planning. Darrow Miller tells of meeting a university student in Japan who read in the Bible that God was building a city. The student thought, *If God is building a city, he must be interested in cities!* For the next four years, she read the Bible to see what it had to say about city planning. This kind of insight should be the norm, not the exception.[78]

We ought to envision so much more for our communities based on Christ's redemption. The gospel demands it. British theologian and missiologist Lesslie Newbigin wrote, "A preaching of the gospel that calls men and women to accept Jesus as Savior but does not make it clear that discipleship means a commitment to a vision of society radically different from that which controls our public life today must be condemned as false."[79]

Redeem Entertainment

Part of community renewal is telling great stories. Jeffrey Katzenberg, former studio chairman of Disney, said, "Each of us in Hollywood has the opportunity to assume individual responsibility for creating films that elevate rather than denigrate, that shed light rather than dwell in darkness, that aim for the highest common denominator rather than the lowest."[80]

It's a good sentiment for Christians to embrace. We're surrounded by entertainment. This, too, needs a touch from God. Fortunately, technology's rapid advance makes this more and more possible. Diane Howard, journalist and dialogue coach for movie actors, thinks that a renaissance of art might be taking place because of new technology that "gives filmmakers and artists access to the best artistic events, performers and directors"[81] through broadcast media and techniques that would have cost too much money just a few years ago. Howard also points to the growing influence of such producers as Mark Burnett and Roma Downey, whose *Bible* miniseries was a blockbuster hit for the History Channel. Their series *A.D. The Bible Continues* was the number one series on Sunday-night television when it was airing.[82]

> People are clamoring for stories that tell the truth, stories that delve into the goodness of creation, the tragedy of fallenness, and the hope of redemption.

People are clamoring for stories that tell the truth, stories that delve into the goodness of creation, the tragedy of fallenness, and the hope of redemption. Screenwriting instructor Robert McKee says, "When culture repeatedly experiences glossy, hollowed-out, pseudo-stories, it degenerates. We need true satires and tragedies, dramas and comedies that shine a clean light into the dingy corners of the human psyche and society."[83] Screenwriter and director Brian Godawa agrees. "Movies may be about story, but those stories are finally, centrally, crucially, primarily, *mostly* about redemption," he says.[84]

Ratings aren't necessarily a good indication of whether a film is redemptive. Some R-rated movies tell the truth redemptively, and some G-rated movies lead people away from the truth. But generally, a movie's rating says something about whether it's family friendly, and family-friendly content is in high demand. Catherine Clinch reviewed the top twenty-five box-office hits of 2011 and found that only four were rated R.[85] In addition, movie-profitability data over a five-year period showed that G-rated films raked in $108.5 million, whereas R-rated films managed $12.7 million in profits. In light of this, Clinch asks commonsensically, "If G-Rated films are 8.5 times more profitable than R-rated films, what is accomplished by under-serving this consumer base?"[86]

This doesn't mean that just because something is family friendly, it's Christian. While gratuitous violence harm us all, just because a film is violent doesn't make it un-Christian. The Bible doesn't flinch at realistic portrayals of human evil. But as Clinch notes, the movers and shakers in Hollywood are increasingly realizing that movies that serve the Christian market well—movies featuring uplifting, redemptive values—also serve the rest of the market well. In her article, Clinch reported on the first *Variety* magazine Family Entertainment and Faith-Based Summit in 2012. In the packed hotel ballroom, Christian filmmakers were able to express to the industry what Christians really want: not so much faith-based films (with overt Christian content) as faith-friendly content that either supports or at least doesn't attack religious faith.[87]

> Hollywood is increasingly realizing that movies that serve the Christian market well—movies featuring uplifting, redemptive values—also serve the rest of the market well.

Redeeming entertainment is a big vision, and it's not just for the movies. Through learning the crafts of writing, moviemaking, and music performance, you can tell great stories that tell the truth and tell the truth about telling the truth. Perhaps it could be a means of earning an income for your family as well. You don't have to have your movies on the big screen or perform to sold-out audiences to make a living at it either. Today's market makes it possible to serve a niche audience very profitably, for example, by making films for people of specific ages or interests, or films for churches and schools looking to teach compelling lessons to children.

It's not just about telling other people's stories, though. To live faithfully in a world determined to amuse itself to death (as Neil Postman put it), we must live our own life stories well.

Christians can tell stories of tragedy that enable our audiences to cleanse themselves of unwanted emotions through the experience of pity or terror. But we can also tell comedic stories that revel in what often seems to be the folly and absurdity of life.[88] Our laughter need not be an act of cynicism. Rather, it can display the value of living heroically even when everything goes wrong.[89] Our hope is this: no matter how crazy life gets, all the pieces weave together in God's plan.

Prepare for Opposition

Reclaiming territory from Satan is a battle not against "flesh and blood" but against principalities and powers (Eph. 6:12).[90] A price must be paid. It will hurt. But it isn't a destructive pain. It's more like childbirth (Rom. 8:22)[91] that hurts like crazy but produces new life. The road to success is through service, and service involves suffering, even as we anticipate a new heaven and a new earth in which suffering will be no more.

> The road to success is through service, and service involves suffering, even as we anticipate a new heaven and a new earth in which suffering will be no more.

We need to count the cost, as did the believers described in Hebrews 11.[92] Talent isn't enough. Hard work and commitment win the day for those equipped through Christ and empowered by the Holy Spirit. Terry Moffitt is a friend of mine who can attest to this. When he served as a city-council member of his town in North Carolina, Moffitt confronted a growing number of sexually oriented businesses in his community. He successfully took a stand against them not by giving rousing speeches but by drafting legislation focused on protecting children and families.

The rigorous licensing provisions Moffitt drafted regulated everything from parking to the serving of alcohol to the protection of performers. Because community members saw how the regulations protected the vulnerable, they pushed sexually oriented businesses to the margins of their community and showed that their "heroes of free expression" claim was a fraud. Most of these sordid businesses shut down, and those planning to open decided not to.

But for Moffitt and his family, the cost was high. Many of the sexually oriented businesses were associated with organized crime. His "meddling" was met with serious death threats. The liberal media piled on with critical articles. But in the end it was worth it: Moffitt says that the legislation he drafted has been adopted in more than eighty communities across the United States. This legislation is restoring honor and decency, protecting children and families, and reducing crime.

Putting It All Together: The Example of Oklahoma City

Renewing a community or building a nation requires people who catalyze and engage in movements rather than in building monuments to themselves or their institutions. We need people who can amass and spend cultural and political capital. These are the culture shapers. We need supportive networks like the Clapham Sect. We also need economic capital, or financing, that expands the movement.[93]

An example of how these forms of capital come together in shaping a community is Oklahoma City, a community of just over 600,000 people in what many of society's elites think of as flyover country. In the past, Oklahoma City was known mostly for the 1995 terrorist bombing of a federal building that killed 171 people, including three unborn children. Even people who lived there considered it to be a dusty, boring town. Gary Pierson, publisher of *The Oklahoman* newspaper, said that after the attack,

> there was every reason for people to give up hope completely.... And our people were at that point. They were at the threshold, looking at the abyss. They said we are going to stand up, we aren't going to give up, and they said it without hesitation, without prompting.... They just did it.[94]

Oklahoma City changed. It's a change I noticed from the moment I arrived at Oklahoma City's shiny, clean, and architecturally interesting airport terminal. The city has sports teams and lots of restaurants, churches, and creative community activities. Entrepreneurs in the energy sector and other business sectors have flocked there. Most important, the citizens of Oklahoma City have banded together to take care of people who need help. They're involved with programs like the Spero Project, a nonprofit that helps churches mobilize to reach underserved populations, and the 111 Project, which organizes churches to recruit foster families for orphaned children.

> **Most important, the citizens of Oklahoma City have banded together to take care of people who need help.**

As Doug Serven, pastor of City Presbyterian Church in downtown Oklahoma City, says that believers "care about Oklahoma City: not just saving souls, but entering into the city and its brokenness and joy, incarnating with the belief that Jesus really does change things."[95]

At the core of these changes is a group of business leaders, government leaders, educators, and pastors who began gathering in a conference room at the headquarters of Hobby Lobby, which operates a nationwide chain of craft stores. Hobby Lobby was founded and is operated by a Christian family whose members care about bringing change to their hometown. Together, the leaders meeting at Hobby Lobby organized local churches to think bigger than just Sunday services. They began identifying barriers that had stopped Oklahoma City from being great. Then they formed action councils to come up with specific, measurable plans.

The Oklahoma City Thunder basketball team is a good example of the city's new spirit. General manager Sam Presti moved to Oklahoma City in 2008 and challenged Thunder players and staff to get involved in the community. At a more poignant level, Presti insists that every new player and staff member tour the Oklahoma City National Memorial and Museum.[96] Superstar player Kevin Durant says,

> As players and citizens of the community, we try to shine a bright light on the city every time we see how we can change the vision of the city—but we also still realize what they've been through and how tough it was to go through that. We want to let everybody know how resilient we are as a city, and how important it is to know what that Memorial means to our state, and the pride we have when we play.[97]

Thanks in part to the Thunder organization, a new initiative has been launched in the state called the Oklahoma Standard, in which Oklahomans are encouraged to commit to one act of honor, one act of service, and one act of kindness during the month of April.

Focusing on human flourishing—and capitalizing on individual and community assets—churches, businesses, schools, and government all working together have changed Oklahoma City. It's a biblical worldview in action.

5. CONCLUSION

> There has never been a better time for a massive movement of the church bringing healing to broken communities and fractured nations.

There has never been a better time for a massive movement of the church bringing healing to broken communities and fractured nations. As the twentieth-century German martyr Dietrich Bonhoeffer said shortly before his death, "The church is the church only when it exists for others."[98] This chapter isn't just an academic exercise. Communities need renewal. Nations need reformation. You're the one to do it, and so am I. The steps to renewal and reformation may be summarized quite simply.

1. Start with what you have, not with what you don't have. Think about your own gifts. Think about who can work with you. Think about your collective spheres of influence. Write down the names of the churches you and your friends attend and ask how you might connect them to a vision for transformation. Who are the experts you know? Who are the persons of influence you know? What financial and creative resources might you have access to in support of a really good idea?

2. Develop your team.[99] A good team includes *teachers*[100] who know how to frame ideas and cast vision, *modelers*[101] who get excited about moving into action, and *connectors*[102] whom many people know and trust. Connectors are especially important. Years ago researcher Stanley Milgram gave letters to 160 people in Omaha, Nebraska. Each contained the name of a stockbroker who worked in Boston and lived in Sharon, Massachusetts. Every letter recipient was asked to write their names on their packets and send them to people they thought would get the packets closer to the stockbroker listed on the recipient's letter. When the letters arrived at the stockbroker's house, Milgram looked at the list of names and found that most of the letters had reached their destination in five steps. This is the origin of the popular idea that everyone in the world is connected by no more than six degrees of separation.[103] Connections are vital. I have a friend, Kay, who, it seems, knows everyone and is known by everyone. Having Kay as an adviser has helped our ministry team immensely when it comes to gaining credibility with others.

3. Make your plan. After you've begun cultivating relationships, take time to pray, fast, and seek wise counsel from people you trust. Spend time with your team asking God to bring his kingdom to your community and do his will in your community (Matt. 6:8–13).[104] Ask someone who is really good at strategic planning to lead your group through a planning process in which you'll establish goals, objectives, and action steps. Most projects start small and get bigger as the people involved grow in their capacity and as more people join the team.

A great hymn by William Fullerton, whom Charles Spurgeon mentored, summarizes well what it means to hope in God in spite of the difficulties we face:

> *I cannot tell how He will win the nations,*
> *How He will claim His earthly heritage,*
> *How satisfy the needs and aspirations,*
> *Of east and west, of sinner and of sage.*
> *But this I know, all flesh shall see His glory,*
> *And He shall reap the harvest He has sown,*
> *And some glad day His sun shall shine in splendour*
> *When He the Saviour, Saviour of the world, is known.*[105]

The Savior has come. We have a redeemer who meets us in our brokenness to bear his redemption first to our own lives and then to our communities, our nations, and the world.

ENDNOTES

1. I don't know who invented this term, but the first use I can find was around 2004. See Paul Dickson, *Slang: The Topical Dictionary of Americanisms* (New York: Walker and Company, 2006), 360.

2. *World Urbanization Prospects: The 2014 Revision* (New York: United Nations/Department of Economic and Social Affairs, 2014), 1, https://esa.un.org/unpd/wup/Publications/Files/WUP2014-Highlights.pdf.

3. *Detroit News* investigation, cited in "Half of Detroit Property Owners Didn't Pay 2011 Taxes," CBS Detroit, February 21, 2013, http://detroit.cbslocal.com/2013/02/21/half-of-detroit-property-owners-didnt-pay-2011-taxes/. See also Kate Abbey-Lambertz, "Detroit's Abandoned Ruins Are Captivating, but Are They Bad for Neighborhoods?," Huffington Post, January 23, 2014, www.huffingtonpost.com/2013/12/30/detroit-ruins_n_4519731.html.

4. FBI's Uniform Crime Report statistics, *Crime in the United States: January–June 2015*, cited in Daniel Fisher, "America's Most Dangerous Cities: Detroit Can't Shake No. 1 Spot," *Forbes*, October 29, 2015, www.forbes.com/sites/danielfisher/2015/10/29/americas-most-dangerous-cities-detroit-cant-shake-no-1-spot/#3e5767a112c8; see also Warren Cole Smith and John Stonestreet, *Restoring All Things: God's Audacious Plan to Change the World through Everyday People* (Grand Rapids: Baker Books, 2015), 48.

5. Alison L. Hill et al., "Emotions as Infectious Diseases in a Large Social Network: The SISa Model," *Proceedings of the Royal Society B* (July 2010): 1–9, http://rspb.royalsocietypublishing.org/content/royprsb/early/2010/07/03/rspb.2010.1217.full.pdf.

6. Miller McPherson, Lynn Smith-Lovin, and Matthew Brashears, "Social Isolation in America: Changes in Core Discussion Networks over Two Decades," *American Sociological Review* 71, no. 3 (June 2006): 353–75.

7. Patrick F. Fagan and Christina Hadford, *The State of the Black Family in America* (Washington, DC: Marriage and Religion Research Institute, 2015), http://downloads.frc.org/EF/EF15B29.pdf.

8. "Christopher Brooks," Evangel Ministries, accessed August 4, 2016, www.evangelministries.org/#!chris-brooks/w75rs.

9. Andy Crouch, "Why Apologetics Is Different—and Working—in the Hood," *Christianity Today*, October 22, 2013, www.christianitytoday.com/ct/2013/november/urban-apologetics-christopher-brooks-detroit.html?saveto=newfolder&start=1.

10. Daniel James Devine, "Michigan's Homeless Makeover," *World* 30, no. 16 (August 2015): 54–56, https://world.wng.org/2015/07/michigans_homeless_makeover.

11. Richard John Neuhaus, "The Gods of Left and Right," *First Things*, March 1999, 63, www.firstthings.com/article/1999/03/the-gods-of-left-and-right.

12. Matthew 28:18–20: "Jesus came and said to [his disciples], 'All authority in heaven and on earth has been given to me. Go therefore and make disciples of all nations, baptizing them in the name of the Father and of the Son and of the Holy Spirit, teaching them to observe all that I have commanded you. And behold, I am with you always, to the end of the age.'"

13. Tim Keller, "To Transform a City: How Do You Know If You're Reaching a City?," *Leadership Journal* 32, no. 1 (Winter 2011), www.christianitytoday.com/le/2011/winter/transformcity.html?start=1.

14. "God Loves Cities and Christians Should Too, Says Tim Keller," *Christianity Today*, October 21, 2010, www.christiantoday.com/article/god.loves.cities.and.christians.should.too.says.tim.keller/26938.htm.

15. Genesis 1:2: "The earth was without form and void, and darkness was over the face of the deep. And the Spirit of God was hovering over the face of the waters."

16. Darrow L. Miller, "Community Renewal," research paper submitted for this chapter, December 9, 2014.

17. Genesis 1:1: "In the beginning, God created the heavens and the earth."

18. Genesis 1:31: "God saw everything that he had made, and behold, it was very good. And there was evening and there was morning, the sixth day."

19. G. Johannes Botterweck, Helmer Ringgren, and Heinz-Josef Fabry, eds., *Theological Dictionary of the Old Testament*, trans. Douglas W. Stott (Grand Rapids: Eerdmans, 2003), 12:92–93.

20. Genesis 3:16–19: "To the woman [God] said, 'I will surely multiply your pain in childbearing; in pain you shall bring forth children. Your desire shall be contrary to your husband, but he shall rule over you.' And to Adam he said, 'Because you have listened to the voice of your wife and have eaten of the tree of which I commanded you, "You shall not eat of it," cursed is the ground because of you; in pain you shall eat of it all the days of your life; thorns and thistles it shall bring forth for you; and you shall eat the plants of the field. By the sweat of your face you shall eat bread, till you return to the ground, for out of it you were taken; for you are dust, and to dust you shall return'"; Romans 1:28–31: "Since [humans] did not see fit to acknowledge God, God gave them up to a debased mind to do what ought not to be done. They were filled with all manner of unrighteousness, evil, covetousness, malice. They are full of envy, murder, strife, deceit, maliciousness. They are gossips, slanderers, haters of God, insolent, haughty, boastful, inventors of evil, disobedient to parents, foolish, faithless, heartless, ruthless."

21. Noah Webster, *American Dictionary of the English Language 1828* (Chesapeake, VA: Foundation for American Christian Education, 1967), http://webstersdictionary1828.com/.

22. Romans 12:1–2: "I appeal to you therefore, brothers, by the mercies of God, to present your bodies as a living sacrifice, holy and acceptable to God, which is your spiritual worship. Do not be conformed to this world, but be transformed by the renewal of your mind, that by testing you may discern what is the will of God, what is good and acceptable and perfect."

23. Darrell L. Bock, ed., *The Bible Knowledge Word Study: Acts–Ephesians* (Colorado Springs, CO: Victor, 2006), 189.

24. Philippians 2:1–8: "So if there is any encouragement in Christ, any comfort from love, any participation in the Spirit, any affection and sympathy, complete my joy by being of the same mind, having the same love, being in full accord and of one mind. Do nothing from selfish ambition or conceit, but in humility count others more significant than yourselves. Let each of you look not only to his own interests, but also to the interests of others. Have this mind among yourselves, which is yours in Christ Jesus, who, though he was in the form of God, did not count equality with God a thing to be grasped, but emptied himself, by taking the form of a servant, being born in the likeness of men. And being found in human form, he humbled himself by becoming obedient to the point of death, even death on a cross"; James 1:2–4: "Count it all joy, my brothers, when you meet trials of various kinds, for you know that the testing of your faith produces steadfastness. And let steadfastness have its full effect, that you may be perfect and complete, lacking in nothing."

25. James 1:4: "Let steadfastness have its full effect, that you may be perfect and complete, lacking in nothing."

26. Matthew 28:18–20: "Jesus came and said to [his disciples], 'All authority in heaven and on earth has been given to me. Go therefore and make disciples of all nations, baptizing them in the name of the Father and of the Son and of the Holy Spirit, teaching them to observe all that I have commanded you. And behold, I am with you always, to the end of the age'"; Romans 16:25–27: "Now to him who is able to strengthen you according to my gospel and the preaching of Jesus Christ, according to the revelation of the mystery that was kept secret for long ages but has now been disclosed and through the prophetic writings has been made known to all nations, according to the command of the eternal God, to bring about the obedience of faith—to the only wise God be glory forevermore through Jesus Christ! Amen."

27. For more, see Thomas A Bloomer, "Calvin and Geneva," in Jim Stier, Richlyn Poor, and Lisa Davis, eds., *His Kingdom Come: An Integrated Approach to Discipling Nations and Fulfilling the Great Commission* (Seattle: YWAM, 2008).

28. Ken Myers, "What Is the Church's Interest in Culture?," Mars Hill Audio, transcript, https://marshillaudio.org/node/345.

29. James A. Swanson, *A Dictionary of Biblical Languages with Semantic Domains: Hebrew Old Testament* (Oak Harbor, WA: Logos Research Systems, 1997), s.v. "*shalom.*"

30. Darrow Miller, *LifeWork: A Biblical Theology for What You Do Every Day* (Seattle: YWAM, 2009).

31. Colossians 2:15: "[God] disarmed the rulers and authorities and put them to open shame, by triumphing over them in [Christ]."

32. Romans 12:4–5: "For as in one body we have many members, and the members do not all have the same function, so we, though many, are one body in Christ, and individually members one of another"; 1 Corinthians 12:27: "You are the body of Christ and individually members of it."

33. Ephesians 3:10–11: "[This grace of preaching the gospel was given to me] so that through the church the manifold wisdom of God might now be made known to the rulers and authorities in the heavenly places. This was according to the eternal purpose that he has realized in Christ Jesus our Lord."

34. Miller, "Community Renewal."

35. Ephesians 4:11–13: "[God] gave the apostles, the prophets, the evangelists, the shepherds and teachers, to equip the saints for the work of ministry, for building up the body of Christ, until we all attain to the unity of the faith and of the knowledge of the Son of God, to mature manhood, to the measure of the stature of the fullness of Christ."

36. Darrow Miller and his coworker Scott Allen have developed lectures on the awesome potential of the church and how the church can inspire community transformation. Their Monday Church, A.K.A. Occupy Till I Come, and LifeWork conferences are offered around the world.

37. Proverbs 16:9: "The heart of man plans his way, but the LORD establishes his steps."

38. Romans 12:2: "Do not be conformed to this world, but be transformed by the renewal of your mind, that by testing you may discern what is the will of God, what is good and acceptable and perfect."

39. Galatians 2:20: "I have been crucified with Christ. It is no longer I who live, but Christ who lives in me. And the life I now live in the flesh I live by faith in the Son of God, who loved me and gave himself for me."

40. Matthew 13:31–33: "[Jesus] put another parable before [his disciples], saying, 'The kingdom of heaven is like a grain of mustard seed that a man took and sowed in his field. It is the smallest of all seeds, but when it has grown it is larger than all the garden plants and becomes a tree, so that the birds of the air come and make nests in its branches.' He told them another parable. 'The kingdom of heaven is like leaven that a woman took and hid in three measures of flour, till it was all leavened.'"

41. Michael Miller, interview by Summit Ministries, quoted in "Want to Win the Culture? Focus on Human Flourishing," *Summit Announcements* (blog), Summit Ministries, November 4, 2013, www.summit.org/blogs/summit-announcements/want -to-win-the-culture-focus-on-human-flourishing/.

42. Cornelius Plantinga Jr., *Not the Way It's Supposed to Be: A Breviary of Sin* (Grand Rapids: Eerdmans, 1996), 10.

43. Andy Crouch, *Culture Making: Recovering Our Creative Calling* (Downers Grove, IL: IVP Books, 2008), 105.

44. Crouch, *Culture Making*, 140–46.

45. For the latest research on families, see the Heritage Foundation's website FamilyFacts.org at www.familyfacts.org.

46. From "Want to Win the Culture?," *Summit Announcements* (blog).

47. Not all missionaries were against colonialism, but no other Westerners were engaged in anti-colonial activity except Christian missionaries. See Vishal Mangalwadi and Ruth Mangalwadi, *The Legacy of William Carey: A Model for the Transformation of a Culture* (Wheaton, IL: Crossway, 1999); see also Glenn Sunshine, "William Carey (1761–1834)," *Christian Worldview Journal*, January 2, 2012, www.colsoncenter.org/the-center/columns/indepth/17309-william-carey-1761-1834.

48. Rodney Stark, *For the Glory of God: How Monotheism Led to Reformations, Science, Witch-Hunts, and the End of Slavery* (Princeton, NJ: Princeton University Press, 2003), 336–37.

49. Jim Liske, quoted in Smith and Stonestreet, *Restoring All Things*, 35.

50. "Every Child Has a Story," Angel Tree, Prison Fellowship Ministries, accessed August 4, 2016, www.prisonfellowship.org /about/angel-tree/.

51. Smith and Stonestreet, *Restoring All Things*, 106. Based on Eric Metaxas, "Prisoners' Children Need You," BreakPoint commentary, October 24, 2014, www.breakpoint.org/bpcommentaries/entry/13/26282.

52. Jill Suzanne Shook, ed., *Making Housing Happen: Faith-Based Affordable Housing Models*, 2nd ed. (Eugene, OR: Cascade Books, 2012), 81–86.

53. Mary Hopkins, "Cooking for Christ," *WORLD* 26, no. 14 (July 16, 2011), https://world.wng.org/2011/07/cooking_for_christ.

54. Angela Lu, "Churches Step into Ferguson's Pain," *WORLD*, November 25, 2014, https://world.wng.org/2014/11/churches _step_into_fergusons_pain.

55. Lu, "Churches Step into Ferguson's Pain."

56. Lu, "Churches Step into Ferguson's Pain."

57. Matthew 25:14–15: "[The kingdom of heaven] will be like a man going on a journey, who called his servants and entrusted to them his property. To one he gave five talents, to another two, to another one, to each according to his ability."

58. Matthew 5:45: "[God] makes his sun rise on the evil and on the good, and sends rain on the just and on the unjust."

59. First Corinthians 1:26–29: "Consider your calling, brothers: not many of you were wise according to worldly standards, not many were powerful, not many were of noble birth. But God chose what is foolish in the world to shame the wise; God chose what is weak in the world to shame the strong; God chose what is low and despised in the world, even things that are not, to bring to nothing things that are, so that no human being might boast in the presence of God"; 2 Corinthians 12:9–10: "[Jesus] said to me, 'My grace is sufficient for you, for my power is made perfect in weakness.' Therefore I will boast all the more gladly

of my weaknesses, so that the power of Christ may rest upon me. For the sake of Christ, then, I am content with weaknesses, insults, hardships, persecutions, and calamities. For when I am weak, then I am strong."

60. For more on this, see Scott Allen and Darrow Miller, *The Forest in the Seed: A Biblical Perspective on Resource and Development* (Phoenix: Disciple Nations Alliance, 2005), www.disciplenations.org/resources/free-downloadable-books-bible-studies/.

61. Galatians 5:22–23: "The fruit of the Spirit is love, joy, peace, patience, kindness, goodness, faithfulness, gentleness, self-control; against such things there is no law."

62. Andy Crouch, *Playing God: Redeeming the Gift of Power* (Downers Grove, IL: IVP Books, 2013), 38–44.

63. E. Calvin Beisner, *Social Justice: How Good Intentions Undermine Justice and Gospel* (Washington, DC: Family Research Council, 2013), 16, http://downloads.frc.org/EF/EF13E133.pdf.

64. Corliss Lamont, *The Philosophy of Humanism* (New York: Frederick Ungar, 1982), 267.

65. Philosopher Paul Kurtz wrote, "We believe … that the more affluent nations have a moral obligation to increase technological and economic assistance so that their less developed neighbors may become more self-sufficient. We need to work out some equitable forms of taxation on a world-wide basis to help make this a reality." Paul Kurtz, *Toward a New Enlightenment: The Philosophy of Paul Kurtz*, eds. Vern L. Bullough and Timothy J. Madigan (New Brunswick, NJ: Transaction, 1994), 43. V. M. Tarkunde, an Indian socialist, suggested, further, that "a cooperative economy in which the workers in an undertaking will be the owners of the means of production employed in that undertaking is undoubtedly the most democratic economic institution conceived so far." V. M. Tarkunde, "An Outline of Radical Humanism," *Humanist* (July/August 1988): 13.

66. Alvin Rabushka, "Taxation, Economic Growth, and Liberty," *Cato Journal* 7, no. 1 (1987), cited in Wayne Grudem and Barry Asmus, *The Poverty of Nations: A Sustainable Solution* (Wheaton, IL: Crossway, 2013), 159.

67. William Voegeli, "Not Leveling with Us," *Claremont Review of Books* 12, no. 3 (Summer 2012): 24, www.claremont.org/crb/article/not-leveling-with-us/.

68. Data cited in N. Gregory Mankiw, *Principles of Economics*, 5th ed. (Mason, OH: South-Western, 2009), 170.

69. Daniel James Devine, "Cultivating Change," World 29, no. 15 (July 2014), https://world.wng.org/2014/07/cultivating_change.

70. Katherine Hussman Klemp, "Give and Take: A Mother Teaches Her Children That Sharing Means Caring," *Sesame Street Parents' Guide*, December 1989, 36–38, cited in Armen A. Alchian, "Property Rights," in David R. Henderson, ed., *The Concise Encyclopedia of Economics*, 2nd ed. (Indianapolis: Liberty Fund, 2007), 424, www.econlib.org/library/Enc/PropertyRights.html.

71. Grudem and Asmus, *Poverty of Nations*, 208–9.

72. George Gilder, *Wealth and Poverty* (Washington, DC: Regnery, 2012), 332. For further discussion of the role of the mind in economics, see Warren T. Brookes, *The Economy in Mind* (New York: Universe Books, 1982).

73. David M. Kennedy, Lizabeth Cohen, and Thomas A. Bailey, *The American Pageant: A History of the American People*, 14th ed. (Boston: Cengage Learning, 2010), 571, quoted in Burton W. Folsom Jr., *The Myth of the Robber Barons: A New Look at the Rise of Big Business in America*, 6th ed. (Herndon, VA: Young America's Foundation, 2010), 122.

74. Folsom, *Myth of the Robber Barons*.

75. Folsom, *Myth of the Robber Barons*, 123–24.

76. See Scott D. Allen, *Beyond the Sacred-Secular Divide: A Call to Wholistic Ministry* (Seattle: YWAM, 2011).

77. Robert L. Thomas, ed., *New American Standard Exhaustive Concordance of the Bible; Hebrew-Aramaic and Greek Dictionaries* (Nashville: Holman Bible Publishers, 1981), s.v. "*abad*" (Strong's no. 5646).

78. Miller, "Community Renewal." For more on this, refer to Miller, *LifeWork*, and the companion website www.mondaychurch.publishpath.org/theology.

79. Lesslie Newbigin, *Foolishness to the Greeks: The Gospel and Western Culture* (Grand Rapids: Eerdmans, 1986), 132.

80. Jeffrey Katzenberg, quoted in Catherine Clinch, "Have Faith … Hollywood Is Trying," Movieguide, accessed August 5, 2016, www.movieguide.org/news-articles/faithhollywood.html.

81. Diane Howard, "Hollywood's New Renaissance and Reformation," MovieGuide, accessed August 5, 2016, www.movieguide.org/news-articles/hollywoods-new-renaissance-reformation.html.

82. Howard, "Hollywood's New Renaissance."

83. Robert McKee, *Story: Substance, Structure, Style, and the Principles of Screenwriting* (New York: Regan Books, 1997), 13.

84. Brian Godawa, *Hollywood Worldviews: Watching Films with Wisdom and Discernment* (Downers Grove, IL: InterVarsity, 2002), 15.

85. Ted Baer's 2012 report to the entertainment industry, cited in Clinch, "Have Faith."

86. Profitability data from the MPAA ratings, 2005–2009. The following chart, derived from Clinch's Movieguide article, vividly supports the claim that family-friendly films are immensely more popular than non-family-friendly ones.

1,000 FILMS OVER 5-YEAR PERIOD, 2005–2009	
% Rated R, PG-13, PG or G	**Average Profit**
Rated R—38%	$12.7 million
Rated PG-13—41%	$59.7 million

Rated PG—18%	$65.5 million
Rated G—3%	$108.5 million
Total—100%	Average—$61.6 million

87. Clinch, "Have Faith."

88. Peter Berger's book on redeeming laughter is an excellent resource for those wanting to tell good stories. See Peter L. Berger, *Redeeming Laughter: The Comic Dimension of Human Experience* (Berlin, Ger.: Walter de Gruyter, 1997), 188.

89. Berger, *Redeeming Laughter*, 194.

90. Ephesians 6:12 (KJV): "We wrestle not against flesh and blood, but against principalities, against powers, against the rulers of the darkness of this world, against spiritual wickedness in high places."

91. Romans 8:22: "We know that the whole creation has been groaning together in the pains of childbirth until now."

92. See, for example, Hebrews 11:36–40: "Some were tortured, refusing to accept release, so that they might rise again to a better life. Others suffered mocking and flogging, and even chains and imprisonment. They were stoned, they were sawn in two, they were killed with the sword. They went about in skins of sheep and goats, destitute, afflicted, mistreated— of whom the world was not worthy—wandering about in deserts and mountains, and in dens and caves of the earth. And all these, though commended through their faith, did not receive what was promised, since God had provided something better for us, that apart from us they should not be made perfect."

93. James Davison Hunter developed and explained these categories—cultural, political, and economic capital—in *To Change the World: The Irony, Tragedy, and Possibility of Christianity in the Late Modern World* (New York: Oxford University Press, 2010).

94. Gary Pierson, quoted in Ian Thomsen, "Tragedy Forges Bond between Thunder, Oklahoma City: Twenty Years after Bombing, Franchise Reflects City's Values," NBA.com, April 19, 2015, www.nba.com/2015/news/features/ian_thomsen /04/19/thunder-and the-oklahoma-standard/.

95. Doug Serven, quoted in Russ Pulliam, "Joining the Big Leagues," *World* 27, no. 5 (March 10, 2012), www.worldmag.com /2012/02/joining_the_big_leagues.

96. Thomsen, "Tragedy Forges Bond"; see also Randy Lee Loftis, "Oklahoma City National Memorial and Museum Aspires to Be Testament to Past, Source of Hope," *Dallas Morning News*, April 18, 2015, www.dallasnews.com/news/local-news /20150418-oklahoma-city-national-memorial-and-museum-aspires-to-be-testament to past-source-of-hope ece.

97. Kevin Durant, quoted in Thomsen, "Tragedy Forges Bond."

98. Dietrich Bonhoeffer, *Letters and Papers from Prison* (New York: Touchstone, 1997), 382.

99. Gary Edmonds, president of Breakthrough Partners, shared these insights as part of a Disciple Nations Alliance Monday Church Conference in Nairobi, Kenya.

100. Teachers are visionaries who are passionate about ideas and shapers who can lend form to ideas. They know that ideas rule the world, and they're driven to communicate those ideas through teaching, writing, social media, films, and many other media. Teachers know they're successful when people are persuaded, set free from false ideas, and moved to action. Vishal Mangalwadi, an Indian Christian philosopher, writer, lecturer, and social reformer as well as the founder of the Revelation Movement, is such a person. Vishal travels the world sharing messages that challenge his listeners to see the world in very different light. See "Vishal Mangalwadi," Revelation Movement, accessed August 5, 2016, www.revelationmovement.com/.

101. Modelers are doers. They can't wait to put ideas into practice. They develop workable models and test ideas. Darrow Miller offers the example of Anna and Nam Ho, who are classic modelers. From the ideas they learned from the Disciple Nations Alliance, Miller's organization, they created a successful model—Truth Centered Transformation (TCT). Their model has been replicated in more than 1,500 churches and communities in their nation. They've seen powerful community renewal take place in a relatively short period of time via this model. Now Anna and Nam have founded the nonprofit Reconciled World to replicate the model in other Asian countries and beyond. See "About: Truth Centered Transformation (TCT)," Reconciled World, accessed August 5, 2016, http://reconciledworld.org/our-programs /truth-centered-transformation/.

102. Connectors bring people and organizations together. They like forming alliances and partnerships and enjoy working with others. Connectors believe the African proverb "If you want to go fast, go alone. If you want to go far, go together." They know they've been successful when the ideas they're working with spread to different networks and spheres of society.

103. Stanley Milgram, "The Small World Problem," *Psychology Today* 1, no. 1 (May 1967): 61–67, http://measure.igpp.ucla .edu/GK12-SEE-LA/Lesson_Files_09/Tina_Wey/TW_social_networks_Milgram_1967_small_world_problem.pdf.

104. Matthew 6:8–13: "Do not be like [the pagans], for your Father knows what you need before you ask him. Pray then like this: 'Our Father in heaven, hallowed be your name. Your kingdom come, your will be done, on earth as it is in heaven. Give us this day our daily bread, and forgive us our debts, as we also have forgiven our debtors. And lead us not into temptation, but deliver us from evil.'"

105. William Y. Fullerton, "I Cannot Tell Why He, Whom Angels Worship," 1920. Sung to the tune of "Londonderry Air."

CHAPTER 18

18

CONCLUSION

1. So ... Should Christians Try to Make a Difference?

Let's pretend you've gained a ride on the Virgin Galactic spaceship we talked about in chapter 1, thanks to a donated $250,000 ticket. You can hardly believe your good fortune as you rocket into space alongside wise-cracking movie stars and billionaire playboys. Suddenly the engines shut off, and you feel something only a few hundred people in all of human history have experienced. Free from the earth's gravity, you gaze out the window at the curve of the earth and the blackness of space beyond. Even the celebrities on your flight are speechless with awe.

From high above the earth's atmosphere, you can see the outline of continents. You can see the brownness of deserts, the greenness of forests, and the blueness of oceans. But are you seeing what is important?

Understanding the Culture has been woven together with one golden strand: what matters most in a biblical worldview is people. Seas and mountains express majesty. The intricacy of the ecosystem inspires wonder. But nothing in creation transcends the significance of the *imago Dei*, the image of God expressed in you and me and everyone around us.

Who God has shown himself to be in nature and the Bible affects not only how we see the world but also how we answer questions about where we came from, who we are, what is real and true, how we should live, and what the future holds.

In turn, how we answer ultimate questions like these affects what we do with culture. Our answers touch every one of the big issues of our day, whether those answers are right or wrong. I firmly believe that God exists and the Bible is true and that these facts provide satisfying answers to our deepest questions. But giving evidence for God's existence and the Bible's truth wasn't the point of this book (if you'd like to explore such evidence, I'd encourage you to read through the first book in this trilogy, *Understanding the Faith*). Rather, *Understanding the Culture* sought to demonstrate that answering our ultimate questions based on God's general revelation in nature and his special revelation in the Bible gives us creative, powerful solutions to society's toughest problems.

> Solutions derived from the Bible's teachings about God, humanity, and the world offer hope and clarity about how to treat people and live together in harmony.

Solutions derived from the Bible's teachings about God, humanity, and the world offer hope and clarity about how to treat people and live together in harmony. They bring peace and wholeness and abundance. They unleash human ingenuity. Most important, they point the way for people to be reconciled to God.

Some Christians have given in to hopelessness. They're in hiding and waiting for a chance to escape. It's a mistake to think this way. No matter the odds, we ought to try to make a difference based on a Christian **worldview**. We know this because of three things God cares about:

1. God cares about his "glory" (Ps. 79:9; Rev. 21:23).[1] In his glory God has made a way for us to be made whole and to live for him (1 Cor. 10:31; 2 Pet. 1:3).[2]

2. God cares that we bear his image (Gen. 1:26–28).[3] Humans have a special place in God's creation.

3. God cares that we love our neighbors (Lev. 19:9–15; Matt. 22:37–40).[4]

The Bible offers many good reasons for making a difference, but these three aspects of God's nature provide guidance on all the issues we've discussed in this book. The other worldviews we examined in *Understanding the Times* all disagree with one or more of these three aspects. Their solutions to society's pressing problems are paltry and unsatisfying in consequence.

CONCLUSION

Equipping us for our task, God has also provided wisdom (Prov. 4:7).[5] He's given us the power to live worthy lives (Phil. 1:27; 4:8).[6] And he has enabled us to speak truth (Prov. 18:21; 25:11).[7] Each chapter of this book has been like a log stacked inside the fire ring of culture. Our job in this final chapter is to light the match. We'll begin by first reviewing what culture is.

2. WHAT IS CULTURE?

Andy Crouch defines **culture** as "what we make of the world."[8] To understand culture, we need to examine its (1) artifacts; (2) institutions; (3) practices; (4) beliefs; (5) moods, styles, and ethos; and (6) metabeliefs.[9] By being thoughtful and observant, we have the opportunity to become "cultural anthropologists" who understand the times and know what steps we humans ought to take next (1 Chron. 12:32).[10]

> *Culture:* the way of life for a group of people; the culmination of human communication and willful activity in a particular civilization.

Yet understanding culture is only the beginning. We also have the opportunity to help *create* it. We are, as James Davison Hunter puts it, "world-makers."[11] In chapter 2, I shared the story of the Chungkai Japanese prison camp during World War II, in which horrifying conditions and brutal treatment pushed captives to adopt a Darwinian, me-first mind-set. At the risk of their own lives, a handful of believers inspired a Christ-like you-first mind-set. It transformed the camp. That mind-set can do the same today.

Worldviews that deny suffering, submit to fate, or coldly envision a world of mere survival of the fittest are unable to harvest the full fruits of this kind of transformation. Real change requires a worldview that recognizes a truth higher than ourselves, puts others first, and fears nothing—not even death. A worldview based on Christ relates to every aspect of culture.[12] Christ isn't against culture; he is in it, transforming it. Because of this, we should take culture seriously. We should seek to create new culture. Culture is part of our mission of spreading the good news.

Understanding the call to transform culture changes how we live. If Christ is indeed a transformer of culture, then we ought to imitate *him* not *culture*. We surrender to God, not to our circumstances. We don't seek to escape this world; we seek to engage it.

Of course, engaging culture takes a great deal of discernment. We risk becoming like the thing we seek to transform. Because of this temptation, Christians often worry about how to respond: Should we condemn culture? Should we admonish those who produce it? Should we ignore it? As it turns out, these are questions Christians have been wrestling with for nearly two thousand years.

3. CHRISTIANITY AND CULTURE: A HISTORY

Christians throughout history have ignored the criticism that Christianity should be tolerated only as a private belief. They've exerted an enormous positive influence as a result.

Christians seek to make a difference because of their beliefs about the cause, nature, and purpose of the universe. These three things—cause, nature, and purpose—are what make up a religion.[13] And because everyone lives as if certain beliefs about these things are true, everyone is religious. Religious belief is to culture what an artistic style, such as impressionism, is to a painting. A painting is the product of an artist's beliefs about the universe, combined with skill. Similarly, a person's religion guides what he or she thinks should or shouldn't be done in the world.

Though all religions—even atheism—are based on beliefs, some religions focus more on what we *do* than what we *think*. Christianity isn't like this. The Bible calls Christians to be mindful (Rom. 12:2).[14] It's not just about right actions. It's about the connection between right actions and right thinking. We're to love God with all our hearts, souls, minds, and strength. This involves thought and belief. We're then to love our neighbors as ourselves, which puts belief into practice (Luke 10:27).[15]

> Christians seek to make a difference because of their beliefs about the cause, nature, and purpose of the universe. These three things are what make up a religion.

Furthermore, Christianity doesn't just focus on *avoiding* what's bad; it also focuses on *pursuing* what's good. Believing rightly is a key to this focus. Yes, we want to regulate traffic and punish crime, but we also want to create art, educate people, and express love to those in need.

Throughout the book, we've seen how Christians, acting on their biblical beliefs,

- advanced human rights,

- applied biblical principles of justice and dignity to fight for the abolition of slavery,

- secured the basis of rights for women and children,

- established modern education,

- formed the practice of modern medicine,

- instituted principles of modern charity,

- built the foundations of modern science, and

- shaped the arts.

Christians have wielded a weighty influence in nearly every aspect of Western culture—and other cultures as well. The Christians who exerted an influence probably didn't realize how their contribution would shape things for generations to come, but it has been clear throughout this book that history's culture shapers influenced the world *because* of their Christian faith, not in spite of it. We, too, ought to choose to live in a way that makes life more worthwhile for others. But how specifically do we do this?

4. Christianity and Culture: A Plan

Christians tend to make the greatest difference in the midst of crisis. Just as starving people appreciate a good meal more than those who've just eaten, cultures that are exhausted, in pain, and fighting insecurity more readily welcome truth.

But if we wait until the moment of crisis, we'll miss many of our greatest opportunities. Difference makers don't wait. Instead, they take two actions. First, they develop a *posture of engagement* in advance. Like a search-and-rescue team that knows every square acre of a wilderness area, Christians familiar with the cultural terrain are more likely to arrive in time to help. A posture of engagement, as we saw in chapter 4, involves three things: (1) "reading" the times accurately, (2) "writing" culture by engaging at an intellectual level, and (3) "entering" culture by forming groups of like-minded people who influence others.

But that's not all. Culture shapers establish a *direction of engagement*. This involves understanding that God made creation good. Human sin is a parasite in this good creation, but through Christ's redemptive sacrifice on the cross, God has broken sin's grip. He is "making all things new" (Rev. 21:5). Culture shapers put their strong sense of direction to work by asking insightful questions, such as,

> Culture shapers put their strong sense of direction to work by asking insightful questions.

- "What is good in our culture that we can promote, protect, and celebrate?"

- "What is missing in our culture that we can creatively contribute?"

- "What is evil in our culture that we can stop?"

- "What is broken in our culture that we can restore?"[16]

Think about how you might answer these four questions. If you're like me, lots of society's problems come to mind, many of which may seem overwhelming. The world's systems seem so permanent, so established. But they really aren't. Take business, for example. Within five years of its founding, Uber blew past elite Fortune 500 transportation companies in market value. It became bigger than FedEx, which had been operating for more than forty years, and Delta Airlines, which had been operating for more than eighty-five years.[17]

Similarly, tiny pro-life ministries like Live Action are giving fits to the huge and lavishly funded proabortion company Planned Parenthood. Everyday people, who are living redemptively, can become culture shapers in ways that might at first seem impossible.

Of course, cultural innovation is never without risks. If good has any value, evil will always try to steal it. A printing press with movable type might be used to print lies as well as truth. A free market that enables us to develop beneficial products also enables people to traffic in abusive sex and drugs. Weapons used to keep the peace can also be used to spark violence.

This is why the Bible warns us not to be taken captive by the philosophies of our day (Col. 2:8).[18]

If we're lazy or insensitive to Jesus, we can be overrun. Sin makes us dumb. It deceives us. A posture of engagement and a God-focused direction of engagement are essential for positive culture shaping.

> A posture of engagement and a God-focused direction of engagement are essential for positive culture shaping.

Yet there's something more. We might have a posture of engagement and a strong direction of engagement but still fail to have a shaping influence. We need to know how to *communicate* truth to others, especially those who don't want to hear it.

5. THINKING AND SPEAKING CLEARLY

Christians haven't cornered the market on doing good. Lots of people from lots of religious traditions have done good things. Christianity is unique, though, in that it accounts for aspects of reality that other worldviews ignore. The first and second books in this trilogy, *Understanding the Faith* and *Understanding the Times*, showcase Christianity's reasonableness and resilience. The Christian worldview not only meets the tests of reason, evidence, and good consequences but also is deeply satisfying on an emotional level, speaking to our hopes and dreams as well as our fears and disappointments.

> *Valid Argument:* a properly formed argument.

Clearheadedness ought to be highly valued as a Christian virtue. We must reason well. We must take words seriously. Instead of making an invalid argument, we must learn to make a **valid argument** to support each conclusion we draw. We must forsake name-calling, defensiveness, and muddled thinking. We're to be transformed by renewing our minds so we can know and do God's will (Rom. 12:2).[19]

Good arguments are those accurately drawn from true premises. They're relevant. They're complete and fair, and they address the points at hand. Bad arguments, on the other hand, attack people or call their motives into question rather than addressing the points at hand. They try to frighten or threaten people or make them feel shame, all while coating reality in a thick layer of triviality (like bumper-sticker pronouncements). Bad arguments confuse definitions of terms. They engage in circular reasoning (assuming in a premise what the arguer is trying to prove in the conclusion). They appeal to invalid authorities (for example, authorities who are unreliable or have a reason to deceive or exaggerate). They appeal to ignorance (saying the claim must be true because no one has proven it false). In short, they trick people into arriving at conclusions that aren't merited based on the evidence provided.

Good arguments build trust, helping an audience make good decisions based on what is *right* rather than feeling coerced into serving someone's selfish interests. Good arguments form a clear message and boldly ask people to act. But in the end, good arguments don't persuade people. People persuade themselves. An old saying applies here: "A man convinced against his will is of the same opinion still." All we can do is provide our audience with good reasons for what we believe. Some will embrace them; some won't. We can't control the outcome, but we can control whether we'll be trustworthy. When people trust us, they're more likely to agree to help.

Being trustworthy is especially important in a culture that is constantly trying to manipulate us. Authentic persuasion avoids manipulation. It pursues what is true. It encourages an emotionally healthy response. It seeks the good of others (Matt. 20:28).[20] It treats others as we would wish to be treated (Matt. 7:12).[21]

It appeals to right motives. Manipulative arguments violate every one of these principles. They lead to propaganda, such as the kind the Nazis used to get people to hate Jews.

Most persuasion doesn't take place in speeches. People who dialogue well *listen* as much as they *talk*. Their goal isn't just to be right. It is to learn—and to help others learn—the truth. They learn to ask good questions (such as "What do you mean by that?"). They see the flaws in wrong views and ask people to consider adopting true ones.

As we think clearly, persuade rightly, and dialogue honestly, we stay focused on one aim: speaking the truth in love. That's how we grow up in Christ (Eph. 4:15).[22]

Once we properly understand what Christ wants, we can turn our attention to some of the big issues we face today. We can be clear eyed about what culture is and how we might influence it, drawing inspiration from those who have gone before and acting with integrity.

> People who dialogue well *listen* as much as they *talk*. Their goal isn't just to be right. It is to learn—and to help others learn—the truth.

In this book, we've looked at the following issues: technology, the arts and entertainment, the value of human life, sexuality, marriage, creation care, politics, religious freedom and persecution, poverty care and cure, the use of force, justice, and community renewal. Each chapter has focused on making good arguments and applying relevant biblical principles—namely, who God is, what it means to bear his image, and how we might love our neighbors better as a result.

Technology was the first issue we tackled. Technology is central to our lives, and it can tempt us to lose focus, isolate ourselves, be superficial, and give in to evil.

6. TECHNOLOGY

Technology makes our lives easier, safer, more comfortable, and more secure. It makes possible the rapid spread of information. More information, however, doesn't necessarily make us wiser. **Wisdom**—not just knowledge—should be our goal. As the late theologian Howard Hendricks reportedly said, "When God measures a man, he puts the tape around the heart, not the head."

Technology has led to a tremendous amount of good in human history. From the time Cain developed techniques for growing crops and Abel developed techniques for tending sheep, humans have used technology to make life easier. Technology is an accelerator. It saves time, which people use to invent more things. This in turn leads to more inventiveness, which grows wealth. This is how humanity went from primitive farming techniques to waterwheels to computers in just a few hundred years.[23]

During this fertile period of imagination, a stark difference emerged between the Christian worldview and other worldviews. Cultures based on non-Christian worldviews had more advanced technology, in some cases. But lacking a concept of God's image in every person, the elites tended to use technology as a plaything rather than a way to make the lives of everyday people better.

> **Cyberculture: the modern values, habits, and social conditions brought about by the widespread use of the Internet.**

Modern technology is in dire need of shifting its focus from a non-Christian worldview to a Christian worldview. Today, computer-based devices have created a **cyberculture** that accelerates both the good and the bad of technology. This cyberculture has driven down costs, saved time, and increased comfort. Unfortunately, it has also distracted us with shallow communication and made it much easier than ever before to forfeit our innocence through degrading, demeaning, perverse content.

Technology isn't neutral. It *does* some things, but it also *undoes* other things.[24] As MIT professor Sherry Turkle puts it, "We make our technologies, and they, in turn, make and shape us."[25] If we fail to cultivate habits of the heart, such as discernment, moderation, wisdom, humility, authenticity, and diversity, we risk losing a sense of what it means to bear God's image well. In the process, we lose sight of what the "good life" is and what it means to be human.[26] Technology doesn't *make* us do anything, but it can seduce us away from God's best for our lives. It tempts us to become unfocused, isolated, superficial, and unable to resist evil.

Ultimately, a Christian worldview rescues technology from itself. It not only helps us save time for the most important things, such as making life better for others, but it also reminds us that it isn't the most important thing. Virtue is. After all, technology may change rapidly, but what makes a person virtuous never changes. Knowing this, we must avoid using technology to hide from reality. We ought to be suspicious of technology that makes life easier while making relationships weaker. Remembering who we are in God's story helps us maintain the balance. This is especially important, since technology, such as smartphones, puts entertainment in front of us twenty-four hours a day, moving us from being informed and amazed to being idle and merely amused.

7. THE ARTS AND ENTERTAINMENT

To muse means "to think," and *a* means "without." **Amusement** *is entertainment without thought.* No one sets out with a goal of becoming apathetic and ignorant. Rather, we cross the line between relaxing **entertainment** and addiction to amusement without realizing we've done so. Entertainment doesn't make us shallow; it reveals our shallowness.

> **Technology may change rapidly, but what makes a person virtuous never changes. Remembering who we are in God's story helps us maintain a balance between technology and "the good life."**

Our amusements also reveal our fear of not finding what we're looking for in life. This is a fear so deep that we find ourselves willing to accept a vision of life hyped by those who make money from writing new songs, inventing new fashions, or producing "groundbreaking" new television shows and movies. By tethering our lives to what is constantly changing, we find ourselves anxious about being ignorant of the latest trends and cultural references. To be "out of it," in a certain sense, is to cease to exist as persons. True, entertainment can help relieve stress and bring us happiness. But it can also enslave our affections, destroy contentment, and make us restless and angry. At that point, we can hardly recognize ourselves.

Entertainment is as old as humanity. Ancient cultures all used stories, music, athletics, and celebrations to express joy and bond people together. The nature of entertainment changed during the Age of Enlightenment, though. People began thinking of the world as a two-story building. The upper story was furnished with feelings and preferences. The lower story was furnished with facts and science. Though the real action took place on the lower story, Enlightenment thinkers believed, they could

> Entertainment can help relieve stress and bring us happiness. But it can also enslave our affections, destroy contentment, and make us restless and angry.

always rise to the upper story when they needed a break from reality. Art became entertainment, which in turn became trivial amusement. Art didn't deepen people's understanding of reality; it was a way of escaping from reality.

The Christian worldview has an answer to the idea of using entertainment to escape from reality: we need to let Christ peel back the layers of our fallenness and bring healing not just to release us from the pain but to give purpose to our lives.

Throughout human history, the arts have helped express human purpose. The highest and best of Western art has Christianity's fingerprints all over it. Shakespeare liberally quoted from the Bible; he trusted his audience's understanding of it to grasp his subtle allusions. The very structure of Western music follows the biblical pattern of creation, fall, and redemption. So, too, great literature reminds us of the horror of sin, the honor of self-sacrifice, and the glory of redemption pictured in a story's ultimate resolution.

This is because the Christian worldview isn't an upper-story or lower-story truth. It's a "whole building" truth: all truth is God's truth, and the story of the world is that God both created and redeemed it through his Son, Jesus Christ. The upper story and the lower story are resolved through the incarnation: God is with us. We ought to care about the arts and entertainment just as we ought to care about everything else.

Still, we must learn to discern the difference between false stories that distract us from reality and true stories that enable us to be fully attentive to it.

But being discerning Christians isn't just about how to be wiser as consumers of culture. It's about how to produce good culture. This takes imagination and hard work. In chapter 7, we learned the story behind the movie *Up*, which filmmakers turned from an upper-story tale about two quarreling rich kids into a whole-building story about honor, caring, hope, and finding significance. Producing a good movie required director Pete Docter to dig deep into his own pain and insecurities to ask, "What is this story *really* about?"[27] To make the final story deeply meaningful, filmmakers had to risk letting go of what made the initial story amusing but trivial.

> The Christian worldview is a "whole building" truth: all truth is God's truth, and the story of the world is that God both created and redeemed it through his Son, Jesus Christ.

We ought to do the same. Why settle for being amused with low-risk, small stories when God is telling a much bigger story that we're part of?

Many today like to think of our culture as residing in the lower story of facts and science. But facts and science apart from an understanding of who God is can mislead us. We can end up missing the whole point of what it means to bear God's image. Indeed, when people embrace facts and science apart from an understanding of who God is, they entirely miss the point of what makes human life special.

8. THE VALUE OF HUMAN LIFE

When two-thirds of college freshmen say they think **abortion** should be legal, we don't have a culture of life.[28] We have a culture of death. Of course, even abortion advocates recognize that abortion destroys human life. But to many people, this doesn't mean an unborn human has value. If nothing outside of the material world exists—if there is no God and no certain truth—then human value comes down to one of two things. First is the **performance view of human life**, which states that people who don't meet certain requirements, such as self-awareness, don't have the value others do. Second is the **utilitarian view of human life**, which says that if those around us stand to lose more than we stand to gain by our existence, then it's better for us not to exist. Both the performance view and the utilitarian view make human value a matter of degree.

> *Utilitarian View of Human Life:* **the belief that a human being's value is measured relative to the value of other human beings (e.g., disabled, malformed, etc.).**

If human value is based *in any way* on degree, then there is no solid basis for all people having equal worth.[29] Unborn humans who are unwanted—and who cannot stand up for their own interests—aren't especially valuable. Those at the very end of their lives are also without value, which is why **euthanasia** (which means "easy death" in Greek) is on the rise. Usually this is achieved through **passive euthanasia**, which involves withholding treatment so that a person will die. Other times it is achieved through **active euthanasia**, in which a physician takes terminal action against a patient.[30] In both circumstances, the intent is for the patient to die. To some, this is hardly controversial: we put suffering pets to sleep out of mercy, so why not apply the same practice to people?

But when we embrace the practice of killing as a legitimate medical treatment, we cross a line of intent. We're then faced with questions like "Who gets to decide who lives and dies, and for what kind of sickness is death a proper treatment?" Once this line has been crossed, people very quickly lose the ability to choose life. In some countries where euthanasia is legal, doctors actively euthanize elderly patients outside of the accepted and legal protocols.[31] Clearly, some doctors have decided that "right to die" means "right to kill."

> *Endowment View of Human Life:* **the belief that all human beings have intrinsic value simply because they are human.**

Christians who believe in the **endowment view of human life** should care because the *imago Dei* is the foundation for valuing human life. Humans are bearers of God's image in their *created* state; being human is, in itself, image bearing. When facing those who make fierce arguments in favor of abortion and euthanasia, we must remember that it's up to those who recognize

God's image in every person—and who are committed to loving their neighbors—to make the case for life. In chapter 8, we looked at many things we can do, from supporting those in crisis pregnancies to refuting anti-life arguments. We need to do what we can, being on the lookout for and taking care of the most helpless in our communities (Matt. 25:40; Gal. 2:10; James 1:27).[32]

Of the two anti-life issues we discussed in chapter 8, the issue of abortion is the one that garners the most attention. Millions of lives are at risk. And the reason has nothing to do with whether terminating pregnancies is medically necessary. It has to do with a revolution that has taken place in America over the past one hundred years, a sexual revolution dictating that nothing—not even the humanity of the unborn—should be allowed to stand in the way of sexual freedom. As a result, sexual brokenness has become epidemic, and the call for Christians to speak truth into this aspect of culture has taken on greater urgency than ever before.

> Sexual brokenness has become epidemic, and the call for Christians to speak truth into this aspect of culture has taken on greater urgency than ever before.

9. SEXUALITY

If the Secularists are right and the material world is all that exists, then human beings don't really have souls. Indeed, we don't even have minds—just brains. Nor is there any reality that exists outside of what we can taste, see, smell, hear, or touch. If only the physical world exists, then our bodies are all we have. And those who hold this worldview insist that because our sexual impulses are our strongest biochemical reactions, sexual expression is how we become authentic persons.

Two aspects of sexual expression are behind the **sexual revolution**: removing the link between God-given design and sexual identity and liberating people from the idea that sexual choices should somehow be governed by morality. The cost has been high. Tens of millions of Americans now live with sexually transmitted diseases (STDs), many of which have no cure. The impact on personal and public morality has been devastating. At its heart, the sexual revolution is a struggle for culture itself.

A Christian worldview has a lot to say about sex. It begins with a surprising fact: God loves sex. In fact, he invented it. If we pay close attention to what God says in the Bible, we can learn to love sex too and find sexual fulfillment in faithful marital relationships.[33]

The sexual revolution promised to set people free, but instead it only enslaved them to disordered sexuality, confusion about sexual identity, **pornography**, and sexual politics. This shifting sexual landscape has displaced the institution of exclusive, permanent man-woman marriage and the stability it provides men, women, and children.

A Christian worldview, as outlined in the Bible, holds up a standard of sexual wholeness. This starts with the creation of male and female in Genesis 1:27, something Jesus also affirmed (Matt. 19:4).[34] Maleness and femaleness were portrayed as important even before Adam and Eve had sex.[35] Hebrews 13:4 says, "Let marriage be held in honor among all, and let the marriage bed be undefiled, for God will judge the sexually immoral and adulterous."

The message of today's culture is that our identity is based upon our sexual urges. The Christian worldview acknowledges that we are sexual beings, but it places our identity in something far beyond biochemistry: God's image in us, redeemed in Christ. Being secure in Christ, we can pursue sexual purity, closeness with God, and self-giving friendship.

Undoubtedly, the call to **sexual purity** is a radical one that includes being open and honest about our sexual urges and failings and experiencing God's grace in our sexual brokenness. The most radical aspect of sexual purity is recognizing that even in marriage, only God can ultimately meet our need for intimacy. Only God can really know us as we want to be known. Only God can love us without condition. Only God offers complete forgiveness. In turn, our capacity for intimacy with him overflows into the ability to share love with others and to receive love from them.[36]

> *Intimacy:* having a close or familiar relationship that meets a deep need of being known and loved.

Intimacy with God isn't just the basis of sexual wholeness; it's also the basis of the good life. And in God's plan, intimacy is the basis of a dying institution that is the bedrock of a stable civilization: the institution of marriage.

10. MARRIAGE

A key indicator of a society's state of health is the state of marriage. Men and women who are married, with children, are a society's most basic stabilizing influence. The Christian worldview has a lot to say about marriage and related topics of love, sex, singleness, dating, kids, family relationships, and life purpose.

Marriage can be defined as "a permanent, comprehensive, exclusive union between a man and a woman that involves the capacity to bear children and raise them in a stable environment." Government has a vested interest in promoting the kinds of marriages that have a uniquely stabilizing influence on society. Man-woman marriage is of that kind. Other kinds of relationships can be stable, of course, such as mentoring relationships. But their impact is short term and localized. They don't create culture and sustain civilizations over time.

> *Natural Law:* the belief that morality can be seen in the natural order of creation and accessed through human reason; the belief that laws are rules based upon on an internal code of morality that all people possess.

The biblical idea of marriage adds enormous depth to what we understand about this institution from **natural law**. The Christian worldview says that God designed marriage. Marriage expresses God's very nature in a way that helps humans flourish.

We bear God's image, in part, through marriage. God is relational: Father, Son and Holy Spirit. God's personal nature and the relationship between the members of the Trinity establish a pattern for the kind of relational depth that makes marriage what it is. Genesis 1:26 quotes God as saying, "Let *us* make man in our image, after our likeness." Then God proceeded to make man (humankind), male and female. Both men and women bear God's image. We are living, moving representations of him. Beginning with God's image, marriage creates oneness. Marriage is such a mysteriously good kind of relationship that in the New Testament, the apostle Paul used it to picture the oneness of Christ and the church.

Today, though, a spiritual battle surrounds marriage. This battle is often fought in the courts, which insist on redefining marriage as something other than a permanent, comprehensive, exclusive union between a man and a woman. Meanwhile, as marriages fail, the cost to society skyrockets. Government is called on to provide the stability that marriage once provided. And government is faltering.

Yet marriage isn't just something husbands and wives should think about. Singles ought to think about the significance of marriage as well, committing to being single with purpose. Adam had purpose in the garden before God created Eve. Before he married, he was busy taking responsibility. The creation story is told in such a way as to demonstrate the significance of singleness in God's design.

> The creation story is told in such a way as to demonstrate the significance of singleness in God's design.

God designed marriage. The family was his idea. We have before us an opportunity to be restorers of the family as God designed it. This has everything to do with how we live as single people or married people. It affects home life, work, child rearing, and stewardship of our time and talents. It affects public policy and citizenship. And most important, it's life affirming. Human life has special value to God. Of course, this is a politically incorrect thing to say these days, when humans are seen as part of the problem rather than part of the solution. This brings us to one of the most controversial topics of our day: how to care for the planet in a way that elevates people rather than diminishes them.

11. Creation Care

No one wants an unhealthy planet. No one thinks cities look nicer when they're polluted. No one is proud of trash piling up in their communities or floating in their rivers. No one rejoices when wild animals die off or the beauty of nature is carelessly ravaged. But what people think ought to be done about the environment says as much about their worldview as it says about the planet's condition. As we saw in chapter 11, many environmental efforts are dominated by special-interest groups that believe people are a cancer on the planet. Saying that people are good and that we ought to have more of them is an unforgivable heresy to these groups.

There seem to be two sides to the environmental movement. One side has embraced **environmentalism** as an alternative to believing in God. The other side is spiritual: nature *is* god, and environmental damage is a spiritual offense. If Christians fail to involve themselves, these two groups will dominate the environmental debate. Christianity asserts that it would be better if humans prospered. Environmental extremism argues that it would be better if humans disappeared. We can't have it both ways.

A properly focused Christian worldview cares for creation. God made it. He reigns over it. He sustains it. God has given human beings **stewardship** over his creation, not to brutalize it but to care for it. Certainly, human sinfulness affects our ability to steward creation.

> *Stewardship:* the process of managing something that has been entrusted to one's care.

But sin doesn't end our responsibility; it intensifies it. Redemption is meant to save us *for* life on this earth, not *from* it.

If, as Psalm 24:1 (NIV) says, "the earth is the LORD's, and everything in it," then we bear God's image best by understanding what God sees in creation and then pursuing his priorities, such as abundance and beauty. Caring for creation, though, doesn't begin with rocks and trees and plants. It begins with people.

Some environmental extremists say that people are the problem. The Christian worldview acknowledges humanity's destructive tendencies, but it also acknowledges that people are part of the solution. When people are free to bear God's image as creators and caretakers, when they're pulled out of poverty and pollution and illness, their influence on the world can be profoundly healing.[37]

Surprisingly, one of the keys to environmental healing is for people to increase their wealth. When people have greater wealth, they can take better care of themselves, their families, and their surroundings. They can put screens on their windows to help avoid disease-carrying mosquitoes. They can afford cooking methods that don't fill their homes with poisonous smoke. They can use their time in creative pursuits rather than stripping trees for firewood. When they don't have to worry about where their next meal will come from, they can turn their attention to cleaning up streams and properly disposing of waste. Those who believe that only the material world exists see wealth as something we get only by ravaging the planet. But the Christian worldview recognizes that wealth is created when we use our minds. The more that people are free to think and dream and create, the fewer natural resources they must consume and the more time and effort they spend living in a way that's healthier for the planet.[38]

> The Christian worldview acknowledges humanity's destructive tendencies, but it also acknowledges that people are part of the solution.

Christians can—and should—care for creation. We can glorify God by studying the majesty of what he has made. We can bear his image by being good stewards of what he has entrusted to us. We can love our neighbors by caring for them and helping them bear God's image more fully. This is the essence of creation care. This last part, caring for people, involves something more than caring for creation. It involves making sure our communities are just and orderly, which moves our discussion squarely into the oft-dreaded realm of politics.

12. POLITICS

We're told that politics and religion don't mix, especially if that religion is Christianity. Many Christians have come to believe that. But wherever two or more people are gathered,

> *Politics:* the study of community governance.

politics—which comes from the Greek word for that which relates to the citizens within a community—will be part of their common life. If Christians want to ensure that people are treated justly, that society is orderly, and that leaders do what they're supposed to do, then we must be involved in politics.

Not getting involved allows people of other worldviews to decide what to do, and they could very well do the wrong thing. Many politicians subscribe to a secular worldview that says God is irrelevant to politics, or a Marxist worldview that says the church—along with businesses and the institution of the family—is to blame for things going wrong. As Islam rises, things become even more complicated. Islam teaches that government ought to be based on Islamic law, sharia, so that everyone will come under the submission of Allah.

Deceived or intimidated by these arguments, some Christians timidly step aside. But that's not the right thing to do. Instead, believers ought to discern a biblical basis for political involvement and then become more involved, not less. Government isn't a necessary evil but a positive good, according to the Christian worldview. On this basis, Christians have played a valuable role through the centuries, especially in developing ideas of representative democracy, the rule of law, and limited government.

The Christian worldview teaches that God is just and that we're made in his image. Thus, all people are equal under the law. Christian monasteries were the first institutions to allow every member an equal vote. The revered legal scholar William Blackstone, a Christian, based the framework of our modern understanding of rights upon *natural laws*—laws that exist because of the way God created the world—and from *Scripture*.[39] America's early leaders agreed and regularly referred to Blackstone's work. Later, American leaders held in high regard the thoughts of men like Noah Webster, author of the 1828 *American Dictionary of the English Language*, who argued that the principles of the Bible are based on unchanging truth.[40]

> Believers ought to discern a biblical basis for political involvement and then become more involved, not less.

Among other things, the Bible tells the truth about sin. Right and wrong and good and evil actually exist, it says, and yet we're free to choose right over wrong and good over evil. We can take responsibility, and this makes society better. Yet because "*no one* is righteous" (Rom. 3:10–11),[41] humans cannot be trusted with too much power. Realizing this, America's founders divided power among three branches of government: the executive, the legislative, and the judicial branches.

Christians should be wise and morally centered rather than gullible. Gullible people aren't clear about what's true, and they care too much about being liked. They're easily misled. Yes, Christians want to be kind. But even if obeying God comes into conflict with obeying man, Christians are called to stand firm and obey God. Society relies on us, as citizens of the kingdom of God, to stand for a higher truth rather than waver in the midst of rapidly changing opinions.

Standing firm is no light decision. For Christians around the world, proclaiming their faith has led to criticism and persecution. Many have been tortured and killed. Especially in Marxist and Muslim countries, people aren't able to practice their religion free from threat. This is an especially significant area where a Christian worldview is urgently needed.

13. Religious Freedom and Persecution

Seven out of ten people in the world live under regimes that severely restrict religious freedom.[42] Christians suffer the worst.[43] Attacks are even accelerating in Western countries, and while these attacks haven't yet led to physical violence or overt persecution, they point to a potentially dangerous—and growing—intolerance of religion. In countries where this has happened, religious persecution and conflict result.[44]

Religious freedom is "the right of all human beings to think as they please, believe or not believe as their conscience leads, and live out their beliefs openly, peacefully, and without fear."[45] This requires **tolerance**. True tolerance, that is. Not the kind of tolerance that implies that everyone is right or that no one is wrong. True tolerance means respecting the dignity of all people, *including* those we think are wrong.

> *Tolerance:* the willingness to recognize and respect the dignity of those with whom one disagrees.

In chapter 13, we saw that while Christians, Buddhists, and Hindu nationalists have all been persecutors, the worst persecution in the last hundred years has been of Christians at the hands of Marxists and Muslims. Although unthinking Christians have at times supported them, Marxist governments are uniformly atheist.[46] Marxist governments routinely crack down on those they feel threaten their power, usually under the cynical guise of protecting the interests of the working class. Christians, unimpressed by leaders who think they are gods, often find themselves targeted.

> *Sharia Law:* the moral and legal code derived primarily from the Quran and the *Sunnah* that governs the lives of Muslims. Sharia addresses a wide variety of subjects, such as diet, hygiene, prayer, contracts, business, crime, and punishment.

Today there are fewer Marxist countries than in the past. But Islam is on the rise, and Muslim countries now lead the world in persecution of Christians.[47] **Sharia law**, Islam's legal code, requires all Muslims to engage in **jihad**, which means resisting anything hindering the advance of Islam.[48] Sharia doesn't explicitly require the persecution of Christians and Jews, unless they are converts from Islam, but persecution is commonplace in practice. Islamic groups like ISIS, claiming devotion to Allah, commit such atrocities as gang rape, public torture, and execution by beheading, shooting, drowning, stoning, and throwing people off buildings. Islamic governments with the power to stop ISIS have made little effort to do so. If ISIS were to have its way, Christianity would be eradicated in the Middle East.[49]

A Christian worldview protects religious freedom not only for itself but for those who disagree with it. Religious freedom is strongly tied to Christian teachings on the soul's immortality, divine judgment, providential acts, the sin nature, moral absolutes, the human capacity to bear God's image, order in the universe, public virtue, and the general teachings of the Bible. In history, Christians have focused on caring for the oppressed, as Jesus taught (Luke 4:18),[50] and sustaining a free and virtuous society that enables **human flourishing**.

The issue isn't just about the freedom to assemble for worship. It's about the right to advocate ideas that may even be politically unpopular, and to do so with others of like mind. This is what it means to have religious freedom, and it's central to living out a Christian worldview.

CONCLUSION

14. Poverty Care, Poverty Cure

The same created attributes of human beings that demand that we stand against religious oppression also demand that we stand against economic oppression. The goal of a Christian worldview is not just caring for the poor but curing **poverty** itself.

Some think poverty can be solved by stripping the wealthy of their largess and redistributing it. But as we saw in chapter 14, poverty isn't just an economic problem. It's also a political, social, and spiritual problem. Well-meaning initiatives aren't enough. Sometimes they make things worse.

None of the other worldviews we've been studying—Secularism, Marxism, Postmodernism, Islam, and New Spirituality—offers a vision of poverty cure quite like that of the Christian worldview. The Bible commands us to care for the poor, and we've noted specific ways of doing so. **Government redistribution** of wealth isn't among them. Rather, poverty is treated on several levels. On the first level, the Bible calls for a personal touch by feeding the hungry, clothing the naked, and giving the thirsty something to drink (Matt. 25:35–40).[51] On the second level, the Bible calls for allowing the poor the dignity of work. Leviticus 23:22, for example, instructs harvesters to leave the edges of their fields unharvested so the poor can glean food for their families.

> *Government Redistribution:* a state-controlled economic policy that taxes the wealthy at a higher rate than others and then reallocates those assets to the poor either through direct subsidies or government-sponsored social programs.

There is a third level of poverty care as well, which is readily derived from God's nature and the way he designed us: creativity and innovation. Recognizing this, Christians over the centuries have made advances in education, medicine, human rights, and technology. These advances have accelerated economic growth. Scores of people have been lifted out of poverty. Indeed, the face of the world has been changed forever.

Such advances are possible because the Christian worldview rejects the idea that the world is a *closed system* with nothing existing outside the universe to bring meaning into it. Rather, it says that God created us with minds that aren't limited in the way physical resources are. A farmer planting corn has only so many varieties of seed to choose from. But *idea* seeds are limitless. People willing to think and work hard can plant them, bring them to fruition, and enjoy the resulting abundance. Our primary resource as God's image bearers is not what's in the ground. It's what's in our minds.

So how might Christians effectively address poverty? First, they can start locally. Those closest to the problem are generally best at solving it. Of course, money is helpful too. But so are friendship, caring, creativity, encouragement, and other resources we possess in abundance.

> The long-term goal, though, isn't just to care for the poor; it's to cure poverty itself. Destroying the stronghold of poverty requires us to "teach a man to think about fishing.

The long-term goal, though, isn't just to care for the poor; it's to cure poverty itself. To do this we need to go beyond the "give a man a fish" mind-set (emergency aid) and even beyond the "teach a man to fish" mind-set (sustainability). Destroying the stronghold of poverty requires us to "teach a man to think about fishing."[52] God has provided people, communities, and nations the assets they need to flourish. In their distress, though, they may not see this and may need other people to come alongside to encourage them. We can be those people, helping them start businesses, build community, improve education, and so much more.

When it comes to poverty cure, everyone has something to contribute. Engineers and architects are needed as well as social workers. Medical personnel are still critical to poverty cure, but so are manufacturers. We need missionaries, but we also need those gifted in economics and finance. Everyone is called. All of our gifts are needed.

Obviously, some things people do for money, such as prostitution and drug dealing, have no place in God's plan for redemption. But throughout history, some Christians have expanded the list of forbidden vocations to include military service and law enforcement. Their reasoning is that Jesus was a man of peace and that the use of force has no place in God's kingdom. This leads to a general pacifism, in which any use of force—including self-defense— is prohibited. Is this the most valid biblical response to war and violence?

15. THE USE OF FORCE

The history of humanity is that of near-constant war, punctuated by brief periods of peace. The human cost has been enormous. In the twentieth century alone, more than 38 million people died in wars, including civil wars, and more than 169 million people died as a result of their own governments using force against them.[53] Every life lost is someone with a soul—someone made in God's image whom others cared for, who had thoughts and ideas, and who will be missed.

> The history of humanity is that of near-constant war, punctuated by brief periods of peace. The human cost has been enormous.

Historically, the use of force to hurt people has often been met by the use of force to protect them. This puts many Christians in a quandary. Jesus said to love one another, even our enemies (Matt. 5:44; John 13:34–35).[54] But do such passages prohibit going to war? Christians have debated this for many centuries. Usually they take one of four positions:

1. **Pacifism.** Neither the state nor Christians should take up arms.

2. **Nonresistance.** While the state may take up arms, Christians must not do so.

3. **Just war.** Christians may go to war on behalf of a legitimate government that has a just cause and intends to secure peace.

4. **Crusade or preventive war.** The state may go to war when a threat is imminent to stop people from committing evil. Christians may participate.

All these views agree that war is an unfortunate evil. Christian theologians and philosophers have historically seen the **just-war theory** as providing a balanced view of how a state may engage in war in the most humane way possible.

The Bible's backdrop is war, just as the world's backdrop is war. Only a tiny fraction of human history has seen complete peace. In the Old Testament, God allowed Israel to conquer the nations around it that threatened its survival. Most of the Bible's teaching related to violence, though, is on securing justice for individuals, not on the principles of war. For example, the sixth of the Ten Commandments states, "You shall not murder" (Exod. 20:13). Criminal punishment revolved around the principle of *lex talionis* (the law of retaliation). "If anyone injures his neighbor, as he has done it shall be done to him, fracture for fracture, eye for eye, tooth for tooth" (Lev. 24:19–20).[55]

In Bible times, it seems common that people were permitted to carry weapons for self-defense. In Nehemiah 4:18, for example, the people carried weapons while rebuilding Jerusalem's wall. Even a few of Jesus's own disciples were armed (Luke 22:38). Everyday people were capable of wielding lethal force but were prohibited from doing so under certain conditions. Exodus 22, for example, indicates that using lethal force against a thief was considered murder. Scripture is clear that God's people aren't to admire men of violence (Prov. 3:31–32)[56] and are to put their trust in God, not in their weapons (Ps. 44:6–7).[57]

> Scripture is clear that God's people aren't to admire men of violence and are to put their trust in God, not in their weapons.

Nothing in the New Testament countermands the Mosaic law in regard to the use of force for defense of one's family or nation. Personal insults don't justify physically harming another person. This much is clear from Jesus's teachings. Other passages say we aren't to take our own revenge (Rom. 12:19), nor should we be quick to strike out at others (Titus 1:7).[58] But to imply that these verses prohibit protecting one's family against physical harm or to say that they condemn war is to stretch them far beyond their context. Many scriptural heroes were warriors, even in the time of Jesus and the apostles. Jesus called the Roman centurion ruling near his hometown a man of great faith (Matt. 8:10).[59] The apostle Peter converted another centurion, Cornelius, to Christianity (Acts 10:1, 30–35).[60] In neither case were these centurions told to give up their military service.

Christians are citizens of the kingdom of God. As such, we ought to be the best citizens of the kingdom of humanity as well, since we recognize a higher authority than the state. We need to hold the state accountable for its actions, including actions taken in times of war. It seems God's main concern for his people is justice, not restraining them from legitimate efforts to punish evil and restore what is right.

> Nothing in the New Testament countermands the Mosaic law in regard to the use of force for defense of one's family or nation.

16. JUSTICE

"Injustice anywhere is a threat to justice everywhere," said Martin Luther King Jr. in his famous "Letter from a Birmingham Jail."[61] King believed that **justice** should be grounded in the permanent rights of each person. This is quite different from the modern concept of justice that is focused on keeping order in society. Given the injustice we see in society today, there's never been a better time to think through what the Bible says about justice and its role in expressing Christ's redemption in culture.

In chapter 16, we discussed the two dominant views of justice. The inherent-rights view asserts that God has granted all people the permanent right to life, **liberty**, and the pursuit of happiness (**inherent-rights view of justice**). The government doesn't grant

> *Liberty:* **freedom from undue restraint.**

> *Right-Ordering View of Justice:* **the belief that justice involves the government seeking to preserve social order.**

these rights; it merely *secures* what God has already granted. The other view—the **right-ordering view of justice**—asserts that God is irrelevant and that our rights come from government, so government leaders must actively organize society in the way they think works best.

The second view dominates today. Most people think God is irrelevant to the pursuit of justice. Even if God exists, which they doubt, we humans are certainly not made in his image. The idea that God could be the source of rights is seen as being out of touch with the complexities of modern society. The Christian worldview, though, insists that acknowledging God's role as creator leads to a much better framework of justice.

The Bible declares that God not only cares about justice but also loves it (Ps. 33:5).[62] In fact, justice is one of his attributes. Jeremiah 9:24 says, "I am the LORD who practices steadfast love, justice, and righteousness in the earth. For in these things I delight, declares the LORD." When you love someone, you intentionally seek his or her good. It isn't enough to try to avoid hurting that person. The biblical idea of justice is like this. It's based on the Hebrew word *tzedek*, which implies purposely seeking to do what's right, not just avoiding what's wrong.

In practical terms, pursuing what is right means protecting the rights of victims and punishing wrongdoing, regardless of the perpetrator's wealth or status. It involves restoring the balance of justice while recognizing the permanent rights of both victims and perpetrators. A movement called **restorative justice** seeks to apply principles consistent with a biblical ethic to the problems in the justice system. Restorative-justice efforts include prison reform to increase prisoners' chances of success as they reenter society, community corrections, victim restitution, encouragement for people to change their ways before they get in legal trouble, and advocacy for youth and those with mental-health issues.

Some of today's most successful restorative-justice programs are openly Christian. They're also highly effective, especially in mentoring young adults and helping rehabilitate those who've gone to prison as punishment for a crime. One program, the InnerChange Freedom Initiative (IFI), has shown that only 8 percent of those who had completed the program ended up back behind bars.[63]

By restoring people to their full capacity as God's image bearers, a biblical view of justice is making a difference. People's rights are taken seriously. Society, in turn, becomes more orderly and peaceful. Justice for all isn't just a dream. Biblical thinking and action turn it into a reality.

Note the personal touch in restorative justice as well as poverty-cure initiatives and many of the other ideas we've discussed. Some of the most effective solutions are hands-on and local. They're based in local communities, where people can get to know one another as persons, not as problems. The gospel renews communities.

17. Community Renewal

The Clapham Sect, a network allied with abolitionist William Wilberforce, led British efforts to end the slave trade and restore decency to society. Wilberforce and the Clapham Sect are an example of how God can use a group of believers committed to working together, giving generously, and persisting in the face of intimidating odds.

The Clapham Sect showed that cultural change is accomplished by going to the top of society, as well as by inspiring everyday people to action—the **grassroots movement**. It's a combined approach that is sometimes called the **grasstops movement**. Effective action thinks big and small. It thinks nationally as well as locally.

As we've seen, though, people at the local level are best able to offer a personal touch. Renewal happens one community at a time. Communities need renewing more than ever, given the plague of financial shortfalls, crime, congestion, waste, ineffective schools, dilapidated housing, pollution, poor health care, inadequate services, homelessness, and corruption.

God cares about communities. We should too. The Bible calls us to move toward the messy, complicated problems we face when we have neighbors, rather than seeking to escape them. In the Old Testament, even when God's people were taken captive, they were told to care for the communities in which they lived. Speaking through the prophet Jeremiah, God said their own well-being would be secured as they pursued the community's well-being (Jer. 29:4–7).[64] The Old Testament word for "well-being" is *shalom*, which means "peace, prosperity, completeness, safeness, salvation, health, satisfaction, contentment, and blessing."[65] *Shalom* is the very best thing that can happen to a person or a community. It is God's heart.

> The Bible calls us to move toward the messy, complicated problems we face when we have neighbors, rather than seeking to escape them.

The Christian worldview naturally lends itself to community renewal, but we have to be purposeful about it. To help people flourish, we must identify and remove barriers that prevent people from living fully as image bearers of God. From a biblical viewpoint, winning isn't about seizing the reins of power as much as it is about creating a robust vision of a flourishing society.

> To help people flourish, we must identify and remove barriers that prevent people from living fully as image bearers of God.

In addition to focusing on bearing God's image, the Bible focuses on loving our neighbors. Being a good neighbor can start with a simple question: "What are the pain points in my community, and how can I help?" We're not out looking for problems, though. Rather, we're looking at the God-given gifts, opportunities, and assets that people in the community possess. Our job is to encourage people as they learn to steward those assets and help their communities solve their own problems.

Of course, community renewal isn't easy. It takes thoughtfulness. It takes good communication skills. It takes work. But by applying principles of community renewal, communities everywhere are becoming safer, more welcoming, healthier, and more prosperous.

18. CONCLUSION

There have never been more Christians in the world than there are at this moment in history. It's time for the church to be the church in the midst of broken communities and fractured nations. Through God's power, we can see what is going wrong in culture and work to transform it. By holding God's glory above all, bearing his image, and loving our neighbors, we can move from being a culture of death to being a culture of life.

> **Through God's power, we can see what is going wrong in culture and work to transform it.**

This seems to be C. S. Lewis's understanding of redemption as communicated in *The Lion, the Witch and the Wardrobe*. Aslan was killed on the stone table, but he rose again. When the children asked what happened, Aslan said,

> If [the witch knew the true meaning of sacrifice], she would have known that when a willing victim who had committed no treachery was killed in a traitor's stead, the Table would crack and Death itself would start working backwards.[66]

Death has been met on the field of battle and turned back. Christ has risen, death is losing its grip, and more and more of God's people, empowered by the Holy Spirit, are catching the vision of making all things new.

Through Christ, we can truly say we live at the greatest moment in history. We celebrate heroes of the past, but it may very well be that some of the bravest, most creative, most heroic Christians to ever live are alive right now. I can be one of them. So can you.

ENDNOTES

1. Psalm 79:9: "Help us, O God of our salvation, for the glory of your name; deliver us, and atone for our sins, for your name's sake!"; Revelation 21:23: "The city has no need of sun or moon to shine on it, for the glory of God gives it light, and its lamp is the Lamb."
2. First Corinthians 10:31: "Whether you eat or drink, or whatever you do, do all to the glory of God"; 2 Peter 1:3: "His divine power has granted to us all things that pertain to life and godliness, through the knowledge of him who called us to his own glory and excellence."
3. Genesis 1:26–28: "Then God said, 'Let us make man in our image, after our likeness. And let them have dominion over the fish of the sea and over the birds of the heavens and over the livestock and over all the earth and over every creeping thing that creeps on the earth.' So God created man in his own image, in the image of God he created him; male and female he created them. And God blessed them. And God said to them, 'Be fruitful and multiply and fill the earth and subdue it, and have dominion over the fish of the sea and over the birds of the heavens and over every living thing that moves on the earth.'"
4. Leviticus 19:9–15: "When you reap the harvest of your land, you shall not reap your field right up to its edge, neither shall you gather the gleanings after your harvest. And you shall not strip your vineyard bare, neither shall you gather the fallen grapes of your vineyard. You shall leave them for the poor and for the sojourner: I am the LORD your God. You shall not steal; you shall not deal falsely; you shall not lie to one another. You shall not swear by my name falsely, and so profane the

name of your God: I am the LORD. You shall not oppress your neighbor or rob him. The wages of a hired worker shall not remain with you all night until the morning. You shall not curse the deaf or put a stumbling block before the blind, but you shall fear your God: I am the LORD. You shall do no injustice in court. You shall not be partial to the poor or defer to the great, but in righteousness shall you judge your neighbor"; Matthew 22:37–40: "You shall love the Lord your God with all your heart and with all your soul and with all your mind. This is the great and first commandment. And a second is like it: You shall love your neighbor as yourself. On these two commandments depend all the Law and the Prophets."

5. Proverbs 4:7: "The beginning of wisdom is this: Get wisdom, and whatever you get, get insight."

6. Philippians 1:27: "Only let your manner of life be worthy of the gospel of Christ, so that whether I come and see you or am absent, I may hear of you that you are standing firm in one spirit, with one mind striving side by side for the faith of the gospel"; Philippians 4:8: "Whatever is true, whatever is honorable, whatever is just, whatever is pure, whatever is lovely, whatever is commendable, if there is any excellence, if there is anything worthy of praise, think about these things."

7. Proverbs 18:21: "Death and life are in the power of the tongue, and those who love it will eat its fruits"; Proverbs 25:11: "A word fitly spoken is like apples of gold in a setting of silver."

8. Andy Crouch, *Culture Making: Recovering our Creative Calling* (Downers Grove, IL: InterVarsity, 2008), 23.

9. Ken Myers originally presented this list at a lecture on culture at the Association of Classical and Christian Schools (ACCS) 2008 Conference, "Recovering Truth, Goodness, and Beauty," Austin, Texas, June 26–20, 2008; see also "ACCS—Ken Myers on Culture," *Mark's Blog*, Every Good Path, July 23, 2008, www.everygoodpath.net/ACCSKenMyersCulture.

10. First Chronicles 12:32: "[The] men [of Issachar] … had understanding of the times [and knew] what Israel ought to do, 200 chiefs, and all their kinsmen under their command."

11. James Davison Hunter, *To Change the World: The Irony, Tragedy, and Possibility of Christianity in the Late Modern World* (New York: Oxford University Press, 2010), 3.

12. An examination of various Christian approaches to culture is found in H. Richard Niebuhr, *Christ and Culture* (New York: Harper and Row, 1951).

13. Dictionary.com, s.v. "religion," http://dictionary.reference.com/browse/religion.

14. Romans 12:2: "Do not be conformed to this world, but be transformed by the renewal of your mind, that by testing you may discern what is the will of God, what is good and acceptable and perfect."

15. Luke 10:27: "You shall love the Lord your God with all your heart and with all your soul and with all your strength and with all your mind, and your neighbor as yourself."

16. Warren Cole Smith and John Stonestreet, *Restoring All Things: God's Audacious Plan to Change the World through Everyday People* (Grand Rapids: Baker Books, 2015), 25–26.

17. Joel Stein, "Baby, You Can Drive My Car, and Do My Errands, and Rent My Stuff …," *Time*, January 29, 2015, http://time.com/3687305/testing-the-sharing-economy/.

18. Colossians 2:8: "See to it that no one takes you captive by philosophy and empty deceit, according to human tradition, according to the elemental spirits of the world, and not according to Christ."

19. Romans 12:2: "Do not be conformed to this world, but be transformed by the renewal of your mind, that by testing you may discern what is the will of God, what is good and acceptable and perfect."

20. Matthew 20:28: "The Son of Man came not to be served but to serve, and to give his life as a ransom for many."

21. Matthew 7:12: "Whatever you wish that others would do to you, do also to them, for this is the Law and the Prophets."

22. Ephesians 4:15: "Rather, speaking the truth in love, we are to grow up in every way into him who is the head, into Christ."

23. "Medieval Inventions," accessed July 12, 2016, www.medieval-life-and-times.info/medieval-life/medieval-inventions.htm.

24. Neil Postman, *Technopoly: The Surrender of Culture to Technology* (New York: Vintage Books, 1993), 5.

25. Sherry Turkle, *Alone Together: Why We Expect More from Technology and Less from Each Other* (New York: Basic Books, 2011), 263.

26. Quentin J Schultze, *Habits of the High-Tech Heart: Living Virtuously in the Information Age* (Grand Rapids: Baker Academic, 2002), 20.

27. "*Up* (2009 Film): Production; Development," Wikipedia, accessed July 15, 2016, https://en.wikipedia.org/wiki/Up_(2009_film)#Development.

28. Results of 2015 CIRP Freshman Survey monograph, cited in "The American Freshman: National Norms Fall 2015," Research Brief, Higher Education Research Institute at UCLA, February 2016, www.heri.ucla.edu/briefs/TheAmericanFreshman2015-Brief.pdf.

29. Francis J. Beckwith, *Defending Life: A Moral and Legal Case against Abortion Choice* (New York: Cambridge University Press, 2007), 139.

30. Agneta Sutton, *Christian Bioethics: A Guide for the Perplexed* (New York: T&T Clark, 2008), 48–49.

31. Wesley J. Smith, *Forced Exit: Euthanasia, Assisted Suicide, and the New Duty to Die* (New York: Encounter Books, 2006), 116–28.

32. Matthew 25:40: "The King will answer them, 'Truly, I say to you, as you did it to one of the least of these my brothers,

you did it to me'"; Galatians 2:10: "Only, they asked us to remember the poor, the very thing I was eager to do"; James 1:27: "Religion that is pure and undefiled before God, the Father, is this: to visit orphans and widows in their affliction, and to keep oneself unstained from the world."

33. In a supreme irony for those seeking sexual satisfaction by bending or breaking the "rules" of Christianity, researchers have found that the greatest sexual satisfaction and pleasure are in the context of a monogamous, formal man-woman marriage. See Edward O. Laumann et al., *The Social Organization of Sexuality: Sexual Practices in the United States* (Chicago: University of Chicago Press, 2000), 364.

34. Matthew 19:4: "[Jesus] answered, 'Have you not read that he who created them from the beginning made them male and female.'"

35. Dale S. Kuehne, *Sex and the iWorld: Rethinking Relationship beyond an Age of Individualism* (Grand Rapids: Baker Academic, 2009), 117–18.

36. Kuehne, *Sex and the iWorld*, 169.

37. E. Calvin Beisner, "What Is the Most Important Environmental Task Facing American Christians Today?," *Mount Nebo Papers*, no. 1 (November 2007): 2, 11–13, www.ccalvinbeisner.com/freearticles/MtNebo.pdf.

38. Beisner, "What Is the Most Important Environmental Task?," 14.

39. Marshall Davis Ewell, ed., *Essentials of the Law*, vol. 1, *A Review of Blackstone's Commentaries with Explanatory Notes for the Use of Students at Law*, 2nd ed. (Albany, NY: Matthew Bender, 1915), 3.

40. Noah Webster, "Advice to the Young," in *History of the United States* (New Haven, CT: Durrie and Peck, 1832), 339.

41. Romans 3:10–11: "No one is righteous, no, not one; no one understands; no one seeks for God."

42. Brian J. Grim et al., *Rising Tide of Restrictions on Religion* (Washington, DC: Pew Research Center, 2012), www.pewforum.org/files/2012/09/RisingTideofRestrictions-fullreport.pdf.

43. Grim et al., "Harassment of Specific Groups," in *Rising Tide of Restrictions on Religion*, 22.

44. Brian J. Grim and Roger Finke, *The Price of Freedom Denied: Religious Persecution and Conflict in the Twenty-First Century* (New York: Cambridge University Press, 2011), 79, 219.

45. Robert P. George et al., *Annual Report of the US Commission on International Religious Freedom* (Washington, DC: U.S. Commission on International Religious Freedom, 2014), 1.

46. See Jeff Myers and David Noebel, *Understanding the Times: A Survey of Competing Worldviews* (Colorado Springs: David C Cook, 2015), especially the chapters on Marxism and theology.

47. Paul Marshall, Lela Gilbert, and Nina Shea, *Persecuted: The Global Assault on Christians* (Nashville: Thomas Nelson, 2013), 123.

48. Islamic scholar Khurshid Ahmad says, "*Jihad* has been made obligatory, which means that the individual should, when the occasion arises, offer even his life for the defense and protection of Islam and the Islamic state." Khurshid Ahmad, *Islam: Its Meaning and Message*, 3rd ed. (Leicester, UK: Islamic Foundation, 1999), 39.

49. Eliza Griswold, "Is This the End of Christianity in the Middle East?," *New York Times Magazine*, July 22, 2015, www.nytimes.com/2015/07/26/magazine/is-this-the-end-of-christianity-in-the-middle-east.html?_r=0.

50. Luke 4:18: "The Spirit of the Lord is upon me, because he has anointed me to proclaim good news to the poor. He has sent me to proclaim liberty to the captives and recovery of sight to the blind, to set at liberty those who are oppressed."

51. Matthew 25:35–40: "'I was hungry and you gave me food, I was thirsty and you gave me drink, I was a stranger and you welcomed me, I was naked and you clothed me, I was sick and you visited me, I was in prison and you came to me.' Then the righteous will answer him, saying, 'Lord, when did we see you hungry and feed you, or thirsty and give you drink? And when did we see you a stranger and welcome you, or naked and clothe you? And when did we see you sick or in prison and visit you?' And the King will answer them, 'Truly, I say to you, as you did it to one of the least of these my brothers, you did it to me.'"

52. Darrow Miller's research for chapter 14, "Poverty Care, Poverty Cure."

53. R. J. Rummel, *Death by Government* (Piscataway, NJ: Transaction Publishers, 1994), 4, 15.

54. Matthew 5:44: "I say to you, Love your enemies and pray for those who persecute you"; John 13:34–35: "A new command I give to you, that you love one another: just as I have loved you, you also are to love one another. By this all people will know that you are my disciples, if you have love for one another."

55. See also Exodus 21:23–25: "If there is harm, then you shall pay life for life, eye for eye, tooth for tooth, hand for hand, foot for foot, burn for burn, wound for wound, stripe for stripe." The formulation of "an eye for an eye" is commonly referred to as the *lex talionis*.

56. Proverbs 3:31–32: "Do not envy a man of violence and do not choose any of his ways, for the devious person is an abomination to the LORD, but the upright are in his confidence."

57. Psalm 44:6–7: "Not in my bow do I trust, nor can my sword save me. But you have saved us from our foes and have put to shame those who hate us."

58. Romans 12:19: "Beloved, never avenge yourselves, but leave it to the wrath of God, for it is written, 'Vengeance is mine, I will repay, says the Lord'"; Titus 1:7: "An overseer, as God's steward, must be above reproach. He must not be arrogant or quick-tempered or a drunkard or violent or greedy for gain."

59. Matthew 8:10: "When Jesus heard [the centurion's reply], he marveled and said to those who followed him, 'Truly, I tell you, with no one in Israel have I found such faith.'"

60. Acts 10:1: "At Caesarea there was a man named Cornelius, a centurion of what was known as the Italian Cohort"; Acts 10:30–35: "And Cornelius said, 'Four days ago, about this hour, I was praying in my house at the ninth hour, and behold, a man stood before me in bright clothing and said, "Cornelius, your prayer has been heard and your alms have been remembered before God. Send therefore to Joppa and ask for Simon who is called Peter. He is lodging in the house of Simon, a tanner, by the sea." So I sent for you at once, and you have been kind enough to come. Now therefore we are all here in the presence of God to hear all that you have been commanded by the Lord.' So Peter opened his mouth and said: 'Truly I understand that God shows no partiality, but in every nation anyone who fears him and does what is right is acceptable to him.'"

61. Martin Luther King Jr., "Letter from a Birmingham Jail," Birmingham, Alabama, April 16, 1963, in Martin Luther King Jr., *Why We Can't Wait* (Boston: Beacon, 1986), chap. 5.

62. Psalm 33:5: "[God] loves righteousness and justice; the earth is full of the steadfast love of the LORD."

63. "InnerChange Freedom Initiative," Prison Fellowship, accessed August 3, 2016, www.prisonfellowship.org/about/reentry-support/innerchange-freedom-initiative/.

64. Jeremiah 29:4–7: "Thus says the LORD of hosts, the God of Israel, to all the exiles whom I have sent into exile from Jerusalem to Babylon: Build houses and live in them; plant gardens and eat their produce. Take wives and have sons and daughters; take wives for your sons, and give your daughters in marriage, that they may bear sons and daughters; multiply there, and do not decrease. But seek the welfare of the city where I have sent you into exile, and pray to the LORD on its behalf, for in its welfare you will find your welfare."

65. James A. Swanson, *A Dictionary of Biblical Languages with Semantic Domains: Hebrew Old Testament* (Oak Harbor, WA: Logos Research Systems, 1997), s.v. "*shalom.*"

66. C. S. Lewis, *The Lion, the Witch and the Wardrobe* (New York: Collier Books, 1970), 160.

CONCLUSION

GLOSSARY

Abad: from the Hebrew for "to serve"; the term also means "to work and worship."

Abortion: any medical procedure or medication that deliberately ends the life of an unborn human being.

Accountability: the act of accepting responsibility for one's actions.

Active Euthanasia: the practice whereby a physician administers a lethal dose of medication with the intent of ending a suffering patient's life.

Ad Hominem: a fallacy in which an argument attacks a person rather than supporting or disproving a conclusion.

Adultery: any sexual activity between a married person and someone who is not that individual's spouse.

Affirmative Action: any effort or policy that seeks to improve the employment or educational status of minority groups by granting them special advantage in the selection process over others.

Age of Enlightenment: an eighteenth-century intellectual movement that emphasized reason, science, and individualism over tradition and religious authority.

Amusement: the state of being entertained without inspiring thought.

Animism: the belief that various spirits inhabit plants, animals, and physical objects.

Anthropic Principle: the theory that the universe contains all the necessary properties that make the existence of intelligent life inevitable.

Apartheid: a government-sponsored policy of segregation and discrimination against South African blacks in the mid- to late twentieth century.

Appeal to Ignorance: a fallacy in which an argument asserts that a proposition must be true simply because it has not been proven false (or vice versa).

Appeal to Pity: a fallacy in which an argument tries to evoke an emotional response rather than establish logical support for its conclusion.

Argument: a set of premises supporting a conclusion.

Argument by Definition: a deductive argument in which a premise establishes a specific definition, while another premise establishes a subject's association with that definition.

Argument by Elimination: a deductive argument in which the first premise presents all possible scenarios, while the second rules out all unreasonable scenarios, and the conclusion is reached by a process of elimination.

Argument from Analogy: an inductive argument that uses a comparison between similar subjects to reach a conclusion.

Art: a physical, visual, or auditory expression of human creativity, skill, and imagination (e.g., paintings, music, plays, and musicals).

Artifact: any man-made thing, both tangible (e.g., works of art and technology) and intangible (e.g., literary forms and philosophical concepts).

Asset-Based Community Development: the process of trying to improve the economic conditions of a community by developing inside resources, such as people's talents and skills.

Atheism: the belief that God does not exist.

Attacking the Motive: a fallacy in which an argument attacks a person's vested interest in the conclusion instead of the person's conclusion.

Axios: from the Greek meaning "recognized as a fitting thing"; translated as "worthy."

Bandwagon: a fallacy in which an argument appeals to popular support of a conclusion instead of building a case for that conclusion.

Begging the Question: a fallacy in which a premise of an argument merely assumes what the conclusion is trying to prove.

Belief: any idea that a person or group holds as a common understanding or conviction.

Benedict Option: the belief that Christians should remove themselves from culture and establish alternative communities to separate themselves from the sinfulness of human culture.

Bourgeoisie: a term used in Marxist theory to describe those who own the means of production.

Capital: any asset that has monetary value.

Capitalism: an economic system in which capital assets are privately owned and the prices, production, and distribution of goods and services are determined by competition within a free market.

Caste System: the Hindu practice of assigning individuals to various static social classes based on one's birth.

Categorical Syllogism: a deductive argument that confers a conclusion from exactly two premises.

Category Mistake: a fallacy that presents things belonging to one particular category as if they belong in another category.

Charity: the act of voluntarily giving time, money, and other resources to help those who are in need.

Chastity: the state of abstaining from fornication and adultery.

Civil Disobedience: the practice of resisting a government's unjust laws.

Cogent Argument: a clear and convincing inductive argument in which the premises lead to a highly probable conclusion.

Cohabitation: an arrangement whereby two people live together in a sexual relationship without being married.

Communism: the Marxist ideal of a classless and stateless utopian society in which all property is commonly owned and each person is paid according to his or her abilities and needs.

Communist Manifesto: a work commissioned by the Communist League and written by Karl Marx and Friedrich Engels, *The Communist Manifesto* is the 1848 political tract outlining the league's goal of and means for eliminating capitalism and achieving a communist society through a proletariat revolution.

Community Discipleship: the idea that God called his followers not just to save souls but also to transform communities.

Community Renewal: any effort taken to restore and rebuild a community so that its people can thrive and prosper.

Conservationism: a movement that supports the conservation of natural resources as a necessity for human thriving and survival.

Contraception: any device, drug, procedure, or technique that is used to prevent pregnancy.

Conversionist: someone who acknowledges the fallen nature of humanity but recognizes the transforming power available through the redemptive work of Christ to restore culture to what is good rather than replacing it with something that is different.

Critical Thinking: the process of analyzing and evaluating arguments for validity and soundness.

Crony Capitalism: an economic system in which businesses that have close relationships with government officials are given unfair economic advantages through some kind of special treatment (e.g., incentives, grants, and tax breaks).

Cultural Anthropologist: one who studies the cultural details of society, such as social institutions, language, law, politics, religion, art, and technology.

Culture: the way of life for a group of people; the culmination of human communication and willful activity in a particular civilization.

Cultural Capital: a culture's enduring and significant ideas.

Cultural Literacy: the knowledge and understanding of a culture that enables individuals to engage and influence that culture.

Cyberculture: the modern values, habits, and social conditions brought about by the widespread use of the Internet.

Darwinism: the theory developed by Charles Darwin asserting that life arose and slowly evolved through the natural selection of favorable variations found within species.

Deductive Argument: any argument built on generally accepted premises necessarily leading to a conclusion.

Deep Ecology: an environmental philosophy based on the idea that all living beings form a spiritual and ecologically interconnected system, which is presently threatened by the harmful impact of human beings; a philosophy that advocates a radical restructuring of society toward environmental preservation, simple living, legal rights for all living creatures, and a reduction in the human population.

Deism: the belief that God exists and created the world but currently stands completely aloof from his creation; the belief that reason and nature sufficiently reveal the existence of God but that God has not revealed himself through any type of special revelation.

Democracy: a system of government in which citizens vote directly for or against particular laws, officials, measures, and so on.

Derek: from the Hebrew for "the way," *derek* refers to the overall direction of a person's life.

Dhimmi: a non-Muslim living in an Islamic state.

Dirigisme: an economic system in which the government exerts control over the private sector and directly manages its investments.

Discernment: the ability to distinguish between truth and error, right and wrong, good and bad, and to prefer what is true, right, and good.

Dispensational Premillennialism: an eschatological doctrine that establishes a sequence of events for the end times, asserting that the anti-Christ will soon rise, the second coming of Christ is imminent, and all things will culminate in a millennial reign of Christ.

Distributive Justice: the belief that a just society should seek to redistribute its citizens' resources equally among everyone.

Doctrine of Original Sin: the orthodox Christian belief that Adam's first sin corrupted the nature of his descendents, leading to humanity's present propensity toward committing sin.

Dominion: the power or right of an authority to rule over a territory or people.

Doxa: from the Greek for "glory"; it also means a "good reputation" or "honor."

Ecofeminism: a political philosophy that links the oppression of women and the exploitation of the environment with the values inherent in what advocates refer to as Western patriarchal society.

Ecology: the branch of biology that deals with how organisms relate to one another.

Economic Interventionism: an economic system in which the government influences aspects of a market economy in an attempt to improve the public good.

Ecumenism: the push to foster unity among various Christian traditions that disagree on key doctrinal issues.

Elastic Good: any good whose demand is highly correlated with price increases and decreases (i.e., as the price increases or decreases, consumer demand responds conversely).

Embryo: an unborn human being who is between four days and eight weeks from conception.

Embryology: the branch of biology that studies the early stages of human development.

Embryonic Stem Cell: a pluripotent stem cell harvested from human embryos.

Endowment View of Human Life: the belief that all human beings have intrinsic value simply because they are human.

Entertainment: an activity designed to hold the interest and attention of an audience.

Environmentalism: a movement that seeks to protect the environment from a perceived threat of human beings.

Equivocation: a fallacy in which a key word in an argument is used ambiguously or in two different senses.

Ethos: from the Greek word for "character"; refers to the moods or styles of a particular group of people that form cultural distinctives.

Euthanasia: the practice whereby a physician intentionally aids in ending the life of a suffering patient.

Evangelicalism: a mid-twentieth-century Protestant movement that sees the essence of Christianity as the gospel: salvation comes by grace through faith in the saving work of Jesus Christ.

Fallacy: a mistake in reasoning that renders an argument invalid, unsound, weak, or ineffective.

Fallacy of Composition: a fallacy based on the assumption that because parts of a whole have certain characteristics, then so must the whole.

Fallacy of Division: a fallacy based on the assumption that because a whole has a certain characteristic, then so must its parts.

False Cause: a fallacy in which a cause-and-effect connection is assumed without sufficient evidence for that connection.

False Dilemma: a fallacy in which a problem is presented as having only two solutions when there is at least one other possibility.

Fascism: a political system usually headed by a charismatic leader and based upon a strong sense of pride, superiority, and veneration of one's state that asserts the right of stronger nations and people to displace or eradicate weaker states.

Fetus: an unborn human being who is at least eight weeks from conception.

Flow: a state in which a person works intently on something fascinating and is able to work in a smooth rhythm, be creative, and recognize afterward that it was a pleasurable experience.

Force: strength or power used to influence or oppress others.

Formalism: an artistic movement that emphasized the formal elements of art, such as line, color, space, and volume.

Fornication: any sexual activity between two people who are not married.

Free-Market Economy: an economy in which economic decisions are freely made by individuals, households, and firms instead of being regulated by the government.

Fundamentalism: an early twentieth-century Protestant movement that sought to defend orthodox Christianity against the challenges of liberalism, modernism, and Darwinism by requiring strict adherence to a set of "fundamental" doctrines.

Gnosticism: a second-century heretical Christian movement that taught that the material world was created and maintained by a lesser divine being, that matter and the physical body are inherently evil, and that salvation can be obtained only through an esoteric knowledge of divine reality and the self-denial of physical pleasures.

Government Redistribution: a state-controlled economic policy that taxes the wealthy at a higher rate than others and then reallocates those assets to the poor either through direct subsidies or government-sponsored social programs.

Government Subsidy: any financial benefit that the government gives to an individual or group of people.

Grassroots Movement: an approach to change that mobilizes people in local communities in an effort to bring about positive social transformation.

Grasstops Movement: an approach to change that mobilizes people in local communities (bottom up) and seeks to influence government policy (top down) in an effort to bring about positive social transformation.

Gratitude: the quality or feeling of being thankful.

Greed: the selfish desire for excessive wealth or power.

Groupthink: a psychological phenomenon that occurs when a group reaches a bad decision because it finds itself striving for unity over reason.

Hadith: the oral history of Muhammad's teachings and rulings, and the actions of his early companions.

Hasty Generalization: a fallacy in which a certain quality of a part is assumed to be a quality of the whole.

Higher Consciousness: the state of awareness wherein individuals realize their divinity and the divine interconnectedness of all things.

Hippocratic Oath: attributed to Hippocrates in the fourth or third century BC; the pledge taken by physicians outlining the obligations and proper ethical conduct of those who treat patients.

Human Flourishing: the idea that true human fulfillment comes from the pursuit of truth, virtue, and beauty.

Human Rights: the standards of conduct based on moral principles that express the dignity of humanity; those rights that are inherent to every human being just by merit of being human.

Human Trafficking: the illegal trade and movement of human beings who are bought and sold for some type of coerced labor.

Humanist Manifesto: the title of three manifestos laying out a Secular Humanist worldview: *Humanist Manifesto I* (1933), *Humanist Manifesto II* (1973), and *Humanist Manifesto 2000*. The central theme of all three is the elaboration of a philosophy and value system that do not include belief in God.

Hypocrisy: the practice of claiming to have moral standards that don't match a person's behavior; behaving in a manner contrary to how one believes people should behave.

Idol: any image or substitute representation of God used as an object of worship.

Idolatry: the act of worshipping or valuing something above God; entertaining thoughts about God that are unworthy of him.

Imago Dei: from the Latin for the "image of God"; the idea that human beings were created in God's likeness.

Inappropriate Appeal to Authority: a fallacy in which an argument is built upon the testimony of an individual who is not an authority on the subject at hand.

Inductive Argument: any argument built on specific premises leading to a probable conclusion.

Inelastic Good: any good whose demand is affected very little by price increases and decreases (e.g., food and gasoline).

Infanticide: the deliberate killing of a human child within one year of birth.

Information Technology: the use of computer systems for collecting, storing, accessing, and retrieving data.

Inherent-Rights View of Justice: the belief that justice involves the government seeking to protect the inherent rights of its citizens.

Inklings: an informal group of Oxford scholars who met in the 1930s and 1940s to discuss and develop literary works.

Institution: any organization of cultural significance that preserves or promotes cultural features (e.g., schools, sports leagues, and country clubs).

Intimacy: having a close or familiar relationship that meets a deep need of being known and loved.

Islam: a theistic worldview centered on the life of the prophet Muhammad that derives its understanding of the world through the teachings of the Quran, Hadith, and *Sunnah*.

Islamic Theocracy: a state ruled by Islam and Islamic religious leaders.

Jihad: from the Arabic word translated as "struggle"; signifies both the inner spiritual battle of every Muslim to fulfill his or her religious duties and the outer physical struggle against the enemies of Islam.

Jizya: a tax imposed on *dhimmis* (i.e., non-Muslims) living in Islamic states.

Jus ad Bellum: in just-war theory, a concept dealing with the requirements that constitute a just cause for fighting a war.

Jus in Bello: in just-war theory, a concept dealing with what constitutes ethical behavior in the act of fighting a war.

Justice: the moral principle of equally observing the rights of everyone and treating them fairly.

Just Peacemaking: a movement in Christendom that seeks to identify and encourage practices that can reduce injustice and make conflict less likely.

Just-War Theory: the belief that war is justifiable only if a certain set of criteria is met.

Karma: the belief in Eastern religions that good is returned to those who do good, and evil is returned to those who do evil (either in this life or the next).

Late-Term Abortion: any abortion performed within the second or third trimester of a pregnancy.

Law: the study of ordinances designed to help citizens coexist peacefully.

Legalism: the act of adding to either God's commands or his requirements for salvation; the act of relying on the law for salvation rather than on God.

Legal Positivism: the belief that laws are rules created by human authorities and that there is no inherent or necessary connection between law and morality.

Lex Talionis: the principle that a wrong should be righted with a retributive act equal in degree and kind.

Libertarianism: a political philosophy that upholds individual liberty as that highest good based upon the principle that people should be allowed to do whatever they want as along as they don't infringe upon the rights of others.

Liberty: freedom from undue restraint.

Loaded Question: a fallacy in which a question presupposes an unjustified assumption.

Logic: the study of orderly thinking; the art of formulating conclusions and outlining the reasons supporting those conclusions.

Maharishi Effect: the belief that positive improvement in the quality of life within a community can be brought about by a large group of people collectively engaged in the practice of Transcendental Mediation (TM), first described by Maharishi Mahesh Yogi.

Malthusian Catastrophe: based on the work of Thomas Malthus; any disastrous event brought about by an increase in the human population (e.g., disease, famine, or war), which naturally returns the human population to a state of equilibrium.

Marriage: a lifelong, exclusive union between a man and a woman that involves the capacity to bear children and raise them in a stable environment.

Marxism: an atheistic and materialistic worldview based on the ideas of Karl Marx that promotes the abolition of private property, the public ownership of the means of production (i.e., socialism), and the utopian dream of a future communistic state.

Materialism: the belief that reality is composed solely of matter.

Medieval Inquisition: a series of Catholic courts formed to prosecute and punish perceived heretics in the twelfth and thirteenth centuries in France and Italy.

Meditation: the art of focusing one's mind to induce a higher state of consciousness.

Mercy: receiving forgiveness rather than the punishment one deserves.

Mere Christianity: the idea, based on the work of C. S. Lewis, that Christians can and should work together around their shared beliefs in essential doctrines.

Metabelief: the intuitive sense of being, purpose, and posture toward other people and creation.

Metanarrative: a single, overarching interpretation, or grand story, of reality.

Metaphysics: the branch of philosophy that seeks to understand the nature of ultimate reality.

Microfinance: any venture in which investors give small loans to low-income individuals for the purpose of helping them start a self-sustaining business.

Minimum Mandatory Sentencing: a legal requirement that sets minimum standards of punishment for particular crimes.

Moral Majority: a late twentieth-century political and religious movement founded by Jerry Falwell to further Christian ideals through conservative politics—namely, promoting laws that restrict abortion on demand and protect religious expression in public education.

Moralistic Therapeutic Deism: a term coined by sociologist Christian Smith in reference to the shallow beliefs of many young Christians in the twenty-first century; the belief that God loves everyone and wants them to be happy.

Mosaic Law: the set of laws God gave Moses and the Hebrews following their exodus from Egypt.

Narcissism: the love of or obsession with oneself; selfishness; self-centeredness.

Natural Law: the belief that morality can be seen in the natural order of creation and accessed through human reason; the belief that laws are rules based upon on an internal code of morality that all people possess.

Nazism (aka National Socialism): the totalitarian, fascist, and socialist political system of World War II Germany that sought to establish its perceived racial superiority by eliminating all non-Aryan people and nations.

Need-Based Community Development: the process of trying to improve the economic conditions of a community by giving outside resources, such as money, goods, and aid.

Negative Liberty: the belief that liberty is secured when the government removes unwarranted constraints (e.g., ensuring a right to assembly or guaranteeing free speech).

New Spirituality: a pantheistic worldview that teaches that everyone and everything are connected through divine consciousness.

Nonresistance: the belief that individuals shouldn't resist those who seek to do them harm.

Orthodoxy: sound doctrine.

Orthopraxy: sound practice.

Pacifism: the belief that violence and war are always unjust and conflicts should be settled by peaceful means.

Pan-Islam: the belief that all Muslims should be united under a single Islamic state; the belief that the world should be united under a global Islamic state.

Partial-Birth Abortion: a medical procedure in which a living fetus is partially extracted from the birth canal before being exterminated.

Passive Euthanasia: the practice whereby a physician withholds treatment with the intent of ending a suffering patient's life.

Pedophilia: a psychiatric condition in which an adult has abnormal sexual desires for prepubescent children.

Performance View of Human Life: the belief that human beings have value only if they meet certain conditions (e.g., self-awareness, rationality, sentience, etc.).

Perigrinatio: a pilgrimage from which one does not expect to return.

Personal Autonomy: the belief that individuals should have the freedom to decide what is right for their own lives and live in whatever manner brings them the most happiness.

Physician-Assisted Suicide: the practice whereby a physician writes a lethal prescription that is intended to end a suffering patient's life.

Platonic Humanism: the idea that because the world came from God, studying the world can lead us back to God.

Plea Bargaining: an arrangement between a criminal and the courts whereby a defendant pleads guilty in exchange for a lesser punishment.

Political Correctness: the censoring of language, ideas, acts, or policies that are perceived to discriminate or alienate minority social groups.

Politics: the study of community governance.

Polyamory: from the Greek for "many lovers"; the practice of having more than one lover at a time.

Polygamy: the practicing of having more than one spouse at the same time.

Porneia: from the Greek for "sexually immoral acts," which include fornication, adultery, homosexuality, incest, and bestiality.

Pornography: any written or visual materials containing explicit sexual acts intended to elicit lustful desires in place of emotionally bonding with another human being.

Positive Liberty: the belief that liberty is secured when the government acts to remove inequality between people or people groups (e.g., enforcing affirmative action or passing minimum-wage laws).

Positivism: the idea that sensory experience, interpreted through logical thinking, forms the only basis for knowledge.

Postmodernism: a skeptical worldview, founded as a reaction to modernism, which is suspicious of metanarratives and teaches that ultimate reality is inaccessible, knowledge is a social construct, and truth claims are political power plays.

Poverty: the state of not having the money or resources to regularly meet one's basic needs (e.g., water, food, clothing, and shelter).

Practice: any traditional activity or observance by which people express the value of certain cultural features (e.g., holidays, weddings, and funerals).

Preemptive War: attacking an enemy whose aggression is imminent but has not yet occurred.

Premise: a basic statement in an argument that is used as support for a conclusion.

Preventive War: a war started to prevent another state from acquiring the capabilities to attack.

Progressivism: the belief in human progress; the belief that political systems can be used to create economic prosperity, minimize risk, and advance society.

Proletariat: a term used in Marxist theory to describe the working-class wage earners who do not own the means of production.

Proletariat Morality: the belief that whatever advances the proletariat and communism is morally good, and whatever hinders them is morally evil.

Propaganda: any biased, selective, misleading, or manipulating information circulated with the goal of changing opinions and influencing action toward a particular position or cause.

Purity: the condition of being free from immorality.

Pygmalion Effect: a psychological effect whereby the confidence of an arguer makes the persuasion of those listening more likely.

Quran: the central holy book of Islam that Muslims believe to be the literal word of God, recited verbatim from God to Muhammad through the angel Gabriel.

Realism: an artistic movement that emphasized portraying the world truthfully without embellishment, exaggerated emotion, or romantic idealism.

Red Herring: a fallacy in which an irrelevant issue is raised in an argument to avoid the issue at hand.

Rehabilitation: any attempt to change a criminal's tendency to commit crimes so that the individual will be less likely to reoffend when he or she is reintroduced into society.

Religion: a system of belief that attempts to define the nature of God and how human beings can understand and interact with the divine; any system of belief that prescribes certain responses to the existence (or nonexistence) of the divine.

Religious Freedom: the universal right of human beings to think, live, and worship as they feel convicted by their religious beliefs, without fear of persecution.

Religious Persecution: the restriction or punishment of any religious group or individual for one's religious beliefs and practices.

Repentance: the act of admitting our transgressions, seeking forgiveness, turning away from evil, and pursuing what is good.

Republic: a system of government in which citizens elect agents to represent the interests of those who elected them.

Restorative Justice: the practice of pursuing justice between a victim and a perpetrator.

Retributive Justice: the belief that a just society should focus on punishing criminals rather than rehabilitating them or removing the root causes of crime.

Revolution: an overthrow of an established order, system, or state.

Right: a guarantee that what belongs to someone will not be unjustly taken.

Right-Ordering View of Justice: the belief that justice involves the government seeking to preserve social order.

Romanticism: an artistic movement that emphasized the emotional elements of art and rejected the more traditional artistic elements, such as order, harmony, and balance.

Sadism: the condition, based on the work of the Marquis de Sade, whereby someone receives pleasure, especially sexual pleasure, by inflicting pain or humiliation on others.

Sadomasochism: the act of deriving pleasure from either inflicting (sadism) or receiving (masochism) pain during sex.

Salem Witch Trials: a series of trials that led to the execution of twenty individuals accused of witchcraft in late seventeenth-century colonial Massachusetts.

Scare Tactics: a fallacy in which an argument's strength is built on the fear of negative consequences for not agreeing with its conclusion.

Scientific Method: a process of empirical inquiry that seeks to understand the phenomena of the physical world through hypothesizing, observing, measuring, experimenting, predicting, and testing.

Secular Humanism: a religious and philosophical worldview that makes humankind the ultimate norm by which truth and values are to be determined; a worldview that reveres human reason, evolution, naturalism, and secular theories of ethics while rejecting every form of supernatural religion.

Secularism: an atheistic and materialistic worldview that advocates a public society free from the influence of religion.

Secularization: the movement of a culture away from religious identification and values as religion loses cultural relevance and significance.

Self-Interest: the desire to make sure one's own needs are met.

Sex Trafficking: a form of human trafficking that uses violence, debt, abduction, and fraud to coerce human beings to work in the sex trade.

Sexual Purity: the condition of being free from sexual immorality.

Sexual Revolution: a 1960s Western social movement that celebrated advances in contraception, encouraged sexual experimentation, and promoted sex outside of marriage.

Shalom: from the Hebrew for "peace, prosperity, and wellness"; a concept that implies harmony in creation and with one's neighbors as well as a right relationship with God.

Sharia Law: the moral and legal code derived primarily from the Quran and the *Sunnah* that governs the lives of Muslims. Sharia addresses a wide variety of subjects, such as diet, hygiene, prayer, contracts, business, crime, and punishment.

Sin: any action or inaction that violates the will of God.

Sin of Commission: the failure to avoid what God commands us to avoid (e.g., theft, gossip, and adultery).

Sin of Omission: the failure to act as God commands us to act (e.g., loving and forgiving others).

Slippery Slope: a fallacy in which a claim is made with insufficient evidence that if a certain action is taken, it would eventually lead to dire consequences.

Social Contract: the belief that individuals within a society form either an implicit or explicit agreement with their government, whereby citizens forfeit some freedoms in exchange for safety.

Social Gospel: a late eighteenth-century, early nineteenth-century postmillennial movement popular among liberal Protestants that sought to eradicate social evils like poverty and racism in the belief that this would usher in the second coming of Christ.

Social Safety Net: any collection of government programs intended to assist individuals who fall on hard times and keep them out of poverty (e.g., welfare, unemployment insurance, and universal health care).

Socialism: an economic system based on governmental or communal ownership of the means of production and distribution of goods and services.

Sound Argument: a valid argument with true premises.

Spanish Inquisition: a series of Spanish courts formed to preserve Catholic orthodoxy against perceived heresies in the fifteenth century.

Sphere Sovereignty: the belief formulated by Abraham Kuyper asserting that God ordained certain spheres of society, such as family, church, and state, and that society functions best when each sphere is properly managing its own area of responsibility.

Stem Cell: an undifferentiated cell that has the ability to replicate and develop into another kind of cell (e.g., skin cell, blood cell, or nerve cell).

Stewardship: the process of managing something that has been entrusted to one's care.

Straw Man: a fallacy in which an argument is misrepresented in a way that makes it easier to refute.

Suttee: an ancient Hindu practice of burning a widow alive on the funeral pyre of her deceased husband.

Technology: the application of techniques employed to solve human problems.

Technopoly: a term coined by Neil Postman referring to any culture that assumes that technology is the highest human good.

Terasem: a cyberreligion, founded by Martine Rothblatt, that teaches that human beings will someday be able to attain immortality by downloading data from their brains (i.e., mind files) and uploading this information into some form of robot.

Texts: a culture's media (e.g., books, movies, and works of art).

Theory of Forms: a type of philosophical idealism, formulated by Plato, positing that everything we experience in this world is simply an imperfect instantiation of an eternal and perfect ideal that exists in the world of the forms.

Tob Meod: a Hebrew phrase translated as "very good"; the very best thing possible; the ultimate superlative of good.

Tolerance: the willingness to recognize and respect the dignity of those with whom one disagrees.

Tort Law: the area of law governing remedies for those wronged by others, such as through negligence.

Totalitarianism: a highly centralized system of government in which the state retains and exerts complete authority over its citizens and seeks to regulate every aspect of people's lives.

Traditional Marriage: the belief that society benefits most when marriage is defined as a monogamous and lifelong union between one man and one woman, oriented toward having children.

Tragedy of the Commons: a situation in which a natural resource becomes exploited because it is collectively shared by individuals seeking their own self-interest.

Tu Quoque: a fallacy in which a person's conclusion is rejected because he or she doesn't live as if the conclusion is true.

Two-Kingdoms Theology: based on an idea expressed by Martin Luther, two-kingdoms theology distinguishes between the kingdom of God (i.e., the church) and the kingdom of humanity (i.e., the state), contending that Christians should not promote their religious views outside the kingdom of God.

Universal Enlightened Production: the belief that an individual's financial success is directly proportional to his or her level of enlightenment; the belief that positive thought creates wealth.

Utilitarian View of Human Life: the belief that a human being's value is measured relative to the value of other human beings (e.g., disabled, malformed, etc.).

Utilitarianism: the belief that we ought to do whatever maximizes happiness and reduces suffering for the greatest number of people.

Valid Argument: a properly formed argument.

War on Poverty: the set of government programs initiated by president Lyndon Johnson to reduce poverty in the United States.

Weak Analogy: a fallacy in which a comparison is made between things that aren't comparable in relevant respects.

Wisdom: the ability to think and act with good judgment.

Worldview: a pattern of ideas, beliefs, convictions, and habits that help us make sense of God, the world, and our relationship to God and the world.

Zakat: the third pillar of Islam establishing a mandatory donation of 2.5 percent of a Muslim's annual net income.

Zero-Sum Game: any situation in which one participant's gain (or loss) is proportionally offset by another participant's loss (or gain).

INDEX

- A -

abad, 486

abandonment, 371–72

ABCD (asset-based community development), 403, 481, 482

Abdalati, Hammudah, 392

Abélard, Peter, 51

The Abolition of Man (Lewis), 103

abortion, 21, 22, 71–72, 203–4, 212, 216–17, 341, 361, 470–72, 506, 507
    (See also crisis pregnancy centers; Planned Parenthood; pro-life advocacy)

abundance, 309

Abwehr (German military intelligence organization), 324

Acacius of Amida, 70

accommodation, 56

accountability, 162, 246, 339

accuracy, 121

accused, dignity of, 451

action, in persuasive messages, 133

Action Institute, 402, 477

active euthanasia, 211, 506

Acton, Lord, 333, 366

Ad hominem fallacy, 126

A.D. The Bible Continues (television miniseries), 487

Adams, John, 336–37, 365

Administrative Justice (AJ), 452

administrative laws, 450

Adrian VI (pope), 74

adultery, 247–48, 263

Advent, 161

affections, 177–78

Affordable Care Act of 2010 (ACA), 366

Afghanistan, 363, 413

Africa, poverty in, 385–86, 400, 402

African American community, 470–72, 480

after-birth abortions, 212

Against Heresies (Irenaeus), 300

Age of Enlightenment, 176, 229, 298, 505

Agricola, Rudolph, 74

AIDS, 240

Airbnb, 105

al-Baghdadi, Abu Bakr, 364

Albigensians, 357

Alcorn, Randy, 236

Alcuin of York, 73–74

Algeria, 364

Alliance Defending Freedom (ADF), 372

alliances, 162

Alone Together (Turkle), 150, 156

alternative enculturation, 474

Alternatives to Marriage Project, 277

America. See United States

American Dictionary of the English Language (Webster), 511

The American Pageant (Bailey), 485

American Protestantism, 19

American Psychological Association (APA), 280–81

American Veda (Goldberg), 331

Americans United for Life (AUL), 221

Amish tradition, 50

- B -

Bach, Johann Sebastian, 80

Bacon, Francis, 79

Bacon, Roger, 79

bad arguments, 125–31, 502

bad habits, 192–93

bad information technology, 149–50

Baehr, Ted, 92, 108, 183

Bailey, Thomas, 485

Baillie, John, 91

Bainton, Roland, 414–15

Baker, Hunter, 327–28

Baker, Joe, 221

bandwagon fallacy, 127

Bannerjee, Krishna Mohan, 68, 72, 74

Baptist Missionary Society, 468

Baptist Press, 21

Baptist tradition, 52, 75, 365

Barfield, Owen, 96

Battin, Margaret, 212

Baudrillard, John, 185–86

Bauer, Peter T., 303

Bauerlein, Mark, 153, 374

Baumeister, Roy, 193

beauty, 57–58, 249, 306

Becket Fund for Religious Freedom, 372

Beckwith, Francis, 208, 214–15, 218

Beckwith, Michael Bernard, 393

Begbie, Jeremy, 179

begging-the-question fallacy, 128

Beguines, 357

Beisner, E. Calvin, 299, 303, 310, 390–91, 398, 483

Belarus, 360

beliefs, 47, 48–49, 64–66, 120, 500
(See also unbelief)

Bell, Daniel, 430

Ben-Hur (Wallace), 80

Benedict Option, 50–51

Bengali renaissance (nineteenth century), 69

Bentley, Toni, 243

Berger, John, 185, 186

Berry, Wendell, 314

bestowed worth, 213

Bible Institute of Los Angeles (B.I.O.L.A.), 19

Bible (television miniseries), 487

biblical beliefs, 500

biblical worldview, 498

Bieber, Justin, 14

The Biggest Loser (television show), 90

Bill of Rights (US Constitution), 440

Billington, James, 153

bioethics, 209–10

Biola University, 19

bipolar disorder, 458

birth control, 396

Biscet, Oscar Elias, 360–61

The Black Book of Communism (Courtois), 359–60

Black Death, 358

Black Panther Party, 438

Black Swan (Taleb), 191

Blackstone, William, 336, 511

blame, 272–74

Blamires, Harry, 94

blasphemy, 356, 363, 364

Blough, Paton, 458

capitalism, 234, 264, 392, 393

Capra, Frank, 116, 117

Captivated (documentary), 152–53

Carell, Steve, 181

Carey, William, 74, 468, 478

caring, 12–18

Carolingian Empire, 73

Carpenter, Humphrey, 58

Carson, D. A., 242

Carson, Rachel, 292, 294, 311

Carter, Jimmy, 21

Casler, Lawrence, 263

caste system, 69

categorical syllogism, 124

category mistake, 66

Cathedral of Notre-Dame, France, 80

Catholic Charities, Massachusetts, 367

Catholic Church. See Roman Catholic Church

Cathy, Dan, 367–68

Catmull, Ed, 194

cell-phone minutes as currency, 147

Center for Biological Diversity, 305

Center for Ecoliteracy, 304

Centers for Disease Control and Prevention (CDC), 203, 240

ceremonial laws, 237, 334, 450

change, 194, 475–76

Chaput, Charles, 368

charity, 76–77

Charlemagne (king of France), 73, 74

Chartres Cathedral, France, 81

chastity, 242, 247–48

Chesterton, G. K., 82, 91

Chick-fil-A, 367–68

child pornography and prostitution, 234

children, value of, 282–83

children's rights, 71–73, 261–63, 276, 280–81

China, 361–62

Christ-above-culture view, 52–53

Christ-against-culture view, 50–51

Christ and culture in paradox view, 53–54

Christ and Culture (Niebuhr), 49–50

Christ-of-culture view, 51–52

Christ-the-transformer-of-culture view, 54

Christian Action Council, 22

Christian conservatism, 20–24

Christian mission, 55–56

The Christian Observer (journal), 468

Christian Science Monitor, 23

The Christian Virtuoso (Boyle), 79

Christianity and culture, history, 499–500

Chungkai (Japanese prison camp), 38–39, 42, 499

church, 269–70, 325, 329, 341–42, 371, 414–15, 472, 475–76
(See also specific religious traditions)

Churchill, Winston, 204

Cialdini, Robert, 139

Cicero, 326

CiRCE Institute, 95

circular reasoning, 128, 502

cities, 469–70, 474

citizenship, 343–45

City of God (Augustine), 64, 70, 415

"the City on the Hill," 473

civic or civil laws, 237, 334

civil disobedience, 345

Civil Rights Act (1964), 438

dispensational premillennialism, 20

distractive driving, 149

distress, 108

distributive justice, 445–49

diversion programs, 453–54

Divine Comedy (Dante), 80

division, fallacy of, 130

divorce laws, 278

Dixon, A. C., 19

Do Hard Things (Harris & Harris), 282

Docter, Pete, 195, 505

doctrine of original sin, 449

domination, 268

dominion, 298, 299–300

Don't Waste Your Life (Piper), 192

Dostoyevsky, Fyodor, 82

Douglass, Frederick, 71, 219

Douthat, Ross, 109, 340

Downey, Roma, 487

Downtown Pregnancy Center, Dallas, Texas, 221

Dreher, Rod, 50–51, 94, 228, 236

drugs, illegal, 456

Duchamp, Marcel, 81

Duhigg, Charles, 140, 192

The Dumbest Generation (Bauerlein), 153

dumbing-down effect, 157–59

Dunham, Lena, 233

Durant, Kevin, 490

Durant, Will, 341, 364

Dust Bowl era (1930's), 295

Dutch Reformed tradition, 51

Dutt, Clemens, 329

Dworkin, Andrea, 248

Dykstra, Craig, 160

Dyson, Hugo, 96

- *E* -

Eagle River, Alaska, 51

Earthkeeping in the Nineties (Wilkinson), 298

Easter, 161

Eberstadt, Mary, 242

ecofeminism, 294

ecology, 294

economic democracy, 483

economic growth, 483–84

economic interventionism, 312

economy, management of, 388–90

ecumenism, 20

Eden, Dawn, 248

educating versus informing, 138

education, 73–75, 148–49

Edwards, Jonathan, 473

EEOC (Equal Employment Opportunity Commission), 367

egalitarian universalism, 68

ego, 331

Egypt, 52, 75, 363

Eichmann, Adolf, 98

Einstein, Albert, 16, 79

elastic goods, 389

Elder, Linda, 120

Eli Lilly, 369

Eligius (saint), 70

Eliot, T. S., 42, 57, 82, 91, 188

Elliot, Elisabeth, 243

Elliot, Jim, 243

Ellis, Havelock, 229, 230

Ellison, Marvin, 232

Ellul, Jacques, 135, 155

Elon, Amos, 98

email messages, 148

embryology, 213

embryonic stem cells, 210

embryos, 209–10

Emmons, Robert, 190

emotional capital, 481

emotions, 104

empathy, 158

To End All Wars (Gordon), 38–39

end-of-life technologies, 212

endowment, 214

endowment view of human life, 207, 506

endurance, 437–39

enduring evil, 428

engagement in culture, 98–109, 117, 501

engaging culture, 39–42

Engels, Friedrich, 264

entertainment, 173, 486–88, 504–6

entertainment culture, 173–79

Enuma Elish creation myth, 99

environmental disaster prophecies, 303–4

environmental issues, 293

Environmental Protection Agency (EPA), 292

environmentalism, 293–94, 509

Equal Employment Opportunity Commission (EEOC), 367

equality, 334–35, 446–49

Equiano, Olaudah, 70–71

equivocation fallacy, 128

Erasmus, Desiderius, 74

Erickson, Millard J., 270

Eritrea, 359

erotic justice, 232

ethos, 48, 131

Euler, Leonhard, 79

euphemisms, 120

euthanasia, 210–13, 506

Euthyphro (Plato), 118

Evangel Ministries, Detroit, Michigan, 470–72

evangelicalism, 21–23

Evans, Rachel Held, 232

Evans, Tony, 342

Every Young Man's Battle (Arterburn & Stoeker), 241

everyday economics, 392

evil, 98, 101, 153–54, 421, 424, 425, 428, 450–52, 501

exclusivity, 274

excuses, 108

Exline, Julie, 193

extreme poverty, 387

Eyck, Jan van, 81

Eyes of Honor (Welton), 249

– F –

face-to-face talk, 149

Facebook, 152

FaceTime, 148

fairness, 121, 446

the Fall, 100–102

fallacies, 126–31

fallacious attacks, responding to, 220

fallacy, defined, 126

fallacy of composition, 130–31

fallacy of division, 130

- *H* -

Khan, Tim, 413

Khrushchev, Nikita, 360

Kidd, Thomas, 357

killing, 65, 210–13
  (See also murder)

Kim Il Sung, 361

Kim Jong-Eun, 361

kindness, 398–99

King, Martin Luther, Jr., 65, 93, 345, 437–38, 515

Kinnaman, Dave, 25

Kinsey, Alfred, 230, 240

Kirkendall, Lester, 205

Kirkpatrick, Melanie, 361

Kissling, Frances, 204

Klusendorf, Scott, 214, 221

Knights Templar, 357

Know, John, 473

Koch, Kathy, 151

Kollontai, Alexandra, 264

Koop, C. Everett, 22

Kostamo, Leah, 293, 301, 308, 309

Kotter, John, 42

Koukl, Greg, 136–39

Krishna, 185

Kuehne, Dale, 233, 236, 238, 248, 249–50

Kurtz, Paul, 153, 205, 327, 328, 329

Kutcher, Ashton, 14

Kuyper, Abraham, 340, 343, 374

- L -

La Ferrara, Eliana, 182

Laats, Adam, 128

L'Abri (Switzerland), 56

laity, 475

Lake Superior, North America, 311

Lake Victoria, Africa, 311

Lamont, Corliss, 483

language, 43–45, 119–20
  (See also communication)

The Language of God: A Scientist Provides Evidence for Belief (Collins), 80

Laos, 360

Las Casas, Bartolomé de, 372

The Last Christian on Earth (Guinness), 55

last resort, 426

late-term abortions, 204

Latimer, Hugh, 375

law of retaliation, 418

laws, 237–38, 260, 271, 278, 280, 326, 328, 332, 334–37, 344, 345, 362, 372, 418–19, 440–42, 450, 451, 457, 478–79, 508, 511, 512, 515

Lawson, Deodat, 358

leaders, 324

Leadership Journal, 472

Leaf, Caroline, 181

Leal, Donald, 312–13

Lecrae (hip-hop artist), 107

Lee, Marc Alan, 431

legal positivism, 328, 441–42

legislator, 336

Leifman, Steven, 459

Leland, John, 365

Lenin, Vladimir, 330

Lent, 161

lesbian, gay, bisexual, or transgendered (LGBT), 231–32, 233

"Letter from a Birmingham Jail" (King), 438, 515

- M -

Making Sense of Your World (Phillips, Brown & Stonestreet), 117–18

malaria, 291–93

Malaysia, 396

Malcolm X, 438

maleness, 241, 507

Malthus, Thomas, 310, 395

Malthusian catastrophe, 310

Mangalwadi, Vishal, 66, 159

manipulation, 121, 134–35, 182, 503

Mao Tse-tung, 361

Marcion, 53

market-basket approach, 313

market power, 482–86

marketing, 188–89

Marks, Loren, 281

marriage, 43, 177, 228, 229, 231, 235, 238, 240, 241, 243, 259–84, 470–72, 477, 507, 508–9

Mars Hill Audio Journal (Myers), 44

Marsden, George, 19

Marshall, Bruce, 242

Marshall, Paul, 362, 363

Martens, Elmer, 297

Martinson, Robert, 459

Marvel Comics, 82

Marx, Karl, 264, 329, 391

Marxism, 184, 234, 264, 277, 329–30, 358, 359–62, 391, 511, 512

Marxist-Leninist theory, 330

Mary I (queen of England), 375

Maslow, Abraham, 101

Masterpiece Cakeshop, Denver, Colorado, 192–93

material world, 300–301

materialism, 230, 298, 360, 476

materialists, 482–86

Mather, Increase, 358

Mauren, Kris Alan, 402

Maxwell, James Clerk, 79–80

May, Rollo, 177

McBrayer, Justin, 127–28

McDowell, Josh, 236

McDowell, Sean, 43, 246–47, 268–69

McGinnis, Alan Loy, 162

McIlhancy, Joe, Jr., 241

McKee, Robert, 194, 487

McMahan, Jeff, 208–9

meaning, 18

media addiction, 152–53

mediation, 454

Medici family, 341

medicine, 75–76

medieval inquisition, 357

meditation, 331

Medved, Michael, 173

Meek, Esther Lightcap, 93

Meilaender, Gilbert, 213

Memphite creation myth, 99

Menino, Thomas, 367

Mennonite tradition, 50, 422

mental-health advocacy, 458–59

mentors, 193–94

mercy, 76, 163

mercy killing, 210–13

Mere Christianity (Lewis), 106, 231

Meredith, Martin, 385, 390

Messiah (Handel), 80

metabeliefs, 48–49

metamorphosis, 473

Mustol, John, 298, 306

myelination, 190

Myers, David, 232

Myers, Ken, 44

mystery, 269

- N -

- P -

pacifism, 414, 421, 422–23, 514

paganism, 332

Paine, Thomas, 365

Pakistan, 363

Palestinian Territories, 364

Palmer, Parker, 32

Pamerleau, Susan, 459

pan-Islam, 332, 362

Papa, Matt, 194

Paradigm Project, 405

Paradise Lost (Milton), 80

Paraguay, 479

paranoia, 272

Paris, Jenell, 242

Park, Michael Alan, 307

partial-birth abortions, 204, 219

Pashukanis, E. B., 330

Passion and Purity (Elliot), 243

passive euthanasia, 211, 506

pathos, 131–32

Patient Protection and Affordable Care Act of 2010 (PPACA), 366

Patrick (saint), 70

patronage, 76

Patterson, Eric, 430

Paul, Richard, 120

PayPal, 105

peace, 414, 418, 423, 424–25, 427, 429, 446

Pearcey, Nancy, 78, 176, 188

pedophilia, 234

peer pressure, 103

Pelser, Adam, 104

people, 16–17, 302–6, 345–46, 470–72, 498, 510

PEP (Prison Entrepreneurship Program), 459–60

Percival, Sir Thomas, 75

Percy, Walker, 82

performance view of human life, 207–9, 506

perigrinatio, 73

permanence, 274

pernicious laws, 457

persecution, religious, 356–59, 511–12

personal autonomy, 231–32

personal legacy, 13

personal retribution, 420–21

personally relevant messages, 134

persuasion, 131–35, 139, 502–3

persuasive messages, 132–33

persuasive words, 119

Pew Forum on Religion and Public Life, 354

Pew Research Center, 359

Phillips, Adam, 264–65

Phillips, Jack, 192–93

Phillips, Wendell, 375

Philo of Byblos, 99, 118

Phips, Sir William, 358

physical capital, 481, 482

physical force, 417–21

physical violence, 424

physician-assisted suicide, 211

Pierard, Richard, 371

Pierson, Gary, 489

Pieters, Albertus, 419

Pietists at Halle, 75

---

procreation, 281

productivity, 308–9

productivity loss, 149

progressivism, 294–95

proletariat, 264, 329, 359

proletariat morality, 359

promiscuity, 240

propaganda, 134–35, 503

property crimes, 456

property rights, 339

proportionality, 398

proportionate means, 426

prosperity, 17, 388–90

prostitution, 234

"the Protestant Rome," 473

prudence, 54, 95

psychosis, 458

public policy and marriage, 275–77

public regulation of marriage, 275

Public Rights/Private Conscience Project, 368

Pullman, Philip, 183

Puritan England, 473

Puritan New England, 473

Puritan tradition, 70

purity, 245–46

purposefulness, 190

Putnam, Robert, 401

Pygmalion effect, 132

- Q -

Qatar, 369

Quaker tradition, 50, 70, 414–15, 422

Queen Latifah, 43, 49

queer theory, 233

questions, asking, 136–37

Quintilian, 139

Quo Vadis (Sienkiewicz), 80

quod omnes tanget, 335

Quran, 266, 362

- R -

Rabushka, Alvin, 483

race riots, 470

racial issues, 470–72, 480

Rae, Scott, 139, 213

rain forests, 305

"*raison d'etat*," 421

Ramabai, Pandita, 72, 74

Ramsay, James, 71

Randall, Joseph, 206

rape, 218–19, 234, 266

Ratio Christi, 221

rationalism, 176

Rauch, Jonathan, 278

Rauschenbusch, Walter, 19

Rawlings-Blake, Stephanie, 445–46

Rawls, John, 447–48

re-formed, 473

Reader, Mark, 328

Reagan, Nancy, 210

Reagan, Ronald, 22, 210, 444

realism, 176

realpolitik, 421

reasoning, 118–21, 128, 502

rebellion, 101

reconciliation, 246–47, 283–84, 414

Red Cross, 77

Spurgeon, Charles, 417, 491

St. Matthew Passion (Bach), 80

Stalin, Joseph, 204, 330

Stanley, Andy, 243

Stanmeyer, William, 337–38

Star Wars (movie), 159, 182, 185

Stark, Rodney, 58, 66, 72, 76, 78, 300, 335, 356–57

State Department, 363, 373

state (government), 275–76, 419–21, 440

statistical form of an argument, 125

STD (sexually transmitted disease), 228, 240, 507

steamroller tactic, 138

Steeves, Rouven, 415, 430

stem cell research, 210

stem cells, 209–10

Stenger, Victor J., 128, 129

Stetzer, Ed, 23, 31

Stevens, Leonard A., 136

stewards of creation, 155–56

stewardship, 293, 299–300, 383–84, 509

Stewart, Kenneth, 372

Stewart, Lyman, 19

Stoeker, Fred, 241, 246

Stone, Linda, 151

Stonestreet, John, 24, 43, 99, 103, 105, 108, 109, 179, 187, 188, 231, 235, 242, 246–47, 263, 270, 309, 340, 479

Storer, Morris, 328

Stott, John, 302

Stowe, Harriet Beecher, 71

straw-man fallacy, 127

Strom, Bruce, 452

structure of creation, 56

Struthers, William, 232

Students for Life of America (SFLA), 221

styles, 47–48

subsidiarity, 339–40

subsidies, 390, 404

subsistence, 403–5

substance view, 214

Sugihara, Chiune, 69

suicide, 211, 240

Sullivan, Andrew, 232, 374

Summerville, John, 179

Summit Ministries, 345

Sunshine, Glenn, 66, 67, 68

superficiality, 152–53

supplemental measure (SPM), 385

suspicion, 131

suttee (or sati), 69, 72, 478

Sutton, Agneta, 211

Sutton, Willie, 96

Swiss Reformers, 473

Switzerland, 56

symbols, 43–44

Syria, 364

- *T* -

Tactics (Koukl), 136–37

takers, 12, 32

taking the roof off, 138

Taleb, Nassim Nicholas, 191–92

Tanenhaus, Sam, 130

tax policy, 389–90, 403, 483–84

teams, 490–91

technocracies, cultures, 157

The Technological Society (Ellul), 155

technology, 14, 45, 104–5, 145–95, 205, 209–10, 211, 246, 304, 310–11, 369, 470–72, 503–4

technopoly, 157

Technopoly (Postman), 162

"Telling the World Its Own Story" Neuhaus, 92

temperance, 54

temple tax, 282

temporal minutes, 161

temptation, 417

Ten Commandments, 205, 230, 418, 515

Terasem (cyber-religion), 153–54

terrorist organizations, 364

Tertullian, 50, 422

text messaging, 146–47, 148

texts, defined, 93

Thatcher, Margaret, 303

Thaxton, Charles, 78

theism, 423

A Theology for the Social Gospel (Rauschenbusch), 19

theology of expertise, 157

theory of forms, 67

therapeutic cloning, 210

Thicke, Robin, 43

thinking, 94, 104, 117–21, 181, 502–3

Thomas Aquinas. See Aquinas, Thomas (saint)

Thomas, Cal, 402

Thomas, Clarence, 279–80

Thomas, Pete, 89–90

Thomas, Robert, 96

Thomson, Judith Jarvis, 218

Thor (movie), 82

Thor of Norse mythology, 82

Thornton, Henry, 468

thoughtful intentions, 91

thoughtlessness, 163–64

Three Essays on the Theory of Sexuality (Freud), 229

throw-away mentality, 309

time, 161

Tinka Tinka Sukh (radio show, India), 182–83

TM (Transcendental Meditation), 331

tob meod, 25, 260

Tocqueville, Alexis de, 230–31, 337

Todd, Pat, 454

Tokyo Christian Women's University, 72

tolerance, 356, 512

Tolkien, J. R. R., 58, 96, 102, 314, 374

Tolle, Eckhart, 331, 393

Tollefsen, Christopher, 213

tool-using cultures, 157

Tooley, Michael, 208, 217

Torah, 334

Torrey, R. A., 19

tort law, 344, 451

totalitarianism, 330

toxic thinking, 181

Tozer, A. W., 343

traditional marriage, 261, 275, 278–79

tragedy of the commons, 311

trans-formed, 473

Transcendental Meditation (TM), 331

"To Transform a City" (Keller), 472

transformation, 460–61

Transformers (movie), 127

transforming culture, 38–39, 55–58

transparency, 339

Treaty of Utrecht (1713), 70

Tren, Richard, 292

Trinity, 158, 161, 270, 296, 297, 474, 508

trust, building, 131–32

trustworthiness, 502–3

truth, 104, 117, 136, 176, 186, 279, 339, 499, 505, 511

Truth and Reconciliation Commission (TRC), 454

Tsuda College, Japan, 72

Tsuda Umeko, 72

tu quoque fallacy, 126

Tubman, Harriet, 71

Turkey, 80, 364

Turkle, Sherry, 150–51, 153, 154, 156, 158, 164, 178, 504

Turkmenistan, 360

Tutu, Desmond, 454

Twenge, Jean, 26

Twitter, 148

two-kingdoms theology, 22

The Two Towers (Tolkien), 102, 374

Two Treatises of Government (Locke), 68

tWorld, 249–50

typed notes versus written notes, 149

- *U* -

Uber, 105, 501

Uganda, 369

Umbreit, Mark, 454

Umeko, Tsuda, 74

un-formed, 472

unalienable rights, 69, 207

unbelief, 101
    (See also beliefs)

UnChristian (Kinnaman & Lyons), 25–26

understanding, 29

Understanding the Faith (Myers & Noebel), 12, 117, 498, 502

Understanding the Times (Myers & Noebel), 12, 117, 184, 295, 311, 312, 327, 367, 422, 498, 502

unfairness, 279–80

Unfettered Hope (Dawn), 162

unfulfilled desires, 178

United Nations, 329, 455

United States, 364
    (See also US entries)

United Way, 77

Universal Declaration of Huma Rights (1948), 355

universal enlightened production, 393

universal forms, 67

universe, 29, 78, 99–100

universities, 74

University of Northwestern, 19

unjust laws, 345

Unmarried Equality, 277, 278

Up (movie), 194–95, 505

upper-story truth, 176, 505

Urban Ministries, Atlanta, Georgia, 480

US Bill of Rights, 440

US Commission on International Religious Freedom (USCIRF), 364, 373

US Constitution, 338, 365, 440, 442, 453

US Declaration of Independence, 207, 328, 334, 336, 441, 442

US Department of Health and Human Service (DHS), 366

US Department of State, 363

US Environmental Protection Agency (EPA), 292

US International Religious Freedom Act of 1998 (IRFA), 356

US State Department, 363, 373

US Supreme Court, 279

USSR. See Soviet Union

utilitarian view of human life, 207–9, 506

Uzbekistan, 360

- V -

Valenti, Jack, 184

valid arguments, 124, 502

values, 155

van der Bijl, Andrew, 345–46

Vanderbilt, Cornelius, 485

Vanhoozer, Kevin, 42, 66, 92, 93–94

vengeance, 425–26

victim-impact panels, 454

victim-offender mediation, 454–55

victims, 443–44, 446–47, 451, 453, 455

Victory Trade School (VTS), Springfield, Missouri, 480

Vietnam, 360

Viguerie, Richard, 444

Vines, Matthew, 232, 239

violence, 177–78, 413–14, 424, 515

Violence-Free Zone program, Washington DC, 458

violent crimes, 456

Virgin Galactic spaceship, 14–15, 497–98

virginity, 248

virtue, 30, 95, 190, 477, 504

visualization, in persuasive messages, 133

Vitoria, Francisco de, 372, 422

vocation, 477, 486

Voegeli, William, 233, 484

Voice of the Martyrs, 373

volitional capital, 482

voting, 344

Voxer, 148

- W -

Waldensians, 357

Wallace, Lew, 80

Wal-mart, 369

Wapshott, Nicholas, 387

war and warfare, 413–15, 425–27, 514

War: Four Christian Views (Clouse), 421

The War of Art (Pressfield), 191

War of the Spanish Succession (1701-1714), 70

war on poverty, 328, 386–87, 389–90

Ward, Gary, 265

Ward, Glenn, 80, 185

Warfield, B. B., 19

Warren, Mary Anne, 217

Washburn, Kevin, 160

Washington, George, 337

wastefulness, 309, 310

waterwheels, 147

Watson, Paul, 302

Watt, James, 159

Watts, Craig, 129

Watts, Jay, 211, 217

"the way," 58

weak-analogy fallacy, 130

wealth and wealth creation, 339, 510
    (See also redistribution of wealth)

weapons, 419, 515

Webster, Noah, 337, 511

- X -

- Y -

- Z -

THE CLASSIC ON APOLOGETICS AND WORLDVIEW — REWRITTEN FOR THE NEW GENERATION!

Summit Ministries is the gold standard of worldview and apologetics studies. Their classic *Understanding the Times* has been completely rewritten and split into two volumes to help a new generation know and defend their Christian faith.

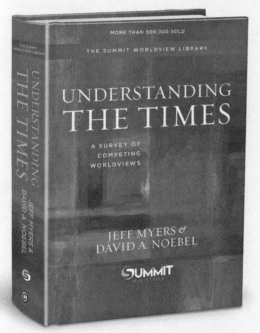

Understanding the Times: A Survey of Competing Worldviews is a landmark guide to understanding the most significant religious worldviews operating in Western Civilization: Christianity, Islam, Secularism, New Spirituality, and Postmodernism. It equips today's generation to know and defend their Christian faith against the onslaught of skepticism and doubt.

Get a FREE 7-day devotional based on this book at bit.ly/understanding-the-times

Understanding the Faith: A Survey of Christian Apologetics is the definitive resource for understanding how God's Word can be both true and authoritative in a relativistic world. With only 17 percent of today's believers able to articulate and defend their Christian beliefs, this book is a required resource for every family.

Get a FREE 7-day devotional based on this book at bit.ly/understanding-the-faith

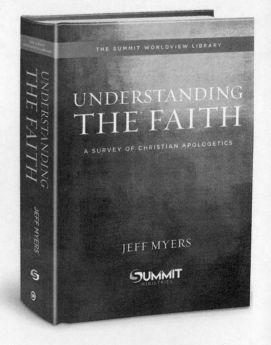

DAVID C COOK
transforming lives together

Available everywhere books are sold